Washington Printing Office

Notes of Hearings before the Committee on Pacific Railroads of the Senate of the United States on the Subject of the Indebtedness

Of the Pacific Railroads to the Government

Washington Printing Office

Notes of Hearings before the Committee on Pacific Railroads of the Senate of the United States on the Subject of the Indebtedness
Of the Pacific Railroads to the Government

ISBN/EAN: 9783744746441

Printed in Europe, USA, Canada, Australia, Japan

Cover: Foto ©Suzi / pixelio.de

54TH CONGRESS, 1st Session. } SENATE. { DOCUMENT No. 314.

GOVERNMENT DEBT OF THE PACIFIC RAILROADS.

NOTES OF HEARINGS

BEFORE THE

COMMITTEE ON PACIFIC RAILROADS

OF THE

SENATE OF THE UNITED STATES

ON THE

SUBJECT OF THE INDEBTEDNESS OF THE PACIFIC RAILROADS TO THE GOVERNMENT.

IN THE SENATE OF THE UNITED STATES,
June 9, 1896.

Resolved, That the hearings had before the Select Committee on the Pacific Railroads, not heretofore printed as documents, be printed for the use of the Senate.

Attest: WM. R. COX, *Secretary.*

WASHINGTON:
GOVERNMENT PRINTING OFFICE.
1896.

GOVERNMENT DEBT OF THE PACIFIC RAILROADS.

NOTES OF HEARINGS BEFORE THE COMMITTEE ON PACIFIC RAILROADS OF THE SENATE OF THE UNITED STATES ON THE SUBJECT OF THE INDEBTEDNESS OF THE PACIFIC RAILROADS TO THE GOVERNMENT.

WASHINGTON, D. C., *February 1, 1896.*

The committee met at 10 o'clock a. m.

Present, the chairman (Mr. Gear) and Senators Stewart, Davis, Frye, and Faulkner.

The chairman stated that the counsel and secretary of the Union Pacific Railroad Company were present and that the committee would be glad to hear what they had to say.

UNION PACIFIC RAILROAD COMPANY.

STATEMENT OF MR. WINSLOW S. PIERCE.

Mr. WINSLOW S. PIERCE, counsel for the reorganization committee of the Union Pacific Railroad Company, addressed the committee. He said:

Mr. CHAIRMAN AND GENTLEMEN: I assume that what the committee will want me to do is to give a brief summary of the reorganization proposed to the security holders of the Union Pacific Railroad Company. The reorganization committee consists of Louis Fitzgerald, Jacob Schiff, Chauncey M. Depew, T. Jefferson Coolidge, jr., Marvin Hughitt, and Oliver Ames, second. The committee was organized for the purpose of submitting to the security holders a plan for the settlement of its debt. It was organized at the request of a large number of security holders. As this committee is aware, its plan was promulgated upward of a year and a half after the time that the Union Pacific Railroad went into the hands of receivers, becoming utterly insolvent and bankrupt. The receivers were appointed in a main cause, instituted by stockholders and creditors, and subsequently in mortgage foreclosure suits covering divisions of the Union Pacific Railroad. The first of the series was that instituted under the Union Pacific first-mortgage lien extending from Omaha to Ogden. Subsequently the trustees of the Kansas Pacific consolidated mortgage (a mortgage covering the entire division and including the terminus at Kansas City and the terminus at Denver, Colo., 394½ miles) filed a foreclosure bill, and that part of the property was placed in the hands of the same receivers. At about the same time the same officers, as trustees of the Denver Pacific first mortgage (extending from Denver to Cheyenne and constituting 1,800 miles), filed their bill of foreclosure and receivers were appointed in the same way.

The CHAIRMAN. The same receivers?

Mr. PIERCE. Yes. The Kansas Pacific consolidated mortgage was anterior to the first mortgage on the general line. At the outset there were only three receivers, who had been appointed in the main cause by Judge Foster. The receivership was, on the application of the Government, without entry of formal appearance, extended so as to embrace the five receivers. Messrs. Clark, Mink, and Anderson were the original receivers, and Messrs. Doane and Coudert were the receivers appointed at the instance and by the request of the Attorney-General. The Government lien extends from a point in the city of Omaha (exclusive of the terminals in that city and of the Omaha Bridge) to the western terminus of the main line of the Union Pacific—a point 5 miles west of Ogden.

Senator FRYE. Has there been any adjudication as to whether the Government lien covers any of these terminals?

Mr. PIERCE. The Supreme Court has held that the lien is coterminous with the parts of the line. The line was drawn very sharp with reference to the Kansas Pacific. That Kansas Pacific line extends from the initial point as fixed in the act (a straight line between the two States of Kansas and Missouri) to a point 394 miles west, that being the extent of road on which subsidy bonds were issued. From that point on to Denver no subsidy bonds were issued, and on that part of the road there has been no Government lien. Then, again, between Cheyenne and Denver there is no Government lien.

These two parts of the main line of the Union Pacific Railroad constitute a mileage of 350 miles on which there is no Government lien. In addition to the other property of the Union Pacific Railroad that is excluded from the Government lien are the Omaha Bridge, the terminus in Kansas City, the terminus at Omaha, the terminus at Denver, the lands granted in aid of construction, and probably the equipment of the property.

The property thus excluded from the Government lien is of very large value. On that property there rest two mortgages—a first mortgage on what is known as the Omaha Bridge; and on the Kansas City terminus, the Denver terminus, and the 350 miles of road not included within the Government lien, as well as on the entire Kansas division, there rests the Kansas Pacific consolidated mortgage, which is junior to the first mortgage issued, junior also to the Government lien, and junior to the Denver extension mortgage.

Senator FRYE. How as to the Omaha terminals?

Mr. PIERCE. They are not covered by the Government lien. They are covered by the first mortgage, and they are possibly also covered by the sinking-fund mortgage, the sinking-fund mortgage being junior to the first mortgage and to the Government lien on the main line, but being an exclusive mortgage on the remaining unsold lands granted in aid of the construction of the Union Pacific main line.

Senator FRYE. On those unaided portions of the Union Pacific Railroad—on the Omaha terminus, the Denver terminus, and the Omaha Bridge—how does the indebtedness secured by the mortgage compare with the actual cost?

Mr. PIERCE. The indebtedness secured by the mortgage in the case of the Omaha Bridge is much less than the cost of construction. After the bridge had been completely built at a very large cost, it was to a great extent destroyed, and had to be rebuilt. The cost, therefore, has been very large.

Senator FRYE. I change the question so as to make it apply to the value, not the cost.

Mr. PIERCE. I think there is in no man's mind any doubt that the Omaha Bridge bonds will not represent anything in excess of the value of the bridge. On the contrary, they are probably below the actual value of the bridge. The bridge and terminals would aggregate a very large value, running well up into six or seven or eight or nine millions. I have here no accurate estimate of values, but that estimate is in course of preparation at the request of a member of the House committee, and I will furnish the same statement to the Senate committee. The Omaha Bridge and approaches are called 5 miles, roughly.

The indebtedness on the main line from Omaha to a point 5 miles west of Ogden, at which point there is no terminus, it being the point of junction with the Central Pacific under an arrangement with the Union Pacific——

The CHAIRMAN. For which the Central Pacific pays the Union Pacific $20,000 a year?

Mr. PIERCE. Yes. The mortgage which is prior to the Government's lien on the line between Omaha and Ogden is $27,299,000. The mileage is a little over 1,000 miles (1,040). There is now outstanding from the first mortgage on the Omaha Bridge $508,000, and on the second mortgage $1,056,000, a portion of which, $322,000, is held by the receivers, thus reducing the real amount of the debt on the Omaha Bridge renewal mortgage to about $900,000.

The sinking fund 8-per-cent mortgage secures bonds now outstanding to the amount of $3,330,000. These are the mortgages on the main line and on the Omaha Bridge. Subject only to this first mortgage on the main line proper is the Government lien for an equal amount, $27,229,000.

Senator FRYE. That does not include interest?

Mr. PIERCE. No; that is the principal. The entire amount of the principal of the Government debt is $33,539,512, the excess over the amount which I first stated being the Government debt resting on the Kansas division, $6,303,000.

Senator FRYE. The interest on that being nearly $7,000,000?

Mr. PIERCE. The interest may be stated at about nineteen millions and a half, after deducting the sinking fund payments, which have been pretty large on the Union Pacific. I think that the figures made by the Government officials and those made by the receivers do not materially diverge.

Senator FAULKNER. About fifty-two millions in all?

Mr. PIERCE. Yes, about fifty-two millions. That is, with interest, after deducting the sinking fund. After the application of the sinking fund, the debt for principal and interest will be about $52,000,000.

Now, upon the Kansas division, out to the 314-mile post, Government bonds were issued at the same rate per mile as the first mortgage. The entire amount issued and outstanding, including these first-mortgage bonds, is $6,303,000 of each debt. I do not know that I should trouble the committee with any elaborate statement of these figures, as it is inconceivable that they should be borne in mind as the result of a mere oral statement.

The plan of reorganization contains a statement of the securities proposed to be issued by the new company. It also gives the amount of outstanding securities of the old company for which it is intended to make provision.

The CHAIRMAN. With accrued interest?

Mr. PIERCE. The interest on the first-mortgage bonds is taken care of by a syndicate which finances the reorganization. The Government interest it is proposed to take care of by the issue of securities. The plan of reorganization provides a pretty wide margin of approach through which it is proposed to take care of the Government indebtedness. The proposition is to issue a mortgage of one hundred millions to cover not only the aided part of the Union Pacific property, but also the unaided part of the property—the lands, the terminals, the equipments, the bridges, etc., all the property that now belongs to the Union Pacific and that is subject to the lien of any of its mortgages on physical property. All this is to be embraced in the reorganization by a provision of new bonds—4 per cent fifty-year gold bonds. The cardinal principle of the reorganization scheme is that no new 4 per cent bonds shall be issued in exchange for a security where the old mortgage does not contribute the full value. I want to impress that upon the minds of the committee, because it is a fundamental consideration.

The Government of the United States will not complain that 4 per cent bonds are issued in exchange for the $33,000,000 of first-mortgage debt, which is ahead of the Government lien, if the interest is reduced; nor will the Government of the United States complain if, in the offer that we make to it, we press the Government debt up to an equality with the first mortgage. Therefore these two elements will be found eliminated from the consideration of the justice of this scheme of reorganization. The only question beyond that is whether the new property (new as far as the Government is concerned) that is contributed to this new first mortgage is of a value equal to the nominal amount of bonds to be issued against it. In the statement which I propose to make, at the request of the House committee, it will be made to appear that not only is this so—that is, that the value of this property is as great as the amount of bonds to be issued against it—but that it is largely in excess of that amount, so that the new property contributed to the mortgage increases the value of the Government lien and of the lien of the first-mortgage bonds. The only dilution of the security is in the proposition of pressing the Government up to an equality with the first-mortgage bonds.

Senator FRYE. You say that you propose to issue one hundred millions of bonds. I suppose that this syndicate proposes to take possession of the entire Union Pacific Railroad—its terminals and all its property?

Mr. PIERCE. Yes.

Senator FRYE. And then to pay off all the present incumbrances by issuing $100,000,000 of new bonds?

Mr. PIERCE. Yes; clean them all up.

Senator FRYE. Over what number of miles of railroad do the $100,000,000 of bonds extend?

Mr. PIERCE. Over the railroad proper—1,827 miles, plus the mileage which the reorganization committee will avail itself of, and which is now embraced in mortgage trusts.

Senator FRYE. Does that statement include the terminals?

Mr. PIERCE. It does not. It does not include any of those elements of value, except the 350 miles of the road outside of the Government lien and the 270 miles of branch lines. All these other properties (which are valued at about $18,000,000) and the lands given to the railroad are subject to mortgages.

The CHAIRMAN. There are mortgages issued on the land?

Mr. PIERCE. Yes.

The CHAIRMAN. The same as on the Omaha Bridge?

Mr. PIERCE. Yes; they are all covered by mortgages. I suppose this is as brief a way of stating it as any other way. Thirteen millions of bonds are proposed to be reserved for extraordinary requirements, for unforeseen contingencies, and for future corporate use.

Senator FRYE. That is, out of one hundred millions of bonds, you reserve thirteen millions.

Mr. PIERCE. Yes; thirteen millions are to be reserved for the corporation.

The CHAIRMAN. Will they be held in the Treasury?

Mr. PIERCE. Yes; unless there is some controlling emergency at present and before the reorganization is completed, but that is not expected. $32,842,000 of the new 4 per cent bonds will be issued for the present first mortgage, which is senior to the Government lien, and $33,539,000 will be attributed to the Government, for the purpose of taking care of the Government debt in some way. They will underwrite them or treat them in some way so as to dispose of the Government debt. That leaves a surplus of $20,618,000 in bonds to be accounted for. These bonds it is proposed to issue against the securities which are now outstanding, covering property that is not included in the Government lien; and if that property has a value greater than the amount of the bonds issued, that phase of the reorganization plan is beyond exception. The property to be covered by this $20,618,000 of bonds is the Omaha Bridge, the terminals at Kansas City and Denver, the lands and land contracts (valued at $19,000,000), 600 miles of road, including 350 miles of main line, and also the equipment.

Senator FRYE. Do you get in the terminal at Omaha Bridge?

Mr. PIERCE. Yes; the terminals at Kansas City, Denver, and Omaha. I have no statement of the actual value of the bridge or of the terminals. I have seen the statement of the value of the land in the receiver's report.

Senator FRYE. I think the receivers made a statement in their report of the value of all this property.

Mr. PIERCE. If we assume that the 350 miles of main line is worth $20,000 a mile (and we can not very well assume it to be worth less than that, as the Government lien is subject to about $20,000 a mile), there is a value of $7,000,000 there. Then assume the lands to be worth what the receivers value them at——

Senator FAULKNER. Is that valuation less the mortgages?

Mr. PIERCE. No, sir. I am speaking of the property. We take care of the mortgages under the reorganization scheme; and the only point that the committee need consider is, whether the property contributed bears a proper relation of value to the new bonds issued against it.

Senator FRYE. You say that the $100,000,000 will be fairly represented by property owned by the Union Pacific Railroad?

Mr. PIERCE. Yes; it was with that view that I tried to divide these bonds up into three classes, so that the committee would take them up in their separate classes and see clearly whether each class of bonds represented the actual value of the property contributed. The first class is the bonds issued in exchange for the first-mortgage bonds; second, the bonds issued to cover the Government claim, and, third, the bonds representing property not covered by the Government lien. We have not proposed to the Government that it shall take those bonds, but our purpose has been to make our plan so flexible that we can meet any just proposition coming from the Government, as I assume that propositions will be made that will bear a proper relation to the financial possibilities of the property and that will be relatively just.

The CHAIRMAN. And all these separate properties are to be merged in the general mortgage of $100,000,000?

Mr. PIERCE. Yes.

Senator FRYE. You intend to keep them on the same dead level?

Mr. PIERCE. Certainly.

Senator FRYE. And, your corporation having that in view, you propose that the United States shall make a settlement of the indebtedness of the Union Pacific Railroad at some price?

Mr. PIERCE. Yes.

Senator FRYE. The proposition to come from you and to be accepted by the Government, or to come from the Government and be accepted by you?

Mr. PIERCE. Yes, sir; I do not mean to say that it shall be necessarily payable in money, but on some terms.

Senator FRYE. If you have 4 per cent bonds based upon security ample to cover the amount, what is the difference between paying the Government debt in these bonds and paying it in actual money procured by the sale of the bonds?

Mr. PIERCE. This plan contemplates the issue of bonds applicable to the Government debt as respects the principal of that debt and not as respects the accrued interest. There is a further phase of the plan.

Senator FRYE. Your proposition simply covers the principal of the Government debt.

Mr. PIERCE. The plan includes the distribution of the new fifty-year 4 per cent gold bonds and then the distribution of stock to the common stockholders. For the purpose of making this plan a financial success and of meeting the interest on the first-mortgage bonds which requires to be paid the stockholders are called upon to pay an assessment of $15 a share, and a majority of them have already consented to do so. For that we issue preferred stock. The feature of the plan appertaining to the Government debt is this: Bonds reserved for settlement of the debt to the United States and for extraordinary requirements, $35,755,000, and $20,864,000 of preferred stock; or say, in round numbers, an amount of 4 per cent bonds equal to the principal of the Government debt and an amount of preferred stock equal to the interest on the Government debt. These are reserved as a fund by which we hope to be able to settle with the Government.

Senator FRYE. The only advantage that this preferred stock has is that dividends shall be paid upon it prior to dividends being paid on the common stock.

Mr. PIERCE. Yes; up to 4 per cent per annum.

The CHAIRMAN. You did not answer Senator Frye's question, as to the difference between paying the bonds to the Government and paying cash to be procured by the sale of the bonds.

Mr. PIERCE. I thought that my explanation would cover that. If the Government should desire to participate in this plan of reorganization by taking bonds and stock, that would be satisfactory to the reorganization committee. Objection to that has been made and it has been urged upon us that the Government does not want to be a stockholder. Now, if the bonds are to be underwritten they would have to be underwritten at the price at which the Government would be willing to sell them. That is to say, the market for so large an amount of bonds would be very limited. It would be a very large venture and it would be difficult therefore to market the bonds at what they would be worth to the Government as an interest-bearing investment.

Senator FRYE. You have figured out somewhere, I take it, an ascertainment of what you estimate to be the value of all this property over which this $100,000,000 is to be extended. What is all that property worth, according to your own estimates? Is it worth $150,000,000?

Mr. PIERCE. Our own estimates would not make it as much as that. The road is a seasoned road, a good road, but it is very difficult to reach the cost of duplicating it. That would be an element requiring consideration. The main line is bonded now to the amount of about $50,000 a mile.

Senator FRYE. That would show it to be worth $100,000,000.

Mr. PIERCE. No; a little over $50,000,000.

Senator FAULKNER. How about the rolling stock?

Mr. PIERCE. The rolling stock is probably not subject to the Government lien.

Senator FAULKNER. What we are trying to get at is an estimate of the value of the property.

Mr. PIERCE. These items are on my memorandum.

Senator FRYE. What I want to get at is this: Suppose I want to buy a bond and suppose you have a 4 per cent bond to sell. Of course the first inquiry I make is, What is there behind that bond on which I may reasonably count? Now, you say that everything connected with the road will not be worth $100,000,000, but you are going to issue bonds to the amount of $100,000,000. How do you propose to make those bonds good to the people who are to buy them, if they find on inquiry that there is not sufficient property behind the bonds?

Mr. PIERCE. They have already bonds on the property in most cases; and our settlement is with those who (like the Government) have already their interest in the property.

Senator FRYE. Suppose we, in behalf of the Government, say, "No, we don't want to have anything to do with your infernal road; we have had enough of it; we want to settle this debt, and we will settle it for so much money." Suppose we say that we will settle it for $30,000,000. Now, in order to get the $30,000,000 you have to sell bonds.

Mr. PIERCE. Precisely.

Senator FRYE. How do you propose to make those bonds good to a purchaser if, on examination, he finds that there is not property enough behind them to justify that amount of bonds?

Mr. PIERCE. We do not anticipate that contingency. The additional properties put into the mortgage will make these bonds salable at some reasonable price. We do not expect to sell them at par, nor do we expect to be able to sell any large amount of them at a price beyond 90 or 80.

The CHAIRMAN. You propose to bond the road at its utmost earning ability to pay 4 per cent. The foundation of the mortgage is the earning ability of the road to pay 4 per cent on these bonds?

Mr. PIERCE. Yes.

Senator FRYE. Do you not now make a proposition to the Government that you will give the Government so much in 4 per cent bonds and so much in preferred stock for a full settlement of all the indebtedness, or that you will give to the Government so much money for a full settlement?

Mr. PIERCE. I do not think that these are the only possibilities. They should be presented as simply alternatives. In the House committee, when a question something like that was asked me, I told them that the reorganization committee would include the principal of the Government debt in first-mortgage bonds at 3 per cent, and would then give a second lien on the property for the amount of interest—say $20,000,000 at 2 per cent—so that at the end of fifty years the interest obligation would be discharged.

The CHAIRMAN. In other words, there would be no compounding of interest?

Mr. PIERCE. No compounding of interest.

Senator STEWART. Has the interest on the first-mortgage bonds been in default since the road went into the hands of receivers?

Mr. PIERCE. The interest on the first-mortgage bonds has been in default, and there is now a default upon a large amount. The last coupon that has been paid on the first-mortgage bonds on the main line was paid the other day out of the earnings of the property.

Senator DAVIS. Do you mean on the Government bonds?

Mr. PIERCE. No; I mean the interest on the first-mortgage bonds.

Senator STEWART. State the aggregate amount of the default in interest.

Mr. PIERCE. Two coupons on the first-mortgage bonds to the amount of $1,632,000; and then there are four coupons in default on the eastern and middle division bonds.

Senator STEWART. Have you cash on hand to meet that default?

Mr. PIERCE. Yes; but there was not, when I left New York, cash enough on hand to justify the application for the payment on the main line. On the eastern and middle divisions we expect to pay a coupon very shortly.

Senator STEWART. My inquiry was to find out as to how the road is doing now.

Mr. PIERCE. We are pressing the application for payment of the coupons as rapidly as the earnings of the road seem to justify.

Senator DAVIS. The appearance of the Government entered in the Union Pacific suit is merely special?

Mr. PIERCE. On the face of the record it seems to me that it is an absolute appearance in the Ames case.

Senator DAVIS. Has the Government answered in that case?

Mr. PIERCE. No; it has not answered. The position of the Government has been, so far, an attempt to avoid appearance, but to get so far into the suit as was necessary in order to get receivers who should represent the Government's interests.

Senator DAVIS. On the face of the record it is a question.

Mr. PIERCE. Yes; as to whether the Government has actually appeared in the Ames case. In our case (the first-mortgage foreclosure case) there has been no appearance whatever on the part of the Government.

Senator FRYE. But the Government participated in the appointment of the two additional receivers.

Mr. PIERCE. The first appointment was of Messrs. Clark, Mink, and Anderson, but the Attorney-General came in in the Ames case and made application for the appointment of two others.

Senator FRYE. Those appointments were made on the application of the Attorney-General, representing the United States.

Mr. PIERCE. Yes. The only additional suggestion that I want to make is this. The reorganization committee has received the assent of a very large majority of all the security holders of the Union Pacific Railroad to its plan of reorganization. These have handed in their securities, and have deposited them with the reorganization committee; so that that committee acts with the consent of about 65 per cent of all the outstanding bonds of the Union Pacific and of a large majority of the stock of the company. The purpose of this suggestion is to show that while, heretofore, there has been no opportunity for the Government to deal with the security holders of the Union Pacific Railroad Company in a compact body, that opportunity exists now. They are all linked together, and have conferred a common authority on this reorganization committee, so that now, if the Government were simply a bondholder, and if there were no complications by reason of the Government being a government, we would have no difficulty in completing the matter and reorganizing the property. The only difficulty lies in the fact that we are dealing with the Government of the United States, and not with a class of bondholders who would have fewer complications and embarrassments than so large a body as the Government has. If the situation could be reduced to one in which we were dealing exclusively with the security holders of the company, and if the Government could take the same position from a business standpoint as the other bondholders take, we could close the reorganization within a very short time.

The CHAIRMAN. You spoke about stock in the settlement. What do you value that stock at?

Mr. PIERCE. It is impossible to put any value on it, Mr. Chairman. The stock is to be issued to first-mortgage bondholders, in part as a bonus to induce them to accept this reduction of interest.

The CHAIRMAN. How much stock is to be given to each bondholder?

Mr. PIERCE. Fifty per cent.

The CHAIRMAN. Practically the preferred stock will control the future of the road.

Mr. PIERCE. The maximum issue is expected to be $75,000,000 of stock.

The CHAIRMAN. Of course that would control the future of the road.

Mr. PIERCE. Yes, sir.

Senator FRYE. Has the syndicate which you represent presented any bill to Congress?

Mr. PIERCE. No, sir.

Senator FRYE. Is there a bill pending from the Union Pacific Railroad Company covering this plan?

Mr. PIERCE. There is a bill pending, but not under this plan of reorganization.

The CHAIRMAN. Do you represent the receivers?

Mr. PIERCE. Not the receivers, but the reorganization committee.

Senator DAVIS. The receivers do not object to this plan, do they?

Mr. PIERCE. No; I think not. I think that, on the contrary, they are more favorable to it than is generally supposed. It is generally supposed that it is not one of their functions to hasten the reorganization, but I do not think they would be actuated by that idea.

THE CENTRAL PACIFIC RAILROAD COMPANY.

Mr. Collis P. Huntington, president of the Southern Pacific Railroad, stated that Mr. Tweed was present as counsel for the Central Pacific Railroad Company and had something to say to the committee.

STATEMENT OF MR. TWEED.

Mr. TWEED said:

Mr. CHAIRMAN AND GENTLEMEN OF THE COMMITTEE: The situation of the Central Pacific Railroad Company is, in some respects, somewhat more simple than that of the Union Pacific Railroad Company. It is simpler in respect of the lines of road covered by the first obligation. It is simpler, in some respects, in regard to the liens which affect the various portions of the road. And possibly, also, the matter is somewhat simplified by the fact that the Central Pacific Railroad

Company is to-day a going concern, meeting readily all of its obligations as they accrue, and threatened only (I suppose it is threatened) by the rapidly approaching maturity of the subsidy bonds issued by the Government and by the obligations on the part of the company which accrue and attach as the Government, from time to time, meets its obligations on these subsidy bonds.

But, apart from that question of its relation to the Government subsidy bonds and to the obligations arising in respect of those bonds, the company is a going concern, meeting fully the conditions of its loan and meeting all its existing obligations in relation to the first mortgage and to the other mortgages on its property. And, as I say, it is threatened only by the imminence of the obligations arising as the Government pays off its subsidy bonds. So that, if it is feasible on proper terms to make an arrangement with the Government in respect to these obligations existing from the company to the Government on those subsidy bonds, there will be no disturbance of other interests that relate to or grow out of or are affected by the Central Pacific Railroad Company. Everything will go through without disturbance of the bonds, or stock, or any other interest connected with it, provided only that suitable arrangements can be made with the Government for giving to the Government whatever there is to give to it, by reason of the obligations we are under to the Government. I have prepared here a simple statement which perhaps will aid the committee in some respects in relation to the Central Pacific loans, and the several liens that exist upon them, dividing these liens between the aided and nonaided lines.

The aided lines, in respect of which the obligations of the Government attach, and in respect of which—primarily at any rate—the first mortgage of the company attaches, are the line from Sacramento running to a point 5 miles west of Ogden and the line running from Sacramento to San Jose. These roads are stated severally, because at the time the mortgage bonds were issued and the subsidy bonds were issued they were owned by separate companies, the Central Pacific Company owning the line from Sacramento to Ogden and the Western Pacific Company owning the line from Sacramento to San Jose, the first 737 miles in length and second 123 miles in length. The Central Pacific and Western Pacific, however, have been since consolidated into the present Central Pacific. These two lines are now amalgamated by the consolidation which took place in 1870, and they represent the obligations of the company so far as the first-mortgage bonds and the subsidy bonds are concerned. On the line from Sacramento to Ogden the first-mortgage bonds to which subsidy bonds are subordinate are $25,883,000. The United States subsidy bonds of course are for a like amount. On the line from Sacramento to San Jose the first-mortgage bond amounts to $1,970,000, with a like amount of subsidy bonds. But, by reason of circumstances which are well known to the committee, a large amount of interest has accrued on these subsidy bonds which has not yet been reimbursed to the Government. I have set the amount of it (taken from the Government debt statement of October 1, 1895) at $32,868,669.

The CHAIRMAN. In the event of a settlement it would have to be predicated on the amount that will be due to the Government at the maturing of these bonds?

Mr. TWEED. I think, Mr. Chairman, that the settlement which we will make will have to be predicated, as between the Government and ourselves, on the running forward to maturity of all the bonds, with the interest that will be paid up to that date. The Government will have 6 per cent interest to pay on those subsidy bonds until 1898 and 1899;

and, of course, in making a settlement the figures will have to be based on the amount which the Government will have to pay. But, as it stands to-day, you may say that the first mortgage represents $27,800,000 on this property from Ogden to Sacramento and from Sacramento down to San Jose, and that the second lien, represented by the subsidy bonds and interest, represents about $64,000,000.

Senator DAVIS. These subsidy bonds being on 860 miles of road?

Mr. TWEED. On 860 miles of road. The Senator will recollect that the occasion of this comparatively large mileage charge on the Central Pacific Railroad was the distribution of subsidy bonds made under the acts of 1862 and 1864 in reference to the rate of issue on different portions of the line, classified with reference to the character of the country and the difficulties of construction, these rates being $16,000, $32,000, and $48,000 a mile. And it was on account of the exceptional difficulties of construction that these large rates of subsidy were predicated. Of course that is exaggerated when we come to add the accrued and unreimbursed interest which has arisen in relation to those subsidy bonds.

That represents the situation, primarily, of the Government to-day in regard to the aided lines—860 miles of road, with $27,800,000 ahead of the Government debt, and with $64,000,000 due to the Government on subsidy bonds. Of course I should qualify this statement by saying that there is in the Treasury a sinking fund which should be applied in diminution of this $64,000,000. That sinking fund, amounting to $6,250,000, reduces the Government charge net to about $58,000,000.

The CHAIRMAN. Based on present calculations?

Mr. TWEED. Yes; that, if run forward to the maturity of the debt will reach a figure which I have prepared and can refer to. It will bring it to a little over $60,000,000. But the problem which you will have to deal with in reference to this matter is practically that situation. I am confining myself to the aided lines, and without reference to the nonaided lines. So far as the aided lines go, with reference to which the lien attaches under the acts of 1862 and 1864, there are 860 miles of road with a debt of $27,000,000 ahead of the Government debt and with $60,000,000 representing the principal and interest of the Government debt.

Now, in addition to the aided lines on which the lien attaches, the Central Pacific Railroad Company is the owner of certain nonaided lines; and in reference to these nonaided lines I may say that they were originally separate and distinct lines, and were taken into the Central Pacific by consolidation, each being at the time of the consolidation subject to its own first-mortgage lien—for instance the San Joaquin Valley line, from Lathrop to Goshen, running south, and the California and Oregon line, from Roseville to Oregon boundary, running north. Both these lines were organized by different companies as separate enterprises. Each one had issued its own first-mortgage bonds, which were outstanding. And in that situation (with their own first-mortgage bonds already issued and sold) these companies were consolidated into the Central Pacific, so that the Central Pacific acquired the nonaided lines subject to all the existing mortgages resting upon them. That is accurate as a general statement, and perhaps ought to be qualified in one way, that at the time of the acquisition of the California and Oregon line, from Roseville north to the Oregon boundary, a part only of the road had been, in fact, constructed, and that further bonds were issued (but under the old mortgage) as against the new mileage. The first mortgages on these nonaided lines to which the

Central Pacific Railroad Company became subject were $765,000 on the line from Oakland to Niles, 24 miles; $6,080,000 on the line from Lathrop to Goshen, 146 miles, and $10,340,000 on the line from Roseville to Oregon boundary, 296½ miles.

I stop here in my statement to mention the land grant, estimated at 8,000,000 acres, on which there rests primarily the balance of the old Central Pacific land mortgage of 1870. Senators will recollect the provision of the acts of 1862 and 1864, which required a sale or disposition of the granted lands within three years after the completion of the road, which provision, the Supreme Court held, required a mortgage to be made on the land at that time. In 1870 the land mortgage was made. Ten millions is the figure of it that I have in my mind. That mortgage has now been reduced, by reason of the sale of lands, etc., to $2,615,000, and perhaps a little below that figure. That is a mortgage which is gradually eating itself up as fast as the land can be sold to retire the bonds.

That brings us down to the one blanket mortgage which now rests upon these properties, subordinate, of course, to all the mortgages and liens to which I have already referred—I mean the Central Pacific 5 per cent bonds of 1889—to the amount of $16,000,000. That mortgage covers all these local lines, and terminal properties, and real estate in San Francisco, Oakland, and Alameda, the steamers, ferryboats, and everything—that is, all the San Francisco and adjacent terminal property; for, as I rather think the Senators know already, the Central Pacific aided line, running from Ogden to Sacramento and running from Sacramento around at a distance from San Francisco down to San Jose, does not reach San Francisco at all. The Niles and Oakland line carries it up to San Francisco; so that you may say that the great terminal of the property is at San Francisco. Then the other two nonaided lines are the two arms—one extending north to the Oregon line, and the other south, through the San Joaquin Valley, and as far as Goshen.

Now, that represents the situation, as it is to-day, of the various lines of the company and of the various liens resting on them. The company is in a position in which it is able to carry all that burden currently, subject only to the possibility of making an arrangement with the Government, of a suitable character, by which its obligations to the Government can be properly provided for.

That raises, of course, the question how much there is to pay with; how much this property earns and can be fairly expected to earn in the future. I think that we all agree at the outset that whatever there is of reasonably to be anticipated earnings from this property shall go, and is to go, to the Government in fulfillment of the obligations of the company to the Government in such form and manner as Congress may determine; but that that fund, whatever it is, is to go to the benefit of the company, either by capitalization or by annual payments, in whichever way it is determined by Congress that these contributions shall be made. But I should say myself (subject to your opinion) that in looking at this question two things should be considered—that the payment should be such a one as (looking to the earnings of the railroad in the past, looking at the general situation, the hope of better things in the future, the uncertainties of the future, the possibility of poorer things, but also the possibility of the growth and prosperity, to a certain extent, of the railroad interests of the country) shall be satisfactory to the company and as shall make it certain that there shall be no failure to carry out any plan which is now inaugurated.

We should look at it with a view of determining accurately what may fairly be expected in the future. This is a mere suggestion for your consideration—as to whether it is not better for the Government that, in the green years, there should be some chance, some hope, of return to the stockholding interest; some opportunity of better things, in order that there may be an underlying interest, with at least something to hope for when we come to the dry years. If there is a loss and an insufficiency in certain years (as of course there will be), we should know that we assumed that there must be dry years, and that there must be an underlying interest to carry us over those dry years. But these are mere suggestions which I make to you for your consideration, and in order that you may give them such weight as you may deem proper.

The amounts which we have paid to the Government in the past, under the requirements of the acts of 1862 and 1864, and of the Thurman Act of 1878, have been for the last six years as follows, beginning at 1890. (This is the whole Government requirement—the half that goes to the bond and interest account, the portion that goes to the sinking fund, and the 5 per cent net earnings account, embracing everything which up to the present we are called upon to pay to the Government):

1890	$523,000
1891 (a very exceptional year which has not returned again)	613,000
1892	577,000
1893	584,000
1894	599,000
1895 (about)	600,000

Making for the six years an average of $583,000 as the contribution which we have made to the Government.

During these years the net earnings of the property (after taking out these Government requirements) have been as follows:

1890	$898,611
1891	2,444,000
1892	861,000
1893	784,000

1894 and 1895 were years of unusual depression, the net earnings being in 1894 $144,000 and in 1895 $42,000. That was a very dry year.

Senator FRYE. You are giving the net earnings of what?

Mr. TWEED. Of the whole Central Pacific aided and unaided lines.

Senator FRYE. Is there any way by which you are able to give the net earnings of that part of the Central Pacific on which the Government has a lien?

Mr. TWEED. I have not the information here, but I have no doubt it can be given. There must be a segregation of the accounts that will enable me to state that. But I have given the income of the whole Central Pacific property; because I thought that whatever proposition is made to you by us must be a proposition relating to all the property, and must embrace all the property that the Central Pacific Railroad Company controls—not only this trunk line that goes from Ogden to San Jose, but the head of the line in San Francisco which controls it, and also those two arms, one north and the other south, which are feeders and distributers for the road.

The CHAIRMAN. Still I think it desirable that the net earnings of the line from Ogden to Sacramento and from Sacramento to San Jose should be stated.

Mr. TWEED. I shall have that statement prepared and sent to the committee; and perhaps it would be fair for me to say something in connection with it. It is, that the value of the feeders of the road, as compared with the trunk line, is not precisely shown by the distribution of actual traffic on the line, because the trunk, without the arms, would carry much less traffic than it does, in point of fact, carry when feeders and distributors are auxiliaries to it. And if we take (as of course we must take, in making such a statement) the transportation on the trunk line of the road, we should include in it much traffic that comes to the main line by reason of the arms, branches, or auxiliaries on either hand.

Senator DAVIS. I think it is prorated on the mileage basis.

Senator FRYE. The Central Pacific is now leased to the Southern Pacific. I do not mean that you shall give us the earnings of the Central Pacific as distinct from the Southern Pacific, but the actual earnings of that part of the Central Pacific on which the Government has a lien.

Mr. TWEED. I think that, under the lease, that very statement is required as between the Central and Southern Pacific companies. I have no doubt, however, that by reason of its relations to the Government and the ascertainments which have to be made under the Thurman Act not only as to Government transportation, but also as to the 25 per cent of net earnings, that distinction is kept in the accounts. The 25 per cent of net earnings is a theoretical factor under the Thurman Act, although it has ceased to be a practical factor lately, because the second half of the Government transportation has been larger than the 25 per cent of net earnings amount to, so that we settle upon the basis of one-half Government transportation and not on the basis of net earnings. Still, for the purpose of ascertaining the 25 per cent of net earnings, I have no doubt that the figures can be found which represent precisely the earnings on the aided lines.

Now, these are the statements of the whole property. I have given the net earnings and I have given the amounts paid under the Government requirement. The average for six years of the Government requirements was $583,000, and the average net earnings for the same six years over and above the Government requirements were $812,000. That includes the exceptional earnings of 1891, and I must certainly submit to your consideration that the exceptional and abnormal earnings of a single year are hardly to be considered, even in connection with averages. But I have taken the average for the six years, including that abnormal year.

Senator FRYE. Is not the lowest year of the six years almost as abnormal as the highest?

Mr. TWEED. No; I am sorry to say it is not. If it were, the doctrine of averages should apply. So I have stated the average of net earnings for the six years from 1860 to 1865 as $812,000, and the average of the amount paid to the Government under the Thurman Act as $583,000. The earnings for the two years 1894 and 1895 are very much below what the earnings should be, but taking five of these years and leaving off the year 1891 the result is $546,000 of net earnings and $577,000 of Government requirements.

Senator STEWART. You have got in two pretty dry years. What evidence is there that there will be any green years?

Mr. TWEED. I do not know anything but what has been.

Mr. HUNTINGTON (president of the Southern Pacific Railroad). These were rather financially than climatically dry years.

Mr. TWEED. Whatever has been found to be the really normal condition of the past will be returned to in the future, depending upon the development of the country.

Now, that, as I say, represents what seems to me a fair average, $546,000 of net earnings plus $577,000 of Government requirement. That makes $1,125,000, so that from eleven to twelve hundred thousand dollars a year may be considered as representing (if we judge the future by the past) the fairly-to-be-estimated earnings of this property.

But there is one other element which it seems to me the committee should consider in connection with this matter. That is that in a few years the first-mortgage bonds of the company, which are now carrying 6 per cent interest, and the subsidy bonds of the Government, which mature from now to the end of the century, can be extended at a rate of interest lower than that which they now carry, and in that way the company will be able to make a saving, or additional earning, by reason of the diminution of fixed charges.

The CHAIRMAN. At what rate of interest do you estimate that the bonds can be extended?

Mr. TWEED. It is a difficult thing to estimate. I should say they certainly could be extended at 5 per cent interest. Of course it all depends on the condition of the money market at the time, at what rate of interest the Government bonds are going, etc. There are a thousand things that affect the question—the financial situation, commercial prosperity, or, as you may state it briefly, the loaning value of money. I should say that we may estimate that we can do it at 5 per cent. I should certainly hope that we could do it at 4½ per cent. I can not say that my hopes extend lower than that.

Senator DAVIS. Your figures show that it will take close work to pay interest on the Government bonds.

Mr. TWEED. I think there would be just enough left to pay 2 per cent on the $60,000,000 of principal and interest that we owe to the Government. That is where we come to. Judging the future by the past, there is just enough net earnings to pay 2 per cent on the $60,000,000 of the Government bonds. But there is to be taken into account the saving of interest by the extension of the company's bonds. If we have to pay but 5 per cent interest where we now pay 6 per cent, we shall save $278,000 a year. If we can extend the bonds at 4½ per cent we shall have a saving of a little over $400,000 a year. But the difficulty, so far as we are concerned, is that it is not an operation which we can make when we want to, or as if the maturity of the bonds was far off and we had the right to select our own time for their extension. It is an operation forced upon us at a particular time.

Senator STEWART. That is, at the maturity of the bonds?

Mr. TWEED. Yes; and we have got to do it under the money conditions then prevailing. So that, after all (assuming that the amount of Government debt is $60,000,000), we will pay 2 per cent interest on that; and then, if I were making a suggestion myself, I should say that there should be a provision for the annual or semiannual reduction of the principal of the debt by the amount which we shall save on the refunding of the first-mortgage bonds. Of course, as to that saving there is this difficulty; it will take us two or three years in which to do it. A bond issue of $30,000,000 can not be extended without cost to the syndicate, and that is going to involve a certain amount of expenditure in connection with the operation.

So that, in a certain way, it may be said that this saving of 1 or 1½ per cent is not a saving beginning to-day, but a saving beginning in the next century, and is subject, in a certain way, to those charges which will be absolutely necessary in realizing that diminution.

But, based upon the figures I have referred to, it seems to me that we come practically to about this: Two per cent on the aggregate amount of the principal and interest of the Government debt, and then an annual contribution to diminish the principal of the new Government bonds by reason of the 1 or 1½ per cent which we shall be able to save on the first-mortgage bonds, according to the prevailing money condition.

Senator DAVIS. Do you calculate on discharging the principal of the new bonds at the end of the term?

Mr. TWEED. I have not figured that out to see, but I should think that we ought to do it, or at least to pay so much of the principal that, at the maturity of the new bonds, it should be seen that the balance unpaid was so trifling as that it would amount to the same thing. As the years go by, the Central Pacific Railroad Company will have certain amounts of money with which to make these payments. As to how it shall seem wise to you that this shall be done, we must only be certain that whatever operation we set out in may be fairly and reasonably expected to be carried out to its completion.

Senator STEWART. Have you any fixed opinion what other payment can be made to the Government in addition to the interest on these 2 per cent bonds?

Mr. TWEED. I state it, inferentially, in a certain way. We are looking at it to-day with the uncertainties of the money question. Perhaps we can pay $250,000 a year, or 1 per cent. Of course we are now in a time of financial difficulty—in a time when it is difficult to float bonds at a low rate of interest. If we had to do it to-day we could not, I think, save more than 1 per cent on extending the first-mortgage bonds. And yet we have got the advantage or the disadvantage of the course of financial matters between now and 1899, and it may be that within that time we can extend those bonds at 4½ per cent. Of course, if we were going to make the estimate for to-day, we would have to make it at 5 per cent. That would be all that we could now anticipate, and that would save us just $278,000 a year.

The CHAIRMAN. Will you file with the committee the figures you have referred to?

Mr. TWEED. Yes.

[They are appended to Mr. Tweed's statement.]

Senator FRYE. Can you give to the committee an idea of the additional security which you propose to give to the Government? The security which the Government now holds is not worth a cent. The proposition is that there shall be additional security given for the carrying out of this contract which you intimate may be made. Have you given any estimate as to the value of that security?

Mr. TWEED. I have not; and for this reason: It is easy to make estimates, but no two experts will agree upon them. I think that, after all, the way to determine the value of railroad property is by what it earns. I could give you an estimate of the value of this property, but I do not think it would advance you a particle; for, after all, what you have got to look at is what is to come out of this property. The Government, of course, could not sell the bonds for what they would be really worth to the Government; it would be so much more economical for the Government to take the money as it comes.

Senator FRYE. When do the Government bonds become due?

Mr. TWEED. They are maturing from now on until 1899.

Senator FRYE. These are 6 per cent bonds?

Mr. TWEED. Yes.

Senator FRYE. Of course the Government could take up those subsidy bonds by issuing new bonds at 3 per cent?

Mr. TWEED. Undoubtedly. I have taken the principal of the subsidy bonds and have added the interest on all those bonds to June 30, 1896.

The CHAIRMAN. What do you make the amount?

Mr. TWEED. The amount without the application of the sinking-fund payments is $66,618,000, and after the application of the sinking-fund payments is $60,222,000. I have taken the principal of the subsidy bonds to the Central Pacific and the Western Pacific, $27,855,680, and have added to it the interest to maturity, $49,248,924, making the total debt with interest to maturity, $77,104,604.

Then as the average date of maturity of this debt has been fixed by the Interior Department as the 8th of December, 1897, I have discounted this $77,000,000 at 2 per cent per annum, and brought it to the 1st of July, 1896, making an amount equal to about $75,000,000. That is to say, $75,000,000 put at interest on the 1st of July, 1896, would, at the average date of the maturity of the bonds, realize to the Government the whole aggregate amount which the Government will have paid out on the principal and interest of the bonds; and I have deducted from that aggregate amount the credits to the bond and interest account, which leaves the debt on June 30, 1896 (without the application of the sinking-fund payments), at $66,618,000; or, deducting the amount of the sinking-fund payments, at $60,222,000. I should not like to guarantee the accuracy of my figures, but the principle, I think, is right.

The following are the two tables presented by Mr. Tweed:

Central Pacific lines and properties, and existing liens thereon.

Description of Central Pacific lines and properties.	Miles	First-mortgage bonds to which subsidy bonds are subordinate.	United States subsidy bonds.	First-mortgage Western Pacific bonds.	First-mortgage San Joaquin Valley bonds.	First-mortgage California and Oregon and Central Pacific successor bonds.	Central Pacific land-grant bonds of 1870.	Central Pacific 5 per cent bonds of 1889.
Aided lines:								
Sacramento to 5 miles west of Ogden	737.50	$25,883,000	*$25,885,120					
Sacramento to San José	123.14	1,970,000	†1,970,560					
Nonaided lines:								
Oakland to Niles	24.31			$765,000				
Lathrop to Goshen	146.08				$6,080,000			
Roseville to Oregon boundary	296.50					$10,340		
Local lines, terminal properties, and real estate in San Francisco, Oakland, and Alameda, steamers, ferry-boats, and equipment of ferries								$16,000,000
Land grant, estimated at 8,000,000 acres							$2,615,000	

* Balance of interest paid by United States and unreimbursed; to November 1, 1895, $33,868,069.31.
† Balance of interest paid by United States and unreimbursed; to November 1, 1895, $3,077,685.14.

Central Pacific Railroad (including Western Pacific).

Principal of bonds advanced:		
To Central Pacific	$25,885,120.00	
To Western Pacific	1,970,560.00	
Total		$27,855,680.00
Interest thereon to maturity, at 6 per cent per annum:		
Account of Central Pacific	45,786,454.67	
Account of Western Pacific	3,462,469.74	
Total		49,248,924.41
Total debt, with interest to maturity		77,104,604.41
The present worth of $77,104,604.41 as of July 1, 1896, discounting said amount at 2 per cent per annum, for the period between the average date of maturity (December 8, 1897) and the 1st day of July, 1896, is		74,951,983.45
Less credits to bond and interest account:		
To December 31, 1895	8,170,740.57	
Estimate for six months to June 30, 1896	163,000.00	
		8,333,740.57
Debt as of June 30, 1896, without application of sinking-fund payments		66,618,242.88
Deduct amount in the sinking-fund account:		
To December 31, 1895	6,259,127.15	
Estimate for six months to June 30, 1896	137,000.00	
		6,396,127.15
Debt as of June 30, 1896, after application of sinking fund		60,222,115.73

STATEMENT OF MR. COLLIS P. HUNTINGTON.

Mr. C. P. HUNTINGTON, president of the Southern Pacific Railroad Company, said:

Mr. CHAIRMAN AND GENTLEMEN OF THE COMMITTEE: I desire to say a word—not to improve on what Mr. Tweed has said. I organized and built the Central Pacific, and we have kept it a live, going property. We have no floating debt. We commenced with wooden bridges, and they are now all steel and iron. We are getting the road nearly ballasted, and there is a good deal of money that we have been paying and that helps the question; so that we are really better off than we seem. I want to pay a hundred cents on the dollar of our debt, and to pay as much as we can at fixed times and in fixed amounts until it is all paid. I would like to make a statement hereafter, showing that we are a little better off really than we seem to be. That power to-day will be very much more in the future than in the past.

Senator FRYE. That will be very agreeable news to the committee.

Mr. HUNTINGTON. We have no floating debt; everything is free, and we have done a good many things.

The CHAIRMAN. You have made the road permanent?

Mr. HUNTINGTON. Yes; everything is permanent, and we are out of debt, excepting this mortgage, and we have done a good deal in the way of clearing off several little mortgages. When the time comes I wish to come before you and to take half an hour of your time, but not in thrashing out old straw. I want to tell you how clean the matter is. I do not believe that any of you think I have stolen; but that is what our friends, the enemy in California, represent. I do want to talk for the builders of the Central Pacific road and for its financial affairs from the start to the present time.

Senator FRYE. They do say that you have paid a large sum of money to Mr. Sutro to tempt him to stop this threatening in the papers. Is there any truth in that?

Mr. HUNTINGTON. I have nothing to do with that. He wanted me to build a road to his place. I said I could not do it. He asked me to lunch, and he said, "I want to talk to you; I want you to build a road to my place from the Central Pacific road" (8 miles, I believe). I said, "I cannot do it now; I will sometime." He said, "I am going to fight you." I said, "Commence your fight now, damn you. I have nothing more to say." So I got up from the table, and went away. In a general way I have a good many things to say to the committee.

The CHAIRMAN. We want to hear the proposition which you, as president of the company, may make.

Mr. HUNTINGTON. I have got some figures to present to the committee afterwards.

The CHAIRMAN. We will have another meeting next Saturday, in this room, and then we will be able to give you all the day.

THE SIOUX CITY AND PACIFIC RAILWAY.

STATEMENT OF MR. DAVID T. LITTLER.

Mr. DAVID T. LITTLER, of Springfield, Ill., counsel for the Chicago and Northwestern Railway Company, presented the case of the Sioux City and Pacific Railway. He said:

MR. CHAIRMAN AND GENTLEMEN: I am here as counsel for the Chicago and Northwestern Railway Company, but I suppose my employment takes in the Sioux City and Pacific Railway. If the committee is to sit again a week from to-day, I would much rather present the matter then than do it now. Will that suit the committee?

Senator FRYE. For what road do you desire to speak?

Mr. LITTLER. The Sioux City and Pacific Railroad.

Senator FRYE. With a debt of about three or four million dollars to the Government?

Mr. LITTLER. Yes.

Senator FRYE. I am in favor of taking anything for that debt which you wish to give.

Mr. LITTLER. This bill, gentlemen, is so simple that I hardly think it necessary to take up the time of the committee, and if a brief general statement will answer the purpose of the committee I will make it now.

Senator FRYE. You may just as well make it now. The committee will not be bothered a great deal by this matter.

Mr. LITTLER. I will not go into every detail or into figures, although I have them at hand, and am perfectly familiar with the history of the corporation from the first shovelful of dirt thrown up to the time when the United States Railway Commission made its report.

This road belongs practically to the Chicago and Northwestern Railway Company, which owns substantially all its stock; and while I am not prepared to give the names of the owners of the first-mortgage bonds, I expect that if inquiry were made it would be found that many of those who are stockholders of the Chicago and Northwestern road own the first-mortgage bonds of the Sioux City and Pacific. However, for the purposes of this bill it is wholly immaterial who owns them.

The CHAIRMAN. This Sioux City and Pacific Railroad line is part of the line on which the Chicago and Northwestern gets into Sioux City?

Mr. LITTLER. Yes.

The CHAIRMAN. And part of it is operated to connect St. Joseph and St. Paul?

Mr. LITTLER. Yes. I have a report here containing a map which will show these things perfectly.

The CHAIRMAN. The part of the road lying in Nebraska is a part of the Elkhorn division, is it not?

Mr. LITTLER. I think so. The line runs from Sioux City, Iowa, to California Junction, 70 miles in round numbers; then it goes to Fremont, Nebr., far enough to make 101 miles of road.

The CHAIRMAN. Not owning the bridge?

Mr. LITTLER. No, sir; not owning the bridge. I drew the bill which is now before the committee. I am not very proud of it; I am willing that the committee shall amend and perfect it if it needs amendment; but the general features of the bill I think are pretty good. The United States Government can only act through officers and agents. My client proposes (if this bill appointing three commissioners with absolute power to settle and adjust the Government loan, subject only to the approval of the President of the United States, should become a law) to pay you the cash. The Government has got to have an agent to deal with us. This Congress and this committee have not time to go into a dicker with my client for the purpose of ascertaining the value of this lien, and for that reason we offer this bill. If you can conceive of a more sensible and business-like way of disposing of it, we will be glad to accept your plan.

The CHAIRMAN. This bill provides for three commissioners to make a settlement and adjustment of the debt?

Mr. LITTLER. Yes.

The CHAIRMAN. And on their verdict and judgment being approved, your company proposes to pay the money?

Mr. LITTLER. That is exactly what we propose. The question is not complicated, as is that of the Union Pacific or the Central Pacific. I am sorry for those fellows who are not able to come up and say, "We will pay you the cash." But they are not doing that. My bill does not provide for more than three commissioners, because I do not think it necessary to load a cannon in order to shoot a snowbird. I think, however, that there ought to be one little amendment added to this bill. My experience is that even three men can not agree unanimously on any proposition of law or fact.

That proposition will be favored by an examination of the report of the United States Pacific Railway Commission, which had control of the entire bond account system of the Pacific railroads. It was unfortunately true that the minority of that commission disagreed with Mr. Anderson and myself in reference to every question of fact, as well as to every question of law, so that the importance of a small commission can hardly be overestimated. But in order to prevent a failure in this legislation, I think it would be well to amend this bill and provide that the commission, or a majority of it, should have power to settle this indebtedness, subject to the approval of the President of the United States.

Senator DAVIS. That is right.

Mr. LITTLER. I think that is right.

Senator FRYE. Does your bill provide for arbitration?

Mr. LITTLER. It provides for the appointment of three commissioners with absolute power to settle the indebtedness, subject only to the approval of the President of the United States.

Senator FRYE. With an agreement on your part that the Chicago and

Northwestern Railroad Company shall pay whatever this commission will find due to the Government?

Mr. LITTLER. I am not going to make that broad statement. I do not know what sort of a commission you will give us. But I will say right now that we will pay all the money that the best witnesses in the United States, the most competent witnesses, the best engineers, the best accountants, the best railroad builders, the best business men, will say that the Government lien is worth; we will do that. But I am not going to tell this committee that we will take the chance on the appointment of a commission, and will let that commission understand that we are under obligation to pay all that it says the thing is worth. We will pay all that the evidence shows the Government lien to be worth; and that is all that Congress ought to ask at our hands. If you give us an unreasonable commission, we can not help it. We will tender in cash every dollar that the Government lien is worth in equity.

Senator FRYE. I should recommend Governor Pattison as chairman of the commission.

Mr. LITTLER. I give notice here, now, that we would not accept his views. I think the committee will agree with me that the proposition is a very simple and proper mode of disposing of this small matter. I would like the committee, as I say, to amend the bill so as to provide that a majority of the commission shall have power to settle it. With that amendment I think the bill ought to pass. I do not see how any reasonable man can object to it. I can furnish you in great detail every fact in relation to the construction of the road, and can bring it down to date, but I do not choose to encumber you with it, because that will be part of the duty of the commission. The question for this committee is whether the plan proposed is a proper mode to pursue in order to secure a settlement or payment of this claim on behalf of the Government.

The CHAIRMAN. That is probably true so far as this committee is concerned, but this bill will be a matter of debate, and the members of the committee should be fortified by all the evidence that you can suggest. In other words, we should have an engineer's estimate of the cost of the road, and also of its earnings, so as to be able to show to Congress what that cost and those earnings have been, and thereby enable Congress to judge of the propriety or feasibility of adopting the settlement which you propose.

Mr. LITTLER. I can have all these facts prepared and I will do so. And if the furnishing of these will be taken by the committee in lieu of further oral remarks, I will do it.

The CHAIRMAN. That is all that the committee desires.

Mr. LITTLER. I will furnish a statement showing the cost of the construction of this road, the amount of its first mortgage, and the amount of its second mortgage; and I will show that the road has never paid a cent of interest; that it was of no account in the first place; that it was unwise legislation ever to have authorized the subsidy by the Government. There was less excuse for the legislation creating this indebtedness than for any legislation which ever passed the Congress of the United States.

The CHAIRMAN. I differ from you in that. The policy of the Union Pacific Railroad Company was to build a great main line, which was done. Then from the hundredth parallel there was to have been a road built by the northeast to Minnesota and by the southwest to Kansas. The confidence of the Government was abused in the fact that this road was built in a southeasterly direction instead of a southwesterly direction.

Mr. LITTLER. I am talking about the road as it was built, and I am condemning the policy of the Government in so framing a law as to allow a road to be built in the wrong direction.

The CHAIRMAN. Mr. Lincoln's confidence was abused in recognizing the company which built that road.

Mr. LITTLER. I am sorry I drew out the chairman on that point, for it is not an important issue. I am not here to criticise the conduct of the gentlemen who built that road. The practical question is, how much the Government can get out of its loan to the company.

The CHAIRMAN. I agree with you.

Mr. LITTLER. Well, I will furnish the committee with a statement of the present financial condition of the road, showing what it cost in the first place, and probably showing what the Government lien is worth now. We are going to take testimony, we are going to subpœna the ablest engineers and railroad builders, and we are going to pay every dollar which that class of witnesses will say the property is worth, and nothing more.

The CHAIRMAN. That is simply a matter of evidence.

Mr. LITTLER. Yes, sir; it is a matter of evidence which this committee has nothing to do with.

The CHAIRMAN. Therefore we want this statement in regard to the earnings of the road, etc.

Mr. LITTLER. I will give all that to you, and yet I do not know what the committee will want it for.

The CHAIRMAN. The committee knows what it needs it for.

Adjourned until Saturday February 8, at 10 a. m.

WASHINGTON, D. C., *February 8, 1896.*

The committee met at 10 o'clock a. m.

Present, Senators Gear (chairman), Stewart, Wolcott, Frye, Brice, and Morgan.

UNION PACIFIC.

STATEMENT OF MR. WINSLOW S. PIERCE—Continued.

Senator WOLCOTT. I have been reading in your testimony this plan of reorganization which, I take it, you are familiar with as counsel.

Mr. PIERCE. Yes.

Senator WOLCOTT. Do you take the position that the Government lien is one that can be foreclosed?

Mr. PIERCE. Yes, sir.

Senator WOLCOTT. Your position is that the Government must either come to the front and do something, or else that the owners of the first-mortgage bonds may foreclose the Government out of its interest in the property?

Mr. PIERCE. Yes; may foreclose the Government just as it might foreclose individuals.

Senator WOLCOTT. The Government has received the ordinary notice which any other creditors would have received?

Mr. PIERCE. Yes; a monition to the Government notifying it of the pendency of the proceedings that have been taken.

Senator WOLCOTT. Do you think that the Government is in the position of any other creditor, and that if the Government fails to protect the liens in advance of its own the holders of the first-mortgage bonds may foreclose upon the Government interest?

Mr. PIERCE. Yes, sir.

Senator WOLCOTT. So, therefore, this offer that you are making to the Government on behalf of the reorganization committee is not because the presence of the Government is essential to your reorganization plan, but is so that the Government may be advised and warned that if it desires to protect its lien it must come forward and do something?

Mr. PIERCE. Not exactly so. In the statement addressed by the chairman of the reorganization committee to the chairman of this committee the purpose of the reorganization committee in that respect was stated. It was stated there, if I recollect aright, that while the reorganization committee's view was that the Government could be foreclosed, and that no outstanding right of redemption would be left open, the committee would consider it better to agree with the Government on some just and equitable solution of the matter—some fair adjustment of the Government's claim against the property.

Senator WOLCOTT. Just as I understand. Not because it was essential, but because it was equitable.

Mr. PIERCE. Equitable, and also essential from a business standpoint.

Senator WOLCOTT. From a point of view of citizenship?

Mr. PIERCE. No; I say from a business standpoint—that it is, above all odds, a better plan that there should be an adjustment of the debt, so that no question of this character should be raised and pressed to an extremity.

Senator WOLCOTT. It would not be essential to bring in the Government, if it were not necessary.

Mr. PIERCE. It would be far the better course to agree with the Government about questions of this kind than to have a question of this kind litigated. Undoubtedly the position that we take upon that point is not shared universally. I believe it to be the opinion of most lawyers (certainly of those with whom I have discussed the question) that we are correct about this; but it is obviously inexpedient to leave a question of that kind open.

Senator WOLCOTT. You think that the opinion of the lawyers is not shared by the laymen?

Mr. PIERCE. I do not know as to that.

Senator WOLCOTT. But though the opinion of lawyers is that the Government can be effectively foreclosed you thought it a matter of prudence that the Government should be given an opportunity to come in?

Mr. PIERCE. Yes, sir.

Senator STEWART. Do you construe the statutes creating the lien as sufficient authority for a citizen to sue the Government and to bring the Government into court?

Mr. PIERCE. Our view upon that point is, that when the Government subordinated its lien to that of the first-mortgage bondholders, it did so deliberately and in terms effective for that purpose. The Government then consented to all remedies that were necessary for the protection of this prior lien; and an indispensable element of such priority would be the right of foreclosure. And unless there was a concealed purpose on the part of the Government, that right of effective foreclosure was undoubtedly impliedly granted.

Senator WOLCOTT. In view of that, this reorganization committee has been organized, and I notice that you state on page 6 of your testimony "that the interest on the first-mortgage bonds" (I am quoting from your testimony) "is taken care of by a syndicate which finances the reorganization. The Government interest it is proposed to take care of by the issue of securities." When you speak of the syndicate financing the reorganization what do you mean?

Mr. PIERCE. That the syndicate shall take care of the financial requirements under the plan—such, for instance, as the accrued interest of the first-mortgage bonds. The cash requirements of the plan——

Senator WOLCOTT. I will come to that later. How is this syndicate to be compensated for its financiering?

Mr. PIERCE. The reorganization agreement and plan provides for an assessment of the capital stock and an application of the assessment to meet the financial requirements of the plan. That is one method. Another method is, that as the court shall direct the payment of coupons those that have been taked up by the syndicate, or on account of the syndicate, will be, of course, paid.

Senator WOLCOTT. I see that your financial plan contemplates granting to the reorganization committee $6,000,000 of preferred stock. Is that a bonus?

Mr. PIERCE. Compensating the syndicate and bankers. The plan proposes giving to the syndicate and bankers that amount of preferred stock as compensation for their services.

Senator WOLCOTT. Are there bankers as well as a syndicate in this matter?

Mr. PIERCE. Yes.

Senator WOLCOTT. What do the bankers do that the syndicate does not do?

Mr. PIERCE. The bankers furnish the money provided through the syndicate.

Senator WOLCOTT. Do they control the syndicate?

Mr. PIERCE. Yes; in the sense of managing its financial operations.

Senator WOLCOTT. These bankers are?

Mr. PIERCE. Kuhn, Loeb & Co.

Senator WOLCOTT. Then the bankers control the syndicate. In what sense?

Mr. PIERCE. I should rather use the term "manage." It is in the sense of organizing the syndicate and controlling its financial operations, making calls for assessments of money that may be necessary from time to time to meet its financial obligations under the plan.

Senator WOLCOTT. Do the bankers direct the operations of the reorganization committee?

Mr. PIERCE. No, sir.

Senator WOLCOTT. They simply direct the operations of the syndicate?

Mr. PIERCE. Yes; and, in a measure, the reorganization committee directs their action and that of the syndicate. There are some provisions of the plan relating to the matter which I do not remember.

Senator WOLCOTT. What are Kuhn, Loeb & Co. to receive besides the six millions of preferred stock for their services?

Mr. PIERCE. The provisions relating to that matter are found on pages 17 and 18 of the plan of reorganization.

Senator WOLCOTT. Having the book before you, tell me how Messrs. Kuhn, Loeb & Co. are to get this six millions of preferred stock.

Mr. PIERCE. They do not get six millions of preferred stock.

Senator WOLCOTT. What do they get?

Mr. PIERCE. The provision is—

Six million dollars of preferred stock are to be turned over as compensation to the syndicate, of which the bankers are to retain one million as their own compensation.

Senator WOLCOTT. Is that all that they get?

Mr. PIERCE. That is all that they get as bankers. The provision is that the expenses of the reorganization are to be borne through the issue of securities that have only a contingent interest in the profits of the railroad.

Senator WOLCOTT. You mean the securities that come ahead of the stock?

Mr. PIERCE. The preferred stock—having only a contingent interest in the earnings.

Senator WOLCOTT. There is also a provision for seven millions of preferred stock to meet any extraordinary calls prior to the reorganization. Is that also in the control of the syndicate and bankers?

Mr. PIERCE. Prior to the reorganization?

Senator WOLCOTT. So I understand. "Reserved for equitable organization and for corporate uses, $7,000,000." That amount must be applicable to the syndicate.

Mr. PIERCE. No, sir.

Senator WOLCOTT. What is meant by "reorganization and corporate uses?"

Mr. PIERCE. Reorganization uses are those which may arise unprovided for and of an extraordinary character, all of which can not be foreseen in the preparation of a plan of this kind. "Corporate uses" would be those which would be proper to the corporation hereafter—such, for instance, as the issue of securities in extension of the property, if that should be deemed a wise course to pursue. There is a multitude of other uses which will occur to you, being familiar with corporate matters, but all of which should be provided for in any security to be issued by such a provision as would not admit of the use of the security for other than legitimate corporate purposes.

Senator WOLCOTT. It appears that this reorganization plan contemplates the issue of one hundred millions of 4 per cent bonds, seventy-five millions of 4 per cent preferred stock, and six millions of common stock.

Mr. PIERCE. Yes.

Senator WOLCOTT. Of these 4 per cent bonds you are to give the Government the principal of its debt, $33,000,000?

Mr. PIERCE. I should rather state it in this way. In the first place, the amount of securities you mention are the authorized amounts, including some in excess of present requirements. The provision as respects the Government is that a certain amount of securities shall be reserved as a resource for the purpose of making some adjustment of the debt. We do not know, and have not assumed, that the Government is willing to receive the principal of its debt in bonds and the interest paid by the Government in preferred stock, but these funds are reserved as a margin of resources.

Senator WOLCOTT. I understood you to say that that was the feature of your plan.

Mr. PIERCE. If I did say it, it should be with that explanation.

Senator WOLCOTT. I read from page 10 of your testimony:

> Senator FRYE. Your proposition simply covers the principal of the Government debt.
>
> Mr. PIERCE. The plan indicates the distribution of new fifty-year 4 per cent gold bonds and then the distribution of stock to the common stockholders. For the purpose of making this plan a financial success, and of meeting the interest on the first-mortgage bonds which requires to be paid, the stockholders are called upon to pay an assessment of $15 a share, and a majority of them have already consented to do so. For that we issue preferred stock. The feature of the plan pertaining to the

Government debt is this: Bonds reserved for settlement of the debt to the United States and for the extraordinary requirements $35,755,000 and $20,864,000 of preferred stock. Or, say, in round numbers, an amount of 4 per cent bonds equal to the principal of the Government debt and an amount of preferred stock equal to the interest of the Government debt.

Is that what you stated?

Mr. PIERCE. Yes; I have no doubt I stated that, because it is not inconsistent with the facts.

Senator WOLCOTT. Is not that your plan?

Mr. PIERCE. Our plan is to reserve, of the securities to be issued, $35,755,280 of the first-mortgage bonds and $20,864,000 of preferred stock as a fund or resource applicable to the settlement of the Government debt. You will find in that very presentation of the matter from which you are reading that I proposed to the committee a settlement of the debt, which would be wholly inconsistent with the construction you have placed upon that language. That proposition is (involving some slight modification of the plan) that the principal of the Government debt shall be included in a first mortgage at 3 per cent; then that the bonds issued to the Government shall rank in all other respects with the 4 per cent bonds issued and that the interest on the Government debt shall be considered a new principal and shall be paid off from year to year in fifty years, at 2 per cent a year, without interest.

Senator WOLCOTT. You say:

The feature of the plan pertaining to the Government debt is this: Bonds reserved for settlement of the debt to the United States and for extraordinary requirements, $35,755,000, and $20,864,000 of preferred stock. Or, say, in round numbers, an amount of 4 per cent bonds equal to the principal of the Government debt and an amount of preferred stock equal to the interest on the Government debt. These are reserved as a fund by which we hope to be able to settle with the Government.

Mr. PIERCE. Precisely so—as a fund from which, or through which, the Government debt can be settled. Perhaps I should use the word "resource" instead of "fund."

Senator WOLCOTT. Then you propose to settle the Government debt on the basis of 4 per cent bonds for principal and preferred stock for the interest paid by the Government.

Mr. PIERCE. No; we propose to settle with the Government by the use of those securities, and by the use of other resources, if need be. Those securities are to be set aside, primarily, for the purpose of securing a resource to settle with the Government. If the Government shall receive 4 per cent bonds for the principal of its debt and preferred stock for the interest we will settle the matter in that way.

Senator WOLCOTT. You spoke two or three times in your testimony last Saturday of the Government debt being underwritten. You say on page 11 of your testimony:

If the bonds are to be underwritten they will have to be underwritten at the price which the Government would be willing to sell them for.

Then you say that—

the scheme contemplates the issue to the Government of the bonds themselves or of the proceeds of the bonds.

Mr. PIERCE. The scheme admits of either of those plans.

Senator WOLCOTT. I suppose that you have some digested notion in this plan. Do you desire the Government to take the bonds or the proceeds of the bonds?

Mr. PIERCE. We desire to meet any proposition of the Government or to suggest any proposition which, after investigation, we believe will meet the approval of the Government, within the limits of the financial possibilities of the property based upon this plan. In other words, we have made no sort of a hard and fast rule.

Senator WOLCOTT. Have you made any sort of a soft and slow rule? Have you made any plan of settlement that you wish the committee to consider as your plan of settlement? If so, please tell us what it is.

Mr. PIERCE. In the first place, we would issue to the Government 4 per cent bonds for the amount of the principal of its debt, and preferred stock for the amount of the interest on its debt. That is one method of settlement with which we would be content, if it be satisfactory to the Government. A second method would be the issue of 3 per cent bonds to the Government, embraced in a first mortgage, and the issue of a second mortgage, not to bear interest, but to be paid off at the rate of 2 per cent a year for the interest on the debt.

The CHAIRMAN. That would be equal to a duebill for the annual 2 per cent, payable every year, without interest.

Mr. PIERCE. Yes, sir; or we would be willing to pay a lump sum of money equal to the value of the lien, as ascertained by those who are competent to judge of its actual cash value, as a fair proposition.

Senator WOLCOTT. Have you made any proposition of that sort to the committee?

Mr. PIERCE. No, sir; not a definite one. I did say to the House committee that we would probably be able to pay 50 per cent on the total amount due to the Government.

Senator WOLCOTT. That would be less than the principal of the debt.

Mr. PIERCE. That would be somewhat less than the principal of the debt. We would also be willing to settle on such a reasonable sum as might be determined by a commission appointed under a law of Congress, that should be charged with the duty of ascertaining the fair cash value of the Government's claim and lien. I make this suggestion in order to meet the suggestion which you have made, that we have presented nothing definite. I ought to go on and add this. This seems to be a very definite proposition, and would afford a good deal of latitude for fair dealing between the Government and the reorganization committee.

Senator WOLCOTT. The scheme here does not contemplate the payment of any cash sum, does it?

Mr. PIERCE. No; but you will observe that all of the suggestions which I have made are consistent with the suggestions in the plan of reorganization—that there is to be a balance reserved for the purpose of settlement; that is, a resource through which we may be able to meet the Government on any of the settlements proposed.

Senator WOLCOTT. I have not been making the slightest objection as to inconsistency.

Mr. PIERCE. I stated to the House committee what I want to state here, that we felt that, in this matter, while we could afford to lay down in our plan of reorganizatoin such provisions for the distribution of new securities to meet such of the outstanding obligations of the company as were peremptory and fixed, that course was not respectful toward the Government. Therefore we have undertaken to leave this latitude for dealing with the Government.

Senator WOLCOTT. I read from your testimony on pages 12 and 13:

> The additional properties put into the mortgage will make these bonds salable at some reasonable price. We do not expect to sell them at par, nor do we expect to be able to sell any large amount of them at a price beyond 90 or 80.

So that, if the Government should settle at your suggestion by taking 4 per cent bonds for the principal of its debt, you would give it a security, which would be worth only 80 cents on the dollar in the market.

Mr. PIERCE. You have quoted my statement correctly. I had not supposed that I had put so large a value as that on a large block of bonds.

Senator WOLCOTT. Would you now put the value of such a large block of bonds at 70 per cent?

Mr. PIERCE. I do not know that I would be justified in putting any value upon them. That is a matter of surmise and speculation. A very large block of 4 per cent bonds, even fairly secured, would not sell at the rate that a few bonds on the market would sell at.

Senator WOLCOTT. But you would not call this a speculative bond?

Mr. PIERCE. No.

Senator WOLCOTT. How do you deal with the sinking fund in your reorganization plan?

Mr. PIERCE. We have treated the sinking fund as being an amount applicable to the reduction of the debt; and, in our statement of the debt, we have made a statement for the deduction of the sinking fund. The statement of debt, however, I believe, is excessive as made in our plan of reorganization. More recent figures would put principal and interest of the Government debt, after deduction of the sinking fund, at about $52,000,000.

Senator WOLCOTT. Is there any ulterior agreement respecting this reorganization whereby the Missouri Pacific Railway Company is to have the Kansas Pacific branch, and the Chicago and Northwestern Railroad Company is to have the Union Pacific after the reorganization?

Mr. PIERCE. None whatever.

Senator WOLCOTT. Mr. Gould is represented on your reorganization committee, and the Vanderbilt interest is also represented on it.

Mr. PIERCE. I do not know how far that statement is correct. Mr. Depew, president of the New York Central, and Mr. Hughitt, of the Chicago and Northwestern Company, are on the reorganization committee; but I should not have said that either the Vanderbilt or the Gould interests particularly were directly represented upon the committee, although there are on the committee men who are friends, and, in some instances associates, of both those interests.

Senator WOLCOTT. As to the earnings of this Union Pacific Railroad Company. If you continued to pay interest on your first-mortgage bonds you could not very easily foreclose the Government, could you? I mean if you paid interest and principal on the first-mortgage bonds as they matured.

Mr. PIERCE. No, sir.

Senator WOLCOTT. If the road, out of its earnings, continued to pay interest on the first-mortgage bonds, and the principal as it matured, you could not foreclose the Government interest, could you?

Mr. PIERCE. No, sir.

Senator WOLCOTT. You have $1,600,000 interest unpaid on those first-mortgage bonds?

Mr. PIERCE. On the Union division an amount of interest is in default, something like $1,600,000.

Senator WOLCOTT. You are not familiar with the earnings of the road under the receivers, I suppose?

Mr. PIERCE. Somewhat.

Senator WOLCOTT. Do you not know, as a matter of fact, that if the receivers had not diverted the earnings of the road to other purposes, such as paying off the floating debt, the road would have been able, out of its own earnings, even in bad years, to pay the interest on its first-mortgage bonds?

Mr. PIERCE. I can not say that I know that. I represent before Congress, exclusively the holders of the securities of the property. I should add to my answer, in relation to the amount of interest in default on the first-mortgage bonds, that there is also an amount of principal in default.

Senator WOLCOTT. I read from your testimony on page 16:

> Senator DAVIS. The receivers do not object to this plan, do they?
> Mr. PIERCE. No; I think not. I think that, on the contrary, they are more favorable to it than is generally supposed. It is generally supposed that it is not one of their functions to hasten reorganization. But I do not think they would be actuated by that idea.

Do you speak authoritatively for the receivers? Is there a supposition that the receivers are opposed to this reorganization?

Mr. PIERCE. I suppose that what I had in mind at that time was the suggestion which I heard some time ago—I think in the House committee; perhaps a laughing suggestion—that receivers, as a rule, were not eager to bring about reorganization. It was rather in reference to that thought that I made the suggestion that in this case I felt quite confident that the receivers would be very glad to have a reorganization of the property.

Senator WOLCOTT. Differently from other receivers?

Mr. PIERCE. I do not know that I would say that. That criticism upon receivers was not mine.

Senator WOLCOTT. You think that receivers generally would be in favor of reorganization of the property under them?

Mr. PIERCE. I have not qualified myself as an expert on that point.

Senator WOLCOTT. Certainly you spoke as if receivers were not generally favorable to new schemes.

Mr. PIERCE. I have explained how that thought arose in my mind. My own idea about it is this: That while I have been connected with a number of reorganizations, I never had any experience of obstacles being interposed by receivers. As a rule they have been honest men—men whose attention was directed to the best interests of the property intrusted to their care, and therefore I never found them opposed to reorganization.

Senator WOLCOTT. What reorganizations have you been connected with?

Mr. PIERCE. The St. Louis and Southwestern organization, the Missouri, Kansas and Texas Company, and the National and Great Northern, and perhaps others.

Senator WOLCOTT. So you really are an expert in reorganization; and, in your experience, you have not found receivers anxious to delay reorganization?

Mr. PIERCE. I did not mean to draw upon myself such a compliment.

Senator MORGAN. How many Government directors are there in the Union Pacific Railroad?

Mr. PIERCE. Five, I believe.

Senator MORGAN. They derive their powers entirely from Congress?

Mr. PIERCE. The corporate powers of the company are derived partly from Congressional legislation and partly from State legislation.

Senator MORGAN. The organization under which these Government directors act derives its powers from the United States statutes?

Mr. PIERCE. The Union Pacific Railroad Company was created under an act of Congress exclusively. I do not know of any powers that it derives from State legislation. The Kansas Pacific Railway Company was originally created by Territorial legislation as the Leavenworth, Pawnee and Western Railroad Company and derived its powers from the State.

Senator MORGAN. I have not had an opportunity of reading your plan of reorganization. Does it contemplate a new charter from the United States Government?

Mr. PIERCE. There is no provision in the plan of reorganization for that. It should have a new charter from the Government.

Senator MORGAN. Still, that is not a part of the plan of reorganization?

Mr. PIERCE. It is not so provided.

Senator MORGAN. Do you know any authority which the Government of the United States has given, in any of its statutes, for being sued or for having a mortgage forclosed?

Mr. PIERCE. The authority to which I referred a moment ago in answer to Senator Stewart's question. I never have had, personally, any doubt that consent to sue is involved in the act of Congress subordinating the Government lien.

Senator MORGAN. In what court has this Government ever consented to be sued?

Mr. PIERCE. You mean in what specific court?

Senator MORGAN. Yes.

Mr. PIERCE. There is no specific consent by the Government to be sued in any particular court, but the implication would be (if there was consent under the terms of the act) that it would be in any court of competent jurisdiction—I believe the court where the property is situated.

Senator MORGAN. In any district or Federal court?

Mr. PIERCE. In the Federal court of the district in which the property is situated.

Senator MORGAN. If you were going to prepare a bill to foreclose the Government of the United States in the case of the Union Pacific, what jurisdiction would you select?

Mr. PIERCE. I should select the United States circuit court in the district of Nebraska, inasmuch as the corporation had its home there—the original corporation was commenced there; and I think that view has had additional force by reason of the decision in the Northern Pacific case.

Senator MORGAN. If you could not find jurisdiction in that court you would not be able to find it anywhere, would you?

Mr. PIERCE. By reason of the fact that the road runs through several districts?

Senator MORGAN. Or by reason of any fact?

Mr. PIERCE. I would find it in any district through which the road ran with the lien upon its property. In this case the main bill should be filed in Nebraska, and ancillary bills in other districts.

Senator MORGAN. What are the ancillary bills to which you refer?

Mr. PIERCE. Bills in aid of an original bill filed in the court of primary jurisdiction.

Senator MORGAN. The ancillary bill being filed in a separate court?

Mr. PIERCE. Yes, filed in a separate court.

Senator MORGAN. Do you know of any statute which authorizes any proceedings like that?

Mr. PIERCE. I do not know any such statute, and I do not suppose that any statute is necessary for that purpose.

Senator MORGAN. What would be necessary?

Mr. PIERCE. That, I should think, would be a rule of practice and proceeding which the Supreme Court of the United States would have power to announce, and announce effectively.

Senator MORGAN. Has any such power been announced by the Supreme Court of the United States?

Mr. PIERCE. The Supreme Court has recognized the right of comity in courts where the property runs through several districts.

Senator MORGAN. Is there any such doctrine of comity in the United States law?

Mr. PIERCE. I think so.

Senator MORGAN. Can you point to a statute which refers to comity as comprising part of the jurisdiction of any court or a union between the jurisdictions of any two courts?

Mr. PIERCE. No; but I think that without difficulty I can cite you a number of decisions which recognize the rule of comity.

Senator MORGAN. Will you refer the committee to them?

Mr. PIERCE. I can state now where a very excellent discussion of the subject is had. It is in the case of the trustees of the Short Line first-mortgage bonds of the Utah Northern Company before Judge Gilbert, in the ninth circuit. I should be very glad to send you a memorandum of that case.

Senator MORGAN. Is there any other case?

Mr. PIERCE. Judge Ballinger concurred with Judge Gilbert. There are a number of cases cited in that decision, all having the same drift.

Senator MORGAN. Can you cite any decision from the Supreme Court of the United States?

Mr. PIERCE. The case of Miller against Dowd is an authority on the general proposition of the right of dealing with a property that runs through several districts. Then, in the case of Cox against the Texas Pacific, I remember that the primary jurisdiction in the district court of Louisiana was recognized. I think, however, that the decision of Judge Gilbert, covering a reference to a number of other cases, will meet your inquiry.

Senator MORGAN. In whose name would you bring the suit for the securities which you represent?

Mr. PIERCE. In the name of the trustees of the mortgage. The cases are already pending.

Senator MORGAN. That is a private suit by private individuals against the United States.

Mr. PIERCE. It is a private suit in the sense that the individuals are private parties. They are, however, trustees of the mortgage, and are the proper parties to institute suit for the foreclosure of the mortgage.

Senator MORGAN. But not against the United States.

Mr. PIERCE. It is for the foreclosure of the lien; and of course, for a decree under which the effective sale of the property free from all equities or redemption in the junior bondholders (in this case the United States) shall take place. In that suit the United States is named.

Senator MORGAN. Was there an appearance on the part of the United States?

Mr. PIERCE. There was indirectly an appearance in the original Ames bill.

Senator MORGAN. Do you claim that that court has jurisdiction, in virtue of that suit, of the lien of the United States?

Mr. PIERCE. I think that that court has jurisdiction of the property; and that involves the right to decree a sale of the property free from all equities of redemption in the United States or in any other junior bondholder.

Senator MORGAN. Without reference to the fact that the United States Government never consented to be sued?

Mr. PIERCE. I think that is so, without reference to the question of consent at all. The United States has dealt with this property as a lien holder. The theory of foreclosure, it seems to me, is to give all parties notice who may have a right of redemption, and if, within the time, they fail to resort to their right of redemption, the legal effect of that is for estoppel. That doctrine would apply equally to the United States as to other parties. In addition to that, I have already said that it seems to me that the right of foreclosure is necessarily given by the terms of the act, and by the practical construction given to that act by subsequent acts of Congress.

Senator MORGAN. Then you have all the power you need to foreclose the mortgage of the United States?

Mr. PIERCE. I have always thought so.

Senator MORGAN. You do not need any assistance of legislation by Congress to reach the legitimate conclusion of foreclosing this lien?

Mr. PIERCE. Legislation of Congress directly on that point would, no doubt, put an end to any possible debate about it, but yet I do not think it necessary.

Senator MORGAN. You think that you have got all the authority you need?

Mr. PIERCE. Yes.

Senator MORGAN. Do these bills undertake to sell the franchise?

Mr. PIERCE. They undertake to sell the franchise. They undertake to sell all the mortgage rights.

Senator MORGAN. What, then, would become of the Government directors after the foreclosure? You would not sell the directors also?

Mr. PIERCE. No; I hardly think we would attempt that.

Senator MORGAN. What would become of the right of the United States to keep and maintain five directors in that corporation after you had sold the corporation out?

Mr. PIERCE. I should not assume that any such right existed.

Senator MORGAN. You would assume that you had extinguished that right?

Mr. PIERCE. That right would be extinguished.

Senator MORGAN. Then you would repeal the act of Congress which requires directors to be appointed in that corporation, would you?

Mr. PIERCE. No; I would carry out the act of Congress.

Senator MORGAN. In what way?

Mr. PIERCE. By the enforcement of the first lien. I do not think that that would involve the carrying out of all those particular relations existing between the Government and the old company.

Senator MORGAN. You think, then, that you would have extinguished all the rights of the United States in maintaining directors for this company?

Mr. PIERCE. I should say that, when the property was sold under the first lien created by act of Congress, the property would be sold, free and clear of any obligations of that character.

Senator MORGAN. What would become of the right of the United States to the transportation of its soldiers, munitions of war, mails, and such things as that? Would that right be sold also?

Mr. PIERCE. They are to be transported "at reasonable rates." I believe that is the provision of the act.

Senator MORGAN. Well, whatever the provision is.

Mr. PIERCE. The duty of transportation would be a common-law obligation of the company.

Senator MORGAN. I am asking you what you propose to do? What becomes of the right of the United States to the transportation of its mails, soldiers, officers, and munitions of war after you have sold out the road and it has gone into private hands?

Mr. PIERCE. I have no doubt that the right of the United States to the use of the road would subsist after the sale. I have no doubt that that is the right of the United States with reference to any road. Of course, it need not become a practical question, because the transfer provides for that, and the legislation of Congress can reserve that right to the United States.

Senator MORGAN. I do not understand that you need any legislation of Congress. You say that you have got all the power you want. Therefore you can sell this lien of the United States, foreclose it, wipe it out, with all its incidents, and leave the company which may buy the road, or the men who may buy it, to deal with the United States hereafter on the principle of the common law.

Mr. PIERCE. I think I have explained, that legislation in this matter is desirable from the standpoint of the Government and from the standpoint of the security holders.

Senator MORGAN. Would you not say that it was indispensable?

Mr. PIERCE. No, I can not reach that conclusion. I can not reach the conclusion that there is anything in the exercise of this remedy given by Congress that is inconsistent with the remedy itself—that is, that would block the entire purpose of the legislation. I do not believe that the enforcement of the remedy would raise such inconsistencies as would make the act giving the prior lien valueless.

Senator MORGAN. Suppose that all the members of the syndicate purchasing the property are aliens—living in Germany—would that alter the feature of the case in your estimation, or would it leave us, in a national sense, exposed to a very great difficulty?

Mr. PIERCE. I have no idea that that would be the case.

Senator MORGAN. Could it not be the case? Could not a German syndicate buy the property as well as an American syndicate?

Mr. PIERCE. It is not contemplated that the syndicate shall buy the property.

Senator MORGAN. Could not anybody buy it?

Mr. PIERCE. The reorganization committee would probably be the purchasers; or a committee designated by it, as purchasing trustees.

Senator MORGAN. You have got a bill to make sale of this property and all its belongings, including its franchises, and of course the purchasers can get what you sell. Now, if the purchasers should be aliens resident in Germany, would they acquire all the rights which you mention under this decree?

Mr. PIERCE. No purchaser of the property would be qualified who is disqualified under our laws from purchasing such property in this country. If he were qualified under our laws to make the purchase, he would have all the rights that were sold.

Senator MORGAN. Is not an alien creditor qualified under our laws to buy property here? Is not that a universal right?

Mr. PIERCE. I am not able to say whether that is a right which applies in this country or not.

Senator MORGAN. Have you ever heard of a case where an alien was refused the right to purchase property in this country?

Mr. PIERCE. I am very clear that the general rule is that he may, and that he may be able to hold it afterwards. In some States he is not able to, but as a rule he can enforce his lien and sell out the property.

Senator MORGAN. If it became an escheat he could not hold it, I suppose?

Mr. PIERCE. I am quite certain that in some of the States there is legislation that prevents an alien from holding property.

Senator MORGAN. What becomes of the property in that case?

Mr. PIERCE. I have not followed that out. I am not able to give an opinion on that subject.

Senator MORGAN. The point I was trying to arrive at was whether or not, in the existing state of the law, any provision in the statutes of the United States enables you to proceed to a final decree of foreclosure and sale of this property independent of any further action on the part of the United States Government, or whether Congress must not come to your assistance if you expect to do anything toward realizing your money by a sale of the property.

Mr. PIERCE. Our view is that we can foreclose the first-mortgage loan; but as to Congress coming to our assistance, another and a practical question arises. The Government of the United States is the holder of a very large interest in this property. There is absolutely no occasion for foreclosure. The matter should be one of agreement. We know how difficult it is to deal with a large body like the Government. But this is a practical question, and there ought to be no difficulty in reaching a business conclusion of the matter. Therefore the necessity and propriety of legislation.

Senator MORGAN. But you do not think it is a part of the pressure you can use, to bring that about, that you have got already all the rights you require?

Mr. PIERCE. You mean, to put a pressure upon Congress?

Senator MORGAN. Yes.

Mr. PIERCE. I have not referred to the matter in any such light as that, and I should be sorry to have the committee think that we were taking any such position.

Senator WOLCOTT. Do you require legislation?

Mr. PIERCE. I think we do. We require Congress to designate the terms on which it will settle this debt, and we should ask legislation as to the charter.

Senator WOLCOTT. But you have not done so up to this time.

Mr. PIERCE. No; but when we prepare a bill we will prepare it with such provisions as we think will best carry out the reorganization and the adjustment which must be made with the Government.

Senator FRYE. As a matter of fact, no bill has yet been presented to Congress embodying your proposition?

Mr. PIERCE. No, sir.

The CHAIRMAN. As a matter of fact you have made no direct proposition?

Mr. PIERCE. None, except what we suggested last Saturday.

The CHAIRMAN. You stated that in your scheme so much was set aside of bonds and stock for adjustment with the Government. You do not specify, and you have not specified, any given amount of bonds or stock, or any proposition except that general statement.

Mr. PIERCE. Except that I have suggested that the amount of the principal of the Government debt should be embraced in a new 3 per cent mortgage and that a second mortgage should be given for the interest at 2 per cent a year without interest.

The CHAIRMAN. What do you make that amount?

Mr. PIERCE. About $52,000,000—$33,000,000 for the principal of the debt and the balance for the interest.

Senator WOLCOTT. That would leave the hundred millions of 4 per cent bonds ahead of it.

Mr. PIERCE. It would leave an authority for a mortgage of a hundred millions, but not so large an amount would be issued.

Senator STEWART. If I understand you, it will be necessary, in order to reach your remedy, for you to foreclose, and you think that the right to foreclose is implied in the statute—is that it?

Mr. PIERCE. I think that the right to foreclose is implied in the statute.

Senator STEWART. Take any other contract. The fact that a contract is made with an individual, and that the Government enters into an obligation, would not imply the right to enforce that contract in the courts.

Mr. PIERCE. Not to the same extent as in this case. Here the attention of the Government was invited to a particular transaction, and parties were invited, on the faith of a first mortgage, to advance very large sums of money, running up to $33,000,000, for the purpose of the construction of the road. Now, unless we are to impute to the Government a studied purpose to conceal, and unless we are to impute to it bad faith, the purpose of the Government was (and that purpose would be effectively carried out by the courts) to give an enforceable first-mortgage lien.

Senator STEWART. Does not the enforcement of all contracts upon the Government rest entirely upon the supposed good faith of the Goverment? The fact that the contract is made does not imply that there is any remedy in Congress to enforce it. In fact, there is none. In all ordinary contracts with the Government you have to rely upon the Government to carry them out unless the Government with its own consent comes into court.

Mr. PIERCE. That would be so ordinarily, but this particular transaction is outside of the contemplation of that rule. The act of 1887 refers to the first mortgage as an enforceable lien. It speaks of a time when the first lien may be enforced and it makes provisions for the action of the Attorney-General and of the Secretary of the Treasury in the event that the first lien shall become enforceable.

Mr. Pierce asked the committee whether it desired to put any further questions to him.

Senator FRYE. I think that Mr. Pierce is fairly entitled to a certificate entitling him to practice in the Supreme Court of the United States.

Mr. PIERCE. Then I am dismissed with that benediction.

STATEMENT OF MR. E. ELLERY ANDERSON.

Mr. E. ELLERY ANDERSON, one of the Government directors of the Union Pacific Railroad Company, said:

I have attended, Mr. Chairman, in answer to your invitation, with an expectation more of answering any questions that may be put than of presenting any views of my own.

Senator WOLCOTT. You are one of the Government directors of the Union Pacific Railroad, as well as one of the receivers?

Mr. ANDERSON. Yes.

Senator WOLCOTT. You laid before the Secretary of the Interior the suggestions of the board of Government directors as to the treatment to be accorded to the Union and Central Pacific railroads in connection with their Government debt?

Mr. ANDERSON. The Government directors filed their report. I have here a copy of it.

Senator WOLCOTT. In that report you made a recommendation as to the method of treatment of those roads?

Mr. ANDERSON. I believe we did.

Senator WOLCOTT. That recommendation contemplated that the Government should find a way of paying the first-mortgage bonds and the interest upon them, and should then foreclose and let the highest bidder take the property, the Government fixing a minimum as an upset price?

Mr. ANDERSON. That was substantially what we recommended, except that our recommendation contemplated the foreclosure of both the liens of the Union and Central Pacific at the same time.

Senator WOLCOTT. Yes; that there should be a foreclosure of both liens at once. Do you still favor that method?

Mr. ANDERSON. I favor reaching an adjustment at a fixed price, if possible. If the parties can not come to an agreement, it is my opinion that the largest return the Government can obtain is by a foreclosure of both properties, and an offer to the investors of the United States of a complete railroad from the Missouri River to the Pacific Ocean.

Senator FRYE. But the Central Pacific is not in default at all, is it?

Mr. ANDERSON. As to the Central Pacific, I understand that the currency bonds, in a large amount, have become due. Whether the application of the sinking fund has been actually made or not, I am not informed. The sinking fund is reported so as to prevent a default in the public debt statement of the 1st of February as not being then applied, or as being intact. If that is so, the Central Pacific must be in default.

Senator WOLCOTT. Is it your opinion that such a consolidation of proceedings and sale of both properties would bring to the Government the principal and interest of its debt?

Mr. ANDERSON. It is not.

Senator WOLCOTT. Do you think it would bring less than the principal and interest of the debt?

Mr. ANDERSON. I know it will.

Senator WOLCOTT. Explain what you mean by saying you know it will.

Mr. ANDERSON. I have been connected with the Union Pacific Railroad Company very intimately for several years, and I am very familiar with its earning powers, its physical characteristics, and its advantages for business; and it is my judgment that the sale of both the Union and Central Pacific roads will not bring a sum sufficient to pay all prior liens upon the property, and also to pay the principal and interest due to the Government of the United States.

Senator WOLCOTT. Have you the same technical and special knowledge of the Central Pacific and its prospects?

Mr. ANDERSON. I have not.

Senator WOLCOTT. So, when you say you "know" that the sale of these properties would not pay the Government debt, you mean that you know it of the Union Pacific, but not of the Central Pacific?

Mr. ANDERSON. No; I do not.

Senator WOLCOTT. What do you mean?

Mr. ANDERSON. My knowledge of the Central Pacific, while not as accurate as my knowledge of the Union Pacific, is still sufficiently definite to enable me to make the statement that I make. The Senator will remember that in 1887 I was one of the commission appointed to examine into the condition of all the bond-aided Pacific roads, and at that time I became extremely familiar with the condition of all of them. I do not know the Central Pacific nearly as well as I do the Union Pacific.

Senator WOLCOTT. You heard Mr. Pierce's testimony to-day?

Mr. ANDERSON. Yes.

Senator WOLCOTT. Did you hear the several plans that he suggested tentatively?

Mr. ANDERSON. I know what he said about an allotment or reservation of bonds and stock, and about the proposition for a lump sum of money, and about an allotment of 3 per cent bonds as a part issue of a general mortgage, together with a second mortgage to run without interest and to be applied to the payment of the interest due on the Government debt.

Senator WOLCOTT. Are you favorable to that scheme of reorganization?

Mr. ANDERSON. I am favorable to an adjustment. As a receiver, I do not conceive it to be a part of my functions to advocate earnestly particular schemes until I shall have fully matured my own views and ascertained the views of the Government.

Senator WOLCOTT. Speaking as receiver, and as one familiar with the property, have you an opinion as to Mr. Pierce's schemes, and as to whether it would be wise for the Government to embark on any one of them?

Mr. ANDERSON. I have a general idea as to what the Government can get out of the Union Pacific.

Senator WOLCOTT. Can you apply that language to Mr. Pierce's proposal and give us the information that we ought to have as to what plan, if any, the Government should accept?

Mr. ANDERSON. The Government holds on the Union Pacific a lien representing a certain amount of principal advanced and a certain amount of interest paid and not reimbursed. The amount of these two sums approximates $53,000,000 after deducting about $15,000,000 now in the sinking fund under the Thurman Act. My opinion is that the sole question involved, in considering the suggestions of the reorganization plan, is to determine fairly what the lien is worth. I do not regard the rights of the Government against stockholders or trustees, who are claimed to have misapplied funds of the Union Pacific, or to have violated their duties, as entering at all into this computation; not because I do not think that persons ought to be held responsible for wrongs done, but because it is not a tangible asset that can be dealt with.

Senator MORGAN. You do not think that anything would come of it in the way of money?

Mr. ANDERSON. I do not. Too many years have passed and the claims have grown too old and too weak. Regarding, then, the property of the Union Pacific itself as the natural source from which reimbursements may be expected, there are two things to be determined in order to reach a conclusion as to what is a fair value of the Government assets. They are, first, the available value of the property, and, second, the amount that must be deducted or taken out before the Government can realize anything at all. The answer to the question as to the value of the Union Pacific property is not an easy one. That value is affected by a great many considerations which bear upon its earning powers, those considerations being the tendency of freight and passenger rates to decrease and fall all the time (which has been a persistent factor for many years past), the extreme competition of other railroads serving parts of the same community, and many other circumstances, such as the decreased salable value of things that are produced in the West; all of which considerations militate against the earning powers of the railroad.

Senator WOLCOTT. Have you any objection to stating what these militating forces are?

Mr. ANDERSON. I have stated three of them, the decreasing rates, the competition of other roads——

Senator MORGAN. What other roads?

Mr. ANDERSON. There are to-day eight or ten transcontinental lines, whereas twenty years ago there was but one. These are competing roads—the Southern Pacific, the Burlington, the Santa Fe, the Southern Pacific, the Missouri Pacific, the Texas Pacific, and others—all of these railroads being factors to divide the business; and therefore it is harder for the railroad which formerly used to make large profits to maintain its position as an earning carrier of freight and passengers, and harder for it to earn the same amount than when the competition was less.

Senator MORGAN. Does the Southern Pacific Railroad hold any exceptional connection with this subject?

Mr. ANDERSON. The Southern Pacific, by its connection with the Atlantic Seaboard, drains a very large amount of business through its southern connections, which, if the Central Pacific were united to the Union Pacific, would undoubtedly serve to increase the earning powers of the Union Pacific. What I was saying was in reference to ascertaining the fair value of this property, looking at it in several ways. The Union Pacific embraces about 1,900 or 2,000 miles of road. Estimating the value of that road at $25,000 a mile, it would give fifty millions as the value of the railroad, equipment, and rolling stock.

The CHAIRMAN. Do you include terminals in that?

Mr. ANDERSON. No, sir. To which there should be added, perhaps, fifteen or twenty millions to represent not only terminal facilities but the land ownership—not embraced in the land grant, but railroad ownership at Council Bluffs, Omaha, Kansas City, Denver, and Cheyenne, which, in addition to the ordinary facilities of terminal points, embrace very valuable shop plants, fully equipped and representing a a very large amount of money. So in this way you may reach an approximate value of $70,000,000 for this Union Pacific property. Another way to look at it would be based on the estimated value of those very securities which Mr. Pierce proposes to issue. He talked of an issue of ninety millions at present. I limit myself to the amount issued, because I assume that the bonds that are not issued at present would be issued for value and would therefore increase the valuation. So, to reach the valuation based upon the bonds and stock, if you take the ninety millions issued and predicate a market value of 75 per cent for these 4 per cent bonds you would have about $67,000,000.

Senator STEWART. Estimating them as gold bonds.

Mr. ANDERSON. Senator, "sufficient for the day is the evil thereof." I am only dealing with the railroad, and am estimating these bonds as currency bonds. To this sixty-seven millions would have to be added the fair value of seventy-five millions of preferred stock, which would perhaps be from twenty-five to thirty millions, estimating that preferred stock as salable at from 30 to 40 per cent. The common stock I do not consider as having any available money value. Its only value would be for purposes of control. These figures together would give about $92,000,000 for this property as quite the market value of the securities. If you look for the same information based upon the earning powers of the property, you find that the Union Pacific Railroad Company after payment of all operating expenses, after payment of taxes, and coming down to the fund available for interest, earned about $4,300,000 in the year 1894. The earnings for 1895 are somewhat better. But during the year 1895 the receivers have abstained from some peculiar expenditures which were made in 1894—a large amount for new rails. So that perhaps the net earnings in 1895 would be rather a larger figure than it would be safe to assume as representing the real earning powers of the property.

The CHAIRMAN. Are the new rails charged to construction?

Mr. ANDERSON. No, sir; everything is charged to operating expenses. We do simply a cash business. Taking the estimated earnings as between $4,000,000 and $4,200,000, an industrial capitalization (that is, a capitalization to be used for trade purposes) would be regarded as being such an amount as at 6 per cent would produce that income, say, $80,000,000. Then if you take the valuation of eighty millions for the property you will have, at 6 per cent, a net income of $4,800,000. So that whether you value this property by the lien (with the addition of terminals), or whether you value it by the market value of the lot of securities to be issued, or whether you value it on the basis of its fair earning powers, you reach the conclusion that the fair market value of the Union Pacific Railroad Company is something between $75,000,000 and $80,000,000. That is the fair way to look at it.

Senator BRICE. What mileage do you estimate for the Union Pacific line?

Mr. ANDERSON. About 1,900 miles. If this is a fair way to look at it, then the remaining element to be determined, in order to answer the question whether the reorganization plan suggestions are fair suggestions or not, we would have to deduct from the valuation as reached the amounts which must be taken out in order to arrive at the value of the Government lien. These amounts are, first, the first-mortgage bonds, some $35,000,000 on the aided portion of the road; then the first-mortgage bonds on those parts of the Union Pacific Railroad Company that are not included in the bond-aided portion, that is to say, the first-mortgage bonds between a point 394 miles west of Kansas City and Denver, and thence to Cheyenne. In addition to that an adjustment would have to be made with the holders of securities on that portion of the railroad which the Government intends to acquire. Or, at any rate, we must ascertain what claims would have to be taken out of that seventy-five or eighty million dollars before reaching the value of the Government lien. Without going into them in detail, I would say, from such examination as I have given to it, that the total amount so required for first mortgage on parts of those additions and for other mortgages which are claims upon parts that are not aided, and are not first mortgages, would be about $50,000,000.

Senator STEWART. Does that cover terminals?

Mr. ANDERSON. It covers everything that would have to be taken out of the value in order to determine the fair value of the Government lien. Taking that $50,000,000 from the $85,000,000, or the $92,000,000 of your new securities as representing the fair value of the road, would give you a basis of value representing the lien of the Government as being worth from $30,000,000 to $40,000,000.

Senator WOLCOTT. Would you recommend the Government to accept that in cash?

Mr. ANDERSON. I would.

Senator WOLCOTT. Do you consider that better than the offer of securities?

Mr. ANDERSON. I consider it better.

Senator WOLCOTT. Would you consider it wise and good for the Government to accept that offer?

Mr. ANDERSON. I would.

Senator WOLCOTT. If, therefore, the Government can do better than that, it would be wise, of course, to postpone our acceptance of it. Suppose, for instance, the Government can have security for a greater amount than that as a first mortgage, would you then think it wise to accept it?

Mr. ANDERSON. That presents a different question. It depends upon who makes the offer and how it is secured. If somebody offers the Government forty millions, of course it is better to take that forty millions than to take thirty-five millions.

Senator WOLCOTT. Taking that view, that $35,000,000 would be an offer which the Government should accept, you base it upon the earning capacity of the property, do you?

Mr. ANDERSON. I have based it on all the facts I have given, which lead me to the conclusion that the difference between the value of the property and the claims which would have to be paid and adjusted does not exceed $35,000,000.

Senator WOLCOTT. You think that this sum of $35,000,000 it would be wiser for the Government to accept than it would be to follow the Government directors' scheme of putting up enough money to cover the prior indebtedness and to sell the property?

Mr. ANDERSON. I have not said that.

Senator WOLCOTT. I ask you, do you think so?

Mr. ANDERSON. The report of the Government directors is based upon the suggestion of the combined foreclosure of the two properties. The explanations that I have given to the committee this morning are based solely on the question of adjusting the Union Pacific Railroad debt, without reference to the Central Pacific at all.

Senator WOLCOTT. Do you consider the Central Pacific a better security for the advances of the Government than the Union Pacific?

Mr. ANDERSON. I think that the Central Pacific and the Union Pacific, if sold together, would bring more money than the Central Pacific sold by itself, and the Union Pacific sold by itself.

Senator WOLCOTT. Do you think that the lien which the Government holds on the Central Pacific has a greater money value than the lien which it holds on the Union Pacific?

Mr. ANDERSON. I do not.

Senator WOLCOTT. If this $35,000,000 is the full amount that the Government can expect to receive from the Union Pacific, and if it could do equally well with the Central Pacific, would you think it a wiser proposition to accept these sums than it would be to proceed upon the plan suggested by the Government directors?

Mr. ANDERSON. I think it would, because the plan suggested by the Government directors is, of course, somewhat problematical in its outcome and issue; whereas an offer of, say, $65,000,000 in cash, in gold eagles, placed upon this table, would have the tempting characteristic of being an absolute certainty not liable to accidents and disappointments.

Senator WOLCOTT. The net earnings of the Union Pacific Railroad (of the Government-aided portions of it) are about how much?

Mr. ANDERSON. The net earnings of the Union Pacific in 1894 (including the Government transportation in that sum) were $4,300,000, but that includes the aided and the nonaided parts of the road.

Senator WOLCOTT. Have you had anything to do with the application of earnings?

Mr. ANDERSON. A good deal.

Senator WOLCOTT. Would it have been possible for the receivers to have kept the interest on the first-mortgage bonds paid?

Mr. ANDERSON. If they had refrained from putting new rails upon the property, and from keeping the property in a good state of repair, it would have been possible.

Senator WOLCOTT. If you had paid the interest on the first-mortgage bonds, would you have been compelled to leave the road in bad repair?

Mr. ANDERSON. We would have skimped the road a good deal.

Senator WOLCOTT. Has there been no diversion of the earnings of the road to any other purpose than for new rails and repairs?

Mr. ANDERSON. There has been no application of earnings for any purpose except on application to, and under the direction of, the court. (To Senator Wolcott.) What do you mean by the diversion of earnings?

Senator WOLCOTT. The testimony of Mr. Pierce shows that you now have in contemplation the payment of back interest. There has been default in the payment of coupons, because the amount of money which would otherwise have been paid for them has been put into new rails and repairs.

Mr. ANDERSON. We have plenty of money on hand. The judge in charge of the property has required the receivers, before parting with their funds in order to pay mortgage interest, to satisfy him very clearly that the road has been kept up, that all the operating obligations have been met, and that sufficient funds have been retained to assure the continuance of that policy for six months in the future.

Senator MORGAN. You mentioned that in 1895 the net income of the road had increased?

Mr. ANDERSON. Yes.

Senator MORGAN. About how much?

Mr. ANDERSON. I have not got the December figures yet, but I think that the net income for the year will show about $5,000,000.

Senator MORGAN. That has been entirely under the administration of the court?

Mr. ANDERSON. Yes; the property has been administered under the court since October, 1893.

Senator MORGAN. Has the net profit continued to increase all the time since the property has been administered by the court?

Mr. ANDERSON. It has not; it went into the slough of despond in 1894.

Senator MORGAN. Has the court found it necessary to put any debt upon the road in order to meet this falling off in the income?

Mr. ANDERSON. No; there are no certificates or no suggestion of a necessity for certificates.

Senator MORGAN. And no money has been advanced or borrowed?

Mr. ANDERSON. No; none at all. We have a large deposit on hand to-day.

Senator MORGAN. You have not the balance sheet with you?

Mr. ANDERSON. I have the report of 1894, but that does not give the information you request.

Senator MORGAN. So that, at the worst stage of the road since the receivers have been appointed, there has been enough net income to keep the road in repair and to meet obligations?

Mr. ANDERSON. Yes; and to meet a considerable part of the interest on the bonds.

Senator WOLCOTT. Do you share the view of Mr. Pierce, that the Government may be foreclosed of its interest?

Mr. ANDERSON. After a full opportunity for the Government to appear in court and assert its right?

Senator WOLCOTT. The same as any individual?

Mr. ANDERSON. My opinion is of little value. The question, for ultimate solution, would have to go to the Supreme Court of the United States. My own opinion is that a decree of sale, issued by a court of competent jurisdiction after full service and notice on the United States, and at the expiration of such period as the court should see fit to fix for the Government to appear and plead, and after decree of sale duly entered, and after a sale being regularly had, the title to all the property, rails, rolling stock, and terminals would pass to the purchasers free from any lien whatever.

Senator WOLCOTT. What as to the franchise?

Mr. ANDERSON. I do not think that the purchasers could operate the railroad without organizing themselves into some corporate form, either under the permission of the United States or under permission of the States where the road is located.

Senator WOLCOTT. But you do not think that it would necessarily require Government assistance?

Mr. ANDERSON. You mean to pass the title to the property?

Senator WOLCOTT. Yes.

Mr. ANDERSON. I do not.

Senator WOLCOTT. Either to the property or to the franchise?

Mr. ANDERSON. I do not say as to the franchise. My opinion is that the purchasers could not operate the railroad as a corporation without the assistance of an act of Congress or of an act of the States in which the road is operated.

Senator WOLCOTT. But if they could procure an act of the States in which the road is operated they would not need an act of Congress.

Mr. ANDERSON. They would have their own rails and their land and their rolling stock; and if the States of Nebraska, Colorado, and Wyoming should choose to organize them as a corporation, I see no reason why not.

Senator WOLCOTT. There are five receivers of the Union Pacific Railroad, are there?

Mr. ANDERSON. Yes.

Senator WOLCOTT. Are their duties divided?

Mr. ANDERSON. Yes.

Senator WOLCOTT. State how they are divided.

Mr. ANDERSON. Mr. S. H. Clarke is the operating receiver. He is constantly on the property, and has charge of all those questions with which you, gentlemen, are familiar, everything being under his direction and control. Mr. Mink and myself have charge of the financial side of the management and of an enormous variety of legal questions and complications that present themselves from time to time and have to be disposed of. We also participate with Mr. Clarke in questions of some difficulty in relation to traffic contracts, or in relation to questions of operation, and we visit the property from time to time. Messrs. Coudert and Doane were appointed at the request of the Government, and take an active part in the discussion of general questions relating to the administration of the property. Mr. Coudert assists us on many questions, both legal questions and business questions. He is with us from time to time. That is the substantial distribution of the work.

Senator WOLCOTT. You spoke of the traffic being diverted from the Union Pacific line by competing lines as an element of value, and you mentioned the Missouri Pacific, the Southern Pacific, and other lines. Are there not lines which do not run across, but that run near the Union Pacific line, and compete with it?

Mr. ANDERSON. Yes; there is a great competition in all forms of business. Local lines compete for local business.

Senator STEWART. One line competing as far as Ogden?

Mr. ANDERSON. There are lines in course of construction, and they all seem to have an ambition to reach the Pacific, just as every American citizen has an ambition to become President.

Senator STEWART. You suggest that if the Central Pacific and the Union Pacific were sold together, the line would be more valuable than if they were sold separately?

Mr. ANDERSON. Yes.

Senator STEWART. Would that be because it would have a monopoly as against those other roads that are attempting to get to the Pacific Ocean?

Mr. ANDERSON. There would be no monopoly; but the Union Pacific, controlling the Central Pacific, would be protected from the plans of construction which now exist in those several other roads, and would also be able to take for itself a larger portion of the California business than it now obtains. Our relations to the Central Pacific are friendly and pleasant in many ways; but they naturally take all they can by the Southern road, and only give us what is necessary to preserve friendly relations with us; whereas, if we owned the Central Pacific, we would take very much more business than the Central Pacific now gives us.

Senator STEWART. But the Union Pacific controls the short line to Portland, Oreg.?

Mr. ANDERSON. No, sir; the Oregon Navigation Company has been a separate corporation since July, 1894.

Senator STEWART. How far does the short line extend?

Mr. ANDERSON. To Huntington, about 400 miles from Portland.

Senator STEWART. Then the Union Pacific does not control the Oregon Navigation Company? That is under different management?

Mr. ANDERSON. Entirely. I may add that the short line will probably move out of the system in consequence of bankruptcy. It is now in the process of foreclosure.

Senator STEWART. That line does not come into the reorganization plan?

Mr. ANDERSON. It does not come into Mr. Pierce's reorganization plan; but it would affect the interest of the Union Pacific Company very much indeed if the short line passed from it into the hands of a hostile organization.

Senator STEWART. But if the short line should pass into the same management, it would be a pretty strong organization?

Mr. ANDERSON. Even without the short line, the Central Pacific and Union Pacific alone would be a splendid property. I am not merely giving my own opinion on that point, because I am quite familiar with railroad men, and I am giving their opinion. That is the opinion of Mr. Clarke, our operating administrator.

Senator STEWART. That would somewhat damage the prospects of these ambitious roads that are trying to get to the Pacific Ocean, would it not?

Mr. ANDERSON. It would prevent their poaching upon our preserves.

The CHAIRMAN. There have been heretofore, between the Union Pacific and those roads that you have mentioned, close running arrangements and good railroad comity?

Mr. ANDERSON. Railroad comity is always as problematical as court comity. We have friendly relations, but they are disturbed occasionally.

The CHAIRMAN. Is it not a fact that a large number of persons having interests in the Union Pacific Railroad are also interested in other lines?

Mr. ANDERSON. Yes; in the short line.

The CHAIRMAN. You spoke of an arrangement whereby both the Union Pacific and the Central Pacific should be foreclosed coming under one ownership and management.

Mr. ANDERSON. Yes, sir.

The CHAIRMAN. If the Government bid it in that would result in Government ownership of the line and in Government operation of the line?

Mr. ANDERSON. Not necessarily. In the report of the Government directors the suggestion is made that if the upset or minimum price is not bid the operation of the road shall remain in charge of the court until the next session of Congress, when further action can be taken.

The CHAIRMAN. That would be virtual ownership of the road by the Government.

Mr. ANDERSON. So it is to-day. It is Government ownership to-day in that sense. One of the departments of the Government is running that road.

The CHAIRMAN. It has been claimed by a good many persons that by virtue of the fact that the Government was a creditor of these corporations these lines can not be foreclosed by the first-mortgage holders on the general principle that you can not sue the Government. Is it your opinion that a suit brought by the first-mortgage bondholders would hold as against the Government?

Mr. ANDERSON. I have already said that I think a regular decree of sale would pass the right to the property free from the Government lien?

The CHAIRMAN. Not including the franchise?

Mr. ANDERSON. The legal title to the franchise would merge, but the road could not be used or operated by the purchaser without the assistance of the Government.

The CHAIRMAN. Without the consent of the Government?

Mr. ANDERSON. Without a charter from the Government or from the States.

The CHAIRMAN. Then, in other words, the purchaser buying under the foreclosure would simply hold the property?

Mr. ANDERSON. Unless he could get some authority from some sovereign power to use it.

Senator BRICE. Do you hold that this sale would cut off the equities of redemption in the Government, in case the Government saw fit at a future time to redeem it?

Mr. ANDERSON. I have stated what I think, but individual opinions are of little value. That is my opinion, however. Let me say, in explanation of the question of Senator Stewart to Mr. Pierce, that the distinction between contracts made by the Government under authority of law which are not enforceable by process of law, and the present case is, that the title of the first-mortgage bondholders is directly declared by the act of Congress to be prior to that of the Government, and the Government lien declared to be subordinate, whereas, in the case of a contract, the rights of the parties are clearly, at most, equal, and there can be no indication by the Government that it intends to put its rights below the rights of the other party to the contract.

Senator BRICE. With respect to the sale under the first mortgage and to the purchase at such sale by some individuals, is it not usual, where there is a lack of power in the final organization, for the purchaser to operate as purchaser, and would he not be compelled in that case to continue the operation of the road in all respects precisely as it was operated by the receiver or company, until some action is taken by the Government or by the States?

Mr. ANDERSON. I presume that the court (and I have known it to do so) would continue the operation of the road until the purchaser was prepared to undertake to discharge the rights which the public has to have, the railroad property administered so as to carry passengers and freight.

Senator BRICE. The purchaser would be obliged to fulfill his functions as a common carrier. Let me ask you as to the Union Pacific Railroad Company. I understood Mr. Pierce to state the underlying first-mortgage bonds to amount to a total of $33,532,000.

Mr. ANDERSON. That is the amount of the underlying first-mortgage bonds on the bond-aided portion of the railroad.

Senator BRICE. Therefore there was an equal amount of Government bonds issued, secured by a second lien on this same portion of the road?

Mr. ANDERSON. Yes.

Senator BRICE. Making $33,532,000 more, on which there has accrued about $35,000,000 of interest, making some sixty-eight and a half millions, having no reference as yet to the sinking fund?

Mr. ANDERSON. I have not the gross figures in my head. I should have supposed the interest to be more than that.

Senator BRICE. Then $35,000,000 of interest is not an overestimate?

Mr. ANDERSON. No.

Senator BRICE. All the other classes of bonds which it is proposed, under the scheme which Mr. Pierce has submitted, amounts to a total of $33,762,000. That would make a total bonded indebtedness of $135,000,000, or about that sum, would it not?

Mr. ANDERSON. I have no doubt. But I have not Mr. Pierce's plan in my head, nor before me, and I do not know what he has included in it.

Senator BRICE. Then this seems to be subject to a reduction of about fifteen millions, or the amount of the sinking fund?

Mr. ANDERSON. Do I understand you to be quoting from page 6 of the plan?

Senator BRICE. From pages 6 and 7—excluding the collateral trust bonds which are not included in this scheme of reorganization.

Mr. ANDERSON. Do you exclude also the collateral trust notes?

Senator BRICE. I exclude them. They are marked in the margin as "not embraced in reorganization."

Mr. ANDERSON. What is the total you have reached?

Senator BRICE. One hundred and thirty-five million dollars, or more.

Mr. ANDERSON. That includes the entire Government debt?

Senator BRICE. It does.

Mr. ANDERSON. And the funded debt which is included in the reorganization scheme?

Senator BRICE. Yes.

Mr. ANDERSON. Then what is your question?

Senator BRICE. That is subject to a reduction of about $15,000,000 from the sinking fund?

Mr. ANDERSON. The net Government debt is ascertained by reducing from the gross Government debt the amount of the sinking fund.

Senator BRICE. Inasmuch as that has not been done, I prefer to deal with it as a separate item, because the sinking fund may or may not produce the sum estimated. What is the nominal amount of the sinking fund?

Mr. ANDERSON. The sinking fund of the Union Pacific Railroad Company is $15,000,000, fourteen millions in bonds and one million in cash.

Senator BRICE. And that would leave one hundred and twenty millions of debt?

Mr. ANDERSON. Yes; assuming $135,000,000 to be accurate.

Senator BRICE. Is this railroad of 1,825 miles capable of earning, one year with another, 4 per cent upon $120,000,000?

Mr. ANDERSON. It is just able, but it would be close work.

Senator BRICE. Tell the committee the present conditions of this litigation, with reference to any imminent danger of a decree of foreclosure on the part of the first-mortgage bondholders; in what courts are bills for foreclosure pending; what stage have they reached, and what probability is there of an early decree?

Mr. ANDERSON. The best answer to those questions is in the report of the Government directors, which contains specific reference to all the suits pending and a discussion of the questions which the Senator has put to me.

Senator BRICE. Has anything occurred since that time in the way of advancing those proceedings?

Mr. ANDERSON. I think not.

Senator BRICE. Or by way of interest payment on the part of receivers or of the company reducing the liability to a decree?

Mr. ANDERSON. There have been interest payments, but there have been also fresh defaults.

Senator BRICE. So that the situation, on the whole, has not substantially changed since the date of that Government report?

Mr. ANDERSON. It has not. It is not my opinion that there is any immediate danger of a decree being attempted to be obtained.

Senator BRICE. In case the Government should direct its proper officer to appear in those suits and consent to a foreclosure decree being entered, is there anything in the proceedings which would prevent that being done?

Mr. ANDERSON. Nothing whatever.

Senator BRICE. Then a speedy decree, with the assistance of the Government, might be obtained, and a perfect title to the property transferred to a purchaser?

Mr. ANDERSON. That is undoubtedly so.

Senator BRICE. If there was a proposition made to the Government by a purchaser to pay off the first-mortgage bonds and take the title, and if he would give to the Government a first lien on the entire property now covered by the Government lien for the full face of the Government debt, including interest at a reasonable rate, would that be a good proposition for the Government to accept?

Mr. ANDERSON. That would depend on the rate of interest.

Senator BRICE. Say 3 per cent, secured by a first lien.

Mr. ANDERSON. On the whole 1,400 miles known as the bond-aided portion of the Union Pacific, I think that would be a good proposition.

Senator BRICE. If the rate of interest was larger than 3 per cent, your opinion would be still strengthened?

Mr. ANDERSON. Yes, sir.

Senator BRICE. Suppose the rate of interest was 2 per cent, with a sinking fund secured by a first mortgage?

Mr. ANDERSON. I do not think that that would be as good as a cash payment of $35,000,000.

Senator FRYE (to Senator Brice). You exclude from that question the terminals?

Senator BRICE. No, sir; I include all.

Senator FRYE. The terminals are not a part of the bond-aided road.

Senator BRICE. I include the property now covered by the Government lien.

Senator WOLCOTT (to Mr. Anderson). If a mortgage drawing 3 per cent interest on the 1,400 miles covered by the Government loan would be a good proposition for the Government to accept, better than thirty-five millions in cash, please tell us why a mortgage drawing 2 per cent, covering the whole amount of principal and interest with a sinking fund, is not better than 50 per cent of the amount in cash? Does the difference of 1 per cent furnish a reason why the Government should settle at 50 cents on the dollar?

Mr. ANDERSON. It does. A 2 per cent bond is only worth two-thirds of a 3 per cent bond. A 3 per cent bond such as you describe may be worth 60 cents on the dollar, and a 2 per cent bond would be worth only 40 cents on the dollar, as the security is not very good.

Senator STEWART. In speaking of that security, do you exclude the terminals?

Mr. ANDERSON. I answered the Senator's question just as it was put. In my own mind I think it quite a grave question whether the terminals are now covered by the Government lien or not.

Senator STEWART. In your mind you did include the terminals?

Mr. ANDERSON. I did not. I can not say that my mind acted on that question positively; but, since my attention has been called to it, I should rather, for safety's sake, assume that Senator Brice's question applied solely to the line itself, and excluded the terminals.

Senator STEWART. The Government would be much better secured if the lien included the terminals?

Mr. ANDERSON. Certainly; outside of the mere value of the terminals for the purpose of conducting business those at Council Bluffs, Denver, and Kansas City are of great value.

Senator MORGAN. If this road should be sold for a lump sum it would be necessary to get rid of these suits, or else to get a decree of foreclosure pro forma?

Mr. ANDERSON. I think not. If the reorganization people who own the bonds choose to pay the United States $35,000,000 for an assignment of its lien and of all its rights, I do not see that the United States would have anything to do with the suits. I do not know what their proposition is.

Senator MORGAN. In such a case they would go on and execute their charter powers, running the road just as it is run now?

Mr. ANDERSON. If I was advising the reorganization committee, I should couple the payment of the $35,000,000 to the United States with a provision intended for the benefit of all parties: that permission should be given to the persons making this payment to purchase all the property under foreclosure and to extend a new charter to the company, with such rights, powers, and privileges as might be deemed proper and just; and I should couple the extension of these rights and powers with such safeguards as to the rights of the company and to the management of the property as Congress might think proper.

Senator MORGAN. I suppose you have not considered the question whether, in getting a new charter, it would be necessary also to get the consent of the States through which the road runs?

Mr. ANDERSON. I have considered that question to some extent, and I do not think it necessary to obtain the consent of the States.

Senator MORGAN. There might be a serious difference of opinion about that, and, if there was, that would be a vital question to be settled, would it not?

Mr. ANDERSON. Not vital on the question of paying $35,000,000.

Senator MORGAN. No; but on the question of conducting the road afterwards.

Mr. ANDERSON. I think that the parties who make the payment would take the risk of that. We all take risks in this world.

Senator MORGAN. Suppose it should become necessary to get rid of these lawsuits. In order to complete the plan of the payment of a lump sum, and to transfer the property to the keeping of a new company, do you think that that could be accomplished by any means within your mind? Do you know any means by which it could be done?

Mr. ANDERSON. I only know the fact that the reorganization committee states that it has on deposit a majority of all the bonds represented in any of their litigations; and, if that be so, the reorganization committee can, of course, control all the litigations.

Senator MORGAN. Would the ownership of a majority of the bonds give to that majority the legal right to make some arrangement to which the holders of the remainder of the bonds have not consented?

Mr. ANDERSON. No, sir; the remainder may insist on continuing the proceedings for foreclosure.

Senator MORGAN. If you owned $10,000 of bonds and I owned $5,000, do you think you would have a perfect right to control me in the matter?

Mr. ANDERSON. No; I withdraw my statement about the reorganization committee controlling the outstanding bondholders. They could insist on continuing the proceedings for foreclosure and sale?

Senator MORGAN. Then the outstanding bondholders may be insisting on one proposition and the other parties insisting on a different one?

Mr. ANDERSON. Yes; it often happens that a minority of bondholders desire foreclosure, and that a majority desire to stop foreclosure proceedings, or vice versa.

Senator MORGAN. Would not that very fact make it necessary for the court to interpose its authority and make a decree, to which these people would be bound to render obedience, so that their interest should go along with the interest of the majority?

Mr. ANDERSON. I should say that there will have to be a decree of sale, and a sale of the property, whether the minority bondholders are willing to discontinue proceedings or not. The matter can not get along without a foreclosure, because the Union Pacific Railroad Company has pending against it something like fifteen millions worth of claims arising out of contracts.

Senator MORGAN. So that, in any event, there would have to be a prosecution of these lawsuits to a final decree, and a settlement in court of all the equities of all the parties interested?

Mr. ANDERSON. That is my opinion.

Senator MORGAN. The road, as I understand you, is more prosperous under the present management than it was formerly?

Mr. ANDERSON. I do not think so. It is more prosperous somewhat, I suppose, in 1895 than it was in 1894.

Senator MORGAN. How does 1895 compare with 1892?

Mr. ANDERSON. It does not rival 1892; 1892 eclipses it completely. So do did 1891, and so did the first half of 1893.

Senator MORGAN. But there is a great recovery of prosperity?

Mr. ANDERSON. I wish I could see it. The percentage of increased gross earnings since the 1st of November, 1895, is perhaps 5 or 6 per cent greater as compared with the same part of 1894, which was the lowest point of our Government career.

Senator MORGAN. Still, the prospect of success is increasing?

Mr. ANDERSON. If they have good crops in that region, and can find markets for them, the road will improve and its earnings will increase.

Senator MORGAN. You depend for that on the increased development and the good fortune of the people of the region tributary to the road?

Mr. ANDERSON. Yes, sir.

Senator MORGAN. And on that alone?

Mr. ANDERSON. Good management is of course a factor, but the prosperity of the country served by the railroad is the dominating and controlling figure in determining the prosperity of the railroad itself.

Senator MORGAN. To which you think something might be added, if the road formed a really friendly connection with the Central Pacific?

Mr. ANDERSON. Yes, sir. The relative prosperity of the Union Pacific might come from its controlling more of the freight business of California and more local business than at present. Then it would make much more money than it does at present.

Senator MORGAN. What does the little increase of prosperity which you speak of come from? Does it come from good management or from increased resources?

Mr. ANDERSON. I would not call it an increase of prosperity. That is too dignified a name.

Senator MORGAN. Then call it an increase of the sum of gross earnings.

Mr. ANDERSON. The increase runs perhaps from $50,000 to $100,000 a month.

Senator MORGAN. What does it come from?

Mr. ANDERSON. I can not tell without analyzing the passenger and freight returns.

Senator MORGAN. It is not due to better management, is it?

Mr. ANDERSON. No; I think we managed that road quite as well when it saw its worst days as we do to-day.

The CHAIRMAN. Is there any lessening of the expenses?

Mr. ANDERSON. Yes; of course, the expenses naturally go down when the gross business decreases, and we have also decreased them by a careful attention to a number of things under our control.

The CHAIRMAN. You have been more careful than formerly, have you?

Mr. ANDERSON. We have abstained from expending money for rails, when we would have been willing to spend it if money had been perfectly easy; we have abstained from any extravagance.

Senator STEWART. Are you able to estimate roughly the railroad's proportion of through freight and local business?

Mr. ANDERSON. I would not undertake to state those figures, but they will be called for, and I will have them for the committee on my return from New York.

Senator STEWART. You have the figures accessible?

Mr. ANDERSON. Yes.

Senator WOLCOTT. You do not mean to say, of course, that 2 per cent bonds are worth only half as much as 3 per cent bonds, without having relation to the amount of the sinking fund?

Mr. ANDERSON. I do not think that the sinking fund has anything to do with it.

Senator WOLCOTT. Does it not add to the market value of the bonds?

Mr. ANDERSON. You were asking me to compare 3 per cent bonds with 2 per cent bonds.

Senator WOLCOTT. With a sinking fund, you said that 2 per cent bonds were not as good as 50 cents on the dollar in payment of the Government debt, and you said that 2 per cent bonds were only two-thirds as good as 3 per cent bonds. Do you make that statement without taking into consideration the sinking fund?

Mr. ANDERSON. I meant that if the bond has a long time to run, say fifty years, a 2 per cent is only two-thirds as good as a 3 per cent bond.

Senator WOLCOTT. Do you consider a fifty-year 2 per cent bond, with a fair sinking fund, worth only 50 per cent as much as a 3 per cent bond?

Mr. ANDERSON. If the 3 per cent bond, without a sinking fund, is perfectly well secured, a 2 per cent bond, even with a sinking fund, is worth very little more than half of a 3 per cent bond, if the period be long enough. In a fifty-year bond it would be worth something more, for the period is not long enough. You can compute the exact value of a 2 per cent bond running one hundred years as compared with a 3 per cent bond running the same period and you will find that while there is a difference, arising out of the fact that the period is not indefinite in favor of the 2 per cent, which makes it worth a little more than two-thirds, the difference is extremely small; it is less than three-fourths.

Senator BRICE. The fact that interest is paid during the whole time does not change the character of the answer you gave to me?

Mr. ANDERSON. Not at all.

Senator MORGAN. Are you familiar with the great sweep of country tributary to the Union Pacific Railroad?

Mr. ANDERSON. I have been over it very often, but I am not familiar with it in the sense of understanding its traffic relations.

Senator MORGAN. Is there a large immigration to that country now?

Mr. ANDERSON. Not in Nebraska. Nebraska is the most unhappy corner in the United States. For the last two years the crops have been disastrous. I have heard Mr. Clarke estimate the number of people who left Nebraska in 1894 as high as 100,000. I speak of western Nebraska. The Snake River country is a beautiful country, and there is quite a large settlement out there. There is quite a large area of beautiful land on the Snake River. It is not over 3,000 feet above the level of the sea, and in that respect it is much more desirable than the land in Wyoming and Utah.

Senator MORGAN. They are making those lands valuable by irrigation?

Mr. ANDERSON. Yes.

Senator MORGAN. Would you not say that this country has progressed compared to what it was twenty years ago?

Mr. ANDERSON. Yes, taking it as a whole, I would. There are some parts where progress has not been appreciable.

Senator MORGAN. Would you say that it would be a safe calculation that a railroad, properly conducted, for the next hundred years would be a very useful and profitable property in that country?

Mr. ANDERSON. It would be a very useful property.

Senator MORGAN. What would be your estimate of its profits?

Mr. ANDERSON. That depends so much on the considerations of management and competition and of prices of products grown in that country that I can not form any estimate.

Senator MORGAN. Placing up all difference of management, etc., against the influx of population and the known fertility of the soil with the aid of irrigation, what would you say would be the profit to a railroad company which would get this property at $35,000,000 during the next hundred years?

Mr. ANDERSON. I am not able to form any estimate. I think it would be a good property.

Senator MORGAN. Do you think it would be an enormous one?

Mr. ANDERSON. No, sir.

Senator MORGAN. Can you state any reason why there would not be a great profit in it at $35,000,000?

Mr. ANDERSON. The whole property would cost the people embarking in the enterprise something like $100,000,000. I only say that, judging from the experience of the Santa Fe road, the Union Pacific, the Central Pacific, and a number of other railroads which have for the last twenty or thirty years expected to reap profits from the development of the West, there has been a great disappointment, and most of those roads have gone into the hands of receivers. The future may be no better than the past has been.

Senator MORGAN. But after they have passed into the hands of receivers, they seem to be able to pay interest on their first-mortgage bonds?

Mr. ANDERSON. Yes; but that is not exactly making an enormous fortune.

Senator MORGAN. You say that there are about $13,000,000 in suit against the Union Pacific Railroad Company?

Mr. ANDERSON. There are large claims existing against the Union Pacific as a corporation which can not be adjusted except through the intervention of a foreclosure and sale.

Senator MORGAN. These claims are presented to different tribunals, are they not?

Mr. ANDERSON. No, sir; they never have been presented in court. There is not a sufficient expectation of return to make them worth presenting.

Senator MORGAN. Has there been no order of court to creditors to come in and prove their claims?

Mr. ANDERSON. The court directs the receivers to pay all the obligations of the corporation as a going concern; that is, all that have accrued within six months prior to our appointment. All the obligations of this nature we have paid.

Senator MORGAN. But there has not been a creditors' bill to invite creditors to prove their claims?

Mr. ANDERSON. No. The original stockholders' bill has been superceded by the foreclosure bill; there are five or six foreclosure bills. That is the present attitude of the matter.

Senator MORGAN. You do not mean that there are five or six foreclosure bills in the same court?

Mr. ANDERSON. No, they are in different courts, but they are nearly all within the eighth circuit. The same receivers have been appointed in all the bills, so as to preserve the integrity of the property as far as possible.

Senator MORGAN. The five or six foreclosure suits are being conducted, I suppose, in perfect harmony?

Mr. ANDERSON. Do you mean as far as the administration of the property is concerned?

Senator MORGAN. I mean in harmony between the courts

Mr. ANDERSON. Yes; we have no different interests between the courts.

Senator MORGAN. Which court is considered the mother court; which sends out the decrees for the rest of them?

Mr. ANDERSON. The eighth circuit.

Senator MORGAN. And the other courts, without differences, have adopted these decrees and registered them?

Mr. ANDERSON. In the ninth circuit we filed ancillary bills, and the ninth circuit acquiesces in all the proceedings taken in the eighth circuit. It appoints the same receivers and facilitates their operations in every way. The case which Mr. Pierce referred to was a case arising out of an application to appoint a separate receiver for the Oregon Short Line. In that case Judge Gilbert delivered an opinion in which he made a statement in regard to a state of comity as between different courts, and made an application of that principle to that very application for a receiver.

Senator MORGAN. No court of the whole group has undertaken to set up for itself or to set up its own jurisdiction over these bills except the mother court?

Mr. ANDERSON. No, sir; that is correct.

Senator MORGAN. But you have no security that no court will do it?

Mr. ANDERSON. No, sir; we have no security from the court.

Senator MORGAN. There is nothing to constrain these other tribunals to regard the decrees of the mother court?

Mr. ANDERSON. No, sir.

Senator MORGAN. So that in the winding up you may have difficulties?

Mr. ANDERSON. We do not anticipate them.

Senator BRICE. The Union Pacific Road, with which these reorganization plans deal, is all within the eighth circuit, is it not?

Mr. ANDERSON. I have been answering in regard to all the foreclosure suits in which we have been appointed receivers, the Oregon Short Line as well as the Union Pacific.

Senator MORGAN. This main company, the Union Pacific, has an interest in all these litigations?

Mr. ANDERSON. No, sir—or an interest so remote that it counts for nothing. Let me explain: The Oregon Short Line and some of the other roads were constructed under the auspices of the Union Pacific. The Union Pacific furnished the capital, and the bonds and stocks issued in payment went first to the Union Pacific as the constructor. But in order to provide for them, the Union Pacific collateral trusts were formed, and all these stocks and securities are held in these collateral trusts. The collateral-trust mortgages are not counted as part of the debt to the Government, but the amount due on them will entirely absorb all the stocks and bonds which represent any control of the other roads, so that the Union Pacific, as such, has no interest in the Oregon Short Line which could be counted as an asset of any value at all. All that it has is an owner's equity, which would remain after the obligations were discharged.

Senator MORGAN. Looking at the necessity of retaining these cases in court until a final decree is made (no matter what arrangement), are you aware that a number of learned gentlemen of the legal profession insist very earnestly that what are called the second-mortgage bonds are really first-mortgage bonds?

Mr. ANDERSON. You mean that the Government lien has priority of the first mortgage?

Senator MORGAN. Yes.

Mr. ANDERSON. I am not aware of a claim quite in that shape, but I am aware that a claim has been made that some of the first-mortgage bonds issued by the Union Pacific are open to attack.

Senator MORGAN. I have been informed that both these questions arise.

Mr. ANDERSON. I have not heard that anybody has claimed that the Government lien is prior to the lien which is known as the first-mortgage bonds of the Union Pacific.

Senator MORGAN. I am assured that such an insistence is expected to be made. In that event it would not be ever possible to get this matter settled except by a decree of the court?

Mr. ANDERSON. I have already stated that I do not think that the relations of the creditors of the Union Pacific, as they seem to-day, can possibly be settled except through the intervention of a final decree and sale.

Senator MORGAN. A mere assignment of the first mortgage would not have the effect to settle these questions?

Mr. ANDERSON. The assignment of the Government lien in consideration of a lump sum of $35,000,000 being paid would not terminate the litigation.

Senator MORGAN. It would merely let the Government out?

Mr. ANDERSON. It would only let the Government out.

Senator BRICE. Do I understand you to say that the gross earnings of the Union Pacific were somewhat larger in 1895 than they were in 1894?

Mr. ANDERSON. I said that the net earnings were larger.

Senator MORGAN. How about the gross earnings?

Mr. ANDERSON. I think they were about the same.

Senator BRICE. I find a statement of net earnings of the Union Pacific on page 9 of this book (The Plan and Agreement to Reorganize the Union Pacific Railroad), showing that the net earnings in each of the nine years from 1885 to 1895 were more than $6,000,000, after subtracting the taxes, except for the calendar year 1894, when the net earnings were $4,315,000; and I understand you to say that the net earnings for the calendar year 1895 have been about five millions?

Mr. ANDERSON. Yes, sir.

Senator BRICE. My inquiry is why the receivers, in the three years in which the road earned more than twice the amount required to pay the interest on the first-mortgage bonds, should have allowed the first-mortgage bonds to become foreclosable, the receivers applying the earnings to some other purpose, so as to afford an opportunity to the first-mortgage bondholders to keep out the Government?

Mr. ANDERSON. I answered that question to the committee in 1895, and I refer this committee to that answer for details. I would say, however, in explanation of the question, that while $4,315,000 represents the amount of our net earnings, a sum amounting to $1,200,000, which forms a part of that $4,315,000, is never actually received by the railroad. It enters into the account of earnings and is charged as part of the receipts; but it is held by the Government of the United States as being the earnings of the Union Pacific for the transportation of troops and munitions of war, and under the provisions of the Thurman Act it is credited, part to the bond and interest account and part to the sinking fund. So that that reduces what I should call the fund available for interest to something like $3,000,000.

The CHAIRMAN. The sum returned by the Government is about $1,200,000 annually?

Mr. ANDERSON. Yes; eleven or twelve hundred thousand dollars. Now, if you examine the amount falling due for interest, and especially if you consider the fact that in the first three months after our appointment we paid interest rather more rapidly than we should have done because an item of $600,000 on the first-mortgage bonds of the Northern Division became due within two months after our appointment, so that we had to meet that out of two months' earnings (two poor months), you will see that the whole amount received by us was not sufficient to prevent the bonds becoming foreclosable because of the failure to meet coupons at maturity.

Senator BRICE. I wish that at your leisure you would put that in such terms as would make it a clear answer to the statement (which confuses any attempt to judge of that matter) that the receivers have not paid interest, and that they have not done so for some other reason than a desire to properly administer their trust, as, for instance, a desire to force a foreclosure.

Mr. ANDERSON. The receivers are absolutely strangers to any desire of that kind, as well as to the suggestion which has been made that they might abstain from favoring the adjustment in order to retain their office. Such a statement is really not worthy of discussion.

Senator WOLCOTT. You did not understand that there was any such suggestion made by me?

Mr. ANDERSON. Not by you; but I heard that that suggestion had been made. This subject of the application of money to pay interest should be taken in connection with the disposition of the balance which the receivers have in cash. To-day we have a large balance of money on hand, which Judge Sanford does not permit us to apply to the payment of interest without making full provision for the care and custody of the property, and to prevent the possibility of any division of the road receiving more than its fair share, as against another division.

Senator BRICE. It is fair to the receivers, and is absolutely necessary to the committee, that the apparently large surplus over the amount required to pay the interest on the first-mortgage bonds should be explained in connection with the failure to keep up interest payments.

The CHAIRMAN. In other words, to remove the inference which the public would draw.

Senator BRICE. And after hearing the statements made by Mr. Anderson and Mr. Pierce that the Government could be foreclosed of all its interest in the property by reason of that failure to pay interest on the first-mortgage bonds.

Mr. ANDERSON. It is rather by reason of the maturity of some of the first-mortgage bonds.

Senator BRICE. By reason of anything which entitles the holders of the first-mortgage bonds to a decree.

Mr. ANDERSON. I think that the overdue interest could be easily managed if the bonds had not begun to mature. It is the maturity of the bonds which is the serious question.

THE CENTRAL PACIFIC.

STATEMENT OF MR. HUNTINGTON—Continued.

Mr. HUNTINGTON said:

I expected to have some figures this morning, but I did not get them, and therefore would prefer to wait. I organized the Central Pacific Railroad and pretty nearly built it. I was going to say just a word to the committee. Our Government bonds were sold for gold, and did not realize more than 40 cents on the dollar, and we used the gold to build the road. The physical obstructions to be overcome from Sacramento, in crossing the Sierra Madre Mountains to the big bend of the Truckee (138 miles), was said by good engineers to make that part of the road more expensive than the whole 1,032 miles between Ogden and Omaha. Everything was very expensive there and in California. After the road was finished we had to build the snowsheds, and there was 198,800,000 feet of lumber used in that work. I have seen ten locomotives, frequently, behind a snowplow, and we have had out as many as fifteen hundred men in clearing the road of snow. We have paid some of our bonds, have kept the road clean, and paid all our current debts. We are not in default to anybody. The Central Pacific is in good hands, and whatever Congress will agree to in the matter of the Government debt will be done.

Senator MORGAN. Why did you not use silver instead of gold when you built the road?

Senator STEWART. Silver was at that time worth 3 cents on the dollar more than gold.

Mr. HUNTINGTON. We have no mortgage on our rolling stock; everything has been paid and kept clean, and we are willing to pay a hundred cents on the dollar of the Government debt if we get a chance.

SIOUX CITY AND PACIFIC RAILROAD.

STATEMENT OF MR. LITTLER—Continued.

Mr. DAVID T. LITTLER, counsel for the Chicago and Northwestern Railroad Company, addressed the committee. He said:

The bill before the Senate authorizes the appointment of three Commissioners with power to adjust and settle the claim of the United States against the Sioux City and Pacific Railroad Company.

The Sioux City and Pacific Railroad Company is one of the subsidized roads, under the acts of Congress of 1862 and 1864. The subsidized portions of this road, both as to bonds and lands, extend from Sioux City, Iowa, to California Junction, in said State, a distance of 69.75 miles, and from the latter point to Fremont, Nebr., a distance of 32.02 miles, making a total length of subsidized road of 101.77 miles.

That portion of the road from California Junction to Missouri Valley is 5.84 miles in length, and was not subsidized.

The bond subsidy of this road was at the rate of $16,000 per mile; making, in the aggregate, $1,628,320. This subsidy, by the acts of Congress, is made subordinate to the first mortgage of the company, which was also for $16,000 per mile, or $1,628,320.

The Government subsidy bonds bear date as follows:

March 6, 1868	$792,000
March 30, 1868	320,000
March 3, 1869	576,320

Interest began to run on the first issue March 10, 1868; on the second issue, March 30, 1868, and on the third issue, March 3, 1869.

The land grant to this company amounted to 60,000 acres. The company received under this grant 4,343.11 acres in the State of Iowa and 37,055.12 acres in the State of Nebraska, making a total of 41,398.23 acres.

Senator Brice, chairman of the Committee on Pacific Railroads, in his "partial report" on the Pacific railroads, of date January 28, 1895, in speaking of this company, said:

> This road was never of any consequence as a part of the Union Pacific system; in fact, as the commission of 1887 said, "the road is of but slight importance and it is no part of any complete system of railroads."

From the time of the completion of this road up to 1884 its history is unimportant and wholly unimportant to be considered in connection with the bill under consideration. In 1884 it passed under the control of the Chicago and Northwestern Railway Company by the purchase and transfer to the latter of nearly all its capital stock and is now a part of that company's through line from Omaha to St. Paul.

For a more detailed history of the Sioux City and Pacific Railroad Company, from the date of its organization up to the present time, reference is made to the report of the honorable Commissioner of Railroads to the Secretary of the Interior, which brings the history of the company down to the 1st of January, 1895.

On page 90 of the above report the financial condition of the company is stated up to June 30, 1895, and is as follows:

ASSETS.

Cost of road, fixtures, and equipments	$5,749,007.31
Fuel, material, and stores on hand	46,732.64
Accounts receivable	40,920.87
Due from other companies on account of traffic	7,971.83
Half Government transportation on aided road, applied to bond and interest account	86,281.03
Government transportation on nonaided road, applied to bond and interest account	21,255.99
Due from United States, unsettled accounts	263,951.87
Cash on hand	170,933.58
Total	6,387,055.12

LIABILITIES.

First-mortgage bonds	$1,628,000.00
Interest on same, due and accrued	1,140.00
Interest on same, accrued, not due	48,840.00
United States subsidy bonds	1,628,320.00
Interest on same, paid by United States	2,636,687.89
Interest on preferred stock, accrued, not due	2,957.51
Pay rolls and vouchers	48,110.00
Total debt	5,994,055.40
Capital stock	2,068,400.00
Total stock and debt	8,062,455.40
Deficit	1,675,400.28

Revenue and expenditures for year ended June 30, 1895.

REVENUE.

Earnings	$437, 428. 68	
Profit and loss	3, 832. 82	
Total		$441, 261. 50

EXPENDITURES.

Operating expenses	$294, 173. 87	
Interest on first-mortgage bonds	97, 680. 00	
Interest on other funded debt	97, 699. 20	
New construction	64. 14	
New equipment	47. 75	
Interest on preferred stock	11, 830. 00	
Total		$501, 494. 96
Deficit		60, 233. 46

The United States Pacific Railroad Commission in discussing the financial resources of the Sioux City and Pacific Railroad Company in connection with the form of the bill drawn by the Commission for the purpose of settling the Government indebtedness, on page 128 of its report, states among other things—

It is very doubtful whether the above-named company could meet the requirements of the proposed bill.

The financial history of this road from beginning to end clearly establishes the proposition that the subsidizing of the road was an unfortunate venture for the Government. As already stated it is really no part of the great system of roads which connected the Pacific Ocean with the Missouri River. The road has never been able to pay any portion of the principal of the subsidy bonds, nor any considerable part of the interest.

The facts presented not only justify but require Congress to provide some means by which the Government can settle and ascertain the value of its lien upon the property of the company. The Chicago and Northwestern Railway Company is willing to pay in cash the value of that lien as it may hereafter be established by testimony to be taken by the Commission authorized by the bill under consideration. The bill confers upon the Commissioners absolute power to settle the claim of the Government with the company, subject, however, to the approval of the President of the United States.

Senator FRYE. Did I not report a bill for the settlement of the debt of this road?

Mr. LITTLER. You did, and it passed the Senate without opposition. In view of my experience as a United States Pacific Railroad Commissioner, I think it very important that this bill should be amended so as to authorize a majority of any commission which may be appointed to make a report. There might be one contrary man on the committee.

Senator FRYE. What does the bill require now?

Mr. LITTLER. That there should be a report of the commission.

Senator FRYE. Does not that mean a report of the majority of the commission?

Mr. LITTLER. No, sir.

Senator FRYE. Mr. Coombs desires to ask Mr. Littler some questions in relation to his figures.

Mr. COOMBS (who appears before the committee in opposition to the

Sioux City and Pacific Railroad bill) said: Mr. Chairman, a part of my proposition is that a bill for reorganization is substantially a Chicago and Northwestern proposition, and the matter on which I will ask you to hear me is involved somewhat in the Sioux City and Pacific road. It is of interest to know what its relations may be to this matter. The Sioux City and Pacific Railroad was completed as far as the valley of the Missouri in the spring of 1868, and to Fremont in 1869. I believe, Mr. Littler, it had no bridge across the Missouri River until 1883?

Mr. LITTLER. I think so.

The CHAIRMAN. It has no bridge now; it has a traffic right over the Elkhorn road.

Mr. LITTLER. I do not know the name of the bridge, as it has nothing whatever to do with the case.

Mr. COOMBS. The bridge was built on the application of the Sioux City and Pacific road, and that is one of the points concerning which I want to ask Mr. Littler some questions.

The CHAIRMAN. Is not that called the Blair Bridge?

Mr. COOMBS. Yes. From 1871 to 1879, at the time when ten miles of the Fremont, Elkhorn and Missouri Valley road was built, it was underleased to the Sioux City, was it not?

Mr. LITTLER. You will find a complete answer to that inquiry in the last report of the United States Pacific Railroad Commission. I do not think it at all important or germain to this bill, and did not mention it in my remarks to the committee. You will find the whole history of the road in the report of the United States Pacific Railway Commission.

Mr. COOMBS. The Fremont, Elkhorn and Missouri Valley road, and the Sioux City and Pacific road, are there reports of their operations anywhere?

Mr. LITTLER. Not that I know of.

Mr. COOMBS. Governor Pattison made a report at one time in which he stated that Mr. Blair's books for the construction of the bridge could not be found; are there any books to show what the road cost?

Mr. LITTLER. You will find by reference to the report of the United States Pacific Railroad Commission that we had great trouble in finding what it cost. Mr. Blair presented a little book, about one-eighth of an inch thick, in which the entire proceedings, as far as his road was concerned, were contained. If you turn to our report, you will find what we say on that subject.

Mr. COOMBS. Mr. Pattison further reports that the books of the Sioux City Railroad Company showed that it had paid $260,000 to the Fremont, Elkhorn and Missouri Valley road. Do you know how that is?

Mr. LITTLER. I do not. You will find all the knowledge we had on that subject stated in our report as to the financial condition of the road. We did not agree with Governor Pattison on any question either of law or of fact.

Mr. COOMBS. My suggestion is that the Sioux City and Pacific Railroad money has gone to the Fremont, Elkhorn and Missouri Valley road.

Mr. LITTLER. I do not know; and for the purpose of this bill I do not care.

Mr. COOMBS. In getting at the value of the road it would be well to know something of what it cost, of where the money had gone, and whether the company was insolvent.

Mr. LITTLER. I do not think that the fact that the promoters of that enterprise who handled the Government bonds and the first-mortgage bonds and the land grant may have squandered the money or may have misapplied it has anything whatever to do with the bill before the committee.

Mr. COOMBS. Not a thing; I did not want to drift into that. My inquiry bears on the value of the road and its effect on the country which it was intended to serve.

Mr. LITTLER. Would it not be a good thing for you to appear before the commission provided for in the bill when it is appointed? That is to be the very object of the commission—to find the value of the lien—and the Chicago and Northwestern Railroad Company proposes to pay in cash the value of the lien as it may be established by the commission.

Mr. COOMBS. Perhaps so, Mr. Littler. In 1878 the Fremont, Elkhorn and Missouri Valley Company began an extension which for two years ran over 250 miles of the Sioux City and Pacific Road. About 1883 it had some 31 locomotives and 600 or 700 cars. It stayed under lease for three years, when it disappeared from the Sioux City and Pacific Road, and that was the first year that the Elkhorn, Fremont and Missouri Valley Road reported an equipment. It had then 78 locomotives and 2,000 cars. What I am getting at is whether Mr. Pattison was right in saying that the books showed $260,000 paid to the Fremont, Elkhorn and Missouri Valley Railroad, and whether they paid $544,000 for cars in 1883 and 1884, and whether, three years afterwards, the cars disappeared from their list?

Mr. LITTLER. I can not answer that question. You will find all the testimony which was taken by the Pacific Railroad Commission in seven volumes, and if you have the enterprise to peruse these volumes, you will find all that was proven before that Commission, and you will find whether Governor Pattison told the truth or whether Mr. Anderson and myself told the truth.

Mr. COOMBS. Is there anyway by which I can find out whether that statement is true?

Mr. LITTLER. Allow me to ask you in what capacity you appear? Is it as amicus curiæ of the committee?

The CHAIRMAN. Mr. Coombs's object, as I understand, is to get an amendment to this Sioux City and Pacific Railroad bill directing a communication of the roads leading west with the Sioux City, and eventually with the Union Pacific.

Mr. COOMBS. You are right.

Senator WOLCOTT. I understand, also, from his opening statement, that he considers Mr. Littler's measure unwise.

Mr. COOMBS. I think that my suggestion will be that the only color there is for the reorganization committee is the Chicago and Northwestern Railroad Company, and that the Sioux City and Pacific Railroad and Fremont, Elkhorn and Missouri Valley road are both absolutely Chicago and Northwestern roads, although they were built as part of the Union Pacific. There seems to have been a large amount of money and rolling stock which has gone over from the Sioux City road to the Fremont, Elkhorn and Missouri Valley road.

Senator FRYE. Do you desire an amendment to the bill touching the Sioux City road as well as the Union Pacific?

Mr. COOMBS. No; I only want to keep the whole matter together.

Senator FRYE. You mean that the Sioux City proposition is part of the whole proposition?

Mr. COOMBS. Yes.

The CHAIRMAN. We have no evidence of that. Can you provide us with evidence of it?

Mr. COOMBS. I know only what I can state when the committee will be kind enough to hear me.

Senator FRYE. You want to be heard on this bill as well as the other?

Mr. COOMBS. I do not care.

Senator STEWART. Are you opposed to that mode of settling the matter?

Mr. COOMBS. In a way, I am; the combination which exists to-day is remarkable. The Chicago and Northwestern Railroad is a large factor in a great combination of railroads. It reaches half of the country west of Chicago, and within its radius are all the principal points—Sioux City, Omaha, Denver, Minneapolis, and St. Paul; and it has one branch which stretches away off into the West, within a hundred miles of the new transcontinental line, which would be a competitor of the Union Pacific system. All of the freight of that vast half circle of country is gathered up by this road, and it is the interest of the owners of this road to carry this freight to Chicago; four out of seven of the members of the executive committee of the Chicago and Northwestern road are Vanderbilt people. The Lake Shore road, which takes the freight from Chicago east, is part of the same property; so is the New York Central—so that that combination controls everything and takes all the freight.

Senator STEWART. How does that injure the country?

Mr. COOMBS. The Union Pacific and the Chicago and Northwestern roads, mainly in combination, have so arranged that that country is herringboned by fifteen or twenty roads. The Chicago and Northwestern not only has control of the combination I have indicated, but has had for years a contract with the Union Pacific, by which every pound of freight originating at or destined for any point reached by the other is exchanged between them, to the exclusion of all other roads. And I say four of the seven directors of the Chicago and Northwestern road are representatives of the Vanderbilt interest. They include two members of the reorganization committee—Mr. Hughitt and Mr. Depew. A third member of the reorganization is Oliver Ames, 2d.

Senator BRICE. What do you want? Do you want part of the fund realized from any settlement to be applied to the completion of the Sioux City road?

Mr. COOMBS. That is our proposition.

The CHAIRMAN. Was there not a provision in the House bill last year (the Riley bill) that any railway that would make a physical connection with the Union Pacific should have the same treatment as any other road?

Mr. COOMBS. Yes; there was such an item debated before the House committee last year.

The CHAIRMAN. Did not the House committee last year agree to report a bill with that amendment in it?

Mr. COOMBS. Yes; and in three days afterwards there was a memorial received from the Union Pacific people saying that they would not accept a bill with such unusual restrictions in it.

The CHAIRMAN. But still, the committee did report a bill with that amendment?

Mr. COOMBS. Yes, the Riley bill was reported; but its report was immediately followed by a notification from the Union Pacific Company that it would not accept a bill with such unusual restrictions in it.

Senator WOLCOTT. Will any bill containing that restriction answer your object?

Mr. COOMBS. I think it is of consequence that in any settlement with the Chicago and Northwestern the Sioux City and Pacific should be taken into account, and that as much relief as possible from that source will be turned to it. I am making these disconnected statements so that it shall not be said that I sat still and listened to the figures of Mr. Littler which I should have questioned at the time. If I may also refer to Governor Pattison's minority report, it was said in it that Mr. Blair offered a million of dollars over and above the first-mortgage lien. (To Mr. Littler:) Do you know whether that was so?

Mr. LITTLER. If it was so, you will find it in Mr. Blair's testimony, taken by the United States Pacific Railroad Commission. That testimony is contained in seven volumes, and every volume is indexed; so, you can find it

Mr. COOMBS. There appears from 1885 to the present time, in Poor's Manual, apparently, a payment of Government interest on the Sioux City subsidy bonds by the Chicago and Northwestern road, and there is a deficit account amounting to $1,600,000. Are you sufficiently familiar with the finances of the company to know whether that is so?

Mr. LITTLER. No, sir. You will find the accounts of that company with the United States Government approved by the actuary of the Treasury, who stated the accounts on correct principles, and you will find exactly the amount due on all accounts whatever up to the day of that statement.

Mr. COOMBS. Do you know whether the Sioux City and Pacific Railroad did build the bridge across the Missouri?

Mr. LITTLER. I know that it did not build it as a corporation. It may be that some of its stock or bonds went to build it. The Chicago and Northwestern and other roads did build it.

Mr. COOMBS. Is the Sioux City and Pacific Railroad still paying dividends on its preferred stock?

Mr. LITTLER. I think that very likely, it is; but these are all matters which our report shows.

Mr. COOMBS. The last number of Poor's Manual shows $350,000 belonging to this road in the hands of the Government.

Mr. LITTLER. I can not state from memory whether it is right or not. I have not had occasion to refer to that subject since 1887 until I was retained as counsel by the Chicago and Northwestern Railroad Company to prepare this bill.

Senator FRYE. Does the Union Pacific Railroad Company desire to be heard any further before the committee in regard to its proposition?

Mr. PIERCE. Yes, sir; and to submit the draft of a bill.

The CHAIRMAN. And when will you submit it?

Mr. PIERCE. I should like to be heard in the latter part of next week, if convenient to the committee.

The committee adjourned until Friday, February 14, at 10 a. m.

WASHINGTON, D. C., *February 14, 1896.*

The committee met at 10.30 a. m.

Present: Senators Gear (chairman), Stewart, Wolcott, Frye, Brice, and Morgan.

THE UNION PACIFIC.

STATEMENT OF MR. WINSLOW S. PIERCE—Continued.

Mr. Pierce said:

Mr. CHAIRMAN AND GENTLEMEN OF THE COMMITTEE: Since the last session of the committee at which I was present, and in the light of the experience of that session, I became very strongly impressed with the conviction that it would be a most difficult, if not an impracticable, task for the committee to take such testimony and to make such inquiry and investigation as would give to it all the data that it would require in order to form, or to accept the form of, a funding bill or of a fixed sum bill; and I have therefore prepared for submission to the committee a bill providing for the creation of a commission. I think that it will at least have the merit of being suggestive to the committee and of affording a basis for discussion and consideration.

This bill provides for—

(1) Appointment by the President, subject to approval of the Senate, of a commission of three members to investigate, determine, and report to the President the fair cash value of the claim and lien of the United States.

(2) Authority to the commissioners to subpœna and examine witnesses, to have process of courts, to appoint a secretary; fixes compensation of commissioners and secretary and makes maximum appropriation $50,000.

(3) Report of commissioners or a majority, subject to approval of President, to be conclusive as to sum which, together with the amounts appropriated for commissioners' expenses, etc., may be paid for claim and lien of the United States; the Secretary of the Treasury upon such payment to execute instrument of assignment of lien and claim, reserving sinking fund.

(4) Authority to purchasers to organize new company, empowered to acquire and operate the lines and property of the Union Pacific Railway Company, with such corporate powers as are necessarily involved.

(5) Repeal of provisions of prior acts which would be inapplicable to the reorganized company under the new conditions, but reserving the Government's preference right to transportation of mails, troops, munitions of war, etc.

(6) Authority and direction to the Attorney-General, in default of payment of amount fixed by commission, to foreclose the lien of the Government, and upon sale to bid the amount of the indebtedness to the United States.

(7) Reservation of remedies to the United States and of power to alter, amend, or repeal.

Senator MORGAN. Is there a provision in that bill for the commission to make a contract with the purchasers of the road?

Mr. PIERCE. The third provision of the bill is the one to which that inquiry is addressed. It provides that the report of the commission shall be conclusive as to the sum to be paid, subject, however, to the approval of the President. It provides the time within which the commission shall report, and the time within which, after that report, the sum found by it shall be paid.

Senator MORGAN. It does not provide for the negotiation of contract between the purchaser and the Government? It merely provides a sum to be paid.

Mr. PIERCE. A sum to be paid; and the purchasers or their assignees or nominees are to organize as a corporation for the purpose of acquiring the Union Pacific.

Senator MORGAN. That is, the purchaser under foreclosure?

Mr. PIERCE. The purchasers of the claim of the Government. The reorganization committee will go on and foreclose on the property under their own mortgage.

Senator MORGAN. Your bill is on the line of Senator Thurston's bill?

Mr. PIERCE. Not entirely. I think there are some elements of similitude between them. This bill provides for the establishment of a commission to do these things.

Senator STEWART. It provides for the sale of liens without foreclosure, subrogating the purchaser to all the rights of the Government.

Mr. PIERCE. Precisely.

Senator STEWART. Does it provide for immediate payment in cash?

Mr. PIERCE. It provides that the commission shall report on or before July 1, 1896, and that the amount fixed by the commission shall be paid on or before January 1, 1897.

Senator MORGAN. Is there any reason why that arrangement should not extend so as to include both roads?

Mr. PIERCE. I think not. Some provisions of the bill may be peculiarly applicable to the Union Pacific, on account of reorganization, but I have no doubt that the provisions of the bill can be adapted so as to cover the Central Pacific.

Senator MORGAN. So that one commission should take charge of the whole subject.

Mr. PIERCE. Yes, sir.

The CHAIRMAN. Do the parties whom you represent object to the joint arrangement?

Mr. PIERCE. Not if the general provisions of the bill can apply to both roads; but it appears almost impracticable to deal with the two properties in a single measure. This bill, if it should meet the approval of the committee, would eliminate the necessity for prolonged discussion here, and for the inquiry, the preliminary steps of which were taken at the early session of the committee. I have with me a number of copies of the proposed bill, and I will hand them to the chairman and the members of the committee.

Senator MORGAN. From whom does that proposition come which you submit?

Mr. PIERCE. It is suggested by us on behalf of the reorganization committee, but rather as a proposition and basis of discussion than as a complete measure.

Senator MORGAN. It is something to which the reorganization committee gives its assent and its preference, beyond any measure which we may attempt to enact here for the sale of this road or the funding of its debt on the basis that you argued the other day. It is a substitute for that.

Mr. PIERCE. I can not say that the reorganization committee would give its preference to this bill over that. The difficulty in the way of reaching conclusions in legislation of this character is so great that we supposed that this might probably be the best way of reaching a conclusion, and for that reason we suggest it.

Senator FRYE. Is there anything in this bill which binds, or can you provide a bill which will bind the reorganization committee to accept and pay whatever the commission reports?

Mr. PIERCE. We can include a provision binding the reorganization committee to do this; but I do not think that a provision of that kind would be acceptable. The commission might fix seventy millions as the value of the Government lien, or some other exaggerated sum; but, of course, it is not to be supposed that it would do that.

Senator FRYE. Your proposition simply allows the commission to be appointed, and to go on and ascertain the probable value of this indebtedness of the Union Pacific to the Government?

Mr. PIERCE. Yes.

Senator FRYE. And to report their finding to the President?

Mr. PIERCE. Yes.

Senator FRYE. And if the President approves, that shall be found to be the value of the indebtedness?

Mr. PIERCE. Yes.

Senator FRYE. But it does not, and it can not, by law, make any provision by which the people whom you represent shall accept the judgment of the commission and pay the money.

Mr. PIERCE. No; but the company which I represent, holding 75 per cent of the bonded indebtedness of the Union Pacific and 90 per cent of the capital stock of the company, is in a better condition to bid for the property or to accept the conclusions of the commission than any other interest would be in. Therefore, there is a reasonable probability that the finding of the commission (which we assume will be just) will be accepted by the reorganization committee; but if the reorganization committee does not accept it it will retire from the matter and the Government will go on and exercise its rights to the extreme, no doubt. That is the theory of the bill.

Senator MORGAN. I was not here the first day that you made your statement to the committee. Have you given anywhere the list of names of the gentlemen who comprise this reorganization committee?

Mr. PIERCE. Yes; the names appear on the pamphlet of the reorganization plan, which I have already submitted. I will see that you are furnished with one.

Senator MORGAN. Please do so; I have not seen it.

The CHAIRMAN. What percentage of the securities of the Union Pacific interest does your reorganization committee represent?

Mr. PIERCE. Our reorganization committee represents very nearly 75 per cent of all the bonds, and I should say 90 per cent of the stock. That is their actual deposit with the committee.

The CHAIRMAN. Then 25 per cent of the securities and 10 per cent of the stock do not give their assent to the method proposed by the reorganization committee?

Mr. PIERCE. They have not yet deposited their securities.

The CHAIRMAN. Do not some of them seriously object to the reorganization plan?

Mr. PIERCE. I know of no objections to the reorganization plan, except one, and that is indicated by a circular signed by a man named Rogers. What his relations are to the security holders I am not able to state.

The CHAIRMAN. Does he not claim to represent five or six millions?

Mr. PIERCE. I have seen a statement in the newspapers of there being such a claim, but I do not understand that any securities have been deposited with him.

Senator MORGAN. Do you know what proportion of these gentlemen who compose the reorganization committee are nonresidents or aliens?

Mr. PIERCE. I do not think that any are nonresidents or aliens.

Senator MORGAN. They are all Americans?

Mr. PIERCE. So far as I know. I am quite certain as to all except one. There are no aliens among them. However, the committee itself would not necessarily be the purchaser of the road, but would constitute a new committee.

The CHAIRMAN. Do I understand you to mean that the owners of the securities are not aliens or nonresidents?

Mr. PIERCE. I can not tell about that. I know that a good many of those securities came from abroad.

Senator MORGAN. I put that question only for this reason: It might very naturally be expected, if control of the road should pass into the hands of foreigners, that complications would arise between us and them, and foreign Governments might be expected to see that the rights of their subjects were not frittered away or improperly interfered with. That is my reason for putting the question. I want to get the whole subject before the committee.

Mr. Pierce presented the bill submitted by him. It is as follows:

A BILL to amend an act entitled "An act to aid in the construction of a railroad and telegraph line from the Missouri River to the Pacific Ocean, and to secure to the Government the use of the same for postal, military, and other purposes," approved July first, eighteen hundred and sixty-two; also to amend an act approved July second, eighteen hundred and sixty-four; and also an act approved May seventh, eighteen hundred and seventy-eight, both in amendment of said first-mentioned act, and other acts amendatory thereof and supplemental thereto; and to provide for the settlement of claims growing out of the issue of bonds to aid in the construction of certain of the railroads, and to secure the settlement of all indebtedness to the United States of certain companies therein mentioned.

Whereas the subsidy bonds issued by the United States in aid of the construction of the railroad of the Union Pacific Railroad Company were, pursuant to the acts of Congress of the United States approved July first, eighteen hundred and sixty-two, and July second, eighteen hundred and sixty-four, issued to the amount of twenty-seven million two hundred and thirty-six thousand five hundred and twelve dollars, and the subsidy bonds of the United States issued in aid of the construction of the railroad of the Kansas Pacific Railway Company (originally incorporated under the name of the Leavenworth, Pawnee and Western Railroad Company) were issued pursuant to the provisions of the said last-mentioned acts to the amount of six million three hundred and three thousand dollars, and the amount of said subsidy bonds and interest thereon, subject to deductions by reason of interest payments and credits and the due application of the sinking fund created and existing under the act of Congress of May seventh, eighteen hundred and seventy-eight, constitute, pursuant to the provisions of said acts, an indebtedness of the said companies, respectively, and of the Union Pacific Railway Company, successor by consolidation to said companies, to the United States, which indebtedness is secured by lien upon certain portions of the railroad lines of said companies as in said acts provided; and

Whereas all the lines of railway and railroad property of the Union Pacific Railway Company are in the hands of receivers appointed by the circuit court of the United States for the eighth circuit in proceedings now pending therein, and the Union Pacific Railway Company is in default in the payment of two million three hundred and ninety thousand one hundred dollars of interest upon the first-mortgage bonds covering those parts of its railroad upon which the indebtedness to the United States on account of said subsidy bonds is a lien, and also in default in the payment of eight million seven hundred and fifteen thousand dollars of the principal of said first-mortgage bonds, and bills of complaint have been filed for the foreclosure of the mortgages securing the said bonds; and

Whereas the public interest requires the enactment of legislation having for its object the complete settlement of the indebtedness of the Union Pacific Railway Company to the United States, and, in the alternative, the protection and enforcement of the lien of the United States securing the said indebtedness:

Be it enacted by the Senate and House of Representatives of the United States of America in Congress assembled, That three commissioners be appointed by the President of the United States, subject to the approval of the Senate (not more than two of said commissioners to be members of the same political party), to investigate and determine and to report to the President of the United States the fair cash value of the claim and lien of the United States in respect of the indebtedness owing to the United States by the Union Pacific Railroad Company, the Kansas Pacific Railway Company, and the successor company, the Union Pacific Railway Company, on account of the subsidy bonds issued by the United States in aid of the construction of the railway or parts of the railway lines of the said companies, the said United States reserving and keeping all moneys and securities and accumulations in the United States sinking fund applicable to said companies.

SEC. 2. That said commissioners shall have power to take testimony, to subpœna and examine witnesses, and to send for persons and papers; and it is hereby made the duty of the circuit courts of the United States for the several districts in which said commissioners may be sitting as a commission, on request of said commissioners, or any one of them, to issue subpœnas or other process to the United States marshal of the proper district, by him to be executed, requiring the attendance of witnesses before said commissioners. Said commissioners shall have power to appoint a secretary with compensation not to exceed the sum of ten dollars per day; and said commissioners shall each receive as compensation for his services the sum of five thousand dollars, together with their necessary expenses, which said expenses shall be itemized and the report thereof, verified by affidavit, submitted to the Secretary of the Treasury; and the sum of fifty thousand dollars, or so much thereof as may be necessary, is hereby appropriated to cover the compensation, expenses, and disbursements of said commissioners, to be paid out of any money in the Treasury not otherwise appropriated, upon vouchers approved by one or more of said commissioners. Said commissioners shall make report to the President of the United States on or before the first Monday of August, eighteen hundred and ninety-six.

SEC. 3. That the report of the said commissioners or a majority of them shall, subject to the approval of the President of the United States, be a conclusive finding and ascertainment of the amount which, together with the amount (not to exceed fifty thousand dollars) of the compensation, expenses, and disbursements of said commission, the said Union Pacific Railway Company, or any reorganization committee thereof which shall hold a majority of the outstanding mortgage bonds and stock of the said railway company, shall be at liberty to pay, on or before January first, eighteen hundred and ninety-seven, in discharge and satisfaction or in purchase of the indebtedness, right, claim, interest, demand, and lien of the United States against the said Union Pacific Railroad Company, the said Kansas Pacific Railway Company, and the Union Pacific Railway Company; and upon the payment, on or before the date last mentioned, by said Union Pacific Railway Company, or by such reorganization committee, of said sum so found and ascertained by said commissioners, or a majority of them, and approved by the President of the United States, and of the said further sum (not to exceed fifty thousand dollars) of the compensation, expenses, and disbursements of said commission, to the Secretary of the Treasury of the United States, the said Secretary of the Treasury is hereby authorized and directed to accept such sum and to cover the same into the Treasury of the United States, and thereupon, by instrument executed by him in behalf of the United States, to satisfy and discharge, or, in the event of the payment being made by such reorganization committee, or by their agents or trustees, to transfer, assign, convey, and release to the parties making such payment, and their assigns, all the indebtedness, right, claim, interest, and demand of the United States against the Union Pacific Railroad Company, the Kansas Pacific Railway Company, and the Union Pacific Railway Company, together with the lien, charge, mortgage, and rights of the United States on or in respect to the railroad and property of the said companies and the revenues thereof, but without recourse to the United States in any event; in either case, however, reserving and excepting all rights of the United States in the sinking fund established under said act of Congress of May seventh, eighteen hundred and seventy-eight, and in the securities therein held, and in the accumulations thereof; and such conveyance and assignment so made shall operate to transfer to and vest in the persons making such payment and purchase, and in their assigns, all rights, claims, and demands of the United States in and to said indebtedness, and in and to the lien and right of enforcement of the lien securing the same.

SEC. 4. That in the event that said indebtedness, claim, demand, and lien of the United States shall be so purchased by such reorganization committee as and in the manner hereinbefore provided, or for and in behalf of such committee by their trustees or agents, the members of such committee or their assigns, together with their associates, not in all to exceed fifteen persons, shall be, and they are hereby created and erected into a body corporate and politic in deed and in law, and they and their successors, by and in the name of *The Pacific Railway Company*, shall have perpetual succession, and shall be able to sue and be sued, plead and be impleaded, defend and be defended, in all courts of law and equity within the United States, and may make and have a common seal; and the said corporation shall have, possess, and exercise all the rights, powers, privileges, advantages, and franchises conferred upon the Union Pacific Railroad Company, the Kansas Pacific Railway Company, the Denver Pacific Railway and Telegraph Company, and the Union Pacific Railway Company, under the several acts of the Congress of the United States of which this act is amendatory, and all the rights, powers and privileges, advantages and franchises conferred upon railway corporations in the several States through which the railroad property of the said corporation hereby created shall extend and be operated, and said company shall also have power and lawful authority to construct, purchase, lease, or acquire, by consolidation or otherwise, branches and extensions not inconsistent with the general laws of the State or States in which such branches and extensions shall be located or situated, including the power to construct or acquire, by purchase, lease, consolidation, or otherwise, such railroads as will enable it to reach Pacific Coast places or points: *Provided, however*, That no such purchase, lease, or consolidation shall be made of or with any competing through lines of railroad extending from the Mississippi or Missouri River to the Pacific Ocean; and shall have power to become entitled to possess, enjoy, operate, and dispose of all the railway lines, rolling stocks, lands, land grants, goods, chattels, franchises, property, and effects whatsoever originally granted to or vested in or afterwards acquired by each of the said Union Pacific Railroad Company, the Kansas Pacific Railway Company, the Denver Pacific Railway and Telegraph Company, and the Union Pacific Railway Company, subject only to any right, title, interest, claim, or demand, if any such there shall then be, prior at law or in equity to the lien, claim, and demand of the United States aforesaid; and for the purposes of acquiring the railroad and property of which said Pacific Railway Company is herein authorized to become possessed, and for lawful corporate purposes, shall have power to make, issue, and negotiate its corporate bonds for an amount not exceeding at any time in the aggregate the present funded indebtedness (including the principal and interest of the said debt to the United States) of the said Union Pacific Railway Company and its said constituent companies, the Union Pacific Railroad Company, the Kansas Pacific Railway Company, and the Denver Pacific Railway and Telegraph Company, and to secure the same by mortgage or mortgages upon its railroad property and assets, and for like purposes to issue its capital stock, classified into preferred and common shares as it may determine, to an amount in the aggregate not exceeding the bonded indebtedness hereby authorized to be issued by the said Pacific Railway Company: *Provided, however*, That said company shall have the power to issue further bonds and stock for future construction and acquisition of railroads and property beyond that now owned by the Union Pacific Railway Company, but only to the amount of the cost of such future constructed or acquired railroads and property; that the purchasers of the said indebtedness to the United States or their assigns and their associates shall meet at the city of Omaha, in the State of Nebraska, within sixty days after the execution and delivery of the said instrument of transfer, assignment, conveyance, and release hereinbefore provided to be executed and delivered by the Secretary of the Treasury of the United States in section third hereof, and shall then and there proceed to perfect the corporate organization of the said Pacific Railway Company as nearly as may be in accordance with the manner provided for the complete organization of the Union Pacific Railroad Company by the provisions of the said act of Congress of July first, eighteen hundred and sixty-two.

SEC. 5. That all provisions of any acts of Congress hereinbefore recited, and of acts amendatory thereof, relating to the appointment of Government directors, to the collection of any percentage of net earnings, and to the withholding or application of any moneys due or to become due from the United States for any services rendered by the Union Pacific Railway Company or either of its said constituent companies to the United States, shall be and be deemed inapplicable to the said Pacific Railway Company, and the same are hereby repealed as to said Pacific Railway Company, and as to any railroad property, assets, and earnings which it may possess, own, operate, enjoy, or receive. And all provisions of such acts, or of any of them, forbidding or restricting the mortgaging or pledging of property are, as to the said Pacific Railway Company, repealed; and said company shall have and possess all the usual powers of borrowing money on its credit, or on the security of any of its property or assets, and of constructing or extending its railway, and of acquiring for such purposes title to land by condemnation proceedings, and such other powers as are or may be granted to and exercised by railway corporations in the respective States in which its said railway is or may be situated: *Provided, however*, That the grants aforesaid are made upon condition that said Pacific Railway Company shall keep its railroad in repair and use, and shall at all times transport mails, troops, and munitions of war, supplies and public stores upon said railway for the Government whenever required to do so, by any Department thereof; and that the Government shall at all times have preference in the use of the same for all the purposes aforesaid at fair and reasonable rates of compensation, not to exceed the amounts paid by private parties for the same kind of service.

SEC. 6. That, in the event of the failure of the Union Pacific Railway Company or of any such reorganization committee to pay, as in the manner and within the time hereinbefore specified, the amount found and ascertained by the said commissioners appointed by this act, and approved by the President, together with the further sum (not exceeding fifty thousand dollars) of the compensation, expenses, and disbursements of said commissioners, the Attorney-General of the United States shall be, and he is hereby, authorized and directed to enforce, by appropriate legal proceedings to be instituted and prosecuted in the circuit court of the United States for the district of Nebraska, which court shall have jurisdiction in the premises both at law and in equity, or in any other court or courts of competent jurisdiction, the said claim and lien of the United States, and in such proceedings to take such action as may be appropriate for the protection of the interests of the United States, and for the foreclosure of its lien by sale or otherwise. Upon such proceedings the property embraced within the lien of the United States shall be sold to the highest bidder, subject to any prior lien or encumbrance thereon, and for a sum not less than the amount so fixed and determined by said commissioners or a majority of them; and at such sale the Attorney-General of the United States, if in his judgment the interests of the United States so require, may bid the amount of said debt to the United States including interest.

SEC. That this act, and each and every provision thereof, shall severally and respectively be deemed, taken, and held as in alteration and amendment of said act of eighteen hundred and sixty-two and of said act of eighteen hundred and sixty-four, and of said act of eighteen hundred and seventy-eight respectively, and of the other acts amendatory thereof and supplemental thereto, and of all of said acts so far as they are inconsistent with this act; nor shall anything in this act be construed or taken in any wise to affect or impair the right of Congress at any time hereafter further to alter, amend, or repeal the said acts hereinbefore mentioned; and this act shall be subject to alteration, amendment, or repeal, as in the opinion of Congress justice or the public welfare may require; and nothing herein contained shall be held to deny, exclude, or impair any right or remedy in the premises now existing in favor of the United States. This act shall be published and printed as a public act, and in all proceedings may be cited as such.

SIOUX CITY AND PACIFIC.

STATEMENT OF MR. COOMBS.

Mr. Coombs said:

Mr. CHAIRMAN AND GENTLEMEN OF THE COMMITTEE: I appear, as perhaps most of you know, in behalf of the Credits Commutation Company, whose counsel I am. It is an organization composed of three or four hundred State, national, and city banks of twenty-two States, whose interests are located at Sioux City, and who are representatives of several larger interests, who think that their interests will be vitally affected by the disposition which you may make of the interest of the Government in these railroad properties.

Senator MORGAN. Point out on the map the line of road you refer to.

Mr. COOMBS. I have mentioned no road as yet; I am about to do so. Before coming directly to that, I would like to make a few preliminary remarks. In undertaking to ask some questions of Mr. Littler the other day I precipitated an avalanche of interrogatories upon myself, and in endeavoring to answer them I fear that some parts of what I said were "to some a stumbling block, and to others a foolishness." And perhaps it would be well for me further to say, as of great consequence, the fact that a quarter of a million in money had gone from the Sioux City and Pacific Railroad to the Fremont and Missouri Valley Railroad, or half a million in rolling stock; and especially was I not trying to raise any credit mobilier question. Some four days were devoted to the discussion of Union Pacific matters in the House last winter, and perhaps half of it was exhausted in arguing upon that matter, and its utter uselessness was demonstrated. It is a worn-out subject.

There is, if you will permit the illustration, a chemical element which we call nitrogen, which is the flirt of chemistry, whose character is want of stability and an affinity for combinations. We become tired of hearing Aristides called The Just, and of Cleon called a leather seller; and in just such a way a man has been accused of stealing Southern spoons until they made him a governor; and if there should appear to be even a representative of any interest of those who were expelled from the House in connection with the credit mobilier on this reorganization committee, that fact might commend itself because, as I say, the people are weary of this thing. Man is a seminitrogenous compound, and I do not propose to argue against chemical reactions. I want to take the situation as I find it, and to deal with the present and show you that the Government was an unconscious interest in doing injustice when these roads were constructed, and that the evil has gone on increasing, and being aggravated, until it has become somewhat unbearable. I wish to ask that in the reorganization of these roads the evil shall be put an end to.

There is a relation between the bill which Mr. Littler has proposed and the other bill, and it irritated me a little that it was thought advisable that his proposition should be presented as the forerunner of the other, as it was said to have no relation to the rest of the situation. Mr. Pierce would have been the first man to have found fault with Mr. Littler's suggestion if it was not certain that it was going to result in harmony with his own plan.

Coming to formulate consecutively propositions concerning which there has been vague and almost infinite discussion and evidence for two years, there are three reasons urged upon you why this property should be cheaply sold. One of them is that your road is paralleled by competing lines; another, that it is a headless trunk having no terminal on the Missouri River and no bridge across it, and the third is that the third mortgages are being assembled beneath you to lift you out of any position you may hold in the property. The connection of the Chicago and Northwestern with all these propositions is what I wish to bring to your attention first. What they call competing lines are as far away north as the Great Northern and the Northern Pacific.

(Mr. Coombs pointed out on the map the positions of the various lines of railroad which were referred to as the competitors and explained their relations to each other and to the Sioux City road.)

Senator BRICE. Who owns that bridge over the Missouri?

Mr. COOMBS. That is what I was trying to find out the other day from Mr. Littler.

Senator STEWART. Where does that red line [indicating on the map cross the Missouri River?

Mr. COOMBS [indicating on the map]. At a place called Blair.

Senator STEWART. Who owns that bridge?

Mr. COOMBS. The bridge was built by the Missouri Valley and Blair Bridge Company. That matter will be worthy of a good deal of investigation and attention when you come to dispose of that property. A subsidy of $16,000 a mile was paid for every consecutive 20 miles of road. One of your Departments permitted a ferry to be used as a temporary expedient, and when authority to build the bridge was applied for it was to be built by the Sioux City and Pacific road. But it turns out that it is claimed to be owned by a company of which Mr. Blair, who built the Sioux City, was also president. The entire first-mortgage bonds of this Sioux City road (the whole $126,000 of bonds) were distributed as a dividend to the stockholders, and the road was, substantially, built with other funds. The subsidy was paid on the representation that the miles were consecutive. The Department of the Interior said that the ferry was only accepted as a temporary expedient, and if the company did not own the bridge, then the road cost scarcely as much as the subsidy bonds given by the Government.

And yet that Sioux City and Pacific road has not been so bad a property. No one in the world has abused it so much as I have, as a part of the Union Pacific system.

Senator STEWART. You state that you represent a large number of banking institutions and investors. Where is their property?

Mr. COOMBS. All located here [indicating on the map].

Senator STEWART. They have got a bridge up there?

The CHAIRMAN. They loaned their money to a company in Sioux City, which, under the high-pressure business of that country, borrowed a large amount of money from these banks and took all the assets of the so-called Credit-Commutation Company in that country, among which was the authority for building a bridge. They put their hands in their pockets and contributed pro rata to build a bridge.

Mr. COOMBS. Yes, sir.

Senator STEWART (to Mr. Coombs). How is their interest affected by any settlement to be made with the Union Pacific?

Mr. COOMBS. That is what I was getting up to. As I was saying, the Sioux City and Pacific Railroad was not so bad a road for the purposes for which it was designed—as a feeder to the Chicago and Northwestern. The latter road has already paid out considerable money. It paid out nearly $300,000 to the Fremont, Elkhorn and Missouri Valley road. The Sioux City has all the time paid interest on its preferred stock. It has nearly $300,000 in the hands of the Government and $350,000 in its own hands; and that is nearly as much as it cost. But the peculiarity about it is that you own to-day in your sinking fund $716,000 of these same first-mortgage bonds. Now, why should you sell it, under these circumstances, to your competitor?

The CHAIRMAN. Do you think it wise for the Government to purchase a railroad and to operate it?

Mr. COOMBS. You are advancing me to a question which I would like to consider a little later. It would be infinitely better for the Government to buy that road, if it is an outlet to a property of a hundred millions and if that property has no other outlet.

The CHAIRMAN. What did the bridge at Sioux City cost?

Mr. COOMBS. About a million and a quarter.

The CHAIRMAN. Is it a wagon road and a railroad bridge combined?

Mr. COOMBS. Everything.

The CHAIRMAN. What railroad operates it?

Mr. COOMBS. Not any.

Senator MORGAN. Can the Government take a mortgage or statutory lien upon a railroad as security for a debt without being in one sense a purchaser?

Mr. COOMBS. Not without being in one sense a purchaser. Before it is actually driven to the wall it ought to buy the property and not be treated as a party incapable of defending itself, and, therefore, to be beaten or cheated out of the property.

Senator WOLCOTT. Are you coming later to what you desire to advocate?

Mr. COOMBS. Yes.

Senator WOLCOTT. I understand that your advocacy of a Government purchase is not the real solution of the question which you intend to submit to the committee.

Mr. COOMBS. Oh, no; but the other is too large a question.

Senator WOLCOTT. I hope you will come to a practical recommendation, if you have any solution to propose.

Mr. COOMBS. My solution, in brief, is one that I think you have got to come to. The competition of these two lines is, I think, inevitably foreshadowed. The parties who are before you have seen that there is to be a union of the properties which they represent, against which it is impossible to contend on any basis but a purchase of the roads by the Government, and I do not think that will be done. I think you are going to close the competition and make a monopoly of all of these lines. What I want is that in compensation for that there shall be a freight competition from Sioux City by the lakes. I think that the Sioux City and Pacific is practically worthless as a part of the Union Pacific, and that we are going to lose that connection.

Senator STEWART. Explain that a little more fully.

Mr. COOMBS. There was an original railroad designed (and the act was passed) from North Platte northwest to Sioux City, to lead to water transportation at the end of the way to the hundredth parallel. As you are sure to lose all competition on the central lines between the Union Pacific and the Chicago and Northwestern, and as nearly all of the States have passed laws against the combination of parallel roads, there would be a great relief from competition between water-borne freights and overland freights.

Senator WOLCOTT. Then you want the Government to build another line of road?

Mr. COOMBS. I want the Government to shift some of its securities.

Senator WOLCOTT. Tell us how.

Mr. COOMBS. I will tell you how. I suppose it goes without saying that the dominating mind in this reorganization proposition is that of the Chicago and Northwestern Railroad Company. Mr. Littler's proposition is not that the commission, which his bill suggests, shall fix the price for which the Northwestern shall own the road, but that the Government shall pay $20,000 to establish a commission which shall be open for the introduction by him of evidence to depreciate your property, and if the findings of the commission are approved by the President, the Chicago and Northwestern road is to have the option to pay the amount or not as it sees fit.

The CHAIRMAN. Can not that difficulty be met by a provision in the law that the matter must be closed within a limited time?

Mr. LITTLER. Another answer to that proposition is that if we do not comply with the proposition, the Government will have the right to proceed with its foreclosure proceedings.

Mr. COOMBS. Oh, yes, the bill can be amended, of course, in half a dozen ways.

The CHAIRMAN. Then the original right would stand.

Mr. COOMBS. Yes; but that is not the bill as it is to-day. It is as if preceding a war with Great Britain we were to give that power an option over our coast defenses, awaiting the outcome of an invasion. The interest which I represent is an interest affected rather than an interest invaded, and the interests that will be affected by the disposition which you make of this large part of the road are most momentous. I take it that this Congress is not the mere collector of debts of a bankrupt or spendthrift predecessor, and that the welfare of the country is as much considered to-day as it was when the Government went into the scheme of aiding railroads in the first instance. The Union Pacific as it was designed, as you know, was inspired by the Government putting forth great efforts to reduce the Confederate States. It perhaps received its only constitutional sanction when presented as a great military highway to repel foreign invasion on either ocean, or on the Gulf or lakes. It was designed from the first that it should spring east from this great north and south trend of the Missouri River [exhibiting on the map] between Kansas City on the south and Sioux City on the north, and that the roads from there north and south should converge at a common point in the Platte Valley in the hundredth meridian. The southern leg of the tripod was to start from Kansas City. At first it was provided that it should run northwest to the hundredth meridian, but afterwards they had it changed, under the act of 1864, so that the road was to continue straight west. They received the same subsidy as they would have done if they had gone northwest to the hundredth meridian, getting $6,000,000 or $7,000,000 for a line ending at the three hundred and ninety-fourth milepost in the prairie.

The Chicago and Northwestern Company, as I said the other day, is a large factor in a great combination of roads owned by, perhaps, the richest family in the world—a family all of whose fortune is invested in railroad enterprises. That road reaches every important point westward from Chicago. It covers this great circumference [indicating on the map], starting at the head of the lakes, sweeping around Duluth, St. Paul, Minneapolis, Sioux City, and Atchison. That is a brief description of a vast power, but that does not cover it. For years it has had arrangements with the Union Pacific by which every pound of unconsigned freight originating at a point on either road and designed for a point on the other road is exchanged between them to the exclusion of every other competitor. The Chicago and Northwestern is practically controlled by the Vanderbilt family, and its interest is to gather up to its own lines all of the freight and traffic originating on the Union Pacific and bound to the east. It transfers its freight at Chicago to the Lake Shore and Michigan Southern road, by which it is hauled to Buffalo, and there it is turned over to the pride of the association—the New York Central—and carried to New York. The reorganization proposition that is before you proposes to perpetuate and continue that operation. It is a great power, but, as I said before the House committee, that is no reason why you should not treat with it, because if you treat with it you are certain that whatever they give you will be good and that they are able to carry out their own trade. You understand that with the reorganization plan carried out that family will control some 20,000 miles of railroad, stocked and bonded to an amount of $1,000,000,000, and with an annual income of $150,000,000. All of the railroads in this country are only stocked and bonded at about $10,000,000,000, and their whole assessed valuation is only $24,000,-000,000. So that this combination, with its 10 per cent of value and efficiency of all the railroads of the country, will represent directly a property equal to 4 or 5 per cent of your whole assessed valuation.

The great founder of the Chicago and Northwestern was Mr. John J. Blair. At the time that the Pacific railroads were under construction Mr. Blair was building a road across Iowa. He ran a survey up the eastern valley of the Missouri River to Sioux City. You would have called it a feeder of, or an extension to, the Chicago and Northwestern, only that Mr. Blair left 5½ miles between the two roads. He called his road the Sioux City and Pacific Railroad, although nobody dreamed of its having any connection with the Pacific at that time. Afterwards, by the act of 1864, the President of the United States was allowed to designate the company which should build the northwestern leg of the Union Pacific from Sioux City, and Mr. Blair persuaded President Lincoln to designate the Sioux City and Pacific. A road by that route, as well as by any other, could be built to join the Union Pacific, and if it had been done, you will see, looking back thirty years, that Sioux City would have wanted a bridge across the Missouri River, and would have been made the largest city of the Northwest.

The CHAIRMAN. Was it not supposed that representations were made to President Lincoln that this road was to be built in the direction originally designed for it?

Mr. COOMBS. President Lincoln was dead before the location was made.

The CHAIRMAN. He had the designation?

Mr. COOMBS. He designated the company but not the location.

Senator STEWART. The map and direction of the road were not made before Mr. Lincoln's death.

Mr. COOMBS. No, sir. After Mr. Lincoln's death, to everybody's surprise (and I think to the ridicule of some who are now living and are acquainted with the facts) this road located its southwestern connection to the Pacific on a previous survey of this feeder to the Chicago and Northwestern. It started at Sioux City to the Pacific and ran southwest toward the Missouri River to a place which, with a sort of grim humor, is called California Junction—perhaps to save the road from discouragement by the fact that it was 25 or 30 miles farther away from California than when it began. There it found a projected extension of the Cedar Rapids road, and cut out the loop. From there it went straight over to Fremont. Now the consequences of this have gone on aggravating from that day to this. There was at that time in the entire Northwestern group of States but 625 miles of railroad, and only 3,200 in the whole United States; but that 625 miles of railroad (all in Iowa) was just as much entitled to consideration as the Hannibal and St. Jo Railroad, or any of them. Its influence was pressing, and if the line had been built I do not hesitate to say that the Union Pacific would not have failed at all. The railroad development of the Northwest has been enormous. There are to-day in that group of States alone 2,900 miles of railroad—within 300 of the number of miles that the whole country had at that time.

(Mr. Coombs pointed out on the map the various groups of railroads in the Northwest and indicated the location of the bridge at Sioux City, which he said the Chicago and Northwestern Company had to build or suffer it to go into the hands of other parties, because the State had voted aid to the bridge.)

The CHAIRMAN. Right west of this great stretch of the Missouri is there a country which consists only of bad lands inimical to business?

Mr. COOMBS. What you say is true to this extent: There is a bad-land range, but after a hundred miles it is not so; when you strike the Platte Valley the lands get better.

The CHAIRMAN. The country above Sioux City is bad lands?

Mr. COOMBS. Yes; above Sioux City, and especially at the first western turn of the river.

Senator BRICE. Please come to the suggestions you have to make to the committee.

Senator WOLCOTT. All this statement of yours is of surpassing interest, but what the committee seeks is some reason why the proposed plan should not be adopted, with some good reason in favor of that which we ought to do. The committee does not want so much history. It is of fascinating interest, but we want something of value. For instance, the story about the building of the bridge thirty years ago is really not of any help to the committee.

Mr. COOMBS. I will pursue any course that the committee desires. I have a proposition to make which perhaps would not be received without some argument. Whether I stated the proposition first and argued it afterwards, or made the argument first, which might lead to it, is immaterial to me. I have said that injustice was done in the location of this Sioux City and Pacific road. The evidence of how the road happened to be built appears to me to be something which should be submitted to the committee. I present this question: The Congress of to-day would not devote itself entirely to the remedying of a wrong done in the past, but would do almost anything for the future, and if the two were combined—if there was an injustice in the past, taken by itself, would not perhaps appeal to you, because Congress could not go on correcting every mistake of its predecessors—the interests of each might be considered. What I want is that in the arrangement which you may make you shall invest a portion of the sinking fund, now in the hands of the Government, for the correction of an evil in the past and for the general welfare in the future.

The CHAIRMAN. Were not the bonds of the sinking fund to apply to the liquidation of the original debt of the Pacific railroads?

Mr. COOMBS. Yes; but they are still the property of the Union Pacific, and it is for Congress to consider what use is to be made of them. I think it is prudent for me to urge and have you consider the comparison between railroad routes and water-borne routes by way of the lakes to the East which this would facilitate.

Senator WOLCOTT. What would facilitate?

Mr. COOMBS. The route from North Platte to Sioux City.

Senator BRICE. How far?

Mr. COOMBS. Two hundred and fifty miles.

Senator BRICE. How much would it cost?

Mr. COOMBS. About $20,000 a mile. It has been surveyed.

Senator BRICE. What right has Congress to build it?

Mr. COOMBS. The same right as it had to build the Pacific Railroads in the first instance.

Senator MORGAN. Has Congress not exhausted its powers in building what it has done?

Mr. COOMBS. You have now a trade in hand. You are to meet Mr. Pierce on a proposition which he says is elastic—not a hard and fast proposition. The reorganization committee is to keep $13,000,000 in its own treasury for corporate purposes and $7,000,000 of preferred stock, and you are to give and take in the trade in many ways. And I want you to let him have the Sioux City and Pacific road. I think, however, that it is wise and fair, and that it will commend itself to the people, for you to establish competition by way of the lakes.

Senator STEWART. What road would give you that connection?

Mr. COOMBS. Half a dozen of them—principally the southwest branch of the Great Northern Railroad. Water-borne transportation is one-twelfth the price of the lowest rate of an overland haul. The Erie Canal has been the dominant factor in bringing down the tolls of the New York Central, and all the other railroads have to follow it.

Senator WOLCOTT. What is your plan?

Mr. COOMBS. Either that a part of the sinking fund shall, in accordance with the original intention, be invested in the first-mortgage bonds of a road from North Platte to Sioux City, or that there be a like provision made for the purpose of constructing such a road.

Senator WOLCOTT. For the Government to construct it?

Mr. COOMBS. For another company to do so.

Senator WOLCOTT. The company which you represent?

Mr. COOMBS. The company which I will represent.

Senator WOLCOTT. Your suggestion is that we shall transfer some of these securities to you that you may construct this road?

Mr. COOMBS. Transfer them in a first mortgage on another road.

Senator WOLCOTT. To the extent of how much per mile?

Mr. COOMBS. Twenty thousand dollars a mile.

Senator WOLCOTT. By way of a subsidy?

Mr. COOMBS. By way of a transfer of a subsidy from one road to another.

The CHAIRMAN. You want the Government to advance $5,000,000 to build 250 miles of road that will cost, presumably, $20,000 a mile?

Mr. COOMBS. Yes.

The CHAIRMAN. In plain English, then, you want the Government to build the road in its entirety?

Mr. COOMBS. I would not say that.

The CHAIRMAN. That is practically the proposition.

Mr. COOMBS. If you put it in that way that is practically the proposition; I hoped that it would not come in that way. Having stated it, I am free to stop now.

The CHAIRMAN. Will you make your proposition in writing?

Mr. COOMBS. If you desire.

Senator WOLCOTT. What is the company that you represent?

Mr. COOMBS. The Credits Commutation Company.

Senator WOLCOTT. What is its capital?

Mr. COOMBS. Its principal capital is the power of assessment which the stockholders have assumed.

Senator WOLCOTT. How much is invested in it?

Mr. COOMBS. I can not tell. It depends on the results of the development of the business in which it is engaged.

Senator WOLCOTT. How much money is invested?

Mr. COOMBS. Perhaps $5,000,000 or $6,000,000.

Senator WOLCOTT. Is it represented at Sioux City?

Mr. COOMBS. No; on railroad enterprises which we pledge the accomplishment of, but which I have not been talking about.

Senator WOLCOTT. Railroads to Sioux City?

Mr. COOMBS. Directly.

Senator WOLCOTT. Does it include some real estate interests in Sioux City?

Mr. COOMBS. I do not think it does. It does in one class of notes.

Senator WOLCOTT. You have a bridge there?

Mr. COOMBS. Yes.

Senator WOLCOTT. Do you desire to utilize that bridge for railroad purposes?

Mr. COOMBS. We do.

Senator WOLCOTT. You have spoken of the bad conduct of the Chicago and Northwest Company, and yet you say in your argument that the committee might let the Chicago and Northwest Company have the Sioux City and Pacific road, provided you get the Government to build this 250 miles between North Platte and Sioux City?

Mr. COOMBS. Yes.

Senator WOLCOTT. Otherwise not?

Mr. COOMBS. Otherwise not.

Senator WOLCOTT. Therefore, practically, what you are desirous that the committee should do is to build up the interest of Sioux City, where your clients have their money invested?

Mr. COOMBS. We are at the front; we are the representative of other cities of the West.

Senator WOLCOTT. Do you mean the cities of Minneapolis and St. Paul?

Mr. COOMBS. Yes.

Senator WOLCOTT. And Duluth?

Mr. COOMBS. Yes.

Senator WOLCOTT. You represent them all officially?

Mr. COOMBS. I know that I am speaking in behalf of their interests. We are at the very front. We are at the great bend of the Missouri River, and a line which bisects that angle would benefit all of us.

Senator WOLCOTT. And anything which benefits Sioux City will indirectly benefit the rest of the world?

Mr. COOMBS. Yes.

Senator FRYE. Mr. Coombs's claim is that when these provisions for the Pacific railways are made, and when the treaty is completed, you are foreclosed absolutely against any railroad competition whatever, and that his road from Sioux City to the one hundredth parallel would open up a competing line for the whole continent.

Senator BRICE. He said that this reorganization committee is directed by the Chicago and Northwest road.

Mr. COOMBS. The road which I want built would open the way from Sioux City to the head of the lakes.

Mr. BRICE. How would you get farther west?

Mr. COOMBS. That is another point which I want to present to the committee. In the House last winter, I urged before the Pacific Railway Committee that the contract existing between the Chicago and Northwest and the Union Pacific shut out all competition, and that no line built by private capital could get a pound of the unconsigned freight between these two roads, and could not make any headway against the combination. The House committee, therefore, put in the bill last year a provision that any road built there should have its proportionate share of the business, and that provision, I am credibly informed, is the one which made the Union Pacific people immediately file a memorial saying that they would not accept the bill with that provision in it. The proposition which I am making in behalf of my people is one which affects Colorado, one that affects California, and one without which there is no relief for any of us. There are ships coming into New Orleans to-day whose single cargo would load 4 solid miles of freight cars; and so too in the ports of New York and Boston; and 50 ships would stall all these railroads.

Senator WOLCOTT. Why should not the Government build a road from Colorado south as well as build your road?

Mr. COOMBS. I would say nothing against it.

Senator WOLCOTT. Then you want yours, as one of the series of roads, to be built by the Government?

Mr. COOMBS. I would have no objection to other roads.

Senator MORGAN. You are familiar with all these projects, do you know any reason why the Government of the United States is under the necessity of assisting and forcing the Union Pacific and the Central Pacific into bankruptcy, or subjecting that property to sale under such conditions as would effect bankruptcy?

Mr. COOMBS. On the contrary, if you ask me that question, I think that the Government of the United States ought to take up the underlying liens on these roads and put the property in the hands of some other corporation or of the same corporation; but the Government should never lose its control over them and should never be driven into such a position as to be unable to take care of itself as if it were a baby.

Senator MORGAN. At the time that the Government exercised the right to charter these companies there was no objection, as I understand it, from any State between the Missouri River and the Pacific Ocean to the exercise of this power?

Mr. COOMBS. I am not aware of any.

Mr. MORGAN. There was one State between the Missouri River and the Pacific Ocean—California. The rest of the region was all Territory, from Omaha on to the boundary line of California. The Government having, in virtue of its sovereign power over the Territories, exercised this right of chartering these companies and of aiding in the construction of these roads, and having reserved to itself certain important powers and rights of jurisdiction over the roads—having made it, in other words, a governmental instrumentality for the transmission of mails, and troops, and provisions, and munitions of war, do you know of any reason why the Government should now surrender all these privileges and rights, and take the risk of regaining them through the consent of the States through which the railroads pass?

Mr. COOMBS. I am guided more in my opinion by what can be done than by what should be done. The majority of the people of the United States do not want the Government to run a railroad. The minority of the people—which is a respectable minority—does want it done, and a fair compromise between these two opinions is to allow the operation of the road by a company with such stringent oversight and control as to prevent oppression and to secure the best interests of all.

Senator MORGAN. To the extent of having four directors in each of these companies the Government is running these railroads?

Mr. COOMBS. The Government is in the railroad business in its most critical stages.

Senator MORGAN. We are now, and have been a long time, running these railroads, as far as Government directors are concerned.

Mr. COOMBS. Yes.

Senator MORGAN. So that the Government of the United States has been the holder of a power which might be converted into a balance of power, through that board of directors, without owning a dollar of stock. That has been our situation, has it not?

Mr. COOMBS. Yes.

Senator MORGAN. Is there any reason why we should yield that power and run the risk of regaining it (if it is important) by the consent of the States hereafter to some new organization which would change the whole programme?

Mr. COOMBS. I do not care to give an opinion on that point. My views would not be very valuable. I have gone, perhaps, as far as I ought to. A railroad can not be run as a highway, as some people in California suggest, and yet complaint of California is not without justice. She pays something like forty millions a year to railroads for transcontinental business.

The CHAIRMAN. Is it not true that the rates charged to-day to California are only about 40 per cent of what they were originally?

Mr. COOMBS. Yes.

The CHAIRMAN. Has not the natural competition from other roads a constant tendency to lower rates?

Mr. COOMBS. Yes.

The CHAIRMAN. Then the point comes whether California, so far as the long haul is concerned, pays a higher rate to-day than is a proper rate on the capital invested in the railroads?

Mr. COOMBS. It is hard to say; I think that California has but one relief. There are three plans suggested for adjusting the difficulty of the Government with these roads. One is the refunding scheme of Senator Frye, which has been the foundation of everything suggested since (the refunding of the Government debt subject to the prior lien). Another plan is the reorganization of the Union Pacific company as presented by the present reorganization committee; and the third is for the Government to buy the roads and to operate them, or put them in the hands of a company which the Government should create. Of these various plans it seems to be quite generally conceded that the refunding plan is best for California or the Central Pacific end of the line, but California can not, of course, have this road run at a loss by the Government, and it seems to me just as well to let the present people take it.

The CHAIRMAN. You have given a good deal of attention to this subject. Is it the result of your observation that if the Government was to own and operate these roads the people of California and the people all the way that are tributary to this line, would be as well served in the matter of freights and general traffic as they are served under the present ownership?

Mr. COOMBS. I do not think so.

Senator STEWART. Why not?

Mr. COOMBS. No more than the people would be better served if the Government was to take the Western Union telegraph line from Ogden to San Francisco and run it as a Government telegraph line in the midst of Mr. Gould's great Western Union telegraph system. That one line of telegraph in the hands of the Government would not be able to serve the public as well as if it was part of the general system. If you were to adopt the system of telegraphing and made it as much a part of the Government business as the post-office system, you might be able to do so, but to project itself into the situation with a single line would not be practicable.

Senator MORGAN. Laying aside every other question and consideration except the usefulness of that part of the road from Sioux City, what would be the disadvantage of selling and disposing of that part of the road to the Union Pacific at a fair price?

Mr. COOMBS. That is, of course, your only way across the Missouri River, and your only way out, and with the bridges at Omaha and Sioux City in the hands of the Union Pacific there could be no railroad competition.

Now, I have a word to say in behalf of our private interest. The people of Sioux City have appreciated this situation, even if it has not been appreciated at Washington. In fact, the United States Railroad Commissioner himself frankly admits, in his report of 1879, that this was a mistake. It is not an idea which originates with us; but Government officials themselves have called attention to it. We at the Northwest, however, have felt it keenly; and, in 1890, an organization was formed of the principal citizens (financially) of Sioux City to break through the environments which seemed to surround the city. They wanted one railroad of 100 miles to the north of Sioux City to join the southwestern branch of the Great Northern coming to the head of the lakes at that point, and another railroad of 120 miles west of Sioux City to penetrate the corn belt of Nebraska and to seek connection with the roads of that section; and they wanted a large terminal in Sioux City, and a bridge across the river, the terminal being suitable to accommodate all the railroads on equal terms.

All of these properties failed in 1893. All of them negotiated loans through one Boston trust company, and that failed too. The road to the north was bonded for $2,000,000; it had cost $2,500,000. The road to the west had cost $2,500,000, and all of its bonds and all of its stock were pledged to certain New York parties to secure $1,500,000.

Senator WOLCOTT. You had watered the stock of the road to the north to the amount of $900,000?

Mr. COOMBS. Yes; the terminals had cost about $2,000,000 and were mortgaged for $2,500,000.

The CHAIRMAN. The terminals were in separate ownership?

Mr. COOMBS. Yes, there had been half a million dollars spent on the bridge and it was under way to that extent. The people of Sioux City impressed their creditors with the value of the idea of breaking through and getting southwestern and northwestern connections, and that idea was about all the collateral and assets which the company had. The people of Sioux City said that if we would come there and build a bridge to connect these properties and rehabilitate them they would vote us a subsidy to the extent of $3,000,000, which was about as much to them as it would be to the people of the United States to pay the national debt.

The CHAIRMAN. And they got their bankers to reassess themselves an additional amount in consideration of that local aid?

Mr. COOMBS. The bankers pooled their losses, but provided, in articles of association, that they might be assessed without limit, and they went on rebuilding the properties (perhaps putting in a million dollars to complete the bridge).

The CHAIRMAN. The tax voted by the citizens of Sioux City themselves went directly to the interest of this banking association?

Mr. COOMBS. If we complete the bridge on or before the 1st day of March, 1896.

The CHAIRMAN. Otherwise not?

Mr. COOMBS. Otherwise not. There is eight or ten millions invested substantially in the proposition I am urging on you. The question concerning the $3,000,000 pledge is before the court of appeals and I anticipate a decision on which we can recover the securities in proportion to the money advanced. If that be so, and if the roads are left as they are, I shall not redeem the terminal, but shall go back to the house lots and the bridge, leaving the terminal as a representative of my folly.

Senator WOLCOTT. When did your company make this investment?

Mr. COOMBS. In 1891 or 1892.

Senator WOLCOTT. Some twenty years after what you consider this great wrong was done?

Mr. COOMBS. Yes.

The CHAIRMAN. Did this banking association own an interest in the North Platte Line to Sioux City?

Mr. COOMBS. Not that I am aware of.

The CHAIRMAN. Or in the packing-house arrangements there?

Mr. COOMBS. We own a packing-house there and a stock yard.

The CHAIRMAN. That was no part of the original scheme?

Mr. COOMBS. I offered a packer there the other day property in good condition which cost $600,000. I offered it to him as a gift if he would come there and kill beef, but it was so doubtful a proposition that he would not take the gift. The interests I am speaking of are substantial, direct, and palpable.

Senator STEWART. Would it be of any use to you to own the Sioux City bridge?

Mr. COOMBS. I can not say that it would be of any use.

Senator STEWART. You do not want to buy it?

Mr. COOMBS. No.

Senator BRICE. What is it worth?

Mr. COOMBS. Its income last year was $15,700.

Senator BRICE. How much is it worth?

Mr. COOMBS. The value of it depends on whether the Missouri Valley and Blair Bridge Company can assert an independent ownership of the bridge. That bridge was bonded for $1,500,000.

Senator BRICE. What would it cost to build that road from North Platte to Sioux City.

Mr. COOMBS. You can answer that question better than I can. The commission of 1887 said that there was no way to get at the value of the bridge. When Mr. Blair was asked he said five millions. He was asked how he made that out, and he said because that much stock and bonds were issued on it. If there ever were any books which showed its cost they have been burned. Mr. Pattison assumed its cost at $2,500,000.

Senator Morgan pointed to certain railroad lines marked on the map and asked Mr. Coombs to state what lines they were, which he did. Pointing to the Omaha bridge, he asked Mr. Coombs who owned it.

Mr. COOMBS. The Omaha Bridge Company owns it.

Senator MORGAN. And that Omaha Bridge Company is under the control of the Union Pacific?

Mr. COOMBS. Yes.

Senator MORGAN. And the bridge is operated by the Union Pacific?

Mr. COOMBS. Yes.

Senator MORGAN. If the Chicago and Northwestern Company could get hold of that bridge would it have both bridges across the Missouri River?

Mr. COOMBS. Yes, decidedly. The reorganization committee will accomplish the one, and Mr. Littler's plan will accomplish the other.

Senator STEWART. Would the Sioux City bridge be of any value to the Union Pacific?

Mr. COOMBS. It would be a very poor way out for the Union Pacific.

Senator STEWART. Its best way out is this Omaha bridge?

Mr. COOMBS. The Union Pacific system was built for Omaha. There is no question about that.

Senator MORGAN. And if we sell the Sioux City bridge we will have no bridge crossing the Missouri River?

Mr. COOMBS. You will have no bridge across the river that you own.

The CHAIRMAN. You mean because the Union Pacific does not own the Omaha bridge?

Mr. COOMBS. The Union Pacific does not even get to the terminal at Omaha.

Senator FRYE. Have you ever drafted an amendment such as you require?

Mr. COOMBS. I drafted an amendment to the bill that went to the House last year. I wish this committee would study the proposition between water haul and overland haul. That is the great proposition in the internal trade of the country for the next fifty years. It is so inconceivably great that I do not think there is any question of legislation before this Congress, and none at any time (I mean in times of peace) which will be of such momentous consequence to the people of the United States, as the direction you will give to the traffic of these great lines of railway and to the lake traffic. You all know the vast interior commerce, sometimes comparing it with foreign commerce. It carries iron ore to the mills of Virginia, it carries the coal of the North, the grain of the West, and the manufactures of the East. That traffic is not evidence of great gain, and great prosperity, and great power so much as it is evidence of a kind of domestic economy. It does the chores of the day. It brings the fuel from the west slope of the Alleghanies and sets the bread from the wheat of Iowa to rise for the New England breakfast table. We do not want any monopoly which will force that traffic to pay high rates or that will impede it. It is worthy the power and consideration of the Government that the way should be kept open, and everything that is done to facilitate it will be a great blessing.

STATEMENT OF MR. LITTLER.

Mr. David R. Littler, general counsel of the Chicago and Northwestern Railroad Company, rose to address the committee.

Senator BRICE. What is the value of this Sioux City Railroad property?

Mr. LITTLER. I never discussed that point.

Senator BRICE. What would your company give to the Government for it?

Mr. LITTLER. I do not know.

Senator BRICE. Will you consider the matter and make a proposition in case we agree to accept a lump sum rather than go through the form of appointing a commission?

Mr. LITTLER. I will try to do so.

Senator BRICE. And will you report to the committee?

Mr. LITTLER. I will try to. I would like to talk about three minutes. I have been greatly entertained and somewhat edified by the lecture on the railroad geography of the United States delivered by the distinguished gentleman who has just taken his seat. I do not want to question his knowledge of the subject, for he seems to be entirely familiar with it, but I want to bring this committee back to earth again, and I want to present the real question before it which is presented in the bill now under consideration. If I understand the burden of Mr. Coombs's complaint it is that he represents a lot of unfortunate bankers who put their money in Sioux City—the future great city of the Northwest. They have gone and made a bad investment there, and lost a lot of money, and Mr. Coombs's argument, stripped of all sophistry and exposed to the naked light, is this: He asks the committee to have the Government build a railroad on that dotted line [indicating on the map] 250 miles in length, and he asks the Government to subsidize that road to the amount of $5,000,000. I admire him for his modesty. In the first place, he is asking at least $5,000 per mile more than it would cost to build the road. There is not a road west of the Missouri River up to the foothills of the Rocky Mountains which could not be built now for $15,000 a mile.

The CHAIRMAN. You should make some allowance for equipment.

Mr. LITTLER. I am talking about what it would cost to construct the road; $15,000 a mile would be a liberal estimate to build it, and $20,000 a mile would build and equip it. But what has all that to do with the question before the committee? Is this committee going to repeat the extravagance and questionable legislation which led to the construction of a line of railroads between the Missouri River and the Pacific Ocean during the war, and the only reason given for which was that it was a war measure? Is this committee or is this Congress going to invoke the war power of the Government to build a railroad 250 miles in length in order to relieve a lot of Boston bankers who were mistaken in their estimate of the improvement and advance of Sioux City? That is the question now before the committee.

Now, as to the bill under consideration and as to the insinuation which has been made, I desire to reply briefly. The learned counsel intimated that, somewhere along the line, in the history of the Chicago and Northwest Railroad Company, that company stole or plundered from the Sioux City road a lot of equipment or rolling stock. I do not know whether there is any truth in it or not. I am tolerably well acquainted with a number of the gentlemen connected with the Chicago and Northwest road, and they have not the reputation of being thieves. I do not believe that it is so. But let us assume that they have stolen the property of the Sioux City and Pacific. The bill under consideration furnishes to the Government ample opportunities to recoup the Sioux City and Pacific for that; and all that we ask is that Mr. Coombs may appear before the commission proposed to be appointed by Congress and make his statement good. We assume that the commission will be worthy of the Congress which creates it, and worthy of the President of the United States who appoints it. We do not ask to be heard in the appointment of that commission. We simply ask that they be men above suspicion. And we invite you, Mr. Coombs, to appear there and make good your insinuation and your assertion against the gentlemen whom I have the honor to represent. And if you shall show that commission that we have robbed the Sioux City Company of its property we will make reparation; and we will expect the commission to add to the value of the Government lien, as it now appears, the value of the property converted or plundered. I am perfectly willing to have the committee amend the bill in any way that will perfect it and attain the ends which we all seek.

Mr. COOMBS. If what I said when speaking rapidly was construed by Mr. Littler into a charge that the rolling stock of the Sioux City and Pacific Company had been dishonorably acquired by anybody I want to take it back.

Mr. LITTLER. You certainly intimated it both to-day and when you spoke a week ago.

Mr. COOMBS. The Fremont, Elkhorn and Missouri Valley Railroad was practically consolidated with the Sioux City and Pacific, but could not be legally consolidated with it because of the law, and the Sioux City and Pacific Railroad, as I understand it, and as I stated, did furnish the equipment which the Fremont and Elkhorn road used.

Mr. LITTLER. All these questions are questions for the commission and not for this committee; and I ask the gentlemen to appear before the commission instead of making their statements to the committee. Mr. Coombs says that these Pacific railroads are managed adroitly before this committee and that this little bill which I introduced a few weeks ago is but the forerunner of another bill, and is a part of the combination, the other bill having been unfolded here to-day in the presentation of the reorganization committee's proposition. I want to state here to-day (and I call upon the counsel for the Union Pacific and upon Mr. Huntington to say whether I am not telling the truth when I say) that, without consultation with either the Central Pacific or the Union Pacific, I drew up this bill as counsel for the Chicago and Northwestern road and presented it on its own merits. I wish it disconnected from any scheme which may embrace the settlement of those other corporations. I do not represent them directly or indirectly, and I do not wish any intimation that there is any combination here in order to carry forward either of the schemes. I am willing that every tub should stand on its own bottom.

Senator STEWART. What have you to say to Mr. Coombs's suggestion that, by disposing of the Sioux City road, the Government may cut itself off from any eastern outlet?

Mr. LITTLER. I do not think there is anything in it. The most complete eastern outlet to the west is the Omaha bridge, and that is all sufficient. It is in the direct line between the East and West, and there is no sense in talking about cornering the Government or the Union Pacific by the Blair bridge, or by any other bridge. The law of competition is sufficient to answer that question. If a time comes when another bridge is needed across the Missouri River, the money to build it will be forthcoming.

The CHAIRMAN. Do you know the distance from Omaha to Duluth?

Mr. LITTLER. No, sir; I am not acquainted with the railroad geography like my friend Mr. Coombs.

CENTRAL PACIFIC.

STATEMENT OF MR. C. P. HUNTINGTON—Continued.

Mr. Collis P. Huntington, president of the Southern Pacific Railroad, appeared again before the committee at the suggestion of Senator Morgan. He was duly sworn by the chairman.

Mr. Huntington said:

Mr. CHAIRMAN AND GENTLEMEN OF THE COMMITTEE: I have placed upon paper some things which I desire to say, and I have no doubt that I will repeat some things which I said before on the same line of argument.

I come before you again, not to argue the case, or perhaps to say anything new, as it is the same old subject on which you have heard me before, and, that being so, I may to some considerable extent repeat what I have already said.

When these roads were built everybody wanted them. They were commenced—particularly the Central Pacific (which was begun a year or two before any of the others built under the acts of 1862 or 1864)—when everything was very high in price. Many of our iron rails cost $140 a ton laid in the track. These have all been replaced by steel, which now can be bought for about $30, and they have some six or eight times the wear that the iron had. For many of our locomotives we paid from $20,000 to $32,500 apiece. Just such engines can be bought now for from $5,000 to $8,000. The freight on them then—as it was on all material which had to be sent around Cape Horn—was three times what it is now, with very high insurance. Labor was high, and that and all material used in the construction of the road, except what was bought on the Atlantic Coast, was paid for in gold. The material bought in California included vast quantities of lumber, as many of the very deep arroyas or canyons were spanned by timber trestles, all of which were removed later, so that now the trains pass over solid banks or steel and iron bridges. All of this material had to be paid for in gold, for some of which we had to pay as high as $2.20 in currency for each dollar in gold.

When the Central Pacific Railroad was built, it was thought that the people who embarked their money and their time in it were taking great risks. Many of the men in New York and Boston of large means I endeavored to get to join us in the building of the road, but no one was willing to join us in the undertaking. Such men as Moses Taylor, William E. Dodge, Commodore Garrison, and many others, I spent hours with in the endeavor to induce them to take an interest, and the reply made by Commodore Garrison was in about the words in which they all answered: "Huntington, the risk is too great, and the profits, if any, are too remote. We can not take the risk." I called upon very many of the rich men of California, like D. O. Mills, Eugene Kelly, John Parrott, and others, but none of them would join us, some saying the risks were too great, and others that we were crazy. All the people of California, however, wanted the road; the Government wanted it, and all those in the East who had friends in California wanted it, so that each could go to the other without the inconveniences and hardships of the long and tedious sea voyage. Finally, the work was done, and all said then that it was well done.

I can truly say that, when the Central Pacific was completed, the value of all the assets that the builders had was not sufficient to pay the debts created in doing the work by several millions of dollars. That debt was carried for a long time, until values appreciated; then the shares and other assets were sold and the debt was paid. After the road was completed, before it could be operated in the winter, on account of the snowstorms in the Sierra Nevada Mountains, some 40 miles of the line had to be covered. It may be said that a building had to be put over the track, and in some places galleries had to be built for many miles at an expense of say $50,000 a mile, as it was necessary to build them of enormous strength to withstand the terrible avalanches of snow and rocks which passed over them and which have been passing over them nearly every winter since. The road has accommodated thousands of people and, I think, has harmed no one. In order to be able to give the committee some idea of the magnitude of this snow-shed construction I telegraphed to our people in San Francisco for definite information and have received the following reply:

Lumber used in original construction of snow sheds, 65,000,000 feet, board measure. No record preserved of lumber actually used in repairs. Total cost of snow-shed repairs from 1873 to date, $2,241,000. Divide this by $17, average actual cost, and we have an approximate estimate for repairs and renewals to date, 131,800,000 feet, board measure, making a total for construction and repairs to date, 196,800,000 feet, board measure.

By the experience obtained in the building of this road the builders went on and built other roads, and in all places where they have built land has appreciated enormously. Land which was selling at $2 an acre is now worth $30, $40, $80, and in some places even $100 an acre, and probably there is no section through which the road was built, where the land was good for anything that has not increased in value more than 100 per cent.

The Central Pacific since its completion—and before, I believe—has, under the acts under which it was constructed, not only fulfilled all its requirements but has had no trouble—neither has the Government—with the Indians through whose reservations we passed. The Piutes, a very powerful tribe, were, before the road was built, at war with the whites, but when the road was completed that trouble ceased, and the Central Pacific, I think, is entitled to the credit of its discontinuance.

We have kept the road in fine physical condition, and I believe it is one of the best-equipped roads for what it has to do in the whole country. I believe it could to-day do twice the business that is done on all the transcontinental lines without any inconvenience, and that is one reason why the company is to-day unable to pay the Government what it owes; that is, because of the small tonnage and low rates. The cutting of rates, the small tonnage, and the dividing of it between the overland lines has brought most of the other roads into bankruptcy and made it impossible for the Central Pacific to pay its great debt when due; but with a reasonable extension of time it can and will pay every dollar of it, principal and accrued interest, and, while this principal amount is being regularly and gradually extinguished, the company will be paying as much interest currently as I think the Government would have to pay if it wished to borrow money on a long bond.

I believe few thought that when this road was built there would be any other transcontinental railroad for many years; but it was hardly completed before the Government gave to the road immediately north of it a subsidy in land larger than the value of the lands and bonds that the Central road received; and south of it another road was chartered, and to this the Government gave as large a grant of land as to the one north of us. Now, with the experience the Government had with the Central—seeing its workings and how it policed the whole country, saving almost entirely the many millions it was costing the Government for taking care of the country before the Central was built—it was probably wise to do what it did in giving these large grants to the other roads, as they would reasonably expect the same results with them as they had seen on the Central line.

Therefore, I think no one questions the wisdom of the sovereign power in doing what was done, even if it received nothing from the bond-aided roads other than this great service that has been rendered and is being rendered and will no doubt continue to be rendered for all time; for the country through which the roads were built was for much of the way too poor for civilized man's abiding place; yet the railroad must for its own sake watch over and police it for the protection of its own property. The land grant that the Central Pacific Railroad Company received was very small in value. There were many good lands in California, but they were all, or nearly all, taken up by Spanish grants. The lands which the company received were nearly all in the Sierra Nevada Mountains and in Utah and Nevada. I think most of the members of this committee know the value—or, I might say lack of value—of those lands, and I think no one will question but that the half with the railroad is worth much more than the whole was without it.

Some criticism of the Central Pacific has recently been made by men who, I believe, stand very well in the community, who charge that the Central Pacific has not done its whole duty toward its railroad connections, particularly the Union Pacific. They claim, for instance, that the Union Pacific Company were compelled to build branches at the west end of the road in order to take the business that the Central Pacific would not do; but the facts show that such criticism is unjust and that the charge has no basis.

I asked Mr. J. C. Stubbs, the head of the traffic department, how this was, and without reading his letter, which is too voluminous, I will leave it with you, requesting its careful consideration; but I shall ask you to be patient with me while I quote its salient points:

(1) Mr. Coombs charges that almost from the beginning of the operation of the Union and Central Pacific railroads there has been a lack of cooperation between them, and that the present deplorable condition of both roads has been brought about by a violation of the understanding, at the time Congress gave its aid, that the various roads were to form a continuous line, working in harmony.

In the first place, the question of revenue had little, if any, influence upon the minds of Congress in granting the aid; for at that time the mining industry was all that promised traffic, and mining produced little tonnage. The later development of agriculture was undreamed of then. What the Government wanted was a line across the continent for the quick transportation of troops and supplies, and to enable the territory inhabited by Indians to be policed. With respect to the through transcontinental traffic, there was from the beginning the heartiest and most effective cooperation between the two companies. The Union Pacific absolutely controlled the west-bound business, which was of much greater importance than the east-bound, until 1883, when other lines, through no motion of the Central Pacific, made connection with it at Ogden.

(2) Mr. Coombs says that, for the last ten years, the Central Pacific has been under the full control of the Southern Pacific, and that the Union has been absolutely at its mercy in the matter of through passenger and freight traffic.

Now, the Union Pacific has been in no degree at the mercy of either the Central or the Southern, for they had no more voice in the control of the traffic than the Union Pacific, or any other company whose road made a part of the through line between the Missouri River and the Pacific Coast. On the question of the effect of competition for the through traffic of the Central Pacific, and as illustrating the various influences which have operated in the diversion of traffic from the Union, I ask the patience of the committee in examining this map, which shows in prominent colors the roads which compete for California traffic. The Union Pacific and its ally, the Chicago and Northwestern, are shown in red; the Central in yellow; the Southern Pacific in green. All the lines which are competitive with the Union and Southern Pacific are shown in blue. The lines between the Missouri River and Chicago which are neutral as between the Union Pacific and its competitors west of the river are shown in green. No intelligent man, after examining it, can justly say that the competition of the Southern Pacific, by reason of leasing the Central, exercises the major influence in diverting traffic from the Union Pacific; nor can it be said that the diversion of California traffic from the Union Pacific exercised the greater influence in bringing about its present distressed condition.

The lines competing for the through traffic are, in the order of their opening for business, the Union Pacific, connecting at Ogden; the Atchison, connecting with the Southern Pacific at Deming; the Texas and Pacific, connecting with the Southern at El Paso; the Sunset Route, connecting with the Southern Pacific at El Paso; the Denver and Rio Grande and Rio Grande Western, the Burlington and Missouri River, the Chicago, Rock Island and Pacific, the Atchison, Topeka and Santa Fé, and the Missouri Pacific—all connecting with the Central Pacific at Ogden; the Northern Pacific, connecting with the Central Pacific at Portland; the Atchison, connecting with the Southern through the Atlantic and Pacific at Mojave, Cal., with the right to run its trains on the Southern Pacific through to San Francisco, if it wishes to run them, and operating its own line through to Los Angeles and San Diego; the Union Pacific and Oregon Short Line, connecting with the Southern through the Oregon Railway and Navigation Company at Portland; the Canadian Pacific, in connection with the Pacific Coast Steamship Company, running steamers between Vancouver and San Francisco, and which also connects with the Northern Pacific, and through it and the line operated by the Central Pacific from Portland, reaching all California points; and, finally, the Great Northern, which connects with the Central Pacific at Portland.

Senator STEWART. Have those roads a right to make rates to San Francisco?

Mr. HUNTINGTON. Yes.

Senator STEWART. Without the consent of the Southern Pacific?

Mr. HUNTINGTON. Yes; we all agree upon rates. The Atchison showed $7,000,000 of unpaid rebates for getting business.

Senator STEWART. Have these other roads the power to fix the rates if you dissent?

Mr. HUNTINGTON. We made arrangements with them long years ago merely that we prorate.

The CHAIRMAN. The road at the point of shipment makes the rate, and you accept it pro rata?

Mr. HUNTINGTON. Yes; the Central Pacific is probably the most liberal road in the United States—or rather the Southern Pacific.

Of the through freight passing to and from the Pacific Coast over the various lines operated in whole or in part by the Central Pacific or Southern Pacific during the ten years ending with 1892, the Central Pacific (Ogden Line) carried 54 per cent against 46 per cent carried by the other lines, while of the passenger traffic for the same period it carried over 58 per cent against all the other lines.

Senator MORGAN. Up to what time was that?

Mr. HUNTINGTON. That was during the ten years ending in 1892.

Senator WOLCOTT. Was that west-bound business?

Mr. HUNTINGTON. East and west. The Union Pacific made all the west-bound rates.

During the first two years of this period, all these lines were operated by the Central Pacific, and for the remaining eight years by the Southern, and in these two years the percentages carried by the Ogden Line were, for freight, 55 per cent, and for passenger, 62 per cent. Since then the Northern Pacific, the Atlantic and Pacific, the Canadian Pacific, and the Southern California roads have become factors; but it seems to me that this fine showing for the Central Pacific gives us the right to claim that it has been accomplished by reason of the common control of both the Central and Southern Pacific lines.

In corroboration of the above, let me say that in 1885 the Transcontinental Association, composed of all the railroad companies interested in the Pacific Coast traffic with the East (to which Mr. Coombs generally refers), agreed to pool the traffic, and, being unable to agree upon the allotment, left it to a board of eminent and practical railroad men, with the result that, after having heard the claims of all parties, they made the following award:

	Per cent.
Passenger traffic:	
To the Ogden lines	61
To the other lines	39
Freight traffic:	
To the Ogden lines	51
To the other lines	49

As to the competition of the Southern Pacific Railroad, which is used by the Union Pacific officials as an excuse for their greatest loss, the records show that the Sunset Route—that is, the steamship and rail line between New York and San Francisco via New Orleans—participates in very little traffic which might be directed over the Ogden lines, except traffic interchanged by California with the Atlantic seaboard, and the sum of that traffic is but 20 per cent of the total traffic interchanged by California with United States territory on the east of the Missouri River, and a portion of that is taken from the Panama and Cape Horn routes at rates so low that the all-rail transcontinental lines do not care to compete for it.

The CHAIRMAN. You take it by virtue of your lower rates?

Mr. HUNTINGTON. Yes; we take it by figuring our rates on merely paying expenses. We take it at rates that would have bankrupted the road if all freights were taken at the same rates. We figured out the train expenses, and took it at something over those expenses. You have got four men upon a train, two brakemen and stoker, and there is oil and fuel and waste and wear; so that we calculated that if we could make $50 on the whole train we would take freight at those rates.

The CHAIRMAN. You had water rates from New York to New Orleans, and then the rates on your line?

Mr. HUNTINGTON. Yes.

The CHAIRMAN. And you took freight at those rates for the purpose of adding to your business at a very small profit rather than not take it at all?

Mr. HUNTINGTON. We took it at rates throwing out the account of interest, taxes, superintendence, etc.—everything but the mere train expenses.

The CHAIRMAN. You took it on the general principle that you would increase your business if you could, even at a small profit?

Mr. HUNTINGTON. Yes; but we could only do it on account of cheap water rates. It seemed that we could make a little over the cost of movement.

Senator STEWART. That did not reach freight in the interior States?

Mr. HUNTINGTON. No; only what lies upon tide water.

Senator MORGAN. What did you give to the Panama Railroad under that arrangement?

Mr. HUNTINGTON. We have not had any arrangement with the Panama Railroad for several years.

The CHAIRMAN. Well, when you did have it?

Mr. HUNTINGTON. The Interstate Commerce Committee has a copy of the contract which we made with the Panama road.

Senator WOLCOTT. Will you file with the committee a full statement of your tonnage and freight rates?

Mr. HUNTINGTON. Yes, I will do so.

Senator MORGAN. How long did that Panama contract continue?

Mr. HUNTINGTON. I do not recollect. I think it was subject to six months' notice.

Senator MORGAN. How long was it actually in operation?

Mr. HUNTINGTON. I do not know; I should think four or five or six years; it may have been more.

Senator MORGAN. State your recollection of the substance of that arrangement.

Mr. HUNTINGTON. I will send a copy of the contract to the committee.

Senator MORGAN. I would like to have it now.

Mr. HUNTINGTON. I haven't got it and I can hardly tell what it was. My impression is that we gave the Panama Railroad Company $70,000 a month for so much space in three steamers—running from $60,000 to $100,000.

Senator MORGAN. You bought the space, whatever it was, in the three steamers at so much a month?

Mr. HUNTINGTON. We hired so much space.

Senator MORGAN. At the rate of $75,000 or $100,000 per month?

Mr. HUNTINGTON. Yes.

Senator MORGAN. Whether you filled that space with freights or not made no difference?

Mr. HUNTINGTON. I think we did fill it. We calculated to fill it.

Senator MORGAN. It made no difference in the agreement, though, whether you actually sent freights on the steamships?

Mr. HUNTINGTON. My impression is that we hired so much space, expecting to fill it.

Senator MORGAN. About how much was that space in proportion to the carrying capacity of the steamship?

Mr. HUNTINGTON. I think it was about 6 tons.

Senator MORGAN. How would that compare with the capacity of the ships?

Mr. HUNTINGTON. My impression is that the ships ran from 1,500 to 2,500 tons.

Senator MORGAN. Inside or outside measurement?

Mr. HUNTINGTON. What we would call net tonnage. The gross tonnage is what the whole will carry, and then they put the engines and machinery in and the balance is called the net tonnage.

Senator MORGAN. And you say that the net tonnage of the steamers was from 1,500 to 2,000 tons?

Mr. HUNTINGTON. I think so.

Senator MORGAN. You are not certain about that?

Mr. HUNTINGTON. It is very difficult to carry those things in one's mind, but the fact is easily ascertained.

Senator MORGAN. To the extent that you thus obtained and monopolized the capacity of these ships, to that same extent you shut out the people of California, Oregon, and Washington from occupying these ships with their freight?

Mr. HUNTINGTON. We carried their goods all together.

Senator MORGAN. To the extent that you monopolized the freight capacity on these ships, you shut out the right of the people of California, Oregon, and Washington to send their freight on those vessels?

Mr. HUNTINGTON. Of course, if we hired the tonnage, I suppose they could not double it on the same vessel.

Senator MORGAN. So that what you meant to haul to the Pacific Ocean was space and not freight?

Mr. HUNTINGTON. We meant to haul freight. The object was this: We wanted to get a certain price for carrying goods. If they cut rates very much they would run into bankruptcy, and it is always unfortunate for capital to be wasted. Most of the overland lines have gone into bankruptcy, and it seems to be more wise in business matters to agree to something which will give a fair return on the capital invested.

Senator MORGAN. I want to know why it was that the people of California and of the whole Pacific Coast were in this way deprived of the opportunity of having the advantage of this line of steamers in carrying their freight to and from New York.

Mr. HUNTINGTON. I do not see exactly how they were. As I say, there is nothing covered up by it. We sent a copy of the contract to the Interstate Commerce Commission. It was a thing which was admitted. It gave the Panama Company some little thing so that it could continue its line without running into bankruptcy.

Senator MORGAN. Who were the owners of this steamship line?

Mr. HUNTINGTON. The Pacific Mail.

Senator MORGAN. Who were the owners of the Pacific Mail?

Mr. HUNTINGTON. Its stockholders.

Senator MORGAN. Who were its stockholders?

Mr. HUNTINGTON. I can not tell you; there are a great many of them. I have none of the stock.

Senator MORGAN. Does the company which you represent have any stock of the Pacific Mail?

Mr. HUNTINGTON. No; I think not. The Central Pacific did not have any and I do not think the Union Pacific had.

Senator MORGAN. Do the owners of the Southern Pacific own stock in it?

Mr. HUNTINGTON. No.

Senator MORGAN. Where was the stock of the Pacific Mail owned chiefly?

Mr. HUNTINGTON. I should think it was owned in New York. The stock is sold there every day.

Senator MORGAN. What companies were represented in that arrangement you have spoken of?

Mr. HUNTINGTON. I think that all the overland railroad companies were represented.

Senator MORGAN. Name them.

Mr. HUNTINGTON. I should say the Northern Pacific, the Great Northern, the Union Pacific, the Central Pacific, the Southern Pacific, the Atchison, and the Texas Pacific, and perhaps some others.

Senator MORGAN. They were all parties to this agreement for the purchase of the tonnage of this steamship line?

Mr. HUNTINGTON. For the purchasing of space.

Senator MORGAN. Was not the purpose of that agreement that freights which would otherwise have gone by sea would go by the overland railroads?

Mr. HUNTINGTON. No; I think that the object was naturally to get prices of freight steady so that bankruptcy could be kept off. I think that was the object of it.

Senator MORGAN. But in order to keep out of bankruptcy, was it not deemed necessary to force the freights into the railroad lines instead of permitting them to go by water?

Mr. HUNTINGTON. No; we always filled the space.

Senator MORGAN. Are you sure of that?

Mr. HUNTINGTON. I do not know that we aways did it. I know that it was calculated we would fill the space.

Senator MORGAN. What arrangement had you at the same time with the Panama Railroad Company?

Mr. HUNTINGTON. It was the one arrangement. Whatever was done was done in the joint interest of the Panama Railroad and the Pacific Mail.

Senator MORGAN. Did the Panama Railroad own the steamship line?

Mr. HUNTINGTON. No.

Senator MORGAN. What did the Panama Railroad get out of that contract?

Mr. HUNTINGTON. It got a certain percentage.

Senator MORGAN. What was it?

Mr. HUNTINGTON. The same as it had upon the through traffic, and the same as it gets now on the through traffic—55 per cent from New York to Panama. The Pacific Mail does not run steamers on this side now.

Senator MORGAN. What difference was made in freights under this arrangement between the freights shipped under your contract and those shipped by the people at large?

Mr. HUNTINGTON. I do not know.

Senator MORGAN. There was some contract, was there not, about differentiating the rates?

Mr. HUNTINGTON. I do not know whether there was or not.

Senator MORGAN. Was there not a great difference in regard to the freights carried by the Panama Railroad under your contract?

Mr. HUNTINGTON. I have no doubt there was.

Senator MORGAN. And you do not know them?

Mr. HUNTINGTON. I must have seen the contract.

Senator MORGAN. I would like to have a full and frank statement about that.

Senator FRYE. Mr. Huntington has offered to produce the contract itself, and I submit that he is not to be cross-examined about facts which are contained in a contract that was in writing when his memory does not extend to them.

Senator MORGAN. Then the examination is not to close until the contract is produced?

The CHAIRMAN. If the contract will show the rates that would be the best evidence.

Mr. HUNTINGTON. If I were in my office I could produce the contract.

The CHAIRMAN. The contract does show the rates?

Mr. HUNTINGTON. I have no doubt it does.

Senator MORGAN. I am not disposed to accept the statement that the contract does show that. At all events, I shall try to exercise my right to cross-examine the witness on the contract when he produces it.

The CHAIRMAN. The point which Mr. Frye wants to make is that the contract ought to be the basis of the examination, and that Mr. Huntington should be able to refresh his memory by looking at it.

Mr. HUNTINGTON. I should like the Senator to have everything connected with the contract and everything I know about it.

Senator MORGAN. Mr. Huntington did not expect that no question would be asked about this contract, and he should have been prepared to answer the questions.

The chairman directed Mr. Huntington to produce the contract when he comes next before the committee.

Mr. HUNTINGTON (3). Mr. Coombs says it is currently reported in California that compulsion is brought to bear upon shippers who wish to ship over the Central line to force them to ship by the Southern.

Outside of the fact that rumor is a bad argument in itself, let me say at once that this charge is false, and that an appeal to the shippers themselves is the quickest refutation of it; and as the Southern Pacific has not been at any time without competition during the period referred to, both by sea and rail, shippers have been free to exercise their choice of routes, and to say that they could be forced over any special route simply shows ignorance of the subject and of the method of soliciting and handling traffic, to say nothing of the well-known independence of shippers under competitive conditions. The Union Pacific has been represented in California by as large a staff of soliciting agents as the Central and Southern Pacific, and all the other competing companies have also been represented.

(4) Mr. Coombs explains the Union Pacific's course in building roads, or entering into alliance with roads already built to the north and south of it, which should act as feeders to the main line east of Ogden, as being necessary to release itself from the clutches of its competitor. This simply anticipates a charge that the Union Pacific has itself been building lines to divert freight from the Central Pacific. Now, the facts are that the Utah Northern was commenced in 1872, some ten or twelve years before the Southern Pacific was built. The Oregon Short Line was commenced before the Southern Pacific was completed; when the Central was then, as it is now, being conducted upon lines of great liberality, while our eastern neighbor, the Union Pacific, charged over the Utah Northern from Ogden to Silver Bow, Mont., first-class, $4.10; second, $4; third, $3.75; fourth, $3.25, per hundred pounds.

When through rates were established between San Francisco and

Silver Bow the proportions received by the two companies were as follows:

	First class.	Second class.	Third class.	Fourth class.
Total rate per 100 pounds	$5.05	$4.55	$4.05	$3.50
Utah Northern (Union Pacific)	4.25	4.00	3.75	3.25
Central Pacific	.80	.55	.30	.25

The disproportionate character of these rates will be better realized when it is noted that the rates received by the Utah Northern were for a haul of 390 miles, while those received by the Central Pacific were for a haul of 883 miles west of Ogden, and they were fixed by the Union Pacific, which then controlled the situation with respect to this through business.

The Oregon Short Line cut off from the Central Pacific all participation in the large and valuable traffic interchanged by Oregon and Washington with the Eastern States by way of the Union and Central, which, before this diversion, was carried via Ogden to Roseville, through to Oregon and Washington. When the Utah and Northern Railroad was completed to Butte, Mont., it passed into the control of the Union Pacific, which instantly began discriminating against the Central Pacific traffic with Montana, which was considerable, in order to force the business over the Union Pacific's rails and extensions, and to divert it from the Central Pacific line over which it had been going; and its efforts were largely successful.

When the Central Pacific first commenced taking coal from the Union Pacific in 1870 we paid that company for coal from the Almy mine $4.15 per ton of 2,000 pounds for a haul of 75 miles mostly down grade to Ogden, or 5½ cents per ton per mile, while coal is hauled on some of the roads in this country for 2½ mills per ton per mile. In fact, very high rates prevailed until the Denver and Rio Grande Western was built to Ogden, and since then we have bought coal delivered there for about half of what we paid for transporting our own coal 75 miles, and the Rio Grande Western hauls it, as I remember, about 125 miles. I do not believe any of the officers of the Union Pacific Company who were familiar with their business have ever made any complaint of our handling their business on the Central Pacific line; and since such great companies as the Chicago, Burlington and Quincy, Rock Island, Chicago and Alton, and others, which were their through connections, reached us at Ogden, we have endeavored to treat them well; and while doing some things for the Union Pacific that we did not do for them, we could not afford, because we did not think it was right for us to refuse to handle the business they brought to us and give something in return for the business so brought.

Let me say here that, as a rule, the Central Pacific has stood with the Union Pacific against other lines in all matters relating to the through traffic, where it could be done without affecting injuriously the public interest. Previous to 1887, the larger part of the time, the traffic between all the lines was pooled, and the share of the Union Pacific was determined either by its own officers or by disinterested parties. If the common control of the Central and Southern restrained the Union Pacific in any degree in its independence of action, that restraint was never any greater than it was upon each and every other competitor; and, far from being harmful to the Union Pacific, it was of incalculable benefit in preventing unrestricted and unregulated competition, which, because of its greater volume of business, would have been more hurtful to the Union Pacific than to any other company. I would be willing to leave it to any court of practical railway managers whether the stability in rates would not have been less constant and effective during the whole period had either the Union or Central controlled the other, or had the two roads been operated as a single interest.

Considerable has been said with reference to a plan which one of the Senators has prepared for the settlement of the debt; and I may be pardoned for saying that, in my opinion, its operation would result not in benefit but in harm to any interest that deserves benefit, as it would retard commerce and trade, and render the stock of both the Union and Central Pacific railroads valueless to their owners. Looking back upon the situation at the time the acts of 1862 and 1864 were passed, and at the temper and sentiment of Congress at that time, I can understand how difficult it must be for Members of Congress whose familiarity with national legislation came at a later date to appreciate just what the position of the Government was toward these Pacific railroad enterprises, and I unhesitatingly say that it was never contemplated by the statesmen of that day that the Union and Central Pacific railroads should form one continuous connected line, to be operated without being permitted to make connections or arrangements for interchange of traffic with any other company or companies which should compete for a common traffic.

The claim is in itself preposterous, as I think I can show you. Neither of these acts can be fairly construed into such a strained signification, and if they had the meaning imputed to them by Senator Thurston, why does the interstate commerce act provide, as in section 3, that "it shall be unlawful for any common carrier to make or give any undue or unreasonable preference or advantage to any particular person, company, firm, corporation, or locality, or any particular description of traffic, in any respect whatsoever," etc., and that "every common carrier subject to the provisions of this act shall, according to their respective powers, afford all reasonable, proper, and equal facilities for the interchange of traffic between their respective lines and for the receiving, forwarding, and delivering of passengers and property to and from their several lines and those connecting therewith, and shall not discriminate in their rates and charges between such connecting lines."

Referring again to the map, let me say that it is to the agency of these powerful competing railroads and their contributions to the traffic of the Central Pacific quite as much as, perhaps more than, to the Union Pacific, that the Central Pacific has enjoyed so large a share of the traffic to and from California. Once close the Ogden gateway, or attempt to place them at a disadvantage as compared with the Union Pacific, and does any member of this committee doubt that they will find some other outlet or connection, and when that is done the value of the Central and Union Pacific as earning properties will at once and permanently be damaged.

Senator STEWART. What do you mean by that?

Mr. HUNTINGTON. If these other roads were shut out from Ogden they would force themselves through and build another bridge of 300 miles long (as it were) across that desert.

The CHAIRMAN. They would only do that if they considered the California business sufficient?

Senator MORGAN. That would not hurt the country?

Mr. HUNTINGTON. Nothing could hurt that country.

Senator MORGAN. It would do it good?

Mr. HUNTINGTON. No, sir.

Senator MORGAN. Is that because the land is intrinsically not fertile or because of want of water?

Mr. HUNTINGTON. If there was water there there would be people there.

Senator MORGAN. It only depends upon the question of human ingenuity to get water there?

Mr. HUNTINGTON. But there is no water in sight. They bring water there by gravity.

Senator MORGAN. Snows fall in that country?

Mr. HUNTINGTON. Not much snow. Five inches of all kinds of water in Nevada in the year.

Senator MORGAN. You do not suppose that that country is always to be a desert?

Mr. HUNTINGTON. I believe that between there and the western passes of the Wahsatch Mountains, if we were to move our railroad away, there would not be in two years' time a thousand people there within 5 miles of the road.

Senator MORGAN. But if you built two lines of railroad there, there would be 2,000 people.

Mr. HUNTINGTON. No; I do not think there would be any more than there are now.

The CHAIRMAN. The capital invested must necessarily depend upon the termini of the roads.

Mr. HUNTINGTON. Yes; that road might as well be a thousand miles in the air so far as any local business is concerned.

Senator MORGAN. I think that these gentlemen from the West are anticipating that some day or other they will have a fine country there by virtue of irrigation.

Mr. HUNTINGTON. I hope they are right, but I do not see where they are likely to get the water.

Senator MORGAN. Take the country 500 miles to the north of the Central Pacific and an equal area of country 500 miles to the south of it; is the intrinsically fertile soil as good in the southern portion as it is in the northern portion?

Mr. HUNTINGTON. No; I should think it was better in the north.

Senator MORGAN. Is it very much better?

Mr. HUNTINGTON. I should think it considerably better. When you get to the Snake River in the north, in here [indicating on the map], I believe the country is very good. Here to the south of it [indicating] it is very poor. There are no agricultural lands in the lower part of Nevada or in the southwestern part of Utah. I had a corps of engineers in Washington County looking out for coal. They didn't find any coal there, and they said there "wasn't any coal and nothing else there." This road here [indicating on the map] lies on the high plateau of Albuquerque. This line here to White River [indicating] lies low, not more than 600 or 700 feet above tide water. It can be irrigated from the Colorado River or from the Gila or from the Salt River, and these rivers can bring any amount of water.

Senator MORGAN. The area south [indicating on the map] is an absolute desert of sage brush?

Mr. HUNTINGTON. Yes; there is some actual timber.

Senator MORGAN. It is fertile land, and what it wants is water?

Mr. HUNTINGTON. Yes.

Senator MORGAN. These lands are as good as the lands to the north?

Mr. HUNTINGTON. I should think so.

Senator MORGAN. And the reason why the lands are better to the north is that there are better opportunities for irrigation, on account of the mountains, and because more snow falls here than falls below?

Mr. HUNTINGTON. Yes; there is much more snow here [indicating] than there is in Arizona.

What, then, will happen to the Government's lien? Will there be any recompense to the Union Pacific division of the "connected continuous line," by additions to its traffic and revenues? Certainly not, because these competitors are not going out of the through business, for that would not be to their own interest or to that of the Government or the public. They will find a new path, and the Central and Union Pacific will not only lose business, but suffer material loss in the average rate obtainable for what is left. These are facts which it will be well for you, gentlemen of the committee, as men of intelligence and business experience, to carefully consider.

It is well to note that the Rock Island and the Burlington could as well have connected with the Union Pacific at Denver as with the Rio Grande and Colorado Midland roads, but the Union Pacific closed its line and forced them to an adverse connection. What has been the result? Instead of these two powerful systems being feeders to the Union Pacific line for about one-half of its length they have become gigantic competitors, and this competition has been the most powerful factor in the diversion of traffic from the Union Pacific line, while at the same time they have been equally potent in collecting and bringing to the Central Pacific traffic which, without their aid, would have gone by the Southern gateways and been lost, not only to the Union but to the Central Pacific also.

Again, the Union Pacific, owning and operating the Utah and Northern, running from Ogden to Butte and Helena, and connecting with the Oregon Short Line at Pocatello for Portland and Puget Sound, also shut out the Rio Grande Western and all its connections from any participation in that business upon fair or living terms; so that it may be assumed that the policy of the Union Pacific has been to cut off all connection and interchange of traffic with roads physically connected with it but which were not under its control. I have already given you an example of this. You must remember that the Chicago, Burlington and Quincy, the Rock Island, etc., could all make connection at Denver with the Santa Fe system and could divert their traffic and send it into California via Mojave without much sacrifice of their revenue. To the Rock Island it would be a matter of indifference whether it carried the traffic to Fort Worth and gave it to the Texas and Pacific, or to Denver and delivered it to its connections for the Ogden route. The Chicago, Burlington and Quincy and the Missouri Pacific could in like manner connect with the Santa Fe, which would no doubt be very glad to open its line to such powerful feeders. In fact, I see no possible advantage which could accrue to the Union Pacific by any such arrangement as is proposed by Senator Thurston, but I do see the great harm and detriment that would result to both of these bond-aided roads, and one thing I believe to be certain—that it would permanently decrease the value of the Government lien.

It does seem to me that it would be better for all interests—of course, including the greater interest of the Government—that the Central Pacific remain, as it were, an open highway to treat all who meet it at Ogden fairly and alike, as it has the physical and financial ability to do—if the Government will make a fair settlement, as I have said—many times the business that would reach it there. The Central Pacific will continue to do as it has done—pay all its debts and endeavor to create harmony among the lines reaching it at Ogden, so as to make not only all the companies, but the patrons of each and every company, satisfied. If there should be one continued line from Chicago to San Francisco, as it is now from Chicago over the Northwestern Railroad to Ogden, these other great companies could hardly expect fair usage from such a line, reaching, as it would, something more than halfway out, when they were refused anything like equal mileage rates from, say, Cheyenne to Ogden, or other points east of the Rockies, for they are strong and important companies, and would be bound to build through from Ogden to the Pacific Coast over a barren country that needs no railroad.

The country between the Wahsatch and the Sierra Nevada mountains is like a bridge, high in the air, so far as business is concerned, and after a new road was completed the competition brought about under such circumstances would probably make it impossible for either road to earn sufficient to pay anything to the Government, and perhaps not even to be able to meet its current and fixed charges outside of the Government claim. So it would be an injury not only to this great Central interest, but to the Northern Pacific, the Great Northern, the Atchison, Topeka and Santa Fe, the Southern Pacific, and the Texas Pacific, and many other roads participating with them in this transcontinental business. In short, the question before you, gentlemen, is whether this road over the desert between the eastern base of the Sierra Nevadas and the western base of the Wahsatch shall be used as a bridge for all the roads reaching Ogden from the East, or used for only one.

As for the rates of fares and freights on the Central Pacific, I am quite sure they are lower than those of any other road in the world operated under the same circumstances. The Central and Southern Pacific west of Ogden have no great tonnage. While the fruit products are fairly large, the miscellaneous freight is not large, as, say, west of the one hundredth meridian lies more than one-half of the acreage of the United States, with not over 4,000,000 of people, while east of that line, on the same or less acreage, there are probably 65,000,000 of people to-day. The Chesapeake and Ohio Railroad, some few years ago, transported, in twelve months, 29,000,000 pounds of freight more than was handled over the, say, 8,000 miles of the Central and Southern Pacific west of Ogden and New Orleans. Notwithstanding this light tonnage, the average rates per passenger per mile for 1894 were 1.946 cents, or less than 2 cents. The average rates per ton per mile for 1894 were 1.171 cents, or less than 12 mills.

For the ten months ended October 31, 1895 (the latest date to which we have this information), the average rates were 1.054 cents, or 10½ mills; which, considering the vast mileage and the high cost of fuel and labor—in fact, almost everything that enters into the operation of these roads is much higher than in any other part of the United States—is phenomenally low, and the roads could not live unless those controlling them were exceedingly watchful and practiced a rigid and intelligent economy, keeping their rolling stock and permanent way in the very best condition, for these are the tools by which the railroad makes its money.

But I have detained the committee too long, and will hurry my remarks to a close. These debts are soon coming due, and I hope you will offer us something, the requirements of which the company can meet. I have been in business for myself sixty years, lacking only a few months, and I have always paid 100 cents on the dollar. While this is not a personal debt of mine, yet I take as much interest in the matter as I would if I were the sole owner and responsible for the Government claim, for the Central Pacific is the first railroad that I ever built, and no fairer or honester work has ever been done. I have nothing to take back and nothing to apologize for in that undertaking, and I do not come here asking equities or eulogies. I only ask on behalf of the Central Pacific Railroad Company that you treat the question of a settlement with the Government on business principles. If these are observed I have no fear of the result.

I would recommend the company to pay as much interest currently as the road could earn over its fixed and operating expenses (other than the Government claim, as all other than the Government claim is perfectly good, there being little or no floating debt), and pay into the Treasury of the United States every six months a fixed sum, until the whole indebtedness, both principal and the interest that has accrued in the past, is paid. As these payments are made, the principal amount due the Government will be steadily diminished, while the property will continue naturally to increase in value, for every house that is built upon or near the line will bring a new patron, and every acre plowed will bring additional tonnage, so that the security will be unquestionably good.

We had hoped that the Government would take 1½ per cent interest on the great debt owing to it by the Central Pacific and require a certain fixed sum paid on the 1st day of January and the 1st day of July of each year until the whole amount, comprising the original principal of the debt and all the back interest, had been finally and fully liquidated. In doing this, I should be satisfied that we had done well by the Government, considering the fact that the road had received so little from the Government business sent over it compared with what it was expected, when the acts of 1862 and 1864 were passed, that the company would get. Up to the time of the passage of those acts, the Government had been paying vast sums for policing the immense area of country between the Missouri and Sacramento rivers.

When the Pacific railroads were completed and in operation, the Government might well say, "We have builded better than we knew, even if we get no interest upon the money loaned toward the construction of this great work, for it was done seven years before the time allowed to the companies for the completion of the undertaking, and in those seven years the Government saved more than all the money loaned to these organizations." So well was it for the Government that it gave freely to the Northern Pacific and to the Atlantic and Pacific land which was of greater value than the bonds and lands granted to the pioneer roads. The Government must have realized that in doing this it was deliberately destroying, or greatly weakening, the security it had on the Central line, because it was taking away from it much of its earning power, from which alone the Government could expect a return of the money loaned, and such was, in fact, the logical result. Yet, who doubts to-day that the wisdom of the statesmen of that time was amply justified when the magnificent development of the great West, due to the onward march of the world's greatest civilizer—the railroad—is considered? For, from the moment of their completion, these roads, like the Central and the Union Pacific, have thoroughly policed the wide expanse of territory which they traverse, without cost to the Government, and have made it possible to settle up the arable lands along their lines.

But we shall have to leave to you, gentlemen of the committee, the method of this proposed settlement, and I have faith to believe that in the proposition you lay before Congress you will not put upon the Central Pacific a burden greater than it can bear. Speaking on behalf of that road, I assure you that we will do all we can, and no corporation or individual can do more than that. Further than that, it is my belief that no other men, or set of men, can do as much for the Central Pacific in clearing off this obligation as its builders can. The record of the road is clean and clear, despite the cries of the noisy few, who, like jackals, howl along its track, and the great mass of the people of California know and appreciate the greatness and the value of the work that we have done. I personally am proud of the record we have made, for we have never failed to fulfill all our contracts with the Government, with States, and with individuals.

Senator MORGAN. You mentioned that under certain conditions or certain methods of dealing with the Central Pacific the other competing lines south of it will be compelled to make their way across this desert country to the Pacific Ocean—to bridge the desert. What motive would they have for getting to that country except for the traffic?

Mr. HUNTINGTON. They would go for the traffic beyond the desert.

Senator MORGAN. Is there enough to justify their building the road through?

Mr. HUNTINGTON. I hardly think there is, but these things are being done continually. They would divide the cost, and when they get to this point [indicating on the map] they would have a thousand miles of haul, which might make up for the haul across the desert.

Senator MORGAN. And each of those roads that would tap the Pacific Coast on the Southern Pacific would perhaps draw a considerable portion of traffic from the Southern Pacific?

Mr. HUNTINGTON. The roads would probably get their proportion of our tonnage, and we would try to return tonnage to them.

Senator MORGAN. Would not that be one of the inducements for the building of this bridge, as you call it, across the desert?

Mr. HUNTINGTON. They would get tonnage.

Senator MORGAN. If tonnage is not there they could not get it?

Mr. HUNTINGTON. No.

Senator MORGAN. Do you think that the prospective growth of the Pacific Coast south of San Francisco would be sufficient to justify these roads in building this bridge across the desert?

Mr. HUNTINGTON. That is a question. But I think that three or four of these great roads would join together and build a road and have a joint ownership of it.

Senator MORGAN. I notice that there are seven great railroads which connect the Pacific Coast with the country to the east of the Rocky Mountain range—the Northern Pacific, the Great Northern, the Central Pacific, the Oregon Short Line, the Union Pacific, the Southern Pacific, the Canadian Pacific, and the Atchison and Topeka. Each of these roads is making a living?

Mr. HUNTINGTON. The Atchison has been in the courts twice. The last time it showed pretty bad, and the first time not much better.

Senator MORGAN. Their being in court does not prove that they are not making a living, does it?

Mr. HUNTINGTON. I had supposed so.

Senator MORGAN. The Union Pacific appears to be making a better living since it has been in court than it was out of the court.

Mr. HUNTINGTON. The Union Pacific has not made the interest on its first-mortgage bonds, I believe, which is the best evidence that it is not doing well.

Senator MORGAN. Still its income is increasing?

Mr. HUNTINGTON. I should hope so, and I believe it is.

Senator MORGAN. Do you think that the competition between these roads is going to result in the bankruptcy of all of them because there is not enough traffic with the Pacific Coast to supply them with business?

Mr. HUNTINGTON. I think perhaps they will have to run very close in order to get past the headlands.

Senator MORGAN. Still they will all survive?

Mr. HUNTINGTON. I really do not know, but I should think they would have pretty hard times. However, not being a prophet or the son of a prophet, I would not like to venture a prediction.

Senator MORGAN. Do you think that the stockholders had better go into bankruptcy than continue to run those roads?

Mr. HUNTINGTON. I have been in mercantile business for fifty-seven years and have been through all the panics. I commenced in a very small way and have seen hard times, but I have never had a piece of my paper go to protest in all that time.

Senator MORGAN. You mean that your genius can survive calamities which others would not survive?

Mr. HUNTINGTON. I would not call it by that name; I would call it untiring perseverance, that works twenty-four hours a day, if necessary. I believe that I have done better than anybody else could for the Central Pacific.

Senator MORGAN. Do you really believe that there is enough of income for these seven railroad lines to sustain prices?

Mr. HUNTINGTON. I believe that they should be paid fair prices. There have been a great many uncomfortable things said by the people of San Francisco. For particular reasons they went and started a line of steamers from San Francisco to Panama. They ran it at great cost. As they say themselves, they made $19,000,000 at a cost of $400,000, and they would have continued if they could have raised the money to carry it on.

Senator MORGAN. Why did they stop?

Mr. HUNTINGTON. I do not know.

Senator MORGAN. But during that time they had pretty severe competition?

Mr. HUNTINGTON. They made their own rates.

Senator MORGAN. They had competition, however?

Mr. HUNTINGTON. They may have had competition.

Senator MORGAN. What was it?

Mr. HUNTINGTON. They had the Pacific Mail and the overland railroads.

Senator MORGAN. In combination?

Mr. HUNTINGTON. I do not know whether there was a combination. They had to go down on their prices.

Senator MORGAN. I understand that you had a contract with the Pacific Mail.

Mr. HUNTINGTON. The contract with the Pacific Mail was six or seven years ago. We had no contract then.

Senator MORGAN. You do not consider it necessary that the Congress of the United States should wreck the Central Pacific?

Mr. HUNTINGTON. I believe it will be the worst thing that the Government could possibly do, and I would awfully hate to have the Government do it. I would rather work twenty years without a dollar than to have the Central Pacific fail in any one thing. The Central

Pacific will pay a fixed sum, and at any time that it fails for six months to do that the Government can go right in and take possession of the property without going to a court or to Congress.

Senator MORGAN. Ought there not be an intimate natural business connection under one management between the Union Pacific and the Central Pacific?

Mr. HUNTINGTON. I believe that that would be the worst thing that could happen. I believe that we can accommodate all other roads better without any such business connection.

Senator MORGAN. Is there any reason against it?

Mr. HUNTINGTON. I think there is.

Senator MORGAN. What is it?

Mr. HUNTINGTON. The Central Pacific has been run better than any of the other Pacific roads.

Senator MORGAN. I am speaking of the future.

Mr. HUNTINGTON. I do not know how to judge of the future except by the past. The competition is certainly sharp enough. It has nearly bankrupted all the roads.

Senator MORGAN. Would it increase the competition to have those two companies under one management?

Mr. HUNTINGTON. Probably not.

Senator MORGAN. Would it increase or lessen the expenses?

Mr. HUNTINGTON. I think it would increase the expenses. I do not think that anybody can run the Central Pacific as well as I can, and keep it in such good condition.

Senator MORGAN. But after you pass away posterity will have to take charge of it.

Mr. HUNTINGTON. You and I will hold on a good while yet.

Senator MORGAN. I hope so; but what I want to know is whether it is not better and cheaper to have a long line of road under one management than to have shorter lines under two managements?

Mr. HUNTINGTON. We have virtually under one management 9,000 miles of road. What broke the Atchison people the first time was the building of a line from Kansas City into Chicago. Before that they gathered freights at three or four different places.

Senator MORGAN. Your answer is instructive but it is not responsive. I would like to know whether you do not think that a line from Omaha to San Francisco under one management can be managed more cheaply and with larger economies than two lines under separate management?

Mr. HUNTINGTON. I do not believe so, because there is a limit to the capacity of one set of people.

Senator MORGAN. You have incorporated a great sweep of organization under your Kentucky charter.

Mr. HUNTINGTON. I say there is a limit.

Senator MORGAN. What is the limit?

Mr. HUNTINGTON. I do not know.

Senator MORGAN. How many miles have you in operation on the Southern Pacific under your Kentucky charter?

Mr. HUNTINGTON. Say about 7,000 miles.

Senator MORGAN. Then that is not the limit.

Mr. HUNTINGTON. I do not think that anybody will work as I do.

Senator MORGAN. It is not 7,000 miles between Ogden and San Francisco; so that that line of railroad is within your limit?

Mr. HUNTINGTON. Yes.

Senator MORGAN. Then your argument does not seem to hold good.

Mr. HUNTINGTON. I hold that we can do that business and manage that road more economically than any other road I know of west of the Missouri River. A gentleman in the other end of the Capitol said that the Central Pacific branches were not worth what they cost. I wish to say that the Central Pacific is altogether a different road from what it was when it was built. We have not a single timber structure, not one. When we built the road we had very large trestles over mountains, and wooden bridges. They are all now iron or steel bridges and the canyons are all filled up where there was not water to prevent their being filled up. We filled them all up so that now the road is running on solid banks over those mountains. I do not think there is an iron rail in the main track. The rails are all steel. The road is pretty thoroughly ballasted. We had on that road when we started $1,500,000 of convertible bonds. They became due and we paid them off. We had $1,500,000 in State-aid bonds and we paid them off when they became due. We renewed the debt on the California and Oregon division for $1,500,000 less than the old mortgage. In short, we have paid oft $20,892,000, and our rates have certainly been low. There is no better test of that than the fact that the price of land is more than ten times as much in California as when we built our road.

Senator MORGAN. Have your local earnings been increasing on the Southern Pacific in Arizona?

Mr. HUNTINGTON. Yes. They are irrigating the country south of the Gila River between Seneca Canyon, east of Tucson, to the river—300 miles. They are irrigating all that country, and they are beginning to produce crops at Phœnix.

Senator MORGAN. There is quite a large population pouring in there, is there not?

Mr. HUNTINGTON. Yes; at Phœnix.

Senator MORGAN. When you were building the Southern Pacific were there any white people living there?

Mr. HUNTINGTON. Very few.

Senator MORGAN. So that that country is prospering?

Mr. HUNTINGTON. Yes.

Senator MORGAN. And the railroad is largely contributory to its prosperity?

Mr. HUNTINGTON. Yes.

Senator MORGAN. And irrigation is a big thing for it?

Mr. HUNTINGTON. Yes. They can get water there by gravity, but there is a great deal of that country where there is no water to be had.

Senator MORGAN. If we got the water in there it would be a rich country?

Mr. HUNTINGTON. I do not know how rich it would be. That would depend upon the people who occupied it.

The CHAIRMAN. Your people built what is called the Western Pacific, commencing at Sacramento and ending at San Jose?

Mr. HUNTINGTON. We completed it; we did not commence it.

The CHAIRMAN. Why was that road built to San Jose instead of to Sacramento, the great emporium?

Mr. HUNTINGTON. That is a little unwritten history. I was here in 1862 when the railroad bill passed. Some of our enterprising men from San Francisco came here and said that the bill would not be passed unless I assured them of the building of the road between San Jose and San Francisco, and I did so. For some reason they were interested in the road from San Jose to San Francisco, 50 miles, and so they fixed a road something like that at Sioux City. They located it from San Jose to Sacramento, which is 173 miles, over Mount Diablo, while there was a line of 92 miles—the tide line. They had got 23 miles of railroad above Niles, and they came to me and said that if I would take the road and finish it I might have it, and I did so, but I never should have laid out a road there; it was a great mistake.

The CHAIRMAN. It was done by other parties?

Mr. HUNTINGTON. It was done by other parties. I do not know what interests they had.

The CHAIRMAN. I see that you operate 5 miles of the road west of Ogden. Why did you not build those 5 miles?

Mr. HUNTINGTON. The Union Pacific distributed our line. We graded down to Ogden and the Union Pacific graded up to Promontory Mountain, 54 miles west of Ogden. They got their track laid, and I told them I would like to have that road from Promontory road down to Ogden, which was not much of a town then. They said they would let me have it down to this place 5 miles west of Ogden. That is as far as we could get; so that we stop there, which was a good deal better for us than to stop on the top of the mountain.

The CHAIRMAN. It is said that the Southern Pacific was built largely, if not entirely, out of the profits of the Central Pacific syndicate. How about that? Was that so or not?

Mr. HUNTINGTON. Not much so. I had been doing business a good deal. I had a good deal of paper out in New York in the panic of 1837, and I took care of it, although I knew a great many rich men in New England and New York who were bitten. That road from San Francisco to Gilroy, 80 miles, the Southern Pacific built mostly on time. Then we built the Southern Pacific on long credit, using bonds as collateral. It issued thirty-eight millions of bonds on 1,000 miles of road. It was a very expensive road. The tunneling through the Sierra Madre cost us about $1,600,000. There are 17 tunnels, and it was a very expensive road to build. We issued bonds to the amount of thirty-eight millions. Our people wanted to have us sell the bonds even as low as 60 per cent in order to pay off the floating debt, and I said: "Never mind the floating debt; I will take care of it; that is my part of the business." A man of the name of Michael Reese, of San Francisco, came to me in New York and laid a contract on my table where he had bought ten millions of these bonds—three millions firm, and the rest at 70, 72½, and 75 per cent. I knew that he was a rich man, a Jew. He wanted to know if he could have the bonds. I said, "I guess so, but not now." He said that he was going to Europe to-morrow, and I said, "All right." "But," said he, "can I have them?" I said, "You can have them the day after the court of last resort says they are yours." He said, "Do you not think it is a good contract?" and I said, "Yes; but you had better let it go."

The CHAIRMAN. Had he these bonds hypothecated?

Mr. HUNTINGTON. No; he had a contract made in San Francisco and I was to deliver them to him in New York; in short, he gave it up and told me that I could keep the contract. He did not get the bonds and he went away, and I kept those bonds until we showed that the road was earning an income on its bonds and something more. Then I sold two millions of them for 90, and so on, until seven or eight millions of them were sold as high as 116. If I had sold the bonds at 60 it would have made a difference of between $12,000,000 and $14,000,000 against the company.

The CHAIRMAN. You operate some nonaided lines?

Mr. HUNTINGTON. Yes.

The CHAIRMAN. Tell the committee the importance of those nonaided lines to the main line of the Central Pacific.

Mr. HUNTINGTON. These nonaided lines are through what may be called the fat parts of California. There is one up the coast and one down the coast. One runs up the San Joaquin Valley and gathers a large tonnage for the main line. There are three branches, and almost every mile of them is through a fat country. The California and Oregon runs by mountains, but there is an immense tonnage of timber there, so that every mile is very valuable for the tonnage which the road covers and takes to the main line. We have a number of feeders in California that do not pay the cost of operation, but that bring a large tonnage to the main line. These feeders are very valuable to the main line even though they do not show much earnings of themselves. In fact, we have about some fifteen little roads in California that were each of them running at a loss, but that are profitable to the main line.

The CHAIRMAN. Do you give these nonaided lines a larger percentage of earnings than you give the Central Pacific?

Mr. HUNTINGTON. No; I think not.

Senator STEWART. The terminal facilities that you have are operated in connection with the Central Pacific?

Mr. HUNTINGTON. Yes.

The CHAIRMAN. The terminals do not belong to the Central Pacific?

Mr. HUNTINGTON. Oh, yes; but they are mortgaged separately.

Senator BRICE. Do you charge an arbitrary rate for the terminals?

Mr. HUNTINGTON. We charge at San Francisco 5 cents a hundred pounds, but that includes the steamboat line.

Senator BRICE. That goes into the treasury of the Central Pacific?

Mr. HUNTINGTON. Yes.

Senator BRICE. There are no separate mortgages by any of the other companies?

Mr. HUNTINGTON. Oh, no.

Senator BRICE. There is no separate charge made for the terminals in San Francisco as against the Central Pacific?

Mr. HUNTINGTON. No.

Senator BRICE. When it comes to the Central Pacific all the earnings go into its treasury?

Mr. HUNTINGTON. Yes; there is nothing that goes out from the Central Pacific.

Senator BRICE. If the Central Pacific was separated from these terminals there would have to be some division of the earnings as between the Central Pacific and the balance of the roads?

Mr. HUNTINGTON. Yes.

Senator BRICE. Under the ordinary rules what percentage for terminal facilities would be charged by a disinterested manager on the business from Ogden to San Francisco?

Mr. HUNTINGTON. Not very much.

Senator BRICE. What percentage would it be?

Mr. HUNTINGTON. It would not be a percentage; it would be an arbitrary.

Senator FRYE. I did not object to the cross-examination of Mr. Huntington on the contract with the Panama Railroad Company, but I desired that Mr. Huntington should have that paper when he was being examined, so that he should not be guessing at its contents. (To Mr. Huntington.) Can you have that paper on Monday?

Mr. HUNTINGTON. I would like to be in New York on Monday.

Senator MORGAN. Bring here on Monday your Kentucky charter; I want to ask you about the directors and about the stockholders both of the Southern Pacific and of the Northern Pacific.

Mr. HUNTINGTON. We have dividend warrants and we are not always able to place the stockholders.

Mr. LITTLER. I want to offer an amendment to my bill so as to meet an objection which Mr. Coombs made. He said that there was no time fixed within which any sum of money that might be found by the commission should be paid. I offer this amendment:

After the word "six," in line 18 of the printed bill, add: and unless said sum so to be found by the commission shall have been paid within thirty days after the approval of said report, the United States shall have the right to enforce any rights it may now have under the laws as they may exist.

Senator FRYE (to Mr. Huntington). Have you a draft of any bill that covers any proposition which you have to make?

Mr. HUNTINGTON. No, sir.

Senator FRYE. The bill which I reported involved an immense amount of calculation and study at the hands of half a dozen auditors. You propose to fix a sum certain to be paid upon the principal and upon the interest?

Mr. HUNTINGTON. I asked Mr. Tweed to get up a bill of that sort, and I do not know whether he has done so yet. Your committees are so much in the habit of adding considerably to what is offered that we hesitate about offering any sum. We want to go up as high as we can.

Senator BRICE. I suggest that Mr. Huntington shall consult with Mr. Tweed and fix upon a sum to be offered to the Government.

Senator FRYE (to Mr. Huntington). I suppose that to secure that agreement you are ready to assign to the Government everything contained in the old bill?

Mr. HUNTINGTON. Everything.

Senator FRYE. And to give the Government all the security that the old bill proposed to give?

Mr. HUNTINGTON. Yes; everything that we have got, personal, real, and mixed.

Senator FRYE. Suppose you fix the payment upon the principal at $2,000,000 a year, and payment on the interest annually at $1,000,000 a year, you will be gradually, as a matter of course, reducing the amount of interest to be paid just as you decrease the principal. I want you to consider whether or not after the lapse of, say, ten or twenty years you can not increase the amount of principal to be paid over that with which you start out, and if so, how much?

Mr. HUNTINGTON. It can be worked out, but we can not pay $2,000,000 a year at the start.

Senator FRYE. I only used that as an illustration.

Mr. HUNTINGTON. We will do the very best we can. We want to pay 100 cents on the dollar, with as much interest as we can pay.

Senator FRYE. I want you to consider the other proposition, whether or not as you decrease the principal and also decrease the interest, you can not increase the annual payments?

Mr. HUNTINGTON. That appears to be reasonable and we will see if we can not work it out. There have been $50,000,000 gathered all over the world for the shares of the Central Pacific, and I would like to hold out a dim hope at least to the stockholders that their shares are worth something.

Senator MORGAN. If the Central Pacific is as good property as United States bonds the stock will be valuable.

Adjourned until Monday, February 17, at 10.30.

WASHINGTON, *February 17, 1896.*

The committee met at 10.30 a. m.

Present, Senators Gear (chairman), Wolcott, Frye, Brice, and Morgan.

UNION AND CENTRAL PACIFIC.

STATEMENT OF MR. FRANCIS W. THURBER.

Mr. FRANCIS W. THURBER, of New York, appeared before the committee and said:

MR. CHAIRMAN AND GENTLEMEN OF THE COMMITTEE ON PACIFIC RAILROADS: I appear before you representing the National Board of Trade and the New York Board of Trade and Transportation to oppose the idea of Government ownership of the Pacific railroads and to advocate the adjustment of the debt due to the Government by these roads on the best terms practicable. I am chairman of the committtee on railroad transportation of the New York Board of Trade and Transportation, and have for many years studied the relations of railroads to the public. I have been one of the most strenuous advocates of holding railroads to a proper and just responsibility to the public. I am chairman of the committee appointed by the National Board of Trade in January, 1895, to present to Congress the views of the National Board of Trade on the subject of Government ownership of railroads and the adjustment of the debt of the Pacific railroads. These were embodied in the following resolutions, unanimously adopted by that body, which, as you are probably aware, is composed of delegates from leading commercial organizations in the United States and is more fully representative of the interests of the business public than any other organization:

Whereas it has been recently proposed that the Government should acquire and operate the Union and Central Pacific railroads, instead of extending its liens thereon; and

Whereas there is, perhaps, no branch of business which so much requires for its successful conduct the stimulus of private interest, coupled with the best administrative ability, as that of railroads:

Resolved, That the National Board of Trade deprecates any movement looking to the Government ownership of railway lines, but strenuously advocates a wise, firm and continuous supervision over the operation and management of these great agencies, in all matters affecting their relations with the public in the conduct of interstate commerce.

Resolved, In the judgment of this board the bonded indebtedness of the Pacific railroads to the Government should be extended on the best terms practicable.

It is doubtless natural that there should be found advocates of the Government ownership of the Union and Central Pacific railroads. There are some people who believe in the Government ownership of all the great agencies of communication and even of mines and other industries, but long and careful study of this subject has convinced me that, in a country and with a Government like ours, any step in this direction would be unwise. Any material increase in the number of Government employees is undesirable, for reasons which are obvious to all who are conversant with our political system. From a commercial point of view it is equally undesirable. Political influence would be brought to bear to carry the products of one section at the expense of the other sections, and it is not improbable that this consideration is at the bottom of some of the agitation regarding the Government ownership of the Pacific railroads.

Republics are proverbially ungrateful, and a study of the history and the relations of the Pacific railroads to the public illustrates how easy it is for the public to forget the benefits to the public of individual effort. The history of the construction of the Pacific railroads is an industrial romance. The difficulties which were encountered and overcome by the great captains of industry who undertook this work entitle them to the consideration and thanks of the American people; and, without excusing the Credit Mobilier scandal or any other abuse which accompanied the progress of this great work, it is safe to say that for every dollar of private benefit accruing to its projectors a thousand dollars of benefit has accrued to the public. The saving to the Government in the transportation of its supplies for the Army, although large, is trifling compared to the saving to the public in transportation charges. Land which was worthless was made accessible and valuable. An empire in extent was opened up, and has crystallized into great and productive States; and yet the pioneers who conceived and executed this great work are frequently denounced as if they were public enemies.

Senator MORGAN. Name those pioneers.

Mr. THURBER. I say the men who constructed the Union Pacific and the Central Pacific railroads.

Senator MORGAN. Who are they? Just name the persons you refer to.

Mr. THURBER. I should say, for instance, Mr. C. P. Huntington.

Senator MORGAN. Who else?

Mr. THURBER. His associates in the Central Pacific.

Senator MORGAN. Name them.

Mr. THURBER. Mr. Stanford and Mr. Crocker, and in the Union Pacific Mr. Oakes Ames. I do not remember all of them, but the men who were the pioneers in that work are the men I refer to.

Senator MORGAN. All right; proceed.

Mr. THURBER. Now, as to the plans which have been proposed for the adjustment of the debt owed by these roads to the Government. The Government mortgage is a second lien. The first mortgage is partly due, and the rest is rapidly maturing. The holders are taking steps to foreclose, and something must be speedily done. By a cooperation of all the interests concerned and extending the time for the payment of the first and second mortgage bonds, the Government can be repaid in full and something remain for the stockholders.

A method for doing this, as regards the Central Pacific, has been formulated in a bill introduced in the Senate by Mr. Frye, of Maine, and in the House by Mr. Smith, of Illinois, the latter being H. R. 3459 of the present Congress. The reorganization committee of the Union Pacific have also submitted to you a plan for that road which seems reasonable. The adjustment of the indebtedness of the Pacific roads to the Government would be an important starting point for placing the railroad interests of the country on a better basis, and this would have an important bearing upon the entire business interests of the country. It will give confidence to capital to embark in new enterprises and start the wheels of industry in every direction.

The importance of the transportation interests of the country as a leader in industrial activity is not generally appreciated. It touches the business interests of the country at every point. This is illustrated by the fact that in 1893 there were about 874,000 men employed on the railroads of the United States; in 1894 this number had fallen to about 780,000; and since 1893 nearly one-fourth of the mileage of the United States has gone into the hands of receivers. The throwing out of employment of an army of 100,000 men was only a part of the difficulty. Not only was the number of those employed decreased, but the incomes of those who remained were lowered. There was a general cut of wages in all grades of the service. Five thousand general officers suffered as well as 100,000 track men, 150,000 shopmen, and over 500,000 other operatives. Wages were lowered directly and time was reduced, bringing about the same result indirectly. Industries depending on railroads for a demand were affected, and many millions of people besides those actually discharged and their dependents found themselves less able to buy the necessaries of life.

During the year ending June 30, 1894, railroad stock, having a par value of $3,660,150,094, or 63½ per cent of the total, received no dividend. During the three years ending December 31, 1894, 9,178 miles of road, capitalized at $494,821,000, were sold under foreclosure. From January 1 to July 1, 1895, these totals were increased by 2,049 miles, capitalized at $149,615,000, and 2,396 miles, capitalized at $100,941,000, each respectively, which went into the hands of receivers and were sold under foreclosure. According to the report of the statistician of the Interstate Commerce Commission for the year ending June 30, 1894, the income of railroads in a section including 52 per cent of the area of the country did not produce enough above the actual cost of operation to pay their fixed charges during that year.

Mr. Chairman, when I began the study of the railroad question twenty-five years ago, I felt that rates were too high and that there was danger of the public being oppressed by the railroads. I ranged the commercial sentiment of the country on the side of Senator Reagan when he was contending for the prohibition of pooling in the interstate commerce bill, but the logic of time and events has convinced both Senator Reagan and myself that the prohibition of pooling was unwise; that we need no longer fear unduly high rates for transportation; that the problem now is to eliminate unjust discriminations and systematize the administration so that shippers may enjoy reasonable, uniform, and stable rates, and carriers may earn a just compensation for the capital honestly invested.

As an illustration of the progressive reduction in the charge for transportation, the average charge for carrying a ton of freight one mile on 13 of the most important railroads of the United States during 1865 was 3.08 cents; in 1870, 1.81 cents; in 1875, 1.36 cents; in 1880, 1.01 cents; in 1885, 0.83 cent; in 1890, 0.77 cent; in 1893, 0.76 cent. These railroads performed one-third of the entire freight transportation during 1893, and from the figures given it appears that 0.76 cent would pay for as much transportation over their lines in 1893 as could have been obtained for 3.08 cents twenty-eight years earlier. This reduction, amounting to three-fourths the average rate for 1865, has been exceeded in that of the lessened price of but few even of those articles in the manufacture of which new inventions have worked the most radical changes.

The entire transportation performed by the railroads of the United States during the twelve years ending June 30, 1894, was equivalent to moving 136,799,677,822 passengers and 807,935,382,838 tons of freight one mile. Had rates averaging as high as those of 1882 been collected upon this traffic, the railroads would have earned $2,629,043,459 more than they actually received in these twelve years.

The rates on the Pacific railroads are now less than one-third what they were when the roads were first constructed, and this is an important argument in favor of treating these roads liberally in the adjustment of obligations which they incurred, based upon earnings at higher rates. The Government has aided the construction of competing lines with enormous land grants, and thus directly aided in reducing the revenues of the Union and Central Pacific railroads, upon which they relied to meet their obligations to the Government. It was doubtless to the public interest, speaking in a broad sense, that this should be done, but the Government should be willing, under such circumstances, to correspondingly modify the obligations which the earlier roads entered into, based upon conditions then existing, and which they had no reason to believe would be changed by the power of the Government being exerted to diminish the income upon which they relied to meet their obligations to the Government.

The Fifty-fourth Congress has a great opportunity to commend itself to the country by promptly passing measures to adjust the indebtedness of the Pacific railroads; and also a fair and reasonable bankruptcy bill. These two measures would go far to restore business prosperity, even if we do not get a solution of the complex and much mooted question of the currency, although it is devoutly to be wished that a wise solution of this question may also be found.

Thanking you, Mr. Chairman and gentlemen, for your patient hearing of my somewhat desultory remarks, I will close.

Senator MORGAN. What institutions, companies, or associations comprise the National Board of Trade?

Mr. THURBER. The leading commercial organizations of the country—the Chicago Board of Trade, the St. Louis Merchants' Exchange, the Cincinnati Chamber of Commerce, the Boston Chamber of Commerce, the New York Board of Trade, and some thirty others scattered all over the country, and representing probably the business of the country.

Senator MORGAN. Are there any of them on the Pacific Coast?

Mr. THURBER. No, sir.

Senator MORGAN. Are any of them west of the Mississippi River?

Mr. THURBER. St. Louis may perhaps be considered so.

Senator MORGAN. Was the St. Louis Merchants' Exchange represented in that meeting where these resolutions were adopted?

Mr. THURBER. Yes.

Senator MORGAN. Who represented it?

Mr. THURBER. Ex-Governor Stanford was the chairman.

Senator MORGAN. Did any body else represent any other board of trade west of the Mississippi River?

Mr. THURBER. I think not.

Senator MORGAN. So that this is entirely an Eastern recommendation?

Mr. THURBER. If you consider the Mississippi valley East, it is.

The CHAIRMAN. Were Milwaukee and Chicago represented there?

Mr. THURBER. Chicago was represented; I do not think Milwaukee was.

Senator MORGAN. Was St. Paul represented?

Mr. THURBER. St. Paul has been represented in the board of trade; but I do not think its representatives were in the last meeting.

Senator MORGAN. Your speech was submitted to the delegates assembled from those different commercial bodies?

Mr. THURBER. The substance of my remarks here was contained in a report adopted by the board unanimously. Every figure that I have given you here was in that report which was submitted by the Committee on Railroad Transportation, of which I am chairman.

Senator MORGAN. The particular speech which you have made to us here now was not submitted to that National Board of Trade?

Mr. THURBER. Yes.

Senator MORGAN. Just as you have presented it here?

Mr. THURBER. With the exception of some allusions to the present situation.

Senator MORGAN. This is not the paper which the Board of Trade adopted?

Mr. THURBER. Substantially, it is.

Senator MORGAN. Is it the very paper?

Mr. THURBER. No, sir.

Senator MORGAN. Point out what you put in it since you submitted it to the Board.

Mr. THURBER. I have simply put in these words: "I appear before you representing the National Board of Trade and the National Board of Trade and Transportation to oppose the idea of Government ownership of the Pacific railroads, and to advocate the adjustment of the debt due to the Government by those roads on the best terms practicable."

Senator MORGAN. Did you put in those words about the ingratitude of republics?

Mr. THURBER. Yes, sir; that is in the report as adopted. The fact is that the paper I have read is nearly verbatim the same, with the exception of where I speak of the reorganization committee of the Union Pacific Railroad. They had not at that time submitted to this committee the plan which they have now formulated. I would be very glad to send you a copy of the report as it was submitted.

Senator MORGAN. Then we can compare and ascertain if this is the report that you made there and that was adopted in substance with your gloss upon it.

Mr. THURBER. I do not know that I have glossed it any.

Senator MORGAN. It looks to me pretty shiny.

Mr. THURBER. I will be very glad to send you a copy of the report verbatim as adopted by the National Board of Trade.

Senator MORGAN. About the ingratitude of republics. Do you think that this Republic has been ungrateful to Mr. Huntington and Mr. Oakes Ames and the promoters of those Pacific railroads?

Mr. THURBER. I think that the people who denounce Mr. Huntington and Mr. Ames and others who were instrumental in giving the country these roads are very unjust.

Senator MORGAN. But that is not the Republic, is it?

Mr. THURBER. Perhaps the phrase "republics are ungrateful" was used because it is familiar.

Senator MORGAN. Would you like to be put down as saying that the whole Republic has denounced Huntington, Ames, and Hopkins?

Mr. THURBER. No, sir; I think not.

Senator MORGAN. It is only the people who denounce them that you include in your remark as to republics being ungrateful. You do not know whether they are Republicans or Democrats?

Mr. THURBER. No, sir.

Senator MORGAN. In what sense do you think that even these people who have denounced Mr. Huntington and Mr. Ames have been ungrateful?

Mr. THURBER. I think so for the reason that they do not appreciate the benefits which they have received from the efforts of these men. They make little of them and condemn them when they should not do so.

Senator MORGAN. Have you yet heard of a man who engaged in the promotion of these railroads who did not come out of it a very rich man?

Mr. THURBER. I do not know that I have.

Senator MORGAN. Have not some of them accumulated very enormous estates?

Mr. THURBER. Whether from that particular source or not, I can not say.

Senator MORGAN. I am not asking you the source.

Mr. THURBER. People who have built the Pacific railroads as a rule are rich men.

Senator STEWART. Did Mr. Ames make or lose money in it?

Mr. THURBER. I think he made money in the long run.

Senator MORGAN. Then, in the sense of enabling these gentlemen to become very rich, the Republic has not been ungrateful.

Mr. THURBER. In the sense that these railroads through their development have made the men connected with them rich, perhaps the Republic has not been ungrateful; but in the sense of indiscriminate fault-finding and censure of these men, I think that any citizen of the Republic who indulges in it is ungrateful.

Senator MORGAN. Then your objection is against liberty of speech and criticism?

Mr. THURBER. No, sir; I think every man should have the right to express his opinion.

Senator MORGAN. I suppose you do not know anything about the circumstances of Mr. Huntington, Mr. Crocker, and Mr. Stanford, and the gentlemen you have mentioned, at the time they entered into this business?

Mr. THURBER. Only what I have heard.

Senator MORGAN. I do not want any hearsay. But you are aware that the estates which these men have or have left are very large.

Mr. THURBER. I have heard so.

Senator MORGAN. Are you aware of any business in which any of these gentlemen have been engaged which would be likely to magnify and build up their estates to that enormous extent except through their connection with these railroads?

Mr. THURBER. I do not know of any business they have ever been associated with, excepting, I believe, that Huntington, Hopkins & Co. were in the hardware business. I do not understand that they made their money in it.

Senator MORGAN. They had one store, at what place?

Mr. THURBER. I do not know; I think in Sacramento or San Francisco.

Senator MORGAN. You hardly think that their hardware business developed into their immense fortunes?

Mr. THURBER. I understand that they made their money in the railroad business.

Senator MORGAN. In these railroads?

Mr. THURBER. Yes; and others.

Senator MORGAN. Are you connected with any railroad?

Mr. THURBER. No, sir.

Senator MORGAN. Have you any stock in any railroad?

Mr. THURBER. No, sir.

Senator MORGAN. You are not a director in any railroad?

Mr. THURBER. No.

Senator MORGAN. Are you an agent for any railroad?

Mr. THURBER. No.

Senator MORGAN. Are you in any railroad employment?

Mr. THURBER. No.

Senator MORGAN. And you are entirely neutral on this subject?

Mr. THURBER. Yes.

Senator MORGAN. And we are to accept your argument as coming from an entirely neutral and unprejudiced source.

You speak of having changed your opinion upon the subject of pooling. Give the committee the ground on which you changed your opinion.

Mr. THURBER. Because the experience of the years since railroad pooling has been prohibited by the interstate-commerce law, has been greater inequality of rates, and the railroads that are complaining of these inequalities say that it is impossible for them to remedy the evil, because they can not enforce agreements with each other, and they say that if they were given the power they could stop those discriminations and inequalities which are so unjust.

Senator MORGAN. Unjust to whom?

Mr. THURBER. Unjust to the shippers.

Senator MORGAN. Why?

Mr. THURBER. Because any preference which one shipper gets over another in the way of business and charges helps to build up the one and break down the other.

Senator MORGAN. Build up one railroad?

Mr. THURBER. No; build up one shipper as against another.

Senator MORGAN. You mean shippers in the same location?

Mr. THURBER. Sometimes in the same location and sometimes in different locations.

Senator MORGAN. If some railroads find themselves able to lower rates to figures which other railroads can not afford to take, do you think that that hurts the shipper?

Mr. THURBER. No, sir; not if all the shippers have the same chance. But what I complain of, and what shippers generally complain of, is that some men get advantages which other men can not get.

The CHAIRMAN. In other words, if A gets rebates which B, living in the same town, does not get, that is to the injury of B?

Mr. THURBER. Yes.

Senator MORGAN. But that is contrary to existing law.

Mr. THURBER. That is true, perhaps; but you can not reach the evil.

Senator MORGAN. Why can not you reach it?

Mr. THURBER. Because it seems impossible to do it. The Interstate Commerce Commission has been trying to do it, but has not been able to do it.

Senator MORGAN. Why not?

Mr. THURBER. I suppose owing to the secret undercutting of rates which the different agents practice. Men who are honest and who wish to do right have assured me that it is an utter impossibility for them to stop these things until they have the right to enforce their contracts on each other, which they are now prohibited from doing.

Senator MORGAN. Take the railroads of the United States as a mass, with all the powers and wealth and opportunities which they enjoy, is not the remark true that the railroads have become stronger than the Government?

Mr. THURBER. I do not think that is true. It may be, in a sense, in the way of controlling political movements.

Senator MORGAN. I am not speaking of political movements. I am speaking of the movement of freight and passengers.

Mr. THURBER. I can hardly say that the Government is engaged in that particular business.

Senator MORGAN. We have enacted a system of law here which has met the approbation of Congress, and has been justified by experience thus far, and has been sustained by many decisions of the Supreme Court in favor of the control, through the Interstate Commerce Commission, of the operations of all the railroads of the United States?

Mr. THURBER. Yes, sir.

Senator STEWART. When they cross State lines?

Senator MORGAN. Yes; all interstate roads. And now the complaint is that the operation of that law is not effectual, because the Interstate Commerce Commission can not execute it, as I understand you.

Mr. THURBER. It is practically true.

Senator MORGAN. And the railroad companies want the power to inflict penalties on each other in order to compel the less wealthy lines to work up to the standard of rates which the wealthier lines have adopted or may adopt?

Mr. THURBER. I do not understand it. I would say that when the freight tariff is established all the lines should observe that tariff and not secretly avoid it by means of discriminations to shippers, giving those shippers advantages over others.

Senator MORGAN. The purpose of the pooling system to which you have been converted is to enable the railroad companies to establish a tariff of rates which no other company shall be allowed to break in upon?

Mr. THURBER. Whatever tariff is established should be uniform and observed by all alike.

Senator MORGAN. In all sections of the country?

Mr. THURBER. Oh, no, sir; the tariff which exists for a certain section. Of course there will be as great a diversity as there are conditions. There is nothing perhaps more elastic than the system of railroad rates in the United States.

Senator MORGAN. That would be to withdraw Government control over the railroads of the country and to relegate that authority to a commission consisting of railroad companies that should have the right to prescribe rates and the right to enforce them against railroads crossing State lines.

Mr. THURBER. You should either do that or strengthen the hands of the Interstate Commerce Commission. You ought to give them five times the appropriation that you do give them, so that they could employ the proper experts and talent. The true policy is to strengthen the hands of the Interstate Commerce Commission; but at the same time do not take away from the railroad companies the ability to enforce their own contracts upon each other, so that if a railroad is dishonest and wishes to evade an agreement which it has gone into, it can be forced to observe it.

Senator MORGAN. If we should quintuple the appropriation for the Interstate Commerce Commission, and if the rascality of the railroads should remain as you describe it, would we make any greater progress in repressing this fraud and wrong than we are doing now with the present meager appropriation?

Mr. THURBER. If you did not accomplish anything, of course you would not.

Senator MORGAN. But you think we would accomplish something?

Mr. THURBER. Yes.

Senator STEWART. I would like to have your view as to how you would frame legislation that would give paramount authority to the Interstate Commerce Commission and at the same time should omit the prohibition to railroad companies of the power to enforce their contracts as against each other. How would you make the two operate together as one system?

Mr. THURBER. I think that the Patterson bill to permit pooling is a very desirable measure in many respects for strengthening the hands of the Interstate Commerce Commission. If we could get that bill passed it would be a long step in the direction of controlling the railroads and giving the Interstate Commerce Commission the proper power, and at the same time it would allow the railroad companies, under the permission of the Interstate Commerce Commission, to make their pooling agreements. The law as it now stands should be amended in accordance with the recommendations of the Interstate Commerce Commission to Congress.

Senator STEWART. The idea is to empower the Interstate Commerce Commission to supervise pooling contracts and to hold the railroad companies under its control?

Mr. THURBER. Yes, and to disapprove of those contracts and annul them when unreasonable.

Senator STEWART. The pooling contracts are for the purpose of allowing railroads a remedy against each other?

Mr. THURBER. Yes.

Senator STEWART. And the two plans are to work together?

Mr. THURBER. Yes.

Senator MORGAN. You spoke of the lands given to these railroad companies as being worthless because they were inaccessible until the railroads were built. Were they in fact worthless, or was it only because they were not accessible?

Mr. THURBER. That is all.

Senator MORGAN. Only that?

Mr. THURBER. Only that.

Senator MORGAN. So that the pressure of immigration westward would finally have made those lands valuable, even without the assistance of the railroads?

Mr. THURBER. Relatively so, perhaps; but in proportion as they were made quickly and easily accessible they were increased in value.

Senator STEWART. Do you mean to say that the lands in the interior could have been utilized to any great advantage without the railroads?

Mr. THURBER. I do not know. Of course their value depends upon the quickness and the cheapness of accessibility.

Senator MORGAN. Does not the value of these lands depend upon their intrinsic productive power?

Mr. THURBER. In getting their products into the market?

Senator MORGAN. Or in finding a market for them at home?

Mr. THURBER. Yes.

The CHAIRMAN. Is it not true that the lands in the western part of Iowa, lands three or four hundred miles west of the Missouri River, would have been in a degree practically useless for farming purposes by reason of the fact that their products could not be hauled to market unless those railroads had been built in that country?

Mr. THURBER. Undoubtedly.

The CHAIRMAN. Would they not have been confined largely to pasturage farming instead of raising grains?

Mr. THURBER. Undoubtedly.

Senator MORGAN. The whole South between Georgia and the western limit of Texas, and as far north as Kansas and Tennessee, was filled up by a very thrifty, active, productive people between the years 1800 and 1840. Was there any railroad running into any part of that country in 1840?

Mr. THURBER. They had rivers there and the country was accessible by water, which the people of the West and Northwest did not have.

Senator MORGAN. With only that advantage?

Mr. THURBER. I think that that perhaps was the chief advantage, although there may be advantages of climate, soil, etc., which the regions I have mentioned before did not enjoy.

Senator MORGAN. What navigable rivers did Texas and Kansas have?

Mr. THURBER. Texas and Kansas did not develop until they had railroads.

Senator MORGAN. They did not?

Mr. THURBER. Not much.

Senator MORGAN. We have to differ about that fact.

The CHAIRMAN. Is it not true that the country spoken of by my distinguished colleague has grown in population and products 400 or 500 per cent since the construction of railroads in that country?

Mr. THURBER. I do not know to what extent they have increased; but they have increased enormously in value and productions since the building of the railroads.

Senator MORGAN. And the western country is also increasing in product and value?

Mr. THURBER. Yes; especially since it has been opened up by railroads.

Senator MORGAN. All the way from the Gulf of Mexico to the Canadian line?

Mr. THURBER. Yes.

Senator MORGAN. And back to the Pacific Ocean?

Mr. THURBER. Yes.

Senator MORGAN. All the way through?

Mr. THURBER. Yes.

Senator MORGAN. Then, while railroads are a great facility, and are, perhaps, indispensable to the development of a country, they are not the whole value of a country, are they?

Mr. THURBER. I do not suppose we could get along without the land.

Senator MORGAN. Could the railroads have got along without the support of the industry and labor of the people?

Mr. THURBER. No, sir; undoubtedly their interests are mutual.

Senator MORGAN. Which is the supreme interest, the railroads or the men who supply the produce to them?

Mr. THURBER. I think that a man is superior to a machine; but a man may not be able to exist if he has not access to the world, and he may not be able to develop a country unless he has the communication to do it with.

Senator MORGAN. Adam and Abraham have done pretty good work in subsisting and multiplying and replenishing the earth without the assistance of railroads.

Mr. THURBER. They were pioneers, undoubtedly.

Senator STEWART. Did not the civilized portions of the human race prior to railroads dwell in the vicinity of water transportation of some kind?

Mr. THURBER. Unquestionably.

Senator STEWART. And were the great interiors of this country penetrated to any great extent by the population until they got railroads?

Mr. THURBER. I think that everybody appreciates the situation.

Senator MORGAN. I appreciate the advantages of railroads, I expect, as fully as you do; but in considering what their advantages are to the wealth of the whole country, I think that the men who are induced by the presence of those instrumentalities of commerce to go out and settle up those lands and open mines and cut down forests are, after all, the real contributors to the railroads, and after them to the wealth of the country. Do you not agree with me?

Mr. THURBER. I do. I think that the country was made for men, and that the railroads were made for men, and not men for the railroads.

Senator MORGAN. In your speech to-day you have not made any allusion as to what is to become of the people who occupy this Western country or as to what advantage is to be gained by them in this legislation. Do you not think that the people out there ought to be the first care of Congress?

Mr. THURBER. I do not think you should neglect the interests of the people in any part of the country.

Senator MORGAN. Ought they not to be the prime care of Congress in any legislation in reference to the dealings of the Government with these railroads in the future?

Mr. THURBER. Yes, I do. I think that the interests of the people should be the first interests in your action; but at the same time it all comes down to a question of what is reasonable. There is reason in everything, and I do not think that the people of the Pacific Coast in wishing the Government to take these railroads are reasonable.

Senator MORGAN. You do not suppose that Congress would be more unreasonable in favor of the people than you are in favor of the railroad companies?

Mr. THURBER. I suppose not.

Senator MORGAN. You are very much opposed to Government ownership and control of those railroads?

Mr. THURBER. Not Government control of them; I am entirely in favor of Government control.

Senator MORGAN. How could the Government control them if it does not own them?

Mr. THURBER. The creation of the Interstate Commerce Commission shows that you have that right and that power.

Senator MORGAN. Is that the control of which you speak?

Mr. THURBER. Yes.

Senator MORGAN. You do not mean that the Government has the right of controlling, for instance, the railroad officers?

Mr. THURBER. No, sir.

Senator MORGAN. Or the employment of railroad agents?

Mr. THURBER. No, sir.

The CHAIRMAN. Nor the ownership of the roads?

Mr. THURBER. Nor the ownership of the roads.

Senator MORGAN. If the Government owned a railroad and submitted the control of it to a board of directors, would the difficulty exist?

Mr. THURBER. I think it would.

Senator MORGAN. Notwithstanding that the Government might delegate the entire authority to make appointments and to give employment to a board of directors without the intervention of any Government officer?

Mr. THURBER. Do you allude to a board of directors appointed by the Government?

Senator MORGAN. I am talking about directors either appointed by the Government or elected by the stockholders.

Mr. THURBER. It is quite a different thing if the directors are elected by the stockholders; but if they are appointed by the Government, political influence at once comes in and you will find one section of the country wanting its products carried at the expense of other sections.

Senator MORGAN. We have got in these Union and Central Pacific Railroad Companies the right to appoint four Government directors in each.

Senator STEWART. Not in the Central Pacific.

Senator MORGAN. Well, in the Union Pacific we have a right to appoint four Government directors and the Government does not own any part of that railroad.

Mr. THURBER. Yes, I understand so. These directors are for looking after the Government interests in that road.

Senator MORGAN. They are there and have the right to vote upon any subject that comes up in the board of directors. They have coordinate and equal powers with the directors elected by the stockholders.

Mr. THURBER. But they are in a minority.

Senator MORGAN. But they are there and the Government of the United States owns no interest in that property, none whatever.

Mr. THURBER. Not directly. Of course the Government has its interest in the securities.

Senator MORGAN. That is a different thing. The Government is a creditor like any other creditor. The Government has had these four directors in that company since it was organized.

Mr. THURBER. I believe so.

Senator MORGAN. Appointed by whom?

Mr. THURBER. By the President, I believe.

Senator MORGAN. Without confirmation by the Senate?

Mr. THURBER. I do not know how that is.

Senator MORGAN. There is no confirmation by the Senate. Has any one of these directors been appointed on political grounds, so far as you are aware, or have you ever heard a suggestion of the kind?

Mr. THURBER. I do not know.

Senator MORGAN. You do not know as to what political parties they belong?

Mr. THURBER. I do not know.

Senator MORGAN. Then the political evil has not given to the Union Pacific a board of directors such as you contemplate would be the case?

Mr. THURBER. No, sir; I think the conditions are entirely different.

Senator MORGAN. Taking the same situation, and the exercise of the same powers precisely, and suppose the Government chooses to amend the charter of the Union Pacific so as to raise the number of the Government directors to a majority—just on the present conditions. Would you then apprehend that political influence would get into the company and control it?

Mr. THURBER. I should think greater danger of it if the Government had a majority of the directors than when it has only a minority.

Senator MORGAN. What is the number of directors in the Union Pacific?

Mr. THURBER. I do not know; about a dozen, I suppose.

Mr. PIERCE. I think there are fifteen.

Senator MORGAN. Well, four is nearly one-third of that number. In a severely controverted proposition in relation to the management of the road, as for instance, creating a further debt, or the election of a president, or of any other officer, if parties in the company directors should be equally divided upon any question of this kind, then the Government of the United States, through its four directors, could come in and cast its vote as a balance of power and carry the question exactly as it desired.

Mr. THURBER. Yes, yes; under such a hypothesis as that.

Senator MORGAN. So that we are now in possession of all the power needed to decide a question on this side or on that side in any controverted or disputed line of policy that might be suggested by the board of directors.

Mr. THURBER. I think you are supposing a state of affairs not very likely to exist.

Senator MORGAN. Suppose I think it is. Will you answer my question? In that case would not the Government of the United States, of its own authority and its own power, without responsibility, without ownership of the road, and in virtue of the powers which now exist, under the charter, be able to cast the decision of such questions on the one side or on the other side of any line of policy which might be suggested in a board of directors?

Mr. THURBER. Yes; I should say so.

Senator MORGAN. Then, with that adaptation of the law as it exists, all the authority needed to control the decisions of the Union Pacific Railroad Company on any question where the directors elected by the stockholders are divided in opinion, exists in the Government?

Mr. THURBER. Yes, sir; if they are divided.

Senator MORGAN. Has any harm come from that?

Mr. THURBER. I do not think there has, so far as I know.

Senator MORGAN. If we had from the beginning a board of directors all appointed by the President and confirmed by the Senate, and if those men had been such honorable persons as the United States furnish in multitudes—men who have got a personal conscience—do you think that a Credit Mobilier could ever have grown up in that company?

Mr. THURBER. I think that you increase the chances of corruption and mismanagement the moment you let an enterprise of that kind get into politics.

Senator MORGAN. Then you think it was the Government influence, probably, and not the influence of those who controlled the company at that time that gave rise to the Credit Mobilier in the Union Pacific?

Mr. THURBER. No; I would not say that.

Senator MORGAN. What would you say?

Mr. THURBER. What I say is, that in my judgment you would find greater abuses under a Government management of railroad business than you do under private management.

Senator MORGAN. Take that specific abuse. Do you believe that the existence of the Credit Mobilier in the history of the Union Pacific Railroad was due in the slightest degree to the presence of Government directors there?

Mr. THURBER. No, sir; I do not think it was.

Senator MORGAN. Do you think it was due to the presence of directors elected by the stockholders?

Mr. THURBER. I think that the Credit Mobilier scandal was a pretty good illustration——

Senator MORGAN. You can answer my question without divergence. Do you think that the Credit Mobilier scandal was due to the directors who represented the private stockholders?

Mr. THURBER. I do not.

Senator MORGAN. What was it due to?

Mr. THURBER. I think that the Credit Mobilier scandal was largely due to the Government having anything to do with the railroad. It has a direct bearing upon and is a direct illustration of what may be expected if we have Government ownership of these transportation lines.

Senator MORGAN. And yet in that particular case you are unable to state that the Government directors in the Union Pacific had any connection with the Credit Mobilier scandal?

Mr. THURBER. Not to my knowledge.

(Mr. Pierce, in correction of his former statement, said that there were fifteen directors in the Union Pacific representing the stockholders and five representing the Government.)

Senator MORGAN. Having exonerated both the Government directors and the directors represented by the stockholders, as you have done, from connection with the Credit Mobilier, will you please inform the committee how it was possible that that Credit Mobilier could have originated and gotten hold of that company as it did without the assistance of some, at least, of the directors of the company?

Mr. THURBER. I am not sufficiently familiar with the details of the history of that thing to judge, but I go upon the general ground that it was through the corruption of public men that that scandal occurred.

Senator MORGAN. You refer, of course, to Congress?

Mr. THURBER. Well, perhaps to Congress; and all who were concerned in it.

Senator MORGAN. There was nobody concerned in it but Congressmen. So that you think that the Credit Mobilier scandal was the result of the corruptions of Congress?

Mr. THURBER. I do not know whether it was a result or a cause. It was simply an illustration that it is not a good thing to get railroads into politics.

Senator MORGAN. These men were not in politics.

Mr. THURBER. They came in contact with politicians.

Senator MORGAN. Did you ever hear of any political question in the United States between the Credit Mobilier and Congress, or between the Credit Mobilier and the board of directors, or between the Credit Mobilier and anybody else. Was there ever a Credit Mobilier party in the United States?

Mr. THURBER. No; but there were a good many men interested in the Credit Mobilier who were in public life.

Senator MORGAN. The Credit Mobilier, when brought into English terms, was a company of construction, was it not?

Mr. THURBER. Subtantially that.

Senator MORGAN. Altogether that?

Mr. THURBER. I think so—finance and construction.

Senator MORGAN. It was simply a company of construction?

Mr. THURBER. Yes.

Senator MORGAN. Could that company ever have got a contract from the Union Pacific without the assent of the board of directors?

Mr. THURBER. I should presume not, although I do not know anything about it.

Senator MORGAN. Then, if there was any fraud on the part of the Credit Mobilier, the board of directors were responsible for it?

Mr. THURBER. Probably.

Senator MORGAN. Which set of directors—the Government set or the Union Pacific set?.

Mr. THURBER. Probably both; I do not know.

Senator MORGAN. You have not heard that the Government directors had anything to do with the Credit Mobilier or with awarding to it the right to construct the road?

Mr. THURBER. I am not sufficiently familiar with the affair to know in respect to its details.

Senator MORGAN. After a review of that situation, would you not conclude with me that if all the directors (the twenty) had been Government directors, selected from the great body of citizens, men of honor, such as we might expect to have appointed by the President and confirmed by the Senate (if we had had twenty Government directors instead of five), the Credit Mobilier would never have seen the daylight?

Mr. THURBER. I can not answer as to that.

Senator MORGAN. What is your opinion as to that?

Mr. THURBER. I think that the character of one set of men is about as good as that of another.

Senator MORGAN. You believe, then, in the degeneracy of mankind, and that all are susceptible to corruption?

Mr. THURBER. No, I do not say that. I believe there is an average human nature; and of the class of men engaged in this enterprise I think that possibly the Government directors were no better than the others.

The CHAIRMAN. Did you ever hear of any opposition among the Government board of directors to making this contract to which Senator Morgan has referred?

Mr. THURBER. I am not so familiar with the details of that scandal. The point I make is this: that the Government ought to be kept out of railroad business.

The CHAIRMAN. Senator Morgan asked you this question: Is it not presumable to suppose that the Government directors gave their assent to the contract when it was made?

Mr. THURBER. Really, I have no knowledge on the subject.

The CHAIRMAN. Is it not presumable?

Mr. THURBER. I think it probable.

Senator MORGAN. Were not the directors of the Union Pacific at that time also the directors of the Credit Mobilier?

Mr. THURBER. I think they were.

Senator MORGAN. Man for man?

Mr. THURBER. I do not know to what extent, but that is my impression.

Senator MORGAN. That they let contracts from themselves to themselves?

Mr. THURBER. Yes.

Senator MORGAN. Do you think that that could have occurred if there had been twenty Government directors, subject to dismissal by the President of the United States upon any hint of improper conduct?

Mr. THURBER. I have no doubt they would have been dismissed for cause.

Senator MORGAN. Do you think it would have occurred—this creation of a Credit Mobilier to make a contract with the directors themselves—do you think that that could have occurred if the twenty directors of the Union Pacific Railroad Company had been all Government directors instead of only five Government directors?

Mr. THURBER. I think that the construction of that work under a system of Government directors would have developed abuses as great as those that occurred.

Senator MORGAN. You have a very convenient way of not answering my question. Please answer it.

Mr. THURBER. Very likely not.

Senator MORGAN. The likelihood would have been in favor of the proposition that it would not have occurred. I think we agree upon that.

Senator FRYE. There never would have been a Pacific railroad at all if there had not been a Credit Mobilier, just as there never would have been a Nicaragua Canal if there had not been such a company. You have in the Nicaragua Canal and Construction Company precisely what the Union Pacific had in the Credit Mobilier.

Senator MORGAN. Not at all. The construction company in the Nicaragua Canal matter is to be a company organized by the Congress of the United States, in which (the bill proposes) the Government shall have a majority of the directors.

Senator FRYE. I am talking of the thing as it is now, where the Nicaragua Canal Company makes a contract with the Nicaragua Construction Company for the latter company to go on and build the Nicaragua Canal, and they did it from necessity, precisely as the Union Pacific, from necessity, went on and had the Credit Mobilier to construct the road.

Senator MORGAN. The bill which we have reported requires that the Government of the United States and the Governments of Nicaragua and Costa Rica shall have a very large majority of the directors, and those directors are put in so as to give these Governments governmental control of the work and to prevent the possibility of a Credit Mobilier, or anything like it.

Senator FRYE. That is your bill. I am talking about the old company.

Senator MORGAN. I am not responsible for the old company. We are trying to arrange that the old company shall not do that thing, if we can make the charter. So here I propose that there shall be no possibility of a Credit Mobilier, or anything of that sort, in the future operation of these railroads. I want to clean them out, to bar them out.

The CHAIRMAN. How are you going to accomplish that?

Senator MORGAN. I will inform the committee when I get through with the testimony. I am now proposing to get the facts on record. (To Mr. Thurber.) Have you studied the history of the Union Pacific and the Central Pacific, in the last two years, closely?

Mr. THURBER. I do not know that I have, closely. I have followed the general trend of the work as it appeared in the public press.

Senator MORGAN. Taking the history of those two roads for the last two years, or three, and comparing that history with the history of two other prominent lines crossing the continent—the Northern Pacific and the Southern Pacific—do you think that the Union and Central Pacific have had a degree of prosperity commensurate with that of the Northern Pacific Railroad in the last three years?

Mr. THURBER. The Northern Pacific has not been very prosperous; the Central Pacific has been more prosperous.

Senator MORGAN. Take the two together—the Union Pacific and the Central Pacific, that transcontinental line—and compare it with the Northern Pacific; which has had the greater prosperity in the last three years?

Mr. THURBER. Speaking broadly, I should say that the Union Pacific and the Central Pacific have done better than the Northern Pacific, although the Union Pacific has not of itself.

Senator MORGAN. Which has had the greater prosperity in the last three years, the Southern Pacific or the Union Pacific?

Mr. THURBER. The Southern Pacific.

Senator MORGAN. Much greater?

Mr. THURBER. It has met all its engagements.

Senator MORGAN. And made money for its stockholders?

Mr. THURBER. I do not know to what extent.

Senator MORGAN. It has a surplus, has it not?

Mr. THURBER. I do not know.

Senator MORGAN. It is a prosperous road, is it not?

Mr. THURBER. It is a solvent road.

Senator MORGAN. And prosperous?

Mr. THURBER. I think it may be called prosperous.

Senator MORGAN. Prosperous, even as compared with the roads from the East to Chicago.

Mr. THURBER. No, sir; I think not.

Senator MORGAN. But still a prosperous road?

Mr. THURBER. Yes.

The CHAIRMAN. Is it not true that a large majority of Western roads, during the last three years, can not be called fairly prosperous?

Mr. THURBER. That is true. The prices of the securities of those roads are, perhaps, a good index of their prosperity, because the prices indicate the profit-making power of the roads.

Senator MORGAN. When did you prepare this speech that you made here to-day?

Mr. THURBER. I had it copied yesterday.

Senator MORGAN. When did you write it?

Mr. THURBER. I took it almost bodily from the report I spoke of.

Senator MORGAN. When did you do that?

Mr. THURBER. In the National Board of Trade which met in Washington.

Senator MORGAN. I am talking about the speech you made here to-day?

Mr. THURBER. The speech is the report, practically.

Senator MORGAN. When did you prepare the paper which you read before us to-day?

Mr. THURBER. I really prepared the whole matter when the National Board of Trade met here in January.

Senator MORGAN. When did you read it to the National Board of Trade?

Mr. THURBER. On the 27th of January.

Senator MORGAN. The whole of that paper?

Mr. THURBER. All excepting the introductory fringes of it.

On motion of Senator Wolcott it was ordered that a minority of the committee shall have the right to sit and hear statements and that the committee shall hold continuous sessions.

The committee took a recess until 2 o'clock p. m.

CENTRAL PACIFIC.

After the recess the examination of Mr. Huntington was resumed.

Senator MORGAN. I have not had the advantage of looking over the report of the examination, so that I must make my examination at greater length than it otherwise would be. In examining you I act on the supposition that you know more about this business than any other living man, and inasmuch as the Senate expects from this committee a report on every material fact connected wih the subject I will have to examine you as the fountain source of knowledge in order to get a number of facts which, perhaps, you will think irrelevant for the moment, but which occur to me as necessary.

Mr. HUNTINGTON. I will be glad to give you, Senator, all the knowledge that I have; but you overestimate my information.

Senator MORGAN. The people of the State which I represent have not any interest of a financial character to the value of a cent in this question, and for that reason I have an absolute neutrality. The first question which I am going to ask you is this: If one man owned or controlled the Southern Pacific from New Orleans to San Francisco, and the Central Pacific from its sea terminus to Ogden, could he not control the business west from Ogden to the Pacific Ocean, except that portion of it which would find an outlet through the Oregon Short Line?

Mr. HUNTINGTON. But temporarily. Perhaps to an extent temporarily. There are a great many railroad properties connected with the Union Pacific which come clear to the Atlantic; and these properties are so large and have such a vast capital that if they did not have fair usage at Ogden they could no doubt build a line through to the Pacific; and therefore the Central Pacific would be a loser, and a very large loser, by being in any way unfair to its railroad connections.

Senator MORGAN. My question is predicated on the existing state of facts, and without reference to whether other railroad companies might build to the Pacific Ocean or not. And I repeat it: If a man owned all the railroads from New Orleans to San Francisco, and from San Francisco to Ogden, would he not be able to control all the business from and to the Pacific Coast, back and forth, except such as might find its way out to the Eastern market over the Oregon Short Line?

Mr. HUNTINGTON. There are so many lines other than those which you mention that, if the Southern and Central Pacifics should put the rates up above fair rates, the Canadian Pacific would take all the business, or the Northern Pacific; or the Atchison and Santa Fe. They run, some of them, to San Diego, Santa Monica, and San Pedro; and all of them to San Francisco; and they have the right to run over the Central Pacific on the same terms as we have from Mojave Station into San Francisco. So if we raised the rates above what was fair, these roads would take the business, and the Union Pacific and ourselves would suffer.

Senator MORGAN. My question assumes that you would charge fair rates, and that your competitors would therefore be compelled to charge fair rates; but still you have not answered the question, which is, whether, if you owned the lines from New Orleans to San Francisco and from there to Omaha, you would not be able to control the traffic to and from the Pacific, except that taken by the Oregon Short Line?

Mr. HUNTINGTON. I wish to answer the question, Senator, as directly as I can. I should say it could be done only temporarily, if it could be done at all.

Senator MORGAN. And why temporarily?

Mr. HUNTINGTON. Because the amount of capital interested in having a free open way to and from the Pacific would build a road to San Francisco or to the connection with the Atchison and Santa Fe road at Golph in a very short time. That is not very far from the road in Utah. It can not be more than three or four hundred miles, and could be built very easily; so that it would take a very short time for us to ruin our own property in this way and not to hurt these roads very much.

Senator MORGAN. Then your answer would be that you could control it unless these other railroads should build a line from some point, at the west of the lakes or east of the Sierra Nevada Mountains, to the Pacific?

Mr. HUNTINGTON. It is just as natural that these great properties should take care of themselves as it is that water should run down hill.

Senator MORGAN. But for that possibility of their building a line of railroad to the Pacific Ocean you would say, I suppose, that the ownership of the lines I have indicated would control the commerce to and from the Pacific Ocean?

Mr. HUNTINGTON. No, I think they would not control it, because there are other ways for the traffic to get in and out. They might go round Cape Horn by steamers, and they will soon have a road through Guatemala. All these routes would be open, and even the farthest one off would take the business if we put prices above what they ought to be.

Senator MORGAN. I am assuming that prices should not be above what they ought to be.

Mr. HUNTINGTON. Then the nearer lines would compete. I understand how to handle property well enough so as not to get in the way of great interests, as we would be (in that case) in the way of thousands of miles of affiliated railroads between the Atlantic Seaboard and Ogden. As a business man I think it would be the most foolish thing we could possibly do.

Senator MORGAN. I want answers to my questions; not arguments. The next question I ask is this: Is not the road from San Francisco to Portland and to other points in Oregon a competitor for the traffic of the Oregon Short Line, between Ogden and the Pacific Ocean?

Mr. HUNTINGTON. To a certain extent. We do very little of that business. If they should put the prices up, we should perhaps do all the business.

Senator MORGAN. What is the name of that road from Portland to San Francisco?

Mr. HUNTINGTON. From San Francisco to the State line it was chartered as the California and Oregon, and the line from Portland to the State line of California is called the Oregon and California. We speak of the whole line in San Francisco as the California and Oregon, and they speak of it in Oregon probably as the Oregon and California.

Senator MORGAN. That line is practically a competitor with the Oregon Short Line for freights and passengers to and from the East?

Mr. HUNTINGTON. They both have an all-rail connection. Of course, on the Central Pacific line we have to pass the Sierra Nevada Mountains twice.

Senator MORGAN. Is there any other railroad which leaves the line of the Union and Central Pacific, and which reaches the Pacific Ocean, except the Oregon Short Line?

Mr. HUNTINGTON. I do not know whether they connect with the Northern Pacific. I do not think they do. There is a line [indicating on the map] which seems to run out of that territory. I should think there was a line running off the Union Pacific.

Senator MORGAN. Which is the shorter line—that between Portland and San Francisco or that between Portland and Ogden?

Mr. HUNTINGTON. It is a longer line from Ogden to Portland than from Portland to San Francisco.

Senator MORGAN. How much longer?

Mr. HUNTINGTON. I have not the exact figures, but I should think it is about 300 miles longer.

Senator MORGAN. Which road has the easiest gradients?

Mr. HUNTINGTON. The Oregon Short Line.

Senator MORGAN. Which is the better-constructed line?

Mr. HUNTINGTON. I presume the Central Pacific. I say so because we build better than anybody else. I have not been over the Oregon Short Line.

Senator MORGAN. You do not know how it is constructed?

Mr. HUNTINGTON. No.

Senator MORGAN. Under what control is the Oregon Short Line now?

Mr. HUNTINGTON. I do not know. I believe the Union Pacific has it. It went into the hands of a receiver, I think. Whatever information I have about it I have got from the newspapers.

Senator MORGAN. Under what control is the California and Oregon?

Mr. HUNTINGTON. The Oregon and California is leased by the Southern Pacific.

Senator MORGAN. It is under the control of the Southern Pacific?

Mr. HUNTINGTON. Yes.

Senator MORGAN. So that the Southern Pacific, in getting the traffic from the part of the coast north of San Francisco, is in competition with the Union Pacific through the Oregon Short Line?

Mr. HUNTINGTON. Do you mean for the San Francisco business?

Senator MORGAN. No; I mean for all the coast business.

Mr. HUNTINGTON. To a very limited extent they may be in one sense considered competitors; but our line is so much longer than theirs that there is very little business done over our line except the local business.

Senator MORGAN. Where do you get the main part of the business which you transact over the California and Oregon road?

Mr. HUNTINGTON. We take it at Portland, mostly. I think there may be some picked up from the Canadian Pacific; but most of the passengers are local passengers, picked up at Portland and taken to San Francisco.

Senator MORGAN. Have you any arrangement with the Canadian Pacific in regard to that traffic?

Mr. HUNTINGTON. I think not at this time.

Senator MORGAN. Have you had?

Mr. HUNTINGTON. I think we had some years ago. The traffic people made these arrangements if they were made, and I think they were. I never knew much about the details of them.

Senator MORGAN. As to the Canadian Pacific, can it penetrate California over your line as far as San Francisco?

Mr. HUNTINGTON. Yes; we give them all fair rates. The Canadian Pacific controls the steamer lines from Vancouver to San Francisco.

Senator MORGAN. That arrangement, while it exists, puts the Canadian Pacific in competition with the Union Pacific?

Mr. HUNTINGTON. Yes; I think that was an arrangement made by all the roads. I do not think we ever had a special arrangement with the Canadian Pacific.

Senator MORGAN. What do you mean by a special arrangement?

Mr. HUNTINGTON. I mean that the Central Pacific and the Union Pacific never made any arrangement with the Canadian Pacific, but the arrangement was made by all the roads engaged in the overland traffic.

Senator MORGAN. Without any consideration?

Mr. HUNTINGTON. There was some agreed percentage, I suppose.

Senator MORGAN. You have no exact knowledge on the subject?

Mr. HUNTINGTON. No, I have not.

Senator MORGAN. Where can I get it?

Mr. HUNTINGTON. I do not know; I expect that it could be got from our people.

Senator MORGAN. Whom do you call "our people?"

Mr. HUNTINGTON. Mr. J. C. Stubbs is our chief traffic man.

Senator MORGAN. If one man controlled the entire line from New Orleans to Portland, Oreg., and from San Diego and San Francisco to Ogden, could he not control the entire traffic south of Portland and west of the Sierra Nevada Mountains between the Atlantic and Pacific?

Mr. HUNTINGTON. I should think that that was very nearly the same question as that which I have answered. Please state it again.

Senator MORGAN. If one man controlled the entire line from New Orleans to Portland, Oreg., and from San Diego and San Francisco to Ogden, could he not control the entire traffic south of Portland and west of the Rockies between the Atlantic and Pacific?

Mr. HUNTINGTON. No; I should think not. The Southern Pacific does not go to San Diego; the Atchison, Topeka and Santa Fe does.

Senator MORGAN. If one man controlled the whole business there, would not that give him control of all the traffic south of Portland and west of the Rocky Mountains?

Mr. HUNTINGTON. No; there are other roads which come in. The Oregon Pacific connects with Willamette River, and runs to Keenawha Bay. They run steamers from there to San Francisco, and that makes a good connection with Portland.

Senator MORGAN. If a man had this control which I speak of (if he had such a sweep of control as that), would not the Oregon Short Line and the line from Albuquerque be at his mercy?

Mr. HUNTINGTON. No; I should think not.

Senator MORGAN. Why?

Mr. HUNTINGTON. If he was a wise man he would let everybody use his line.

Senator MORGAN. I am not speaking of wise men; I am speaking of one who had the wisdom of cupidity; I want to know what power he would have?

Mr. HUNTINGTON. If one man had all the avenues of trade he could control the trade; but that is not the case, and even then he could only control it temporarily.

Senator MORGAN. I just want to know what would be the power in the hands of one man having this control, to absorb the traffic and to put this railroad company from Albuquerque to Mojave and the Oregon Short Line in his power?

Mr. HUNTINGTON. If a man owned all the roads I can not pretend to say what he would do.

Senator MORGAN. I do not put it on the question of ownership, but on the question of control.

Mr. HUNTINGTON. Control would be the same thing as far as operation is concerned. If he controlled, of course it is no matter how he controlled.

Senator STEWART. Does that question include the control of the Atlantic and Pacific, and of the Oregon Short Line, and of the other roads which come through to the Pacific Ocean?

Senator MORGAN. My question includes the entire line from New Orleans and Portland, Oreg., to San Diego, San Francisco, and Ogden.

Senator STEWART. There is no line running from San Diego to Ogden direct.

Senator MORGAN. I know; I want to know whether, if a man had that control, he would not have the control of the Pacific and Atlantic traffic—the traffic to the East and West—and whether, in such conditions and under such circumstances, he would not be the master and ruler of the Albuquerque and Mojave road, and also of the Oregon Short Line?

Mr. HUNTINGTON. If he controlled all these roads he would have the control of the position temporarily.

Senator MORGAN. He would not want much more, would he, to control the traffic across the continent between the Atlantic and Pacific?

Mr. HUNTINGTON. He would have a very poor property if he attempted to control it to the disadvantage of other companies.

Senator MORGAN. But he would not want much else in the way of power, would he?

Mr. HUNTINGTON. He would have the power but temporarily.

Senator MORGAN. I want to know about the conditions which exist, not about those which are prospective and conjectural.

Senator STEWART. Would it include the Northern Pacific, which goes to deep water, and the Oregon Short Line, which also goes to deep water?

Senator MORGAN. My question includes the Oregon Short Line and the road from Albuquerque to Mojave. I want to know whether these roads would not be in a box and at the mercy of a man who owned the railroads from New Orleans to San Francisco and San Diego and out to Omaha?

Senator STEWART. Would that affect the Canadian Pacific with a line of steamers to San Francisco and San Diego?

Mr. HUNTINGTON. It seems to me, Senator Morgan, that it is so easy to get around that that if I was charging anything more than fair rates they would run steamers from San Francisco, which is a very cheap way of transporting persons and property.

Senator MORGAN. I am not counting on the competition of rates, but I am counting on the advantages which a man would have who controlled the line from New Orleans to San Francisco and San Diego, and then from San Francisco and San Diego to Omaha over lines such as those from Albuquerque to Mojave and the Oregon Short Line. I want to know what the material power of such an aggregation of control in the hands of one man would be for the purpose of holding down and keeping in check these competitive roads?

Mr. HUNTINGTON. I suppose we have only one way of judging of the future, and that is by the past, and I do not think that one great railroad ever dared, up to this time, to shut up another. When the Southern Pacific had a road to El Paso, the Texas Pacific arrived there, and we gave them the same rates as we charged ourselves. When the Atchison, Topeka and Santa Fe got to Mojave (about 400 miles from San Francisco), we at once gave them the best rates—best for them and best for ourselves. We thought so because they have been there ever since, for a number of years, and if we had not given them the best rates, of course they would have moved on.

Senator STEWART. Assuming the question asked you by Senator Morgan that one party owned the road from Portland——

Senator MORGAN. No, that is not my question; from New Orleans.

Senator STEWART. Would the ownership of the road from New Orleans to San Diego interfere with the traffic of the Atlantic and Pacific to San Francisco, over the Central Pacific, according to present contracted prices?

Senator MORGAN. From New Orleans to San Francisco and San Diego, and from San Francisco and San Diego to Omaha. That is the line I am talking about being in the control of one man.

Senator STEWART (to Mr. Huntington). Would that interfere with the Atlantic and Pacific going to San Francisco under existing contracts?

Mr. HUNTINGTON. It would not.

Senator STEWART. Would that interfere with the Atchison and Topeka going to San Diego?

Mr. HUNTINGTON. Certainly not. We have nothing to do with that line at all.

Senator STEWART. Would that interfere with the Oregon Short Line going to Portland and running a line of steamers from Portland to San Francisco?

Mr. HUNTINGTON. Not in the least.

Senator STEWART. Would that interfere with the Northern Pacific, which runs to Puget Sound and which runs steamers from there down the coast?

Mr. HUNTINGTON. It would not.

Senator STEWART. Would it interfere with the Canadian Pacific, which runs across the continent and has a line of steamers at its terminus?

Mr. HUNTINGTON. No.

Senator STEWART. None of them would be blocked up by means of the ownership of the road from New Orleans to Portland and to Omaha?

Mr. HUNTINGTON. No.

Senator STEWART. All these ways would still be open?

Mr. HUNTINGTON. Oh, yes.

Senator FRYE. And the Great Northern?

Mr. HUNTINGTON. Yes; I omitted that.

Senator MORGAN. The Senator from Nevada thinks that my question involves the ability to block up these roads. It does not. I am speaking of your ability to compel the Oregon Short Line and the road from Albuquerque to Mojave to make freight terms with you and to come to your terms whenever you want to raise the rates.

Mr. HUNTINGTON. The Union Pacific would take its freight by steamer from San Francisco to Portland and would then use the Oregon Short Line, and we could not interfere with that at all.

Senator MORGAN. When they reached Portland and were met there by the same rates as the Southern Pacific rates, could you not, if you owned these roads that I have mentioned, compel the Oregon Short Line and the road from Albuquerque to Mojave to come to your terms, no matter whether these terms suited the people or not?

Mr. HUNTINGTON. Oh, no.

Senator MORGAN. Would it not give you the ability of forcing these other roads to raise their rates?

Mr. HUNTINGTON. Oh, no.

Senator MORGAN. State why.

Mr. HUNTINGTON. They can take goods from San Francisco on steamers to Portland, there put them on the Oregon Short Line and take them to Ogden, and they would have a good line.

Senator MORGAN. How would that line, with two breakages of traffic, compete with your line?

Mr. HUNTINGTON. The Southern Pacific has two breakages of traffic to New York, and yet it does considerable business.

Senator MORGAN. But a line which has competition with the Southern Pacific to New York has to make the same breakages of traffic you have.

Mr. HUNTINGTON. Yes; but they have all-rail lines across the continent and it is about three or four thousand miles shorter.

Senator MORGAN. If I did not know that you were a very public-spirited man, in favor of the people having fair rates, I would be afraid of trusting this power to you.

Mr. HUNTINGTON. I am sorry for it, because "out of the abundance of the heart the mouth speaketh." I never would have thought that of you.

Senator MORGAN. Thought what?

Mr. HUNTINGTON. What you have said.

Senator MORGAN. I have said that if I were not satisfied that you were a friend of the people I would hate to put that power in your hands.

Mr. HUNTINGTON. Excuse me, I take that back, all I said.

Senator MORGAN. You would not be afraid to trust yourself with it?

Mr. HUNTINGTON. No; I would rather trust myself than anybody else I know of.

Senator MORGAN. What roads are under the control of the Southern Pacific Railroad Company?

Mr. HUNTINGTON. I do not know that I can name them all. It controls the Oregon and California; but it is by a lease which can be broken at any time. Then it controls the San Francisco Northern, and the Southern Pacific of California. We consolidated a good many of those little roads in California under the Southern Pacific Railroad of California, and I can not tell you just how many of them there are. We control the California Pacific. The Northern California is not consolidated with the Southern Pacific Company. There is a distinction between the Southern Pacific Company and the Southern Pacific of California. We control the Southern Pacific of California, the Southern Pacific of Arizona, the Southern Pacific of New Mexico, the Louisiana Western, and the Morgan, Louisiana and Texas in Louisiana. As I remember, that is all.

Senator MORGAN. You have no road east of New Orleans under the Kentucky corporation?

Mr. HUNTINGTON. No.

Senator MORGAN. Have you had any?

Mr. HUNTINGTON. No; I think not.

Senator MORGAN. So that this line in its outer terminals begins at New Orleans and goes to Portland, Oreg.?

Mr. HUNTINGTON. Yes; I think so.

Senator MORGAN. And in its reach it consolidated the various minor lines which you have been speaking of?

Mr. HUNTINGTON. Yes; there were quite a number of short lines in California which could not be run as separate lines, and we consolidated them for the sake of economy.

Senator MORGAN. You are speaking of consolidation, and I am speaking of control; I want to know what lines the Kentucky company owns or controls in the West. You have not mentioned the Central Pacific.

Mr. HUNTINGTON. No. The Southern Pacific has leased the Central Pacific. That is a short lease, subject to abrogation at any time.

Senator MORGAN. You have not bought all these other roads; you lease them, too, do you not?

Mr. HUNTINGTON. No; the Southern Pacific of California controls them; that company was organized to economize the workings of these roads, and they exchanged shares with the Southern Pacific Company so that most of these lines are owned by the Southern Pacific Company.

Senator MORGAN. But that is not the case as respects the Central Pacific?

Mr. HUNTINGTON. No.

Senator MORGAN. These other roads which you control are not owned by this Kentucky company under this programme of exchanging shares. I speak of roads which you do not own, but which you control. Have you mentioned them all?

Mr. HUNTINGTON. I think I have mentioned them all. There are some little roads in California which I may have left out, but I think not.

Senator MORGAN. Are you the president of the Kentucky company?

Mr. HUNTINGTON. Of the Southern Pacific Company? Yes.

Senator MORGAN. Then it seems you ought to know what railroads you are president of.

Mr. HUNTINGTON. I am president of the Southern Pacific Company. Each of those small companies keeps up its organization, but it is not an expensive organization. At one time there were very many more than there are now, but I do not recollect them all. When I want to know a thing in the office I ring the bell and see the man who does know it.

Senator MORGAN. Then we are examining the wrong man. I want to examine the man who knows all about it. If you will give me the name of the man who does know I will send for him.

Mr. HUNTINGTON. I think I know all that I suppose is material.

Senator MORGAN. That is what I supposed when I set out to examine you. Who is the president of the Southern Pacific of California?

Mr. HUNTINGTON. Mr. Charles F. Crocker, as I remember.

Senator MORGAN. What is the length of that line?

Mr. HUNTINGTON. The Southern Pacific of California? We are adding a little to it almost every day. I think it is about 1,600 miles.

Senator MORGAN. Who is the president of the San Francisco Northern?

Mr. HUNTINGTON. I do not know that I can answer that question.

Senator MORGAN. It has a president?

Mr. HUNTINGTON. Yes.

Senator MORGAN. And a board of directors?

Mr. HUNTINGTON. Yes.

Senator MORGAN. What are the terminals of that road?

Mr. HUNTINGTON. San Francisco and Tehama, I should say.

Senator MORGAN. That is in the direction of Portland?

Mr. HUNTINGTON. Yes.

Senator MORGAN. What line lies between that and Portland?

Mr. HUNTINGTON. The California and Oregon.

Senator MORGAN. What are the terminals of that road?

Mr. HUNTINGTON. Roseville and Coles.

Senator MORGAN. Does that road get to Portland over its own line?

Mr. HUNTINGTON. No; the Oregon and California takes it up there.

Senator MORGAN. What are the terminals of the California and Oregon?

Mr. HUNTINGTON. The same southern end, Coles, and at the north, Portland.

Senator MORGAN. Who is president of that line?

Mr. HUNTINGTON. I do not know; I can send you his name to-morrow.

Senator MORGAN. Who is president of the California and Oregon?

Mr. HUNTINGTON. Mr. Requa; that is, part of the Central Pacific.

Senator MORGAN. It is consolidated with the Central Pacific?

Mr. HUNTINGTON. Yes.

Senator MORGAN. Has it a separate board of directors?

Mr. HUNTINGTON. No.

Senator MORGAN. What is the length of that line?

Mr. HUNTINGTON. Two hundred and ninety-seven miles.

Senator MORGAN. Does it run through a good country?

Mr. HUNTINGTON. Yes; most of the way it is very good.

Senator MORGAN. What is the length of the line which is called the Oregon and California?

Mr. HUNTINGTON. It is about 800 miles.

Senator STEWART. Do you mean the whole line?

Mr. HUNTINGTON. We have lines through the Willamette Valley which all belong to this organization, something between seven and eight hundred miles.

Senator STEWART. Of roads in Oregon?

Mr. HUNTINGTON. Yes.

Senator MORGAN. Will you state what companies have made what you call an interchange of stock with the Southern Pacific?

Mr. HUNTINGTON. The Southern Pacific of California, the Southern Pacific of New Mexico, the Southern Pacific of Arizona, the Morgan Company, and the Louisiana and Western.

Senator MORGAN. These companies have all made an interchange of stock with the Southern Pacific?

Mr. HUNTINGTON. Yes.

Senator MORGAN. Have they given up their separate organizations?

Mr. HUNTINGTON. No.

Senator MORGAN. To what extent has this exchange of stock been made?

Mr. HUNTINGTON. Substantially, all of their stock.

Senator MORGAN. That is to say, that they would give you an amount of stock of their respective roads equal to the amount of stock which they get in the Southern Pacific?

Mr. HUNTINGTON. Yes; on a graded basis of value—not necessarily share for share.

Senator MORGAN. Are these the only roads which have made this interchange of stock?

Mr. HUNTINGTON. The Galveston, Harrisburg and San Antonio of Texas is another.

Senator MORGAN. After that interchange of stock took place, the roads were practically one as to ownership from New Orleans clear up to San Francisco?

Mr. HUNTINGTON. A majority of the shares were, I think.

Senator MORGAN. The stockholders of the Southern Pacific of New Mexico were stockholders in your road?

Mr. HUNTINGTON. Yes; they exchanged their shares, and the shares were put in a trust. We took the shares of the Southern Pacific of New Mexico and we put them in the hands of a trustee.

Senator MORGAN. Was that a permanent arrangement made under the authority of the law, or was it a mere contract or deal, made under the authority of a trust?

Mr. HUNTINGTON. I suppose it was legal. The Southern Pacific was authorized to buy the shares and they bought them.

Senator MORGAN. I do not know whether it was a mere private contract or whether the law authorized it.

Mr. HUNTINGTON. The law authorized it.

Senator MORGAN. Do you mean the laws of the different States and Territories from which these several roads derived their charter power?

Mr. HUNTINGTON. I do not know that there was an article in any special law authorizing a man to sell his own. I did not understand that there was an owner of a share of stock who had not the right to sell it; and the Southern Pacific had a special right, by legislation, to buy it, or to buy anything.

Senator MORGAN. That would cover the case; then the relations existing between these different corporations and the corporation of the Southern Pacific is that the Southern Pacific is the real owner of the stock of each of these corporations, without their having broken up their separate legal organization, or their boards of directors?

Mr. HUNTINGTON. It can not be that.

Senator MORGAN. It is not, then, a real, actual consolidation?

Mr. HUNTINGTON. Oh, no.

Senator MORGAN. So that the Southern Pacific does not seem, in the eyes of the law, as the legal representative of all the rights and powers of each of these companies thus included within its organzation?

Mr. HUNTINGTON. As I understand it, the companies would seem like any other shareholders, neither more nor less.

Senator MORGAN. Which of the roads of California that are under lease to the Southern Pacific are not included in these arrangements for the interchange of stock?

Mr. HUNTINGTON. I am inclined to think that the Southern Pacific Company has the majority of the shares of all the companies in California; that the board of directors of the Southern Pacific controls all of them except the Central Pacific.

Senator MORGAN. Has the Southern Pacific any stock of the Central Pacific?

Mr. HUNTINGTON. I think not.

Senator MORGAN. But the individuals in the Southern Pacific have stock of the Central Pacific?

Mr. HUNTINGTON. Yes.

Senator MORGAN. To what extent?

Mr. HUNTINGTON. Not very great.

Senator MORGAN. Give a percentage.

Mr. HUNTINGTON. I do not know really. I have not looked at the books. It is a dividend-warrant stock, like a bond with coupons. We found in dealing in that stock all over the world that it was inconvenient for holders of it to have to get their dividends in the ordinary way, and we set to work to fix up something like a bond, so that dividends are paid on dividend warrants just like coupons, and so we have them made in that way.

Senator MORGAN. In whatever way you contrive to get the ownership represented, about what is the percentage of the stock of the Central Pacific which is owned by the stockholders of the Southern Pacific?

Mr. HUNTINGTON. I do not know. It is not very large. We have had to part with these Central Pacific shares to pay the old indebtedness, and we have not got very many shares. I am not a large shareholder.

Senator MORGAN. Is there any stock issued by the Kentucky company?

Mr. HUNTINGTON. To the Central Pacific?

Senator MORGAN. To anybody?

Mr. HUNTINGTON. Oh, yes.

Senator MORGAN. That company has issued stock?

Mr. HUNTINGTON. It has issued stock for shares.

Senator MORGAN. How much stock has that company issued?

Mr. HUNTINGTON. I think something over one hundred millions.

Senator MORGAN. You are president of that company?

Mr. HUNTINGTON. Yes.

Senator MORGAN. Are you the president of the Southern Pacific of California?

Mr. HUNTINGTON. No.

Senator MORGAN. Who is?

Mr. HUNTINGTON. Mr. Charles F. Crocker.

Senator MORGAN. Who is the president of the Central Pacific?

Mr. HUNTINGTON. Mr. Requa.

Senator MORGAN. For what was this $100,000,000 of stock issued? Was it for cash paid in?

Mr. HUNTINGTON. No; it was issued for stock.

Senator MORGAN. Was there no cash paid in?

Mr. HUNTINGTON. Whatever the charter called for was done. Perhaps there was no cash called for or paid in.

Senator MORGAN. Then it was a corporation based upon the shares of other companies?

Mr. HUNTINGTON. Yes; it was a corporation to economize the workings of many roads. It was organized for that purpose.

Senator MORGAN. How much stock have you got in the Kentucky corporation?

Mr. HUNTINGTON. I may have five or six millions.

Senator MORGAN. Is there any larger stockholder than yourself?

Mr. HUNTINGTON. I do not know. I should not wonder if Governor Stanford had more stock than I have.

Senator MORGAN. Have you a list of the stockholders in the Kentucky company?

Mr. HUNTINGTON. Yes. I have not got it with me.

Senator MORGAN. Is it in town?

Mr. HUNTINGTON. No; but I can get it very easily.

Senator MORGAN. Have you the book which shows to whom the shares belong?

Mr. HUNTINGTON. No, we have not got that. It is a dividend-warrant stock, like a coupon bond.

Senator MORGAN. Is it not an extraordinary arrangement to issue stock and to have no books to show who the stockholders are?

Mr. HUNTINGTON. No.

Senator MORGAN. Is there no transfer book?

Mr. HUNTINGTON. Oh, yes.

Senator MORGAN. If I understand this peculiar arrangement, it is like a coupon bond which can be transferred by delivery?

Mr. HUNTINGTON. Yes.

Senator MORGAN. Not registered?

Mr. HUNTINGTON. No; there is a great convenience in this.

Senator MORGAN. But a great inconvenience to those who want to find out who own the stock.

Mr. HUNTINGTON. I do not see what object anybody would have, if there are so many shares out, to know where they are.

Senator MORGAN. The creditors might be very hungry to find out who owned the stock, and the Government of the United States might want to know it, too. Inasmuch as no money was paid for the stock of the Kentucky company, what was paid for it?

Mr. HUNTINGTON. There was an exchange of stock.

Senator MORGAN. And you got five millions, or more?

Mr. HUNTINGTON. Yes.

Senator MORGAN. What did you give for that?

Mr. HUNTINGTON. I had some shares in the Louisiana company (the Morgan company), and I had some in the Western Pacific Company (a good many), and I had some in the Texas and New Orleans; I had some in the Galveston, Harrisburg and San Antonio; I had some in the Southern Pacific of New Mexico; I had some in the Southern Pacific of Arizona; some in the Southern Pacific of California; some in the San Francisco Northern, and some in the Oregon and California. I had some in all of these companies.

Senator MORGAN. Did you have any in the Central Pacific?

Mr. HUNTINGTON. Yes.

Senator MORGAN. Did you transfer that stock?

Mr. HUNTINGTON. No.

Senator MORGAN. Have you got it yet?

Mr. HUNTINGTON. Yes.

Senator MORGAN. How much?

Mr. HUNTINGTON. Not a great many shares. I suppose I have got four or five thousand shares.

Senator MORGAN. How much money would that represent on the face value?

Mr. HUNTINGTON. One thousand shares represent $100,000.

Senator MORGAN. And you have got four or five thousand shares, about $500,000?

Mr. HUNTINGTON. Yes.

Senator MORGAN. Was anybody admitted into this Kentucky company except persons who were shareholders in those roads you have been just mentioning and which were put under the control of this company?

Mr. HUNTINGTON. No, I do not think so. If anybody wanted shares, of course they could buy them.

Senator MORGAN. It was a grouping of the shares of the shareholders of these respective companies, delivered into the treasury of this Kentucky company, and in place of these shares this warrant stock which you speak of (transferable by delivery) was issued to the various shareholders?

Mr. HUNTINGTON. Yes; it was a transfer.

Senator MORGAN. So that the man who put in his shares of these various companies into the Kentucky company, and got his warrant stock, was no longer a stockholder in these various companies?

Mr. HUNTINGTON. No.

Senator MORGAN. It was a cancellation of his ownership of stock in these various companies?

Mr. HUNTINGTON. Hardly a cancellation. The stock was put in the hands of trustees. The business was done directly between the company and the shareholders.

Senator MORGAN. Has anybody who owns this ambulatory stock (this warrant stock) the right to go to the treasury of the Kentucky company and demand that his shares in the other companies which he put in there should be delivered to him on the surrender of his warrant stock?

Mr. HUNTINGTON. Oh, no; it does not belong to him.

Senator MORGAN. Does this arrangement for the warrant stock absorb all the stock of these railroad companies?

Mr. HUNTINGTON. I think not all, but a large majority of it.

Senator MORGAN. Was not the plan to have enough in the hands of the respective stockholders to qualify them under the law to become directors?

Mr. HUNTINGTON. That we had to do.

Senator MORGAN. It was your plan to work down to that scale?

Mr. HUNTINGTON. It was subject to everybody to exchange or not to exchange.

Senator MORGAN. Your plan was to convert the stock of all these corporations into this warrant stock so that the Kentucky corporation would become the representative in law and in fact of the interests which these gentlemen had in these respective roads; what is that short of a purchase of these roads?

Mr. HUNTINGTON. I suppose it is a purchase. The object was not to change shares, but to get up an organization to economize the working of the roads to the farthest possible extent, and to aid the people of the country through which these roads pass by giving them the lowest possible rates of freight.

Senator MORGAN. We may assume that for all practical purposes except the question of legal organization the Kentucky company is the owner of these roads, and is entitled to the proceeds of the roads and entitled to officer them.

Mr. HUNTINGTON. That would go, I suppose. It would follow the shares.

Senator MORGAN. It is entitled to manage and does manage the actual business of all these roads?

Mr. HUNTINGTON. It manages the traffic.

Senator MORGAN. Has the Kentucky company assumed the debts of all of these corporations?

Mr. HUNTINGTON. I think so. We always kept our road pretty clean, without any floating debt.

Senator MORGAN. So that whatever mortgage rested on these properties, or whatever floating debt may have been incurred in the operation of these roads, have become now the debt of the Kentucky company?

Mr. HUNTINGTON. Not necessarily, as I understand it, although I am not learned in the law. I would take a mortgage to bind whoever held the stock. The mortgage would hold the property; and if the owners did not pay, the mortgagee would take the property.

Senator MORGAN. I want to know whether you did assume the debt or not?

Mr. HUNTINGTON. I think not.

Senator MORGAN. Then your Kentucky company does not feel obligated to pay the debts included in any mortgage given by either of those companies absorbed by it?

Mr. HUNTINGTON. I do not know; but I think not, to any considerable extent. Of course, if the debt was not paid, the mortgagee would take the property.

Senator MORGAN. Have you not been going on paying the debts of the companies?

Mr. HUNTINGTON. Yes, we have paid the debts currently. I do not know that any of the mortgage debt has been due yet on the Southern road. We never have defaulted.

Senator MORGAN. Have any of the bonds become actually due on any of these roads?

Mr. HUNTINGTON. I think not upon any that are worked by the Southern Pacific.

Senator MORGAN. You mean by the Kentucky road?

Mr. HUNTINGTON. Yes. I think not; but if any has become due we issue another to take its place.

Senator MORGAN. Suppose that a creditor of one of those strangulated companies wished to proceed to foreclose his mortgage, and that the property of the company was not worth enough to pay the mortgage debt; what would happen?

Mr. HUNTINGTON. Exactly what you mean by a strangulated company I do not quite understand.

Senator MORGAN. I will explain after awhile.

Mr. HUNTINGTON. I do not see the point exactly.

Senator MORGAN. If it be more convenient, I will call it a company choked down.

Mr. HUNTINGTON. We have not any of those, and I do not exactly know how to answer your question.

Senator MORGAN. Suppose that one of those companies, which should be unfortunate enough not to be able to conduct its own business but had to merge itself into this great Kentucky corporation, should not be able to pay the mortgage debt resting on its property, has the Kentucky corporation made any engagement by which it pays that debt?

Mr. HUNTINGTON. I suppose they would stand just like any other stockholder. I do not know of any difference between them and any other stockholders in relation to a transaction of that kind.

Senator MORGAN. In the betterments of the road, in the improvements and repairs between New Orleans and the northern terminus—say Portland, Oreg.—are these betterments charged up to each particular company separately, or are they put into one general account?

Mr. HUNTINGTON. I think that when we once build a road, and the construction account is closed, the repairs go to the current expenses.

Senator MORGAN. In this Kentucky company?

Mr. HUNTINGTON. Yes.

Senator MORGAN. I want to know whether the current expenses of these other companies are paid by the Kentucky company.

Mr. HUNTINGTON. They are paid by the operating company, so far as I know.

Senator MORGAN. That is the Kentucky company?

Mr. HUNTINGTON. Yes.

Senator MORGAN. So that if one of these roads was subjected to some great misfortune, the loss of a bridge or otherwise, the Kentucky company would make the repairs and charge it to its own account.

Mr. HUNTINGTON. I do not know. I think that any extraordinary expenses of that kind (just how far I do not know) would be borne by the Southern Pacific Company, just the same as by any other shareholders.

Senator MORGAN. So that, for betterments and repairs and the loss of profits, you do not keep a separate account in the books of the Kentucky company with each of these separate organizations?

Mr. HUNTINGTON. I understand that we do.

Senator MORGAN. And then you charge up whatever losses fall upon them?

Mr. HUNTINGTON. Not necessarily; we like to know how the account stands.

Senator MORGAN. You do it for information and not for business.

Mr. HUNTINGTON. We do it because it is a proper thing to do.

Senator MORGAN. Is there any charge against either of those companies for the losses which may be sustained on its particular account?

Mr. HUNTINGTON. It would be well to know just how it was; I think that is the way we do it.

Senator MORGAN. Well, what is the way you do it?

Mr. HUNTINGTON. We pay all those things which go to the current expenses, although there may be some small things which are not covered in.

Senator MORGAN. Is not this whole line of railroad, represented by the Kentucky company, kept as one line, and are not all the earnings of the whole line credited to the Kentucky company, and all the charges and expenses charged to it?

Mr. HUNTINGTON. We keep an account of the earnings and expenses of the separate companies.

Senator MORGAN. Do you charge it up to them?

Mr. HUNTINGTON. The bookkeeping shows how it is. The operating company pays the ordinary operating expenses.

Senator MORGAN. You do not seem to know how it is.

Mr. HUNTINGTON. I think I do.

Senator MORGAN. If you know it you can state it. I want to know whether you keep a separate account against each one of these companies.

Mr. HUNTINGTON. We do; I am pretty sure of that.

Senator MORGAN. In which account you charge them with all the expenses of operating.

Mr. HUNTINGTON. I think it runs just as though you and I owned the shares instead of the Southern Pacific owning them.

Senator MORGAN. Do you charge the companies with the salaries of the officers?

Mr. HUNTINGTON. They do not get much salary. I do not think they get any salary.

Senator MORGAN. Well, the other expenses. Do you charge them with the expenses of the repairs of track?

Mr. HUNTINGTON. That is current expenses, and the Southern Pacific company pays them as shareholders in those companies. They are run just as though the shares belonged to Senator Morgan and myself.

Senator MORGAN. These accounts, I suppose, are stated annually?

Mr. HUNTINGTON. Yes.

Senator MORGAN. At the end of the year, if any one of these companies is found to have absorbed more of the money of the general company than it was entitled to (after deducting expenses of repairs and keeping the line in order), could you state an account against that company, and sue it, to recover the balance in favor of the general company, or not?

Mr. HUNTINGTON. I do not know. I think that none of these things have occurred yet. We have had no extraordinary repairs.

Senator MORGAN. Is it possible that such a thing might occur under the arrangement absorbing the stock and virtually putting control of all the lines in the Kentucky company?

Mr. HUNTINGTON. I do not think that the Southern Pacific Company has any power because it holds these shares, any more than any other private shareholder has.

Senator MORGAN. To come directly to the point, is not the Kentucky company the owner of these lines of railroad from end to end, from New Orleans to Portland, Oreg.?

Mr. HUNTINGTON. Not all the way. It does not own any shares of the Central Pacific. I think it has a majority of the shares of the other companies.

Senator MORGAN. Is not this Kentucky company regarded as the owner of these lines of railroad from New Orleans to Portland, Oreg., except the Central Pacific?

Mr. HUNTINGTON. The Southern Pacific has a majority of the shares of the various companies. I do not know that that carries any more rights than other shareholders have.

Senator MORGAN. But in so far as it owns a majority of the shares the Kentucky company is the owner of these lines?

Mr. HUNTINGTON. Yes; it has a majority of the votes.

Senator MORGAN. Can either of those intermediate corporations give orders to any man who runs a train or performs any other kind of work on the line thus under the control of the Kentucky company?

Mr. HUNTINGTON. Yes.

Senator MORGAN. Please name an instance in which the orders of any of the intermediate companies would be respected?

Mr. HUNTINGTON. My opinion is that the Galveston, Harrisburg and San Antonio road is running with its own officers.

Senator MORGAN. Is any other company doing so?

Mr. HUNTINGTON. I guess that the Texas and New Orleans is.

Senator MORGAN. Any other?

Mr. HUNTINGTON. I do not think now of any other.

Senator MORGAN. Then, with these two companies the Kentucky company made special arrangements, differing from the arrangement with the others?

Mr. HUNTINGTON. Yes; I think so.

Senator MORGAN. You found it necessary, in order to get their cooperation, to make a special arrangement with these companies that their own officers should run their line.

Mr. HUNTINGTON. That is a fact, I think.

Senator MORGAN. By virtue of the fact that you made a special arrangement for that purpose.

Mr. HUNTINGTON. I do not know how it is, but it is so.

Senator MORGAN. Does this corporation pay any dividends on its stock?

Mr. HUNTINGTON. I am sorry to say that it does not.

Senator MORGAN. Has it paid all of its current expenses?

Mr. HUNTINGTON. It has. It is one of the cleanest corporations in the country, I think.

Senator MORGAN. Has it paid the interest on its bonds?

Mr. HUNTINGTON. It has never defaulted a coupon on any bond.

Senator MORGAN. Has it reduced traffic charges and made the work more economical over the whole extent of the line than when the roads were running separately?

Mr. HUNTINGTON. Oh, yes.

Senator MORGAN. Very materially?

Mr. HUNTINGTON. Yes.

Senator MORGAN. What would be the percentage of reduction?

Mr. HUNTINGTON. I think that prices have gone down. Last year the rates were less than 12 mills per mile per ton, and I think we used to get 2½ cents a mile.

Senator MORGAN. That is a reduction of freight.

Mr. HUNTINGTON. And there was a reduction of expenses to correspond. We practice the most rigid economy.

Senator MORGAN. Are you earning more than your necessary expenses?

Mr. HUNTINGTON. We always have a little to the good.

Senator MORGAN. What is the amount of the reserve fund?

Mr. HUNTINGTON. It is very little.

Senator MORGAN. About how much?

Mr. HUNTINGTON. About one million dollars, or so.

Senator MORGAN. Where is that money kept?

Mr. HUNTINGTON. It is kept in San Francisco and along the road.

Senator MORGAN. It is kept in different banks and places where you may want to use it?

Mr. HUNTINGTON. Yes.

Senator MORGAN. Where is the business office of the Kentucky company?

Mr. HUNTINGTON. We keep an office in Kentucky and we keep an office in San Francisco. The working office is in San Francisco.

Senator MORGAN. Have you an office in New York?

Mr. HUNTINGTON. Yes; we keep an office there.

Senator MORGAN. The head office is in New York?

Mr. HUNTINGTON. I think it can hardly be called the head office. The president lives in New York, but the working office is in San Francisco.

Senator MORGAN. In which of those offices are the reports collected?

Mr. HUNTINGTON. Of course you can get the reports in the New York office or the San Francisco office.

Senator MORGAN. I want to know to which office these different employees of the railroad, big and little, are required to report.

Mr. HUNTINGTON. To the office at San Francisco.

Senator MORGAN. So that the San Francisco office is the main office of the company.

Mr. HUNTINGTON. It is the main office for the operations of the company.

The CHAIRMAN. Are you required by law to keep an office in San Francisco?

Mr. HUNTINGTON. I presume so. We do keep it there.

Senator MORGAN. The statute under which you are operating is, I understand, a Kentucky statute.

Mr. HUNTINGTON. Yes.

Senator MORGAN. And that supplies all the law which controls your action?

Mr. HUNTINGTON. I hardly know how to answer that question. We have the right to buy shares, with other things. We buy them and own them, and the ownership of these shares, of course, takes control of the property.

Senator MORGAN. The legislatures of Arizona, Louisiana, New Mexico, and California have not contributed any powers to this Kentucky company? It gets all its powers from the Kentucky legislature?

Mr. HUNTINGTON. We got the power to buy shares.

Senator MORGAN. Whatever powers you have you got from the Kentucky legislature.

Mr. HUNTINGTON. The companies have franchises from the several States to run the roads.

Senator MORGAN. Has any legislature, besides the Kentucky legislature, given any official recognition of the existence of the Kentucky company?

Mr. HUNTINGTON. No; not that I know of.

Senator MORGAN. So that the powers of that company come from the Kentucky legislature. Do you do any business in Kentucky?

Mr. HUNTINGTON. We have an office there.

Senator MORGAN. Do you do any business there?

Mr. HUNTINGTON. No; we are not allowed to build roads in Kentucky. We can buy a charter of a road in Kentucky, or we can buy shares of a road in Kentucky, but we have no power to go to work as an organization and build a road in Kentucky.

Senator MORGAN. So that, in getting your charter, Kentucky prohibits you from building a road in that State.

Mr. HUNTINGTON. It is a charter to go anywhere in the world and do business where we had a right to do it. We merely went to the legislature of Kentucky and got a charter; but that charter of itself gives us no right to build a railroad in Kentucky.

Senator MORGAN. On the contrary, it positively prohibits you from doing so.

Mr. HUNTINGTON. I think so. The charter was drawn, to a certain extent, under our supervision, and we did not suppose that the legislature would give us a right to build a railroad under a charter of that kind. If we wanted to build a road there, I have no doubt that the legislature would give us authority to build it; but it did not.

Senator MORGAN. Then you had a railroad charter in Kentucky with the prohibition against your building a railroad in that State?

Mr. HUNTINGTON. We did not have the right to go over the State and build railroads where we liked.

Senator MORGAN. Did not the Kentucky legislature refuse to give you any charter at all until you consented not to build a railroad?

Mr. HUNTINGTON. Not at all. We would not ask a roving charter to go anywhere and build a railroad, and I do not suppose any State in the Union would grant it. At the same time I am certain that we could go to the Kentucky legislature and get the right to build a railroad in Kentucky, reasonably located, from point to point.

Senator MORGAN. You say the stock of the Central Pacific has been taken up by this Kentucky company?

Mr. HUNTINGTON. Excuse me. The Southern Pacific Company has no stock in the Central Pacific.

Senator MORGAN. None at all?

Mr. HUNTINGTON. No.

Senator MORGAN. No stockholder of the Central Pacific has ever exchanged his stock with the Southern Pacific?

Mr. HUNTINGTON. No; I am sure of it. No stockholder of the Central Pacific was ever asked to exchange it.

Senator MORGAN. You never would permit that?

Mr. HUNTINGTON. We would not ask it to be done.

Senator MORGAN. All of the control of this great line of railroad, reaching from Portland, Oreg., to New Orleans, including the lateral roads, is in a corporation chartered in Kentucky, with one office in New York and one in San Francisco (the main office)?

Mr. HUNTINGTON. Yes.

Senator MORGAN. What business is done in the New York office?

Mr. HUNTINGTON. Some considerable part of the executive business is done there. A majority of the board of directors is in San Francisco. We buy material in New York. I have always bought the material for all the roads myself. There is something coming up every day in New York that has to be attended to. All the coupons and warrants are paid in New York.

Senator MORGAN. Has this Kentucky company also connection by sea with other companies?

Mr. HUNTINGTON. No; the Southern Pacific has not.

Senator MORGAN. It has no business connections by sea?

Mr. HUNTINGTON. It has ships running on the Gulf of Mexico and it has ships running to New York.

Senator MORGAN. Take the Occidental and Oriental Line of steamships. Is that under the control of the Kentucky company?

Mr. HUNTINGTON. No; we have nothing to do with the Pacific Ocean.

Senator MORGAN. And you have no contract or business arrangement with any ships on the Pacific?

Mr. HUNTINGTON. I think not. The Occidental and Oriental Line is controlled by the Union Pacific and the Central Pacific.

Senator MORGAN. Now, as to the Atlantic. You do own lines of ships that run from New Orleans to New York?

Mr. HUNTINGTON. Yes.

Senator MORGAN. How many ships have you?

Mr. HUNTINGTON. I think twenty, all belonging to that company.

Senator MORGAN. What company do you mean?

Mr. HUNTINGTON. The Southern Pacific Company.

Senator MORGAN. I call it the Kentucky company.

Mr. HUNTINGTON. We always call it the Southern Pacific Company.

Senator MORGAN. And you have twenty ships?

Mr. HUNTINGTON. Yes.

Senator MORGAN. Steamships?

Mr. HUNTINGTON. Yes; we have no sailers.

Senator MORGAN. What is about the burden of these ships?

Mr. HUNTINGTON. The carrying capacity of the heavier ones is about 5,000 tons.

Senator MORGAN. The probable average is 4,500 tons?

Mr. HUNTINGTON. No; they would not average over 4,000 tons. And we have a line to Vera Cruz.

Senator MORGAN. So that you have 80,000 tons of steamships in your control?

Mr. HUNTINGTON. No; I do not think they would average 4,000 tons. I question if they would average over 3,000 tons.

Senator MORGAN. Do you build your ships or do you buy them?

Mr. HUNTINGTON. We built four of the larger ones at Newport News. Some we built in Philadelphia, and some in Wilmington.

Senator MORGAN. These ships are, out and out, the property of the Kentucky company?

Mr. HUNTINGTON. Of the Southern Pacific Company; I think so.

Senator MORGAN. Were they built on credit or were they built for money?

Mr. HUNTINGTON. Partly money and partly credit.

Senator MORGAN. How much money and how much credit?

Mr. HUNTINGTON. I should have to go back to the accounts for that.

Senator MORGAN. Well, about how much?

Mr. HUNTINGTON. We generally made certain payments upon them, and we usually got twelve months on part of them.

Senator MORGAN. You are not in debt for them now?

Mr. HUNTINGTON. No.

Senator MORGAN. They are all paid for?

Mr. HUNTINGTON. Yes.

Senator MORGAN. What are they worth?

Mr. HUNTINGTON. I suppose that twelve of them are worth somewhere about $400,000 apiece.

Senator MORGAN. And the other eight?

Mr. HUNTINGTON. They are not worth so much.

Senator MORGAN. Three hundred thousand dollars apiece?

Mr. HUNTINGTON. No; I think that two or three of them are worth $300,000 apiece, and some of them are not worth more than half that.

Senator MORGAN. Out of what funds were those vessels paid for by the company?

Mr. HUNTINGTON. I think we issued some bonds for a part of them.

Senator MORGAN. You have taken those bonds up?

Mr. HUNTINGTON. No; I think not.

Senator MORGAN. How many of these bonds have you outstanding?

Mr. HUNTINGTON. I do not know.

Senator MORGAN. About how many?

Mr. HUNTINGTON. I should think about $2,500,000 in bonds.

Senator MORGAN. That covers pretty well the whole cost of the ships, does it not?

Mr. HUNTINGTON. No; not of the whole 20 ships. It would be $6,000,000 or $7,000,000.

Senator MORGAN. Are the running and other expenses, and everything connected with these ships, credited to the Kentucky company?

Mr. HUNTINGTON. Yes; I should say so.

Senator MORGAN. Just as the railroads are?

Mr. HUNTINGTON. Yes.

Senator MORGAN. So that they are, practically, an extension of the railroads by sea?

Mr. HUNTINGTON. Yes.

Senator MORGAN. Have you any more ships besides these twenty that you speak of?

Mr. HUNTINGTON. Not as owning them.

Senator MORGAN. You have got some others leased?

Mr. HUNTINGTON. We have an arrangement for ships between New Orleans and Europe. We have certain arrangements for transportation.

Senator MORGAN. This Kentucky company has business arrangements for the freight of ships to Europe?

Mr. HUNTINGTON. Only for a portion of the year—during the cotton season.

Senator MORGAN. Is that a profitable arrangement?

Mr. HUNTINGTON. Freights are so low now that we do not make much.

Senator MORGAN. So that, under the powers of the Kentucky legislature, this railroad company from New Orleans to Portland has twenty ships to New York and some ships under contract to Europe?

Mr. HUNTINGTON. Mr. Hutchinson made the contracts. I do not think that I ever saw the contracts. He said he had made an arrangement which he thought would facilitate matters.

Senator MORGAN. You have through arrangements for freight from San Francisco to Europe over this line?

Mr. HUNTINGTON. Not to any considerable extent.

Senator MORGAN. Have you got through arrangements for freight between New York and New Orleans on these lines and all the way through to the West?

Mr. HUNTINGTON. Yes; we do a good deal of business between the Gulf States and Texas in the way of taking cotton to Japan.

Senator MORGAN. So that steamers on the line starting at New Orleans bring you in competition with all the overland lines running to the ocean?

Mr. HUNTINGTON. Yes; the overland lines would not amount to much in competition.

Senator MORGAN. That is your competition?

Mr. HUNTINGTON. Yes.

Senator MORGAN. If you could extend that line of railroad from San Francisco to Ogden, it would be a very important feature, would it not, to that great line of transcontinental American and foreign trade?

Mr. HUNTINGTON. That is a very good business of the road now. It has been, and I presume will continue to be.

Senator MORGAN. You would like to have a contribution of the traffic from Ogden to San Francisco, and to throw into this line the immense traffic to New York and across the Atlantic Ocean?

Mr. HUNTINGTON. We do not do business in that way. I do not think it would pay.

Senator MORGAN. If it pays you to put these other lines in connection with the Southern Pacific, why would it not pay you to put the Central Pacific in connection with it?

Mr. HUNTINGTON. The Central Pacific starts 1,500 miles from Chicago, which is a great city. That is about the central point of the eastern traffic. From Ogden to San Francisco, call it 900 miles. From San Francisco to New Orleans is 2,518 miles, and from New Orleans to Chicago is some 1,200 miles; so that would be some 4,600 miles against 1,500 miles. Our coal costs us three times as much as the coal on the roads between Ogden and New York; so that it would be rather forcing things to send freight that way.

Senator MORGAN. Then you think that it would be rather a detriment to you than an advantage to have the Central Pacific?

Mr. HUNTINGTON. I do not see how it would be a detriment. The Central Pacific has business of its own.

Senator MORGAN. Would it not be an advantage to the Southern Pacific to have it?

Mr. HUNTINGTON. I do not think it would.

Senator MORGAN. It would be neither a detriment nor an advantage. It would be a dead center. What is the inclination in your mind as to having the Central Pacific line connected with this big sweep of enterprise?

Mr. HUNTINGTON. I never have thought of it in that connection. But as a property in itself, it is a good property.

Senator MORGAN. I want to know whether it would be a detriment or a benefit to your line to have the Central Pacific connected with it.

Mr. HUNTINGTON. If the Central Pacific was not there——

Senator MORGAN. But it is there, and likely to remain there. Would the connection of the Central Pacific with your great enterprise have a tendency to be injurious to that other line or contributory to it in the way of advantage?

Mr. HUNTINGTON. I think it would be rather beneficial to have it there.

Senator MORGAN. Very beneficial?

Mr. HUNTINGTON. Beneficial, so far as that.

Senator MORGAN. Your company without the Central Pacific is a very rich and powerful company, is it not? I mean this Kentucky company.

Mr. HUNTINGTON. It is a very good company; but as to its being a rich and powerful railroad company, it is not. West of the hundredth meridian we have more than half the acreage of the country and not over 4,000,000 of population, while east of it there are 66,000,000 of population.

Senator MORGAN. If you wait for it to grow up you would be likely to have 100,000,000 of people west of one hundredth meridian?

Mr. HUNTINGTON. I would like to see those figures.

Senator MORGAN. Your company has first-class credit?

Mr. HUNTINGTON. Yes; our credit has always been very good.

Senator MORGAN. You can command a hundred millions in the market at any time you want to?

Mr. HUNTINGTON. I should hate to try that and fail. I never did fail, and I should hate to try to raise a hundred millions.

Senator MORGAN. You could command fifty millions?

Mr. HUNTINGTON. No; nobody could command fifty millions in any railroad organization in the world. I believe I could command, on my personal credit, as much as anyone.

Senator MORGAN. Is there any other railroad company which has as valuable assets as you have and is entitled to the same sort of credit as you can get?

Mr. HUNTINGTON. You can not build up the credit of a railroad with the sort of mileage that we have got (so much of the road running through sagebrush) to the same extent as you can with railroads at the North.

Senator MORGAN. Is there any other railroad company (especially any company in the transcontinental trade) which has a credit better than your organization?

Mr. HUNTINGTON. Well, I believe that anything which we want to do capitalists would have faith that we would do; but there is the great Pennsylvania Central and the great New York Central. I should not suppose that you could put another terminal in New York such as the New York Central has there for $100,000,000.

Senator MORGAN. If the United States Government is ever forced to the disagreeable humiliation of being compelled to sell the Central Pacific, or the Union Pacific, or both, do you not think you would be a pretty fair competitor in bidding in the market for them?

Mr. HUNTINGTON. There would be a place in the bidding where would stop.

Senator MORGAN. Where would that be?

Mr. HUNTINGTON. I could not tell you now.

Senator MORGAN. But there would be a place where you would stop?

Mr. HUNTINGTON. Yes.

Senator MORGAN. You would be certain to be in the fight, would you not?

Mr. HUNTINGTON. Yes; but I should stop.

Senator MORGAN. You could not stop without going on first.

Mr. HUNTINGTON. I probably would go on as far as anyone, but nobody could buy either of these properties, in my opinion, and pay a big price for them. Still, they are a going property, and if they were properly handled, and close economy observed, and care taken in their operation, the Central Pacific could pay all its debt to the Government. We would have to work pretty hard; but, with an extension of about fifty years, the road could pay 2 per cent currently on the Government debt.

Senator MORGAN. In my six years of experience on this committee I have not been so fortunate as to hear anyone suggesting that these roads could ever be sold for their actual value, or that they could even be sold for the money which would replace them. I conclude, therefore, that whenever they are sold they will be sold at a low figure, and I have concluded, in the next place, that, whatever they are bought for, they would have to be bought by men who would have the ability to control a very large amount of money. And I have concluded, in the third place, that when they are sold and bought they will fall into the hands of some great railroad corporation of the country; and in that view of the case I have thought of you as a competitor, in the full expectation that if there had to be a sale of these roads you would come in and buy.

Mr. HUNTINGTON. C. P. Huntington will make a dreadful effort to take care of himself, and would like very much to pay 100 cents on the dollar to the Government. That would give him more satisfaction than any work he has ever done, and he would also like to pay as much as could be taken out of this road to pay the interest on the Government debt. I should go right to work to see what I could do. I know the country west of the Wahsatch Mountains better than any other man.

Senator MORGAN. Do you think that you could sit still with all this power in your hands and see your pet railroad sold at a sacrifice without making a bid for it?

Mr. HUNTINGTON. No; I should make a bid for it. But if the United States, after all that I have done for this road, should now sell it out and give me no consideration at all, I should say that I could not help it.

Senator MORGAN. Would you not be willing in some sense to recoup what you did for the Government by what the Government has done for you?

Mr. HUNTINGTON. The Government has done nothing for me; I have done more for the Government than the Government has done for me. I am an American citizen and am proud of the country. We built this railroad in seven years—three years less than the time allowed—and within those three years the Government saved more money in transportation and in policing that country than the whole cost of the road to the Government. The building of the Central Pacific road is the best thing and the cleanest thing which has ever been done in this country.

Senator MORGAN. You did pretty well for yourself in this matter.

Mr. HUNTINGTON. It is well enough to talk in that way. When I went into the railroad business I was a rich man, and I have been poor ever since. If a man wanted to borrow $100,000 from me before I went into the railroads, I could let him have it; but since then I have been a borrower all the time. I started into the Central Pacific with honesty of purpose.

Senator MORGAN. I am not questioning your honesty of purpose.

Mr. HUNTINGTON. I went to New York and to Boston and went among my old friends and asked them to invest money in this enterprise, and they said, "Huntington, we do not want to go into it, but if you guarantee the interest on these bonds for ten years we will take them." I said, "I will guarantee them, because if the Central Pacific ever stops short of completion C. P. Huntington will be so badly broken that they never will spend any time in picking him up."

Senator MORGAN. We have got all these statements about the absorption of roads into the Kentucky company, and about the debts being paid on everything by the Central Pacific as they matured, and that there has been a general comparative prosperity on your side of the continent down there. Now it becomes my duty to question you on some other points. Certain citizens of California have made a complaint and have addressed a memorial to the Congress of the United

States in reference to the Central Pacific and the Southern Pacific, in which they make certain statements. I want to lay these statements before you one by one and see whether or not you admit them or whether you deny them. They are not my statements. I know nothing about them. I happen to be from a section of the country which is entirely impartial, and which is rather more inclined to lean to you than to anybody else, because you did help New Orleans. These statements come from a committee appointed by the Anti-Funding and Foreclosure Convention held at the Metropolitan Temple in San Francisco, January 18, 1896. I will give you a chance to say whether they are true or not; and I am glad that you have an opportunity of making your statement on oath. It was for that purpose that I insisted upon witnesses being sworn before this committee.

I will not bother you now with the preamble in which they refer to the embarrassment which they are under because of the management of the roads, nor will I discuss the fact that they insist that the situation in connection with these roads is one (owing to its involvements and entanglement and to the great number of collateral roads that are included in the situation); that can not be solved and finally adjusted in any other way than through judicial action. They insist on that as one of the points. They say it can not be done by a contract of sale, and that it can not be done in any other way than through judicial action, and therefore they oppose any proceeding except a proceeding in foreclosure of the mortgage at the instance of the United States Government. They are in favor of a foreclosure of the mortgage and against any contract and sale, and for those reasons generally stated, they say, as to the facts of the case that it is not true that the Central Pacific is an honest debtor or that it is entitled to favorable treatment at the hands of the Congress. They say, "the facts are that in 1861 the Central Pacific Railroad Company was incorporated under the laws of California. The constitution of California prescribed then, as now, that every stockholder of a corporation or joint stock association shall be individually and personally liable for his proportion of its debts and liabilities." Are you aware that this is a part of the constitution of California?

Mr. HUNTINGTON. I am not learned in law. The question, I believe, is in the courts. My own impression is that we are not responsible. If we are, we are; that is all. But I have no idea that we are.

Senator MORGAN. They say that that question was decided by the supreme court of California in the case of French *v.* Teschemacher, the interpretation being as follows: "It is unconstitutional for the legislature to relieve a stockholder of a corporation of his individual liabilities." They then insist that as every stockholder of the Central Pacific Railroad Company, under the constitution of the State of California, is bonded for his proportionate share of all the debts and liabilities of the corporation, no act of Congress can now be passed which will legally relieve him from such responsibility. So they object to our attempting to heal up this controversy by making a new arrangement.

Mr. HUNTINGTON. That is the opinion of Adolph Sutro. I do not know that it should have considerable weight.

Senator MORGAN. There are other gentlemen here besides Adolph Sutro. There is M. M. Estee.

Mr. HUNTINGTON. Has he signed it?

Senator MORGAN. Yes.

Mr. HUNTINGTON. And he and Sutro are together? These men——

Senator MORGAN. I do not want to get on your private quarrels. The memorial is signed by M. M. Estee, Henry E. Highton, A. Caminetti, Adolph Sutro, J. L. Davie, E. M. Gibson, and Marion Cannon.

Mr. HUNTINGTON. I know them all. They all have a grievance.

Senator MORGAN. At the same time, the memorialists have stated facts. They say: "The admitted facts show that, practically, four men living in Sacramento, in the State of California, namely, C. P. Huntington, Mark Hopkins, Charles Crocker, and Leland Stanford, incorporated the Central Pacific Railroad Company and essayed to build its road. None of these men were capitalists."

Mr. HUNTINGTON. We four men had to do with the building of the road.

Senator MORGAN. They say that you had the company incorporated in order to build the road.

Mr. HUNTINGTON. I did myself most of the work of getting the organization up.

Senator MORGAN. They say, "None of these men were capitalists." Were any of you capitalists at that time?

Mr. HUNTINGTON. I do not know what constitutes a capitalist.

Senator MORGAN. About what was the value of the estate of each of these gentlemen at that time?

Mr. HUNTINGTON. Mr. Hopkins was worth several hundred thousand dollars. The Stanford brothers were worth, I guess, several millions.

Senator MORGAN. Is it a guess?

Mr. HUNTINGTON. I never saw a catalogue of what they were worth; but they were rich men; how rich, I do not know. Mr. Crocker was a thrifty merchant there.

Senator MORGAN. The memorialists state here, "The assessed valuation of all their property did not reach $250,000."

Mr. HUNTINGTON. We were men who were largely in trade, and in a good way. I do not know what the assessed valuation of our property was.

Senator MORGAN (reading). "The people of California, although few in number, are generous to a fault. And the most munificent grants and donations ever made by a government or a people to a private citizen or corporation were at that time made to the Central Pacific Railroad Company. The following is a statement of some of the principal grants and donations of land and money made. Congress granted to this corporation every other section of land for 20 miles on each side of its contemplated road for the whole length thereof, and also on the Oregon branch of that system, amounting in the aggregate to 10,000,000 acres, of the value of fully $12,500,000." Did Congress make a donation of that value?

Mr. HUNTINGTON. I do not know what the value was. The land is not sold, excepting as it is mortgaged. I do not think we have sold over one-fourth of it; but we have sold the best of it.

Senator MORGAN. Was there as much as 10,000,000 acres of land granted?

Mr. HUNTINGTON. I should think that in the two grants there were.

Senator MORGAN (reading). "It is reported that they have already obtained about that amount in sales of those lands."

Mr. HUNTINGTON. We have never obtained anything like that; perhaps two-thirds of it.

Senator MORGAN (reading). "The Government fixed the value of its own adjoining land at $2.50 an acre." Has the Government held on to that price?

Mr. HUNTINGTON. Yes; that is now the Government's price for the adjoining land.

Senator MORGAN (reading). "At the same time the Government issued to that company its mortgage bonds in the sum of $27,000,000 (in round numbers), which now amount, principal and interest, to at least $58,000,000."

Mr. HUNTINGTON. That is about correct. We had Government bonds to the amount of twenty-seven millions and something; and, as I stated the other day, they were sold and we bought gold for them. A good many of these bonds did not net us $40 on the hundred.

Senator MORGAN (reading). "In addition thereto the State of California guaranteed the interest on $1,500,000 of the bonds of the company, and also granted to it 30 acres of land in the city of San Francisco of great value, which, with another undivided interest of 30 acres more, is now mortgaged for $12,283,000."

Mr. HUNTINGTON. I do not think there is anything in that. This land was in Mission Bay, in 30 feet of water; and the filling it up cost as much as the land is worth now. It was very expensive filling.

Senator MORGAN (reading). "The several counties of the State contributed to the company in money and property $1,500,000."

Mr. HUNTINGTON. We got $300,000 from Placer County and $400,000 from the city of Sacramento, which we have paid back.

The CHAIRMAN. These counties loaned their credit to the company?

Mr. HUNTINGTON. They gave us some bonds, which we sold, and afterwards paid for.

Senator MORGAN. Did you do that with all the counties?

Mr. HUNTINGTON. There were no counties except Placer and Sacramento. The city of San Francisco gave us $400,000.

Senator MORGAN. That makes one million and a half?

Mr. HUNTINGTON. No; it makes eleven hundred thousand.

Senator MORGAN (reading). "The city of Sacramento deeded to it its river front of the estimated value of $1,000,000."

Mr. HUNTINGTON. It was of no practical value; it never was.

Senator MORGAN. The city made a deed of it to the company?

Mr. HUNTINGTON. We acquired an easement there, which any railroad company could get. We did not get the fee of the property.

Senator MORGAN. Are you using that easement now?

Mr. HUNTINGTON. No; I do not think so.

Senator MORGAN. They say that it was of the estimated value of $1,000,000?

Mr. HUNTINGTON. Oh, no; it is not so because these fellows say so. There was no particular value to it. It was an easement which any railroad company could get, and we used it for two years, and then we came in with our line of road above that. It was of no particular value; of no money value.

The CHAIRMAN. This 30 acres given by the city of San Francisco was land lying in the bay?

Mr. HUNTINGTON. Yes; in Mission Bay, 30 feet deep.

The CHAIRMAN. You say that it cost you as much to fill it up as the land is worth now?

Mr. HUNTINGTON. More than it is worth now. Nobody would have taken it and filled it up then.

The CHAIRMAN. What is it worth now?

Mr. HUNTINGTON. It may be worth $1,000,000.

The CHAIRMAN. What about the half interest in the 30 acres more?

Mr. HUNTINGTON. The Southern Pacific has 30 acres and the Central Pacific has 30——

Senator MORGAN. In the start the Southern Pacific and the Central Pacific were owned by the same parties?

Mr. HUNTINGTON. When that land was granted we had nothing to do with the Southern Pacific. That road was made by other men entirely. There was nobody in the Southern Pacific who was in the Central Pacific.

Senator MORGAN. When you bought it?

Mr. HUNTINGTON. When we bought it—along in the seventies, sometime.

Senator MORGAN. You say you had nothing to do with building the Southern Pacific?

Mr. HUNTINGTON. They had built it to Gilroy, and then we bought it.

Senator MORGAN. Who bought it?

Mr. HUNTINGTON. I did the dickering, and paid for it partly in money and partly in credit.

Senator MORGAN. Who were the men that bought it?

Mr. HUNTINGTON. Stanford, Crocker, Hopkins, and myself.

Senator MORGAN. Nobody else?

Mr. HUNTINGTON. My impression is nobody else.

Senator MORGAN. Then you bought the Southern Pacific road of California?

Mr. HUNTINGTON. We bought the Southern Pacific road from San Francisco to Gilroy.

Senator MORGAN. So that, approximately, this statement is correct?

Mr. HUNTINGTON. This 30 acres of land is. I do not know where they got the other.

Senator MORGAN. They say that you have got more than 10 miles of the water front of the bay of San Francisco, forming the entire harbor of Oakland and parts of the harbors of Alameda, Berkeley, and San Francisco, which is of the estimated value of not less than $10,000,000.

Mr. HUNTINGTON. Well, the Central Pacific never had anything to do with it, except that the Central Pacific had certain grounds which it needed for depot purposes. The Central Pacific had nothing to do with the Oakland water front.

Senator MORGAN. Did anybody obtain the entire harbor of Oakland and parts of the harbors of Alameda, Berkeley, and San Francisco? Has anybody got that water front?

Mr. HUNTINGTON. We own shares in the Oakland Water Front Company. I own some myself. The Southern Pacific or the Central Pacific does not own any of it that I know.

Senator MORGAN. Does it cover 10 miles of water front?

Mr. HUNTINGTON. I do not think it covers half of it.

Senator MORGAN. Does it cover 10 miles of the water front of the bay of San Francisco, forming the entire harbor of Oakland and parts of the harbors of Alameda, Berkeley, and San Francisco?

Mr. HUNTINGTON. I think the Oakland Water Front Company owns 3 or 4 miles.

Senator MORGAN. And you own stock in that company?

Mr. HUNTINGTON. Yes.

Senator MORGAN. Who else owns stock in it?

Mr. HUNTINGTON. There is quite a great number of shareholders.

Senator MORGAN. Who holds the majority of that stock?

Mr. HUNTINGTON. Lloyd and Levis.

Senator MORGAN. Who owns the majority of that stock now?

Mr. HUNTINGTON. I should think these four men own a majority of the stock. They never got any money out of it, and it is not worth any $10,000,000.

Senator MORGAN (reading). "It also obtained from Wells, Fargo &

Co. $1,500,000 of their stock in consideration of favorable transportation facilities accorded to said company." Is that a fact?

Mr. HUNTINGTON. I do not think it was that much. I think it was $1,300,000.

Senator MORGAN (reading). "The foregoing grants reached the enormous amount in value of $57,000,000, which is much more than the entire cost of the road." Can you state what was the entire cost of the Central Pacific road?

Mr. HUNTINGTON. No; but it cost more than that—very much more.

Senator MORGAN. More than $57,000,000?

Mr. HUNTINGTON. Very much more.

Senator MORGAN. Have you ever known what it cost?

Mr. HUNTINGTON. Oh, yes, yes. First we started with some contractors from Sacramento to Newcastle, 31 miles.

Senator MORGAN. Who were they?

Mr. HUNTINGTON. One was C. D. Smith, and Hubbard. These are the only two names I remember. I had no interest in those contracts whatever.

Senator MORGAN. Had you any interest in any contract to build the Central Pacific road?

Mr. HUNTINGTON. No; I had no interest in the contracts. I had some little interest in the Contract and Finance Company. After the first contractors failed to do the work Charles Crocker took the contract and went on and started to build the road. I do not know who was with him early. He thought that he could do it, but by and by he found that he could not. I tried to get some rich men in New York and Boston to go in with him; but they said no; they could not go into an open copartnership with unlimited liabilities. Then the Contract and Finance Company was organized. When that was organized I tried to get men in New York and Boston to go into it; but they all said that the risks were too great and the profits too remote. There never was work done so closely as that. We had hard work to get the money to pay for it, selling Government bonds for currency and taking the currency and buying gold.

Senator MORGAN. You have mentioned Mr. Crocker as one of the gentlemen who had an interest in the contract for the construction of the Central Pacific road. Had you any interest in it?

Mr. HUNTINGTON. I had none except in the Contract and Finance Company.

Senator MORGAN. Had Mr. Stanford any interest in the Contract and Finance Company?

Mr. HUNTINGTON. I think so; I am quite sure he had.

Senator MORGAN. Had Mr. Hopkins any interest in the Contract and Finance Company?

Mr. HUNTINGTON. I think so.

Senator MORGAN. So they all had an interest in the contracts of the Contract and Finance Company except yourself?

Mr. HUNTINGTON. I do not understand; not in contracts.

Senator MORGAN. You had no interest and they had no interest in actual contracts?

Mr. HUNTINGTON. No; I am sure they had not.

Senator MORGAN. Only through the Contract and Finance Company?

Mr. HUNTINGTON. Only through the Contract and Finance Company.

Senator MORGAN. They say here that you got donations also on the Central Pacific line for town sites, depot purposes, and other kinds of property.

Mr. HUNTINGTON. No doubt we got considerable for depot purposes. Everybody wanted us to go into a particular place, and everybody was anxious for the road to go through his farm.

Senator MORGAN. They say here that "soon after the construction of the Central Pacific Railroad Company, C. P. Huntington and his three associates incorporated another company under the name of the 'Contract and Finance Company,' and the same men were the owners of, and represented, both the Central Pacific Railroad Company and the Contract and Finance Company." Is that true?

Mr. HUNTINGTON. Yes; it is true that we organized it, but I was in New York at the time.

Senator MORGAN. Is that statement true?

Mr. HUNTINGTON. I was not there at the time; I do not think I had anything to do with it at the start. I think I had something to do with it later. I did not have anything to do with the organizing.

Senator MORGAN. Did the same men comprise the two companies?

Mr. HUNTINGTON. Mr. Crocker was in it.

Senator MORGAN. And Hopkins?

Mr. HUNTINGTON. Yes.

Senator MORGAN. And Stanford?

Mr. HUNTINGTON. Yes.

Senator MORGAN. And you?

Mr. HUNTINGTON. I do not think I had anything to do with it at the start.

Senator MORGAN. But you had stock in it?

Mr. HUNTINGTON. I had stock in it later.

Senator MORGAN. How much stock had you?

Mr. HUNTINGTON. I do not know how much.

Senator MORGAN. In proportion to the whole amount of capital stock, how much had you?

Mr. HUNTINGTON. I do not know; Mr. Hopkins was a partner of mine, and I always looked to him to see after our interests.

Senator MORGAN (reading). "The directors of the Central Pacific Railroad Company contracted with themselves to complete the road of that company under the name of the Contract and Finance Company."

Mr. HUNTINGTON. They did not contract with themselves. They may have contracted with the Contract and Finance Company, but not with themselves.

Senator MORGAN. That depended on the fact of there being the same membership in the two companies?

Mr. HUNTINGTON. I do not know how they were intermingled.

Senator MORGAN. Were not the two organizations composed of the same membership?

Mr. HUNTINGTON. I think that the same men were in the Central Pacific and in the Contract and Finance Company. I never saw the books of the Contract and Finance Company.

Senator MORGAN. You are not prepared to deny this statement?

Mr. HUNTINGTON. I deny it on the general assumption that these men never told any truth that I ever heard of.

Senator MORGAN. That may do for you, but not for the committee. The committee does not know them.

Mr. HUNTINGTON. But I do.

Senator MORGAN. I am very thankful that I do not.

Mr. HUNTINGTON. I think you need be.

Senator MORGAN. Do you know M. M. Estee, one of these men?

Mr. HUNTINGTON. I know him, unfortunately.

Senator MORGAN. Then I do not understand you to deny this statement made by these very credible and reliable gentlemen?

Mr. HUNTINGTON. I do not know anything about it; I never saw the books of the Contract and Finance Company.

Senator MORGAN. Do you not know, just as well as if you had read every line in every book of the company, that you owned stock in this Contract and Finance Company?

Mr. HUNTINGTON. I am very sure I did.

Senator MORGAN. How much?

Mr. HUNTINGTON. I do not know.

Senator MORGAN. Did not you and Crocker and Stanford and Hopkins own the whole of it?

Mr. HUNTINGTON. No.

Senator MORGAN. Name any man who owned any stock in this company except you four.

Mr. HUNTINGTON. I will not say that even Mr. Stanford owned any.

Senator MORGAN. You have said so.

Mr. HUNTINGTON. No; I said I believed he did. I do believe he did, although I never saw the books.

Senator MORGAN. These men state facts, and if the facts damage you——

Mr. HUNTINGTON. It would be very damaging if they could damage me.

Senator MORGAN. You have the opportunity to state now, on oath, whether they have stated these facts correctly or not. That is all you should desire; but I do not understand that you do. They say further here, "They charged their own prices for the work, and when finished they held most of its assets and someone else owned most of its debts. Under these conditions it is apparent that the asserted cost of the road was about three times as much as its actual cost."

Mr. HUNTINGTON. Do they say that anybody owned any debts which they did not get paid?

Senator MORGAN. No, sir.

Mr. HUNTINGTON. That is important, I should think.

Senator MORGAN. I am merely putting to you what they say; I am not arguing this statement or making it; I am putting it to you just as they make it, and you have the opportunity of answering it just as you desire. (Repeating.) "They charged their own prices for the work, and when finished they held most of its assets and someone else owned most of its debts."

Mr. HUNTINGTON. There was no doubt that when the road was completed there were large debts, but they were paid.

Senator MORGAN. Did you own any of these debts?

Mr. HUNTINGTON. No.

Senator MORGAN. Who did?

Mr. HUNTINGTON. I can not tell now. We owed Speyer & Co. largely. That was a banking house in New York and Europe. We owed a great many debts in New York, but they were all paid in time, as soon as we got the money.

Senator MORGAN. Were these debts contracted in your service for your benefit, by those contractors under you?

Mr. HUNTINGTON. I got money for the Contract and Finance Company and sent it out to them.

Senator MORGAN. Is it true that "the directors of the Central Pacific Railroad Company contracted with themselves to complete the road of that company, and that they charged their own prices for the work?"

Mr. HUNTINGTON. The prices were not unreasonable, because I do not believe there was another set of men in the country who would have taken the contract to build that road, which Stanford and Crocker and the other men did, and they would not have taken it, only that I told them I would get some of the rich men of New York and Boston to go into it with them. I think I must have spent a hundred evenings in arguing the matter with rich men in New York and Boston, but they all gave the same answer.

Senator MORGAN. Was it to get the money to work out your contract that you talked with them?

Mr. HUNTINGTON. It was to build the road.

Senator MORGAN. Was it to get the money to work out your contract?

Mr. HUNTINGTON. It was to build the road.

Senator MORGAN. That will not do.

Mr. HUNTINGTON. I had no contract to build the road.

Senator MORGAN. You did not undertake to build the road or any part of it?

Mr. HUNTINGTON. I started in, and in that way we built the road.

Senator MORGAN. I am talking about the obligation to build it.

Mr. HUNTINGTON. The Contract and Finance Company agreed to build the road, I have no doubt.

Senator MORGAN. Did you agree to build the entire road?

Mr. HUNTINGTON. Yes; to build the entire road.

Senator MORGAN. That was what the Contract and Finance Company agreed with the Central Pacific—to build the entire road?

Mr. HUNTINGTON. Yes; until we met the Union Pacific road.

Senator MORGAN. This Contract and Finance Company had a contract with the Central Pacific to build this road clear through until it met the road of the Union Pacific?

Mr. HUNTINGTON. I think so; I never saw the contract, but I am satisfied there was such a contract.

Senator MORGAN. And the road was built under that contract?

Mr. HUNTINGTON. Yes, as I understand it.

Senator MORGAN. The prices at which the road was built were fixed by whom?

Mr. HUNTINGTON. I presume by the directors of the Cental Pacific.

Senator MORGAN. Were they not the same men as constituted the Contract and Finance Company?

Mr. HUNTINGTON. Mr. Crocker was not a director of the Central Pacific; Mr. Stanford and Mr. Hopkins were.

Senator MORGAN. So that the same men who owned the Central Pacific contracted with the Contract and Finance Company, which they also controlled, and fixed the prices at which the road was to be built?

Mr. HUNTINGTON. Yes.

Senator MORGAN. The memorialists say here that "the bonded indebtedness which the United States assumed and agreed to pay is but a small part of the actual nominal indebtedness of the corporation. According to Poor's Manual for 1895 the total liabilities of the Central Pacific Railroad Company reached the vast sum of $202,491,584, while under the estimates made by the United States Railroad Commission in 1888 the total cost of building and equipping the Central and Western Pacific railroads did not exceed $40,000,000."

Mr. HUNTINGTON. Anybody who understands the case can know that the road was not built for any such money. The share capital of a railroad is always the gambling element in building railroads in this country. I think that three-fourths of the roads in this country have been built because there was a speculative element in the shares, and I think that the speculative element in railroads has broken more men in this country than anything else.

Senator MORGAN. Aside from the indebtedness to the United States, and aside from the first-mortgage bonds of the company, what was the indebtedness of the Central Pacific at the time it made the junction with the Union Pacific?

Mr. HUNTINGTON. There were $60,000,000 of shares in face value and $27,000,000 in bonds.

Senator MORGAN. I am excluding that. How much did the company owe at the time of its junction with the Union Pacific, aside from its debt to the United States and aside from the first mortgage?

Mr. HUNTINGTON. It had out 600,000 shares of stock; that was all.

Senator MORGAN. How much money did that represent?

Mr. HUNTINGTON. It represented $60,000,000, I think.

Senator MORGAN. Were these shares sold at par?

Mr. HUNTINGTON. No.

Senator MORGAN. What were they sold at?

Mr. HUNTINGTON. At all sorts of prices. The shares of the Union Pacific changed hands at from 5 to 8 per cent, and the shares of the Central Pacific exchanged hands at about the same. We bought quite a lot of them at 12½ per cent.

Senator MORGAN. What were they worth at the time they were issued?

Mr. HUNTINGTON. I do not believe they could have been sold in New York for 5 cents on the dollar.

Senator MORGAN. Did you issue them to the Contract and Finance Company or did you issue them for money?

Mr. HUNTINGTON. We issued them because we thought they would have some value.

Senator MORGAN. Did you sell them for fun or for money?

Mr. HUNTINGTON. For money.

Senator MORGAN. What did you get for them?

Mr. HUNTINGTON. For some we got 19 per cent, and some went as high as 85 per cent.

Senator MORGAN. Money actually paid in?

Mr. HUNTINGTON. Yes.

Senator MORGAN. Did you buy any of them?

Mr. HUNTINGTON. No.

Senator MORGAN. You never bought a share of the Central Pacific stock?

Mr. HUNTINGTON. No; I think not.

Senator MORGAN. Did Crocker buy any of them?

Mr. HUNTINGTON. No.

Senator MORGAN. Did Stanford?

Mr. HUNTINGTON. No; I think not.

Senator MORGAN. Did Hopkins?

Mr. HUNTINGTON. I think not.

Senator MORGAN. None of these four gentlemen bought any shares of stock in the Central Pacific?

Mr. HUNTINGTON. No; I think not.

Senator MORGAN. They got them into the hands of other people?

Mr. HUNTINGTON. Yes.

Senator MORGAN. How much money did they get for the shares sold to other persons?

Mr. HUNTINGTON. I do not know; probably $30,000,000.

Senator MORGAN. You and Crocker and Stanford and Hopkins took shares in the Contract and Finance Company?

Mr. HUNTINGTON. The Contract and Finance Company took so many shares and so many bonds, and built the road. That is the usual way. They took payment in shares and bonds.

Senator MORGAN. In what bonds?

Mr. HUNTINGTON. In the Government bonds and in the first-mortgage bonds.

Senator MORGAN. How many bonds did the Contract and Finance Company take?

Mr. HUNTINGTON. I think it took them all.

Senator MORGAN. How many shares of the Central Pacific?

Mr. HUNTINGTON. Six hundred thousand shares.

Senator MORGAN. Which you gentlemen took?

Mr. HUNTINGTON. I did not take any of them. The Contract and Finance Company took them.

Senator MORGAN. This construction company took all of the bonds issued and indorsed by the United States, and all of the first-mortgage bonds, and $60,000,000 of stock in payment upon its account for building the road?

Mr. HUNTINGTON. Yes.

The CHAIRMAN. In other words, you got a dollar in stock for every dollar in bonds?

Mr. HUNTINGTON. The company took so much for doing the work.

Senator MORGAN. Counting the bonds at par, and the stock at par, how much money would that represent as payment made to you by the Central Pacific for building the road?

Mr. HUNTINGTON. That is easily figured out, I suppose. But the bonds and stock were not figured at par, we sold Government bonds for 85, and we bought gold at over 2 to 1, and we sold our own bonds at about par in currency.

Senator MORGAN. You will have to stay here a long time before you get me away from my question. Treating the Government bonds at par, and the first-mortgage bonds at par, and the stock at par, how many dollars would they all amount to?

Mr. HUNTINGTON. One hundred and sixteen million dollars.

Senator MORGAN. What was the cost, in your account rendered, of the building of this railroad from end to end?

Mr. HUNTINGTON. I have not got the figures, but it was so much that we could not begin to pay our debts when the road was completed, and we had to carry our debts on private credit. It was several years before we could pay the debt.

Senator MORGAN. Did you never cast a balance between the amount of money due from this Contract and Finance Company and the amount of bonds and stock which you got?

Mr. HUNTINGTON. I question if I ever did.

Senator MORGAN. Although you are a good business man?

Mr. HUNTINGTON. I am; but I am like the Dutchman who said that he never kept books, but that he knew how much he owed and how much he had to pay it.

Senator MORGAN. I want to know how much was to be paid to the Contract and Finance Company and how much you got for it. How much did the work cost?

Mr. HUNTINGTON. I can not say.

Senator MORGAN. You had a final settlement, I suppose, between the Contract and Finance Company and the Central Pacific Company?

Mr. HUNTINGTON. Yes.

Senator MORGAN. In that financial settlement what was the amount of your account for building that road?

Mr. HUNTINGTON. I can not say. I was not in California at the time.

Senator MORGAN. Do you state now before this committee that you do not recollect?

Mr. HUNTINGTON. I do not recollect.

Senator MORGAN. Can you come within a million dollars of it?

Mr. HUNTINGTON. No; it is over twenty years ago.

Senator MORGAN. Can you get within $5,000,000 of it?

Mr. HUNTINGTON. I have not any figures in my head now.

Senator MORGAN. Do you wish the committee to adjourn to give you a chance to reflect on it?

Mr. HUNTINGTON. No.

Senator MORGAN. I will take your statement within $5,000,000. State to the committee within $5,000,000 what that railroad cost under the contract with the Contract and Finance Company.

Mr. HUNTINGTON. It must have cost, as I put things together, somewhere in the neighborhood of $80,000,000 or $90,000,000 in money.

Senator MORGAN. So that these men are not more than $10,000,000 wrong in their statement?

Mr. HUNTINGTON. They say $40,000,000, I believe. I am only surprised that they have not said $10,000,000.

Senator MORGAN. Are the books of the Contract and Finance Company in existence?

Mr. HUNTINGTON. I do not think they are.

Senator MORGAN. What became of them?

Mr. HUNTINGTON. I do not know.

Senator MORGAN. Were they not destroyed?

Mr. HUNTINGTON. I do not think I ever saw the books of the Contract and Finance Company.

Senator MORGAN. Have you ever made any inquiry about them?

Mr. HUNTINGTON. I do not think that I have.

Senator MORGAN. Do you not know that they were destroyed?

Mr. HUNTINGTON. No; I do not.

Senator MORGAN. Do you not believe that they were?

Mr. HUNTINGTON. I believe they were.

Senator MORGAN. By whom?

Mr. HUNTINGTON. I do not know; when the work was all over I told Mark Hopkins, who had a whole room full of books and papers and stuff in the building, to sell them for old paper stock.

Senator MORGAN. It would have been inconvenient for the Contract and Finance Company to have a set of books which showed them indebted under the constitution of California.

Mr. HUNTINGTON. I never thought of that.

The CHAIRMAN. Was that provision of the constitution of California in operation at that time?

Mr. HUNTINGTON. I do not know exactly; I think it was.

Senator MORGAN (reading from the constitution of California). "Each stockholder of a corporation, or joint stock association, shall be individually and personally liable for his proportion of its debts and liabilities." That is in the thirty-sixth section of the fourth article of the constitution of 1849.

Mr. TWEED (counsel for the Central Pacific). You are aware, Senator, that in the Stanford case the circuit court of California and the circuit court of appeals have both held that there was no stockholder's liability under the laws of California at that time. The case has been argued before the Supreme Court of the United States last month and has not yet been decided; but the decisions of the courts up to the present time have been that there was in fact no stockholder's liability under the law of California existing at that period.

Senator MORGAN (to Mr. Huntington). Suppose that those who were compromised by the existence of those books put them out of the way?

Mr. HUNTINGTON. I do not think that was ever thought of.

Senator MORGAN. But the books are gone?

Mr. HUNTINGTON. I think so.

Senator MORGAN. And destroyed?

Mr. HUNTINGTON. I do not think I ever saw the books of the Contract and Finance Company. I was here on this side nearly all the time, and I am quite sure that I never saw them.

Senator MORGAN. It is an unusual event, is it not, for gentlemen who are engaged in contracts and enterprises which cover accounts amounting to $100,000,000 or more to want to preserve the records of their transactions rather than to destroy them?

Mr. HUNTINGTON. No; I think not. It is not unusual with me to destroy anything which is not of use. I want to get these things out of the way.

Senator MORGAN. You can see how much trouble it would have saved us if these books had been preserved.

Mr. HUNTINGTON. I do not know.

Senator BRICE. This is a very important matter, and is a very complicated and difficult matter, but it is a separate matter from that which we commenced to hold this investigation about. We commenced to hold this investigation about bills for the settlement of the debts to the Government of the Central Pacific and the Union Pacific. The liabilities of the stockholders is a different question, and must be met by a different report, and I suggest to the chairman that he should separate these two inquiries. In one of them I am interested and in the other I am not. I have no objection in the world if Senator Morgan and the citizens of California can make Mr. Huntington and others pay their share of the indebtedness of the company, but I am concerned about the terms of the settlement which we ought to make with each of these companies in the pending bills.

Senator MORGAN. I am not concerned with the settlement until certain facts are developed. We want to know what are the complications which the court will have to deal with before the settlement is made.

The CHAIRMAN. Is not that a matter for the courts to find out?

Senator MORGAN. Yes; but I am going now, as a member of the Senate, to inform my conscience and judgment as to whether I shall vote for a contract to Mr. Huntington, or whether I shall vote to put him in court.

The committee here adjourned until to-morrow at 10.30 a. m.

WASHINGTON, D. C., *February 18, 1896.*

The committee met at 10.30 a. m.

Present: Senators Gear (chairman), Stewart, Brice, Frye, and Morgan.

CENTRAL PACIFIC.

EXAMINATION OF MR. C. P. HUNTINGTON—Resumed.

The examination of Mr. COLLIS P. HUNTINGTON, president of the Southern Pacific Railway Company, was resumed.

Senator MORGAN. I will continue where I left off yesterday, Mr. Huntington, in the examination of statements made at a public meeting in San Francisco, to which I called your attention in part yesterday. They say that Mr. Huntington and his associates, at different times, organized three companies with which to carry on their railroad business. First, the Contract and Finance Company; second, the Western Development Company; and third, the Pacific Improvement Company. Did you organize such companies?

Mr. HUNTINGTON. There were such companies organized.

Senator MORGAN. For the purpose of enabling you to carry on railway business in California?

Mr. HUNTINGTON. Yes; railway and other business.

Senator MORGAN. I believe you said that the books of the Contract and Finance Company had disappeared in some way and were not to be found?

Mr. HUNTINGTON. I said that I did not know where they were, and that I presumed they had been sold for old paper stock or burned up. I do not know that.

Senator MORGAN. How much do you know about it; what is the extent of your knowledge on that subject?

Mr. HUNTINGTON. I never saw the books of the company and was never in the office of the Contract and Finance Company. But from common report, which, I may say, was gathered from the atmosphere, perhaps, I have come to the conclusions which I have stated.

Senator MORGAN. Have you relied on the atmosphere for information as to a fact so important as that?

Mr. HUNTINGTON. It was not so very important after the company was closed up.

Senator MORGAN. Whether important or not, have you relied on the atmosphere for your information about it?

Mr. HUNTINGTON. I think I have got some better information from the atmosphere and from common report sometimes than from other sources.

Senator MORGAN. In this particular case have you relied on common report and on the atmosphere for your information?

Mr. HUNTINGTON. I never saw the books of the Contract and Finance Company, and therefore——

Senator MORGAN. Mr. Huntington, it will take a long time for you to dodge this question. You had better come right to the answer.

Mr. HUNTINGTON. It would take me a longer time to tell what I do not know.

Senator MORGAN. Do you know now, and do you state on your oath, that you rely on common rumor for your information?

Mr. HUNTINGTON. I do, for this matter as to the Contract and Finance Company.

Senator MORGAN. Have you not been informed of it by any of your associates in that company?

Mr. HUNTINGTON. I never was told that their books were destroyed, or were burned up, or were sold.

Senator MORGAN. Have you not been informed of their being, in some way or other, put away?

Mr. HUNTINGTON. No; I never have been.

Senator MORGAN. Those books contained transactions to the extent of many million dollars?

Mr. HUNTINGTON. Yes; they must have, I think.

Senator MORGAN. They contained information of all the particulars and details of those transactions?

Mr. HUNTINGTON. I should say so.

Senator MORGAN. They included, I suppose, the contracts between the Contract and Finance Company and the railroad company?

Mr. HUNTINGTON. I should say so.

Senator MORGAN. They contained statements of all the money received from the Central Pacific for the construction of the road?

Mr. HUNTINGTON. I suppose so.

Senator MORGAN. They included evidence of all the payments made by the Central Pacific to the Contract and Finance Company?

Mr. HUNTINGTON. I can not say as to that, but no doubt they did include a large proportion of it.

Senator MORGAN. Was a history of any part of the company's transactions kept anywhere else except in the books of the Contract and Finance Company?

Mr. HUNTINGTON. A major part of them would have been kept in those books.

Senator MORGAN. Would they be kept anywhere else?

Mr. HUNTINGTON. I do not know.

Senator MORGAN. Then why do you say the major part of them were?

Mr. HUNTINGTON. Because I do not know that all of them were.

Senator MORGAN. You profess not to know that any of them were?

Mr. HUNTINGTON. I know from common report, or, as I say, from the atmosphere, which seems to be a more comprehensive term.

Senator MORGAN. You stated yesterday, if I understood you, that you advised that the best disposition to be made of these books and papers was to burn them up.

Mr. HUNTINGTON. Yes; I told Mr. Hopkins that.

Senator MORGAN. Why?

Mr. HUNTINGTON. Because the business of the company was closed up.

Senator MORGAN. Are you accustomed to burn your books and papers after you close a transaction?

Mr. HUNTINGTON. Yes; after a certain time.

Senator MORGAN. How long after?

Mr. HUNTINGTON. General book accounts are kept until after the law of limitation expires.

Senator MORGAN. As soon as the transaction is without the law of limitation you burn your books?

Mr. HUNTINGTON. Not always.

Senator MORGAN. There are some exceptional cases, it appears. What exceptions can you call to mind at this moment?

Mr. HUNTINGTON. I do not know; I should say there are many.

Senator MORGAN. State what general transactions you have had in which you have burned your books.

Mr. HUNTINGTON. We have burned very few in our mercantile accounts. It is a continuous business, from decade to decade, and the accounts are very old before we burn them. But when a company is disincorporated I do not see any object in keeping its books.

Senator MORGAN. To what person did you give the advice to burn these books?

Mr. HUNTINGTON. To Mark Hopkins.

Senator MORGAN. How did you and Mr. Hopkins happen to get into conversation on that subject?

Mr. HUNTINGTON. As I remember, there was a room in the building occupied by these books and papers of the Contract and Finance Company, and I said to Mr. Hopkins, "As the company is disincorporated, why not clear the stuff out?"

Senator MORGAN. Where was that building?

Mr. HUNTINGTON. No. 56 K street, Sacramento, on the south side of K.

Senator MORGAN. Did you burn up the contents of any other room there?

Mr. HUNTINGTON. I do not think there was any other room with a finished, complete business.

Senator MORGAN. What did you do with that room after the papers were burned up?

Mr. HUNTINGTON. I can not say. It was put into use immediately.

Senator MORGAN. Did you have any great use for house room in that building?

Mr. HUNTINGTON. I am quite sure that all the rooms were occupied.

Senator MORGAN. Was it a matter of great importance to you that you should have the use of that particular room?

Mr. HUNTINGTON. Perhaps the rent of the room may have been important as one item of expense, for I always watch little things.

Senator MORGAN. Was that a rented house?

Mr. HUNTINGTON. Yes.

Senator MORGAN. I suppose you could have rented a room close by?

Mr. HUNTINGTON. If there had been any reason for keeping the papers of a disincorporated company, I suppose the company could have rented another room.

Senator MORGAN. In your discussion with Mr. Hopkins about the burning up of these papers was anything said about the constitution of California, and about the possibility of the liability of stockholders under that constitution individually for the debts of the company?

Mr. HUNTINGTON. No; I am pretty sure there never was. The fact is that these are matters that the legal department of the company always attends to. Anything of that kind I do not have anything to do with myself. It is passed over to the legal department.

Senator MORGAN. But if the Government of the United States, or any other creditors of the Central Pacific or of the Contract and Finance Company, had desired to enforce an obligation against the stockholders of either of these respective companies, these papers would have been important evidence, would they not?

Mr. HUNTINGTON. I do not know whether they would or not.

Senator MORGAN. Their absence would have been very convenient for you, would it not?

Mr. HUNTINGTON. That I do not know; I should turn that matter over to the legal department.

Senator MORGAN. Did your lawyer advise you to burn those books and papers?

Mr. HUNTINGTON. No.

Senator MORGAN. Then you did not turn that over to the legal department?

Mr. HUNTINGTON. No; I merely said to Mr. Hopkins that I would clear out the room. I was there only temporarily.

Senator MORGAN. Those books and papers were not any particular inconvenience to you, were they?

Mr. HUNTINGTON. No; not to me. My office was in New York.

Senator MORGAN. So, then, you advised that these papers be destroyed?

Mr. HUNTINGTON. It was hardly advice. I simply said to Mr. Hopkins, "If you want the room, why not clear it out?"

Senator MORGAN. It was a little casual remark?

Mr. HUNTINGTON. Not a serious thing.

Senator MORGAN. But it became serious when the papers were burned.

Mr. HUNTINGTON. I do not know that they were burned.

Senator MORGAN. I should like to have those papers before the committee.

Mr. HUNTINGTON. I should like very much to furnish them, but I do not know how to get them.

Senator MORGAN. I see in this memorial adopted by the California Anti-Funding Convention that they state that they represent——

Mr. HUNTINGTON (interrupting). Excuse me; who are "they"?

Senator MORGAN. They state that they represent a large public meeting.

Mr. HUNTINGTON. Yes; it was a meeting of 52 persons. They called for delegates from all the counties of the State, and I believe there were delegates from five counties. It was a Sutro meeting. But the call was very loud and very long and far spread.

Senator MORGAN. There was a public meeting held January 18, 1896, at the Metropolitan Temple, San Francisco, and that meeting appointed James H. Barry, Charles C. Terrill, and John M. Reynolds a committee on the funding bill to prepare an address.

Mr. HUNTINGTON. I wonder are they on the tax list of San Francisco.

Senator MORGAN. They may not be, but you know it is written that the poor shall inherit the kingdom of heaven.

Mr. HUNTINGTON. I do not know.

Senator MORGAN. And I expect you will never find out.

Mr. HUNTINGTON. We will see.

Senator MORGAN. Yes, we will see. Do you know these gentlemen, or either of them?

Mr. HUNTINGTON. I do not know that I do. Please to name them again.

Senator MORGAN. James H. Barry, Charles C. Terrill, and John M. Reynolds.

Mr. HUNTINGTON. I take it they were not among the merchants or bankers.

Senator MORGAN. They may be common people.

Mr. HUNTINGTON. I do not mean common people.

Senator MORGAN. They say:

On Saturday evening last, on two days' notice, during one of the heaviest storms of the season, a public meeting was held at Metropolitan Temple in this city (which was crammed to its utmost capacity and from which not less than 15,000 people were turned away) to protest, among other things, against any funding of the Pacific Railroad debt.

The strength and unanimity of sentiment, the earnest determination of the audience, which represented every shade of politics, even the press could not adequately describe.

No counterpart to the scene has ever occurred in this city since 1861, when, at the intersection of Market and Montgomery streets, 23,000 men resolved to maintain the union of these States with their lives, their fortunes, and their sacred honor.

At that meeting, without a dissenting voice, the following resolutions were adopted.

Resolved, By the people of San Francisco, in mass meeting assembled, that we enter our solemn protest against the passage of any funding bill whatever, and hereby appeal to the Speaker of the House to protect us by not giving a special order for a day to the Pacific Railroad Committee; and further

Resolved, That we appeal to each individual member of the House of Representatives not to overlook the 200,000 protests filed against the bill by the inhabitants of the Pacific Coast.

Have you been entirely unaware of that meeting?

Mr. HUNTINGTON. To this extent: That I have no more idea that there were 15,000 people there than that there were 15,000,000 there.

Senator MORGAN. It was a very large meeting.

Mr. HUNTINGTON. I do not think it was. I heard about it.

Senator MORGAN. Are you aware that this memorial came from the Pacific Coast?

Mr. HUNTINGTON. Have you the envelope that it came in?

Senator MORGAN. I have not.

Mr. HUNTINGTON. I think there was printed on it a red line with the words: "Huntington on his way to Washington to bribe Congress." There is nothing in all that one-half as earnest as Adolph Sutro was when he told me that if I did not build a road to his place, where he had a drinking saloon, a bath house, a gambling house, and rooms upstairs, and build it at once, he would fight me in Washington and fight me everywhere else. That was in earnest.

Senator MORGAN. Now, you have brought Adolph Sutro into the case, and you will not hear the last of him until you have answered all your accusations against him. I have not brought him in.

Mr. HUNTINGTON. He signs that paper.

Senator MORGAN. No; he does not. That is the paper issued by the first meeting. Here is the paper issued by the second meeting, and it is signed M. M. Estee, Henry E. Heighton, A. Caminetti, Adolph Sutro, J. L. Davie, E. M. Gibson, and Marion Cannon.

Mr. HUNTINGTON. As uncanny a crowd as a farmer ever found by his henroost at night. All these charges emanate from the same parties.

Senator MORGAN. The next company that they speak of your organizing was the Western Development Company.

Mr. HUNTINGTON. That was an organized company.

Senator MORGAN. Who organized that company?

Mr. HUNTINGTON. I should think David Colton and Mr. Crocker and Mr. Miller—I should think largely—and Mr. Hopkins. I do not know exactly. It was an organized company.

Senator MORGAN. Were you in it?

Mr. HUNTINGTON. I think I was.

Senator MORGAN. Was Mr. Stanford in it?

Mr. HUNTINGTON. I think he was.

Senator MORGAN. Then you omitted two of the most important names in it. Was there anybody else in it?

Mr. HUNTINGTON. I do not think there was. There were not more than five or six or seven.

Senator MORGAN. Have you told all of the membership of that company so far as you recollect?

Mr. HUNTINGTON. There may have been others.

Senator MORGAN. You said that Mr. Miller was in it.

Mr. HUNTINGTON. I think that D. H. Miller was in it. That company was a convenience for building railroads and ships and many other things. Those things could not be done by an open copartnership.

Senator MORGAN. What railroads did this Western Development Company build?

Mr. HUNTINGTON. I think it built the San Francisco Northern. I am not positive. I think they had to do with the Monterey road. That was a road commenced by others and not completed; and they finished it and changed it. It was a crooked narrow-gauge road, and they made it a straight and standard gauge road.

Senator MORGAN. Be good enough to point out those roads on the map.

[Mr. Huntington pointed out on the map the two roads referred to.]

Senator MORGAN. How far does that road run?

Mr. HUNTINGTON. Something like 200 miles.

Senator MORGAN. What is its northern terminus?

Mr. HUNTINGTON. Tehama.

Senator MORGAN. That is not part of the Oregon and California road, is it?

Mr. HUNTINGTON. No; I think that that was built by the Pacific Improvement Company. They commenced to build this road from Portland down, and they failed, and they let us complete and finish it. We only built up to Redding, and there we stopped for some time.

Senator MORGAN. Is this road, or the road to Monterey, a part of the Central Pacific system?

Mr. HUNTINGTON. Yes.

Senator MORGAN. It belongs to the Central Pacific?

Mr. HUNTINGTON. The road from Redding to Coles belongs to the Central Pacific?

Senator MORGAN. How about the Monterey line?

Mr. HUNTINGTON. That belongs to the Southern Pacific.

Senator MORGAN. Were both built by the same company?

Mr. HUNTINGTON. I think so.

Senator MORGAN. That is to say, by the Western Development Company?

Mr. HUNTINGTON. No; I say that the northern one was built by the Pacific Improvement Company, and the southern one by the Western Development Company.

Senator MORGAN. Then they are both the property now of the Central Pacific system?

Mr. HUNTINGTON. No. The one from Redding to Coles belongs to the Central Pacific, and the one from Salina to Monterey to the Southern Pacific, system.

Senator MORGAN. They say in this memorial that the books can not now be found nor the history of the company traced.

Mr. HUNTINGTON. Which of the companies?

Senator MORGAN. Of the Western Development Company.

Mr. HUNTINGTON. I do not know. I think that the books are in California.

Senator MORGAN. Where are they kept?

Mr. HUNTINGTON. In San Francisco, I should say.

Senator MORGAN. In what place in San Francisco?

Mr. HUNTINGTON. I should say in the building on the corner of Market and Fourth streets. We have two pretty large offices in San Francisco; one on the corner of Market and Fourth and one on the corner of Thompson and Fourth.

Senator MORGAN. Are there many books and papers connected with the Western Development Company?

Mr. HUNTINGTON. I do not know.

Senator MORGAN. They did a good deal of business, did they not?

Mr. HUNTINGTON. Yes; they did considerable business.

Senator MORGAN. Their transactions are all outlawed, are they?

Mr. HUNTINGTON. I do not know. I should think so.

Senator MORGAN. But their books have not been burned nor destroyed within your knowledge?

Mr. HUNTINGTON. I do not know.

Senator MORGAN. Are they in the way?

Mr. HUNTINGTON. I do not know. We may have more room now than we had then.

Senator MORGAN. You did not discover that they were in the way when you were burning the books of the other company?

Mr. HUNTINGTON. They did not exist at that time. Yes; I guess the Western Development Company was organized then.

Senator MORGAN. You have not stated to the committee whether the books and papers of that company are in existence or not.

Mr. HUNTINGTON. I am not positive.

Senator MORGAN. Do you believe that they are accessible to this committee if we wanted to send for them?

Mr. HUNTINGTON. I think so; I do not know.

Senator MORGAN. The Pacific Improvement Company; what was that instituted to do?

Mr. HUNTINGTON. The same as the others.

Senator MORGAN. Who were the stockholders in it?

Mr. HUNTINGTON. Substantially the same.

Senator MORGAN. Were they not exactly the same?

Mr. HUNTINGTON. No.

Senator MORGAN. What difference was there?

Mr. HUNTINGTON. Mr. Colton was not in that company, and I think Mr. Hopkins was not. I do not know whether he was living when that company was organized or not.

Senator MORGAN. But, except those gentlemen, the stockholders in that company were the same as the stockholders in the Western Development Company and in the Contract and Finance Company?

Mr. HUNTINGTON. Substantially, I should say. You see these companies were organized for the purpose of building railroads and ships and various things. There were some people in the Contract and Finance Company—Mr. E. B. Crocker and some others, I think, and I think one of the Stanfords other than Leland—and they died, and then the company was closed up. It is an easy thing to organize companies under the laws of California, and old interests were dropped out. Some time, Senator, if you build railroads you will find that when men drop out and can not work you have to leave them out and organize another company, so that the men who do the work shall have whatever benefit comes from it.

Senator MORGAN. Yes, I understood that a freezing-out process was necessary in this business.

Mr. HUNTINGTON. I never heard the expression used in that way before. When a man gets so that he does not work he should not have pay, either living or dead.

Senator MORGAN. Did the Contract and Finance Company, or the Western Development Company, or the Pacific Improvement Company build any railroads that are not connected with the Central Pacific?

Mr. HUNTINGTON. The Contract and Finance Company built the Central Pacific. I think the whole of it except that part from Redding to Coles on the Oregon and California line; I think that that was built by the Pacific Improvement Company. I am pretty sure that it was.

Senator MORGAN. Did the Contract and Finance Company build any other railroads?

Mr. HUNTINGTON. Not for the Central Pacific.

Senator MORGAN. Did it build any railroads except for the Central Pacific?

Mr. HUNTINGTON. I have mentioned the Monterey branch. The Pacific Improvement Company built most of the roads of the Southern Pacific—perhaps not most, but they built the last roads that were built for the Southern Pacific; I suppose 500 or 600 miles.

Senator MORGAN. The controlling stockholders, and almost all the stockholders of these three companies, were the same parties, were they not?

Mr. HUNTINGTON. Hardly that, Senator.

Senator MORGAN. How was it?

Mr. HUNTINGTON. Mr. Colton went out, and Mr. E. B. Crocker went out, and I think some others. They died, I think.

Senator MORGAN. The controlling men in each of those corporations were the same, were they not?

Mr. HUNTINGTON. Yes; they were the same set that built all these roads.

Senator MORGAN. And they furnished the capital?

Mr. HUNTINGTON. Yes; they furnished the credit.

Senator MORGAN. Their credit was the capital?

Mr. HUNTINGTON. It is so in all these great undertakings.

Senator MORGAN. Were these roads built before or after the completion of the Central Pacific?

Mr. HUNTINGTON. They were built after the completion of the Central Pacific, I think. We completed the Central Pacific in 1869, on the 10th of May, as I recollect, and I think that all the railroads in California that we have constructed were built after that.

Senator MORGAN. And these two other companies—the Western Development Company and the Pacific Improvement Company—were organized for the purpose of building these additional roads?

Mr. HUNTINGTON. They were organized to build whatever was wanted to be built. They were bright, active men, and the building of railroads was in their line, and they were the only men there to do it.

Senator MORGAN. And these roads were built by men who at that time owned the Central Pacific?

Mr. HUNTINGTON. Yes; substantially. They owned the shares of the Central Pacific, or held them as collateral. The Contract and Finance Company built the road, and they took the shares and sold them.

Senator MORGAN. That is to say, the Contract and Finance Company having built the Central Pacific, the stock of the Central Pacific, all of it, was held by the Contract and Finance Company as collateral to secure the debt of the Central Pacific to the Contract and Finance Company for building the road?

Mr. HUNTINGTON. Perhaps that would not be just the proper way to state it.

Senator MORGAN. Well, you state it the other way.

Mr. HUNTINGTON. As I said yesterday, I think that the Contract and Finance Company took the bonds and stock of the Central Pacific and agreed to build the road.

Senator MORGAN. That is plain enough.

Mr. HUNTINGTON. The Contract and Finance Company did not take all the capital stock of the Central Pacific, which was $100,000,000.

Senator MORGAN. How much of the stock did the Contract and Finance Company take?

Mr. HUNTINGTON. Sixty million dollars.

Senator MORGAN. After they had built the road they held this $60,000,000 of stock as collateral?

Mr. HUNTINGTON. I do not think they held it as collateral. They were the owners of the stock, I suppose. There was such a contract made. Mr. Hopkins was living at that time, and was a pretty nice man, and I trusted all these things to him.

Senator MORGAN. When the railroad was completed the stock of the Central Pacific was paid over to the Contract and Finance Company in discharge of the debt of the Central Pacific to the Contract and Finance Company for building the road, to the extent of $60,000,000?

Mr. HUNTINGTON. It was not paid over in bulk, I suppose.

Senator MORGAN. I did not ask about its being paid in bulk. I want to know whether it was paid over.

Mr. HUNTINGTON. The whole $60,000,000 did not go to the Contract and Finance Company. Mr. Crocker and others took some of the shares.

Senator MORGAN. How much was paid over to the Contract and Finance Company?

Mr. HUNTINGTON. I do not know, because Mr. Crocker had a good deal of the shares.

Senator MORGAN. Was $60,000,000 paid over in stock to the Contract and Finance Company?

Mr. HUNTINGTON. Sixty million dollars was the whole amount then issued.

Senator MORGAN. The balance of the $100,000,000 of stock had not been issued?

Mr. HUNTINGTON. No.

Senator MORGAN. How much of this stock was paid for this debt of the Central Pacific to the Contract and Finance Company?

Mr. HUNTINGTON. We usually made contracts in building roads to take so much of bonds and stock and to do a fair amount of work.

Senator MORGAN. I am not asking you for the manner of dealing; I am asking how much was paid.

Mr. HUNTINGTON. I do not know.

Senator MORGAN. About how much?

Mr. HUNTINGTON. I do not know. I should say probably half of the stock of the Central Pacific, or perhaps two-thirds.

Senator MORGAN. Or perhaps four-fifths?

Mr. HUNTINGTON. I should think not; still, there may have been.

Senator MORGAN. Then, between one-half and four-fifths of the $60,000,000 of stock of the Central Pacific was paid for this work?

Mr. HUNTINGTON. I should guess that that was so.

Senator MORGAN. How much was paid in bonds of the Central Pacific Company?

Mr. HUNTINGTON. I think the Construction and Finance Company took all of the bonds. We had great difficulty in getting men in to help us.

Senator MORGAN. I do not want to go wandering on about the private history of this company.

Mr. HUNTINGTON. I thought you did. I thought that that was what you wanted.

Senator MORGAN. I want to know how much of the bonds of the Central Pacific Company (the first or second mortgage bonds) this Contract and Finance Company took from the Central Pacific Company in payment for the work they did in building the road?

Mr. HUNTINGTON. For building the whole road the Central Pacific paid the proceeds of its bonds, and so much stock to different parties, but mostly to the Contract and Finance Company. I do not know any better way of stating it than that. I did not count the shares.

Senator MORGAN. Who did any work there in the building of the Central Pacific road except the Contract and Finance Company?

Mr. HUNTINGTON. There were seven contractors between Sacramento and Newcastle.

Senator MORGAN. Were any of these bonds paid to either of these seven contractors?

Mr. HUNTINGTON. I think there were.

Senator MORGAN. Have you no recollection of it?

Mr. HUNTINGTON. No; I was not there, except on one occasion.

Senator MORGAN. I do not care whether you were there. Do you know whether bonds were paid to them or not?

Mr. HUNTINGTON. I think so; I am quite sure of it.

Senator MORGAN. How much was paid to any or all of them in these bonds?

Mr. HUNTINGTON. I do not know; we had great difficulty in getting men to do the work.

Senator MORGAN. Are you answering the question, or are you excusing yourself from answering?

Mr. HUNTINGTON. I want to explain.

Senator MORGAN. State the facts first.

Mr. HUNTINGTON. After these seven men had finished their contracts we had serious difficulties on account of the labor. We let the contract to Charles Crocker & Co. We thought that they could do it, but we very soon found that they could not. I hoped to get some one to go in with them in New York or San Francisco, but I could not get anyone to do so. They said they would not go into an open copartnership, but that if our people got up a construction company they would take shares in it. We were all tired before they got the road over the Sierra Nevada Mountains. We tried to get in some capitalists in New York and Boston, but they all gave the same reply. They said, "Huntington, the risk is too great and the profits, if any, are too remote. We can not take the risk."

Senator MORGAN. Let me see if I understand you. You got the charter for the Central Pacific and then you got authority from Congress to issue these bonds, and you got the guarantee of the United States for how many millions?

Mr. HUNTINGTON. $27,300,000.

Senator MORGAN. These bonds being the assets for building the Central Pacific, you commenced by contracting with some companies for a portion of the road in California?

Mr. HUNTINGTON. No; I am not sure whether we got the other roads then.

Senator MORGAN. These roads were not built under the act of Congress?

Mr. HUNTINGTON. Yes. They met us here in Washington and they said that we must assign that part of the road between Sacramento and San Francisco to them, and that the Central Pacific would not get the charter unless we did assign that portion. Everybody in California wanted to come home to see the old folks, and the old folks wanted to go out there.

Senator MORGAN. I do not want to listen to all that.

Mr. HUNTINGTON. I want to give the details. We took the road after they had got the other road well along. They had some trouble in building it. We should not have located it where it is if we had had the locating of it.

Senator MORGAN. I want to see if I understand you. I understood you to say that before the Contract and Finance Company took charge of this road a portion of the railroad that is now the Central Pacific was built.

Mr. HUNTINGTON. That is right.

Senator MORGAN. How much of it?

Mr. HUNTINGTON. I do not know. As I recollect, they were away up above Cisco. Mr. Crocker took the contract to go to Station No. 137.

Senator Morgan interrupted Mr. Huntington.

Senator FRYE. Why can not Mr. Huntington be permitted to go on and give his answer?

Senator MORGAN. Because he will not answer.

Senator FRYE. I see no reason for stopping him.

Senator MORGAN. I do, and I am conducting this examination according to my ideas until the committee overrules me.

Mr. HUNTINGTON. I would like to make all this very plain.

Senator MORGAN. You have an opportunity to make it entirely plain. When the Contract and Finance Company took the contract to complete the road from the end which had not been built to Ogden, or to a junction with the Union Pacific, were there any contractors on that part of the road which had not been built?

Mr. HUNTINGTON. Mr. Crocker, as I was going to say, took the contract from Newcastle to section 137. He got up to about Cisco. We were laboring pretty hard——

Senator MORGAN (interrupting). You need not go on that side issue. I want the facts.

Mr. HUNTINGTON. I am giving the facts. We got up on that contract to about Cisco, and I think it was about there that the Contract and Finance Company took up the work. That is 92 miles from Sacramento.

Senator MORGAN. How far between that and Ogden?

Mr. HUNTINGTON. About 742 miles.

Senator MORGAN. That is the portion of the road covered by the Contract and Finance Company?

Mr. HUNTINGTON. Yes.

Senator MORGAN. Did anybody else have anything to do with it?

Mr. HUNTINGTON. I think not.

Senator MORGAN. For building that portion of the road what did the Contract and Finance Company get?

Mr. HUNTINGTON. I do not know. I think they got the bonds and some few shares.

Senator MORGAN. You got all of the bonds of the company for this 742 miles of road?

Mr. HUNTINGTON. I think so, but not all of the $27,300,000. The whole line from San Jose to Ogden is, I think, 865 miles—that 123 miles and 742, as I recollect.

Senator MORGAN. You had not then built any of those "feeders?"

Mr. HUNTINGTON. I do not think we had built any then.

Senator MORGAN. After they got the whole thing completed the Contract and Finance Company was paid up for its contract?

Mr. HUNTINGTON. I do not think we did pay them up at that time. That is, we did not sell the securities for some years after that. We sold the bonds. I do not think I saw any bonds of the company since six months after the road was completed.

Senator MORGAN. As you have stated it, the contract between the Central Pacific and the Contract and Finance Company was that the Contract and Finance Company was to receive its payment in bonds and stock?

Mr. HUNTINGTON. That is correct.

Senator MORGAN. It was to receive no money?

Mr. HUNTINGTON. No. I think there was no money.

Senator MORGAN. Then, when they completed their work they got their payment in bonds and stock of the Central Pacific?

Mr. HUNTINGTON. Yes; they got it in the usual way. The engineer made estimates for every 20 miles, and when that section was completed the debt was paid.

Senator MORGAN. The debt of the Central Pacific to the Contract and Finance Company was paid?

Mr. HUNTINGTON. Yes. I think the Central Pacific issued bonds, the same as the Government did, for every 20 miles.

Senator MORGAN. It is quite an easy question for you to answer, whether the Central Pacific complied with its contract and paid you for this work in bonds and stock?

Mr. HUNTINGTON. I think they did. I said so before.

Senator MORGAN. Then after that you organized two other companies for the purpose of building other lines in California?

Mr. HUNTINGTON. Yes; they came in, not at the same time, but each in its own time.

Senator MORGAN. After these transactions?

Mr. HUNTINGTON. Yes.

Senator MORGAN. You organized these two other companies?

Mr. HUNTINGTON. Yes; we organized three, or four, or five companies.

Senator MORGAN. I want to know how many railroads or parts of railroads ("feeders") were built by you and your associates to connect with the Central Pacific, and when each one was built, and what was the name of each?

Mr. HUNTINGTON. We bought, I think, a dozen roads in California. All of them had failed, I think, when we bought them and could not meet their obligations.

Senator MORGAN. Connected with the Central Pacific?

Mr. HUNTINGTON. No.

Senator MORGAN. I have not asked you about any roads bought by you that were not connected with the Central Pacific.

Mr. HUNTINGTON. I do not know of any except those which we built. They were the Oregon branch, the San Jose branch, and the Niles branch. I do not know of any other. We bought a road, a small road, near Galt, a narrow-gauge road; but that did not connect with the Central Pacific. It crossed the Central and went down to Stockton Slough.

Senator MORGAN. I do not want the whole story of those roads. I want to know——

Mr. HUNTINGTON. I am giving you an explanation. The next road—the Stockton and Copperopolis—came down to Stockton and crossed the Central Pacific and went down to the water at Stockton, and made connection with steamers there.

Senator MORGAN. Did you build that road?

Mr. HUNTINGTON. No; we bought it.

Senator MORGAN. What did you give for it?

Mr. HUNTINGTON. I think we gave $500,000 in bonds of the road.

Senator MORGAN. What bonds?

Mr. HUNTINGTON. Bonds of the Stockton and Copperopolis road. It was owned by people in Holland who had $1,000,000 in 8 per cent bonds that were issued on it.

Senator MORGAN. And you bought these people out?

Mr. HUNTINGTON. No; we gave them $500,000 in 5 per cent bonds for their million of 8 per cent bonds and the stock.

Senator MORGAN. What 5 per cent bonds did you give them?

Mr. HUNTINGTON. The 5 per cent bonds of the Stockton and Copperopolis road.

Senator MORGAN. Then there were bonds issued by that road?

Mr. HUNTINGTON. Yes.

Senator MORGAN. You agreed with them to take the corporation and to issue $500,000 in 5 per cent bonds?

Mr. HUNTINGTON. No; we gave them $500,000 in 5 per cent bonds for their $1,000,000 in 8 per cent bonds, and all the stock.

Senator MORGAN. Then you took that road and agreed with these stockholders that you would take up their bonds at 50 per cent of their face value and give them, instead, bonds issued by the Stockton and Copperopolis road?

Mr. HUNTINGTON. Yes.

Senator MORGAN. Who guaranteed those bonds?

Mr. HUNTINGTON. I do not think they were guaranteed at all, except that I told them that they would be good.

Senator MORGAN. For whom was this deal made? Was it made for the private persons engaged in these various companies, or was it made for the Central Pacific Company?

Mr. HUNTINGTON. It was made for the private persons.

Senator MORGAN. Has that property ever passed into the ownership of the Central Pacific?

Mr. HUNTINGTON. No; never.

Senator MORGAN. Is it now being run as a separate corporation and by separate directors?

Mr. HUNTINGTON. It is now a part of the Southern Pacific, I think. It is connected with the Southern Pacific at Merced.

Senator MORGAN. That, then, is a line which crosses the Central Pacific and runs to the Southern Pacific?

Mr. HUNTINGTON. It crosses the Central Pacific from the steamboat landing at Stockton, goes to Milton, and runs at the west base of the Sierra Nevada to Merced, about 100 miles.

Senator MORGAN. And there it lapses into the Southern Pacific?

Mr. HUNTINGTON. Yes.

Senator MORGAN. Then this deal was not made in the interest of the Central Pacific, but in the interest of the Southern Pacific?

Mr. HUNTINGTON. No; the Southern Pacific, I think, at that time was not as much of a corporation as it is to-day.

Senator MORGAN. That is very likely, but that does not answer the question.

Mr. HUNTINGTON. I said it was not.

Senator MORGAN. I asked you the question, whether the deal was not made in the interest of the Southern Pacific?

Mr. HUNTINGTON. I do not think it was.

Senator MORGAN. Was it made in the interest of the Central Pacific?

Mr. HUNTINGTON. My impression is that it was made in the interest of the Western Development Company. That is what that company was organized for.

Senator MORGAN. And for the benefit of neither the Central Pacific nor the Southern Pacific?

Mr. HUNTINGTON. No; but the Central Pacific has benefited by it, and so has the Southern Pacific; because, instead of running to the water, we bring the stuff to Milton, I believe.

Senator MORGAN. Now let us leave that road and come to the next road that you built to connect with the Central Pacific, under the powers contained in the charters of either of those companies, the Western Development Company or the Pacific Improvement Company.

Mr. HUNTINGTON. We had no right to build roads under those charters. We had no charters to build roads, excepting as we bought and controlled them.

Senator MORGAN. It was a sort of universal improvement company?

Mr. HUNTINGTON. Perhaps we might call it so.

Senator MORGAN. Then, when you found some railroad company in existence, or when you found a railroad laid out, this Pacific Improvement Company went to work and built it for them?

Mr. HUNTINGTON. We had the right to buy.

Senator MORGAN. I ask you one question and you commence at another different place. I repeat the question. When you found a railroad company chartered, the line surveyed and ready for the operation of building, this Western Development Company, or the Pacific Improvement Company, went to work——

Mr. HUNTINGTON. They did not operate at the same time.

Senator MORGAN. Well, this Western Development Company went to work and took the contract and built the road?

Mr. HUNTINGTON. If they took the contract, of course they built the road. They did not take everything that was offered.

Senator MORGAN. I am talking about the roads that were actually built, and that are connected with the Central Pacific road. In regard to those roads that had been actually built, and that connected with the Central Pacific, did the Western Development Company become the company of execution, and did it build the road?

Mr. HUNTINGTON. Yes; I think so.

Senator MORGAN. Tell the next road, in order of point of time, that was built? You have mentioned the Stockton and Copperopolis.

Mr. HUNTINGTON. I think we went to building the Southern Pacific. The California Pacific we bought.

Senator MORGAN. You do not understand that the Southern Pacific was ever connected with the Central Pacific except physically?

Mr. HUNTINGTON. All the roads in California are connected physically.

Senator MORGAN. I am speaking of those roads in California that were built as feeders to the Central Pacific. Was the Southern Pacific built as a feeder?

Mr. HUNTINGTON. Not at all. The Southern Pacific and the Central Pacific started off in different directions.

Senator MORGAN. But the Southern Pacific and Central Pacific are connected at one end?

Mr. HUNTINGTON. Yes; at San Francisco.

Senator MORGAN. The Southern Pacific was not built as a feeder to the Central Pacific?

Mr. HUNTINGTON. No.

Senator MORGAN. What was the next road built as a feeder to the Central Pacific and actually connected with it?

Mr. HUNTINGTON. I do not know that any roads were built as feeders to the Central Pacific.

Senator MORGAN. You mentioned two or three roads that were built by this Western Development Company. What was the next one after the Stockton and Copperopolis?

Mr. HUNTINGTON. I can not say exactly. I do not think that we built a road especially to connect with the Central Pacific, but merely to accommodate certain localities.

Senator MORGAN. With outlets to the Central Pacific?

Mr. HUNTINGTON. Or to any railroad.

Senator MORGAN. I am talking about outlets to the Central Pacific. What was the next road you built with such outlet?

Mr. HUNTINGTON. I do not think of any other; and these were not built for that purpose.

Senator MORGAN. You have already mentioned the Copperopolis and the Southern Pacific.

Mr. HUNTINGTON. Yes; but they were not built as feeders.

Senator MORGAN. What other roads did you build?

Mr. HUNTINGTON. As feeders?

Senator MORGAN. No.

Mr. HUNTINGTON. We built a road from Bakersfield to Asphalt.

Senator MORGAN. Had this road connection with the Central Pacific?

Mr. HUNTINGTON. No; with the Southern Pacific. I do not think we built any others as feeders to the Central Pacific.

Senator MORGAN. Or having a direct connection with it—one end of the road joining with the other—call it direct or indirect?

Mr. HUNTINGTON. I do not think of any. The Sacramento and Placerville road connected with the Central, but it was built to run with the California Pacific across the river to Sacramento.

Senator MORGAN. Does that road connect with the Central Pacific?

Mr. HUNTINGTON. It crosses it at Sacramento, but it does not belong to us. The people who built it work in harmony with those who built the California Pacific.

Senator MORGAN. To whom does that road belong now?

Mr. HUNTINGTON. I think to the California and Northern.

Senator MORGAN. To whom does the California and Northern belong?

Mr. HUNTINGTON. To the shareholders—the Southern Pacific, I think.

Senator MORGAN. The California and Northern belongs to the Southern Pacific, and that is a Kentucky corporation?

Mr. HUNTINGTON. Yes; I call it the Southern Pacific Company.

Senator MORGAN. In the bills that you have presented here you have offered to give a mortgage on certain railroad properties in addition to the Central Pacific line.

Mr. HUNTINGTON. They differ from the aided line. I mean these three branches.

Senator MORGAN. What three branches?

Mr. HUNTINGTON. The branches from Roseville to Coles, and from Lathrop to Fresno, and from Niles to Oakland.

Senator MORGAN. Take the Lathrop and Fresno. Does that connect with the Central Pacific?

Mr. HUNTINGTON. It is part of the Central Pacific.

Senator MORGAN. Who built that line?

Mr. HUNTINGTON. It was built by the same organization.

Senator MORGAN. When?

Mr. HUNTINGTON. It was commenced in 1871 and was completed within a reasonable time.

Senator MORGAN. It was commenced after the Central Pacific had been built?

Mr. HUNTINGTON. Yes.

Senator MORGAN. And paid for?

Mr. HUNTINGTON. I should think so.

Senator MORGAN. Then we have another.

Mr. HUNTINGTON. That is part of the Central Pacific.

Senator MORGAN. I am talking about those roads or parts of roads that were added to the Central Pacific after that road was completed and paid for.

Mr. HUNTINGTON. It is a part of the road.

Senator MORGAN. I am talking about the roads added to the Central Pacific after the Central Pacific had been built and paid for.

Mr. HUNTINGTON. The road between Ogden and San Jose is the Central Pacific. The road from Lathrop to Fresno was built first, and then the next, as I recollect, was the road from Roseville to Coles.

Senator MORGAN. Take the road from Lathrop to Fresno. Was that built under a separate charter?

Mr. HUNTINGTON. I think not. I am quite sure it was not.

Senator MORGAN. You have a habit of saying, "I think." What makes you think so?

Mr. HUNTINGTON. That work was done in California. I am quite sure that I have never seen the papers. I would not like to say it was positively so. I wish, as you are particular, to be particular also.

Senator MORGAN. You know whether it was built under the charter of Congress or of the State?

Mr. HUNTINGTON. My impression is that it was built under the charter of the Central Pacific.

Senator MORGAN. Under the charter granted by Congress?

Mr. HUNTINGTON. No; not especially.

Senator MORGAN. Then by what authority?

Mr. HUNTINGTON. The authority of the State of California.

Senator MORGAN. Then it was a separate company acting under a charter from the State of California?

Mr. HUNTINGTON. The Central Pacific was also built under a State charter as well as under the legislation of Congress of 1862 and 1864, which gave it certain rights. Just how far these rights extended I do not know, but it was commenced under a California charter. The grant of Government lands was given to the Central Pacific of California, the charter being created under the laws of that State.

Senator MORGAN. And that was the charter adopted by the United States Government?

Mr. HUNTINGTON. Yes.

Senator MORGAN. And there has been no charter since that for the road from Lathrop to Fresno?

Mr. HUNTINGTON. No; we changed the name. The charter of the Oregon road was granted to another company entirely.

Senator MORGAN. Keep to the Lathrop Company.

Mr. HUNTINGTON. My opinion is—and still I am in doubt about it when I think of the other—I can not say.

Senator MORGAN. Was that road from Lathrop to Fresno built by a separate board of directors, different from the board of directors of the Central Pacific, or was it built by the board of directors that managed and controlled the Central Pacific?

Mr. HUNTINGTON. If it was the same organization, of course it was the same board of directors; if it was not the same organization, the directors may have been mixed. Still I think it was built by the Central Pacific under its California charter.

Senator MORGAN. Was it built by the Central Pacific under the order of that body corporate that it should be built?

Mr. HUNTINGTON. Yes; I am pretty sure that that is so.

Senator MORGAN. And ever since it has been built it has been considered a part of the Central Pacific?

Mr. HUNTINGTON. It was always a part of the Central Pacific.

Senator MORGAN. What is the length of it?

Mr. HUNTINGTON. As I recollect, 146.3 miles.

Senator MORGAN. About how much a mile did it cost to build it?

Mr. HUNTINGTON. I think the mortgage upon it is $40,000 a mile.

Senator MORGAN. How much a mile did it cost to build it?

Mr. HUNTINGTON. I can not say. It cost probably $40,000 a mile.

Senator MORGAN. Is it through a mountainous country?

Mr. HUNTINGTON. No.

Senator MORGAN. Does it cross rivers?

Mr. HUNTINGTON. There are a great many expensive rivers to be crossed.

Senator MORGAN. The road was built with wooden bridges?

Mr. HUNTINGTON. Yes.

Senator MORGAN. And those have been replaced with iron bridges?

Mr. HUNTINGTON. Yes.

Senator MORGAN. Do you state that it cost $40,000 a mile to build that line?

Mr. HUNTINGTON. I think so. You see the company did not get par for those bonds. Some of them sold at 60 per cent.

Senator MORGAN. I do not want to wander through the whole history of the company. I want to know as to this particular enterprise. Did you pay out bonds?

Mr. HUNTINGTON. I think $40,000 a mile.

Senator MORGAN. What did you do with those bonds?

Mr. HUNTINGTON. We used them, I suppose, to build the road.

Senator MORGAN. Were they paid over to any construction company?

Mr. HUNTINGTON. I think they were paid either to the Pacific Improvement Company or to the Contract and Finance Company.

Senator MORGAN. They were paid to one of those two companies?

Mr. HUNTINGTON. I think so.

Senator MORGAN. You did all the work and got all the bonds?

Mr. HUNTINGTON. I should think so, but they were used finally to build the road.

Senator MORGAN. Where are those bonds now?

Mr. HUNTINGTON. I do not know; I have not seen one of them since the road was built.

Senator MORGAN. Did you ever own any of them?

Mr. HUNTINGTON. No; I never owned one of them.

Senator MORGAN. Were they sold in the market?

Mr. HUNTINGTON. Yes.

Senator MORGAN. To anybody who would buy them?

Mr. HUNTINGTON. Yes.

Senator MORGAN. At what rate?

Mr. HUNTINGTON. I should say they averaged 87 or 88 or 90.

Senator MORGAN. Were they protected by any guaranty from the Central Pacific Company?

Mr. HUNTINGTON. They were a bond of the Central Pacific, and therefore the company was responsible for them.

Senator MORGAN. The company was responsible for what?

Mr. HUNTINGTON. Responsible for those bonds.

Senator MORGAN. And still is responsible for them?

Mr. HUNTINGTON. Yes.

Senator MORGAN. Is that mortgage still overhanging that road?

Mr. HUNTINGTON. It is.

Senator MORGAN. For the whole amount?

Mr. HUNTINGTON. No; there is a sinking fund.

Senator MORGAN. Have any of the bonds been actually taken up?

Mr. HUNTINGTON. Bonds have been taken up that are in the sinking fund.

Senator MORGAN. To what amount?

Mr. HUNTINGTON. To whatever amount the requirement was· I do not know.

Senator MORGAN. Have you no idea?

Mr. HUNTINGTON. Well, no; I can get the amount.

Senator MORGAN. Was there a separate stock issued on that road?

Mr. HUNTINGTON. No; I think not. There is none outstanding now, and I am quite sure there never was.

Senator MORGAN. The stock of the Central Pacific covered that property?

Mr. HUNTINGTON. It is a part of the Central Pacific if the Central Pacific built it, and I am inclined to think it did.

Senator MORGAN. Then that road was really owned by the persons who owned the Central Pacific?

Mr. HUNTINGTON. Yes; it was owned by the shareholders of the Central Pacific.

Senator MORGAN. And it was really built by the same persons?

Mr. HUNTINGTON. The same persons as who?

Senator MORGAN. As owned the stock of the Central Pacific?

Mr. HUNTINGTON. No; I do not think it was built by the same persons. It was built by a company.

Senator MORGAN. I am talking about the persons engaged in both companies.

Mr. HUNTINGTON. I think so. There may have been some persons in one who were not in the other.

Senator MORGAN. But, in effect, they were virtually built by the same persons?

Mr. HUNTINGTON. They were built by two organizations—one trading with another. I would not say they were the same persons. I am quite sure, however, that some of them are the same.

Senator MORGAN. If they were not the same, state those who were in the one company and not in the other.

Mr. HUNTINGTON. I do not know.

The committee here took a recess until 2 p. m.

After the recess the examination of Mr. Huntington was continued.

Senator MORGAN. Are there any other roads built by either of those two companies on account of or as part of the Central Pacific?

Mr. HUNTINGTON. No; I think not.

Senator MORGAN. Did the Central Pacific contribute any money or bonds or property of any kind to the construction of either of those lines that we have been mentioning that run into and form a part of the Central Pacific road?

Mr. HUNTINGTON. Yes; bonds were issued by the Central for the road from Lathrop to Fresno or Goshen. I think the road runs up to Goshen, which is, I think, the southern end of it, instead of Fresno.

Senator MORGAN. Each of those roads that you speak of is considered the property of the Central Pacific?

Mr. HUNTINGTON. They are part of the Central Pacific property, the same as the line to San Jose.

Senator MORGAN. But I do not understand that you know whether they were built under a separate corporate organization or whether they were built under the corporate organization of the Central Pacific.

Mr. HUNTINGTON. I think they must have been built under the organization of the Central Pacific.

Senator MORGAN. And by the order of the Central Pacific?

Mr. HUNTINGTON. They must have been.

Senator MORGAN. So that you always considered the Central Pacific Company liable for the debts of those additional roads?

Mr. HUNTINGTON. Yes, responsible for all of them.

Senator MORGAN. When you add those roads that have been built, since the main trunk of the Central Pacific was completed, to the mileage, what is the amount of the mileage of the entire Central Pacific road?

Mr. HUNTINGTON. As I recollect, it is something over 1,300 miles; between 1,300 and 1,400.

Senator MORGAN. The Central Pacific has no leased roads?

Mr. HUNTINGTON. No.

Senator MORGAN. The Southern Pacific has a number of leased roads?

Mr. HUNTINGTON. Yes.

Senator MORGAN. All of those roads about which we have been speaking to-day are now under lease to the Southern Pacific or belong to the Southern Pacific?

Mr. HUNTINGTON. I may be wrong about their being leased. They are operated by the Southern Pacific; but just how far they are owned, or whether they are all owned or not, by the Southern Pacific, I do not know. My recollection is that the San Francisco Northern is not owned by the Southern Pacific.

Senator MORGAN. It is leased to the Southern Pacific?

Mr. HUNTINGTON. If not owned it is leased.

Senator MORGAN. But all the roads that we have been speaking of either belong to or are leased by the Southern Pacific?

Mr. HUNTINGTON. I think they have all been consolidated south of San Francisco into the Southern Pacific Company. In the State of California, and east of there, the Southern Pacific Company controls them by ownership.

Senator MORGAN. Is the Pacific Improvement Company still an organization?

Mr. HUNTINGTON. Yes.

Senator MORGAN. Does that company own any stock of the Central Pacific?

Mr. HUNTINGTON. Not that I know of, and I would be likely to know if it did.

Senator MORGAN. Does it hold any stock of the Southern Pacific?

Mr. HUNTINGTON. I think it does.

Senator MORGAN. How much?

Mr. HUNTINGTON. I do not know.

Senator MORGAN. About how much?

Mr. HUNTINGTON. I think they have, if I recollect right, 15,000 or 16,000 or 17,000 shares.

Senator MORGAN. How much a share?

Mr. HUNTINGTON. One hundred dollars.

Senator MORGAN. Those gentlemen say in their memorial: "The same company, we are informed, own, or claim to own, the railroad's interest in the bridge at Sacramento."

Mr. HUNTINGTON. I think that that belongs to the California Pacific. We did not build the California Pacific. The bridge was built as a wagon-road bridge, and then, as I remember, it was strengthened, and the California Pacific road ran over it. Now, the California Pacific has built a new bridge just below the other, and I think they are running over it to-day, or if not to-day, they will be running over it very soon.

Senator MORGAN. Then that bridge does not belong to the Pacific Improvement Company?

Mr. HUNTINGTON. No; it belongs to the California Pacific.

Senator MORGAN. And the California Pacific belongs to the Pacific Improvement Company?

Mr. HUNTINGTON. No.

Senator MORGAN. Has it got any interest in the stock of the Pacific Improvement Company?

Mr. HUNTINGTON. I am not sure. I am inclined to think that it has a little, but I am not sure. It isn't very much.

Senator MORGAN. These men say that the same company own or claim to own the railroad's interest in the bridge at Sacramento.

Mr. HUNTINGTON. I am not surprised that they say that, because it isn't true.

Senator MORGAN. Also, that the same company owns the ferryboat *Piedmont* that plies between Oakland and San Francisco, and that forms part of the Central Pacific Railroad Company's line.

Mr. HUNTINGTON. I do not think that the Pacific Improvement Company has any interest in it.

Senator MORGAN. Or did have?

Mr. HUNTINGTON. I do not know that it did have, but I am quite sure that it has not now.

Senator MORGAN. Who owns the ferryboats on that part of the line?

Mr. HUNTINGTON. The Central Pacific owns a part of them, and the California Coast Line Railroad—I think that is what it is called—owns some.

Senator MORGAN. Those boats that are used by the Central Pacific; who owns them?

Mr. HUNTINGTON. They are owned by the Central Pacific; some of them run to Oakland and some to the other side of Alameda Creek.

Senator MORGAN. These memorialists say that this company—the Pacific Improvement Company—owns the river steamers *Modoc* and *Apache*. Is that so?

Mr. HUNTINGTON. I do not think it does.

Senator MORGAN. They say that the company owns the railroad office building at the foot of Fourth and Townsend streets in the city of San Francisco. Is that so?

Mr. HUNTINGTON. The Pacific Improvement Company did own that building at the corner of Fourth and Townsend streets.

Senator MORGAN. Who owns it now?

Mr. HUNTINGTON. My impression is that the Pacific Improvement Company owns it now; I am not certain.

Senator MORGAN. They say that the same company (the Pacific Improvement Company) owns the Del Monte Hotel at Monterey. Is that so?

Mr. HUNTINGTON. That is so; I am quite certain.

Senator MORGAN. They say that the same company owns the principal part of the lands formerly belonging to the old company in and around North Berkeley, and the depots at Sacramento and Los Angeles. Is that so?

Mr. HUNTINGTON. I hardly think so, and I know it isn't, if they say it is.

Senator MORGAN. Can you not give a better reason?

Mr. HUNTINGTON. That is a very good reason, but I do not think the Pacific Improvement Company has any interest in the Sacramento and Los Angeles depots.

Senator MORGAN. Who owns the Los Angeles depot?

Mr. HUNTINGTON. The Southern Pacific Railroad Company.

Senator MORGAN. And the depot at Sacramento?

Mr. HUNTINGTON. The Pacific Improvement Company had nothing to do with that.

Senator MORGAN. To whom does the depot at Sacramento belong?

Mr. HUNTINGTON. To the Central Pacific Company—the large one. There is a smaller depot there that belongs to the Sacramento and Placerville Company. It is now owned by the San Francisco Northern.

Senator MORGAN. They say that the same company also owns the Central Pacific Railroad wharf at San Pedro. Is that true?

Mr. HUNTINGTON. I am quite sure it is not. The wharf was built by the Northern Pacific Company.

Senator MORGAN. They say also that the same company formerly owned or assumed to own the Oakland water front and the Mission Bay property. Is that true?

Mr. HUNTINGTON. I do not think the Pacific Improvement Company ever owned it.

Senator MORGAN. They say that it owns the coal mines in the State of Washington and in Mexico, from whence the Central Pacific obtains its coal. Is that true?

Mr. HUNTINGTON. It does not own any coal mines in Mexico; and the Central Pacific gets very little coal from there. The coal that we get there is mostly used in Mexico.

Senator MORGAN. What do you say as to the coal mines in the State of Washington?

Mr. HUNTINGTON. I think that the Pacific Improvement Company owns coal mines there.

Senator MORGAN. And sells its coal to the Northern Pacific?

Mr. HUNTINGTON. I think so.

Senator MORGAN. Does the Northern Pacific get its chief supply of coal from those mines?

Mr. HUNTINGTON. More than it gets from any other source, perhaps. Those are very large mines.

Senator MORGAN. They say that the Pacific Improvement Company nets two millions a year from the coal it supplies to the Southern and Central Pacific Railroad companies. Is that so?

Mr. HUNTINGTON. It nets very little. I can not say what the amount is. They sell coal to the railroads there for, I think, two-thirds of what the coal is selling for in the market.

Senator MORGAN. Would they net from the coal sold to these two roads two millions a year?

Mr. HUNTINGTON. No, nor half of it; I do not think they would net one-fourth of it. The coal that we bought from everywhere up to four years ago was costing us \$6 or \$7 a ton, but now we have got the price down.

Senator MORGAN. Has the Central Pacific or the Southern Pacific, or both of them, any interest in the street railroads of San Francisco?

Mr. HUNTINGTON. I think not.

Senator MORGAN. To whom do these street railroads belong?

Mr. HUNTINGTON. To the shareholders; they have a great many shareholders. The Market Street Company owns perhaps most of the street railroads of San Francisco, and it has a great many shareholders. The different roads were consolidated, and their shareholders came in and took shares in the consolidated company. The Central Pacific and the Southern Pacific, I think, have no interest in these street railroads, and I do not think they ever did have. At least I have no recollection of their having.

Senator MORGAN. The Central Pacific and the Southern Pacific, if I understand you, either own or control a line of steamers from San Francisco to New York by the way of Panama?

Mr. HUNTINGTON. No; the people who control the Union Pacific and the Central Pacific own the steamers. Neither company has any shares in them.

Senator MORGAN. They have freight arrangements with that company?

Mr. HUNTINGTON. Yes; they were organized mostly to run in connection with them, to pick up as much trade as we can from eastern Asia. The steamship company does not own any steamers; it charters them.

Senator MORGAN. These men say that Mr. Huntington and his associates destroyed a part of the so-called Record Book of Corporation Debts, which book they were required by law to keep. Was there such a record book kept by the Contract and Finance Company?

Mr. HUNTINGTON. I should say so, if the law required it to be kept. We were very particular about such things.

Senator MORGAN. Was that record book destroyed with the rest of the papers?

Mr. HUNTINGTON. I do not know.

Senator MORGAN. If you wanted to find such a record as that, would you know where to go for it?

Mr. HUNTINGTON. No. If I wanted it, I should inquire about the office for it.

Senator MORGAN. Would you expect to find it?

Mr. HUNTINGTON. It depends upon what it was. If it was a record book of a part of the operations of the road, I should think it went with the other papers; but if it was something which the statute of the State required to be kept, I would expect to find it.

Senator MORGAN. But you do not know whether it now exists or not?

Mr. HUNTINGTON. I do not.

Senator MORGAN. These memorialists say that for fifteen years last past the Central Pacific Railroad Company and the Southern Pacific Company have owed taxes to the State of California always amounting to from $500,000 to $1,500,000, and that for four years of that time they owed $400,000 to the school fund of the State. Is that true?

Mr. HUNTINGTON. I do not know. They overtaxed us very much, as we thought, and we went to the courts and the courts sustained us, deciding that we were right. They taxed, for instance, the Summit Tunnel, and we thought that it was not a hole to be taxed, and we went into the courts about it. They did many things like that.

Senator MORGAN. What became of that suit; has it been ended?

Mr. HUNTINGTON. Oh, yes. There is a fragment of it somewhere in the courts now.

Senator MORGAN. Was that a suit which involved $535,000 of a tax due by the Southern Pacific and Central Pacific to the State of California, and for taxes levied and assessed for the year 1887 on which a suit was pending in the State courts which has now been transferred to the United States court?

Mr. HUNTINGTON. One case has been decided. It went to the Supreme Court and was decided in our favor. I think there is another case either in the Supreme Court or on its way there.

Senator MORGAN. The Government of the United States, I suppose, has been paying interest regularly on the bonds issued to the Central Pacific Company?

Mr. HUNTINGTON. I suppose so.

Senator MORGAN. What is the rate of interest?

Mr. HUNTINGTON. Six per cent.

Senator MORGAN. When do the first of these bonds mature?

Mr. HUNTINGTON. A few matured last year.

Senator MORGAN. Were they paid?

Mr. HUNTINGTON. I understand so.

Senator MORGAN. Paid by the Government of the United States?

Mr. HUNTINGTON. No; they were paid out of the sinking fund.

Senator MORGAN. Payment was made by the Government of the United States, although it may have been made out of the sinking fund?

Mr. HUNTINGTON. They naturally took the bonds out of the sinking fund to pay for them.

Senator MORGAN. And all the bonds of the Government now outstanding pay 6 per cent interest?

Mr. HUNTINGTON. Yes.

Senator MORGAN. And the Government has been paying 6 per cent interest from the beginning of the transaction down to date?

Mr. HUNTINGTON. As I recollect the contract, that is so.

Senator MORGAN. Between man and man, if one is paying out money under an agreement for another during a long series of years, the party for whom the money is paid would naturally, on the final settlement of the account, have to pay interest on it?

Mr. HUNTINGTON. I do not know. That depends upon various things. When the law was passed originally the Government was to pay the interest, and nothing was due to the Government until the maturity of the bonds.

Senator MORGAN. Do you admit that the Central Pacific is in debt to the Government of the United States for the interest that it has been paying?

Mr. HUNTINGTON. I suppose so. That is one of those things which the legal department of the company always attends to.

Senator MORGAN. The sinking fund was provided as a means of recouping or reimbursing the United States?

Mr. HUNTINGTON. Yes. We were about preparing a sinking fund; in fact, we had got a resolution passed through the board of directors of the Central Pacific for a sinking fund, but when the Thurman law was passed we stopped it. The money that went to the sinking fund established by that act was invested in Government bonds at as high as 135; so that we got very little interest on that investment, whereas we could have invested the money at 6 per cent.

Senator MORGAN. In the proposition that you submit here for settlement by getting an extension of the date, do you include the interest paid by the United States on these bonds?

Mr. HUNTINGTON. What was proposed was, that you find out what the whole sum would be on the 1st of July next, adding the interest up to the maturity of the bonds in 1899, and then treat that as a fixed debt due to the Government.

Senator MORGAN. In making up this aggregate of indebtedness, do you include in your proposition not only the interest paid by the Government, but the interest due on that interest?

Mr. HUNTINGTON. I do not think so. That is a thing for the law to decide. But the law was, that the debt did not become due until the maturity of the bonds. You see that the Government saved very largely by the building of those roads. The Government had paid $1,750,000 to Wells, Fargo & Co. for carrying a little bit of mail between the ends of the road until they were completed, and when the roads were completed we carried upon them five hundred times the weight of mail, and probably more, and I do not think that we got over $300,000 a year for carrying five hundred times the weight of mail. Then in one year (1854 it may have been) the Government paid over $18,000,000 for keeping things reasonably quiet in and about Utah.

Senator MORGAN. In the meantime the Government has supplied you with power to carry more than 500 tons of weight.

Mr. HUNTINGTON. Yes; but that is what was paid.

Senator MORGAN. I want to know whether, in the proposition you submit here, you include in the aggregate indebtedness of the Central Pacific to the United States the interest which the Government has paid on those bonds, and interest upon that interest?

Mr. HUNTINGTON. I should say not; I do not know why, in the world, we should, as I understand the law.

Senator MORGAN. You think that the Government of the United States was paying this interest upon a debt that it owed, not upon a debt that you owed?

Mr. HUNTINGTON. It was paying it not only for a consideration, but for a good consideration.

Senator MORGAN. Was that the sole consideration that induced the Government to put the second-mortgage bonds ahead of the first?

Mr. HUNTINGTON. Yes.

Senator MORGAN. You think it was the same thing?

Mr. HUNTINGTON. About the same thing.

Senator MORGAN. You have been here with several propositions for the settlement of this transaction at different times, have you not?

Mr. HUNTINGTON. Hardly that. I have been here a number of times to have some arrangement made with the Government—something so that I could see that we had reached the beginning of the end of a settlement. I have said frequently that I wanted to pay the Government 100 cents on the dollar on the principal of the debt, and as much interest as we could pay currently—as much as we can get out of the road after the current expenses and after the fixed expenses are paid, and these have to be paid.

Senator MORGAN. You do not wish to occupy the attitude of making any proposition to the Government?

Mr. HUNTINGTON. The proposition is that, in general terms.

Senator MORGAN. I was asking whether you had made any proposition?

Mr. HUNTINGTON. That is the proposition—to pay 100 cents on the dollar, as soon as we can, by making fixed payments at fixed times, until it is all paid; and if we ever get so as not to be able to pay, and there is a default of six months in payment, the Government may go in without legislation, and without court proceedings, and take the property, and the whole of it. That has been my proposition.

Senator MORGAN. You have made two or three propositions, have you not?

Mr. HUNTINGTON. Substantially in this way. Some years ago we proposed that the Government should pay off the Government debt and the first-mortgage debt and put them in a hundred-year bond, and I would guarantee that the Government would have the money in sixty days.

Senator MORGAN. Your first proposition was for a seventy-five-year bond, was it not?

Mr. HUNTINGTON. Perhaps it was.

Senator MORGAN. And the second one you raised to a hundred-year bond?

Mr. HUNTINGTON. The earnings of the road had been growing less and less every year, so that it would require a longer time to pay the debt.

Senator MORGAN. The third proposition is the one embraced in Senator Frye's bill?

Mr. HUNTINGTON. That is the proposition. I can hardly tell what is in it.

Senator MORGAN. That is the proposition which you now submit?

Mr. HUNTINGTON. That so much is to be paid to the Government.

Senator MORGAN. In more than one hundred years?

Mr. HUNTINGTON. No; not more than one hundred years, if you commence with a fixed sum to-day.

Senator MORGAN. That would be equal to an extension of the whole amount; and you change the rate of interest in each of these propositions.

Mr. HUNTINGTON. Yes. I thought that 1½ per cent was enough, but I afterwards thought I would let that go.

Senator MORGAN. What is the rate of interest in your present proposition?

Mr. HUNTINGTON. I do not see where we can pay more than 2 per cent. There is nothing in sight that will allow us to do it. I have looked the matter over very carefully.

Senator MORGAN. Does Senator Frye's bill contemplate paying 2 per cent interest?

Mr. HUNTINGTON. I think so.

Senator MORGAN. Your first proposition was 1½ per cent, or was it 1 per cent?

Mr. HUNTINGTON. It was 1½ per cent. I did not see my way clear to offer any more. Of course, we will have a little less interest to pay on the first-mortgage bonds when we extend them.

Senator MORGAN. If the Congress of the United States should not accept your proposition as couched in the bill of Senator Frye——

Mr. HUNTINGTON. I do not know what that bill is exactly.

Senator MORGAN. Whatever your last proposition was. You asked us to print it at the last session, and we did so.

Mr. HUNTINGTON. I know there was such a bill, but I can not tell who originated it.

Senator MORGAN. The bill was prepared by your counsel and brought here, and we had it printed. Suppose that the present Congress passed a bill accepting your proposition just as you make it, what authority have you to show us that you have the right to make it?

Mr. HUNTINGTON. I represent, pretty largely, the Central Pacific Railroad Company, and we have talked the matter over. We have talked it in this way: that we will do anything we can, but we do not want to agree to a thing that we can not do.

Senator MORGAN. Would such questions, under your charter and by-laws, have to be disposed of at a stockholders' meeting or at a meeting of the board of directors?

Mr. HUNTINGTON. I suppose at a meeting of the board of directors.

Senator MORGAN. Unless it is a very peculiar organization, I should think that such a question should be decided by the stockholders. Do you think that the board of directors has authority to sell out that railroad property?

Mr. HUNTINGTON. I do not understand that we are selling it out. I think we have a right to do whatever is necessary to do under the bill before your committee.

Senator MORGAN. Conceding, for the sake of argument, that you have got such right, has the board of directors ever taken any special action on this subject?

Mr. HUNTINGTON. I do not know that we have, because we saw no necessity, but I have talked it over with every member of the board.

Senator MORGAN. With Government directors and all?

Mr. HUNTINGTON. We have no Government directors.

Senator MORGAN. You have come to an agreement among yourselves formally?

Mr. HUNTINGTON. We have talked it over.

Senator MORGAN. You are not here for the purpose of representing mere gossip among the board of directors?

Mr. HUNTINGTON. No. What I say goes will go.

Senator MORGAN. Why do you think it will go?

Mr. HUNTINGTON. Because it always has gone.

Senator MORGAN. Is it not because you have the controlling interest in the corporation?

Mr. HUNTINGTON. No; but because they know that I take the greatest care of the property. I never had a controlling interest.

Senator MORGAN. What interest have you in the Central Pacific?

Mr. HUNTINGTON. A stock interest.

Senator MORGAN. How much stock interest do you own in that company?

Mr. HUNTINGTON. Not a great deal.

Senator MORGAN. Whether much or little—how much?

Mr. HUNTINGTON. I have not a great deal. I may have—I do not know; it may be four or five thousand shares.

Senator MORGAN. Not more than that?

Mr. HUNTINGTON. Not more than 6,000.

Senator MORGAN. And that is left after the six millions which you have disposed of to the Kentucky company?

Mr. HUNTINGTON. The Southern Pacific Company has no shares of the Central Pacific.

Senator MORGAN. How many shares of the Central Pacific has the Stanford estate got?

Mr. HUNTINGTON. I do not know; it has got considerable.

Senator MORGAN. More than you have got?

Mr. HUNTINGTON. Oh, yes.

Senator MORGAN. And these four other gentlemen?

Mr. HUNTINGTON. I do not think they have as much as the Stanford estate.

Senator MORGAN. How many shares of the Central Pacific are voted in the election of directors?

Mr. HUNTINGTON. Usually about two-thirds, from 60 to 70 per cent.

Senator MORGAN. Is that voted on proxies?

Mr. HUNTINGTON. Largely. Shareholders would hardly go to California from all over the United States and Europe.

Senator MORGAN. Are these proxies bought or hired?

Mr. HUNTINGTON. I never have bought or hired any myself, and I do not think any of our people have. The work has been done so well from start to finish that the stockholders are very well satisfied, I think.

Senator MORGAN. Like the men who in getting big dividends on bank stock do not think it is their business to investigate how the bank is going on?

Mr. HUNTINGTON. I have not much bank stock.

Senator MORGAN. Do you, and the estates which belong to those who are dead, control a majority of the Central Pacific stock to-day?

Mr. HUNTINGTON. I do not think we do.

Senator MORGAN. So that you have the power to elect yourselves to office only by proxies?

Mr. HUNTINGTON. The stockholders know pretty well who are to be the board of directors. That is generally understood.

Senator MORGAN. Then the election of directors is merely pro forma?

Mr. HUNTINGTON. No; not that. The stockholders elect such men as suit them. If they want a change in the board of directors, they can have it.

Senator MORGAN. Has not this road, from the time it was first built till this day, been practically under the control of the same men who built it?

Mr. HUNTINGTON. Yes; I think so. I think they have done more than anyone else to control the property.

Senator MORGAN. The road has been practically, from the beginning up to date, under the control of the same set of gentlemen?

Mr. HUNTINGTON. Yes; I should think so. Rotation in office in going properties of this kind would not do. They have to keep the men who are accustomed to the work and who know how to do it.

Senator MORGAN. I call your attention to-day to a statement made here on the authority of a number of gentlemen at a great mass meeting held in San Francisco about a year before the meeting was held, at which Mr. Sutro and his associates addressed a memorial to Congress. This statement is testified to by James H. Barry, Charles C. Terrill, and John M. Reynolds, a committee which represented the meeting of citizens. They say:

> Our railroad communication with other parts of the Union has been and is controlled by four men (and their heirs) whose united fortune in 1862 did not exceed half a million.

Is that a fact?

Mr. HUNTINGTON. Do you mean a fact about the half a million?

Senator MORGAN. I mean the whole statement [reading it again].

Mr. HUNTINGTON. Well, there isn't any truth in it, not in the least part. The Atchison, Topeka and Santa Fe Railroad connects with San Francisco the same as we do. They do not run their traffic in from Mojave, for the reason that they can not run it as cheap as we do the business for them. That is, we distribute up the business at Mojave and one engine takes it to San Francisco. That company is right in the market there, the same as we are.

Senator MORGAN. With all the same advantages?

Mr. HUNTINGTON. I do not know any advantages which we have that they do not have. They have a contract to run over our line, and they have their offices in San Francisco, and go for freight the same as we do.

Senator MORGAN. You can stop that whenever you wish to?

Mr. HUNTINGTON. No; we have a contract with them.

Senator MORGAN. But you can stop the contract?

Mr. HUNTINGTON. That would be suicidal.

Senator MORGAN. Why?

Mr. HUNTINGTON. Because they would run down to Santa Monica with their goods, and send them by steamer to San Francisco and put them on the Union Pacific road, and take them over it to Chicago.

Senator MORGAN. You would not be very much frightened by such competition as that?

Mr. HUNTINGTON. There is no superior competition than that. It is shorter by water than by rail.

Senator MORGAN. Why do they not do that rather than get you to take their cars on?

Mr. HUNTINGTON. It is more convenient for them to get their cars taken on. We have no advantage over them. If we undertook to prevent them sending on their cars or to refuse to give them as good accommodations as we have, they would do what I say.

Senator MORGAN. Here is a statement which they make, but it is rather a piece of declamation than a statement of facts.

Mr. HUNTINGTON. It is just as good as any other statement they make.

Senator MORGAN. Not quite. They say:

> These men were lavishly endowed by the people in their municipal, State, and Federal capacities, with land and money aggregating quadruple the cost of building the said roads. They have drained our people of every dollar they could extract by excessive freights and fares; they have through the power thus given them entrenched their own monopoly and established and made monopolies subservient to their interests; they have obstructed the development of the State, and by the addition of extortion and fraud have accumulated the unprecedented sum of fully two hundred millions of capital.

Mr. HUNTINGTON. That is all a lie, and if they had not known it to be a lie they would not have written it.

Senator MORGAN. These men say that they represent thousands and thousands of people.

Mr. HUNTINGTON. The only thing that surprises me is that they do not say they represent millions and millions.

Senator MORGAN. Do you know these three men, Barry, Terrill, and Reynolds?

Mr. HUNTINGTON. No; but I know the strain about poor Dog Tray who had been in company with bad dogs.

Senator MORGAN. They say that, at that public meeting, not less than 15,000 people were turned away who could not gain admission to the Metropolitan Temple.

Mr. HUNTINGTON. Oh, there were no 15,000 or 1,500 people there. I wish you would read that paragraph again; it is interesting.

Senator Morgan again read the paragraph commencing, "These men were lavishly endowed by the people," and he asked Mr. Huntington whether that was true.

Mr. HUNTINGTON. That is a lie.

Senator MORGAN. How wide is the lie?

Mr. HUNTINGTON. They do not know anything about it.

Senator MORGAN. Give your statement about it. What is your statement?

Mr. HUNTINGTON. Let me take the book. [After getting the book and reading the paragraph beginning "These men were lavishly endowed by the people."]

Senator MORGAN said: That is the statement which you say is a lie?

Mr. HUNTINGTON. I do, decidedly; and if it were not a lie these men would not have written it. That is my opinion.

Senator MORGAN. Can you give an approximate statement of how much the people have endowed you with, so that we can see how broad a lie these men have been telling?

Mr. HUNTINGTON. The city of San Francisco gave us $400,000. The State of California paid the interest on a million and a half of our bonds for twenty years. I do not think of anything else they did for us that has been of any use. They gave us the right to go on the levee at Sacramento, but we went off from there and went on the other side of the slough. That levee was free to anybody there. They gave us 30 acres of land in Mission Bay, San Francisco, but we never have got the interest on the money that it cost us to fill it up, from that day to this. And that is what these men put down at $40,000,000. I do not know anything that we got from the State of California, except that the State paid the interest for twenty years on a million and a half of our bonds. The city of San Francisco gave us $400,000 in bonds. I sold those bonds in the East in the neighborhood of par, and they would not have brought over 60 cents in gold. That is $240,000. The State paid the interest on a million and a half of our bonds for twenty years. And I know well enough that that road cost us something about eighty or ninety million dollars. I am talking now about what I know.

Senator MORGAN. I thought you were doing that all the time. Have the charges on freights that you have been making on the goods to the East or West been excessive?

Mr. HUNTINGTON. The people of New Jersey and of Delaware complain that the prices we make on fruit from California to New York are so low that they can not compete with the California fruit raisers; that answers that part of the charge. Last year our charge for freight was less than 12 mills a ton a mile. We began with over 2 cents a mile. When we built the road through the San Joaquin Valley, land there was offered to me at $1.25 an acre which has been selling since the road has been built at from $10 to $100 an acre. Does that look like injuring the farmer? Up the Salinas Valley we built 200 miles of road. There was an estate of 40,000 acres there which we could have bought at $5 an acre, but when the road was built one part of that farm was sold at $40 an acre, and another part at $25 an acre. Mr. Althorpe told me he would sell me a farm on the Soledad at $2.50 an acre—some 20,000 acres. The next time I went back there, we had crossed the Calendario Creek, and he offered it to Mr. Stanford at $5 a acre. I asked Stanford to buy it, as it was beautiful land, but he would not. The next time I was there the governor had not bought the land, and when we had crossed the Elkhorn Slough he asked Althorpe what he would sell the land for, and he said $40 an acre. That is the way we served the farmers of California, and they do not complain when we move tonnage for less than 12 mills a ton per mile and passengers at less than 2 cents a mile. The trouble is with these fellows they have got nothing out of us and they will not unless they work for it. They have been discharged employees.

Senator MORGAN. Any of these three?

Mr. HUNTINGTON. I do not know them at all. All of these things I know. There is no guesswork about it.

Senator MORGAN. I suppose you know that the farmers and all business men of California have made the same complaint, that the arrangement which you made with the Panama Railroad and Steamship Company running from San Francisco to the coast, by which you bought space in those ships, worked to their injury?

Mr. HUNTINGTON. I never heard of their making any complaint.

Senator MORGAN. They had a right to make a complaint.

Mr. HUNTINGTON. I suppose they had a right if they wished.

Senator MORGAN. They had a just right to complain.

Mr. HUNTINGTON. No; it was done merely to conserve the property and to get something out of the road.

Senator MORGAN. Was not the effect of it to cut these people off from the steamboat business which you monopolized?

Mr. HUNTINGTON. No; we gave lower prices than they had been paying.

Senator MORGAN. Then, according to your statement, there was very little use in making this monopolistic arrangement and paying this enormous sum to the steamship company in order to get the haul?

Mr. HUNTINGTON. I did not control the Panama line then. I did not have an interest in it. It was a legitimate thing—such a thing as is done all the time. Everybody who travels in western Europe knows that the railroad rates there are very much higher than they are here, although everything else is so cheap there. Although between Liverpool and London the population is so dense that you can hardly get out of sight of a great smokestack, I paid $7.50 railroad fare from Liverpool to London, 198 miles, one of these points being a city of 5,000,000 and the other a city of 1,000,000 inhabitants.

Senator MORGAN. Did you ever admit freight to be carried between San Francisco and Panama in the steamers or the ships in which you bought a space at a lower rate than was paid on the railway?

Mr. HUNTINGTON. We always made a difference.

Senator MORGAN. Did you in the first instance?

Mr. HUNTINGTON. Always.

Senator MORGAN. What was the difference in the rates?

Mr. HUNTINGTON. The difference now, I think, is 75 cents and 60 cents on the dollar.

Senator MORGAN. I am talking of the space that you bought in those steamships, for which you paid how much?

Mr. HUNTINGTON. We paid, I think, $6 a ton.

Senator MORGAN. How much a month, or by the year?

Mr. HUNTINGTON. Seventy-five thousand dollars a month.

Senator MORGAN. For space in those steamships between Panama and San Francisco?

Mr. HUNTINGTON. Yes.

Senator MORGAN. Did you admit the freights of the people into that space at rates as low as you charged on your railroad?

Mr. HUNTINGTON. Lower.

Senator MORGAN. Why did you do that?

Mr. HUNTINGTON. Because there is a differential. There is insurance and delay and other things, so that if there was not a differential no one would ship goods in that way.

Senator MORGAN. Then the advantage in favor of steamship lines is a very decided one to the people, according to your statement?

Mr. HUNTINGTON. Please state that again.

Senator MORGAN. The advantages in favor of the people who produce on the Pacific Coast, and who have to seek a market abroad, on those commodities which will bear sea transportation must be very great if the freight is lower than by the railroads and if the differentials are in their favor.

Mr. HUNTINGTON. The freights must be less by the steamship lines than by all rail, otherwise people would not ship by them, of course, because there is a certain risk and a certain length of time consumed.

Senator MORGAN. If you permitted the people of California to ship their goods in the space you had bought at $75,000 a month, I can not see why you should make such an arrangement as that, when even then the people could take that space and ship in it on lower rates than they could on your railroads.

Mr. HUNTINGTON. There is always a differential in favor of the railroads. Take the Pennsylvania road and the New York Central, and they have a differential in their favor. I do not think any other roads would get so much.

Senator MORGAN. Was it not a fact that those steamers went practically empty?

Mr. HUNTINGTON. Oh, no.

Senator MORGAN. On this space that you paid for, did they go fully freighted?

Mr. HUNTINGTON. I do not know that they always did. The spirit of the arrangement was to fill all the space.

Senator MORGAN. I can not understand why you made the arrangement.

Mr. HUNTINGTON. We had made rates to New York, and some companies cut those rates. One concern that failed last year had seven millions of unpaid rebates. We wanted to avoid all that, but that could not be done altogether. Mr. Thurber, I think, said that one-third of all the railroads of the country were in bankruptcy, caused largely by secret rebates.

Senator MORGAN. And your purpose was to prevent other roads cutting rates?

Mr. HUNTINGTON. It was to get a uniform rate of freight fair to the shipper and fair to the transportation companies.

Senator MORGAN. And to prevent other roads from cutting?

Mr. HUNTINGTON. That is the result.

Senator MORGAN. What roads were in the arrangement?

Mr. HUNTINGTON. I do not think I could call them all—the Canadian Pacific, the Great Northern, the Northern Pacific, the Union Pacific, the Southern Pacific, the Central Pacific, and the Atchison, Topeka and Santa Fe.

Senator MORGAN. So that you were practically protecting yourselves against a railroad war of rate cutting against all of those roads?

Mr. HUNTINGTON. We have to do that.

Senator MORGAN. I want to know why you did it.

Mr. HUNTINGTON. We did it so as not to have our property wasted and not to have to go into bankruptcy; that is what we did it for. If we could have always trusted companies to agree upon rates and to observe them we would do so.

Senator MORGAN. Did you succeed in breaking up this cutting of rates?

Mr. HUNTINGTON. No; I see that one railroad company has over seven millions of unpaid rebates out.

Senator MORGAN. What company is that?

Mr. HUNTINGTON. The Atchison, Topeka and Santa Fe.

Senator MORGAN. Then you did not succeed, even after paying this $75,000 a month, in keeping rates up?

Mr. HUNTINGTON. That arrangement did not run very long before the railroads gave notice to quit.

Senator MORGAN. How long did it run?

Mr. HUNTINGTON. About three years, I think.

Senator MORGAN. You do not think it was more than that?

Mr. HUNTINGTON. No; it was about three years, perhaps a little more than that.

Senator MORGAN. Where is the contract under which that agreement was made?

Mr. Huntington produced the contract, as follows:

This agreement, between the Transcontinental Association, an association consisting of the following railroad companies, namely, the Southern Pacific Company; the Atchison, Topeka and Santa Fe Railroad Company; the Atlantic and Pacific Railroad Company; the California Central Railway Company; the California Southern Railroad Company; the Burlington and Missouri River Railroad Company; the Denver and Rio Grande Railway Company; the Denver and Rio Grande Western Railway Company; the Northern Pacific Railroad Company; the Oregon Railway and Navigation Company; the Missouri Pacific Railway Company; the Texas and Pacific Railway Company; the Oregon Short Line Railway Company; the Union Pacific Railway Company; the St. Louis and San Francisco Railroad Company; the Chicago, Kansas and Nebraska Railway; Denver, Texas and Fort Worth Railroad, and the St. Paul, Minneapolis and Manitoba Railway Company, which association is now represented by James Smith, its chairman, party of the first part, and the Pacific Mail Steamship Co., a corporation created by and existing under the laws of the State of New York, party of the second part, made and entered into this first day of October, 1889, witnesseth:

First. That the said party of the first part, in consideration of the undertakings and agreements of the said steamship company hereinafter contained, undertakes, promises, and agrees to and with said steamship company, to guarantee, and does hereby guarantee, that the gross earnings upon through freight and passengers between New York and San Francisco to be provided to said steamship company by said party of the first part shall be seventy-five thousand ($75,000) dollars per month. All the gross earnings of said steamers from through business between New York and San Francisco each way shall go to and belong and be payable to said party of the first part or credited upon its said guarantee to said steamship company.

Second. In consideration of said guaranty, of said party of the first part, the said Pacific Mail Steamship Company covenants, promises, and agrees to and with the said party of the first part that it, the said steamship company, will, at its own cost and expense, dispatch and run from the port of New York for Aspinwall not more than three nor less than two through steamers per month, and not more than three nor less than two steamers connecting therewith from Panama to San Francisco, and from the port of San Francisco for Panama not more than three nor less than two through steamers per month, and not more than three nor less than two steamers connecting therewith from Aspinwall to New York, and that said steamship company will permit said party of the first part to fix the rates at which all through freight between New York and San Francisco and all passengers shall be transported by the vessels of the steamship company from the port of New York to the port of San Francisco, and from the port of San Francisco to the port of New York, and will furnish room on each of said steamers from New York and San Francisco, respectively, and their connecting steamers for the transportation of, and will transport from New York to San Francisco and from San Francisco to New York all and only such passengers and such freight as may be obtained under rates fixed by said party of the first part, to an amount as to freight not exceeding six hundred tons of two thousand pounds each, in case it runs two steamers per month, and four hundred tons, in case it runs three steamers per month, upon any one steamer, it being understood that the deficiency of excess of said six hundred tons or said four hundred tons, respectively, of cargo upon any one steamer may be added to or taken from, as the case may be, the cargo of any other vessel sailing in same direction within the same calendar month, the intent being that the steamship company shall carry monthly an average of six hundred tons per vessel in case two steamers per month are run, or a monthly average of four hundred tons per vessel in case three steamers per month are run.

All above steamers to be first class and equal to those now maintained, and in case of the loss of a steamer or its withdrawal for any cause, the Pacific Mail Steamship Company shall as soon as possible furnish a steamer of equal capacity and rating. In the event of failure on the part of said steamship company to furnish proper and adequate facilities for the transportation of at least one thousand two hundred tons of freight each way per month, at the rate of at least four hundred tons per vessel, then the guaranty herein provided for shall be reduced pro rata.

The steamship company is to bear and pay all the expenses and charges of every kind of transporting such goods, passengers, and freight from New York to San Francisco and from San Francisco to New York, including all charges and expenses of every kind in the ports of New York and San Francisco, and all supplies of passengers with food and sleeping accommodation, giving them proper accommodation according to class, and to continue to use all efforts to obtain first class and other passengers as heretofore.

Third. The understanding and intention of this agreement is, that the party of the first part shall, through agents appointed by itself, have entire and exclusive control of all the through business of the said steamship company between New York and San Francisco each way, and that no through freight or passengers shall be taken except at prices to be fixed by the party of the first part and by its consent, it being understood that said control shall be exercised through the established agencies of said steamship company. If the said steamship company shall have room or capacity for more than six hundred tons, in the event of its running two steamers per month each way, or for more than four hundred tons, in the event of its running three steamers per month each way, of through freight on any steamer, and the party of the first part shall desire to fill it, the said party of the first part shall be at liberty to do so at rates fixed jointly by duly authorized representatives of the parties hereto, the party of the first part to have one-half of the freights on such excess and the steamship company the other half.

Fourth. The Pacific Mail Steamship Company shall render to the party of the first part an account or statement of the transactions for through business of each month on or before the tenth day of the succeeding month, showing the amount claimed to be due from the party of the first part under this agreement, and on or before the thirtieth day of the succeeding month the chairman of the party of the first part shall draw his draft in favor of the Pacific Mail Steamship Company upon each of the railroad companies constituting the party of the first part for the portion payable by it to said steamship company on account of the aggregate amount payable by the party of the first part to the said steamship company according to the foregoing provisions hereof. The portions of such aggregate amount payable from time to time by the respective companies forming the party of the first part shall be such as has been or may be fixed or prescribed among themselves; and each of the said companies forming the party of the first part shall be liable for its own portion of such aggregate amount, but none of such companies shall be liable for the portion payable by the others or any other of such companies.

Provided, nevertheless, that in the event of default in payment by any one or more of the companies constituting the party of the first part of its proportion herein provided for, it shall be optional with the party of the second part to terminate this agreement on giving ten days' notice to the party of the first part through its chairman.

The party of the first part, or any other companies constituting the same, may, at any time on demand, examine the books and accounts of the said steamship company for the purpose of obtaining full details as to freight and passengers transported by said steamship company under this agreement and verifying the accounts and statements of the steamship company.

Fifth. It is mutually understood and agreed that this contract shall be deemed to have commenced on the first day of October, 1889, and to include the earnings from through business on steamers sailing on and after that date, and as to each and all of the foregoing provisions shall continue in force thereafter until ninety days after written notice of the intention to terminate the same shall have been given by either party to the other, with this exception, that if the exclusive contract between the said steamship company and the Panama Railroad Company, so far as it refers to the business of the steamship company between San Francisco and New York, is broken or changed in any respect, or if any other competing line by rail or vessel shall be established between the waters of the Atlantic and Pacific Oceans, either overland or via the Isthmus of Panama, that shall affect the through business, concerning which this agreement is made, then the said party of the first part may abrogate and terminate this agreement at any time or not, as it may elect.

Sixth. In regard to the freight and passengers received by the steamship company at San Francisco, for transportation to Europe via Panama, it is understood that the class of business to be taken and the rates to be charged thereon shall be the subject of conference and mutual agreement between the San Francisco agency of the Pacific Mail Steamship Company and the San Francisco general agent of the party of the first part to the end that the interests of both parties may be fully protected.

In witness whereof the party of the first part has subscribed its name hereto by its chairman, and the said steamship company has caused its corporate seal to be hereto annexed, attested by its secretary, and its name to be signed hereto by its president, the day and year first above written.

[SEAL.]

JAMES SMITH,
Chairman Transcontinental Association.

GEORGE J. GOULD,
President Pacific Mail Steamship Company.

Attest:

JOS. HELLEN,
Secretary pro tem.

Senator MORGAN. I see that it is signed by James Smith, chairman Transcontinental Association, on the one part, and George J. Gould, president Pacific Mail Steamship Company, on the other part.

Mr. HUNTINGTON. Yes.

Senator MORGAN. Your guaranty appears to be that the gross earnings upon through freight and passengers between New York and San Francisco to be provided to this steamship company by the railroad companies shall be $75,000 per month. These railroad companies constituted the Transcontinental Association?

Mr. HUNTINGTON. Yes.

Senator MORGAN (reading from the contract):

All the gross earnings of said steamers from through business between New York and San Francisco each way shall go to and belong and be payable to said party of the first part or credited upon its said guaranty to said steamship company. In consideration of said guaranty of said party of the first part, the said Pacific Mail Steamship Company promises and agrees that it will, at its own cost and expense, dispatch and run from the port of New York for Aspinwall not more than three nor less than two through steamers per month, and not more than three nor less than two steamers connecting therewith from Panama to San Francisco, and from the port of San Francisco or Panama not more than three nor less than two through steamers per month, and not more than three nor less than two steamers connecting therewith from Aspinwall to New York, and that said steamship company will permit said party of the first part to fix the rates at which all their freight between New York and San Francisco and of passengers shall be transported by the vessels of the steamship company from the port of New York to San Francisco, and from the port of San Francisco to the port of New York, and will furnish room on each of said steamers from New York and San Francisco, respectively, and their connecting steamers for the transportation of and will transport from New York to San Francisco and from San Francisco to New York all and only such passengers and such freight as may be obtained under rates fixed by said party of the first part to an amount as to freight not exceeding 600 tons of 2,000 pounds each in case it runs two steamers per month, and 400 tons in case it runs three steamers per month upon any one steamer, the intent being * * * that the steamship company shall carry monthly an average of 600 tons per vessel in case two steamers per month are run or a monthly average of 400 tons per vessel in case three steamers per month are run.

* * * * * * *

The understanding and intention of this agreement is that the party of the first part shall, through agents appointed by itself, have entire and exclusive control of all the other business of the said steamship company between New York and San Francisco each way, and that no through freight or passengers shall be taken except at prices to be fixed by the party of the first part and by its consent, it being understood that said control shall be exercised through the established agencies of said steamship company.

Now, Mr. Huntington, without going through this paper, it appears to be a contract under which the party of the first part, representing several railroad companies, has a right to fix the freight upon a certain amount of tonnage on each of those vessels?

Mr. HUNTINGTON. Yes; that is it.

Senator MORGAN. Which was the largest amount—occupying nearly the entire carrying capacity of the ship. The object of that was to be enabled, in competition with those steamships, to keep up the rate of charges on your railroads and on the railroads represented in this agreement without cutting.

Mr. HUNTINGTON. Yes; the object was to make us able to get paying rates.

Senator MORGAN. And this arrangement between the railroad companies represented by Mr. Smith, and the steamship company represented by Mr. Gould, put it in the power of Mr. Smith and of the roads he represented to fix the rate of freights both on the steamship line and on the overland lines to any figure they saw proper?

Mr. HUNTINGTON. Any price that was fair and right.

Senator MORGAN. He was not controlled in any way by that consideration.

Mr. HUNTINGTON. We could not raise the rates upon grain tonnage, which is a low-priced tonnage, and which goes around Cape Horn.

Senator MORGAN. It goes that way now?

Mr. HUNTINGTON. Yes; tonnage where the cost per pound is small.

Senator MORGAN. Was not the effect of this arrangement to put all the freight south of San Francisco, going and coming, under the control of these particular railroads?

Mr. HUNTINGTON. It extended over the whole coast. The Northern Pacific reached Seattle, the Union Pacific reached Portland, the Oregon and California reached Tehama Bay, and the Atchison and Topeka ran to San Diego.

Senator MORGAN. How did it happen that this combination of railroads and steamship lines found it expedient to abandon their contract?

Mr. HUNTINGTON. I suppose it was on account of the cutting of rates. That is why these agreements have always gone up.

Senator MORGAN. Cutting of rates by whom?

Mr. HUNTINGTON. By some of the railroad lines.

Senator MORGAN. Not by some of those included in the agreement?

Mr. HUNTINGTON. I think so. If they had all agreed upon a fair rate, and had all held to it, it was a very fair and proper thing to have done. I did not have much to do with the making of that agreement.

Senator MORGAN. The companies that came into the agreement—some of them—broke away from it?

Mr. HUNTINGTON. I assume that, because notice was given to withdraw from the agreement.

Senator MORGAN. The withdrawal was not caused by competition from the Canadian railroads or from the Northern Pacific?

Mr. HUNTINGTON. No; the Northern Pacific was in the agreement, and I think the Canadian Pacific was in it.

Senator MORGAN. Then it was not competition from that quarter?

Mr. HUNTINGTON. It may have been. There was a screw loose somewhere.

Senator MORGAN. It was not the competition from the companies that were outside of the agreement, but from those that were inside, that caused you to have to break it up?

Mr. HUNTINGTON. I should say so.

Senator MORGAN. Did the Panama Railroad have anything to do with causing you to throw up this agreement?

Mr. HUNTINGTON. I think not.

Senator MORGAN. Did not that railroad company raise the rates for transportation across the Isthmus?

Mr. HUNTINGTON. The Isthmus rates we had nothing to do with.

Senator MORGAN. Did not the Panama Company notify you, or notify Mr. Smith, that it would no longer be bound by that agreement?

Mr. HUNTINGTON. I think not.

Senator MORGAN. And that they would levy their usual charges?

Mr. HUNTINGTON. I think not.

Senator MORGAN. And was not the result of it that you had a lawsuit in New York about it?

Mr. HUNTINGTON. No; we never had a lawsuit about it.

Senator MORGAN. Was not a suit in contemplation?

Mr. HUNTINGTON. That was on an old contract of 1872; not for San Francisco business at all, but on the west coast of the coast of Mexico and with the small republics south of it,

Senator MORGAN. That was a different contract?

Mr. HUNTINGTON. Yes.

Senator MORGAN. How long did that 1872 contract run?

Mr. HUNTINGTON. I think it ran some twenty years.

Senator MORGAN. Who had that contract?

Mr. HUNTINGTON. It was between the Pacific Mail Steamship Company, by Col. W. Park, I think, on the one side, and the Panama Railroad Company on the other. I do not know who its president was.

Senator MORGAN. Was the Central Pacific interested in that contract which ran for nearly twenty years?

Mr. HUNTINGTON. No; none of the Pacific roads had anything to do with it.

Senator MORGAN. That was a contract for the purpose of keeping down competition?

Mr. HUNTINGTON. Not between San Francisco and New York. As I remember, they gave a certain price over the isthmus—a certain price per month.

Senator MORGAN. So that neither the Central Pacific or the Southern Pacific had any connection with that agreement?

Mr. HUNTINGTON. Not at all. It was before the Southern Pacific was commenced. It was in 1872.

Senator MORGAN. Did you make your money back which you paid to this steamship company, $75,000 a month?

Mr. HUNTINGTON. I suppose so.

Senator MORGAN. You heard no complaint about not making it back?

Mr. HUNTINGTON. I never heard any. It seemed a proper thing to do to get fair rates.

Senator MORGAN. How much money, in the aggregate, was paid to this steamship company presided over by Mr. George J. Gould during the continuance of this contract?

Mr. HUNTINGTON. $75,000 a month, and it ran about three years. That would make $2,700,000.

Senator MORGAN. You collected that, of course, out of the people of California?

Mr. HUNTINGTON. If we did the business, we collected our freight upon it. We always do so before we deliver the goods.

Senator MORGAN. So that the loss of that sum fell upon them?

Mr. HUNTINGTON. I do not understand that there would be a loss in paying honest freights on goods.

Senator MORGAN. If a man can buy a thing to-day at $20, and if the price to-morrow is $30, and he must have it, he loses $10. The people of California had no market that they could reach except by water or by land. They were confined to one of those means of reaching the market, and if they had to pay $75,000 a month for the privilege of carrying their goods on the railroads, I would suppose that they lost $75,000 a month.

Mr. HUNTINGTON. The price of land in California has gone up tenfold. That seems to have a bearing upon this same thing. We have got several millions of dollars in shares of the company, and we haven't got a dividend on them for twenty years.

Senator MORGAN. The price of mineral lands has been very much increased?

Mr. HUNTINGTON. I never owned a share of mining stock in my life, and I do not know about mineral lands. I know that we never got any dividends on shares in a property where we have put a great deal of honest money.

Senator MORGAN. Do you say that you have never got any dividend on the shares of the Central Pacific?

Mr. HUNTINGTON. No; I say the Southern Pacific.

Senator MORGAN. Then you have received no dividend on the shares of the Southern Pacific?

Mr. HUNTINGTON. No.

Senator MORGAN. From the beginning down to date?

Mr. HUNTINGTON. No. I remember that at one time Senator Stanford, learning that we had made $2,000,000 on our capital of a hundred millions, proposed to pay a dividend of 2 per cent, but I said no; that the money was going into rolling stock.

Senator MORGAN. So that instead of dividing this money you put it into railroad property?

Mr. HUNTINGTON. We improved the property.

Senator MORGAN. Still, the shares of stock ought to have had some increase in the last twenty years.

Mr. HUNTINGTON. Just as land has had. Land which twenty years ago was worth, in the neighborhood of these railroad lines, $1.50 an acre, is now worth $100 an acre. That does not look as if we were hard upon the farmer.

Senator MORGAN. Who are the real owners of the Southern Pacific Railroad now?

Mr. HUNTINGTON. There are a great many.

Senator MORGAN. Who are the large ones?

Mr. HUNTINGTON. Three or four parties have most of the shares. There are a great many holders in California. These are the same parties who began railroad improvement by building the Central Pacific. They have been in it steadily for thirty-five years.

Senator MORGAN. They always kept together?

Mr. HUNTINGTON. They always kept right on.

Senator MORGAN. So that, if they did not divide profits in the form of money, they did it it in the development of their property?

Mr. HUNTINGTON. We kept building, and shall probably continue to the end.

Senator MORGAN. So your roads have increased in the value of the property and not in money?

Mr. HUNTINGTON. That is a fair statement. We must have a good permanent way and a good rolling stock, or we can not do any business.

Senator MORGAN. How much money have you put into railroading in California derived from other parts of your fortune or from other business?

Mr. HUNTINGTON. I have been in the railroading business largely and have made a good deal of money. The State of Virginia gave me a railroad. It fell into my hands very much because others who undertook it failed before they reached a market. The road from Richmond, Va., to Covington cost twenty millions. I finished it to Cincinnati, and when it was all done it represented a little more than $70,000,000 in stock. Then I got the Big Sandy line. They told me they would give me that road if I would finish it, and I did. I made a first-class property of it and made a good deal of money by it. Then there was the Chesapeake and Ohio Railroad, 400 miles from Lewiston to Memphis. That road remained unfinished so many years, without iron being put upon it, that the bridges rotted and fell down before I took the road in hand. I took that road when its bonds were selling in Frankfort and Amsterdam at 18 and 20 cents on the dollar, and I bought a good many of the bonds at 18 and 20 cents on the dollar. I bought the stock almost by the pound; it appeared to be good for nothing. I bought the road and finished it and made a first-class road of it, and I sold the road at what it was worth. When I got from 95 to 109 for my bonds—and there were a good many of them, too—I sold them cheaper, considering the value of the road, than when I got them at 25 cents, and they were not worth that. So that I sold them cheaper than I bought them. I bought the Kentucky Central road in about the same way. It was an old road, pretty well run down, and I built it. From Paris to Livingston, 70 miles, it was a very heavy road to build. Other parties had begun to build it, but they got out of money, and I bought the shares for cash, many of them at 10 and 12 per cent. I completed that road and sold my shares—45,000 of them—for 55. So with various roads. Chattaroy road, running up the Big Sandy River, is another of the roads that I took in hand. I commenced to build that road. I paid $54,000 to put 2 miles of it in order crossing Blaine Creek. I put in a new bridge and made a straight line of it without grade, and that cost me $54,000. I bought a road through the canyon, paying cash for it, and I sold that seven years ago. I had thirteen roads on this side of the Mississippi and south of the Ohio and Potomac. I built an elevated road in Louisville. Nearly all of these roads were broken-down, worthless property, and I made first-class property of them, selling them for really cheaper than I bought them, because they were paying interest on everything when I sold, and they were absolutely worth nothing when I bought. I picked up the old Atlantic and Pacific road and bought it for almost nothing. I could have bought the whole of it, land grant and everything, for a trifle when it reached Vinita, but our people said that the thing was too big. I put all the profit that I made in these great works into railroads in California, except what I put into the shipyard at Newport News.

Senator MORGAN. So that you had the capacity to build all these great works because your credit was very good?

Mr. HUNTINGTON. My credit was good, and I was entitled to have a good credit. I worked many hours a day, and at nights when necessary. All that money has gone west of the Mississippi, and it is, most of it, in shares on which I have no dividends.

Senator MORGAN. In what companies?

Mr. HUNTINGTON. In all the companies.

Senator MORGAN. They are summed up in the eight millions of the shares of the Kentucky company, to which you transferred your stock in the other companies?

Mr. HUNTINGTON. No, I sold the shares and took the money and invested it here and there.

Senator MORGAN. Do you mean that you took all this immense accumulation of wealth and invested it in railroads west of the Mississippi?

Mr. HUNTINGTON. I bought shares.

Senator MORGAN. Do you own them now?

Mr. HUNTINGTON. I own the Southern Pacific shares.

Senator MORGAN. You said yesterday that you had exchanged the shares you held in those various companies west of New Orleans for shares in the Southern Pacific Company.

Mr. HUNTINGTON. That was right; I say it now.

Senator MORGAN. After making this accumulation in the East in all these railroad transactions, you took your money out West, and took those shares and exchanged them for stock of the Southern Pacific?

Mr. HUNTINGTON. Yes.

Senator MORGAN. So that eight millions represents what you put into that company?

Mr. HUNTINGTON. I did not say that.

Senator MORGAN. You said that you had eight millions in stock, and that you took it to the Kentucky company and expended it for warrant stock of that company.

Mr. HUNTINGTON. It did not all go there. We have a large mileage in Mexico.

Senator MORGAN. All this accumulation was very probably based on your credit.

Mr. HUNTINGTON. You may say that. It was not all done at one time. One road was sold after another.

Senator MORGAN. But the basis of your credit came from the handling of those subsidy bonds of the United States and of the first-mortgage bonds of the Central Pacific.

Mr. HUNTINGTON. I had a considerable amount of paper out in New York in 1837. I went to Mr. Platt, No. 12 Maiden Lane, and paid him what I owed him, about $3,000, and he said, "Mr. Huntington, that is all right. Perhaps you would like to know that you are the only man who has paid a note to me for the last three months."

Senator MORGAN. Still, I do not think you were a very rich man when you got hold of this railroad in California, and I should like to know just how much you were worth when you took up the building of that road.

Mr. HUNTINGTON. I can not tell you.

Senator MORGAN. Were you worth a million of dollars?

Mr. HUNTINGTON. We ought to have been.

Senator MORGAN. Who are "we"?

Mr. HUNTINGTON. I question whether I was worth a million dollars.

Senator MORGAN. You surely know what you were worth at the time, or something like it.

Mr. HUNTINGTON. No, it was largely in property, and you can not tell what property is worth until you sell it.

Senator MORGAN. Your property was not worth much as a basis of credit if you could not realize upon it.

Mr. HUNTINGTON. A man's credit is not so much on what a man has got as upon what he is able to do.

Senator MORGAN. You think that the opportunity afforded to you by this contract between the Central Pacific and the Contract and Finance Company did not amount to so much in your career, but that your success was due to your genius?

Mr. HUNTINGTON. I would not call it genius; I would call it an untiring application to business, working at all hours of the day and night, and always practicing a very strict economy.

Senator MORGAN. You came out with $119,000,000 on the face value of bonds and stocks for which you had expended probably $70,000,000 or $80,000,000 in making the road. Is that your statement?

Mr. HUNTINGTON. The $119,000,000 that you speak of was not worth the $90,000,000 that it cost to build the road.

Senator MORGAN. So that you lost money by building the road?

Mr. HUNTINGTON. We did, until the securities appreciated; and then we paid all our debts and had something to the good, not a great deal. If anybody had given me $1,000,000 I would not have done it right over again.

Senator MORGAN. It was there that your genius came to your relief—

the Government not having furnished you with enough money to build the road.

Mr. HUNTINGTON. No, it was a kind of staying power. I was not as rich when we ran our locomotives from Promontory Point to Ogden as when we started to build the road, because we did not have enough out of all these assets to pay our debts. I understand these things pretty well.

Senator MORGAN. I think I can understand them, too, if I can get them all down in proper sequence, but I have not been able to do that. When did the Central Pacific enter under the control of the Kentucky company?

Mr. HUNTINGTON. I do not know. That is easily ascertained. I should say ten or twelve years ago.

Senator MORGAN. It went in under lease?

Mr. HUNTINGTON. Yes.

Senator MORGAN. Have you got a copy of that lease?

Mr. HUNTINGTON. I have not.

Senator MORGAN. Is it easily accessible?

Mr. HUNTINGTON. I think so.

Mr. TWEED. It is published among the proceedings of the Interstate Commerce Commission, and it has also been published in the report of the Commissioner of Railroads. It is a public document.

Senator MORGAN (to Mr. Huntington). At the time that this lease was made, did you have a meeting of the board of directors of the Central Pacific?

Mr. HUNTINGTON. I should say so; I am quite sure we had. I do not know that I was there.

Senator MORGAN. Did the board of directors authorize the making of that lease?

Mr. HUNTINGTON. I should say so.

Senator MORGAN. You do not know as a legal question whether the Central Pacific Company had a right to do that under its charter from the United States Government?

Mr. HUNTINGTON. No, I do not; but we are partially working under the charter from the State of California. We have a right under that charter, I am pretty sure.

Senator MORGAN. So that you derive the powers of your corporation from the California charter, as it has been incorporated in and amended by the United States charter?

The CHAIRMAN. Would the incorporation of those powers in the United States statute interfere with any powers exercised by that company prior to that act?

Mr. HUNTINGTON. No.

Senator MORGAN. Then you had authority under your State charter to make this lease—for ninety-nine years, was it not?

Mr. HUNTINGTON. No; as I recollect, it was a contract, to run for five years, and then there could be a readjustment if it worked hard ship for either company.

Senator MORGAN. But the lease ran for ninety-nine years?

Mr. HUNTINGTON. I do not think so; I am not sure.

Senator MORGAN. I think you so stated in your examination.

Mr. HUNTINGTON. No, I think not. There was to be a readjustment at the end of five years; that is my recollection.

Senator MORGAN. So that the contract would run indefinitely?

Mr. HUNTINGTON. I think it ran ten years, and that it then was readjusted.

Senator MORGAN. What I wanted to know was whether the board of directors authorized the making of this contract by any resolution?

Mr. HUNTINGTON. I think it did.

Senator MORGAN. Who made the contract?

Mr. HUNTINGTON. I should say it was made by the boards of directors of the two companies.

Senator MORGAN. Did you make it?

Mr. HUNTINGTON. I think I did.

Senator MORGAN. Did you sign it?

Mr. HUNTINGTON. I am not sure. The vice-president or myself, no doubt, did sign it.

Senator MORGAN. Were you the president of the Central Pacific at that time?

Mr. HUNTINGTON. No; I was the vice-president. I have been vice-president of the company since its organization.

Senator MORGAN. You say that the lease ran on for five years, and that it was then changed?

Mr. HUNTINGTON. I am not sure of that; but I am very sure that there is a provision of that kind in the lease.

Senator MORGAN. I want to know about the fact.

Mr. HUNTINGTON. I am not able to say.

Senator MORGAN. You do not know whether there was any change made at the end of the first five years?

Mr. HUNTINGTON. I do not know; I am inclined to think there was none.

Senator MORGAN. How much was to be paid for the annual rent of the Central Pacific, under the contract?

Mr. HUNTINGTON. That I can not say. The Southern Pacific had to pay the interest on the bonds, to take care of the property, and to pay the current expenses.

Senator MORGAN. Do you mean the interest on the debt to the Government?

Mr. HUNTINGTON. No; but the interest due on the bonds.

Mr. LITTLER. The Southern Pacific paid the Central Pacific $1,200,000 a year rent.

The CHAIRMAN. The rent to be increased afterwards?

Mr. LITTLER. There was a sliding scale in the lease. The lease is set out in full in our report (the report of the United States Pacific Railroad Commission).

The CHAIRMAN. What you meant by a sliding scale was that the two companies had the right to increase or reduce the rent?

Mr. LITTLER. Yes.

The CHAIRMAN. And the Southern Pacific did reduce the rent?

Mr. LITTLER. I will not state that.

Mr. HUNTINGTON. I do not think the Southern Pacific reduced the rent. It changed the terms of the lease, as I remember.

Senator MORGAN. You say that this lease continued in operation for ten years?

Mr. HUNTINGTON. I think so. If I wanted to know I would send for the contract. It seems to me that the contract could not be changed except at the end of every period of five years; I do not think that there was a readjustment at the end of the first five years.

Senator MORGAN. Did the Kentucky company undertake to keep the road in repair during the first five years?

Mr. HUNTINGTON. I do not know what the Southern Pacific Company really did do, but it is all set forth in the contract; I can not carry these things in my head, and it is not necessary. I never bother myself to carry things in my head when I know that I can send into another room and get the information.

Senator MORGAN. At the end of the first five years was any change made in the stipulations of the lease?

Mr. HUNTINGTON. I can not say. If you will excuse me, Senator, I have answered that three times.

Senator MORGAN. But you know whether the amount of the rent was reduced?

Mr. HUNTINGTON. No; I am pretty sure it was not; but I can not say positively.

Senator MORGAN. At what time was this contract to terminate?

Mr. HUNTINGTON. That I can not say.

Senator MORGAN. Has it ever been terminated?

Mr. HUNTINGTON. We are working under a different contract; it may be the same, and it may not be.

Senator MORGAN. You do not recollect about that?

Mr. HUNTINGTON. No; I should have thought that it was changed, and that there was another contract made, but it may not be so.

Senator MORGAN. Was it not changed, and was not the amount stipulated to be paid less than the amount which had been paid previously?

Mr. HUNTINGTON. I think that it was changed so that whatever the Southern Pacific Company made on the Central Pacific over the expenses went to the Central Pacific.

Senator MORGAN. But you do not remember when that change was made?

Mr. HUNTINGTON. No, I do not; I would not naturally remember.

Senator MORGAN. I will read to you a portion of the statement made by you before the Senate Committee on Pacific Railroads on the 6th of February, 1894:

> Senator MORGAN. Who owns the Central Pacific now?
>
> Mr. HUNTINGTON. It belongs to a great number of shareholders; there are so many of them that I do not know who they are; I suppose there are 25,000 of them altogether.
>
> Senator MORGAN. I mean, who has control?
>
> Mr. HUNTINGTON. We control it; that is, the present board of directors, representing over 5,000 shareholders, perhaps.
>
> Senator MORGAN. It has never been transferred, on long lease or otherwise, to any other corporation?
>
> Mr. HUNTINGTON. No. We leased it to the Southern Pacific Company for $1,360,000 (as I have it in my mind now, and I think that is correct), with the proviso that whenever one company was getting the advantage in the contract, at the end of any period of five years the contract could be renewed or changed, or something, so that one company would not be at the expense of the other. This last year it lost considerably. Now the lease is with the Central Pacific, taking all that it earns up to 6 per cent upon the capital, and anything beyond that, which I do not expect to live to see, is divided, half to the Southern Pacific and half to the Central. That is the present lease.
>
> Senator MORGAN. There is a subsisting lease on that road now to another company; what company is that?
>
> Mr. HUNTINGTON. That is the Southern Pacific.
>
> Senator MORGAN. Has the Southern Pacific gone into any scheme of consolidation with any other company?
>
> Mr. HUNTINGTON. The Southern Pacific controls something near 7,000 miles of road by ownership.
>
> Senator MORGAN. Through what corporation has that arrangement been effected?
>
> Mr. HUNTINGTON. The corporation in Kentucky.
>
> Senator MORGAN. Is that still subsisting?
>
> Mr. HUNTINGTON. Yes, sir.
>
> Senator MORGAN. So that the lease which subsists now upon the Central Pacific is under the control of the Kentucky corporation?

Mr. HUNTINGTON. Yes, sir; but they make nothing out of the lease, as I stated, all the earnings going to the Central Pacific.

Senator MORGAN. How long is that lease to last?

Mr. HUNTINGTON. I think it is the old lease, which will expire at the end of five years; but there can be no hardship now, because the Central Pacific gets all that it earns.

Senator MORGAN. What is the outside length of the term of lease?

Mr. HUNTINGTON. Five years; that is, it can be renewed or abrogated at the end of any period of five years.

Senator MORGAN. Every five years for how many years?

Mr. HUNTINGTON. I have not the lease with me, but I think it can be abrogated at the end of any period of five years.

Senator MORGAN. The contract is to run in that way for ninety-nine years, is it not?

Mr. HUNTINGTON. I do not think it is.

Senator MORGAN. It is some very long period, is it not?

Mr. HUNTINGTON. I think not; I think it can be abrogated or changed at the end of any period of five years.

Senator WOLCOTT. How long will it last?

Mr. HUNTINGTON. I suppose if neither party called it would probably last forever; but I think it is subject to change or abrogation by either party at the end of any period of five years.

Senator MORGAN. Then it is a contract for sale, subject to alteration at the end of every period of five years.

Mr. HUNTINGTON. It is hardly a sale; that is, we did not contemplate anything of that kind. We find that the object of the Southern Pacific Company was to save an expense of keeping up the organization of (I think) some forty different roads. Excepting the Central Pacific and one or two others on the main line between Portland, Oreg., and New Orleans, I think the Southern Pacific owns the stock of all the companies; if not all, probably most of them.

Senator MORGAN. What is the name of that Kentucky corporation?

Mr. HUNTINGTON. It is called the Southern Pacific Company.

Senator MORGAN. That controls, really, in the manner you have stated, all of the properties of which you have been speaking?

Mr. HUNTINGTON. All excepting the Central Pacific. The contract can be abrogated, and I will guarantee that that shall make no trouble if my proposition be accepted.

Senator MORGAN. I am speaking of the present legal situation.

Mr. HUNTINGTON. Well, I do not know what the legal situation might be. You can tell by reading a copy of the lease.

Senator MORGAN. Has not the board of directors of the Kentucky company—the Southern Pacific Company—the rightful control over all the properties you have been speaking of here this morning?

Mr. HUNTINGTON. No; I think not the Central Pacific, and I think not the California Pacific.

Senator MORGAN. The point I want to get at is this: Did you find that paying $1,360,000 a year for the lease of the Central Pacific was a losing deal?

Mr. HUNTINGTON. As I recollect, the Southern Pacific lost considerably by it.

Senator MORGAN. How did you ascertain that loss?

Mr. HUNTINGTON. I suppose the bookkeeping shows it.

Senator MORGAN. But how was it ascertained?

Mr. HUNTINGTON. We found that we paid out more than we received.

Senator MORGAN. You paid out $1,360,000 a year, and found that you lost money. You ascertained, I suppose, that the income of the Central Pacific had fallen away during that five years?

Mr. HUNTINGTON. Yes; that was the way of it.

Senator MORGAN. And when the income of the Central Pacific had thus fallen away, you concluded that you would let that company have that and no more, and if the earnings were more than 6 per cent on the capital stock you would divide the surplus with it?

Mr. HUNTINGTON. Yes; that is how I recollect it.

Senator MORGAN. In that period of five years did the earnings of the Kentucky corporation (the Southern Pacific) decrease in like proportion?

Mr. HUNTINGTON. I do not know. I presume that they did.

Senator MORGAN. I do not want presumption. I want to know the facts.

Mr. HUNTINGTON. Well, I can not say whether they did or not; but usually, when the earnings of one road fall off, it is because the business is poor over the whole line. As a rule, if one runs short they all run short.

Senator MORGAN. At the time you consolidated or united all these companies in that Kentucky company you knew the income of each company over and above its fixed charges?

Mr. HUNTINGTON. I presume we did.

Senator MORGAN. And the transfer of the stock that you owned in those companies into this warrant stock of the Kentucky company was based on the calculation that you would get as much money out of that stock as out of the other?

Mr. HUNTINGTON. That was the natural conclusion. It was an operation to make it possible to operate the roads at the lowest rates so as to build up the country through which the roads passed.

Senator MORGAN. To build up the country or to build up the roads?

Mr. HUNTINGTON. To build up the country. What we want to do is to build up the country; and when we increase the traffic, then we begin to make money. I think we would double the business on any one of our roads if we could get the rates down 25 per cent, and we would make more money.

Senator MORGAN. If your object was to build up the country, I suppose you succeeded; for the country is building up rapidly.

Mr. HUNTINGTON. It is to the interest of the company to get a good road, and to build up the country as fast as possible.

Senator MORGAN. Was it not your real, main purpose to make money by economizing?

Mr. HUNTINGTON. We have to do that, or we would not make both ends meet.

Senator MORGAN. Then your object was either to make money or to save money?

Mr. HUNTINGTON. Yes.

Senator MORGAN. I should like to know from you whether your object in making this arrangement with the Central Pacific Company was not to make money?

Mr. HUNTINGTON. Not altogether. Of course we had that object in view in a general way.

Senator MORGAN. Was it in part to make money?

Mr. HUNTINGTON. It was in part to make money, and to build up the country along the road. We thought that in the end that would result satisfactorily.

Senator MORGAN. You worked for glory as well as for money?

Mr. HUNTINGTON. No; I never worked much for glory.

Senator MORGAN. To get down to plain facts, I put the question to you in this form: After you formed this arrangement which was completed in the organization of the Kentucky company, and after you had made this lease of the Central Pacific, did not the income of the Kentucky company increase during the first five years of this lease over the aggregate of the several companies of which it was formed?

Mr. HUNTINGTON. I should suppose it would. I do not recollect the figures; but I should say it would naturally increase, as the facilities for doing business were so much better.

Senator MORGAN. About how much were they increased?

Mr. HUNTINGTON. I do not remember. I do not recollect whether even they did increase; but I think they did.

Senator MORGAN. Was the increase very considerable?

Mr. HUNTINGTON. It goes up and down.

Senator MORGAN. Was it satisfactory?

Mr. HUNTINGTON. Sometimes, probably, it was.

Senator MORGAN. Was it more satisfactory to the parties concerned than the previous arrangement had been by which each company conducted its own business?

Mr. HUNTINGTON. Yes; it was more satisfactory than when these companies—perhaps forty of them—were working separately.

Senator MORGAN. It was more satisfactory and more profitable. How did you ascertain that the Central Pacific, during those first five years, was receiving from the Kentucky company more than it ought to receive?

Mr. HUNTINGTON. We kept, of course, a debit and credit account, and we knew, of course, how things were going.

Senator MORGAN. Was it not in consequence of the fact that the income of the Central Pacific was constantly decreasing, and that during those five years it decreased very materially?

Mr. HUNTINGTON. No; I think not.

Senator MORGAN. Why do you think not?

Mr. HUNTINGTON. I do not know why it should; that is all. I do not pretend to carry these figures in my head.

Senator MORGAN. If the income of the Central Pacific during those first five years did not decrease very materially, what excuse had you for cutting down the amount of money you were paying to it?

Mr. HUNTINGTON. I do not know.

Senator MORGAN. It is all a mystery to you, is it?

Mr. HUNTINGTON. There was some good and sufficient reason. Probably some of the shareholders thought it would be better for them to take the earnings of their road.

Senator MORGAN. Do you not know that, during the first five or ten years of the lease, the income of the Central Pacific continually ran down?

Mr. HUNTINGTON. No, I do not know it; but it is easily ascertained.

Senator MORGAN. Tell us how we can ascertain it.

Mr. HUNTINGTON. I think I can write to California for the figures.

Mr. LITTLER. You will find all these figures in the annual reports of the Central Pacific taken from the books of the company, showing the gross and net earnings of the company from the time it began operations.

Senator MORGAN (to Mr. Littler). Do these reports show an increase or decrease during the first five years of that lease?

Mr. LITTLER. I do not remember.

Senator MORGAN (to Mr. Huntington). I will assume that, during the first five years of this lease, the income of the Central Pacific did run down, and did run down materially. I will assume further, that it was because of this fact, and not because of any burden from the lease with this Kentucky company, that the terms of the contract were changed so that the Central Pacific should not receive any more than it earned. In that intermediate period who actually controlled the freight which came to the Central Pacific from the direction of Oregon and from the direction of the Pacific Ocean, or any other direction in California, and which found its way across the continent through the Central Pacific and the Union Pacific roads?

Mr. HUNTINGTON. These things are usually done by an agreement between the companies interested in the business.

Senator MORGAN. I am not asking what is usually done. I am asking who controlled that business.

Mr. HUNTINGTON. I have very little doubt that that was the way it was done—at agreed rates.

Senator MORGAN. Was it not entirely in the power of this Kentucky company to direct that this freight should pass over the Central Pacific road, or should pass over the Southern Pacific road, just as that company proposed, except shippers otherwise ordered?

Mr. HUNTINGTON. There has been sharp competition, and most of the railroad companies have had their own agents in California seeking business. We did not control that business, because shippers got the best rates they could. I think that half a dozen railroads from Chicago had agents in San Francisco soliciting freight.

Senator MORGAN. The great company which you controlled, running from New Orleans to Portland, Oreg., and having an agent in San Francisco, was trying, I suppose, to get all the freight and all the passengers it could?

Mr. HUNTINGTON. I suppose that our agents were working for business.

Senator MORGAN. That is what they were there for?

Mr. HUNTINGTON. Yes; and all the other companies were working for the same thing.

Senator MORGAN. Who was the agent for the Central Pacific all that time?

Mr. HUNTINGTON. Mr. Stubbs was at the head.

Senator MORGAN. He was not the agent for both companies, was he?

Mr. HUNTINGTON. I do not know.

Senator MORGAN. Who was your agent at that time?

Mr. HUNTINGTON. I do not know; Mr. Gray was at the head of the traffic department there.

Senator MORGAN. You have said that Mr. Stubbs was the freight agent for the Central Pacific. Who was the freight agent for your company?

Mr. HUNTINGTON. I have stated that Mr. Stubbs was at the head of the traffic department for the Southern Pacific, and he may also have been at the head of the traffic department of the Central Pacific; I do not know. There was a Mr. Snurr, a Mr. Platt, and a Mr. Gray.

Senator MORGAN. You had a head agent for both roads?

Mr. HUNTINGTON. I think very likely.

Senator MORGAN. You can not tell who they were?

Mr. HUNTINGTON. No; I have nothing to do with those men.

Senator MORGAN. You have named five or six men. Who was the head man?

Mr. HUNTINGTON. Mr. Stubbs.

Senator MORGAN. For the Central Pacific?

Mr. HUNTINGTON. No; I think for the Southern Pacific, and perhaps for the Central Pacific.

Senator MORGAN. So it rested with Mr. Stubbs to say whether he would send freight over the Southern Pacific road or over the Central Pacific road?

Mr. HUNTINGTON. Perhaps so; but there is a very small percentage of California business which comes to New York. The largest part of the tonnage stops in the Mississippi Valley.

The CHAIRMAN. If it rested with Mr. Stubbs to send freight either by one road or the other, that was simply in reference to unconsigned freight?

Mr. HUNTINGTON. Yes; of course every shipper has the direction of how his freight goes.

The CHAIRMAN. The shippers would be the judges?

Mr. HUNTINGTON. Yes.

Senator MORGAN. We have got to the point where Mr. Stubbs is the freight agent of both roads, and it rested entirely with Mr. Stubbs to say whether freight should go over the Central Pacific or over the Southern Pacific?

Mr. HUNTINGTON. Unless the shippers give directions, with most of the business there, the railroads are looking to see where the freights shall go after they get to Ogden. The Chicago and Burlington, and the Chicago and Rock Island, and the Chicago and Northwestern, and various other companies, are watching for freight.

Senator MORGAN. I am not trying to follow you in your statement. I am trying to get at a particular fact.

Mr. HUNTINGTON. But I want to show you how that business is handled.

Senator MORGAN. I want to know if Mr. Stubbs was the man who had the power, as freight agent of both these roads, to determine whether the freight should go one way or the other, unless it was consigned and was so marked by the shippers?

Mr. HUNTINGTON. I suppose he would have, but the facts are that very little of this trade comes to New York. I suppose he found out what the shippers wanted. We send nearly all the freight over the Central Pacific.

Senator MORGAN. Who employed Mr. Stubbs?

Mr. HUNTINGTON. He was employed by the Central Pacific when the Southern Pacific leased the Central Pacific. He was originally in the employment of the Central Pacific.

Senator MORGAN. Then when the Southern Pacific leased the Central Pacific Mr. Stubbs became an employee of the Southern Pacific, or the Kentucky company?

Mr. HUNTINGTON. Yes.

Senator MORGAN. So that Mr. Stubbs was the actual agent of the Southern Pacific Company and controlled the freight over the Southern Pacific and the Central Pacific at his will, except in the case where the shipper otherwise directed; that was true?

Mr. HUNTINGTON. I should say that that was naturally the case.

Senator MORGAN. Being employed by the Kentucky company, was he there to work against the interests of that company or in favor of them?

Mr. HUNTINGTON. He was there to work in favor of the Kentucky company and of the Central Pacific. Certain things went one way and certain things another, and the shippers, I suppose, nearly all direct their own freight.

Senator MORGAN. You had stock in the Southern Pacific (the Kentucky company) to the amount of probably $10,000,000?

Mr. HUNTINGTON. No, I do not know how much I had.

Senator MORGAN. And in the Central Pacific you had none at all?

Mr. HUNTINGTON. Oh, yes; I had some. I always had stock in the Central Pacific.

Senator MORGAN. How much?

Mr. HUNTINGTON. Four or five thousand shares.

Senator MORGAN. But your great interest was in the direction of the Southern Pacific?

Mr. HUNTINGTON. I had more money in the shares of the Southern Pacific than in the shares of the Central Pacific.

Senator MORGAN. You had more money in every way?

Mr. HUNTINGTON. I had no money excepting the shares.

Senator MORGAN. Had it not been one of your leading purposes in building that Southern Pacific road, and in getting steamers across the Atlantic, to give that road all the advantage you could?

Mr. HUNTINGTON. I have had an ambition to get a European trade at a price which would pay our fruit growers to send their fruit to western Europe. That has been an ambition of mine for a good many years.

Senator MORGAN. And your ambition (that is to say, your interest, stimulated by your pride) had led you to be too warmly a friend and advocate for business on the Southern Pacific?

Mr. HUNTINGTON. Not for any but legitimate trade.

Senator MORGAN. For any trade which you could get?

Mr. HUNTINGTON. We take goods on that line.

Senator MORGAN. It is a very much longer line than the line of the Central Pacific, is it not?

Mr. HUNTINGTON. The Central Pacific is the shortest line to New York.

Senator MORGAN. I am speaking of the line between New Orleans and Portland.

Mr. HUNTINGTON. The Southern Pacific does not do much business from Portland.

Senator MORGAN. It is farther from San Francisco to New Orleans than from San Francisco to Ogden, is it not?

Mr. HUNTINGTON. Oh, yes.

Senator MORGAN. Very much farther?

Mr. HUNTINGTON. Yes; twice as far.

Senator MORGAN. So that the long haul was over the Southern Pacific line?

Mr. HUNTINGTON. Yes.

Senator MORGAN. And it was to your interest, was it not, to have the long haul?

Mr. HUNTINGTON. It might be, or it might not be. In the article of fruit, that nearly all went the other way.

Senator MORGAN. If you had found that Mr. Stubbs had set himself to work to divert freight from the Southern Pacific and to send it across the Central Pacific you would have dismissed him, would you not?

Mr. HUNTINGTON. No, I should not. I do not know why I should. He is there to attend to that business.

Senator MORGAN. Would it not be because he was making you lose money all the time?

Mr. HUNTINGTON. Not necessarily.

Senator MORGAN. Would it not be a losing business for the Southern Pacific to have an agent in San Francisco who would divert freights from that road and send them by the Central Pacific?

Mr. HUNTINGTON. There are a good many things which go over that way. The Central Pacific has carried more than 50 per cent of all the business from San Francisco—50 per cent of the business on all the railroad lines, including the connection with Portland, Puget Sound, and Seattle.

Senator MORGAN. Was not the Southern Pacific in competition with the Central Pacific at the time that this lease was binding and in force?

Mr. HUNTINGTON. To a certain extent, yes.

Senator MORGAN. They were competing roads?

Mr. HUNTINGTON. To a certain extent.

Senator MORGAN. As much so as any other roads?

Mr. HUNTINGTON. No; I should think not. They might cut rates and all that against each other.

Senator MORGAN. Was not that competition the real reason why the income of the Central Pacific ran down so much that the Southern Pacific could not afford to pay it $1,300,000 a year?

Mr. HUNTINGTON. No; I do not think so.

Senator MORGAN. What was the real reason?

Mr. HUNTINGTON. The general shrinkage in rates. Properties have gone down steadily.

Senator MORGAN. Did the general shrinkage of rates affect the Central Pacific any more than it affected the Southern Pacific?

Mr. HUNTINGTON. I should think not.

Senator MORGAN. Then how could it be the general shrinkage of rates which reduced the income of the Central Pacific and did not reduce the income of the Southern Pacific?

Mr. HUNTINGTON. If that is a fact I can not account for it.

Senator MORGAN. Was it not your interest, and the interest of every man concerned in the Kentucky company, to get trade away from the Central Pacific and to bring it over this line?

Mr. HUNTINGTON. No, I think not; we worked those properties so as to do the fair and proper thing by each. A considerable part of our tonnage which we take from New York over the Southern Pacific is low-priced tonnage. Such things as nails, pig iron, bar iron, and the like, we take from New York through to the coast. It is on these low-priced articles that we have competed with the vessels round Cape Horn. The railroads from New York are very strong companies, and we have to work in harmony with them, otherwise, and if we took what did not legitimately belong to the Southern Pacific, these companies would cut rates all to pieces.

Senator MORGAN. Does any part of the traffic which you bring out on these steamers from New York to New Orleans, or from across the Atlantic to New Orleans, and thence to San Francisco, go across the Central Pacific?

Mr. HUNTINGTON. No, it can not reach the Central Pacific. The freight of a steamer coming to New Orleans from Europe can hardly find its way up the Central Pacific; it does not belong there.

Senator MORGAN. So that all the advantages of the line of about twenty steamers between New Orleans and New York, and across the Atlantic Ocean, go to the competing line and not to the Central Pacific?

Mr. HUNTINGTON. The stuff which we mostly direct to New Orleans from western Europe is, I think, generally consigned through, and goes through all the way on the Southern Pacific. I do not know any particular business from western Europe which we bid for.

Senator MORGAN. I am speaking about the business between New York and San Francisco by steamers which land at New Orleans, where the business takes your railroad lines.

Mr. HUNTINGTON. We pick up a good deal of business along tide water, but we can not get more than about just so much.

Senator MORGAN. The advantage of all of this business goes to the Southern Pacific, which competes with the Central Pacific?

Mr. HUNTINGTON. Yes. It competes with it like all the other lines, but not to the same extent. The great through tonnage which is picked up is west of the Alleghanies.

Senator MORGAN. You have been vice-president of the Central Pacific from the time it was built until to-day. State something which you have ever done to increase the freights and travel on the Central Pacific road.

Mr. HUNTINGTON. There are probably a dozen roads to New York that have through connection with San Francisco, and all of them solicit that business. We have one agent in New York, and the New York Central has one and more, and the Pennsylvania has one, and the Baltimore and Ohio has one.

Senator MORGAN. I am speaking of any particular efforts which you have made to increase the traffic of the Central Pacific Railroad Company.

Mr. HUNTINGTON. I never go out soliciting trade.

Senator MORGAN. My question is not as narrow as that. My question is, What have you done as vice-president of the Central Pacific in order to increase the traffic on that road?

Mr. HUNTINGTON. We have our agents, who take business.

Senator MORGAN. I want to know what particular effort you have made.

Mr. HUNTINGTON. We depend largely for business on these other roads. There is no interest which we could have quite equal to that of the Pennsylvania or the New York Central.

Senator MORGAN. I understand you, by your evasion of my question, to mean that you have not taken any steps; that you have not, as vice-president of the Central Pacific, taken any particular steps to increase the traffic between San Francisco and the Central Pacific?

Mr. HUNTINGTON. Well, I have not taken any steps to increase it the other way. I did everything I could; I put the best rolling stock that we could have on the road, and the Central Pacific is the best surfaced road in the United States. That is all that the executive officer of a road can do.

Senator MORGAN. I shall just assume that your evasion of the question means that you have not done anything.

Mr. HUNTINGTON. I have not intended to evade the question. The executive department of a railroad company has nothing to do but to keep its property in the best possible condition to do the business. There is no better surfaced road in the United States than the Central Pacific.

Senator MORGAN. You have stated that a good many times; thirty or forty times. Are you an officer of the Kentucky company?

Mr. HUNTINGTON. Yes.

Senator MORGAN. What office do you hold in that company?

Mr. HUNTINGTON. I am its president.

Senator MORGAN. What have you done in behalf of that company, as its president, to extend its traffic?

Mr. HUNTINGTON. I have kept the road in first-rate condition.

Senator MORGAN. Is that all?

Mr. HUNTINGTON. That is all.

Senator MORGAN. I thought you made rather a boast of it that you had built twenty ships for that line.

Mr. HUNTINGTON. No; I said there were twenty ships on that line.

Senator MORGAN. Did you not say that you had made contracts for building them?

Mr. HUNTINGTON. No; I said that I had built four of them.

Senator MORGAN. And that you had made contracts also for the pur pose of extending the trade of the Southern Pacific across the Atlantic Ocean direct?

Mr. HUNTINGTON. Yes; I think Mr. Hutchinson has done it under my orders.

Senator MORGAN. Do you not claim credit for establishing that line of twenty steamers?

Mr. HUNTINGTON. No; that line of steamers has been running thirty years.

Senator MORGAN. Did you not claim credit for it yesterday?

Mr. HUNTINGTON. No; I claimed credit for the good condition of all the property, and I said that we had some very fine steamers running between New York and New Orleans.

Senator MORGAN. That is not any answer. Answer me whether or not you did not yesterday claim credit for having established, in behalf of the Southern Pacific (the Kentucky company), a line of steamers between New York and New Orleans, and also one across the Atlantic Ocean?

Mr. HUNTINGTON. I might have taken some credit for it, and probably I am entitled to some; but the line across the Atlantic is to send goods to Europe at certain seasons of the year, particularly during the cotton season.

Senator MORGAN. Were not both these steamship arrangements made by your personal assistance?

Mr. HUNTINGTON. Not the arrangement for the European line; Mr. Hutchinson did that.

Senator MORGAN. Under your direction?

Mr. HUNTINGTON. No; I had been trying to get a line of steamers there for a number of years, but Mr. Hutchinson said that he thought the best way was to charter steamers during certain parts of the year.

Senator MORGAN. To sum the matter up, have you not been very active and efficient in extending the trade of the Southern Pacific (the Kentucky company) both by land and sea, and more particularly by sea, between New York and New Orleans and across the Atlantic Ocean?

Mr. HUNTINGTON. Yes; I have been endeavoring for a long time to get a good line from New Orleans to Europe.

Senator MORGAN. That was in the interest of your Southern Pacific Company?

Mr. HUNTINGTON. Yes; to a certain extent.

Senator MORGAN. Being vice-president of the Central Pacific Company and president of the Kentucky company, you have bestowed your energies and abilities (admittedly very great) on the betterment and improvement of the condition of the Southern Pacific line, and you can not state what you have done as vice-president of the other corporation to help it at all?

Mr. HUNTINGTON. I kept the road in first-rate condition, putting in iron bridges where we had wooden ones, and ballasting the road.

Senator MORGAN. Have you done that, or has it been done by your subordinate officers?

Mr. HUNTINGTON. It has been done under my general direction.

Senator MORGAN. Have you kept the Southern Pacific road in as good a condition?

Mr. HUNTINGTON. I think so. We try to keep all our roads in a good condition, and I never thought of keeping the Southern Pacific road in a better condition than the Central Pacific road.

Senator MORGAN. Have you really expected that the Central Pacific

Company could have any prosperity when its guardian and builder was in competition with it, and, when as president of another road, he was continually profiting by the freight which the Central Pacific lost?

Mr. HUNTINGTON. I believe that the Central Pacific has been handled as well and better under my management than it would have been under any other management.

Senator MORGAN. How has it done, in comparison with the Southern Pacific?

Mr. HUNTINGTON. It is not better nor worse than the Southern Pacific in its physical condition. It is probably a little better than the Southern Pacific because it is an older road.

Senator MORGAN. I am talking about its earnings?

Mr. HUNTINGTON. I have never directed any of the operating departments to take freight away from the Central Pacific and to send it by the Southern Pacific.

Senator MORGAN. But you knew perfectly well that it was done.

Mr. HUNTINGTON. No; and I have told them further to send fruit by the Central Pacific. It is about the same distance from El Paso by each road, but I do not think that one car of fruit from El Paso has gone by the Southern Pacific for every fifty cars which have gone by the Central Pacific.

Senator MORGAN. The fruit from Southern California would have to come to San Francisco?

Mr. HUNTINGTON. Oh, no; I am speaking of the country south of Madre Mountain which takes in the best fruit country in California, particularly as to oranges. I think that forty-nine fiftieths of the fruit cars from that country have gone over the Central Pacific.

Adjourned till Thursday, February 20, at 10.30 a. m.

WASHINGTON, D. C., *Thursday, February 20, 1896.*

The committee met at 10.30 a. m.

Present, Senators Gear (chairman), Stewart, and Morgan.

THE CENTRAL PACIFIC.

EXAMINATION OF MR. C. P. HUNTINGTON—Continued.

Senator MORGAN. It is impossible for me to conduct Mr. Huntington's examination in proper consecutive order without going over matter which has perhaps been thoroughly explained, until I can have access to the printed report of the stenographer as to what has been already testified to; but, preparing for the proper and consecutive order of the examination, I will take up at this point another branch of it, and when I get the printed matter I will continue the examination of Mr. Huntington in the consecutive order which I have undertaken to follow.

I will ask you, preliminarily, Mr. Huntington, to state as nearly as you can the exact amount of stock which you now own in the Central Pacific Railroad.

Mr. HUNTINGTON. I stated, I think, that I owned over 6,000 shares.

Senator MORGAN. Representing in face value over $600,000?

Mr. HUNTINGTON. Yes.

Senator MORGAN. What is the largest amount of stock in that railroad which you have ever owned?

Mr. HUNTINGTON. I do not know that I have ever owned more than that. I had an interest in the Contract and Finance Company.

Senator MORGAN. You do not think that you have ever personally owned more than $600,000 of this stock?

Mr. HUNTINGTON. I never had more than that standing in my own name. I am not prepared to say that I had ever so much as that.

Senator MORGAN. What was the largest amount you owned at any time, or that you had a right to, as a member of the Contract and Finance Company?

Mr. HUNTINGTON. I do not know. Mr. Hopkins kept all those accounts; he was the bookkeeper of the concern, and whatever he said always went with me. I never saw the books of the Contract and Finance Company.

Senator MORGAN. Were all the memoranda of the ownership of the stock and the distribution of the stock of each stockholder in the Contract and Finance Company kept on the books of that company?

Mr. HUNTINGTON. I think so. The Central Pacific stock was sold largely, and the debts of the Contract and Finance Company were paid out of the proceeds of the sale, so that it did not really come into my hands.

Senator MORGAN. Was there ever any distribution of the assets of the Contract and Finance Company?

Mr. HUNTINGTON. Yes.

Senator MORGAN. When was that made?

Mr. HUNTINGTON. I do not recollect the date. I should say along in the seventies.

Senator MORGAN. Did that include a distribution of the bonds and stock of the Central Pacific Company?

Mr. HUNTINGTON. There was no distribution. They were sold to pay the debts of the Contract and Finance Company, which debts were incurred, according to my recollection, by the building of the Central Pacific road.

Senator MORGAN. And out of their sale the Contract and Finance Company paid its debts?

Mr. HUNTINGTON. Yes.

Senator MORGAN. About how much?

Mr. HUNTINGTON. It is a long way back, and so many things have come on since. When a matter is settled I have always allowed it to drop out of my mind.

Senator MORGAN. Can you not make an approximate statement? State according to the best of your recollection.

Mr. HUNTINGTON. I do not recollect. As I said, Mr. Hopkins always attended to those matters as long as he lived, and I had very little to do with the accounting. I had great confidence in Mr. Hopkins. He did the bookeeping and handled all the money.

Senater MORGAN. You were careful to get what was coming to you out of the Contract and Finance Company?

Mr. HUNTINGTON. Whatever Mark Hopkins said was mine I never looked into any farther.

Senator MORGAN. You got what he said was yours?

Mr. HUNTINGTON. I have no doubt I did. I do not recollect ever refusing anything.

Senator MORGAN. Was the sum so inconsiderable that you paid no attention to it?

Mr. HUNTINGTON. No; I think not.

Senator MORGAN. Was it not a very large sum?

Mr. HUNTINGTON. No; after paying the debts of the Contract and Finance Company, I do not think it was very large.

Senator MORGAN. Did it amount up to the millions?

Mr. HUNTINGTON. It may have been, perhaps, more than two or three millions, altogether.

Senator MORGAN. Was it in money, stocks, or bonds?

Mr. HUNTINGTON. It must have been money. I do not think I ever owned 200,000 of the bonds of the Central Pacific, and I never owned but one of the Government bonds. I would not swear positively that I ever owned a Central Pacific first-mortgage bond. They were sold, and I sold them, but not as my own. The money was taken to pay the current bills, and, later on, the debts of the company.

Senator MORGAN. Can you refresh your mind by any means to show how much you got out of this division from the Contract and Finance Company after its accounts were settled?

Mr. HUNTINGTON. These accounts were settled, I think, perhaps twenty years ago, and it has been the habit of my life to carry things currently in my head while they are going on, and when a thing is finished to drop it out of my mind. I could not keep both the old and the new; and the new seemed necessary to keep.

Senator MORGAN. You gave a deposition before this United States Pacific Railroad Commission of which Mr. Littler was president?

Mr. HUNTINGTON. Yes.

Senator MORGAN. Have you ever examined that deposition since?

Mr. HUNTINGTON. I do not think I have.

Senator MORGAN. Did they get it all down right there?

Mr. HUNTINGTON. I do not know. I do not think I ever saw it. If I signed it I probably read it over.

Senator MORGAN. You examined the report of the majority of that commission?

Mr. HUNTINGTON. I suppose so.

Senator MORGAN. And of the minority, too.

Mr. HUNTINGTON. I do not think I did; it is possible that I did.

Senator MORGAN. There was a report by Mr. E. Ellery Anderson and D. E. Littler, commissioners on the part of the majority, and by Governor Pattison on the part of the minority. I suppose you have read Pattison's report?

Mr. HUNTINGTON. No; I do not think I ever did. As I understand it, he copied the Sam. Brannan complaint. I do not believe I ever read it.

Senator MORGAN. Then you do not know whether Governor Pattison copied the Sam. Brannan complaint or not, only from common report?

Mr. HUNTINGTON. No.

Senator MORGAN. That would be hardly a proper way to treat the report of a sworn commission.

Mr. HUNTINGTON. It depends upon who the commissioners were.

Senator MORGAN. If they were such men as Pattison would you think it a fair way to treat their report?

Mr. HUNTINGTON. I do not know. I do not know enough about Pattison to wish to speak about him.

Senator MORGAN. Did you never examine the majority report?

Mr HUNTINGTON. I do not know whether I ever read it; I may have read it.

Senator MORGAN. Before you get rid of this examination I will ask you to pay very special attention to the report of the majority and also of the minority. I want to see whether or not these gentlemen have misrepresented you. If they have, it is important for you to read their reports and correct them.

Mr. HUNTINGTON. I am glad, Senator, to see that you are looking out somewhat for my interest.

Senator MORGAN. I am looking out for the interest of everybody concerned. I have no reason to be partial. I have no interest for you and none against you. You know that.

Mr. HUNTINGTON. I should hope so.

Senator MORGAN. And I live in a State which has not one stiver of interest in this controversy—which will be neither benefited by your successes nor injured by your disappointments.

Mr. HUNTINGTON. That is a good thing. We all have an interest in the right and the wrong, and I suppose that the State of Alabama has also.

Senator MORGAN. Therefore, in my investigation of this subject, I am trying to act impartially as a member of this committee, which wants to get at the truth and nothing else. I hope that all the facts which can be shown in your favor will be shown. I will not try to suppress them.

Mr. HUNTINGTON. I do not believe you would.

Senator MORGAN. I want to ask you about some points in this report this morning with the view of getting at facts. This book that I hold in my hand is volume 2, Senate Executive Document, first session, Fiftieth Congress. I read from page 70. Is this a true statement:

About the time of the completion of the construction of the thirty-first section the act of July 2, 1864, was passed. Under this act the donations to the company were vastly increased and it was authorized to mortgage the railroad for an amount equal to the Government aid and to give such mortgage a priority of lien. Messrs. Stanford, Huntington, Hopkins, and Crocker were at this time directors of the Central Pacific and had absolute control of its affairs.

Is that right?

Mr. HUNTINGTON. We were directors, I think. I am not sure about Mr. Crocker; but I am pretty sure that I was a director. In fact, I know I was, and I am sure that Stanford and Hopkins were.

Senator MORGAN. The main point is that you had absolute control of its affairs. Is that true?

Mr. HUNTINGTON. No; I would not be prepared to say that it was true. I think that the directors consisted of nine or seven. We had the largest interest. You may say we did control. Perhaps it would be proper to say that we actually could control. If we were four, and the board consisted of seven members, why, we had control. If the board consisted of seven members, and we were but three, we could hardly be said to control the board.

Senator MORGAN. If there were nine directors, five being the majority to control, you still did control it.

Mr. HUNTINGTON. What we said would have gone. We were the active men who were putting all our power into it.

Senator MORGAN. The commissioners say further:

The board numbered nine. The other members were James Bailey, T. D. Judah, L. A. Booth, D. W. Strong, and Charles Marsh, who were entirely under the control of the four persons named above.

Is that true?

Mr. HUNTINGTON. No; Lucius A. Booth was one of the best men in California, as independent as we were. Charles Marsh was a good man and a wealthy man. He was a good miner and engineer. Dr. Strong was a good man. I do not think he had any great deal of money. James Bailey was a man of means. Mr. Judah had less money. He was a man that I had talked about as engineer. They were all men of prominence in California, and men who were not controlled by any one, I guess, but themselves. They were all good men.

Senator MORGAN. Were they still entirely under the control of the four persons named above?

Mr. HUNTINGTON. No; they were not.

Senator MORGAN. But what the four persons named above said went?

Mr. HUNTINGTON. I think it would have been likely to go because they were putting money in pretty largely. What we recommended would have been pretty likely to be acquiesced in, but not unless it met with their judgment and approval as a thing that ought to be done.

Senator MORGAN. They say that "on the 24th of December, 1862, Charles Crocker resigned and voted to award the contract to five directors. This was the contract that was completed in March, 1866?"

Mr. HUNTINGTON. I should think very likely that it was.

Senator MORGAN. Were you a member of that Charles Crocker & Co.'s construction company?

Mr. HUNTINGTON. No.

Senator MORGAN. Had you no interest in it?

Mr. HUNTINGTON. No.

Senator MORGAN. This contract, the commissioners say, could not be found.

Mr. HUNTINGTON. I was there when that contract was let. I think I was there when the first seven contracts were let. I am quite sure that is one of the contracts that were let to build the road from Sacramento to Newcastle, 31½ miles.

Senator MORGAN. The commissioners then proceed to give a very detailed account of each of the contracts that was made to different persons; and they set out the testimony of several witnesses to show what these contracts were and what work was done under them, and they proceeded as follows:

> Leland Stanford testified that Charles Crocker had no partners, but it appears from his own evidence (vol. 5, p. 2637) that all of the stock received by Charles Crocker under these contracts was turned over to the corporation known as the Contract and Finance Company, in which Stanford, Huntington, Hopkins, and Crocker were substantially the sole stockholders.

Is that correct; is that true?

Mr. HUNTINGTON. They may have been turned over. Mr. Crocker did not complete that contract. He could not get any partners. I worked very hard to get them myself in California, New York, and Boston, but the capitalists that I spoke to said they would not go into an open copartnership and be responsible as individuals for large amounts. So it suggested itself to me that they had better organize some company where a man would know what his responsibility was if he took any stock in it. I am very certain that Crocker did not finish his contract. That contract was to build from Newcastle to Camp 127 or 128, some 100 miles of the most expensive part of the road, and I think perhaps that he did turn it in. The Contract and Finance Company took the work up, and he turned it over to that company. I can not say that that was so, but it is my impression that it was so.

Senator MORGAN. Where was this Contract and Finance Company chartered?

Mr. HUNTINGTON. It was chartered under a statute of California.

Senator MORGAN. The commissioners proceed to say:

> The amount of stock so turned over was about $14,000,000.

Mr. HUNTINGTON. They could not guess anything about it.

Senator MORGAN. You can not deny that statement?

Mr. HUNTINGTON. I can not deny it or affirm it; I do not know that I ever heard the figures before.

Senator MORGAN. The commissioners go on to say:

It is clearly established by the evidence that these four gentlemen were at all times equally interested in the results of these contracts, and that, whether the formal relation of partners existed between them or not, it was understood and agreed between them that they should share equally in all the profits of the enterprise.

Is that true?

Mr. HUNTINGTON. No; I do not think there was any such agreement as that. I had an interest in the Contract and Finance Company. I have no doubt about that. I recollect now (after refreshing my mind) that when Mr. Hopkins telegraphed me at Boston about taking stock in the Contract and Finance Company, I sent him a dispatch in these words: "Take as little as you can and as much as you must." A queer wording, perhaps, but that happens to flash across my mind now. We were in dead earnest about building the road.

Senator MORGAN. "Take as little as you can" of what?

Mr. HUNTINGTON. Of the stock of the Contract and Finance Company. We were always in hope of getting others in to take stock.

Senator MORGAN. You did not get anybody in?

Mr. HUNTINGTON. Not here. We did not get any great capitalists in. I spent probably one hundred nights in New York and Boston discussing the matter with rich men.

Senator MORGAN. The commissioners proceed to say:

The contract was awarded by the votes of Crocker & Co. to Crocker & Co.

Mr. HUNTINGTON. The record would show that. I should have voted for it if I had been there; but my impression is that I was not. If I had been I should have voted for the contract.

Senator MORGAN (reading).

The profits arising out of these contracts were divided among these four persons; and this same singular feature will be found to pervade all contracts for construction, for repairs, for branch lines, for leases of the auxiliary lines, for the express business, for the sale of material, and for the sale of coal; as to all of which, through the intervention of construction companies, express companies, or development companies (in which these four persons were substantially the only stockholders), all of the contracts have been awarded by the votes of Stanford, Huntington, Hopkins, and Crocker.

Mr. HUNTINGTON. We were the parties who stood in all the time and did what we had to do. I was unfortunate in not getting other people in.

Senator MORGAN. Have you any facts to state in contravention of the statement made by the commissioners which I have just read?

Mr. HUNTINGTON. I do not think there was any distribution made at all. We kept everything, as I understand, and we had to go on with the work. That is what was the matter. We could not get anyone in with us that we wished to get in. I labored almost day and night for seven years, back and forth. I would go to California and stay there ten days, and then I would come back to New York and be gone only thirty days, during which time I would have made 1,400 miles of stages and stayed ten days in California.

Senator MORGAN. The commissioners proceed to state some deductions or conclusions from the facts which they have recited in their report. They say, on page 72 of this volume:

In the opinion of the commission, the course pursued in this respect is wholly indefensible. The agreement of the company when it received the munificent aid extended.

by the United States was to repay the loan and so much of the interest as had not been repaid by transportation or percentages of net earnings at the expiration of thirty years. The course pursued by Stanford, Huntington, Hopkins, and Crocker was necessarily absolutely destructive of any possible security. This result will appear more clearly as the detail of the contracts effected is developed.

Mr. HUNTINGTON. Well now, in a general way, if Senator Morgan will allow me——

Senator MORGAN. You are at liberty to say what you want.

Mr. HUNTINGTON. The road was built on $44,000,000 of assets, and I do not believe that any other set of men in the world could have got through without bankruptcy, because I do not think that any other set of men would have put in the days and nights on the work which I did; and if I had not had good credit we never would have made the landing and never would have completed the road. I know that almost as well as I know anything of that character.

Senator MORGAN. When you say that the road was built for $44,000,000, do you mean that that was the amount you had done it for; that is what the road cost—$44,000,000?

Mr. HUNTINGTON. It cost more.

Senator MORGAN. Why did you refer to putting in $44,000,000 of assets if that amount was not what it cost?

Mr. HUNTINGTON. I will tell you how I arrive at it. I am speaking about credit as a part. We had $28,000,000 of Government bonds. We sold them at not over par—we sold them at considerably less than par. I think I sold some of them in the neighborhood of 85.

Senator MORGAN. Did you sell them at rates lower than the Union Pacific Company sold theirs?

Mr. HUNTINGTON. No; I think we got a little more. We did not get 60 cents in gold for them. It was the same also with the $28,000,000 of first mortgage bonds. We mortgaged our land for $10,000,000, and if we sold those bonds at par, getting 60 cents in gold for the currency, that would be $6,000,000 we received from the land-grant bonds. The capital stock of $60,000,000 could not be sold at 10 cents on the dollar. We put it at 10 cents. I do not believe it could have been sold at 5 cents when the road was built. The Union Pacific shares all changed hands (and its stock stood as well as the Central) at an average of less than 8 cents on the dollar. I was offered a majority of the Union Pacific shares myself at 8 cents, but I did not have the money to buy them, and if I had I should not have bought them. That figures up $43,444,000. When we got through we could not commence to pay the debts of the Contract and Finance Company from the assets we had. We could not have come within millions of it, but we carried the debt along, and carried it pretty easily. In completing the road I got money cheap. I did not pay anything like what the Union Pacific did; but after the road was built and the collaterals disposed of, I had to borrow money at 10 per cent. Finally the time came when the Contract and Finance Company sold its Central Pacific shares, so that we got out of debt, and had something to the good. We had something to pay us for the great work we had done; and if I had been offered millions I would not have undertaken the same contract and have made the same landing again.

Senator MORGAN. Are you through with that statement?

Mr. HUNTINGTON. Yes.

Senator MORGAN. Let me see if I understand you. Your estimate is upon gold values for all the things that you got at the time.

Mr. HUNTINGTON. I strike an average. I did pay 122 for a large lot of gold. I strike the average at 60 cents, and that would be rather above than below the average.

Senator MORGAN. Did you sell any of your Government bonds at 60 cents on the dollar for gold?

Mr. HUNTINGTON. I did not sell them for gold at all. I sold them for currency; and it is certain that I sold some of them at 85 for currency. They were a new thing and nobody seemed to want them.

Senator MORGAN. You are speaking of the Government bonds?

Mr. HUNTINGTON. Yes.

Senator MORGAN. How about the company's first mortgage bonds?

Mr. HUNTINGTON. We sold them for currency, and bought gold. We paid for our rails and engines in currency; but all the work was done in California, and had to be paid for in gold. Not a cent of currency appeared anywhere in our transactions there.

Senator MORGAN. Why did you sell these bonds for currency?

Mr. HUNTINGTON. Because that is what we took. We said that we would take so many dollars, and they paid us in currency, of course.

Senator MORGAN. Who paid you?

Mr. HUNTINGTON. The people who bought the bonds; A, B, and C. We did not mention gold. When we wanted gold we bought it. Currency was not used in California at all. Gold was the currency of the State.

Senator MORGAN. So that in Calfornia what payments you made for materials and labor were made in gold?

Mr. HUNTINGTON. On what part of the road?

Senator MORGAN. On the road down as far as Ogden.

Mr. HUNTINGTON. Yes; that is my recollection.

Senator MORGAN. You did not use currency at all?

Mr. HUNTINGTON. I do not think we paid any currency. So many dollars there meant so many dollars in gold.

Senator MORGAN. What were the United States bonds worth at that time in gold?

Mr. HUNTINGTON. A man in Berlin told me the other day that he bought some Government bonds at that time for 36; that is, they cost him 36. When we first got our subsidy bonds nobody knew what to do with them. They did not take them for currency.

Senator MORGAN. What debts of the Central Pacific Company were outstanding at the time of the completion of the road, aside from its bonded debt?

Mr. HUNTINGTON. My impression is, not much. The Contract and Finance Company carried the burden.

Senator MORGAN. The Central Pacific Company proper did not really owe any debts at the time of the completion of the road except the debt to the United States Government and to the first-mortgage bondholders.

Mr. HUNTINGTON. That is one way to put it. The Contract and Finance Company agreed to build the road.

Senator MORGAN. But did the two companies have separate establishments; or, if they were just the same, I want to get at that fact?

Mr. HUNTINGTON. The Contract and Finance Company contracted, as I understand and believe, to build the road for so much stock and so much bonds (which were all the bonds), and when the Central Pacific Company paid the interest on their bonds that was their pay, and the business of the Contract and Finance Company was to build the road as per contract.

Senator MORGAN. You seem to identify the Contract and Finance Company with the Central Pacific.

Mr. HUNTINGTON. I do not know why. In making the contract the Contract and Finance Company had half of the trade and the Central Pacific had the other half. The Central Pacific had the contract to take care of the bonds and the Contract and Finance Company to build the road.

Senator MORGAN. Then the debts which you speak of as being outstanding at the time of completing the Central Pacific road between a point within 5 miles of Ogden and its western terminus were debts which were owing by the Contract and Finance Company.

Mr. HUNTINGTON. I do not see how it could be otherwise, if I am correct in my construction, as I believe I am.

Senator MORGAN. I do not think we have any difficulty about that.

Mr. HUNTINGTON. The Contract and Finance Company contracted with the Central Pacific to do a certain work, for which the Central Pacific gave certain amounts from time to time as the work went on.

Senator MORGAN. But, as between the Central Pacific and its stockholders, and as between the Government of the United States and the Central Pacific, the Central Pacific Company at the time of its completion was out of debt, excepting for its first-mortgage bonds?

Mr. HUNTINGTON. I do not recollect. That is thirty years ago. The Contract and Finance Company may have finished the work at the eastern end of the road, and still there may have been many things to be done.

Senator MORGAN. If there was any debt resting against the Central Pacific at the time of its completion, state what it was and the amount.

Mr. HUNTINGTON. I do not know that there was any debt, but there may have been. The Contract and Finance Company agreed to build the road in certain ways, and I presume it did so and finished the contract. I mean to say that it was not a continuing contract to keep the road up forever; but the road had to be accepted by the Government officials, and when it was accepted that closed that section of the road up, as between the Contract and Finance Company and the Central Pacific. After that the Central Pacific Company may have wanted more rolling stock, and it may not have. But when the Government accepted a section of the road the business on that section was closed as between the Central Pacific and the Contract and Finance Company. After that whatever was needed to be done—for instance, if there came a great freshet and washed away a bridge—in fact the American bridge was burned up——

Senator MORGAN. Then the Central Pacific had to keep it up?

Mr. HUNTINGTON. I do not know who else there was to do it.

The CHAIRMAN. Was the Central Pacific a completed road, ballasted, etc., by the Contract and Finance Company?

Mr. HUNTINGTON. No.

The CHAIRMAN. It was just completed so far as building the track and laying the rails?

Mr. HUNTINGTON. Yes; the Government was to accept the road, and it was ballasted just as all roads are ballasted, with the best material at hand.

The CHAIRMAN. Was that a part of the contract?

Mr. HUNTINGTON. It was not a part of the contract to ballast the road except with the materials that we had at hand.

The CHAIRMAN. You put in the ballast that the country afforded?

Mr. HUNTINGTON. Yes; now we haul the ballast sometimes a hundred miles, but we could not do that when we were building the road.

We agreed to build such a road as the Government would accept, and it was a good road.

Senator MORGAN. At the time of the completion of the Central Pacific road in the manner you have described, how much did the Contract and Finance Company owe?

Mr. HUNTINGTON. I do not know.

Senator MORGAN. About how much?

Mr. HUNTINGTON. I do not know how much, but it was in the millions.

Senator MORGAN. Two or three or four millions?

Mr. HUNTINGTON. A good deal more than that.

Senator MORGAN. Five or six or seven or eight millions?

Mr. HUNTINGTON. I can not say. My impression is that the Contract and Finance Company owed considerably more than $10,000,000.

Senator MORGAN. Has that all been paid?

Mr. HUNTINGTON. It has been all paid.

Senator MORGAN. How?

Mr. HUNTINGTON. By selling what we had to sell; but mostly shares of the Central Pacific.

Senator MORGAN. You held on to the bonds of the Central Pacific and sold its shares?

Mr. HUNTINGTON. We sold bonds currently. We had no bonds except perhaps some few land-grant bonds. I do not think we had a Government bond or first-mortgage bond when the road was completed, but we may have had a few. I am very certain, however, that I never owned a Government bond which the Central Pacific received from the Government, and I have no recollection positively of owning any first-mortgage bonds of the company, but I think I did. I think I took some of them from the Contract and Finance Company.

Senator MORGAN. Estimating that the debt of the Contract and Finance Company at the time of the completion of the Central Pacific road amounted to $10,000,000 and that you paid it, and paid it mostly in cash——

Mr. HUNTINGTON. I paid it in cash. We sold the shares.

Senator MORGAN. What shares, and to whom did they belong?

Mr. HUNTINGTON. They belonged to the Contract and Finance Company.

Senator MORGAN. What shares were they?

Mr. HUNTINGTON. Shares of the Central Pacific Company.

Senator MORGAN. Estimating the debt of the Contract and Finance Company at $10,000,000, how many shares of the Central Pacific did you have to sell in order to raise that amount?

Mr. HUNTINGTON. The Contract and Finance Company had some fifty odd millions in shares of the Central Pacific stock.

Senator MORGAN. How much did you sell of those shares?

Mr. HUNTINGTON. I can not say exactly. In the neighborhood of half of them.

Senator MORGAN. Then you sold in the neighborhood of $25,000,000 of the shares of the Central Pacific?

Mr. HUNTINGTON. Yes.

Senator MORGAN. And these you sold at about 50 cents on the dollar?

Mr. HUNTINGTON. We sold those shares, I think, all the way as high as 85 and as low as 10.

Senator MORGAN. Then, after you got through selling shares and paying up this $10,000,000 of debt you still had shares of the Central Pacific to divide?

Mr. HUNTINGTON. No; I think they were all sold.

Senator MORGAN. You had money to divide?

Mr. HUNTINGTON. It was money, I think.

Senator MORGAN. You do not know how much?

Mr. HUNTINGTON. No; I do not know.

Senator MORGAN. The books of the company are not in existence, and you can not find out?

Mr. HUNTINGTON. No; the books of the company are not in existence. I would like very much, Senator, that you could look them over.

Senator MORGAN. I would not like it. I do not like to investigate things which are of no more importance. I do not like to investigate the grave, either for events or things, for the purpose of satisfying my curiosity.

Mr. HUNTINGTON. I never have disturbed myself much about yesterday or to-morrow.

Senator MORGAN. I do not think you have. I will go back to the report of the United States Pacific Railroad Commissioners in order to give you an opportunity to explain things. On page 72 they say:

The railroad was constructed between section 138 and Promontory Point by a corporation know as the Contract and Finance Company. That company was formed ostensibly for the purpose of inviting the cooperation of outside capital. It was alleged that the personal liability which attached, under the laws of California, to the ownership of the stock of the Central Pacific deterred many persons from taking any part in the enterprise; and the object of forming the Contract and Finance Company seems to have been to obviate that difficulty by causing the construction to be done through that company. (See evidence of Huntington, vol. 1, p. 10; Stanford, vol. 5, p. 2624.) That company was formed in 1867. Its capital stock was $5,000,000. This stock was divided into three equal shares, which were issued to William E. Brown, T. J. Milliken, and B. R. Crocker. The stock so taken was understood by the incorporators to be held for Stanford, Huntington, Hopkins, Charles Crocker, and E. B. Crocker, and the three incorporators who became the managers of the company represented these five persons.

Do you dissent from that statement in any particular as a matter of fact?

Mr. HUNTINGTON. I do not think that I ever heard that these people were shareholders. If I heard they were, it has gone entirely out of my mind. I was in New York nearly all the time.

Senator MORGAN (reading).

Subsequently E. B. Crocker's interest was assigned to the other four parties in interest, so that they each owned a quarter interest in the Contract and Finance Company. (See evidence of Stanford, vol. 5, p. 2638.)

Mr. HUNTINGTON. Stanford understood it thoroughly. I knew E. B. Crocker. He was a worthy citizen; but if I ever did know that he had an interest in the Contract and Finance Company, it has gone out of my mind.

Senator MORGAN (reading).

In December, 1867, a contract was submitted by Leland Stanford to the board of directors of the Central Pacific Company, on behalf of the Contract and Finance Company, to construct the road from section 138 to Promontory Point. There were present at that meeting Stanford, E. B. Crocker, Mark Hopkins, and E. H. Miller, jr. The board accepted the contract on the terms proposed. (See evidence of E. H. Miller, jr., vol. 5, p. 3062.) The terms of the contract were substantially $86,000 per mile, one-half payable in cash, the other half payable in stock. For this the Contract and Finance Company was to complete the road, build all the depots, station houses, turntables, roundhouses, furnish all the equipment, freight shops, and machinery shops, and everything necessary to the running of the road.

Is that right?

Mr. HUNTINGTON. Some of it is new to me; but in a general way it is right. About the cash part, I had forgotten about that; but no doubt it is correct. These bonds must have been sold, and that is the way the money was raised to pay the cash that was paid. As far as I recollect, I should have said that the Contract and Finance Company agreed to build the roads for the bonds and stock; but if Governor Stanford says it was so, I have no doubt it was so.

Senator MORGAN. The sales of bonds that were made—were they made by the Contract and Finance Company or by the Central Pacific Company?

Mr. HUNTINGTON. I sold the bonds myself and accounted to the company.

Senator MORGAN. Which company?

Mr. HUNTINGTON. If they belonged to the Central Pacific, I accounted to the Central Pacific company. The accounting was made correct; there is no doubt about that. But I should have stated, as I said before, that the contract was made to build the road in the usual way; that is, to take the bonds and stock and to do the work.

Senator MORGAN. I see on the same page:

Under this contract the road was constructed between the points indicated, a total of 552 miles, at a cost of $23,726,000 in stock and $23,726,000 in gold. It is a noticeable fact that Mr. Miller testifies that at the time he voted for this contract and at the time he voted for the Crocker contract and its extension, he was not informed that the directors of the Central Pacific were also beneficiaries under the contracts. (See evidence of E. H. Miller, jr., vol. 5, pp. 3061, 3062.) The commission has made diligent effort to ascertain the actual cost of the railroad to the Contract and Finance Company; and, in their opinion, have arrived at a conclusion which can not be far from the truth. An accurate answer to this question would be shown by the books of Charles Crocker & Co. and of the Contract and Finance Company. These books were not produced, and, in the opinion of the commission, were purposely destroyed by direction of Stanford, Huntington, Hopkins, and Crocker. The evidence on this point appears to be conclusive.

Mr. HUNTINGTON. Is that the Pattison report?

Senator MORGAN. No; it is the report of the other two commissioners.

Mr. HUNTINGTON. I do not know anything about that, but it is not correct.

Senator MORGAN. I do not know whether it is or not.

Mr. HUNTINGTON. Well, I do.

Senator MORGAN. In what respect is it not correct?

Mr. HUNTINGTON. If the books were destroyed, I do not know anything about it, but I do not think they were. If they were destroyed, they were either sold for waste paper or burned up without respect to that. About the building of the road, nobody in the world could know anything about the cost or guess anything of the cost. We shoveled snow in the mountains there one winter. We hauled rails across the mountains on sleds to get down into the country where there was no snow. We did it at very great expense, and nobody could know anything about the cost. The commissioners could only get their information as they do out there now. Most business men have something to do. But the Sutro Examiner Combination or the Examiner Sutro Combination (I do not know which is the head and which the tail) always have leisure, and they rushed out to give information to the commissioners. I wish to say that under oath, because that is my opinion.

Senator MORGAN. You mentioned the Lambard and Brannan suit, suggesting that perhaps Mr. Pattison had copied it.

Mr. HUNTINGTON. I imagine so from what I heard of his doings in California.

Senator MORGAN. I want to read to you what the majority of the commission say about that:

In 1870 suits were brought or threatened by Charles A. Lambard, Samuel Brannan, and others, against Stanford, Huntington, Hopkins, and Crocker, as owners of the stock of the Central Pacific Railroad Company, alleging that those persons had been guilty of many violations of their duties as directors, and that they had voted profitable contracts to themselves; that by means of these contracts they had procured possession of substantially all of the assets of the company remaining after the expenditure of the actual cost of construction. The commission do not mean to intimate that all of the charges contained in these complaints are sustained by the evidence; but it does appear that the four persons named did vote contracts to themselves, under which large profits were made and divided. The allegations contained in these complaints were such as would compel men of honor, if these allegations were false, to defend themselves at any cost. It appears from the evidence that all these suits were settled, and that the stock owned by the plaintiffs was bought at rates varying from $400 a share to $1,000 a share. (See evidence of Stanford, vol. 5, p. 2641; vol. 6, pp. 2775, 2779.)

You may make any statement you see proper about that.

Mr. HUNTINGTON. Their information was picked up on the street corners, I have no doubt.

Senator MORGAN. By the commission.

Mr. HUNTINGTON. And there is no truth in that report. We could not get men to join us in the contract. There never was a man who tried harder and who used up his time and ability to a greater extent than I did to get somebody to come in and share and share alike with us in building the road. But not a man of any importance would come in. They all made about the same reply; they would not take the responsibility of undertaking to build the road. When the Contract and Finance Company completed the road there was not enough by several millions to have paid its debts created by the building of the road, notwithstanding anybody's report. That I know. I am speaking of things which I myself know; and a cleaner piece of work never was done.

Senator MORGAN. That is what I want to get at—what you know.

Mr. HUNTINGTON. I do know that. As to the sale of stocks, I do not know anything about it except by common report that there were some shares sold. These fellows in San Francisco charged us with every crime in the catalogue except one, and I told them to put that in, too; that is, piracy on the high seas. I told them to add that.

Senator MORGAN. They did not do it, I suppose, because there is no water in that country.

Mr. HUNTINGTON. Oh, yes; there is plenty of water. I say, knowing all about it, that we could not pay the debts created by the building of the Central Pacific, by many millions, out of any proceeds that we could get from the assets.

Senator MORGAN. How did you pay the debts?

Mr. HUNTINGTON. By borrowing the money.

Senator MORGAN. How did you pay the borrowed money?

Mr. HUNTINGTON. The stock appreciated, and we sold it.

Senator MORGAN. And it was out of the advance of value which you created by your personal efforts?

Mr. HUNTINGTON. The property appreciated. The road was a good road. The showing was sufficient to warrant the prices obtained. But after the Government gave great subsidies to the Northern Pacific, and to the Southern Pacific, and to the Atlantic and Pacific, so that these great roads divided the volume of business and cut the rates in two, the value of the shares of the Central Pacific was destroyed, and the prices went down.

Senator MORGAN. That will be the subject of a separate inquiry.

Mr. HUNTINGTON. It is a part of the whole thing.

Senator MORGAN. I will get you to state about what month and what year the Central Pacific and the Union Pacific made through connection with each other?

Mr. HUNTINGTON. It was on the 10th of May, 1869.

Senator MORGAN. You then went into regular traffic across the continent with your line of road?

Mr. HUNTINGTON. Yes.

Senator MORGAN. Did you have a sufficient equipment at that time to do all the business?

Mr. HUNTINGTON. I should say so. Business grew, and we kept putting on additional equipment. When the road was completed we had equipment enough to do the business offered. Of course we were adding to it all the time.

Senator MORGAN. That was four or five years after the termination of the civil war?

Mr. HUNTINGTON. Yes, four or five years.

Senator MORGAN. So that the existence of the war did not have any particularly stimulating effect on the income of the road?

Mr. HUNTINGTON. No; I do not think that it affected the income of the road in one way or the other. The main work in building the road had to be done in 1867. The Sierra Nevadas were the great obstacle. The Rocky Mountains were ugly, but not so bad as the Sierra Nevadas.

Senator MORGAN. What is the fiscal year of the Central Pacific Company?

Mr. HUNTINGTON. I believe it is the calendar year.

Senator MORGAN. So that we will commence now in 1870 when the road was in full operation. What was the stock of the Central Pacific worth in 1870?

Mr. HUNTINGTON. I do not know. The stock could have been sold for 10 cents, I know, in 1869.

Senator MORGAN. It then had not gone into operation?

Mr. HUNTINGTON. Yes; it went into operation on the 10th of May, 1869.

Senator MORGAN. Between 1870 and 1880 was there not a rapid increase in the value of the stock?

Mr. HUNTINGTON. Yes.

Senator MORGAN. How did it go?

Mr. HUNTINGTON. I think between 70 and 80. I think I sold some at 85.

Senator MORGAN. Did that stock ever command a premium in the market?

Mr. HUNTINGTON. Not to my knowledge. I sold it a good deal in blocks to brokers in New York. We did not offer a share in the New York market ourselves.

Senator MORGAN. But did not the price go up in the market?

Mr. HUNTINGTON. Yes; it went up considerably; I do not know how high.

Senator MORGAN. Did it go above par?

Mr. HUNTINGTON. I do not recollect; it may have. I sold enough to get out of debt.

Senator MORGAN. The stock of the Union Pacific went away above par, did it not?

Mr. HUNTINGTON. Yes; a good deal above par.

Senator MORGAN. It went higher than the Central Pacific?

Mr. HUNTINGTON. Yes.

Senator MORGAN. At what time did the Central Pacific have this high rate of value?

Mr. HUNTINGTON. I do not know; I should think I would say in the eighties.

Senator MORGAN. In 1885, probably?

Mr. HUNTINGTON. No; I should say from memory that it dropped off before 1885.

Senator MORGAN. As soon as you got the stock high enough in the market you let it go?

Mr. HUNTINGTON. As we saw our way to pay our debts we did it. We always did that.

Senator MORGAN. How much debt did the Contract and Finance Company have at the time of the completion of the railroad?

Mr. HUNTINGTON. I think I have answered that two or three times—something about ten millions.

Senator MORGAN. I thought perhaps that by asking you again you would be able to state just how much it was.

Mr. HUNTINGTON. No; it has not come to me exactly.

Senator MORGAN. I hope it will after awhile.

Mr. HUNTINGTON. I will be much pleased if it does to give you the exact figures.

Senator MORGAN. You had $10,000,000 of debts to pay and you had how much stock to pay these debts with?

Mr. HUNTINGTON. I think we had over $10,000,000 debts to pay, and we had something over $50,000,000 stock of the Central Pacific Railroad.

Senator MORGAN. So that if you got the stock up to an average of 80——

Mr. HUNTINGTON. We did not get any such average as that.

Senator MORGAN. Well, up to an average of 50 cents on the dollar——

Mr. HUNTINGTON. I think it probably averaged 50 cents on the dollar.

Senator MORGAN. So that you had, at least, $25,000,000 in gold with which to pay this $10,000,000 of debt.

Mr. HUNTINGTON. Up in the eighties gold and currency had got together again, I think.

Senator MORGAN. So that, by continuing your debt and running your credit, you got the advantage by time in the depreciation of gold as well as the appreciation of Government bonds and securities? You got that advantage?

Mr. HUNTINGTON. Yes. We had to wait, and we did very well by waiting.

Senator MORGAN. The way I count it, I find that $25,000,000 was made by the operations of the Contract and Finance Company in the building of that road.

Mr. HUNTINGTON. I do not understand your figures, Senator.

Senator MORGAN. My figures are that you got about $80,000,000 of stock and sold it for 50 cents on the dollar.

Mr. HUNTINGTON. How much stock do you say we got?

Senator MORGAN. Eighty million dollars.

Mr. HUNTINGTON. Only $50,000,000.

Senator MORGAN. Not more than $50,000,000?

Mr. HUNTINGTON. That is what the Contract and Finance Company got.

Senator MORGAN. Fifty million dollars of stock which you sold at 50 cents on the dollar?

Mr. HUNTINGTON. We sold some of it as low as 18 cents on the dollar.

Senator MORGAN. You said you sold it at an average of 50 cents. Put the amount at the lowest possible figure, $15,000,000——

Mr. HUNTINGTON. Put it at $10,000,000.

Senator MORGAN. I don't think I can do that.

Mr. HUNTINGTON. According to my recollection we had something to the good after those nearly twenty years of waiting. We got some pay for the waiting.

Senator MORGAN. If I were a partner, stating an account with you, I would not compromise on that account for $25,000,000. How much money did you pay out of your own pocket in this business, not counting your genius or your labor but your money?

Mr. HUNTINGTON. I can not say. We were doing a very large hardware and mercantile business, and we used to lend money pretty largely. We put in a considerable amount. Mr. Hopkins was attending to those things, and when the company was short and we could spare them $100,000 or $200,000, and sometimes more than that, we did so.

Senator MORGAN. Did you pay any money which you did not get back in money?

Mr. HUNTINGTON. Oh, yes; certainly we did.

Senator MORGAN. State how much.

Mr. HUNTINGTON. I do not know. I wish Mr. Hopkins were alive.

Senator MORGAN. So do I. It would save a great deal of trouble.

Mr. HUNTINGTON. He kept all the accounts.

Senator MORGAN. I suppose so. You have some general idea, however, of your own business?

Mr. HUNTINGTON. I was in New York and dreadfully busy all the time, working days and nights, and Mr. Hopkins attended to matters in California.

Senator MORGAN. But when the Contract and Finance Company borrowed from your business house $15,000 or $20,000 or $100,000 you kept a memorandum?

Mr. HUNTINGTON. No doubt.

Senator MORGAN. And it was on your mind?

Mr. HUNTINGTON. Perhaps so. I indorsed paper in New York individually frequently.

Senator MORGAN. Can you tell the committee how much money you put into this railroad programme out of your own pocket and which you never got back from the Contract and Finance Company?

Mr. HUNTINGTON. No, I can not; but we did put in enough money to make a great success of the building of the road, so far as the road was concerned.

Senator MORGAN. Speaking of yourself personally, how much did you put in, and how much did the company fail to pay you back?

Mr. HUNTINGTON. I can not say.

Senator MORGAN. Can you state now that you did put money in there which you did not get out when the road was finished?

Mr. HUNTINGTON. Oh, yes.

Senator MORGAN. How much?

Mr. HUNTINGTON. I can not say, but I know that we put in considerable money.

Senator MORGAN. Get as near as you can to the amount.

Mr. HUNTINGTON. I have no personal means of knowing.

Senator MORGAN. It is twenty years ago and the books have been burned up?

Mr. HUNTINGTON. It is more than thirty years ago.

Senator MORGAN. Of course you can not be exact, but I would like you to be as exact as you can be.

Mr. HUNTINGTON. I would take great pains to satisfy the committee on that point, and if it made any difference to any human being I would sit up day and night to try to find it out, but I do not think it does.

Senator MORGAN. I think it is a very legitimate inquiry, to ascertain how much money you made out of this business.

Mr. HUNTINGTON. Well, I have been at work sixty years, and I have always made something each year.

Senator MORGAN. I have no doubt of that.

Mr. HUNTINGTON. And I have always been using my money and using my credit.

Senator MORGAN. In the operations of this railroad which, the commission says, was owned by you four gentlemen?

Mr. HUNTINGTON. I do not think that anybody else should have half the credit that we have.

Adjourned until to-morrow, Friday, February 21, at 10.30 a. m.

WASHINGTON, D. C., *Friday, February 21, 1896.*

The committee met pursuant to adjournment. Present, Senators Gear (chairman) and Morgan.

THE CENTRAL PACIFIC.

EXAMINATION OF MR. C. P. HUNTINGTON—Continued.

Senator MORGAN. When concluding the examination yesterday I was asking you some questions based on the report of the United States Pacific Railroad Commission, which was sent out to investigate these two railroad companies, and my questions were predicated on the majority report of E. Ellery Anderson (the gentleman who testified here the other day) and David T. Littler, and not on the minority report of Mr. Pattison. On page 73 of their report, speaking of an examination made by the Wilson committee into the condition of these railroad companies or in relation to one of them—the Central Pacific, I suppose (I have not that report before me)—they speak of suits brought or threatened by Lombard & Brannan and others against Stanford, Huntington, Hopkins, and Crocker, alleging that these persons had been guilty of many violations of their charge as directors of the Central Pacific Company, and had voted profitable contracts to themselves; that by means of these contracts they had procured possession of substantially all of the assets of the company remaining after the expenditures of the actual cost of construction.

The commissioners proceed to say that the evidence on which the successful prosecution of such suits would necessarily depend was contained in the books of Crocker & Co., and of the Contract and Finance Company, because the actual cost of construction to that company, compared to the actual payments made by the Central Pacific Railroad Company, would disclose profits divided between Stanford, Huntington, Hopkins, and Crocker. The commissioners say, "They, and they alone, were interested in the suppression of this evidence." Is it true that the actual cost of construction to that company, compared to the actual payments made by the Central Pacific Railroad Company, would disclose the profits divided between Stanford, Huntington, Hopkins, and Crocker?

Mr. HUNTINGTON. I suppose it would. I can not answer that question as to whether it would or not, because I do not have anything before me to judge from or to know whether it would or not. There was no doubt but that we were the great factors in the building of the road; but that we got any profits out of it—anything like what was sufficient to pay for the labor we performed and the risk that we ran in those twenty years' work—I can say most positively that we did not get sufficient to pay us for doing the work. We did the work very largely, and were responsible for it, and we used the money which we were compelled to use, but not to the injury of anyone.

Senator MORGAN. The committee could very much better come to a correct conclusion about that matter if it had a statement of what the profits were.

Mr. HUNTINGTON. As I showed the committee the other day, what we made was the $44,000,000 of gold which we received from the proceeds of all the bonds and the stock, putting the stock at twice its value when the road was completed, and when the stock could not be sold at 5 cents on the dollar; but, after waiting twenty years, we did recoup our money. That commission got its facts, I suppose, from the Sam Brannan complaint—a complaint got up by some briefless lawyers. I am told, and I believe, that they got up a complaint under an agreement by which they were to share whatever plunder they got, call it what you like. I believe that, because I have been told so. I believe that Mr. Stanford did make some settlements, but I believe that they were made from a political standpoint. I never have been in politics myself. The same case exactly they brought against me in New York, as I understand. They said that there was something wrong, something fraudulent. I said to them, "All right, take your suit into court," and I refused to settle. It was in the courts more than twenty years, and the decisions were as clean in my favor by the court of appeals in New York as any decisions that were ever made. I did not give them anything. I knew that I was right. They wanted me to compromise, but I refused to do so. Mr. Beaton came to me to make a compromise, but I refused to make any compromise. It took them twenty years, and then they didn't prove their charge, and no part of it.

Senator MORGAN. Have you not an estimate, even a rough one, as to the actual amount of money you made in your business connection with the Contract and Finance Company in the building of the Central Pacific?

Mr. HUNTINGTON. As I answered that question yesterday, I have not any definite sum in my mind. Mr. Hopkins attended to those things. I made something; I am quite satisfied it could not have amounted to more than $3,000,000 or $4,000,000.

Senator MORGAN. Which you made personally?

Mr. HUNTINGTON. Yes, for twenty years' work.

Senator MORGAN. That is pretty good pay for twenty years' work.

Mr. HUNTINGTON. No; not for the work that I did.

Senator MORGAN. I have been doing as much work for twenty years, and I never got one-twentieth part of that amount.

Mr. HUNTINGTON. When people sit up nights handling things that go into the hundreds of millions, and take the responsibility, they are entitled to be well paid. I would not do that kind of work for any such price as that, not on my own volition.

Senator MORGAN. All the capital that you did this work with, and on which you made this meager sum, was furnished you by the United States Government?

Mr. HUNTINGTON. No.

Senator MORGAN. What part of it was not furnished by the Government of the United States? How much did you put in personally?

Mr. HUNTINGTON. I put in all that I had made in our other business.

Senator MORGAN. How much?

Mr. HUNTINGTON. I can not say; but we put in sufficient to make a great success of the work.

Senator MORGAN. That is no answer to the question, and will not be accepted as an answer. How much money did you put in?

Mr. HUNTINGTON. I can not say exactly. I wish I knew.

Senator MORGAN. You can come within a few hundred thousand dollars, I suppose?

Mr. HUNTINGTON. I do not know how much we put in, but I certainly put in more than $1,000,000, and that was sufficient as a basis for the work. Whatever I did put in was sufficient to make a success of the work.

Senator MORGAN. Do you mean that you put it in to remain permanently, or only as the requirements of the work demanded?

Mr. HUNTINGTON. I put in what we had to put in from time to time. There was not a time that I would not have mortgaged my dwelling house in order to get money to make a success of the work.

Senator MORGAN. Was the money that you put in taken out of your private fortune?

Mr. HUNTINGTON. Yes; I never was a rich man, and I am not to-day. I have got property, but I have been a borrower for the last fifty-eight years.

Senator MORGAN. The money that you speak of putting into this Contract and Finance Company was money that you borrowed, I suppose?

Mr. HUNTINGTON. Some of it was and some was not.

Senator MORGAN. But it must have come out of your private fortune.

Mr. HUNTINGTON. It was private money.

Senator MORGAN. How much money did you take out of your own pocket, or out of your own bank account, and put into that construction company?

Mr. HUNTINGTON. I can not tell. It was taken out again and again, and was loaned and paid back.

Senator MORGAN. Was it not a fact that you merely put in your credit from time to time, and that the company, as fast as it received the money, met the liabilities which you had on your notes discounted in bank?

Mr. HUNTINGTON. No; as I said, I often put in money when money was particularly needed, and I often borrowed money in order to put it in.

Senator MORGAN. Who were the other officers of the company?

Mr. HUNTINGTON. Mark Hopkins was treasurer, and E. H. Miller, jr., was secretary.

Senator MORGAN. Did you ever obtain from them, in the form of a voucher or receipt, any evidence that you had put actual money into that concern?

Mr. HUNTINGTON. Yes; I was a subscriber for stock, and paid in a few thousand dollars on the stock.

Senator MORGAN. How much did you pay on the stock?

Mr. HUNTINGTON. I do not know. It was not very much; I should think not more than about $8,000 or $10,000. That was when they started to organize the company.

Senator MORGAN. Did you ever pay anything else in cash for that stock?

Mr. HUNTINGTON. Yes.

Senator MORGAN. How much?

Mr. HUNTINGTON. Whatever the requirement was. It was all paid for.

Senator MORGAN. An indifferent statement of that sort is no answer to my question.

Mr. HUNTINGTON. I am answering your question the best I can.

Senator MORGAN. I am afraid not.

Mr. HUNTINGTON. I am, and when I say I am, that is what that means.

Senator MORGAN. You can state whether, in addition to the $8,000 or $10,000, you paid any money on that stock.

Mr. HUNTINGTON. Mr. Hopkins attended to these affairs, and I have no doubt he paid in whatever was necessary to be paid in under the statute.

Senator MORGAN. Can you state on oath that you, or Mr. Hopkins on your account, paid any money into that concern except the money necessary to organize it in the first instance?

Mr. HUNTINGTON. Yes; a great deal of money.

Senator MORGAN. How much?

Mr. HUNTINGTON. I don't know; I may have put in several hundred thousand dollars.

Senator MORGAN. In money?

Mr. HUNTINGTON. Yes.

Senator MORGAN. Was that in the form of money lodged with the treasurer of the company for which you took a voucher or receipt?

Mr. HUNTINGTON. I have no doubt of it; but I did not see it.

Senator MORGAN. What has become of these vouchers or receipts?

Mr. HUNTINGTON. I do not know.

Senator MORGAN. Were they burned or destroyed with the books and papers of the Contract and Finance Company?

Mr. HUNTINGTON. I do not know. They may have been sold as paper stock, or they may have been burned up; because, when the whole thing was closed up and the company was disincorporated, it was hardly worth while to cumber up an office with heaps of books and papers of that class of literature.

Senator MORGAN. I never heard it called literature before. You say that you paid into that company—"we," you say. Whom do you mean by "we?"

Mr. HUNTINGTON. I meant Mr. Hopkins and myself. He was doing all the business at that end. He was there, and I was in New York and Boston.

Senator MORGAN. You say "we" put into that company several hundred thousand dollars?

Mr. HUNTINGTON. I referred to myself—to me, personally.

Senator MORGAN. You meant that you had put in several hundred thousand dollars?

Mr. HUNTINGTON. Yes.

Senator MORGAN. Did you pay it on stock?

Mr. HUNTINGTON. I should say so; I don't know what else I could have paid it on.

Senator MORGAN. Did you take certificates of stock when you made your payments?

Mr. HUNTINGTON. I think that that was the way that Mr. Hopkins would have done it.

Senator MORGAN. How many certificates of stock did you get?

Mr. HUNTINGTON. As I said several times, I do not remember, because I do not think I ever counted the shares myself. I had absolute confidence in Mr. Hopkins.

Senator MORGAN. Did you sell these certificates of stock?

Mr. HUNTINGTON. Yes.

Senator MORGAN. To whom?

Mr. HUNTINGTON. I do not know. They were sold at various times, mostly in bulk.

Senator MORGAN. I am speaking of the stock of the Contract and Finance Company.

Mr. HUNTINGTON. And I was thinking of the shares of the Central Pacific. I do not think I ever saw the shares of the Contract and Finance Company.

Senator MORGAN. I do not think you ever did either. You did not state it before if you did. You paid several hundred thousand dollars on the stock of the Contract and Finance Company—you bought stock with the several hundred thousand dollars that you paid in?

Mr. HUNTINGTON. My mind was on the Central Pacific. I never was in the office of the Contract and Finance Company in my life, and I do not think I ever saw the books unless I saw them in masses in the room.

Senator MORGAN. Are you in the habit of turning over your business property—books and bank accounts—to somebody else?

Mr. HUNTINGTON. If I did not trust anybody with my business I could not have been here. I trust a man all in all. I would have trusted Mr. Hopkins before myself; not in integrity; but when it came to the handling of papers if Mark Hopkins said it was right, I assented.

Senator MORGAN. Did Mr. Hopkins have control of your bank account and your financial resources at his will and pleasure?

Mr. HUNTINGTON. I think that if Mark Hopkins had told me that he had sold my dwelling house, and if he had sent me the deed of sale I would have signed it without reading it, I had so much confidence in him.

Senator MORGAN. I suppose Mr. Hopkins at least informed you what he had done with your money?

Mr. HUNTINGTON. When I went out to California, once a year, he said things are so and so, and he handed me a piece of paper. I looked at it and said, "All right." I have always found that it is a better way to trust somebody than to distrust everybody.

Senator MORGAN. Did he inform you from time to time of the sums of money that he took out of your private treasury and put into stock of the Contract and Finance Company?

Mr. HUNTINGTON. Not as a rule. He said: "We did so and so, and we want more money on the work." My desire was that we should not fail before we got beyond the top of the Sierra Nevadas. There was not a time when, if anyone whom I had confidence in had offered to give me half of what the work had cost and to finish it, I would not have said: "Take it."

Senator MORGAN. I do not want to get into that romantic history in the mountains.

Mr. HUNTINGTON. You should know all that I know. I think you would not ask so many questions if you knew all that I know.

Senator MORGAN. I understood you to say that you never owned any stock in the Contract and Finance Company.

Mr. HUNTINGTON. No; I said I supposed I did. I said I did not know how much.

Senator MORGAN. You never sold any?

Mr. HUNTINGTON. No.

Senator MORGAN. Has Mr. Hopkins sold any for you?

Mr. HUNTINGTON. No; I think not. When Mr. Hopkins wrote to me at Boston about organizing a company——

Senator MORGAN. That is getting away back again. There is no occasion for going back there again.

Mr. HUNTINGTON. Well, these questions have been asked five or six times.

Senator MORGAN. You then said that you did own stock in the Contract and Finance Company.

Mr. HUNTINGTON. I said that I had no doubt but that I owned some stock in the Contract and Finance Company.

Senator MORGAN. But you will not say that you did.

Mr. HUNTINGTON. I say I have no doubt that I did.

Senator MORGAN. Do you know that you did?

Mr. HUNTINGTON. I never saw the books.

Senator MORGAN. And you never saw the certificates?

Mr. HUNTINGTON. No; but Mark Hopkins told me, I am sure, that we had stock in the company. I do not think I ever saw a certificate of that stock.

Senator MORGAN. But you are firm in the belief that you did own some?

Mr. HUNTINGTON. Yes.

Senator MORGAN. But you do not know as to the amount?

Mr. HUNTINGTON. I do not know. Very likely it was considerable. When Mr. Hopkins asked me how much stock we would take I telegraphed him: "Take as little as you can and as much as you must."

Senator MORGAN. How much did he tell you he "must" take?

Mr. HUNTINGTON. He did not reply to that telegram. It was not necessary. He had my full authority.

Senator MORGAN. And Mr. Hopkins never informed you how much stock he had taken in the Contract and Finance Company?

Mr. HUNTINGTON. I would not say that he did not. Very likely he did.

Senator MORGAN. What information did he give you as to the amount of stock he took?

Mr. HUNTINGTON. I do not know the amount, and I am not certain that he told me.

Senator MORGAN. About how much stock do you think he took in that company?

Mr. HUNTINGTON. I am sure I can not say.

Senator MORGAN. About how much?

Mr. HUNTINGTON. If I could tell you the one I could tell you the other.

Senator MORGAN. You can inform the committee of the impression on your mind as to the amount of stock that you owned in that company through the assistance of Mr. Hopkins.

Mr. HUNTINGTON. I have not the amount on my mind. I have this on my mind, that I was carrying a load which I hated awfully to carry.

Senator MORGAN. When that company had finished its work in building the Central Pacific how much stock did you own in it?

Mr. HUNTINGTON. In what company?

Senator MORGAN. In the Contract and Finance Company.

Mr. HUNTINGTON. I do not know.

Senator MORGAN. About how much?

Mr. HUNTINGTON. I do not know.

Senator MORGAN. Can you state within a million of how much?

Mr. HUNTINGTON. I would not say.

Senator MORGAN. Within five millions of how much?

Mr. HUNTINGTON. Well, I do not know.

Senator MORGAN. State within $10,000,000 how much stock did you own in it.

Mr. HUNTINGTON. I owned more or less than that.

Senator MORGAN. But you do not know how much it was?

Mr. HUNTINGTON. No; but I am satisfied that it was not more than that. Very likely—I can say, to the best of my knowledge and belief, that it was more than $1,000,000.

Senator MORGAN. Assuming that it was $10,000,000 of stock that you owned at the time the company went up, state whether you paid ten millions in money for it?

Mr. HUNTINGTON. I should say so. I should say we had paid even more than that. We borrowed it largely. We borrowed on our own credit and we made a great success in building the road.

Senator MORGAN. At the time that the Contract and Finance Company was ready to wind up its affairs—at the time it finished the building of the railroad—did that company owe you for any borrowed money?

Mr. HUNTINGTON. I should think I was on their paper, at least, and they may have owed me. The object was to complete the work.

Senator MORGAN. I do not want the object of the company; that is no answer to my question. I am not going to have that any more if I can control it.

Mr. HUNTINGTON. It depends upon the questions you ask what the answers will be.

Senator MORGAN. I want to know if they owed you for any borrowed money at the time they wound up their affairs?

Mr. HUNTINGTON. The Contract and Finance Company owed a great deal of money, just how much I am unable to state. Whether I had borrowed the money myself or whether they had borrowed it and I was on their paper I can not say. It is thirty years ago, very nearly, and things were all finished and I had dropped the matter out of my mind.

Senator MORGAN. If they owed you any money was it money obtained on your credit or money taken out of your pocket?

Mr. HUNTINGTON. I would say, to the best of my recollection, that it was some of both.

Senator MORGAN. How much of each?

Mr. HUNTINGTON. I can not tell the amounts. It is almost impossible for a man doing so much business as I have been from year to year to recollect things that happened thirty years ago and which have been entirely settled up. No man could do it, I think.

Senator MORGAN. Perhaps we had better go back to your deposition given on a former occasion, and to the report of the United States Pacific Railroad commission about it, so as to refresh your memory. The commission says, on page 73 of its report:

In 1873 the disclosures made by the examinations conducted by the Wilson committee excited much public attention and indignation, with reference to similar practices affecting the Union Pacific Railroad Company, through the intervention of the Credit Mobilier. Comparatively little attention was given by that committee to the affairs of the Central Pacific Railroad Company.

Mr. Huntington, however, was examined as a witness. He was examined as to the profits resulting from the construction of the Central Pacific road. He described them as being confined to the stock of the company, and that the share received by him amounted to $1,000,000 of this stock. (See report of the Wilson committee, testimony of Huntington, p. 703.) This evidence was given more than two years after the completion of the Central Pacific Railroad, and Mr. Stanford has testified that each of the parties in interest received $13,000,000 of the stock of the company as his share of the profits. (See evidence of Stanford, vol. 5, pp. 2655, 2656.) Mr. Huntington must, therefore, have known when he was testifying before the Wilson committee that his statement was not a true one.

Mr. HUNTINGTON. If I stated it at the time it was correct.

Senator MORGAN. I give you now, after having recited this matter, a full opportunity to give any explanation that you may desire of this accusation against you.

Mr. HUNTINGTON. I do not fight words thrown into the air by irresponsible committees, as those committees usually were. They picked up their information on the corners of the streets in San Francisco from discharged employees and blackmailers. They got, very likely, the best they could; but we did not go out to gather things thrown into the air.

Senator MORGAN. It appears that the commissioners based their statement upon your deposition and Mr. Stanford's, and that Stanford said that each of the parties in interest received $13,000,000 as his share of the profits.

Mr. HUNTINGTON. The stock of the Contract and Finance Company was only $5,000,000.

Senator MORGAN. This refers to the stock of the Central Pacific Railroad Company.

Mr. HUNTINGTON. That I do not know. Stanford probably knew it if he swore to it. He probably knew whether he got it.

Senator MORGAN. Did he know what you got?

Mr. HUNTINGTON. I do not think he did; Hopkins would have known.

Senator MORGAN. If there was an equal division at the time of the settlement, how could Stanford fail to know whether he got more or less than the balance of you?

Mr HUNTINGTON. I do not know. Mr. Stanford knew very little about the business of the company; but I do not know how he could have made that mistake. He knew very little of the Central Pacific road.

Senator MORGAN. You say that his statement was a mistake?

Mr. HUNTINGTON. I do not say that it was a mistake. I do not know how he arrived at it.

Senator MORGAN. How much did you receive?

Mr. HUNTINGTON. I do not recollect.

Senator MORGAN. Then why do you not believe that Stanford was correct?

Mr. HUNTINGTON. I have no idea that there was such an amount of stock delivered at any time. I do not know just where the Contract and Finance Company commenced. The first seven contractors built from Sacramento to New Castle, 31 miles. Then Charles Crocker & Co. took a contract to build over the mountains, something over 100 miles—120 miles across the Sierra Nevada. They took a contract for that, and I do not think they finished that contract. I think they got some thirteen millions of stock for that. How much of that went to the Contract and Finance Company, when they took up the contract where it stopped, I do not know. If that were so, that would not leave more than forty-five millions of stock at the most. I think it was thirteen or fourteen millions that Crocker received. The other parties I am quite sure got some stock for the building of the first 30 miles. So, how Stanford could have got $13,000,000, I can not say.

Senator MORGAN. I understand you to deny that you got thirteen millions of stock of the Central Pacific Railroad Company as testified to by Stanford?

Mr. HUNTINGTON. I say I do not believe that we did, and I do not believe that there was any such amount of stock to divide after the contract with Charles Crocker & Co. and the other seven contractors. There was only sixty millions of stock altogether.

Senator MORGAN. On page 74 of the report the commissioners state:

The books in question are identified by John Miller, William E. Brown, Daniel Yost, and others, as large journals and ledgers containing several hundred pages each, numbering in all from 12 to 15 volumes, and their disappearance by accident or inadvertence is simply impossible.

Mr. HUNTINGTON. They were probably burned up or sold for paper stock if they were destroyed at all. I have no doubt they were destroyed; for I have asked for them myself within the last five years, and somebody told me they were destroyed.

Senator MORGAN (reading). "Mr. Yost testified that the last he saw of them Hopkins was personally engaged in packing them in boxes." Did you know Mr. Yost?

Mr. HUNTINGTON. Yes.

Senator MORGAN. What sort of a man was he?

Mr. HUNTINGTON. He is dead.

Senator MORGAN. What sort of a man was he when living?

Mr. HUNTINGTON. Well, the best thing he did was to die.

Senator MORGAN. And may be the next best thing that he did was to help get away with those books.

Mr. HUNTINGTON. No; I do not think so. He was a light-weight man. He would not know to-day what he would do to-morrow.

Senator MORGAN. I suppose he knew to-day what he had done yesterday?

Mr. HUNTINGTON. Yes; but he might not tell it.

Senator MORGAN. You have a poor opinion of him?

Mr. HUNTINGTON. I have. I have what is in my mind very strong.

Senator MORGAN. These commissioners go on to say: "These books had been kept for several years by William E. Brown." Did you know him?

Mr. HUNTINGTON. Yes.

Senator MORGAN. What sort of a man is he?

Mr. HUNTINGTON. He is not with us now; he is a very clever man.

Senator MORGAN. How long did you keep him in your employment?

Mr. HUNTINGTON. We did not keep him at all.

Senator MORGAN. But the Contract and Finance Company?

Mr. HUNTINGTON. I do not know that he was in their employ at all.

Senator MORGAN. What did he have to do with this business?

Mr. HUNTINGTON. He was with the governor.

Senator MORGAN. What governor?

Mr. HUNTINGTON. Stanford.

Senator MORGAN. What relations did he have with Stanford?

Mr. HUNTINGTON. He got some money every month, I suppose.

Senator MORGAN. Tripped around after Stanford?

Mr. HUNTINGTON. I can not describe the man; he was a light-weight fellow.

Senator MORGAN. He was at work for Stanford, was he?

Mr. HUNTINGTON. I never knew what he was doing.

Senator MORGAN. Brown, I see, was secretary in 1873, when John Miller succeeded him as secretary and bookkeeper of the Contract and Finance Company. What sort of a man was Miller?

Mr. HUNTINGTON. Miller is living.

Senator MORGAN. What sort of a man is he? Is he a responsible man?

Mr. HUNTINGTON. Well, he was not a very good man. He had one trial, and they cleared him. I went to California and saw a gentleman around the office and asked who it was. They said he was John Miller. Perhaps the next day I asked him what they gave him, and they said $5,000 a year. I said "You give him either too much or too little." They asked me why. I said "In a day or two I will find out what he is doing," and I told Mr. Crocker to put an expert upon his books right away. I waited two or three days, and the expert was not put on; so I said to Crocker, "I will get a man if you do not," and he set a man upon Miller's books. This is a matter of public history there, but I hardly like to tell it. We found where Miller had taken wrongfully something over $700,000 of money of the Contract and Finance Company, and we got but half of it back.

Senator MORGAN. What did you do with him?

Mr. HUNTINGTON. They tried him, and I believe they decided that he was not guilty.

Senator MORGAN. Did the company help him out of it?

Mr. HUNTINGTON. No, not at all; not in the least. We thought he ought to have been found guilty. When Mr. Crocker said that he was a thief, I said, "No; I think he is a pretty clever fellow." He said, "Why?" and I said "Why, because he did not get a wheelbarrow and carry off every brick in the building."

Senator MORGAN. You say that Brown was a pretty good man?

Mr. HUNTINGTON. I do not know much about Brown; he was seemingly a gentleman.

Senator MORGAN. The commissioners say:

Both Mr. Brown and Mr. Miller testified that before Miller took charge of the books William E. Brown prepared a complete and new set, consisting of daybook, journal, and ledger, into which set of books he personally transcribed all the balances of the unclosed accounts contained in the books of the Contract and Finance Company. These books have since been produced before the commission and the fact is as stated.

Have you ever seen those books?

Mr. HUNTINGTON. No.

Senator MORGAN. You have no knowledge what they contained?

Mr. HUNTINGTON. I did not know there were any such books.

Senator MORGAN. You do not know what they contained in relation to your accounts?

Mr. HUNTINGTON. No.

Senator MORGAN. But if Mr. Brown made the transcript, you would suppose that it was fairly done?

Mr. HUNTINGTON. I should be inclined to think so.

Senator MORGAN (reading):

John Miller testified that he saw the books both of the Contract and Finance Company and of Charles Crocker & Co. in their usual place in the rooms occupied by the Contract and Finance Company; that he was personally in charge of the room during the day on which they disappeared; that he left the room for a short time at the lunch hour, leaving Mr. Brown there, and that on his return the books had disappeared. William E. Brown denies any knowledge of their whereabouts or of the circumstances of their disappearance.

Do you know anything about their whereabouts or the circumstances of their disappearing?

Mr. HUNTINGTON. No; I do not.

Senator MORGAN. Are you not the only man living who had an interest in those books?

Mr. HUNTINGTON. Of all the old directors of the Central Pacific Railroad Company I guess that I am. I think that Benjamin Crocker is living, and he had some interest in them, I believe. He was not in the management of the Central Pacific, but I think he had some interest in it.

Senator MORGAN. Mr. Crocker, the commissioners say, "gives it as his opinion that the books were destroyed by Mark Hopkins as having no value."

Mr. HUNTINGTON. The rooms were cumbered up, and I said to Mark Hopkins, "Why not get rid of these books and papers? I would not have the room cumbered up with them."

Senator MORGAN. Where were you when you said that?

Mr. HUNTINGTON. I should think (as my memory runs back) that I was in the hardware and metal store of Huntington & Hopkins, in Sacramento; I should think I was.

Senator MORGAN. Were those books of which you speak in Sacramento or in San Francisco?

Mr. HUNTINGTON. In Sacramento.

Senator MORGAN. You were not in that particular room, were you?

Mr. HUNTINGTON. Not at the time. I do not think I was ever in the rooms of the Contract and Finance Company. I was very busy when I was there.

Senator MORGAN. If you were not in the room how could you know that it was lumbered up?

Mr. HUNTINGTON. It is a mild climate there and the rooms were always open.

Senator MORGAN. How did it become a matter of sufficient importance or significance to you that you should recommend to Mr. Hopkins that this room, which you had never been in, should be emptied of what it contained?

Mr. HUNTINGTON. It is quite natural. I am always watching little things, and I let large things take care of themselves. I suppose it came up out of their wanting more room.

Senator MORGAN. You have stated already that this was a rented room?

Mr. HUNTINGTON. Yes.

Senator MORGAN. Could you not easily have rented another room in Sacramento?

Mr. HUNTINGTON. If we occupied one room with a lot of worthless material we would have to pay rent for it all the same.

Senator MORGAN. And you wanted to save expense?

Mr. HUNTINGTON. Well, I always do that.

Senator MORGAN. These other rooms in the building, were they also littered up?

Mr. HUNTINGTON. There was none of them perhaps littered with dead business.

Senator MORGAN. That means that this business was all wound up?

Mr. HUNTINGTON. I understood that they had wound up.

Senator MORGAN. Absolutely?

Mr. HUNTINGTON. I suppose absolutely would be the word.

Senator MORGAN. No transactions left open at all?

Mr. HUNTINGTON. As I understood, the business was all closed and the company was disincorporated.

Senator MORGAN. Was its charter repealed?

Mr. HUNTINGTON. Yes.

Senator MORGAN. By an act of the legislature?

Mr. HUNTINGTON. No; it might be by an act of the legislature.

Senator MORGAN. Do you not recollect that the charter was dissolved by an act of the legislature?

Mr. HUNTINGTON. I do not.

Senator MORGAN. In what way could you dissolve a charter unless by an act of the legislature, or by a decree of the court?

Mr. HUNTINGTON. I think you can. I thought there was a way to disincorporate a company under the statute. I may be wrong.

Senator MORGAN. How long was it after you had given this advice to Hopkins before these books disappeared?

Mr. HUNTINGTON. I do not know; I would not swear positively that I knew they were taken out of the room at all. I stayed there only two or three days.

Senator MORGAN. Did you ever hear of any of these books and papers being in the hands of any junk dealer or merchant who wanted to use them for wrapping paper?

Mr. HUNTINGTON. I hardly think they would be valuable for wrapping paper. Their most value would be to be ground up and used as paper stock.

Senator MORGAN. Did you have any paper mill there?

Mr. HUNTINGTON. My impression is there was.

Senator MORGAN. If these books and papers had been ground up for paper stock, or if they had been sold to a junk dealer——

Mr. HUNTINGTON. I hardly think they would have been worth anything except for paper stock.

Senator MORGAN. You are not entirely indifferent to public opinion, are you?

Mr. HUNTINGTON. I have often said that, as long as one man in the world thought well of me I would not care what the balance of the human race thought, and that I would not exchange the good opinion of one man for the opinion of the whole human race.

Senator MORGAN. You would take the opinion of that one man?

Mr. HUNTINGTON. I would take the opinion of C. P. Huntington.

Senator MORGAN. You must be a happy man, considering how much C. P. Huntington thinks of you.

Mr. HUNTINGTON. I am; and I go to sleep with great satisfaction.

Senator MORGAN. I am glad you do. The commissioners say:

> Putting all these facts together—the existence of a strong motive on the part of Stanford, Huntington, Hopkins, and Crocker to suppress the books; the impossibility for accounting for their disappearance, except in pursuance of the act or direction of one of these four persons; the evidence of Yost that he saw Hopkins engaged in packing the books in boxes; the evidence of John Miller of their sudden disappearance, and the statement of Mr. Crocker connecting their disappearance with Mark Hopkins—it is impossible to avoid the conclusion that the suppression of these books has been intentional and willful.

Mr. HUNTINGTON. As to that I do not know. But certainly if I had supposed that the books would have been wanted I should not have had them burned, because I am satisfied that there was nothing in the books (although I never saw them) which did not show that the work was well done by the Contract and Finance Company, and that a better work was never done. I should like to have those books to show what great results were brought about for so little. In fact, they would show that the work was done for a smaller amount of assets than such work had ever been done before under similar circumstances.

Senator MORGAN. I am sorry that such a casual remark to Hopkins has deprived you of such valuable testimony.

Mr. HUNTINGTON. I regret it more than you do.

SENATOR MORGAN. The commissioners say further—

in estimating, therefore, the actual cost of construction of the Central Pacific Railroad, of any of the branches which were constructed through contracts with the Contract and Finance Company, of any repairs done by that company or supplies furnished by it, we feel compelled to accept the rule at law which applies to all cases of suppressed evidence, and which raises against the party implicated in the suppression the very strongest presumption that the suppressed evidence, if produced, would testify against the party suppressing the same.

Then the commissioners say:

It is our judgment that the actual cost of construction of the Central Pacific Railroad from Sacramento to Promontory Point and the purchase from the Union Pacific Railroad of 47½ miles, a total distance of 737.5 miles, did not exceed the sum of $36,000,000.

Mr. HUNTINGTON. Now, in the nature of things, Senator Morgan, you can see, I think, that the commissioners did not know anything about it. Nobody could tell anything about it. We had but forty-four millions in gold to do that work with. The work there was paid for in gold, and the like work, in my opinion, was never done better or cheaper. The commissioners did not know anything about it.

Senator MORGAN. But I never have been able to find out from you whether you spent the whole $44,000,000, or whether you had some residuum left after you got through.

Mr. HUNTINGTON. Any set of men who understood anything about the building of railroads, and who understood the difficulties of constructing the Central Pacific road, would see that the work must have been handled remarkably well.

Senator MORGAN. But you are stating now what the road ought to have cost, and would have cost in the hands of ordinarily efficient men, while I am trying to get at the fact of what it actually did cost.

Mr. HUNTINGTON. There are certain results. There is the work and there is what it cost, and there never was so clean a piece of work done in the world. The men who signed that report did not know anything about it and could not know anything about it. We had one avalanche out there that covered up nineteen men.

Senator MORGAN. I do not want to hear all about that.

Mr. HUNTINGTON. But that is part of the history of the road.

Senator MORGAN. That is a diversion from the question.

Mr. HUNTINGTON. I am right on the question.

Senator MORGAN. Very good. Proceed until you have exhausted your statement and I will ask the question again.

Mr. HUNTINGTON. I will hear the question again.

Senator MORGAN. Then I will ask it. How much of this forty-four millions of gold did you actually expend in the construction of the Central Pacific Railroad?

Mr. HUNTINGTON. It is quite safe to say that it was all expended.

Senator MORGAN. Then you claim that you paid out in gold for that road as much as you realized from the sale of the first and second mortgage bonds?

Mr. HUNTINGTON. A good deal of it was not paid in gold. We bought material on this side, and it took a good deal of currency to pay for it.

Senator MORGAN. Your statements have been hitherto all based on gold?

Mr. HUNTINGTON. No, excuse me. I said that all the work and materials in California were paid for in gold. I said that all the payments in California were in gold. I stick to that. But we did not pay for rails in gold. If we had there would not have been money enough.

Senator MORGAN. Then I will change the form of my question so as to cover that new statement. I wish now to know how much money in gold or greenbacks or currency of any kind you realized from the sale of these first and second mortgage bonds.

Mr. HUNTINGTON. I can not say in dollars what we received.

Senator MORGAN. Did you realize more than $46,000,000?

Mr HUNTINGTON. I should think we did, considerably more, in currency.

Senator MORGAN. Did you not realize as much as $46,000,000 in gold?

Mr. HUNTINGTON. We did not put into gold any more than was necessary.

Senator MORGAN. That does not answer the question. I want to know if you realized as much as $46,000,000 in gold.

Mr. HUNTINGTON. I do not know. I would have to go back thirty years and look up the quotations in the New York gold market, and they did not stand two days at the same figure.

Senator MORGAN. I did not expect that your mind would retain the exact amount of gold and currency which you realized, but as to the sum total, I think you should be able to state how much you realized.

Mr. HUNTINGTON. No; I would not carry it in my head. We bought gold as low as we could, and we closed the transaction.

Senator MORGAN. I recall you again to the statement made by the commissioners that the cost of the Central Pacific Railroad did not exceed the sum of $36,000,000.

Mr. HUNTINGTON. They did not know anything about it. What they say was probably what they gathered on the street corners, and it was the best information, probably, that they could get. But it cost more than that, very much more than that.

Senator MORGAN. I have tried on a dozen or twenty occasions to get you tell how much it did cost. I ask you again.

Mr. HUNTINGTON. I can not tell you.

Senator MORGAN. I will ask you, now, finally, so as to get rid of this subject, to state as nearly as you, can what that line of railroad, 737.50 miles, cost for construction and equipment.

Mr. HUNTINGTON. I should say that the road cost (it is merely a guess), from San Jose to Ogden, somewhere about in the neighborhood of between $80,000,000 and $90,000,000. That was part in gold and part in currency.

Senator MORGAN. Take that 737.50 miles from Sacramento to Ogden; what did that cost?

Mr. HUNTINGTON. It is impossible for me to tell what it cost, thirty years after it has been built.

Senator MORGAN. You who are interested in the road to the extent of millions of dollars are unable to state how much it did cost, and yet you say that the commissioners who report that it did not cost more than $36,000,000 based their report upon information picked up on the street corners.

Mr. HUNTINGTON. They must have done so, from their figures. I do not believe that Mr. Anderson or Mr. Littler would have stated anything but what they thought was right.

Senator MORGAN. If it was so difficult for those gentlemen to get at the cost of the road, what must we think about you who are directly interested in it and are unable to state what it did cost?

Mr. HUNTINGTON. What inducement would I have in remembering, thirty years after the road was built, what it cost?

Senator MORGAN. You see that I am simple enough to have an inducement which justifies me in putting the question.

Mr. HUNTINGTON. If I knew I would be glad to tell you.

Senator MORGAN. Then you do not know?

Mr. HUNTINGTON. I do not know, and no man living could begin to tell you the cost, after thirty years.

Senator MORGAN. But it was at the close of these transactions, and when you had finished the road and had it all equipped and in operation, that the division of the stock of the Central Pacific took place, in which division Stanford testifies you each got thirteen millions of stock.

Mr. HUNTINGTON. I do not believe that. I think Governor Stanford was mistaken. I have no idea that he would testify to anything which he did not believe, but he would not be likely to have known very much about it, and I have no idea, either, that the stock was distributed. As I recollect, the stock was sold in blocks, and the whole thing was, I may say, in a pool and never was segregated. I sold the shares, but I never sold a share of my own without the shares of the others being sold too. I am sure that all these blocks of stock belonging to the company were sold and that I never sold a block of my own.

Senator MORGAN. I am giving you a full opportunity under oath to impeach this report of the commissioners.

Mr. HUNTINGTON. I understand, and I am very much obliged to you for it.

Senator MORGAN. The commissioners proceed to say:

> We base this conclusion on the examination of many witnesses as to the actual cost of railroad building and material during the years of construction, on the evidence taken of the character of the country, on the agreed price paid by the Central Pacific to the Union Pacific for 47½ miles of the road between Promontory Point and a point 5 miles west of Ogden; and in reaching this conclusion we have made, in our judgment, full allowance for all that appears in the evidence relating to the peculiar and difficult character of the work, to the excessive cost of building the road over the Sierra Nevadas, to the impediments offered by snow and stormy weather, to the unusual item of cost arising out of the construction of snowsheds, and to the increased cost resulting from the rapidity with which the work was carried on and the necessity of expensive and unusual transportation of all material required for the construction of the road.

Mr. HUNTINGTON. That is very nicely stated.

Senator MORGAN. Is it true?

Mr. HUNTINGTON. Who are the men that they got their information from?

Senator MORGAN. They have given the depositions of all the men.

Mr. HUNTINGTON. Have they given their names?

Senator MORGAN. I can furnish you their names by reference (but it would take an hour or two) to all the depositions which this commission took. The commissioners swore witnesses and they were themselves sworn officers.

Mr. HUNTINGTON. I would like to know the men whose testimony they took.

Senator MORGAN. It will stand you in good stead, inasmuch as you have the opportunity of impeaching this report, to read the depositions. They are all on file.

Mr. HUNTINGTON. I would like to have the names of the men.

Senator MORGAN. I am not here to furnish them to you.

Mr. HUNTINGTON. It is said that we had received forty millions from the State of California, whereas all that we received was $400,000.

Senator MORGAN. That was not in a report made to the Government or made under oath. That was in a report made by gentlemen who had been selected at a public meeting in San Francisco to represent the people of California.

Mr. HUNTINGTON. Fifty-two men. They would have sworn to it.

Senator MORGAN. You say that there were fifty-two men in one of these meetings. I do not know which meeting you refer to.

Mr. HUNTINGTON. I refer to the one in which the State was raked over for delegates.

Senator MORGAN. These gentlemen have stated that there were as many as 15,000 people turned away.

Mr. HUNTINGTON. That is another meeting. I do not think that one-fourth of that number of men ever got together there. At their last great meeting they got fifty-two men, as I was told, and as I believe.

Senator MORGAN. But this is a sworn report, from sworn officers of the Government, made on the sworn testimony of witnesses. In this volume, running from page 4 to page 1010, there are a great number of depositions, among which I find your deposition, and I suppose you had a knowledge of what you swore to.

Mr. HUNTINGTON. I do not think I ever read it, although I may have read it and signed it.

Senator MORGAN. That was the reason for my asking you whether you were entirely indifferent to public opinion, and you said that you were, except as to the opinion of C. P. Huntington.

Mr. HUNTINGTON. I said that when I did the right thing, and was satisfied with myself, then I did not yield to public opinion.

Senator MORGAN. These commissioners, in making their report, state that they had made due allowance for all the difficulties in the way, including the snow shed and the tremendous difficulties that existed in the construction of this very magnificent work, but that, after making allowance for all those difficulties and weighing the testimony (including your own and that of Leland Stanford and of Mark Hopkins) they came to the conclusion that the construction of the Central Pacific Railroad for the distance of 737½ miles, including the 47½ miles purchased from the Union Pacific Company, did not exceed the sum of $36,000,000. Now, if you can show that that statement, or that conclusion, is in any respect unjust to you or to your associates, or in any respect unfair, you have the full opportunity to do it now.

Mr. HUNTINGTON. I say that the commissioners did not know anything about it, but I know all about it in a general way. The work was not done, in my opinion, for more than twice that money. The commissioners did not know what was paid for materials or for freight or for insurance, or for other things.

Senator MORGAN. It was impossible that they could not know anything about it when they had sworn you as a witness and examined you.

Mr. HUNTINGTON. They did not ask me what we paid for rails or what it cost to get timber for the snow sheds. I answered their questions to the best of my ability, but they did not know how to ask the questions; and if I had gone on, it would have taken a month for me to tell them what I paid for railroad ties and sleepers, and bolts, and plates, and spikes, and the material necessary, and for freighting and insurance, or the cost of transferring materials from San Francisco up the Sacramento River and hauling it by teams across the Sierra Nevada Mountains. They did not ask me these questions. If they did, I could have told them pretty nearly; and they would not have set down the total amount at $36,000,000.

Senator MORGAN. Do you really know whether they asked you these questions or not?

Mr. HUNTINGTON. I am pretty sure they did not, if they came to any such conclusion.

Senator MORGAN. If they asked you the questions which covered all these inquiries, your mind was fresher then, and you could have answered them?

Mr. HUNTINGTON. I could tell pretty well to-day, even, because I have been dealing in these things right along and they are more particularly in my line.

Senator MORGAN. We do not want statements that are only "pretty well" true.

Mr. HUNTINGTON. I might not be able to get it exactly, but I could tell pretty nearly, to the best of my knowledge and belief.

Senator MORGAN. You say that the commissioners did not know how to ask the questions?

Mr. HUNTINGTON. They would not have had time to go into the whole question of building the Central Pacific Railroad, the cost of laying the road, laying the rails, and all that sort of thing, not at a thousand but at ten thousand points.

Senator MORGAN. Here are 33 pages of printed matter containing nothing else than the questions asked you and your answers, so that the commissioners must have taken some time in examining you.

Mr. HUNTINGTON. Thirty-three pages of testimony would hardly get on to the edge of it, I think.

Senator MORGAN. The questions asked you relate to very important matters including both money and reputation.

Mr. HUNTINGTON. My reputation they never were looking out for; I take care of that myself.

Senator MORGAN. But when a man is on the witness stand and his reputation is assailed he is always careful, of course, or he ought to be, to protect it. Now, then, while you were in that situation were you holding back in order that the commissioners might put to you the questions which would drive the nail on the head, or were you there to tell the whole story?

Mr. HUNTINGTON. I presume that it struck me at the time that it was not much of their business to know what I had been doing for the last twenty years.

Senator MORGAN. Then you assumed toward the commissioners of the Government an attitude of defiance?

Mr. HUNTINGTON. Not at all. I answered their questions to the best of my ability.

Senator MORGAN. Do you mean to say that if the commission had asked you questions more specific and definite you would have given different answers?

Mr. HUNTINGTON. If they had asked me what rails cost, I would have told them.

Senator MORGAN. Perhaps they did not want to know.

Mr. HUNTINGTON. Perhaps not; I think they were pretty nice gentlemen, two of them.

Senator MORGAN. As to Pattison, you have not any opinion at all, I suppose?

Mr. HUNTINGTON. Pattison may have been a good fellow; I will not say anything about him.

Senator MORGAN. I will ask you to say something about him, and about his report too, before we get through.

Mr. HUNTINGTON. All right.

Senator MORGAN. The commission obtained your statement, and, as I understand from you, your statement did not cover the whole facts, because you did not see proper to disclose them?

Mr. HUNTINGTON. No; you have no reason or business to draw such a conclusion.

Senator MORGAN. If I have no reason to draw such a conclusion, then, of course, your deposition before the commission was the truth, and the whole truth, and nothing but the truth?

Mr. HUNTINGTON. Every question which was asked me I answered to the best of my ability.

Senator MORGAN. But questions which they did not happen to ask you you did not answer, and you did not disclose what you knew about matters germane to these questions.

Mr. HUNTINGTON. I do not think that as a rule volunteer testimony is particularly good.

Senator MORGAN. If it is truth it does not make much difference whether it is volunteer testimony or not.

Mr. HUNTINGTON. Of course a man is not likely to tell anything but the truth when he is under oath.

Senator MORGAN. Do you think that a man, situated as you were on this occasion, should shelter himself behind that excuse and say that he did not answer a question because it was not put in as specific a form as required him to make the statement?

Mr. HUNTINGTON. No.

Senator MORGAN. Are you prepared to say that your former deposition was a full, complete, and honest statement, or that it was an incomplete and untruthful statement?

Mr. HUNTINGTON. I do not say anything about it; I say that whatever questions were asked me I answered to the best of my ability.

Senator MORGAN. And you stopped there?

Mr. HUNTINGTON. Yes; I stopped there.

Senator MORGAN. I read from this report:

> As this investigation is not in the nature of an accounting, it seems unnecessary to detail the facts and the figures. Mr. Stanford's admission is that the $54,000,000 of stock distributed by the Contract and Finance Company was substantially a net profit subject only to the liquidation of an indebtedness of the Contract and Finance Company not exceeding $3,000,000. (See evidence of Stanford, vol. 5, p. 2669; William E. Brown, vol. 5, p. 2979.)

Do you give Mr. Stanford credit for being an honest man, who would tell the truth?

Mr. HUNTINGTON. I think that Leland Stanford would always tell the truth, to the best of his knowledge and belief.

Senator MORGAN. Did he not have knowledge of this matter sufficient to tell the truth?

Mr. HUNTINGTON. He did not. He did not understand what he was talking about when we got through building the road. I do not know how much stock we did have, but I know that the Contract and Finance Company figured up what was due, and found that it would not begin to pay the debts of the Contract and Finance Company; but in making up the figures the other day, to the best of my knowledge, I said that I would be very liberal, and I put the shares of the Central Pacific stock at 10 cents. I do not believe they would have brought 5 cents at the time. I have an idea that if I had offered them at 5 cents a share when the road was finished I could not have sold them at that figure. The Union Pacific shares changed hands, as much as the whole capital, at 8 cents. I was offered a majority of these shares at 7 cents and I would not take them.

Senator MORGAN. Still you said that when you made a settlement of the affairs of the Contract and Finance Company you made some money?

Mr. HUNTINGTON. Yes; but that was ten years later. We carried the debt along, and after the road was built we had to pay more interest on our debt. We paid 10 per cent for some of it, and we held it until the stock appreciated in value; then we sold. But when the road was completed I know that the Central Pacific shares would not have brought 5 per cent, and 10 per cent on these shares would have been needed to pay the debts of the Contract and Finance Company.

Senator MORGAN. You have undertaken to deny the statement of Mr. Stanford that $54,000,000 of stock was distributed to the Contract and Finance Company and was substantially a net profit?

Mr. HUNTINGTON. I do not recollect its distribution. There was quite a lot of stock, and it was sold largely in blocks and the debts were paid, and at the final outcome the balance was distributed.

Senator MORGAN. If you can not make any more definite statement about it than that——

Mr. HUNTINGTON. Is not that pretty clear?

Senator MORGAN. It is pretty clear that you do not know.

Mr. HUNTINGTON. I say that I know the stock would not have brought 10 per cent. I do not believe it would have brought 5 per cent, and that would not have paid the debts which the Contract and Finance Company owed at that time.

Senator MORGAN. Still there may have been $54,000,000 of the stock distributed, even though it was not worth 10 per cent?

Mr. HUNTINGTON. I do not recollect its being delivered.

Senator MORGAN. In the undefined condition of your memory about it——

Mr. HUNTINGTON. My memory is very clear about it.

Senator MORGAN. Yes, as to value, but as to the amount of stock delivered to the Contract and Finance Company, you think it was about $60,000,000?

Mr. HUNTINGTON. I do not think it was so much as that. I told you yesterday that I think it was about $50,000,000.

Senator MORGAN. When you say you think, I want to know what you mean. I am asking you for your recollection of facts.

Mr. HUNTINGTON. The amount of stock was about $50,000,000, which belonged to the Contract and Finance Company, but I think part of it came from the Charles Crocker's unfinished contract. The Contract and Finance Company may have taken (in taking over Charles Crocker's unfinished contract) his shares, possibly all of them, but I think not. In a general way I knew what was going on.

Senator MORGAN. Mr. Stanford seems to have stated in his deposition "that this $54,000,000 of stock distributed by the Contract and Finance Company was substantially a net profit, subject only to the liquidation of an indebtedness of the Contract and Finance Company, not exceeding $3,000,000."

Mr. HUNTINGTON. I do not suppose the Governor knew what the indebtedness was. The indebtedness was twice as much as that in New York. If he said that he positively knew it was $3,000,000 he ought not to have said so.

Senator MORGAN. And you say that you positively know that it was more than $3,000,000?

Mr. HUNTINGTON. Yes.

Senator MORGAN. How much was it?

Mr. HUNTINGTON. It was a large amount—over $10,000,000. I know that the interest which I had to pay on it was much more than I wanted to pay.

Senator MORGAN. Here is another point which the commissioners mention:

The existence of this indebtedness can hardly be said to be satisfactorily proved in the absence of the books It appears, moreover, positively proved from the books of the Central Pacific Railroad Company that during the construction of the road the Central Pacific Railroad Company had paid to the Contract and Finance Company, in lieu of a part of its cash payments, the sum of $6,000,000 in notes. (See Stevens's report, No. 7, vol. 8.) It appears also that in 1871 these notes were still in the possession of the Contract and Finance Company (see evidence of E. H. Miller, jr., p. 3438), and that they were paid by an issue of land-grant bonds delivered to that company at the rate of 86½ per cent, the rate being fixed in this, as in all cases, by the vote of Stanford, Huntington, Hopkins, and Crocker. (See evidence of Stevens, vol. 6, p. 3532.)

Mr. HUNTINGTON. I do recollect something about that. That was a transaction in San Francisco, and it was a matter out there, and not a matter in New York. I had forgotten about it; I am not positive now, but I think I have some recollection of it. That probably is the $3,000,000 which Governer Stanford refers to. The indebtedness in New York was the indebtedness of the Contract and Finance Company. I think that is the way it works out; I think it is.

Senator MORGAN. You do not question the justice of the commissioners' conclusions about it?

Mr. HUNTINGTON. If the Governor says it was done there, he would probably know.

Senator MORGAN. I am speaking about the report of the commission. You do not question that part of it?

Mr. HUNTINGTON. I do not know anything about it myself.

Senator MORGAN. It seems, then, according to this statement and according to other statements, that you took from the Central Pacific all the subsidy bonds of the United States, all the first-mortgage bonds, nearly all the stock, and $6,000,000 in notes?

Mr. HUNTINGTON. No; that is not as I recollect. I think that we took all the bonds, then I think that the Contract and Finance Company was paid in cash so much and in stock so much; so the bonds had to be sold, and the probability is that they did not realize enough to pay the cash part of the payment, and that the deficit came in in that way.

Senator MORGAN. Was the work which was done by the Contract and Finance Company to be paid one-half in cash and one-half in stock?

Mr. HUNTINGTON. Very likely it was so.

Senator MORGAN. And not in bonds?

Mr. HUNTINGTON. I should have said in bonds. I was in New York, and the contract was made in San Francisco.

Senator MORGAN. Did you have the bonds of the Central Pacific Company in New York?

Mr. HUNTINGTON. If the bonds belonged to the Central Pacific Company, I handled them as an officer of that company. I was not a director in the Contract and Finance Company, but I was vice-president of the Central Pacific, and handled the bonds for that company.

Senator MORGAN. Then, as fast as you would sell the bonds of the Central Pacific you would turn over the proceeds to the credit of the Contract and Finance Company?

Mr. HUNTINGTON. No. The Central Pacific would have the credit of the proceeds, and would place the amount in San Francisco according to agreement.

Senator MORGAN. But the transaction was of that character that when the bonds were sold by you the money went to the Contract and Finance Company?

Mr. HUNTINGTON. I should say that that was so.

Senator MORGAN. You paid the amount in New York?

Mr. HUNTINGTON. It had to be paid there; wherever it was paid it made no difference.

Senator MORGAN. When you sold the bonds of the Central Pacific you turned over the proceeds to the Contract and Finance Company?

Mr. HUNTINGTON. I have said no, unless they were their bonds.

Senator MORGAN. I do not know whether they were their bonds or not. What did you do with the money?

Mr. HUNTINGTON. I paid it where it belonged.

Senator MORGAN. Where did it belong?

Mr. HUNTINGTON. If the bonds belonged to the Central Pacific the money went to that company; and if they belonged to the Contract and Finance Company the money went there.

Senator MORGAN. To which company did it belong?

Mr. HUNTINGTON. I am inclined to think that it belonged to the Central Pacific, and that the money went to that company. I kept the accounts and sent them to California at the end of every month.

Senator MORGAN. Were the proceeds of these bonds used for any other purpose than the construction and equipment of the Central Pacific Railroad?

Mr. HUNTINGTON. No; I am quite sure they were not. I do not think the money was ever used except for the construction of the road.

Senator MORGAN. Then you understood from the beginning that the Government subsidy bonds, the bonds which the company issued, and the stock of the company (with some small reservation) and $6,000,000 of notes were intended to construct, complete, and equip the Central Pacific road; and that, when the money on the bonds and stock was realized it was due to the Contract and Finance Company?

Mr. HUNTINGTON. It could not be diverted to any other purpose; but the $6,000,000 of notes, I do not know anything about. That transaction might have come out of a higher price for gold or a lower price for bonds.

Senator MORGAN. You think that the $6,000,000 in notes grew out of the high price of gold?

Mr. HUNTINGTON. Yes; or the low price of bonds.

Senator MORGAN. That is to say, that the bonds held by the Contract and Finance Company were held by them at their face value in payment for their work?

Mr. HUNTINGTON. I do not understand you. The Central Pacific Company agreed to pay the Contract and Finance Company so much money. As I understand, the Contract and Finance Company did not have the bonds. The Central Pacific sold the bonds and paid the Contract and Finance Company so much, in cash, for building the road, and so many shares of stock. The stock went directly to the Contract and Finance Company; but it would seem that the bonds belonged to the Central Pacific, and that the Contract and Finance Company had nothing to do with them. They were sold for cash, and that cash was paid over to the Contract and Finance Company as part payment.

Senator MORGAN. Then the $6,000,000 of notes which this report of the commission says the Central Pacific Company had given to the Contract and Finance Company, in lieu of a part of its cash payment, was the difference between the face value of the bonds and the gold value of the bonds?

Mr. HUNTINGTON. No; I do not say that.

Senator MORGAN. I understood you to say that.

Mr. HUNTINGTON. You are mistaken, or I was mistaken. The Contract and Finance Company did not have anything to do with the face value of the bonds. When the bonds were sold, if the company wanted gold the gold was bought on the account of the Central Pacific Company and was paid to the Contract and Finance Company. The bonds did not sell for par. The first sales, I think, were at 90. They may have been, though, 95. There were not many sold at 90. Some were sold at par, but very few above par, and that was a matter entirely for the Central Pacific Company.

Senator MORGAN. About the $6,000,000 of notes; what was the consideration for these notes?

Mr. HUNTINGTON. They came short, as I understand, of getting gold enough out of those bonds to pay what was due to the Contract and Finance Company, and therefore the Central Pacific gave these notes for the difference.

Senator MORGAN. You mean the difference between the gold value of the bonds for which they were sold and the face value of the bonds?

Mr. HUNTINGTON. It would be a better way to say the difference between what was received from the bonds and what was due to the Contract and Finance Company. What was received from the bonds did not buy gold enough to pay what was due to the Contract and Finance Company. Is not that a better way to state it?

Senator MORGAN. No, sir.

Mr. HUNTINGTON. I can not answer it the other way. We did not get enough from the bonds to pay the gold which we owed to the Contract and Finance Company. I do not see the difference.

Senator MORGAN. I have asked you what the consideration was, and you said you thought it might be that the Central Pacific Company was deficient in money to keep up with the cash payment to the Contract and Finance Company.

Mr. HUNTINGTON. That they did not realize enough from the bonds to pay the gold.

Senator MORGAN. And that, therefore, they gave their notes for the difference between the product of the bonds and the face value of the bonds?

Mr. HUNTINGTON. For the difference between what they got for the bonds and what they owed to the Contract and Finance Company.

Senator MORGAN. The Commissioners say:

> It appears also that in 1871 these notes were still in the possession of the Contract and Finance Company, and that they were paid by an issue of land-grant bonds delivered to that company at the rate of 86½ per cent.

Mr. HUNTINGTON. I do not think I was there at the time; but, if I had been there, that would have been about right.

Senator MORGAN. So that, in addition to all the stock of the company, and all the bonds of the company, the Contract and Finance Company got an additional issue of land-grant bonds at the rate of 86½ per cent?

Mr. HUNTINGTON. That is about right, I should think.

Senator MORGAN. For the payment of the six million of notes?

Mr. HUNTINGTON. I do not remember about the amount.

Senator MORGAN. What was done with these land-grant bonds?

Mr. HUNTINGTON. They were sent to me in New York and I sold them toward paying the debt due to the Contract and Finance Company.

Senator MORGAN. How many of them did you sell?

Mr. HUNTINGTON. I do not recollect how many, but I remember that there were some land-grant bonds sold.

Senator MORGAN. Did you sell them for as much as 86½ per cent on the face value?

Mr. HUNTINGTON. I think so. I think some of them went as low as 81 per cent, but others went higher, and, of late years, they went something over par. I think that is about the right price. I think they sold not much over 90. The bonds that we kept had appreciated.

Senator MORGAN. Are these land-grant bonds still outstanding?

Mr. HUNTINGTON. I think that about eight millions have been redeemed by the sale of lands.

Senator MORGAN. That would be about the amount you would give for the payment of the $6,000,000 of debt.

Mr. HUNTINGTON. We had nothing to do with that. When the bonds were sold they went out and belonged to the holders.

Senator MORGAN. But you got the bonds and sold them?

Mr. HUNTINGTON. We sold them right off as quickly as we could get sale for them. We never had six millions of them; I mean of that issue to the Contract and Finance Company.

Senator MORGAN. The commissioners say in this report that the Central Pacific Railroad Company turned over these land-grant bonds at the rate of 86½ per cent to the Contract and Finance Company.

Mr. HUNTINGTON. Very likely that is right; I do not remember about it.

Senator MORGAN. That would be about $7,000,000. When you sold these bonds you got money for them?

Mr. HUNTINGTON. Naturally.

Senator MORGAN. And they are still outstanding, as far as you know?

Mr. HUNTINGTON. Something over seven millions of the land-grant bonds have been redeemed. They are coming in from time to time. As we sell lands we redeem bonds. I am speaking of the Central Pacific Company.

Senator MORGAN. How many bonds overhang this land grant now?

Mr. HUNTINGTON. Of that issue?

Senator MORGAN. Of all the issues.

Mr. HUNTINGTON. There are, I think, from memory, about two and a half millions of them out. But there are about twelve millions of the 5 per cent bonds.

Senator MORGAN. Overhanging the real estate?

Mr. HUNTINGTON. Yes; a mortgage on the railroad.

Senator MORGAN. These are outstanding now?

Mr. HUNTINGTON. Yes; about $14,000,000 in all.

Senator MORGAN. How many of the bonds have been redeemed?

Mr. HUNTINGTON. Ten millions of the first issue, and some of the others; I do not know exactly how many; as I recollect, there are about twelve millions outstanding.

Senator MORGAN. Then, of the land-grant bond issue (which is a mortgage on the lands granted by the Government), about seven millions of the bonds came into the possession of the Contract and Finance Company?

Mr. HUNTINGTON. I will not say about the amount, only there were some of them I know that did.

Senator MORGAN. And the balance of that issue of bonds (of which there are about $14,000,000 outstanding) were sold in the market?

Mr. HUNTINGTON. They were sold in the market.

Senator MORGAN. What was done with the money?

Mr. HUNTINGTON. As I was saying, there has been a good deal of work done from time to time by the Central Pacific, and the money has been expended on it.

Senator MORGAN. It was carried to the treasury of the Central Pacific and expended in work?

Mr. HUNTINGTON. Yes. There is no iron now in any of the main tracks of the line. They are all steel, and much of it 76 pounds.

Senator MORGAN. Have dividends been declared on the stock of the Central Pacific?

Mr. HUNTINGTON. Yes.

Senator MORGAN. How much have you received in dividends?

Mr. HUNTINGTON. I do not know.

Senator MORGAN. About how much?

Mr. HUNTINGTON. I can not say, but a considerable amount.

Senator MORGAN. I do not know what "considerable" means.

Mr. HUNTINGTON. I do not know how much I have received in dividends. The Central Pacific paid dividends right along from 1873 or 1874 until the competition from the Union Pacific and other roads became so great as to cut rates down.

Senator MORGAN. About how many years was the Central Pacific paying dividends?

Mr. HUNTINGTON. I can not say; about seven or eight years, perhaps.

Senator MORGAN. What was the average amount that you got per annum on your stock?

Mr. HUNTINGTON. It varied. I may have got 10 per cent, but I do not think I did. I was thinking that we got up to the legal rate of interest in California at one time.

Senator MORGAN. I am speaking about the average sum of money which you received in dividends annually from the Central Pacific stock?

Mr. HUNTINGTON. I can not get at the average, and I can not get at the extremes either; but we got considerable.

Senator MORGAN. I am speaking about you, not "we." Did you use the word because you and Stanford and those other men were identified with each other?

Mr. HUNTINGTON. I frequently say "we" when I should say "I," and "I" when I should say "we."

Senator MORGAN. I suppose that you are impressed by the recollection that in all of these transactions all four of you were as one man having an equal interest?

Mr. HUNTINGTON. Nearly the same. I do not think that our interests ran just the same.

Senator MORGAN. But very close?

Mr. HUNTINGTON. I know that we four men stood under and carried the road through when we would have liked to have other men stand under.

Senator MORGAN. What was the average amount of dividends which, during ten years, "we four men who stood under" received from the Central Pacific Railroad Company?

Mr. HUNTINGTON. I do not recollect. It may have been sometimes 10 per cent, but I do not believe it averaged 8 per cent, and it may not have averaged even 6 per cent. The road did very well for some time.

Senator MORGAN. What was the aggregate amount of money which "we four who stood under" received out of the stock annually in the way of dividends?

Mr. HUNTINGTON. You have used the word "we" there, but I have no objection to your doing so. I think we had commenced selling our stock, and I do not know just how much we had; but the road paid very well, and I should think that perhaps I myself may have received in dividends one million or perhaps two millions. I do not know; I was in great operations in other roads at that time. The amount of dividends was considerable, I know.

Senator MORGAN. During the ten years?

Mr. HUNTINGTON. Yes; I do not think that the dividends were running as long as ten years.

Senator MORGAN. I will assume that the dividends ran for ten years and that you got two millions out of them.

Mr. HUNTINGTON. I do not know that I did.

Senator MORGAN. That would be $20,000,000 for each of you during the ten years.

Mr. HUNTINGTON. Not two millions a year, two millions for the ten years; that would be eight millions.

Senator MORGAN. Would you undertake to say that the four gentlemen whom you spoke of, in those ten years or during the years that the Central Pacific Company was paying dividends, only got eight millions in dividends—the four of you?

Mr. HUNTINGTON. I should think we got more.

Senator MORGAN. How much more should you think?

Mr. HUNTINGTON. I do not know; I should think more.

Senator MORGAN. About how much more?

Mr. HUNTINGTON. I do not want to say.

Senator MORGAN. You may not want to say——

Mr. HUNTINGTON. Perhaps that was not the proper word for me to use. We may have got more. Let me see. There were more dividends than that paid—a good deal more. The company paid, I think, altogether $30,000,000 in dividends. No; it could not have been that much. I am not clear in my mind. No; it was not as much as that, but it was considerable. I do not like to state the amount, for I have not got it clear in my mind.

Senator MORGAN. Inasmuch as you are the only survivor of those four gentlemen, I would like you to give your best recollection of how much you four got in dividends out of that road.

Mr. HUNTINGTON. I would not be willing to say that we got more than than $2,000,000 apiece. That would be eight millions, and still we may have got more. There was a good deal more paid by the company, but our stock went out. As we got a chance to sell it, we sold, and I am quite sure, from the prices which we got for the stock, that dividends must have been paid at the time.

Senator MORGAN. Were these dividends forced, or were they the actual honest distribution of the income of the road after the payment of all fixed charges and current liabilities?

Mr. HUNTINGTON. They must have been the legitimate income out of the earnings of the road. At one time the road did very well.

Senator MORGAN. You earned the money, and paid the fixed charges and current liabilities, and then you declared dividends?

Mr. HUNTINGTON. We always did that. I say so more from the rule I have in doing my business than from recollecting the actual facts.

Senator MORGAN. And your difficulty seems to arise from the fact that you do not remember when you began selling this stock?

Mr. HUNTINGTON. Yes.

Senator MORGAN. When do you recollect selling any of the stock that you held?

Mr. HUNTINGTON. I can not say. It was considerably up in the seventies.

Senator MORGAN. Before you sold any of your personal stock?

Mr. HUNTINGTON. Before I sold any of the Contract and Finance Company's stock.

Senator MORGAN. I am not speaking of the stock of the Contract and Finance Company. I am speaking of the Central Pacific Company stock.

Mr. HUNTINGTON. That went out with the contract to build the road. The Central Pacific paid its stock to the Contract and Finance Company for building the road; and also to Charles Crocker and to seven contractors from Sacramento to Newcastle.

Senator MORGAN. So that the stock left the ownership of the Central Pacific and went into the ownership of the Contract and Finance Company?

Mr. HUNTINGTON. Yes; in the usual way.

Senator MORGAN. And after that you got dividends on that stock in favor of the Contract and Finance Company, I suppose?

Mr. HUNTINGTON. Yes; of course. If the Contract and Finance Company owned the shares it must have taken the dividends.

Senator MORGAN. You got the dividends from the Central Pacific and paid them over to the Contract and Finance Company on its stock?

Mr. HUNTINGTON. Of course the dividends were paid over to the owners of the shares.

Senator MORGAN. That means to the Contract and Finance Company?

Mr. HUNTINGTON. Yes.

Senator MORGAN. And you four gentlemen owned the Contract and Finance Company?

Mr. HUNTINGTON. Largely. I do not think we had the last shares.

Senator MORGAN. Do you recollect anybody who had shares in the Contract and Finance Company besides yourselves?

Mr. HUNTINGTON. You read the other day the names of Ben. Crocker and others who had some shares in it. I think that was so; but they were not large shareholders.

Senator MORGAN. Very inconsiderable, were they not?

Mr. HUNTINGTON. Not large; not large.

Senator MORGAN. Got to the Contract and Finance Company, which held all the stock of the Central Pacific?

Mr. HUNTINGTON. Not all. The whole amount of stock issued was $100,000,000. The Contract and Finance Company could not have had over $43,000,000 unless it took over Mr. Crocker's contract. If it did, it had more stock; if it did not, it had not more than $43,000.000.

Senator MORGAN. Whatever the sum was, the Contract and Finance Company got the dividends for the stock.

Mr. HUNTINGTON. The Contract and Finance Company got the dividends on the shares it owned.

Senator MORGAN. Can you state the aggregate amount for the ten years, or for either of the ten years in which dividends were paid on the stock? Can you state the aggregate of the payments which you get on account of dividends from the Central Pacific?

Mr. HUNTINGTON. No; I can not. It came in with other matters.

Senator MORGAN. Have you ever read the report of the United States Pacific Railroad Commission since it was made?

Mr. HUNTINGTON. I do not think I ever read it. I have been very busy about current matters from day to day. I have, perhaps, seen the report, and run it over; but I do not think I ever read it.

Senator MORGAN. There are quite a number of things in that report which I would like to give you an opportunity of replying to.

Mr. HUNTINGTON. Anything that the Senator wants to ask me I will answer. For my own part, I do not care anything for the report, because I am all right, I know; but anything that the Senator wants to ask me I will answer to the best of my ability.

Senator MORGAN. You see, we have got to vote on these matters, and I want to get information about them, and would be very glad for you to give it to us. Here in this official report; and I am sure that the House and Senate will be obliged to adopt it unless you, having the opportunity, can state facts which will turn it down or dispute it. I want to give you a full opportunity to do that, if you choose to avail yourself of it.

Mr. HUNTINGTON. I look upon most of those reports as words thrown into the air. I do not know this report at all, but I have heard it talked about. I was before the Commission three or four days myself.

Senator MORGAN. Do you want to examine this report and to examine your former deposition contained in it, in order that you may make a statement to correct your deposition, or to dispute the report?

Mr. HUNTINGTON. I might look it over, but I do not think I care to do so.

Senator MORGAN. I will assure you that, in the absence of your doing it while you are here under oath, and making a correct statement, the country and the House and the Senate will be inclined to take the report of the Commissioners as containing the truth in full.

Mr. HUNTINGTON. I can not help it.

Senator MORGAN. You can help it if you want to deny it.

Mr. HUNTINGTON. I deny pretty much the whole thing. The Commissioners reported the facts as they got them; but they could not know anything about them.

Senator MORGAN. Are you contented with that broad, sweeping denial of the Commissioners' report without looking at it?

Mr. HUNTINGTON. Perhaps I ought to look it over, but I am a very busy man. The Commissioners bring in the Sam Brannon report (it is of about the same character), and I would hardly care to deny it. I am willing to rest with what we have done. I am willing to rest on the broad statement of the facts that there is the road and that it was built for so much money. Any fair man who understands the situation will see that the work was well done and cheaply done.

Senator MORGAN. I will have the volume placed in your possession.

Mr. HUNTINGTON. I do not believe I will read it all through.

Senator MORGAN. No; but you can read the report of the Commission. It is my duty to leave it with you, and it is for you to say whether you want to answer it or not to answer it.

Mr. HUNTINGTON. I will get some of my folks to read it over and show me any points which have a bearing on this matter.

Senator MORGAN. Do you mean your lawyer?

Mr. HUNTINGTON. Perhaps not a lawyer; somebody in the office. I work about fourteen hours a day, and can not give much time to that kind of literature.

Senator MORGAN. You are not up to my standard of work, for I work eighteen hours a day.

Mr. HUNTINGTON. I think I have averaged more than twelve hours a day for sixty years. I guess that will beat you.

Senator MORGAN. I can go on and carry you through this report, as I have done through a part of it, and can examine you on the different statements which affect your interests, if you desire me to do so. You seem not to wish to examine this report yourself.

Mr. HUNTINGTON. I am sure you mistake me. I would like to examine it, but it will take a good deal of time, and, if you will allow me to say so, I do not think is is particularly profitable reading, because, as I say, I rest on the proof of what I have done, the good work I have done, and what I have done it with. It was remarkable that we did it at all. But I will have this book looked over, and if there are any points in it which I ought to notice, I will.

Senator MORGAN. It is not the points which your lawyer will pick out for you that I want you to attend to.

Mr. HUNTINGTON. I will examine the book carefully, only I do not want to read anything more than is necessary. I will take someone about the office who is familiar with our methods generally, and let him read it. Almost all my people have been with me a great deal.

Senator MORGAN. If you prefer to take this report, read it over, and examine it and your deposition, and then come before this committee and make a statement of the points wherein the Commissioners are correct or wherein they are in error; wherein they are truthful or wherein they are false—we can then get at a precise knowledge of the differences between you and the Commissioners on an examination of these matters.

Mr. HUNTINGTON. You do not mean the Sam Brannan report?

Senator MORGAN. I have not seen the Sam Brannan report.

Mr. HUNTINGTON. It is a beauty. The Commissioners may have seen it.

Senator MORGAN. But if you do not want to do that, I will proceed with your examination.

Mr. HUNTINGTON. I will be guided by what the Senator wants.

Senator MORGAN. No; I have tendered you the opportunity of taking this entire report, and your deposition, and examining them carefully, and marking the points on which you differ from the Commissioners; and you shall have the benefit of your denial or explanation.

Mr. HUNTINGTON. I will be guided by whatever the Senator wants done.

Senator MORGAN. What I want, Mr. Huntington, is to put the Senate of the United States in possession of the facts, and only that. I am not framing an argument for you or against you. I want to give you an opportunity to explain every allegation made against you by everybody.

Mr. HUNTINGTON. It would take me a hundred years, I guess, to do that; for I have had enemies all my life, and I am as proud of my enemies as of my friends. I have always hewed to the line.

Senator MORGAN. Well, sir, if you like to read this report over——

Mr. HUNTINGTON. I will read it myself if Senator Morgan wishes it. I will take it to my library at nights and read it over carefully, and anything that you would care to know about I will look at carefully, and will comment on and answer it all.

Senator MORGAN. That will save you a good deal of time, because, if I conduct this examination throughout as it has been progressing, we will be here day after day; and this examination of the Commission's report by you will be a great economy of time.

Mr. HUNTINGTON. I think I see that you would rather I would do it than be bothered about it yourself, and I will do it.

Senator MORGAN. I do not consider it any bother to me. Unfortunately I have been put in a position here where I am compelled to ask you a great many questions in order to get the facts before the country; and I thought it due to you, and I think so yet, that you should have the opportunity of contradicting, under oath, any part of this report that you can contradict.

Mr. HUNTINGTON. That seems to be fair, and I will do it.

Senator MORGAN. So, Mr. Chairman, in order to give Mr. Huntington that opportunity, I will ask the committee to adjourn.

The committee thereupon adjourned until Friday February 28, at 10.30 a. m.

WASHINGTON, D. C., *Friday, March 6, 1896.*

The committee met at 10.30 a. m., the meeting which had been fixed for Friday, February 28, having failed to take place on account of the indisposition and absence of Mr. C. P. Huntington.

Present: Senators Gear (chairman), Stewart, Wolcott, Frye, and Morgan.

The chairman stated that, before resuming the examination of Mr. Huntington, any other gentleman present who desired to be heard on the subject of the inquiry before the committee had now an opportunity to be heard.

THE UNION PACIFIC.

Mr. JOHN ROONEY, of New York, said that he had had a dispatch this morning from Mr. J. L. Morrison, of New York, counsel for the first-mortgage bondholders of the Union Pacific Company, stating that he could not appear before the committee to-day. He presented, however, copies of the supplemental statement on behalf of the first-mortgage bondholders. This paper was made part of the record, and is as follows:

PACIFIC RAILROAD DEBTS TO THE GOVERNMENT (FIRST AND SECOND MORTGAGES) AND TO INDIVIDUAL FIRST-MORTGAGE BONDHOLDERS. PLAN FOR COMPELLING THEIR CASH PAYMENT, BY FORECLOSURE AND REORGANIZATION, TO BE ADMINISTERED BY GOVERNMENT COMMISSIONERS. THE PRIVILEGE TO BE CONFERRED ON JUNIOR BONDS, AND STOCKS OF THE PRESENT COMPANIES, TO RETAIN THEIR INTERESTS, BY SUBSCRIBING TO NEW ISSUES OF WELL-SECURED OBLIGATIONS, WHOSE PROCEEDS ARE TO BE USED IN PAYING THE FIRST MORTGAGE AND GOVERNMENT DEBTS.

On behalf of first-mortgage bondholders, whose security identifies them in interest with the Government, we have given careful consideration to all the arguments which have been advanced before the committees of Congress. They have satisfied us of the correctness of the plan for the mangement by Government commissioners of the foreclosure and reorganization of these properties; through assessments on subordinate interests, for the cash payment of the first and second mortgages. Indeed, the most notable result of the extended discussions before the committees, seems to be the general conviction that the appraisal of the pecuniary value of these heterogeneous properties, and the bargaining over their price, is a function which a great parliamentary body should reject, and should relegate to administrative officers. Therefore, the practical disposition of this Pacific Railroad problem would seem to be now narrowed to the two following propositions embodied in their respective bills:

First. The plan presented on behalf of first-mortgage bondholders, for the appointment of Government commissioners to collect the first and second mortgages, upon the lines laid down by Congress. The bill requires them to pursue the usual and normal method for realizing on great corporate mortgages—through the certain force of judicial compulsion on junior claims—in order to secure the payment of prior mortgages.

Second. The plan of a syndicate, to authorize commissioners and the President, to assign the Government mortgages at a price fixed by them. We will endeavor to point out the essential differences, both in principle and practice, between these methods of disposing of the Government's property.

The syndicate plan is impracticable as a method for ascertaining the true and full value of the first mortgage and Government interests. This bill is simply the outcome of the successive efforts, made at this session, to obtain advantageous terms for junior bonds and stocks—as will be apparent from the plan which they submitted to the committees—to advance fourth-mortgage bonds to the rank of firsts, and to maintain the present stock interests upon their mere repayment to the syndicate of the amount which it advanced for first-mortgage coupons.

It is impossible for these junior claims to pay the Government, or its commissioners, the full value of its interest, and at the same time secure the desired advantages for themselves. They want to divide the earnings with the firsts and the Government, and not take the secondary chances which their contracts subject them to. It is useless to analyze their different schemes of cheapening the Government's interest, which they have been forced to relinquish. It may suffice to point out that their present bill is merely a covert form for accomplishing the same result. They now propose to substitute, for the ordinary normal method of realizing on a great mortgage interest, the plan of an assignment of the Government mortgages, based on the estimate of commissioners and the President. It would be impossible for any commission to make a proper estimate of such a property in such a way. The estimate which security holders place upon their railroad interests always includes the element of prospective increase of earnings. This is simply the financial reflection of the belief that our country is in course of development.

The magnitude of this element of value is tenfold when applied to the Pacific Railroads—which are, just at present, subject to a diminution of nearly 30 per cent in net earnings—from ten and a half to seven and a half millions of dollars. It would, no doubt, be very desirable for a syndicate to buy the Government's interest on the present reduced basis, and sell it out in a year or two, at the increased price produced by the resumption of prosperity. Yet, this would probably follow if Congress were to pass their bill; for how are commissioners and the President to put a money value on this prospective increase of revenues? It may come at any moment, from a slight increase of rates of freight, or from any of the hundred causes that advance our commercial prosperity. These elements being essentially indeterminate, the result of this commission would necessarily be the sale of the Government's interest at far less than its real value. (It should be added that it would place an unheard of and dangerous power in the hands of administrative officers, however exalted—the power to fix the value of a claim of $165,000,000—the amount of the first mortgage and Government debts.) But it is just this prospective increase in revenues that is represented by the junior interests in the property, and which they wish to retain at the least cost. Hence, their desire for this method of appraising the Government's interest at a minimum price.

BILL FOR GOVERNMENT COMMISSIONERS TO EXECUTE A PLAN, INDICATED BY CONGRESS, FOR THE COMPULSORY REDEMPTION OF THE FIRST AND GOVERNMENT DEBTS AT PAR IN CASH. THE PAYMENTS TO BE MADE BY THE PRESENT JUNIOR BONDHOLDERS, AND THE STOCKHOLDERS, WHO SHALL INVEST THE REQUISITE AMOUNTS IN INTEREST-BEARING MORTGAGE BONDS.

This plan, propounded in the bill which we had the honor to submit, is simply the application to the collection of the Government mortgages of the methods pursued every day by private interests in railroads. Practically, there can be no competitive cash bidding for such colossal properties. The best market of the creditors, requiring the adequate payment of their claims, consists in the junior bonds and stocks, interested to save their equities from foreclosure. In the case of these railroads, the earnings furnish to the junior claimants a desirable investment, which it would be folly for them to reject, at the risk of losing their great interest in the probable increased revenues of these properties.

With these certain elements, based on the present actual earnings of the aided divisions, on which Congress can predicate the Government plan of reorganization, why resort to the aleatory method of authorizing certain officials to assess the value of the Government's mortgages. These properties are worth just what the stocks will pay for them under the pressure of foreclosure. This can not be ascertained except by process of foreclosure—modified as to all junior interests, by providing them with substantial securities to represent their proportions of the redemption of the superior liens. It is upon such an assured basis that this bill proceeds; providing for the execution of the necessary administrative details by commissioners.

The method adopted in this bill is simply the normal course contemplated by the contracts for the benefit of creditors who have stipulated for a superior mortgage, and which is followed by business men every day in the year. Why should the Government alone divest itself of these remedies? These great properties are not worth merely what any three or four worthy officials may declare them, upon problematical data, to be potentially worth; but what the law of the land, acting in its ordinary course upon subordinate and imperiled interests, may actually ascertain it to be worth to them.

In corroboration of the practical nature of this remedy we submit the following concrete considerations, which bear forcibly upon the minds of stockholders called upon to make investments in such new securities as are provided in this plan.

PRESENT INCREASE OF REVENUES.

The recent reports for the completed year 1895 show a rate of increase in Union Pacific earnings which enhances the importance to the stockholders of saving their shares, by paying the Government debts through subscriptions to substituted bond issues of intrinsic value.

Increase of price of junior securities has always followed the payment of heavy assessments and the restoration of the solvency of the companies. In this way the stock has generally promptly recouped itself for its outlay, which in this case would be a result additional to the investment in a desirable security.

SUCCESS OF THE ASSESSMENT PLAN WHEN EMPLOYED BY INDIVIDUAL MORTGAGE HOLDERS NOW INVOKED FOR THE GOVERNMENT AND ITS FELLOW INTERESTS.

The New York Times of February 9 contains such apposite material on this point that we venture to quote from it:

"If the Government had simply asked payment in the same way that a corporation asks payment for an issue of its securities, that is, by certified checks, it would never have been anything but a question of how many times over the loan would have been subscribed. For the sum of $100,000,000 is but a drop in the bucket as compared with the wealth of the country. See the proof of it. Three bankrupt corporations have just called upon certain classes of their security holders for new money, in the way of assessments and otherwise—not to buy Government bonds, but to preserve an equity of more or less doubtful value in these bankrupt properties—and all these demands have already been met or are being met, as follows: Reading, $28,000,000; Atchison, $14,000,000; Erie, $10,000,000. Here is a total of $52,000,000 cash, paid up by a limited number of people, under most discouraging conditions; in the case of the Reading, the new assessment following one of $15,000,000 levied in 1889. We leave out the numerous other assessments of millions levied within the past eighteen months or two years—as the Richmond Terminal, of $18,000,000." Many similar instances could be added.

In the face of these amounts of assessments, raised upon the stocks of roads inferior, in most instances, to these bond-aided properties, and with new stock merely, instead of good bonds, being given to the subscribers, it would be inefficient on the part of the Government not to direct its commissioners to pursue this rightful remedy.

REORGANIZING THE ROADS AS AN ENTIRETY—CONSOLIDATION.

The occasion for contemplating consolidation in the interest of the Government arises from the fact that there is an excess of revenues on the Union Pacific beyond the amount necessary to pay the Government, while on the Central Pacific there is a deficiency. If the surplus on the Union and Kansas Pacific (about $900,000) could be utilized as the basis for capitalizing a further amount of four and a half bonds, twenty millions more of the Central Pacific debt could be paid to the Government. This could be effected by the commissioners providing in the plan for the sales of both roads as an entirety. They could provide for the formation of a single corporation to own both roads. This company should issue mortgage bonds predicated upon the earnings of both lines as an entirety. There would then be $7,500,000 of annual net revenues, ample to apply to the interest at 4½ per cent on $165,000,000 of debt, the net aggregate of the first and Government mortgages on the three roads. The subscription to these bonds by the present stockholders and junior bondholders would furnish the condition for their avoidance of foreclosure and obliteration. Of this amount the commissioners are, by the act, required to reserve $10,000,000 to secure the independent outlet to the Pacific. The present road from San Jose to the Pacific would not be of much value if a new road were built; so that its owners would probably be willing to make a proper arrangement for its use with the new company. But, if it had to be built, the Government commissioners could turn over to the new company $10,000,000 of the interest-bearing bonds, retaining an additional $10,000,000 (to bear interest when earned) as explained in our previous statement.

The practical question would be the distribution of the stock of the consolidated company, as between the present stockholders of the Union and Central. As the Union Pacific would furnish the greater proportion of revenues to the consolidated company, as well as a lesser debt, it would seem that its stockholders should have a proportionately increased amount of the consolidated stock. This could be reached by an arithmetical calculation. There is nothing in the bill, as now drafted, which militates against consolidation. But as it would be so valuable to the Government, we have suggested a clause to cover it, in the list of amendments appended.

PREFERENCE OF PROCEEDINGS ON CALENDARS OF COURTS.

This would insure the utmost promptitude in the disposition of this matter, so that it could be disposed of in sixty to ninety days after the appointment of commissioners, if we are to judge by the celerity with which stockholders have paid similar assessments. An amendment is inserted in our bill to cover this point.

TEMPORARY EMPLOYMENT OF THE ACT OF 1887.—NO SYNDICATE REQUIRED.

The mere affirmance of the act of 1887 by the present Congress would most likely render the execution of its provisions unnecessary, because the first-mortgage bondholders would perceive that it was in the power of the Commissioners to protect the Government. Moreover, the Government plan of reorganization would be acceptable to the first-mortgage bondholders, as it offers them better terms than many of them have already indicated a willingness to accept. In any event, the redemption of the first-mortgage debt accruing in 1896 would be merely temporary until this reorganization was completed, when the new substituted bonds could be sold. The bill enables the Commissioners thus to protect the Government reorganization, either through the act of 1887 or by advances obtained from stockholders who had subscribed to the plan.

This plan is bound to produce the best attainable price for the first and second mortgages.

It must be apparent that the coercive method, adapted in this bill from the prevailing system of railroad reorganization, is certain to produce the best possible price for the prior mortgages. It is not to be supposed, in the nature of things, that the junior interests in these properties are coming forward voluntarily to offer the firsts and the Government the highest price of which the property is susceptible for their interests. As there are just about enough earnings to sustain the capitalization for bringing the firsts and the Government "out whole," it is not surprising to find the juniors and stocks maneuvering to get the prior mortgages to share these present earnings with them, instead of their awaiting a partial resumption of the old scale of revenues. As matter of fact, they will derive considerable advantage from the reduction in the rate of interest upon the new issues, substituted for the present 6 per cent. And with the income bonds (which the Commissioners would likely accord them, in lieu of their present fixed-charge securities, and in addition to the new superior mortgages which they would receive for their subscriptions), they would get all out of the property to which they are equitably entitled. In any event, the Government, through its Commissioners (being its own committee of reorganization), would act directly upon each junior bondholder and stockholder, endeavoring to protect the future of his investment. No syndicate could interpose between the Government and the just payment of more than $100,000,000 into its Treasury, as well as the protection of its prior lienors, the first-mortgage bondholders.

L. J. MORRISON, *Of Counsel.*

AMENDMENTS TO BILL.

Section 1, second line, after "President," insert the words: "not more than two of whom shall be of the same political party, and none of whom shall have been in any manner officially connected with any of said companies."

Section 2, at the end, insert the following words: "All suits to enforce liens on the bond-aided railroads shall, in furtherance of this act, have absolute preference at all stages on the calendars and on hearings in the Federal courts, and the time for return of all process and the filing of all pleadings shall be shortened so that the roads may be sold, under this Government plan of reorganization, not later than October 1, 1896."

Section 3, fourth line, before the word "company," insert the word "consolidated." On the fourteenth line of the same section, after the word "railroads," insert the words, "as an entirety."

Section 4, eighth line, after the word "Government," insert: "This company shall possess all the corporate powers heretofore granted by Congress to the bondaided railroads, and also such powers as may be requisite to enable it to carry out the purposes of this act."

TESTIMONY OF MR. COLLIS P. HUNTINGTON—Continued.

Senator MORGAN. You have had this book with you (the Report of the United States Railroad Commission) for two weeks?

Mr. HUNTINGTON. Yes, about that time.

Senator MORGAN. Have you examined it carefully?

Mr. HUNTINGTON. I have looked over it, in part, carefully; I have been sick; I have not been out of my house six hours since the time I have left here.

Senator MORGAN. Have you found any points on which you wish to raise objections to the report of the Commission?

Mr. HUNTINGTON. I object to the report as a whole. It is a report made without information.

Senator MORGAN. Wherein do you object to it as a whole?

Mr. HUNTINGTON. I have written out some points which I will read to the committee.

Senator MORGAN. I will read it for you. Before reading it, I will ask you whether you object to the facts stated, or to the conclusions of the committee?

Mr. HUNTINGTON. I object, because their conclusions are somewhat contradictory to their statements; but particularly on the ground that they did not and could not know of what they were writing.

Senator MORGAN. They could have known if the witnesses who were brought before them told the truth.

Mr. HUNTINGTON. Probably; but none of the witnesses who came before them knew what the facts were.

Senator MORGAN. Did not Mr. Stanford?

Mr. HUNTINGTON. Stanford knew very little.

Senator MORGAN. You were a witness before the Commission; you had a full opportunity to tell all you knew?

Mr. HUNTINGTON. Yes.

Senator MORGAN. Did you do so?

Mr. HUNTINGTON. Yes.

Senator MORGAN. Then, of course, the Commissioners knew what they were writing about.

Mr. HUNTINGTON. They did not pay much attention to my testimony.

Senator MORGAN. You do not think that they discredited your statement?

Mr. HUNTINGTON. No; I do not mean that.

The following is the paper prepared by Mr. Huntington and handed to the committee as his reply to the conclusions arrived at by the United States Pacific Railroad Commission:

I observe that on page 25 of the United States Railroad Commissioners' report they state that the bonds and stocks of certain leased lines there referred to are chiefly owned by the individual directors in the Southern Pacific Company.

Now, my recollection is that one of the principal leased lines at the time was the California Pacific, with the building of which we had nothing to do, and, as I remember, we never had any of the bonds; and, as to the other roads that we did build, our custom was to carry the bonds until the roads had been worked long enough to show earnings sufficient to pay interest on the bonds, after which they were sold as soon as we could find a market for them, and the debts created in the construction of the road, which meantime had been carried upon our credit, were then paid.

I observe that on the same page the Commissioners say that their review of the history of the affairs of the Central Pacific Railroad Company justifies the assertion that the financial condition of that company has been caused by the incessant depletion of its treasury and misappropriation of its property by those whose sacred duty it was to protect and defend the company.

While I would say that they probably honestly came to that conclusion from what they had been told by parties in San Francisco, yet a greater lie was never printed, for there never was any depletion of the company's treasury or misappropriation of its property; and I will say again that no work was ever built where greater economy was practiced or more care taken in the expenditure of money than in the building of the Central Pacific, and when completed there were not enough of the assets controlled by the builders to pay the debts created in the building of the road, and if the securities taken for such building had not largely appreciated the builders of the road would have been bankrupted by the debts incurred in its construction.

I observe that on page 26 of the report the Commissioners state that the financial inability of the company to meet the requirements of the readjustment bill prepared by the Commissioners was the result of the profligate and wanton dispersion of the assets of the company in dividends and the extravagant contracts made by the company.

What is referred to as extravagant contracts I do not know, as I have no recollection of any extravagant contracts made after the building of the road of any great importance, and they were always made for the best interest of the Central Pacific Company.

As to the dividends, we carried the shares until they began to appreciate and then we commenced selling, and the prices ranged all the way, as I remember, from 19 cents up to 85 cents. These dividends were paid, as is usually the case and as the stockholders had a right to claim should be done, out of the earnings of the property, and only out of such earnings, after the payment of the fixed charges upon the property and the payments of the amounts which the Government by the acts of 1862 and 1864 and 1878 provided should be reserved for repayment of the amount of the Government aid. As I have already stated, we sold our shares in order to enable us to pay the debts incurred in the construction of the road as soon as the shares could be sold at prices sufficient to do this, and the stock was therefore widely distributed while the dividends were being paid.

I observe that on page 50 the Commissioners state that they have reached the conclusion that, with the single exception of the then existing administration of the Union Pacific, all the duties and obligations referred to as assumed by the managers of the roads had been constantly and persistently disregarded, and that the result was that those who had controlled and directed the construction and development of the companies had become possessed of their surplus assets through issues of bonds and stocks and payments of dividends voted by themselves, while the great creditor, the United States, finds itself substantially without adequate security for the repayment of its loans.

In reply to this I would say that the United States expressly provided, in 1862 and 1864, and again in 1878, what security should be reserved for the repayment of its loans, and every dollar of this security was reserved in accordance with the provisions of these acts. We have never heard that the Union Pacific administration, which the Commission refer to as a single exception, ever reserved a dollar more as security for the repayment of its loans than was required to be observed by these acts, which we have fully complied with.

But time has shown how wrong the Commissioners were in their estimate of the results of the Union Pacific administration, which they took so much pains to extol, as compared with the administration of the Central Pacific properties. Time has shown that although the Central Pacific properties were subject to a larger amount of fixed charges on account of the greater physical obstructions which had to be overcome in constructing the road, and although the properties were operated at a great disadvantage, all material being higher and coal used in California being, say, four times as expensive as that used by the Union Pacific, the administration of the Central Pacific has paid all its debts and obligations currently, while the Union Pacific has defaulted even on the interest on her first-mortgage bonds.

As to the statements of the Commission in reference to the construction contracts and the books of the Contract and Finance Company and what became of them I have already testified fully upon my previous examination, and therefore I have not undertaken to correct the statements of the Commission in reference to these subjects. There are many erroneous statements.

I will say, however, that there were no unfair contracts made, and those that were made were so liberal to the railroad company that—I will state here as I have often said—we could get cocapitalists either in San Francisco or in New York or in Boston to share the risks with the builders.

I observe that the Commission refer to the suits which were brought in California by Sam Brannan and others as stockholders of the Central Pacific Railroad Company.

I have already stated that suits of a similar character were brought here in New York, where they were under my direct observation. The suits were defended in all the courts, and we were absolutely and entirely successful, and the plaintiffs were entirely defeated by decisions of the highest courts of the State of New York. As to the suits commenced in California, I can only say that if they had been under my supervision I would have fought them in the same way and with the same results; but the suits were commenced for blackmail and settled by others than myself, and for political reasons about which I knew and cared nothing, and when I heard of it I disapproved the settlement.

I have already stated what an absolutely wild and reckless estimate of the road is contained in the report of the Commission on pages 74 and 75, where it is stated as amounting to $36,000,000. They are mistaken in that. They did not know and could not know anything about the cost of constructing the road, while I knew all about it. While I could not tell to-day just what it cost, my impression is, I might say I believe, that it cost much more than twice the amount named.

Referring to the statement of the Commissioners, page 75, that Mr. Stanford admitted that fifty-four millions of stock held by the Contract and Finance Company were substantially a net profit, subject only to the liquidation of the indebtedness of the Contract and Finance Company, not exceeding $3,000,000, I would say that Mr. Stanford was mistaken; that while I do not know just the amount of the indebtedness of the Contract and Finance Company after the completion of the railroad, I am satisfied it is more than three times three millions, and I do not know how much stock they did have, as I have already testified, I think; that I do not know just how much Charles Crocker did under his contract, but I have a recollection that his contract was turned over to the Contract and Finance Company on account of his inability to meet the requirements of the contract. I do know that the amount of indebtedness remaining unpaid when the road was completed could not have been paid out of the balance of the assets that the Contract and Finance Company held at that time. The fact is that Governor Stanford never knew very much about what the company had or what it was doing. He was always largely in politics and not much in railroading.

As an illustration of the methods adopted by the Commission in ascertaining the cost of work, I would refer to the report at the foot of page 75, where they substituted a wholly unfounded assumption of their own for the testimony of Gen. G. M. Dodge, a well-known and experienced engineer of undoubted ability and integrity, as to the actual cost of construction of the 47½ miles of the road from Promontory to Bonneville Table. General Dodge testified that the cost of this piece of road was $87,000 cash per mile, which would equal $4,132,500, notwithstanding which fact the Commissioners, for their own purposes and without evidence, see fit to estimate its cost at $3,000,000. I have no doubt that General Dodge's statement was right; and it should be understood that there were no important structures on the 47½ miles, and that no rolling stock went with it.

Another illustration of the recklessness (or worse) of the draftsman of the Pacific Railway Commission's report is near the foot of page 73, where reference is made to my testimony, given before the Wilson committee in February, 1873, which was more than a year, I think, before the winding up of the Contract and Finance Company. The draftsman of this report impugns this statement, which I made in February, 1873, and which was a true one, by reference to the testimony of Governor Stanford before the Pacific Railroad Commission, which related to a period long subsequent to the time when I gave my testimony before the Wilson committee, but did not in the slightest degree contradict the testimony which I gave, for, as I have said, it related to a period long subsequent to the time I was testifying to and long subsequent to the time when my testimony was given; and more than all this, as I have already stated, I think Governor Stanford's statement was an erroneous one with reference to any point of time.

I do not know what it refers to, as I am quite sure there was no such amount of stock; but he probably referred to the stock that belonged to the Contract and Finance Company. Yet in that he certainly was mistaken, as no such amount of shares, if any, came to the builders of the road after the liquidations of the debts of the company, although there was some money distributed after the shares were sold and the debts were paid.

As to the building of the Western Pacific, certain portions of it were not very expensive to build; although the work where they crossed the Mount Diablo range was expensive, and also that through the Alameda Canyon, and the bridging was quite expensive. We had to cross between Sacramento and Tracy, and the San Joaquin River, the Tuolumne, the Stanislaus, the McKosmey, and the Calaveras, I think. I think there were three quite important bridges over the Alameda

River, in passing through the canyons by that name, but I do not exactly remember how much of that we built. The parties who located and owned the road and commenced its construction did considerable work, and, I think, built from San Jose into the canyons of the Alameda and then, as I remember, they found that all the resources of the road —bonds and stock—were not sufficient to enable them to complete the work. They gave it up and arranged with our people to complete the road, which we were able to do by our superior credit, which did not compel us to sell our securities until after the completion of the road, which then showed some earning power, which added to the value of the securities. Of course, the difficulties in the way of its construction would not naturally have been noticed by the commissioners, who rode over it probably in a palace car, and possibly did not wish to see any of the great physical difficulties which the builders had to overcome.

As to the construction of the portion of the California and Oregon road, say, 103 miles, from Delta to the Oregon State line, I would say, as I remember it, that $80,000 a mile is as little as I think any conservative parties able to do the work would contract to do it for. Delta is at the foot of the Sacramento Canyon, and from there to the summit or top of the mountain at the divide between the Sacramento and Shasta rivers it was very expensive construction, and the bridges, as I remember, were all of iron, resting on stone masonry. It was very solid, consequently very expensive. I think the constructed line rises to a height of nearly 5,000 feet above the level of the sea, and the road is all expensive; although down Shasta River it is not of so ugly a character as climbing from Delta up to the summit. Then we have to cross the Klamath River, which is a very expensive bridge, and get over Baylis Mountain to the Oregon State line at Coles, in the foothills of the Siskiyou Mountains.

So it seems to me that it was a conservative contract to have agreed to build that road for four and a half millions of bonds and 80,000 shares of the Central Pacific, and particularly so when at the same time the Pacific Improvement Company agreed to acquire the control and secure the completion of the Oregon and California, the acquisition of which was very essential to the Central Pacific, as the California and Oregon would have been of little value between Delta and the State line without connecting there with another and a friendly road to take business to and bring it from Portland, Oreg., on the Columbia River, where it would connect with the great railroad systems of Oregon and Washington. This is particularly true when we consider the expensive character of the work on the Oregon and California between Roseburg and the State line at Coles. The magnitude of that work was the main cause of breaking Ben. Holliday and his associates in the early days, and the Oregon Transcontinental and the associated Villard interests at a later date. The Pacific Improvement Company had to assume the heaviest of all the work from Ashland, on Bear Creek, across the Siskiyou Mountains, to Coles, on the State line.

It would be useless to undertake to discuss the tables which were stated to have been prepared by the accountant of the commission in reference to the cost of construction, and the consideration received in bonds or stock or cash for such construction. I have already shown by my statements how utterly unfounded are the assumptions of this report in respect to the actual cash cost of the construction of the various properties. It is impossible for anyone to carry in his head the cost of railroad materials from a railroad spike up to a locomotive and the varied classifications in the construction of a road, as there are so many articles connected with the building of a railroad that it is not a possible thing for any man to retain in his memory any considerable percentage of them. I have always been satisfied that few men would have built the roads we built out of the assets which we had to build them with, which has been a great gratification to me.

As to the express business on the Central Pacific Railroad I would say that about the time the road was completed an express company was formed in the usual way, and I think Governor Stanford, Lloyd Tevis, Mr. Crocker, and myself started in to provide the means for procuring the facilities necessary to carry on that business. Of course this required a very considerable and expensive equipment outside of the railroad and its equipment and facilities. Afterwards the Wells, Fargo & Co.'s express proposed to consolidate or in some way join interests with us, and that was done, though exactly in what form I do not remember. I do remember having some of the shares, though just how many I could not say, and I sold them, as I did nearly everything that I could realize money on, and used the money to pay my debts.

As to the Rocky Mountain Coal Company, whose properties were at Almy, on the Union Pacific Railroad, some people in California bought it. I do not know who they were at this time, but I am quite sure none of the Central Pacific people had anything to do with it for some time after it was organized; but later it was offered to some of them and a portion of the shares were bought. I had some of them myself—I do not know how many—and they paid dividends for some time; but I think in every case the coal company sold coal to the Central Pacific Railroad Company at less than it could have bought from any other parties, and the existence of that company and its operations constantly tended to diminish the price at which the Central Pacific could purchase coal for use on its line; and just as soon as the Central Pacific could get coal cheaper than we could from the Almy property we did so, and have bought coal largely from the Rio Grande Western. The transaction was a proper and clean one, and there was nothing unusual about it.

There is a great deal said in the report about frauds and wrongdoing, and charging the builders of the road with doing almost everything that was wrong; in fact, much of the stuff published is a rehash of old musty things, and is more like a talk among vicious men not quite sober than the report of a Government commission. I have known from the beginning nearly all that has been done in the building of the road. I have known of the work we had to do and what we had to pay for it, and no better work was ever done than has been done in the building of these roads; and when I say this I say that the interest of the Government has been better cared for in this work than in any other outside work. Of course I do not refer to Government work, as that I do not know anything about.

As to the charge of using money to influence legislation, I will say that no money was ever used by me or by anyone connected with our companies, to my knowledge, for the purpose of influencing legislation, except that from time to time different persons have been employed in the various States and Territories and at Washington to see that the facts in respect to pending legislative matters were thoroughly and fully understood by the legislators who had to pass upon them.

The Commission again refers, on pages 87 and 88, to the dividends which were paid to the stockholders out of the earnings of the Central Pacific Railroad Company. The Commission admitted that these dividends were paid out of the earnings, as shown by the income account of the company, and did not involve any violation of law; and it would seem to follow from their statements in reference to the matter that the stockholders were legally and justly entitled to receive from the company all the dividends which were ever paid; but the fact was, as I have already stated, that the United States prescribed, in 1862 and 1864, and afterwards, in 1878, just what reservation should be made from its earnings for the protection of the Government debt, and we conformed in all respects to the requirements of those laws in reference to that matter. Just before the passage of the Thurman Act we had made arrangements for creating a sinking fund, by way of preparation for the maturity of the Government debt, and if the matter had been left to us to handle a sinking fund would have been created and would have been kept so invested as to pay off a sufficient amount of the Government debt to bring that indebtedness within safe limits; but the Government took the matter out of our hands and passed the Thurman Act and prescribed itself the provision which should be made against the maturity of the Government debt, and we were obliged to accede to the provisions of this act, and have strictly obeyed it. The question of what provision should be made against the maturity of this debt was not left by the Government for us to determine, but was taken out of our hands and determined by the Government itself.

I do not care to enter into a discussion about equities, which appears on pages 91 to 95 of the Commissioners' report. Although I do not see any reason why, still they seem to vex the Commissioners very much. I would hardly expect the Government officers to make any money allowances for them in a settlement, although the great grants given to the roads north and south of the Central Pacific, which were not expected by the Government or anyone else to be completed as soon as they were, destroyed largely the net earnings of the Central line; and in the seven and more years in which the road was completed before the time required the Government probably saved more than it had advanced in bonds to the Union and Central. And these might be reasons why the Government should be a little more lenient in settling with these roads, or consider a bill which would pay all of the indebtedness in an average of, say, fifty years, with as much interest paid currently as could be taken from the earnings for that purpose, as such a settlement would be much better for the Government than if the roads had not been built.

Senator MORGAN. Accepting your statement as true, and you having had an opportunity under oath of giving your deposition before the commission, why has not the commission been able to get the facts on which it based its conclusions?

Mr. HUNTINGTON. I do not know. They did not know anything about the matter, except from what they heard, and they heard mostly from persons who did not know anything. I was in correspondence with people who were there and I knew all about things generally. I was in the building of the Central Pacific road from start to finish; I do not want to go back and change any record which I made.

Senator MORGAN. The question is not so much about your building the road as about what you made out of it.

Mr. HUNTINGTON. We did not make any more than we had a right to make.

Senator MORGAN. I suppose you had the right to make all that you could?

Mr. HUNTINGTON. All that we did make; certainly.

Senator MORGAN. Why is it that you persist in saying that this commission did not know what it was doing, when you had the opportunity, and Stanford had the opportunity, and numerous other witnesses who did know about the transaction had the opportunity, to inform the commission, under oath, of the facts on which the commission was required to act as a judicial investigating body?

Mr. HUNTINGTON. The commission arrived at conclusions which I could not arrive at by the testimony as I read it.

Senator MORGAN. I suppose that you could not arrive at conclusions otherwise than very friendly to yourself?

Mr. HUNTINGTON. I can divide a thing exactly in the center. If I owned half of a thing and somebody else owned the other half I could divide it exactly, and if the knife swerved it would be on my half and not on the other man's half.

Senator MORGAN. As between you and the people, can you make that sort of division?

Mr. HUNTINGTON. I can.

Senator MORGAN. I am going to give you a chance to do it.

Mr. HUNTINGTON. I want you, Senator, to know all that I know.

Senator MORGAN (reading from Mr. Huntington's memoranda):

> I observe that on page 25 of the United States Railroad Commissioners' Report they state that the bonds and stocks of certain leased lines there referred to are chiefly owned by the individual directors of the Southern Pacific Company. Now, my recollection is that one of the principal leased lines at the time was the California Pacific, with the building of which we had nothing to do.

Is that the only one that you except from the findings of the commission?

Mr. HUNTINGTON. That is the only one which we had not anything to do with the building of.

Senator MORGAN. Is that the only one which you wish to except from the findings of the commission?

Mr. HUNTINGTON. I should except to everything the commission has written which is not correct.

Senator MORGAN. Have the commissioners made any incorrect statement about other roads than the California Pacific?

Mr. HUNTINGTON. I think they have.

Senator MORGAN. What others?

Mr. HUNTINGTON. I should have to go and read their report over again. When I read a thing and come to conclusions I put them down and can not carry them in my head.

Senator MORGAN. You can read the report of the commission if you want to.

Mr. HUNTINGTON. I should say, in general words, that their report is wrong.

Senator MORGAN. But you do not undertake, in a general way, or in a special way, to state from your own memory, or otherwise, in what respect the facts are wrong on which the commissioners adjudicated?

Mr. HUNTINGTON. I know this, that the Contract and Finance Company took a certain amount of stock and bonds of the Central Pacific (or of stock and money) to build the road; that the trade which we made was a fair one; that the road was built, and that when we found a way to sell our stock and pay our debts we did so.

Senator MORGAN. You say that it was a fair trade?

Mr. HUNTINGTON. Yes.

Senator MORGAN. You made both sides of the trade?

Mr. HUNTINGTON. No.

Senator MORGAN. Who did?

Mr. HUNTINGTON. If we had all the stock and all the bonds, I do not know who there was to complain. I am assuming that we did have them. If we did, we owned the two sides, and we dealt with ourselves. I think there was some other interest outside of us.

Senator MORGAN. That is to say, that it was the Southern Pacific and the Western Development Company making a trade together, the Southern Pacific and the Western Development Company being in the ownership and control of exactly the same people?

Mr. HUNTINGTON. No; not the same. I do not think that I was in the Southern Pacific a part of the time.

Senator MORGAN. Were you in it at the time you made this contract?

Mr. HUNTINGTON. I do not think I was; but I may have been. We substantially had both sides. We could not get anybody in with us. I tried for years to get somebody to come in.

Senator MORGAN. That is rather an important point, you know?

Mr. HUNTINGTON. It is important with me.

Senator MORGAN. It is important to the country, too. I want to know, and I want you to state as distinctly as you can recollect, what part of the time you were out of the Southern Pacific Company from the beginning of its existence to the present time?

Mr. HUNTINGTON. I do not recollect.

Senator MORGAN. How much of the time were you out?

Mr. HUNTINGTON. I do not recollect. I may have been out part of the time, but I do not recollect.

Senator MORGAN. Were you out of it for a year?

Mr. HUNTINGTON. I may have been out for a year; it may have been less or it may have been more.

Senator MORGAN. Were you out for six months?

Mr. HUNTINGTON. I do not know.

Senator MORGAN. One month?

Mr. HUNTINGTON. I do not know.

Senator MORGAN. One day?

Mr. HUNTINGTON. I think I was out of it many days. If I have got to go and look up my life's history in detail from day to day for the last sixty years, I have not time to do it.

Senator MORGAN. I do not propose to touch any part of your life's history except that which is wrapped up in these railroads, and that part of it, of course, I want to find out.

Mr. HUNTINGTON. If you tell me what you want to know particularly, or tell me of anything which we have wrongfully taken, I will try and explain it to you. I have not wrongfully taken anything. If you want to find out any particular thing I will look it up, but I can not go back for sixty years.

Senator MORGAN. I want to find out those things which you have wrongfully taken, and to find out those things which you have rightfully taken.

Mr. HUNTINGTON. All that I have taken was rightfully taken, and nothing was wrongfully taken.

Senator MORGAN. You have taken all that you could get.

Mr. HUNTINGTON. All that we could get under the contract; and the contract was a fair one.

Senator MORGAN. You do not know whether you were in the company or not when that contract was made for the construction of the Southern Pacific road by the Western Development Company?

Mr. HUNTINGTON. I do not.

Senator MORGAN. Did you not arrange that contract?

Mr. HUNTINGTON. No, I do not think I arranged it; probably I had something to do with it.

Senator MORGAN. Do you not know that you did?

Mr. HUNTINGTON. No, I do not know that I did.

Senator MORGAN. Do you know that you did not?

Mr. HUNTINGTON. No, I do not know. We were doing a great many things, and we did what we knew was right.

Senator MORGAN. There is no use in your using the whitewash brush any longer.

Mr. HUNTINGTON. I am not using a whitewash brush. There is nothing about what we did that needs whitewashing.

Senator MORGAN. Did the Western Development Company take a contract and build the Southern Pacific road?

Mr. HUNTINGTON. Yes, as I recollect it.

Senator MORGAN. Between what points?

Mr. HUNTINGTON. I can not say.

Senator MORGAN. Commencing where?

Mr. HUNTINGTON. That I can not say. We bought the road from San Francisco to Gilroy, 80 miles, and I think we commenced building there.

Senator MORGAN. You commenced to build from Gilroy?

Mr. HUNTINGTON. I think so.

Senator MORGAN. You did not leave a gap?

Mr. HUNTINGTON. No.

Senator MORGAN. Where was the other end of the road which the Western Development Company agreed to build?

Mr. HUNTINGTON. I do not, for the moment, remember.

Senator MORGAN. How far from Gilroy was it?

Mr. HUNTINGTON. The road was built to Yuma.

Senator MORGAN. How far was that?

Mr. HUNTINGTON. Somewhere about 600 miles.

Senator MORGAN. Was it built under that contract with the Western Development Company?

Mr. HUNTINGTON. I do not think that all of it was.

Senator MORGAN. How much of it was?

Mr. HUNTINGTON. I do not know.

Senator MORGAN. About how much?

Mr. HUNTINGTON. I can not say.

Senator MORGAN. You have no opinion, no recollection?

Mr. HUNTINGTON. No, I have not; it was in an open country, where there were few settlers, and where there were no towns most of the way.

Senator MORGAN. How far was the Southern Pacific built?

Mr. HUNTINGTON. It was built to Yuma and the Needles; it stopped there.

Senator MORGAN. Did any other company agree to build any part of this railroad between Gilroy and Yuma?

Mr. HUNTINGTON. My impression is that the Pacific Improvement Company did.

Senator MORGAN. Who owned that company?

Mr. HUNTINGTON. Substantially the same interests.

Senator MORGAN. So that it was a matter of indifference to the gentlemen owning both the companies whether the railroad should be built by the one or the other, as, whatever profit or loss accrued, it fell on the same men?

Mr. HUNTINGTON. I have answered that question. So far as the same men were in the two companies (and I think they were all in them) it would not make any difference.

Senator MORGAN. Nobody came into these companies besides you four men—Crocker, Hopkins, Stanford, and yourself?

Mr. HUNTINGTON. Mr. Colton was in part of the time.

Senator MORGAN. What percentage of interest did Mr. Colton have?

Mr. HUNTINGTON. I do not know; somewhere in the neighborhood of one-sixth.

Senator MORGAN. What did he do with his interest?

Mr. HUNTINGTON. I do not know; he died.

Senator MORGAN. He did not lose it because he died; what has become of it?

Mr. HUNTINGTON. It was settled up by his widow.

Senator MORGAN. Who got it?

Mr. HUNTINGTON. His widow got it.

Senator MORGAN. To whom did she sell it?

Mr. HUNTINGTON. I was not her adviser in the matter.

Senator MORGAN. But still you know?

Mr. HUNTINGTON. I do not.

Senator MORGAN. You do not know to whom she sold it?

Mr. HUNTINGTON. No.

Senator MORGAN. Have you no belief or information as to whom she sold it?

Mr. HUNTINGTON. No; she had some bonds, but what she did with them I do not know.

Senator MORGAN. She may have all that interest now?

Mr. HUNTINGTON. I do not know; I hardly think she has got it; she was in litigation a good deal.

Senator MORGAN. Did you buy her house in San Francisco?

Mr. HUNTINGTON. Yes.

Senator MORGAN. Did you buy her library?

Mr. HUNTINGTON. No.

Senator MORGAN. Did you not take the house with the papers in it?

Mr. HUNTINGTON. I took the house with the wall papers.

Senator MORGAN. No other papers?

Mr. HUNTINGTON. No others that I know of.

Senator MORGAN. And did you not destroy the papers after you bought the house?

Mr. HUNTINGTON. If you charge me with it, I will answer you.

Senator MORGAN. It is charged by men who are probably as good as you or I.

Mr. HUNTINGTON. Oh; they are very good men.

Senator MORGAN. What is your answer?

Mr. HUNTINGTON. I destroyed no papers, and I do not know that such a thing was ever charged, although I suppose that these men in San Francisco, if they had thought of it, would have charged it.

Senator MORGAN. Did you not receive papers which were turned over to you when Mrs. Colton sold you that house, which papers belonged to her husband's estate and were connected with these railroad transactions?

Mr. HUNTINGTON. I did not destroy any papers.

Senator MORGAN. Did any agent of yours do so?

Mr. HUNTINGTON. No; I am sure that nobody did.

Senator MORGAN. Did you buy that house for a residence?

Mr. HUNTINGTON. I did.

Senator MORGAN. Have you lived in it?

Mr. HUNTINGTON. Yes.

Senator MORGAN. When you took possession of it, did you find any of Colton's papers?

Mr. HUNTINGTON. No.

Senator MORGAN. That is the first positive answer which you have given.

Mr. HUNTINGTON. I have answered the same question before, but I answer it now in another way. That is all.

Senator MORGAN. I am glad you are so emphatic. Did you settle your controversy with Mrs. Colton by buying the house?

Mr. HUNTINGTON. No.

Senator MORGAN. How did you settle it?

Mr. HUNTINGTON. I paid her the money for the house about two years ago.

Senator MORGAN. How did you pay for the other part of the business, about which she had that suit against you?

Mr. HUNTINGTON. I think the best way to get at that would be to get the records of the court. I do not know anything about it; I was not there. We settled with Mrs. Colton.

Senator MORGAN. Who are "we?"

Mr. HUNTINGTON. The parties in interest.

Senator MORGAN. Who are they?

Mr. HUNTINGTON. Mr. Stanford and Mr. Crocker and Mrs. Hopkins.

Senator MORGAN. What did you give her?

Mr. HUNTINGTON. We gave her, as I recollect, $200,000.

Senator MORGAN. In money?

Mr. HUNTINGTON. No.

Senator MORGAN. In what?

Mr. HUNTINGTON. In Southern Pacific bonds.

Senator MORGAN. I suppose she has them yet?

Mr. HUNTINGTON. I do not know anything about it.

Senator MORGAN. Now, get back to the contract. We have found out now, to the best of your belief and supposition, that this road between Gilroy and Yuma was built by the Western Development Company, or by the Pacific Improvement Company?

Mr. HUNTINGTON. I think so.

Senator MORGAN. By one or both?

Mr. HUNTINGTON. I think by both.

Senator MORGAN. In building that road, did not the Southern Pacific Company, which belonged to these four gentlemen, make the contract for building the road with either the Western Development Company or the Pacific Improvement Company?

Mr. HUNTINGTON. I should say they did; I think there were other interests in the Southern Pacific at the time.

Senator MORGAN. These other interests were the controlling interests?

Mr. HUNTINGTON. No.

Senator MORGAN. Were not the minor interests very small interests?

Mr. HUNTINGTON. Yes, I should say so; they were not as large as the majority interests.

Senator MORGAN. In making your contract for building this road did you consult the other minor interests?

Mr. HUNTINGTON. All interests, I am satisfied, knew what was being done.

Senator MORGAN. Did you consult this minor interest, or did you make the contract on your own account?

Mr. HUNTINGTON. I can not answer that; but I have no doubt they all knew it.

Senator MORGAN. You mean that you do not know whether they were consulted or not?

Mr. HUNTINGTON. I assume that they were.

Senator MORGAN. Do you know anything about it?

Mr. HUNTINGTON. I presume that they were consulted. I did not do it myself.

Senator MORGAN. That brings me to the point which I left some time ago, when you wandered off. That was, whether you did not really frame the terms of these contracts for building the Southern Pacific road.

Mr. HUNTINGTON. No, I do not think I did; I do not think I framed any of them.

Senator MORGAN. I do not mean that you wrote them out; I mean did you frame them in your mind?

Mr. HUNTINGTON. No; my impression is that they were done in California, and that I was told they were done. I do not think they were done without my knowledge.

Senator MORGAN. Or without your consent?

Mr. HUNTINGTON. I should say that they had my consent.

Senator MORGAN. By whom were these contracts made if they were not framed by you?

Mr. HUNTINGTON. I suppose——

Senator MORGAN. I do not want any suppositions. If you do not recollect, say that you do not recollect.

Mr. HUNTINGTON. I do not recollect. I presume that Judge Sanderson framed them. He was our chief attorney.

Senator MORGAN. Judge Sanderson did not make the contracts.

Mr. HUNTINGTON. He probably drew the contracts.

Senator MORGAN. I am speaking of making them. I am speaking of the negotiation, and the conclusions of this negotiation in the agreement. Who negotiated the contract, who concluded the contract, and who instructed the attorney how to prepare it?

Mr. HUNTINGTON. I think that Mr. Hopkins, probably, in his lifetime, would have had more to do with it than anybody else.

Senator MORGAN. Mr. Hopkins, I understood you to testify, was your universal partner in all of this railroad business?

Mr. HUNTINGTON. He was not my universal partner exactly. He was my partner in the hardware and metal trade.

Senator MORGAN. You have frequently said that he was.

Mr. HUNTINGTON. I may have said so; but he was not my partner in the railroad business. He was a codirector and stockholder with me.

Senator MORGAN. Was he your partner in any of those transactions relating to the railroads?

Mr. HUNTINGTON. No; not in any transactions relating to the railroads.

Senator MORGAN. That is rather an important point. I believe that you said, on some occasions here, that Mr. Hopkins did whatever he pleased, and that whatever he did was all right with you?

Mr. HUNTINGTON. I say that now.

Senator MORGAN. Then it was because he was your universal agent and not because he was your universal partner?

Mr. HUNTINGTON. It was because he was a man in whom I had great confidence. He was a partner of mine in the hardware and metal trade.

Senator MORGAN. Was he your agent to whom you delegated authority to transact for you any and all business connected with these various railroad operations in which he and you were concerned?

Mr. HUNTINGTON. I should say he was not my agent. He was the man who attended to these things and in whom I had so much confidence.

Senator MORGAN. So that he was neither your agent nor your partner?

Mr. HUNTINGTON. Perhaps I should say that he was not. He was my partner in the hardware and metal trade.

Senator MORGAN. He was a man in whom you had such blind faith that you intrusted to him the full disposal and management of your business and accepted what he did without question?

Mr. HUNTINGTON. I would not call it blind faith. I knew Mark Hopkins and trusted him, not blindly, but because I knew he was right.

Senator MORGAN. I am talking about your blind confidence in him.

Mr. HUNTINGTON. It was not a blind confidence; it was a confidence in the man that he would do just what was right.

Senator MORGAN. Did you surrender to him, to the extent you have just said, the full and absolute control of your business in connection with these railroads, so as to authorize him to bind you to any contract he chose to make, to receive any payment which was coming to you, and to dispose of your bonds, stock, or other assets or property in connection with these railroads, without question on your part, and with the understanding with him that he had a perfect authority to do these things?

Mr. HUNTINGTON. As to perfect authority, I would not know how to answer. He had my confidence to do anything for me which he saw fit, and I have no doubt that I should have approved of whatever he did.

Senator MORGAN. You have no doubt that you should have approved; have you any doubt that you did approve?

Mr. HUNTINGTON. No; I am satisfied that I did approve.

Senator MORGAN. Then you made him your agent, by ratification, if not by appointment?

Mr. HUNTINGTON. Just what the word agent may imply I can not say; but I trusted him in everything, and I know that he never failed me in anything.

Senator MORGAN. And the same relations which we have been just trying to describe here extended to all the transactions which you have had, and to all these railroad and construction companies at all times as long as Hopkins lived?

Mr. HUNTINGTON. I think that is true.

Senator MORGAN. Except that you and he were partners in the hardware and metal business?

Mr. HUNTINGTON. Yes.

Senator MORGAN. Did you ever settle up that partnership?

Mr. HUNTINGTON. Yes.

Senator MORGAN. How much money did you get out of it?

Mr. HUNTINGTON. I do not know; we got dividends all the time.

Senator MORGAN. On the final settlement of the business, how much money did you get out of it?

Mr. HUNTINGTON. I can not say. Just before Mr. Hopkins died we reorganized the "Huntington & Hopkins Company."

Senator MORGAN. The Hardware and Metal Company?

Mr. HUNTINGTON. Yes; and we took in three of our clerks.

Senator MORGAN. Was that a corporation or a partnership?

Mr. HUNTINGTON. It was a corporation. It had been a partnership up to that time we took in three clerks; and when the business got a little slow, and a dry rot was getting in, I told Hopkins to sell out, and we did so.

Senator MORGAN. How long did that new corporation last?

Mr. HUNTINGTON. To the best of my recollection it lasted about twenty years.

Senator MORGAN. And when did the dry rot get into it?

Mr. HUNTINGTON. Things got a little slow.

Senator MORGAN. When?

Mr. HUNTINGTON. I can not tell, exactly.

Senator MORGAN. Not very early in the twenty years?

Mr. HUNTINGTON. No.

Senator MORGAN. Not very late in the twenty years?

Mr. HUNTINGTON. Not very late, either. I think in about three or four years.

Senator MORGAN. When the dry rot had worked you out of the business, how much did you get out of it in money or value?

Mr. HUNTINGTON. The stock was $1,500,000, and I think we got about par for the stock.

Senator MORGAN. How much did you get out of it?

Mr. HUNTINGTON. I had about one-tenth interest in it—perhaps more than that or perhaps not as much; I forget.

Senator MORGAN. That, then, was a final settlement of the whole hardware and metal business?

Mr. HUNTINGTON. Yes.

Senator MORGAN. From beginning to end?

Mr. HUNTINGTON. That was the wind-up.

Senator MORGAN. But in the meantime you had drawn out dividends?

Mr. HUNTINGTON. Yes.

Senator MORGAN. How much?

Mr. HUNTINGTON. I do not know. We had done fairly well.

Senator MORGAN. What would you call fairly well for an average annual dividend?

Mr. HUNTINGTON. I do not know. I think we made some 12 per cent per annum.

Senator MORGAN. For thirty years?

Mr. HUNTINGTON. Yes.

Senator MORGAN. What was the capital stock?

Mr. HUNTINGTON. We had $1,500,000 in the corporation.

Senator MORGAN. How much of that capital stock did you take and how much did Hopkins take?

Mr. HUNTINGTON. I forget just what we gave the boys when they came in. We sold out to them, and we trusted them mostly for their shares. I do not know just what the division was. I think that Mr. Hopkins and I had about one-half and that the three boys had the other half.

Senator MORGAN. Did you give the boys one-half?

Mr. HUNTINGTON. I think we did.

Senator MORGAN. They paid up, did they?

Mr. HUNTINGTON. Yes.

Senator MORGAN. So that you and Hopkins got your $1,500,000?

Mr. HUNTINGTON. No; we had our proportion. When Mr. Hopkins died the concern bought his interest.

Senator MORGAN. When you sold the stock to the boys who got the money for it?

Mr. HUNTINGTON. Mr. Hopkins and myself did.

Senator MORGAN. That was $1,500,000 in all?

Mr. HUNTINGTON. No. Whatever they agreed to pay they paid.

Senator MORGAN. At the time you and Hopkins first entered the hardware and metal business how much money did you put in it?

Mr. HUNTINGTON. I do not recollect; I think I had, as I recollect, some couple of hundred thousand dollars.

Senator MORGAN. Which you had put in there?

Mr. HUNTINGTON. No; it was in there. He came in with me in 1855.

Senator Morgan. Did he put in as much as you put in?

Mr. HUNTINGTON. Yes; that was the arrangement.

Senator MORGAN. A couple of hundred thousand for you and the same amount for him would be $400,000?

Mr. HUNTINGTON. Yes; two and two are four.

Senator MORGAN. Did you run the railroad business or the construction business into the hardware and metal business?

Mr. HUNTINGTON. No; I would like to say right here—and perhaps it is proper to say—that Huntington & Hopkins never sold a wheel, an axle, a spoke, or a rail, or anything whatever for the construction of the road, and never had any commission on it.

Senator MORGAN. So that you did not run the railroad business into the hardware and metal business at all in any form or shape?

Mr. HUNTINGTON. No; we may have sold a dozen files or so to contractors, but in any of the great machinery and tools used in building or operating the road Huntington & Hopkins, as a concern, was never interested and never got a farthing.

Senator MORGAN. That corporation did not lend any money to the railroad company, did it?

Mr. HUNTINGTON. We were lending money; we may have.

Senator MORGAN. Did you?

Mr. HUNTINGTON. I think that perhaps in the course of business we did; but I do not know.

Senator MORGAN. How much did you lend to it?

Mr. HUNTINGTON. I do not know.

Senator MORGAN. What makes you think you did?

Mr. HUNTINGTON. I think we did, but I would not swear positively. I have very little doubt that we did.

Senator MORGAN. If the Huntington & Hopkins corporation raised the value of its assets from $400,000 to $1,500,000 how much money did you have in that corporation to put into this railroad company?

Mr. HUNTINGTON. We did not put in all the money that we had. We had various interests.

Senator MORGAN. I am talking about this particular one.

Mr. HUNTINGTON. We made money all the time. In 1854 I made in eight months $854,000 out of the hardware trade myself.

Senator MORGAN. I am trying to find out not what you made but what you put into the railroad business out of the hardware and metal business.

Mr. HUNTINGTON. Enough to make things run smoothly and to pay the debts of the railroad company as they became due.

Senator MORGAN. That is a very delightful answer, stated over and over again. How much money did you withdraw out of the hardware and metal business and put into the railroad in which you and Hopkins were interested?

Mr. HUNTINGTON. I will answer it as I have answered it five or six times, I do not know.

Senator MORGAN. Do you know whether you put any in?

Mr. HUNTINGTON. I am quite sure we did, but I can not tell the dates or the amounts. When the railroad company was short of money they had to scratch around.

Senator MORGAN. Mr. Huntington, you know the difference between putting money into a business and lending money to that business. In your transactions between the hardware and metal business and the railroad company, did you lend money to the railroad company or did you take money out of the hardware and metal business and put it into the railroad business?

Mr. HUNTINGTON. I have no doubt that we did both. These things were done in California when I was in New York. Mr. Hopkins attended to them, and did whatever was necessary.

Senator MORGAN. He was your partner?

Mr. HUNTINGTON. He was my partner in the hardware and metal business.

Senator MORGAN. If he had the right, as partner, to put your money in the railroad business and did do it, did you not continue to be partners to the extent of the money that he put in?

Mr. HUNTINGTON. No; if we lent money to a corporation we took its note to Huntington & Hopkins.

Senator MORGAN. Did you lend money to the Central Pacific Company, or did you put it in?

Mr. HUNTINGTON. I presume it was done in both ways. If we took money out of the business and bought bonds, Mr. Hopkins would always lay by half for me and half for himself.

Senator MORGAN. I am not talking about buying bonds. I am talking about building the Central Pacific, and the Southern Pacific, and other roads; that is what I am talking about; and I wish you would confine your attention to that. Did the hardware and metal company take money out of its business and put it into any of these various enterprises; and if so, into which?

Mr. HUNTINGTON. I can not say. As I have answered a number of times, if we took money out it was charged to the individual.

Senator MORGAN. How do you know?

Mr. HUNTINGTON. Because that is the way to do it.

Senator MORGAN. You say you do not know?

Mr. HUNTINGTON. No; but that is the way to do it. There are certain ways of doing business in a commercial house.

Senator MORGAN. You do not know that the money was ever taken out of the "Huntington & Hopkins" business?

Mr. HUNTINGTON. I am satisfied that it was, but I can not swear to it.

Senator MORGAN. But if it was taken out you know that it was charged to the individual?

Mr. HUNTINGTON. That is the way to do it.

Senator MORGAN. Do you know anything about it?

Mr. HUNTINGTON. That is the only way to do it.

Senator MORGAN. Do you know anything about it?

Mr. HUNTINGTON. I did not know from day to day.

Senator MORGAN. Well, from hour to hour, or from year to year?

Mr. HUNTINGTON. I know that everything was done in a business manner; I did not know from day to day what was done. I was not there; I was in New York.

Senator MORGAN. Then, how do you know that the money which was taken out was charged to the individual accounts?

Mr. HUNTINGTON. That was the only way to do it. After the boys came in they had nothing to do with it

Senator MORGAN. That is a very thin argument; and I would like to get rid of it, and get at some semblance of the facts of this business. I want to know whether you did know that this money which was taken out of the business by Hopkins was charged to his or to your individual accounts?

Mr. HUNTINGTON. It ought to have been.

Senator MORGAN. Do you know that it was?

Mr. HUNTINGTON. I can say nothing more than that it ought to have been and that I have no doubt that it was.

Senator MORGAN. You have no doubt that money was taken out of this hardware and metal business and put into the railroad business?

Mr. HUNTINGTON. I have no doubt that Mr. Hopkins took out money and lent money and bought securities and paid for them.

Senator MORGAN. That is not the question, and you can not dodge it.

Mr. HUNTINGTON. I am not trying to dodge it.

Senator MORGAN. Did Mr. Hopkins put any of the money of the hardware and metal company into the business of building railroads?

Mr. HUNTINGTON. No; I think not. If he took it out it should have been charged to Mr. Hopkins and myself. Huntington & Hopkins may have lent money to the railroad company, and, if so, it would have taken the company's note.

The CHAIRMAN. If you had done that, the amount would have been charged in your cash book to "bills receivable?"

Mr. HUNTINGTON. Certainly.

Senator MORGAN. Was it?

Mr. HUNTINGTON. It ought to have been. Do you suppose I can sit here and give details of business thirty-five years back? That is asking too much of me.

Senator MORGAN. It seems to me that you know some things in your own favor, and that you know nothing against yourself.

Mr. HUNTINGTON. I know some things; and other things I do not know.

Senator MORGAN. Have you not, on various occasions, and in your deposition before the United States Pacific Railroad Commission, stated that Mr. Hopkins was your general partner?

Mr. HUNTINGTON. If I have stated that, I have made a mistake. He was my partner in the hardware and metal business, but not in the railroad business.

Senator MORGAN. Did you settle up all these transactions with the Hopkins estate after he died?

Mr. HUNTINGTON. Yes.

Senator MORGAN. Were the hardware business and railroad business and all the other transactions between you carried into that settlement?

Mr. HUNTINGTON. Not together. They would be entirely distinct.

Senator MORGAN. Were they carried into the settlement?

Mr. HUNTINGTON. Not into the settlement of the hardware and metal business.

Senator MORGAN. No, but into the general settlement.

Mr. HUNTINGTON. There was no general settlement. The widow took the interest and carried on the estate.

Senator MORGAN. Have you never had a settlement with Mrs. Hopkins?

Mr. HUNTINGTON. I think not. There may have been, but I do not think there was.

Senator MORGAN. You had a division of the assets and credits and moneys?

Mr. HUNTINGTON. I think that Mrs. Hopkins kept right on and took her husband's place in the business.

Senator MORGAN. Has she the same business relations with you now that Hopkins had at the time of his death?

Mr. HUNTINGTON. I think so.

Senator MORGAN. So you are conducting the business?

Mr. HUNTINGTON. Yes; she is in the business.

Senator MORGAN. What business?

Mr. HUNTINGTON. Building roads.

Senator MORGAN. You are not building roads now?

Mr. HUNTINGTON. Yes, all the time.

Senator MORGAN. In other words, Mrs. Hopkins represents her husband's interest in the company?

Mr. HUNTINGTON. Yes.

Senator MORGAN. What company is that?

Mr. HUNTINGTON. The Pacific Improvement Company.

Senator MORGAN. Is that company still in operation?

Mr. HUNTINGTON. Yes.

Senator MORGAN. And Mrs. Hopkins still has her interest in it?

Mr. HUNTINGTON. Yes.

Senator MORGAN. And you are still managing it?

Mr. HUNTINGTON. No; Mr. Dalty is president of it. He has all the management of it.

Senator STEWART. Has the representative of Mrs. Hopkins been still carrying on the same business?

Mr. HUNTINGTON. Yes.

Senator MORGAN. Who is that?

Mr. HUNTINGTON. Mr. Russell Wilson. He is the director in the company for Mrs. Hopkins.

Senator MORGAN. He is not the representative of the Hopkins estate, but the representative of Mrs. Hopkins?

Mr. HUNTINGTON. I think the estate is all settled up.

Senator BRICE. Mr. Huntington, you mean Mrs. Stanford, do you not?

Mr. HUNTINGTON. Yes.

Senator MORGAN. I was talking about Mrs. Hopkins.

Mr. HUNTINGTON. Mrs. Hopkins is dead.

Senator MORGAN. She had an administrator?

Mr. HUNTINGTON. Mr. Searles was her husband. I will say for Mrs. Stanford what I said for Mrs. Hopkins. The interest of Mrs. Hopkins is going right along; but it is now owned by Mr. Searles, who was her husband. It is taken care of by General Hubbard.

Senator MORGAN. Mr. Hopkins is dead?

Mr. HUNTINGTON. Yes.

Senator MORGAN. Who was his administrator?

Mr. HUNTINGTON. Mrs. Hopkins.

Senator MORGAN. Did you ever settle your accounts with her?

Mr. HUNTINGTON. I had no accounts with her.

Senator MORGAN. You had no accounts with her?

Mr. HUNTINGTON. Not railroad accounts. I had none.

Senator MORGAN. But you and Hopkins were partners?

Mr. HUNTINGTON. That was in the hardware and metal trade.

Senator MORGAN. Did you settle that?

Mr. HUNTINGTON. That was settled up soon after his death.

Senator MORGAN. By whom?

Mr. HUNTINGTON. Mrs. Hopkins did not want to carry on the business, and Huntington, Hopkins & Co. bought her interest out.

Senator MORGAN. Mrs. Hopkins, then, sold out her interest in the hardware business?

Mr. HUNTINGTON. Yes.

Senator MORGAN. And in the corporation?

Mr. HUNTINGTON. Yes.

Senator MORGAN. To the boys and you?

Mr. HUNTINGTON. To the concern.

Senator MORGAN. As to the railroad business; did you have any settlement with the Hopkins administrator at all?

Mr. HUNTINGTON. I do not know. There may have been some unsettled matters between Mr. Hopkins and myself at the time of his death, and, if so, they were settled up. He died in 1879, as I recollect, and we had then sold out most of our stuff.

Senator MORGAN. When Hopkins died did he have any of your money or property in his possession.

Mr. HUNTINGTON. Very little, if any.

Senator MORGAN. When did he settle with you, before he died?

Mr. HUNTINGTON. I do not recollect. What we sold was stuff that we were carrying to pay the debts of the Contract and Finance Company, largely, and other matters. It was sold and the debts were paid, and there was something left. I think that that was in the Contract and Finance Company. The residuum was there. After paying our debts there was something over and that we divided.

Senator MORGAN. Then, at the time Mr. Hopkins died, he had very little of your property in his possession?

Mr. HUNTINGTON. I do not know that he had any. Possibly there might have been some.

Senator MORGAN. That matter has been settled up?

Mr. HUNTINGTON. Yes.

Senator MORGAN. By whom?

Mr. HUNTINGTON. I suppose that whatever balance there was either way was settled. I may have done it myself.

Senator MORGAN. With whom did you settle, if you did it yourself?

Mr. HUNTINGTON. I think it must have been with Mrs. Hopkins. She was a very capable woman. There was very little to be settled, I am quite sure.

Senator MORGAN. Did Mrs. Hopkins live then at Sacramento?

Mr. HUNTINGTON. No; she lived at San Francisco.

Senator MORGAN. And so the records of the probate court in San Francisco will show what settlement was made?

Mr. HUNTINGTON. I do not know whether they will or not.

Senator MORGAN. When Mr. Hopkins died your interests and his had been separated in all of these several companies?

Mr. HUNTINGTON. About that time there was a market for these stocks, so that we sold a great many, and, I guess, paid off the debts of the Contract and Finance Company.

Senator MORGAN. Your interests were separated; that is to say, they were no longer united?

Mr. HUNTINGTON. We never had any united interests in the railroad; but Mr. Hopkins kept our books, and kept them very strictly, and whatever was due to me was handed over to me.

Senator MORGAN. But in all of these other companies you and Hopkins stood as stockholders?

Mr. HUNTINGTON. Yes.

Senator MORGAN. And your interests in the companies were defined by the amount of stock you held?

Mr. HUNTINGTON. Yes.

Senator MORGAN. So that, in this way, your interests were separate before his death?

Mr. HUNTINGTON. They were always so. We never jointly took any stock in any railroad companies.

Senator MORGAN. What other companies did you and Mr. Hopkins take stock in jointly?

Mr. HUNTINGTON. I do not know. I am quite sure we were in all those construction companies.

Senator MORGAN. As joint owners of stock?

Mr. HUNTINGTON. No; not as joint owners. We were never joint owners in any of the railroad companies or in any construction business.

Senator MORGAN. Your joint ownership, then, was confined to your interests in the hardware and metal company?

Mr. HUNTINGTON. Yes; and to things growing out of that business.

Senator MORGAN. All of these transactions were done outside of this firm?

Mr. HUNTINGTON. Yes.

Senator MORGAN. What property did you have at the time you formed this agreement or partnership with Mr. Hopkins to establish a hardware and metal company, besides that which you put into that company?

Mr. HUNTINGTON. I do not remember at this time, but I always had property. I was a merchandise speculator a good many years, myself—a large merchandise speculator.

Senator MORGAN. Did you have any other active business at that time?

Mr. HUNTINGTON. No; not any that you might say was regular current business.

Senator MORGAN. Did you have any money that you received out of the hardware and metal business at the time of the organization of the Central Pacific Company?

Mr. HUNTINGTON. I had money outside.

Senator MORGAN. How much?

Mr. HUNTINGTON. I can not say.

Senator MORGAN. About how much?

Mr. HUNTINGTON. I do not know; it is a long time ago.

Senator MORGAN. Was it out of the money which you had outside of the hardware and metal business that you found means to put money into the Central Pacific?

Mr. HUNTINGTON. No; we were making money very fast.

Senator MORGAN. I am talking about the time of the organization of the Central Pacific.

Mr. HUNTINGTON. Yes; about 1861.

Senator MORGAN. I want to know what money you had, outside of the hardware and metal business, to put into the Central Pacific?

Mr. HUNTINGTON. I had considerable. I had money; and I presume I had merchandise. I was always buying merchandise in San Francisco.

Senator MORGAN. You did not put merchandise into it?

Mr. HUNTINGTON. No; but merchandise means money.

Senator MORGAN. You did not put real estate into it?

Mr. HUNTINGTON. I might. I had some real estate in Sacramento. The business house belonged to me, and I had some other real estate.

Senator MORGAN. How much money out of your own resources did you actually put into the building of the Central Pacific?

Mr. HUNTINGTON. I do not remember, but it was a very considerable amount.

Senator MORGAN. I am speaking now of the building of the road, from the time you began to the time of its completion.

Mr. HUNTINGTON. I do not know, but I was always able to pay the debts when they became due.

Senator MORGAN. That will not do, Mr. Huntington.

Mr. HUNTINGTON. I am speaking about the general results.

Senator MORGAN. I am not speaking about the general results, but about facts. If you do not wish to state them, say so.

Mr. HUNTINGTON. I am stating them the very best I know how.

Senator MORGAN. You say you put in a large amount out of your own private resources?

Mr. HUNTINGTON. It must have been a very considerable amount.

Senator MORGAN. When did you put it in?

Mr. HUNTINGTON. As the work progressed. Before we got to Newcastle we had to use a large amount of money.

Senator MORGAN. Did you put it in by buying stock of the Central Pacific, or by buying stock of the Contract and Finance Company?

Mr. HUNTINGTON. The Contract and Finance Company was not organized until after the road reached Newcastle.

Senator MORGAN. Then you did not buy stock of the Contract and Finance Company with this money that you put in?

Mr. HUNTINGTON. I did not say that; I think we did.

Senator MORGAN. I am not talking about "we" but about "you." Did you put any money into the Central Pacific or the Contract and Finance Company for which you did not get stock?

Mr. HUNTINGTON. Where we bought stock we got stock; and where we loaned money we got the company to pay for it; and where we bought bonds we paid for them.

Senator MORGAN. Whom do you mean by "we?"

Mr. HUNTINGTON. Mark Hopkins was in my mind, but I will say myself.

Senator MORGAN. Can you not separate between yourself and Mark Hopkins?

Mr. HUNTINGTON. Mark and I were together for a great many years, and I always coupled him with myself. I wish you had known him.

Senator MORGAN. So that if you were not partners you were even closer than partners?

Mr. HUNTINGTON. Yes, I think so.

Senator MORGAN. I would like to know whether, outside of the property which you possessed and held under the firm name as part of the firm property, you put any money into the Central Pacific, and if so how much. I mean you and not Mark Hopkins.

Mr. HUNTINGTON. I can not say. It is thirty-five years ago. I did put some money in, because we took stocks and bonds.

Senator MORGAN. That is not putting money in, is it?

Mr. HUNTINGTON. Why, certainly it is. How would you put it in?

Senator MORGAN. I would suppose you would do it by buying the stock and bonds.

Mr. HUNTINGTON. That is what I am talking about.

Senator MORGAN. And you have now stated that you did not buy any stock or bonds of the Central Pacific Railroad Company, but that the Contract and Finance Company got the stock and bonds for building the road.

Mr. HUNTINGTON. I do not think I made any such statement. I said that the road to Newcastle was built largely by four men.

Senator MORGAN. Did you, as a separate individual, put any money into the stock and bonds either of the Contract and Finance Company or of the Central Pacific?

Mr. HUNTINGTON. Up to Newcastle we built the road and paid for it, and we furnished the money. That is, I furnished my part of the money and put it in stock and bonds, and, probably, some times in the notes of the company. That was, I think, probable. I think that Huntington & Hopkins loaned them money; but when I bought stock I paid for it, and when I bought bonds I paid for them. That is the only way I know of putting money in to build a railroad.

Senator MORGAN. How much stock of the Central Pacific did you buy and pay for?

Mr. HUNTINGTON. I do not know. There were, perhaps, a couple of thousand shares. I think I had about two thousand shares.

Senator MORGAN. Which you bought and paid for individually?

Mr. HUNTINGTON. Which I subscribed for? I think so.

Senator MORGAN. Did you pay up your subscription?

Mr. HUNTINGTON. I should say so.

Senator MORGAN. Did you?

Mr. HUNTINGTON. I say, I should say so.

Senator MORGAN. I ask you if you did?

Mr. HUNTINGTON. I say, I should say so.

Senator MORGAN. You decline to say whether you did or not?

Mr. HUNTINGTON. I am very sure I did. I did not pay it myself, because the last payments were made in installments. The first payment was 10 per cent, and as the work progressed the investments were paid.

Senator MORGAN. How many shares of Central Pacific stock did you get and pay for?

Mr. HUNTINGTON. I think 2,000 shares.

Senator MORGAN. At what rate per share?

Mr. HUNTINGTON. They were $100 shares.

Senator MORGAN. Did you pay in full that amount of money?

Mr. HUNTINGTON. I think so.

Senator MORGAN. Did you ever get your money out?

Mr. HUNTINGTON. Not that amount, probably, but I got some at the end. The stock went up late in the seventies and we sold out and paid the debts incurred in the construction of the road.

Senator MORGAN. The others did the same thing?

Mr. HUNTINGTON. Yes.

Senator MORGAN. What did you four gentlemen do with your shares when you bought them?

Mr. HUNTINGTON. Mr. Hopkins kept mine. I did not carry them about with me.

Senator MORGAN. Did you not capitalize the Contract and Finance Company with these shares?

Mr. HUNTINGTON. As I understood it, these shares had nothing to do with that company. The company never took these shares.

Senator MORGAN. You took them personally?

Mr. HUNTINGTON. Yes; but the Contract and Finance Company never took them.

Senator MORGAN. I did not ask you that question.

Mr. HUNTINGTON. I thought you did.

Senator MORGAN. I asked you if you capitalized the Contract and Finance Company with these shares?

Mr. HUNTINGTON. I do not understand.

Senator MORGAN. What capital did you put into the Contract and Finance Company?

Mr. HUNTINGTON. Money.

Senator MORGAN. How much?

Mr. HUNTINGTON. I do not know.

Senator MORGAN. You say you paid your subscription to the stock of the Central Pacific, 100 cents on the dollar, and then you paid your subscription to the Contract and Finance Company? How much?

Mr. HUNTINGTON. I think the capital of the Contract and Finance Company was $5,000,000. My impression is that we paid in a great deal more than that.

Senator MORGAN. Did you put more than $5,000,000 into the capital stock of the Contract and Finance Company?

Mr. HUNTINGTON. My impression is that we did—very much more.

Senator MORGAN. In money?

Mr. HUNTINGTON. Yes, in money. We had nothing else to put it in.

Senator MORGAN. How did you get the money?

Mr. HUNTINGTON. Borrowed it, largely.

Senator MORGAN. On what?

Mr. HUNTINGTON. On such stuff as we had.

Senator MORGAN. What stuff?

Mr. HUNTINGTON. The bonds of the company.

Senator MORGAN. What bonds?

Mr. HUNTINGTON. The bonds of the Central Pacific.

Senator MORGAN. The Government bonds?

Mr. HUNTINGTON. We may have borrowed money on the Government bonds. We borrowed money until we could sell the bonds.

Senator MORGAN. Then it was not you who were putting money into the Contract and Finance Company, but the Government of the United States?

Mr. HUNTINGTON. No.

Senator MORGAN. Why not?

Mr. HUNTINGTON. The Government gave so many bonds to build the road upon certain conditions. Those conditions were complied with. Then those bonds were ours, to be used for a certain purpose; and for that purpose we used them, and for no other purpose.

Senator MORGAN. Then, in working it back, you built this road and stocked up the Contract and Finance Company on the credit furnished you by the Government of the United States?

Mr. HUNTINGTON. To a certain extent, but on our own credit. We had a great deal of credit of our own.

Senator MORGAN. I want to find out how much individual money (not realized from the sale of stock and bonds of the Central Pacific but coming out of your own pockets) you put in—either one or all of you.

Mr. HUNTINGTON. We put in what you can not buy to-day for $5,000,000. That is, we put in money; but beyond that we put in time, night and day.

Senator MORGAN. It seems to me you are trying to sell it cheaper than $5,000,000, and to buy it yourself. Let me see if I can get at it. I want to try, with all due patience, without irritation, and in a calm, honest, and proper way, to find out what draft the Central Pacific or the Contract and Finance Company made on your private resources for money to carry on its operations in building the Central Pacific road.

Mr. HUNTINGTON. I do not remember, but always enough to make a great success of the building of the road, which could not be done unless we used our own money and our own credit.

Senator MORGAN. Are you willing to say that this Central Pacific road was built on your private resources, and out of your private money?

Mr. HUNTINGTON. Of course not. It could not have been built in that way. We could not have built the road without the first-mortgage bonds and without the Government bonds.

Senator MORGAN. And therefore your private resources were not drawn upon?

Mr. HUNTINGTON. I say that my private resources were drawn upon.

Senator MORGAN. To what extent?

Mr. HUNTINGTON. I can not say.

Senator MORGAN. Aside from the Government credit and the first-mortgage bonds of the company?

Mr. HUNTINGTON. We built the road 31 miles—a very expensive piece of road. Then we got to Colfax, 54 miles—another very expensive piece of mountain road—without anything from the Government; and we were nearly to Cisco before we got any bonds.

Senator MORGAN. Did you get the consent of Congress that you were to have the bonds of the Government and also the first-mortgage bonds of the railroad company for 100 miles in advance of construction?

Mr. HUNTINGTON. No, not that I know of.

Senator MORGAN. Did you not get an act of Congress of that kind?

Mr. HUNTINGTON. No; there was a clause, I think (the tenth section of the act), by which we could draw two-thirds of the amount of the work done; but we never did draw any money in advance until we passed Elcho, near Salt Lake.

Senator MORGAN. After you had progressed in your effort to build this road, and progressed with very marked success, you got an act of Congress which authorized you to sell bonds and to mortgage your road in order to secure the first mortgage bonds for 100 miles in advance of construction?

Mr. HUNTINGTON. I suppose the act is here. My impression is that we had a right to draw on uncompleted work up to two-thirds of the work done. That is my impression; I may be wrong.

Senator MORGAN. No only so, but you got the right from Congress also to dispense with the reserve which was left in the treasury of the company as a security for the ultimate construction of the road, and could do it for 100 miles in advance of the construction. Was that so?

Mr. HUNTINGTON. I do not remember that that was in the act, but whatever it was, we did not use anything more than we were allowed to.

Senator MORGAN. If that was so, where was the occasion or the necessity for the Contract and Finance Company, which had the building of the road, to borrow on your private resources in order to get money?

Mr. HUNTINGTON. There was a necessity at the start, and very likely from time to time.

Senator MORGAN. You say there was a necessity at the start, and very likely from time to time. Well, take the start. How much did you put in at the start?

Mr. HUNTINGTON. We put in money from time to time whenever it was necessary.

Senator MORGAN. I am talking about what you put in at the start.

Mr. HUNTINGTON. We put in whatever the law required.

Senator MORGAN. What was that?

Mr. HUNTINGTON. We organized the company to build the road to the State line; and the law of California required $1,000 a mile to be subscribed. We put in first 10 per cent, and then put in money from time to time as the work progressed.

Senator MORGAN. Ten per cent of what?

Mr. HUNTINGTON. Ten per cent of the face value of the shares.

Senator MORGAN. Of the shares or of the capital stock?

Mr. HUNTINGTON. Of the shares; $1,000 a mile had to be subscribed before we could organize.

The CHAIRMAN. What distance was that?

Mr. HUNTINGTON. 138 miles to the State line.

Senator MORGAN. That was a California requirement?

Mr. HUNTINGTON. Yes.

Senator WOLCOTT. Then you had to pay $138,000 in cash?

Mr. HUNTINGTON. Yes; whatever the law required.

Senator MORGAN. Have you got that money back?

Mr. HUNTINGTON. We may not have got that money back; but we got some money out of the company in the final cleaning up, late in the seventies.

Senator MORGAN. That was a part payment on the stock?

Mr. HUNTINGTON. No; it was on the building of the road.

Senator MORGAN. I am talking about the stock. How much did you pay on it?

Mr. HUNTINGTON. We paid 10 per cent at first, and as the law required from time to time.

Senator MORGAN. Was that a part payment on the stock?

Mr. HUNTINGTON. Of course it was a payment on the stock. The law required payments on the stock, and we paid according to the law.

Senator MORGAN. And you got stock for it?

Mr. HUNTINGTON. Yes.

Senator MORGAN. How much?

Mr. HUNTINGTON. I do not know. Whatever we were entitled to.

Senator MORGAN. That was in the California company?

Mr. HUNTINGTON. That was under the State law.

Senator MORGAN. Then you did not have Central Pacific bonds or stock at that time?

Mr. HUNTINGTON. No; we could not do any business until we subscribed $1,000 a mile and paid 10 per cent of the subscription in advance.

Senator MORGAN. One thousand dollars a mile from what point to what point?

Mr. HUNTINGTON. The distance, as I remember, is 138 miles.

Senator MORGAN. And you paid $1,000 a mile for 138 miles?

Mr. HUNTINGTON. Yes; as I remember.

Senator MORGAN. When you came to the Central Pacific organization, were you required to put in any money?

Mr. HUNTINGTON. I have been talking about the Central Pacific.

Senator MORGAN. I mean the Central Pacific road, on this side of the California State line.

Mr. HUNTINGTON. I think so; I do not know.

Senator MORGAN. You say that you paid the other under the law of California?

Mr. HUNTINGTON. Yes. When we passed the State line of California we were in Nevada, and we paid what was necessary under the law of Nevada.

Senator MORGAN. Did you pay in any money for stock after the road left California, coming east?

Mr. HUNTINGTON. I do not know. Whatever the law required to be done was done.

Senator MORGAN. I do not think there is the least use in the world in wasting time in getting your opinion. What I want are the facts.

Mr. HUNTINGTON. I am giving all the facts I have.

Senator MORGAN. You do not seem to have any recollection of anything?

Mr. HUNTINGTON. I was not there. These things were done currently from day to day by others.

Senator MORGAN. This Commission has stated its judgment and findings upon all of these matters?

Mr. HUNTINGTON. Yes; what they knew about them.

Senator MORGAN. I have been trying to find out whether you know anything contrary to the statements of the Commission?

Mr. HUNTINGTON. I know all about the building of the road. I saw the profiles and studied them. The road was built very cheaply under the circumstances.

Senator MORGAN. Do you undertake to say, with your meager recollection of facts, that the findings of the Commission are untrue?

Mr. HUNTINGTON. My recollection of the building of the road and of what we had to build with is very distinct, and I say that the Commissioners are all wrong in their findings. Where they got their facts I do not know, but there are always plenty of men standing around the street corners in San Francisco to give such information.

Senator MORGAN. You say that your recollection of the facts attending the building of the road and of the resources you built it with are very distinct?

Mr. HUNTINGTON. Yes.

Senator MORGAN. On that announcement I expect to get some facts from you. How long did it take you build the road?

Mr. HUNTINGTON. As I recollect, about seven years.

Senator MORGAN. How many miles did you actually build in those seven years?

Mr. HUNTINGTON. As I have it, 740 miles, or thereabouts.

Senator MORGAN. How much money did you receive from bonds to build the road?

Mr. HUNTINGTON. We received in round numbers $25,000,000 from the Government and $25,000,000 from the first-mortgage bonds. I do not bring in the Western Pacific road.

Senator MORGAN. So you got $50,000,000 in money.

Mr. HUNTINGTON. We go fifty millions in bonds. We did not get par for the bonds.

Senator MORGAN. You got $50,000,000 in money so far as the Government of the United States is concerned?

Mr. HUNTINGTON. We got fifty millions nominal value.

Senator MORGAN. The Government did not have much credit, I suppose?

Mr. HUNTINGTON. It did not for that kind of bonds. They were currency bonds, and gold was high at the time and people did not know what to do with those bonds.

Senator MORGAN. In addition to the bonds, how much stock did you get to build the Central Pacific road?

Mr. HUNTINGTON. There were sixty millions of stock out when we got through. I would say that the building of the road for the bonds and for sixty millions of stock was very cheap.

Senator MORGAN. You say that your recollection is very distinct. I want your recollection.

Mr. HUNTINGTON. I am giving it to you.

Senator MORGAN. How much stock of the Central Pacific Railroad Company did you get in addition to the fifty millions of bonds for building that particular part of the road?

Mr. HUNTINGTON. There were sixty millions of stock out altogether. There was a contract with Charles Crocker & Co., who got, I think, fifteen millions of stock. I am quite sure they did not complete their contract, and then the Contract and Finance Company took it over. How much Charles Crocker & Co. got of the stock of the Central Pacific I do not know. My impression is that the Contract and Finance Company got about fifteen millions of the stock for that work.

Senator MORGAN. How much of the stock of the Contract and Finance Company did you get for that same work?

Mr. HUNTINGTON. I got $1,250,000 of the stock of the Contract and Finance Company. That is, if I had one-fourth share, which I did not have, the amount would have been $1,250,000.

Senator MORGAN. And each of the other four had the same amount?

Mr. HUNTINGTON. Yes. We did not have any of the stock originally. I think that Mr. Ben Crocker and three others subscribed to the stock.

Senator MORGAN. I am appealing to this very distinct recollection of yours.

Mr. HUNTINGTON. You are speaking now of details. I say that so much stock and so much bonds went out for building 765 miles of road.

Senator WOLCOTT. The other two persons that you speak of are Milliken and Brown?

Mr. HUNTINGTON. Yes; I thank you, Senator.

Senator MORGAN. You say that you have a very distinct recollection of the resources you had for building the road?

Mr. HUNTINGTON. I know that fifty millions of stock went out for building the road and fifty millions of bonds. I remember that there was some work to be done, and I saw the profiles for the work over the mountains to the Big Bend of Truckee. We had a general reconnoissance of the rest of the road. We had a close estimate, and we knew that we had so much to build the road with. I said that, with great economy, we could do it. But gold went up, and many things went up in cost; but still, with great economy and hard work, we built the road.

Senator MORGAN. And with good pay?

Mr. HUNTINGTON. Not very good. I would not do it over again for twice that pay. I remember very distinctly what we had to build the road with, but just how that was divided and subdivided I do not know.

Senator MORGAN. Your recollection is a general summary and does not relate to facts.

Mr. HUNTINGTON. These are the main facts. These are factors that we had to deal with.

Senator MORGAN. But I want to know the facts which make up this detailed statement, so that I can see whether your recollection is correct or not.

Mr. HUNTINGTON. I would like you to know, Senator, all that I know.

Senator MORGAN. I think that I have got all that you know. The commissioners found out a great many things about the building of the road, and I want to know whether they differ with you in their conclusions, or whether you feel authorized to contradict what they have found.

Mr. HUNTINGTON. I contradict the report of the commission—pretty much all of it and its conclusions.

Senator MORGAN. Do you contradict the commission on items which you confess you can not state yourself?

Mr. HUNTINGTON. I contradict the commission on this fact. That the work was a great work to do, for what we had to do it with; and when they say that the work could be done for $36,000,000, I say that the commissioners did not know anything about it.

Senator MORGAN. The commissioners have had an opportunity to be instructed and informed by your testimony, and by the testimony of Mr. Stanford and others, given at a much earlier date than this, and when the facts were fresher in your memory than they can possibly be now. You could have made a statement of facts on which they could base their judgment, and I think they did base it upon your statement.

Mr. HUNTINGTON. The commissioners say that the road from Bonneville Table to the summit cost $40,000 a mile. Here is what General Dodge, who is an able and intelligent engineer, says in regard to that question. He testified that it cost $87,000 in cash per mile between Bonneville Table and the summit, which would equal $4,132,500 for the whole distance. General Dodge was there. He was the engineer and knew all about it. The commissioners have put the price at about one-half.

Senator MORGAN. Where is General Dodge now?

Mr. HUNTINGTON. I got this statement from New York. It is an extract from his testimony [presenting a telegram].

Senator MORGAN. Is this telegram from him?

Mr. HUNTINGTON. No; it is from Charles H. Tweed. I told Mr. Miles to ask the question this morning and this information is got, I presume, from General Dodge's testimony.

Senator MORGAN. What testimony are you talking about?

Mr. HUNTINGTON. General Dodge's testimony before the Wilson committee as to the cost of this piece of road. The telegram reads: "Your telegram received; $87,000 cash per mile, which would equal $4,132,000. Charles H. Tweed."

Senator MORGAN. Mr. Tweed is your lawyer?

Mr. HUNTINGTON. Yes.

Senator MORGAN. And you sent Mr. Miles to him?

Mr. HUNTINGTON. No; I told Mr. Miles to ask him the question over the wires.

Senator MORGAN. Who is Mr. Miles—your clerk?

Mr. HUNTINGTON. Yes; my secretary.

Senator MORGAN. And so you told your secretary to ask, by telegraph, what General Dodge had sworn to in a deposition given before the Wilson committee?

Mr. HUNTINGTON. Yes. Eighty-seven thousand dollars a mile from Bonneville Table to the summit. There are no structures on that piece of road, except one bridge over Bear River.

Senator MORGAN. That is part of the mountain road, is it?

Mr. HUNTINGTON. No; it is from Ogden to Promontory Point.

Senator MORGAN. What is the length of that piece of road?

Mr. HUNTINGTON. Forty-eight or fifty miles.

Senator MORGAN. How much a mile in bonds did you get from the Government for that road?

Mr. HUNTINGTON. Thirty-two thousand dollars.

Senator MORGAN. And how much in first-mortgage bonds?

Mr. HUNTINGTON. The same.

Senator MORGAN. That is $64,000 a mile.

Mr. HUNTINGTON. Yes; and I understand the road was not complete at the time we got it.

Senator MORGAN. Why was that part of the road so difficult to build?

Mr. HUNTINGTON. I do not know. Things were expensive. There was a long haul, and we had to pay $10 a day for teams—for the hire of horses and men.

Senator MORGAN. Its expense was not on account of topographical difficulties?

Mr. HUNTINGTON. No; but everything out there was expensive.

Senator MORGAN. Did you build the road from Promontory Point west to any extent?

Mr. HUNTINGTON. Yes.

Senator MORGAN. Did you build it clear through?

Mr. HUNTINGTON. Yes; we did not take that part of the road until we connected at Promontory Point.

Senator MORGAN. You mean that you built the road from Bonneville Table eastward to Ogden?

Mr. HUNTINGTON. No; we bought it from the Union Pacific Company.

Senator MORGAN. Then, what are we inquiring about?

Mr. HUNTINGTON. It is part of the report of the commissioners that that road only cost so much; and the statement of the commissioners is quite in the face of General Dodge's testimony, who said that it cost the Union Pacific Company so much; and no rolling stock went with it.

Senator MORGAN. Then, the Union Pacific Company built that piece of road?

Mr. HUNTINGTON. Yes.

Senator MORGAN. And you wanted to buy it and did buy it?

Mr. HUNTINGTON. Yes.

Senator MORGAN. And you say that the Commissioners have understated the amount of money that you paid for it?

Mr. HUNTINGTON. They have understated the cost of the road.

Senator MORGAN. How much did you pay for it?

Mr. HUNTINGTON. I do not recollect.

Senator MORGAN. Did you pay anything more for it than the Commissioners have stated?

Mr. HUNTINGTON. I think we paid $4,000,000 for it.

Senator MORGAN. Did you pay any more than the Commissioners stated?

Mr. HUNTINGTON. Yes; I know it was more than that.

Senator MORGAN. You do not mean that the building of this 40 miles of road cost you over $4,000,000?

Mr. HUNTINGTON. No; I mean that it cost the Union Pacific Company that much.

Senator MORGAN. But you did not lose any money by buying the road cheaper than the Union Pacific Company built it for?

Mr. HUNTINGTON. No; but this statement of General Dodge's shows the cost of the road.

Senator MORGAN. And the Union Pacific Company sold it to you for less than it cost the company?

Mr. HUNTINGTON. Yes.

Senator MORGAN. Which shows your skill in buying?

Mr. HUNTINGTON. No.

Senator MORGAN. Why did you buy that piece of road?

Mr. HUNTINGTON. Because we did not want to stop on the top of Promontory Mountain. We wanted to come to Ogden, and we should have built the road to Ogden if the Union Pacific Company had not sold us this piece of road.

Senator MORGAN. Would you have skipped the Union Pacific?

Mr. HUNTINGTON. No; but we would have gone alongside of it.

Senator MORGAN. You thought you had a right to build a road parallel to theirs?

Mr. HUNTINGTON. Yes.

Senator MORGAN. And that was your view of it?

Mr. HUNTINGTON. Yes.

Senator MORGAN. You were building your road in a great hurry?

Mr. HUNTINGTON. Yes; we wanted to get into Salt Lake Valley to share that business, which was supposed to be much greater than it actually was.

Senator MORGAN. You do not mean to say that the Union Pacific Railroad Company paid $10 a day for teams in building this piece of road?

Mr. HUNTINGTON. I think so.

Senator MORGAN. Did you ever pay so much for teams?

Mr. HUNTINGTON. I am very certain that we did.

Senator MORGAN. How much time did you save in building that road to a through connection over the time within which you were allowed by act of Congress to build it?

Mr. HUNTINGTON. As I recollect, seven years and three months.

Senator MORGAN. You saved seven years and three months?

Mr. HUNTINGTON. Yes.

Senator MORGAN. You must have been in a great hurry to build it?

Mr. HUNTINGTON. The Union Pacific was trying to drive us out of Salt Lake Valley, and we thought there was great tonnage there.

Senator MORGAN. And the Union Pacific Company did get to Salt Lake Valley before you did?

Mr. HUNTINGTON. Yes.

Senator MORGAN. And you had to buy out the Union Pacific?

Mr. HUNTINGTON. Yes.

Senator MORGAN. So that it was a race of diligence between the two companies as to which would get first to this Salt Lake Valley?

Mr. HUNTINGTON. Yes.

Senator MORGAN. If you had taken that seven years to build the road, would you not have saved much money?

Mr. HUNTINGTON. Yes; I think so.

Senator MORGAN. How much?

Mr. HUNTINGTON. I do not know.

Senator MORGAN. Then, for the advantage of the four men who owned the Central Pacific, you rushed things and had to pay enormous amounts for wagons and other transportation and materials, which amounts you might have saved if you had been a little more temperate and had not been so greedy in regard to the mileage of the road which you wanted to control?

Mr. HUNTINGTON. That is rather a partisan way of putting it. We wanted to get into Salt Lake Valley, and we did get there. Everybody was just hurrying us on. There wasn't a man, woman, or child there who didn't want to come back to the East to visit the old folks at home.

Senator MORGAN. We have had "the old folks at home" several times before.

Mr. HUNTINGTON. It is the second time that I have stated it.

Senator MORGAN. No; I think it is the fifth time. Leaving out "the old folks at home," who were so anxious to get out there and whom you were so anxious to accommodate, and getting back to the question of your anxiety to get into Salt Lake Valley, you wanted as much mileage as possible between the Pacific Ocean and the East under the control of the Central Pacific Railroad Company?

Mr. HUNTINGTON. I do not recollect that that was wanted, but I should think it would have been.

Senator MORGAN. What did you want if you did not expect it to be a large, profitable business?

Mr. HUNTINGTON. Of course, where there are two companies building roads on a joint line, each of them wants to have as much of the road as it can.

Senator MORGAN. Then you were not working for money, but working for glory?

Mr. HUNTINGTON. I do not think we were working for money, really.

Senator MORGAN. But you managed to get it?

Mr. HUNTINGTON. No; I do not think we got pay sufficient for what we did.

Senator MORGAN. I know you do not think so. With all these stories about mileage and about your ambitious scheme to extend the road, you made no mistake about the wisdom or the policy of trying to extend your road as rapidly and as far as you could do it?

Mr. HUNTINGTON. No. As an American citizen, I think it was a good thing to hurry up the road, and it was an economy to the Government. The Government was paying a great many millions of dollars to police that country, which we did as soon as we covered the ground with our road.

Senator MORGAN. Then, in doing this work of patriotism, you were not working against the British, but against other American citizens who were building the Union Pacific road?

Mr. HUNTINGTON. I was figuring upon the general results.

Senator MORGAN. The Union Pacific Company had as good a right to the field as you had?

Mr. HUNTINGTON. Certainly.

Senator MORGAN. So that it was American citizens against American citizens?

Mr. HUNTINGTON. You misunderstand me. I say that, as American citizens, better care was taken of that country than when it was costing the Government seven millions a year to police it.

Senator MORGAN. You still seem to want to take good care of it by owning this road.

Mr. HUNTINGTON. I think that what we have done was a good reason for our having it.

Senator MORGAN. Getting back to "the old folks at home," you found that for the first ten years after you built this long line from Bonneville Table to the Pacific Ocean the road paid well?

Mr. HUNTINGTON. Yes; it paid very well until the Northern Pacific and the Atchison and Sante Fe roads cut in.

Senator MORGAN. The first ten years of its operation the Central Pacific Company paid well?

Mr. HUNTINGTON. Yes; it paid very well.

Senator MORGAN. Did it pay well for the first fourteen years?

Mr. HUNTINGTON. I do not know when these other two roads really got into operation. When they did get into operation freights went down, and tonnage went down, and it was very rough.

Senator MORGAN. Have you examined the Commission's report on that subject as to the income of the competing roads, and as to the influence of the Central Pacific on them?

Mr. HUNTINGTON. I think I looked it over.

Senator MORGAN. Have you any fault to find with the statements of the Commission on that subject?

Mr. HUNTINGTON. I do not recollect now just what those statements were.

Senator MORGAN. They show a very large profit in the operation of the Central Pacific road, beginning with the first year, when they were making perhaps 14 per cent.

Mr. HUNTINGTON. I do not think it was as much as that, but the road did pay very well.

Senator MORGAN. As much as 12 per cent?

Mr. HUNTINGTON. I do not think that there was over 10 per cent at any time.

Senator MORGAN. For the first ten or fourteen years, or for whatever time they have stated, large dividends were paid, so that you found the road immensely profitable during that time?

Mr. HUNTINGTON. I do not know that I would exactly use that language; but the road did well.

Senator MORGAN. Do you know any long road in the United States that has paid its stockholders more than 10 per cent dividends?

Mr. HUNTINGTON. No; I am not very familiar with the dividends paid by other companies.

Senator MORGAN. You have given that matter general observation, I suppose?

Mr. HUNTINGTON. Yes; but I keep myself generally confined to Western roads.

Senator MORGAN. How could you find out how a company was doing unless you had an opportunity of comparing it with other companies?

Mr. HUNTINGTON. I know that a 10 per cent dividend is pretty good, anyway. We were glad when the road began to pay dividends, because then the stock went up, and we sold it in order to pay our debts.

Senator MORGAN. Did you pay your debts out of the dividends you received?

Mr. HUNTINGTON. No; I think we sold the shares and paid our debts out of what we received from them.

Senator MORGAN. You got dividends over and above the debts that were paid. Could there have been any dividends honestly paid unless the honest debts and charges were paid before the dividend was declared? Would it not have been a crime, moral and statutory, to have paid dividends on that road unless you had first satisfied the fixed charges and the current debts?

Mr. HUNTINGTON. I think it would not have been right. I do not think the company declared any dividends when the road was in debt.

Senator MORGAN. You do not think there were any dividends paid except after the payment of all debts and fixed charges of the company?

Mr. HUNTINGTON. No; I said nothing of the kind; you misunderstand me. The Contract and Finance Company was owing the money. I do not think that the Central Pacific Company was owing much, if anything.

Senator MORGAN. That is a side show. I am not talking about the Contract and Finance Company, I want to know about the Central Pacific Company. What was it that prevented you from funding, in good stocks or securities, these 10 per cent dividends paid for ten years (ten times ten equal to one hundred) so as to pay off the first and second mortgage bonds.

Mr. HUNTINGTON. It might have been done, but the only reason for doing it would have been that it was a novelty; no other reason in the world for it. It never was done. We commenced selling shares when the prices went up, and we paid the debts of the Contract and Finance Company, which owned those shares.

Senator MORGAN. You had ten years of 10 per cent dividends.

Mr. HUNTINGTON. We did not have any such thing. I do not believe it.

Senator MORGAN. You said so.

Mr. HUNTINGTON. I said that I think we had dividends as high as 10 per cent one year.

Senator MORGAN. Did you not state that the average dividend was 10 per cent?

Mr. HUNTINGTON. No. Excuse me, Senator, I did not state any average.

Senator MORGAN. What was it?

Mr. HUNTINGTON. I say that the company paid as high as 10 per cent in dividends.

Senator MORGAN. What was the average during the ten years?

Mr. HUNTINGTON. I can not say.

Senator MORGAN. If you can not say, why do you contradict the commissioners?

Mr. HUNTINGTON. I do not think that the commissioners say that the Central Pacific paid 10 per cent dividends for ten years.

Senator MORGAN. Well, if it was only 1 per cent, or 5 per cent, or 8 per cent, why did you not put whatever it was into a sinking fund to meet the debt which you knew you owed to the United States and to the first-mortgage bondholders, so as to extinguish that debt?

Mr. HUNTINGTON. Because these things are never done. The stock was entitled to its dividends when the obligations were met according to law. In 1878 we passed a resolution for a sinking fund for the Government, which sinking fund would have nearly wiped out the debt, but Senator Thurman came here with a bill of his own. I said that we would go on and keep our own sinking fund and pay the Government debt, but Senator Thurman said no; that the Government would keep the sinking fund; and the result has been that that sinking fund, kept by the Government, did not get a new dollar for an old one on its investment. It paid as much as 135 for 6 per cent bonds, and I think it hardly got a new dollar for an old one. I might not have paid off the whole of the debt with the sinking fund that we proposed, but I would have paid enough of it so that we could have easily handled it when it became due.

Senator MORGAN. I have sat here and have had you put that statement on record four or five different times as an excuse for your not making a sinking fund out of your dividends.

Mr. HUNTINGTON. As soon as we could see our way clear to pay our debts we commenced selling Central Pacific stock and paid our debts.

Senator MORGAN. The stockholders got their dividends?

Mr. HUNTINGTON. They were entitled to them.

Senator MORGAN. It is impossible for me to get on the record answers to my questions because of your extreme anxiety to escape answering them. Did the Thurman controversy, which occurred twelve or fourteen years later, prevent you, in the beginning, when you got 10 per cent dividends in one year (perhaps less in another year), from organizing a sinking fund? I mean during the time that elapsed before Thurman got into it?

Mr. HUNTINGTON. I do not know when Thurman got into it. I think his bill was passed in 1878. It was before that that I had a resolution passed in the board for a sinking fund.

Senator MORGAN. Did you create a sinking fund?

Mr. HUNTINGTON. No.

Senator MORGAN. Why?

Mr. HUNTINGTON. Because Senator Thurman took it up and said that he was going to create a sinking fund for the Government.

Senator MORGAN. And when you found that the Government was going to change the law, and to require payment on the net income of the company, without regard to dividends, then you passed a resolution to create a sinking fund?

Mr. HUNTINGTON. Not at all. It was done before Thurman's bill was passed.

Senator MORGAN. How long before?

Mr. HUNTINGTON. Not many months. It was done just at the time that we thought it was well to do something in that way.

Senator MORGAN. Because Congress was getting after you?

Mr. HUNTINGTON. No; we were complying with every requirement of law.

Senator MORGAN. You had that interval of time during three or four months which antedated the Thurman movement, and you did not provide for a sinking fund?

Mr. HUNTINGTON. No.

Senator MORGAN. You paid the dividends?

Mr. HUNTINGTON. Whatever dividends were coming to us we took; but we violated no law, moral or statutory.

Senator MORGAN. Were not dividends enough paid on that stock to have constituted a sinking fund, the principal of which would have been equal to at least two-thirds of the first-mortgage debt and of the Government debt?

Mr. HUNTINGTON. No; I think not.

Senator MORGAN. How much would it have been?

Mr. HUNTINGTON. I do not know how much. If we put in two or three other roads, I suppose it would be less. We followed the statutes.

Senator MORGAN. I do not think I comprehend you.

Mr. HUNTINGTON. If we had called in the first-mortgage bonds before they were due, we would have had to pay a large premium on them. I think that the stockholders were entitled to all the dividends they got.

Senator MORGAN. Did you receive any part of the dividends in money yourself?

Mr. HUNTINGTON. In the last cleaning up, I did receive some money.

Senator MORGAN. In the current business did you receive any dividends in money in your own hands?

Mr. HUNTINGTON. Not directly from the Central Pacific. I had probably some shares of the Central Pacific, but not a great many.

Senator MORGAN. Did you, as an individual man, receive any money in your own hands, or the representative of money, for these dividends or any part thereof?

Mr. HUNTINGTON. I should think I did; I am quite sure I did.

Senator MORGAN. How much do you think you did receive?

Mr. HUNTINGTON. Not a great deal.

Senator MORGAN. How much?

Mr. HUNTINGTON. I do not know.

Senator MORGAN. And when?

Mr. HUNTINGTON. When they were paid to others.

Senator MORGAN. Have you no recollection of having received any particular sum of money as dividends?

Mr. HUNTINGTON. I do not recollect any definite sum, but I have no doubt that I did receive dividends at various times when dividends were paid.

Senator MORGAN. When you are traveling from New York to San Francisco or from San Francisco to New York, do you not know how much your hotel bills are and whether you have paid them?

Mr. HUNTINGTON. Probably I would not know a year afterwards.

Senator MORGAN. Have you not been pretty diligent of late in looking up books and things to see the state of your accounts?

Mr. HUNTINGTON. No.

Senator MORGAN. And yet you knew that you were coming before this committee to ask Congress to put this railroad in your possession?

Mr. HUNTINGTON. I am not reviewing my life's business. I am satisfied with it. We have done, in every case, what the law required.

Senator MORGAN. I would hate to assert that, if I were in your place.

Mr. HUNTINGTON. I do assert it most boldly—that we have done just what the law required. If you say that we have not, and if you will tell me wherein we have not, I will try to explain.

Senator MORGAN. You have got the fullest liberty in the world to explain everything, but I beg leave to say that you are not improving the value of your statements when you decline to give categorical answers to honest questions. If you would do so you would relieve the case very quickly.

Mr. HUNTINGTON. When Senator Morgan asks me to answer questions about things that happened thirty-five years ago, I can only answer in a general way. If I could answer yes or no, I would do so.

Senator MORGAN. After this discourse, argumentation, and general wandering over the field, can you now state that, at any time, you received into your own hands any money that came from the dividends of this Central Pacific Railroad stock?

Mr. HUNTINGTON. I will say, as I have said before, that I think I have. I am quite sure I have.

Senator MORGAN. You can not state it as a fact?

Mr. HUNTINGTON. I know it just as well as I know anything. I am satisfied that I received dividends, but I can not say how much.

Senator MORGAN. If you know it as well as you know anything, can you not state whether you received dividends and how much?

Mr. HUNTINGTON. No; I do not know anybody who could tell exactly what passed thirty years ago.

Senator MORGAN. Awhile ago you said that you could tell exactly what it cost to build the railroad and the resources that you had to build it with.

Mr. HUNTINGTON. I do not know that I used the word "exactly." I said I could tell that it was a great work and could tell what we had to build it with. It had to be done with great economy.

Senator MORGAN. And now you say you know that you have received dividends from the Central Pacific Company in money, into your own hands, and that you can not tell where or how much you received at any time?

Mr. HUNTINGTON. Quite true.

Senator MORGAN. Did you receive any large sums?

Mr. HUNTINGTON. I do not think I did.

Senator MORGAN. Did you receive all that was coming to you?

Mr. HUNTINGTON. I did.

Senator MORGAN. How much was coming to you?

Mr. HUNTINGTON. I can not tell.

Senator MORGAN. How much stock of the Central Pacific did you hold?

Mr. HUNTINGTON. I do not know. It was through the Contract and Finance Company that we got our money.

Senator MORGAN. The Contract and Finance Company seems different from the Central Pacific Company. I admit that it is only a question of bookkeeping; but, at the same time, there is a line of separation in the bookkeeping between the two companies. What do you mean when you say the stock of the Contract and Finance Company?

Mr. HUNTINGTON. I say that the dividends that I received from the Central Pacific Company were received through the Contract and Finance Company. Not all of them. I received some myself. I had some shares of the Central Pacific and sold them just as soon as I needed the money.

Senator MORGAN. Then the Contract and Finance Company were the holders of a large number of shares of the Central Pacific Railroad Company, and received dividends on those shares?

Mr. HUNTINGTON. Yes; when the Contract and Finance Company owned them.

Senator MORGAN. What did that company do with the dividends?

Mr. HUNTINGTON. It paid them out to the shareholders.

Senator MORGAN. From time to time as it received them?

Mr. HUNTINGTON. I presume so; or it may have partly used them in paying some of its debts.

Senator MORGAN. Do you know that the Contract and Finance Company did pay these dividends to the shareholders?

Mr. HUNTINGTON. It paid some, I know; perhaps all.

Senator MORGAN. What did the Contract and Finance Company do with the dividends it received from the Central Pacific Company?

Mr. HUNTINGTON. It used them to pay its debts, if it did not give them to the shareholders.

Senator MORGAN. Did it give the dividends to the shareholders?

Mr. HUNTINGTON. I think that it both paid its debts and gave money to the stockholders.

Senator MORGAN. How much did the Contract and Finance Company pay to you in dividends?

Mr. HUNTINGTON. I do not recollect.

Senator MORGAN. You held stock of the Central Pacific at that time as an individual stockholder?

Mr. HUNTINGTON. Oh, yes.

Senator MORGAN. Without being able to state how much it was?

Mr. HUNTINGTON. Yes.

Senator MORGAN. And the Contract and Finance Company, in which you held stock, also held the stock of the Central Pacific Company?

Mr. HUNTINGTON. Quite right.

Senator MORGAN. And you and Crocker and Hopkins and Stanford owned the Central Pacific Company and the Contract and Finance Company?

Mr. HUNTINGTON. Not all.

Senator MORGAN. Nearly all.

Mr. HUNTINGTON. I think myself that that is substantially so.

Senator MORGAN. You owned all but a slight color.

Mr. HUNTINGTON. We owned the majority of the stock.

Senator MORGAN. There was just a trace left in the hands of other people. In this accidental combination of circumstances the money which was paid on these dividends went to the Contract and Finance Company and was used in its business. Did that Contract and Finance Company take any other contract except for the building of the Central Pacific road?

Mr. HUNTINGTON. I think it did.

Senator MORGAN. What other contracts?

Mr. HUNTINGTON. I do not know. We have been always building roads, and we have generally kept one company in operation until some member died and the company was closed up. When Mr. Colton died and when E. B. Crocker died the company was changed.

Senator MORGAN. I understand you to mean that you are not able to recollect the precise history of all these investments and reinvestments because you had so many companies under your control (I mean you four), and that you are unable to tell what particular company you were employing at a particular time to do a particular job of work?

Mr. HUNTINGTON. Perhaps that is stating it a little partisanly; but in the main it is correct, I should say. There were, however, other interests than those four.

Senator MORGAN. I will take the partisanship and put the truth along with it. Please tell us what roads you did build with these various instrumentalities or corporations.

Mr. HUNTINGTON. I think we built the Oregon branch from Roseville to the State line. I do not know that we built it all the way; that belonged to another railroad company. Originally we had no interest in it. The other company started it, and could not get money to go on with it, and we took it. We built the road from Lathrop to Goshen. I said to Fresno the other day, but I meant Goshen.

Senator MORGAN. Fresno is a mile or two from Goshen?

Mr. HUNTINGTON. It is more than that; and we built the road from Niles to Oakland, and I think the Northern Railway from San Francisco to Tehama, and we built the Southern Pacific.

Senator MORGAN. I will come to something else now. You intended to put in the whole of this statement?

Mr. HUNTINGON. Yes.

Senator MORGAN. You say on page 2:

> I observe that on page 26 of the report the commissioners state that the financial inability of the company to meet the requirements of the readjustment bill prepared by the commissioners was the result of the profligate and wanton dispersion of the assets of the company in dividends and the extravagant contracts made by the company.
>
> What is referred to as extravagant contracts I do not know, as I have no recollection of any extravagant contracts made after the building of the road of any great importance, and they were always made for the benefit of the Central Pacific Company.

I understand that in consequence of your haste in building this road so as to cut out the Union Pacific Company from getting into Great Salt Lake Valley you were compelled to make some very extravagant contracts—hiring teams at $10 a day.

Mr. HUNTINGTON. We paid that much for the best ones in the Central Pacific Company.

Senator MORGAN. You being the company?

Mr. HUNTINGTON. Yes, if you will have it so. Of course I was not the company, but if the Senator wishes it to go on the record in that way I have no objection.

Senator MORGAN. Then you say:

As to the dividends, we carried the shares until they began to appreciate and then we commenced selling.

The shares appreciated, I suppose, because of these large dividends being paid upon them?

Mr. HUNTINGTON. The payment of large dividends would naturally have that effect.

Senator MORGAN. There was only about sixty millions of stock of the Central Pacific issued in all?

Mr. HUNTINGTON. That was all at that time.

Senator MORGAN. And you had all of that except a little margin—a little fringe—you four?

Mr. HUNTINGTON. We had a very large majority of the stock. I mean the Contract and Finance Company.

Senator MORGAN. These shares commenced to appreciate, and appreciated rapidly while the dividends were being paid, did they not?

Mr. HUNTINGTON. They appreciated. That would be the natural effect.

Senator MORGAN. You say, "We carried the shares until they began to appreciate, and then we commenced selling them?"

Mr. HUNTINGTON. Yes.

Senator MORGAN. Why did you commence selling shares when they began to appreciate and when they were paying such heavy dividends?

Mr. HUNTINGTON. Because we were owing money.

Senator MORGAN. Who were owing money?

Mr. HUNTINGTON. The Contract and Finance Company.

Senator MORGAN. How much did the company owe?

Mr. HUNTINGTON. I have not the amount exactly, but to the best of my belief and knowledge, I should say that it owed somewhere from nine to twelve million dollars.

Senator MORGAN. To whom was that money owing?

Mr. HUNTINGTON. That money was owing to various parties, but mostly to bankers and money lenders in New York.

Senator MORGAN. How much was owing to you?

Mr. HUNTINGTON. Not any of it. I may have had my paper out, but it was mere cross paper.

Senator MORGAN. Was any of it owing to you?

Mr. HUNTINGTON. No; except what was to be passed on to be paid to others.

Senator MORGAN. You mean that nothing was owing to you except in your nominal relation as agent to pay it out?

Mr. HUNTINGTON. Yes.

Senator MORGAN. Personally, there was none of it due to you?

Mr. HUNTINGTON. There was, no doubt, some of it due to me.

Senator MORGAN. If any of it was owing to you, do you recollect it?

Mr. HUNTINGTON. I do not recollect any particular piece, but I should say that there was. I always had my paper out individually for the company's debts.

Senator MORGAN. Did you sell this advancing stock (receiving these large dividends) in order to raise money that was due to you?

Mr. HUNTINGTON. No; I should not have sold it for that purpose.

Senator MORGAN. Did you sell it to raise money due to other people?

Mr. HUNTINGTON. I sold it to pay debts—it may have been to myself or to someone else. I sold it because I had to have money to pay debts due to others than myself.

Senator MORGAN. At that time what was the current rate of interest for money in New York?

Mr. HUNTINGTON. I do not know. That was pretty early in the seventies, I think, and we sold stock along up to 78.

Senator MORGAN. Was the rate of interest as much as 5 per cent?

Mr. HUNTINGTON. That is about an average rate there.

Senator MORGAN. You four gentlemen could have carried this $13,000,000 at 5 per cent?

Mr. HUNTINGTON. I can not say.

Senator MORGAN. You would not sell stock that was paying 10 per cent dividends in order to pay debts bearing 5 per cent interest?

Mr. HUNTINGTON. I always pay my debts. I never borrow money to lend it. I would not borrow money at 5 per cent in order to lend it to the best man in New York at 10 per cent.

Senator MORGAN. Were Stanford and Hopkins and Crocker as cautious about their business as you were?

Mr. HUNTINGTON. I do not think they would borrow money to lend. I had the money matters to take care of in New York.

Senator MORGAN. How much of the sixty millions of stock of the Central Pacific did you dispose of among you?

Mr. HUNTINGTON. Most of it.

Senator MORGAN. Nearly the whole of it?

Mr. HUNTINGTON. No; not nearly the whole of it, but pretty large blocks of it.

Senator MORGAN. At the time you were disposing of that stock I suppose you had some consideration of the question as to whether or not the constitution of California held you responsible for the debts of the company because you held the stock?

Mr. HUNTINGTON. We never held much stock. I do not think that we held much stock. In fact, I never thought there was much in that idea, so far as the Government was concerned. I never supposed that it was in sight of the property.

Senator MORGAN. You do not know how it was as to the stockholders and creditors of the company?

Mr. HUNTINGTON. So far as the Government was concerned I did not suppose that it was ever in sight of the property.

Senator Morgan. Still the question was mooted.

Mr. HUNTINGTON. I do not recollect ever having it up.

Senator MORGAN. Can you not assign some reason for selling out this stock?

Mr. HUNTINGTON. To pay debts.

Senator MORGAN. At what rate did you sell the stock?

Mr. HUNTINGTON. We sold it at almost all prices. We sold some as low as 19, and up to 85.

Senator MORGAN. Do you undertake to say that you sold stock at 19 cents on the dollar that was paying dividends at 10 per cent?

Mr. HUNTINGTON. No.

Senator MORGAN. Or paying a dividend at 5 per cent?

Mr. HUNTINGTON. I might sell it when it was paying 5 per cent dividend in order to pay debts.

Senator MORGAN. When did you do it?

Mr. HUNTINGTON. I hardly think that it was paying 5 per cent dividends when we sold it; but I should sell stock to pay debts. Some times, when there is a twist in the money market in New York, people have to pay 1 per cent over night, and I did not want to get into that position.

Senator MORGAN. Was it not your plan to have dividends paid, and then sell stock when it was appreciated in the market?

Mr. HUNTINGTON. No; we sold the stock to pay debts. Some of my people have got Central Pacific stock yet for which they were offered 76½.

Senator MORGAN. I did not know but that the price might be sent up by manipulation.

Mr. HUNTINGTON. There was no manipulation about it; and, if you will excuse me, Senator, that is not a proper word to use either.

Senator MORGAN. I will use it.

Mr. HUNTINGTON. Well, that is all right.

Senator MORGAN. I understand that you sold this stock all the way from 15 to 85?

Mr. HUNTINGTON. I think 19 was the lowest.

Senator MORGAN. When did you get rid of the last of it?

Mr. HUNTINGTON. I do not know. We have not got rid of it all now.

Senator MORGAN. Have you got stock in the Contract and Finance Company?

Mr. HUNTINGTON. No.

Senator MORGAN. When did you get rid of that stock?

Mr. HUNTINGTON. I do not know.

Senator MORGAN. Have you got stock of the Central Pacific Company which you received through the Contract and Finance Company?

Mr. HUNTINGTON. I think so.

Senator MORGAN. Have you got some of that stock for which you subscribed originally, and which never belonged to the Contract and Finance Company?

Mr. HUNTINGTON. I can not say.

Senator MORGAN. Some of the stock of the Central Pacific you have held on to, and other stock of the Central Pacific you have sold. How much did you hold on to?

Mr. HUNTINGTON. I do not know how much I have. I have not got a great deal. Something less than 6,000 shares.

Senator MORGAN. How much of that stock have you sold personally?

Mr. HUNTINGTON. I have sold the balance of it.

Senator MORGAN. I mean on your own account.

Mr. HUNTINGTON. I do not know.

Senator MORGAN. About how much?

Mr. HUNTINGTON. I can not say. I never had a great deal of it outside of the Contract and Finance Company shares.

Senator MORGAN. Are you willing to say that you sold stock of the Central Pacific as low as 15?

Mr. HUNTINGTON. No; I have not said so.

Senator MORGAN. As low as 18?

Mr. HUNTINGTON. No; 19.

Senator MORGAN. Have you sold stock of the Central Pacific at 19 when it was paying a dividend?

Mr. HUNTINGTON. I think so.

Senator MORGAN. Can you tell who the purchaser was?

Mr. HUNTINGTON. I can not. I probably did not know anything about it. I probably never knew. Most of the stock was sold in blocks. Perhaps some of it was sold in small lots. It was given to a broker to sell, and he would bring me a check after it was sold.

Senator MORGAN. If you sold stock at 19 cents on the dollar which was paying a dividend, did you not do it for the purpose of breaking the market?

Mr. HUNTINGTON. No; I never sold a share to break the market, and I never bought a share to put the market up.

Senator MORGAN. Were you in such distress for money that you took stock which was worth par and sold it at 19?

Mr. HUNTINGTON. Certainly not.

Senator MORGAN. Then why did you sell it at 19?

Mr. HUNTINGTON. Because 19 was the market value of it.

Senator MORGAN. When was the stock of the Central Pacific at 19?

Mr. HUNTINGTON. I do not know.

Senator MORGAN. In what year was it at 19?

Mr. HUNTINGTON. I do not know.

Senator MORGAN. The records of Wall street will show that, of course. I want to find out when that thing first occurred—the selling of stock at 19 that was paying dividends.

Mr. HUNTINGTON. I do not know.

Senator MORGAN. Did you ever hear of stock selling at 19 that was paying dividends?

Mr. HUNTINGTON. Yes; the Central Pacific.

Senator MORGAN. Is not that a very remarkable thing?

Mr. HUNTINGTON. No.

Senator MORGAN. Is it a common thing?

Mr. HUNTINGTON. No; it is not common.

Senator MORGAN. You were able to hold this stock?

Mr. HUNTINGTON. I always sell anything that I have when I want money.

Senator MORGAN. I asked you whether you were able to hold the stock.

Mr. HUNTINGTON. I can not tell to-day whether I was able to hold it when I sold it. I do not know that I ever got into a place where I had not something to sell in order to pay my debts.

Senator MORGAN. Have you any doubt now that you were able to hold it?

Mr. HUNTINGTON. I might have sold out something else, probably. I have seen a great many times in my life when I have had to sell something.

Senator MORGAN. Was it before or after the passage of the Thurman Act that you sold Central Pacific stock at 19?

Mr. HUNTINGTON. I think it was after, but I am not sure. It may have been before.

Senator MORGAN. How long after was it?

Mr. HUNTINGTON. It must have been a considerable time after, for the shares at that time were worth more than that.

Senator MORGAN. Did you put the stock on the market yourself?

Mr. HUNTINGTON. I gave it to some broker to sell.

Senator MORGAN. Did you tell him to sell as low as he could?

Mr. HUNTINGTON. I have answered that question, but it is a question which Senator Morgan ought not to ask me. If you want it answered, I will answer it.

Senator MORGAN. I want it answered.

Mr. HUNTINGTON. I did not tell him to sell as low as he could.

Senator MORGAN. Did you tell him to sell as high as he could?

Mr. HUNTINGTON. Probably not. He could not get over the market price, and I probably told him to sell it at the market price.

Senator MORGAN. You did not sell that stock at 19 cents on the dollar when it was paying a dividend?

Mr. HUNTINGTON. I am inclined to think that there was a small dividend on it, but very small.

Senator MORGAN. To all appearance, the stock was worth par, and you sold it at 19.

Mr. HUNTINGTON. I did not say that.

Senator MORGAN. Stock which is paying a dividend would be selling at par.

Mr. HUNTINGTON. Not at all. It would depend upon what the dividend was. It would depend upon many things. If a person wants money and he has got stock to sell which he can spare, he sells it in order to get the money. When stock is selling at 19 or 20 and is paying 2 per cent dividend, that is equal to a dividend of 10 per cent at par.

Senator MORGAN. What effect did the selling of the Central Pacific stock at 19 have on the stock of the Union Pacific at the same time?

Mr. HUNTINGTON. It would not have any.

Senator MORGAN. What effect did it have?

Mr. HUNTINGTON. I do not think it had any effect. The Union Pacific people always attend to their own shares. Probably they sold their stock at the market price. I was offered a majority of the Union Pacific shares once at 7 or 8.

Senator MORGAN. These roads being united joint lines as described by the Supreme Court of the United States—a great national road to be operated as one road—would not your selling stock of the Central Pacific at 19 which was actually paying a dividend have an effect upon the other end of that great national railroad and on the value of its stock?

Mr. HUNTINGTON. I suppose it would.

Senator MORGAN. Did you not sell it on purpose that it would have such effect?

Mr. HUNTINGTON. I have answered that question once, and will answer it again; no.

Senator MORGAN. What purpose did you have?

Mr. HUNTINGTON. To get money.

Senator MORGAN. For what purpose?

Mr. HUNTINGTON. To pay debts.

Senator MORGAN. What debts?

Mr. HUNTINGTON. Debts that I owed.

Senator MORGAN. To whom did you owe them?

Mr. HUNTINGTON. To creditors.

Senator MORGAN. Who were they?

Mr. HUNTINGTON. The men that I borrowed the money from.

Senator MORGAN. You do not mean to tell me who they were?

Mr. HUNTINGTON. I do not know. If I did I would tell you. Things are changing every day.

Senator MOGRAN. Do you not know that this sale of Central Pacific stock at 19 did have an effect on the stock of the Union Pacific?

Mr. HUNTINGTON. No; I think not.

Senator MORGAN. Do you think that that stock stood all up yonder?

Mr. HUNTINGTON. No; I do not know what that stock was selling for.

Senator MORGAN. Did you not know at the time?

Mr. HUNTINGTON. No; and I did not care. I did not want to buy any Union Pacific shares; but the time never came that I did not want the Union Pacific to have the best it could have.

Senator MORGAN. Including the ownership of the Central Pacific?

Mr. HUNTINGTON. If they owned it, of course they would have it.

Senator MORGAN. You always wished the Union Pacific to have the best it could have, including the ownership of the Central Pacific?

Mr. HUNTINGTON. No; I did not say that. I think the Central Pacific has been managed better than the Union Pacific. We have always met our obligations while working under terrible disadvantages. The Central Pacific is as clean as any road that was ever built in America, I do not care who says anything to the contrary.

Senator MORGAN. I want to give you a final opportunity to explain to the committee what stress of monetary embarrassment you were in, or the company of which you were vice-president was in, when you put on the market in this way and sold stock of the Central Pacific at 19 when the stock was paying a dividend.

Mr. HUNTINGTON. Simply my own judgment was that if we wanted money, and if that was the best way to get money, we had to sell the stock.

Senator MORGAN. You spoke of selling it in blocks.

Mr. HUNTINGTON. Not at that price. I do not think I ever sold any so low in blocks.

Senator MORGAN. How much stock did you sell at 19?

Mr. HUNTINGTON. Not a great deal.

Senator MORGAN. How much?

Mr. HUNTINGTON. Probably two or three thousand shares.

Senator MORGAN. Who paid it?

Mr. HUNTINGTON. I never knew. I got a check for it from the broker.

Senator MORGAN. Did not another broker buy it under your directions?

Mr. HUNTINGTON. No; I do not know anything about the crooked ways which Senator Morgan seems to understand. I never bought anything to put shares up, nor sold anything to put shares down.

Senator MORGAN. I have been only two or three times in Wall street, but I have learned about such crooked ways as that.

Mr. HUNTINGTON. I have been in New York for sixty years, and have been in active business down town for thirty-five years, and never bought a thing on speculation in my life. I do not think I ever bought on margin in my life. I never sold a thing on speculation. When I wanted money I have sold something to get it.

The CHAIRMAN. In the sale of stock the transfer is signed in blank and handed to the broker, and he hands it to the buyer, who gets a new certificate?

Mr. HUNTINGTON. Yes.

The CHAIRMAN. Certificates are always transferred in blank?

Mr. HUNTINGTON. Yes.

The CHAIRMAN. And when the holder wants his certificate, he goes to the company that issues certificates of stock and gets it?

Mr. HUNTINGTON. Yes.

The CHAIRMAN. And it is the custom always to transfer in blank?

Mr. HUNTINGTON. Yes. I have always given the certificates to a broker and said to him, "Go and sell these shares on the market." The whole transaction is with him.

Senator MORGAN. And the broker who is instructed to buy the stock goes to the same man and gets it and gives his check for the amount?

Mr. HUNTINGTON. I do not know anything about that. I have never given orders to buy and sell at the same time. I never did anything to put shares up or to put shares down. I have been a railroad builder thirty-five years, and have tried to do the best that I could for the company I was working for in the manipulation of its securities.

Senator MORGAN. What was the lowest point at which you sold Central Pacific stock before the Thurman Act?

Mr. HUNTINGTON. I do not know.

Senator MORGAN. About how low?

Mr. HUNTINGTON. I do not know. I bought once, or the Contract and Finance Company bought, all Charles Crocker's shares of Central Pacific stock at 12½ a share. He went to Europe, and when he came back I told him that we did not want the stock, and that if he took back his interest in the concern as it was I would like to have him do so. He said that he would rather have the money, and I said I would rather he took the shares, and he took them. That was quite a block. The Contract and Finance Company had bought them all at 12½, and when Mr. Crocker came back I asked him to take them back, and he did so. That was two years or more after the road was built.

Senator MORGAN. You say here:

As I have already said, we sold our shares to enable us to pay the debts incurred in the construction of the road as soon as the shares could be sold at prices sufficient to do this, and the stock was therefore widely distributed while the dividends were being paid.

Mr. HUNTINGTON. Yes: that is correct, I believe.

Senator MORGAN. You still hold on to some of it and some of it you sold out at 19?

Mr. HUNTINGTON. There is some stock now in the hands of our people for which 76 was offered.

Senator MORGAN. Did you pay over to the Contract and Finance Company the money which you received from the sale of Central Pacific stock at 19?

Mr. HUNTINGTON. No.

Senator MORGAN. That was your personal money?

Mr. HUNTINGTON. It was my personal money.

Senator MORGAN (reading):

I observe that on page 50 the commissioners state that they have reached the conclusion that with the single exception of the then existing administration of the Union Pacific, all the debts and obligations referred to as assumed by the managers of the roads had been constantly and persistently disregarded, and the result was that those who had controlled and directed the construction and development of the companies had become possessed of their surplus assets through issue of bonds and stocks and payments of dividends voted by themselves, while the great creditor, the Government of the United States, finds itself substantially without adequate security for the repayment of its loans.

In reply to this, I would say that the United States expressly provided in 1862 and 1864, and again in 1878, what security should be reserved for the repayment of its loans, and every dollar of this security was reserved in accordance with the provisions of these acts. We have never held that the Union Pacific administration, which the commission refer to as a single exception, ever reserved a dollar more as security for the repayment of its loans than was required to be reserved by these acts, which we have fully complied with. But time has shown how wrong the commissioners were in their estimate of the results of the Union Pacific administration which they take so much pains to extol as compared with the administration of the Central Pacific properties. Time has shown that although the Central Pacific properties were subject to a larger amount of fixed charges, on account of greater physical obstructions which had to be overcome in constructing the roads, and although the properties were operated at a great disadvantage, all material being higher, and coal used in California being, say, four times as expensive as that used by the Union Pacific, the administration of the Central Pacific has paid all its debts and obligations, while the Union Pacific has defaulted even on the interest of her first-mortgage bonds.

I think that is a fair argument upon that proposition, but it does not contain any statement of facts.

Mr. HUNTINGTON. It states facts as they exist to-day.

Senator MORGAN. The Union Pacific has lost money very largely in consequence of the diversion of traffic from the Central Pacific to the Southern Pacific—do you not think that it has?

(Before Mr. Huntington had answered this question his examination was suspended, Senator Morgan stating that he would look through Mr. Huntington's statement to-night, and would abbreviate the examination to-morrow.)

The act of incorporation of the Southern Pacific Company was put in evidence, as follows:

[Chapter 403.]

AN ACT to incorporate the Southern Pacific Company.

Be it enacted by the General Assembly of the Commonwealth of Kentucky:

SECTION 1. That Henry D. McHenry, Wm. G. Duncan, Samuel E. Hill, Samuel M. Cox, Henry McHenry, jr., and their associates and successors and assigns, be, and they are hereby, created and constituted a body corporate and politic, under the name of the Southern Pacific Company, and as such shall have perpetual succession, and be capable in law to purchase, grant, sell, or receive, in trust or otherwise, all kinds of personal and real property to such amount as the directors of said company may, from time to time, determine; and to contract and be contracted with, sue and be sued, plead and be impleaded, appear and prosecute to final judgments all suits or actions at law or in equity in all courts and places; and to have and use a common seal, and to alter the same at pleasure; and to make and establish such by-laws, rules, and regulations for the government of said company and the conduct of its business as said corporation or the stockholders therein shall deem expedient or necessary for the management of its affairs, not inconsistent with the constitution and laws of this State or of the United States; and generally to do and execute all acts, matters, and things which may be deemed necessary or convenient to carry into effect the powers and privileges herein granted: *Provided*, however, that said corporation shall not have power to make joint stock with, lease, own, or operate any railroad within the State of Kentucky.

SEC. 2. The said corporation is hereby authorized and empowered to contract for and acquire by purchase or otherwise, bonds, stocks, obligations, and securities of any corporation, company, or association now existing or hereafter formed or constituted, and bonds, obligations, and securities of any individuals, State, Territory, government, or local authorities whatsoever, and to enter into contracts with any corporation, company, or association, individuals, State, Territory, government, or local authorities in respect of their bonds, stocks, obligations, and securities, or in respect of the construction, establishment, acquisition, owning, equipment, leasing, maintenance, or operation of any railroads, telegraphs, or steamship lines, or any public or private improvements, or any appurtenances thereof, in any State or Territory of the United States, or in any foreign country, and to buy, hold, sell, and deal in all kinds of public and private stocks, bonds, and securities; and said corporation may borrow and loan money, issue its own bonds or other evidences of indebtedness, and sell, negotiate, and pledge the same, to such amounts, upon such terms, and in such manner as may from time to time be determined by the directors of said corporation; and it may mortgage all or any part of its property, assets, and franchises to secure such bonds and the interest thereon, on such terms and conditions as shall on that behalf be prescribed by its board of directors.

SEC. 3. The capital stock of said corporation shall be one million dollars, divided into shares of one hundred dollars each, which shares shall be deemed personal property, and may be issued, transferred, and forfeited for nonpayment in such manner as the board of directors of such corporation may determine; and no person shall be in anywise liable as a stockholder of said corporation after said capital stock to such amount of one million dollars shall have been paid in in cash, and a certificate to that effect signed and sworn to by the treasurer and a majority of the board of directors of said corporation shall have been filed in the office of the secretary of state of this State; nor shall the said corporation, nor any of the officers or agents thereof, be thereafter bound to make any further returns or certificates: *Provided*, however, that if, after the payment of such capital stock, any part thereof shall be withdrawn for or refunded to any of the stockholders when the property of the corporation is insufficient or will be thereby rendered insufficient for the payment of all its debts, the stockholder receiving the same shall be bound and obliged to repay to said corporation or its creditors the amount so withdrawn or refunded.

SEC. 4. Any two of the persons above named as corporators of said corporation may call the first meeting for the organization of such corporation at such time and place as they may appoint, by mailing a proper notice of such meeting to each of such corporators at least ten days before the time appointed; and in case a majority of such corporators shall attend such meetings, either in person or by proxy, they may open books for subscriptions to its capital stock; and whenever five hundred thousand dollars shall be subscribed and ten per cent of said subscriptions shall be paid in cash, the stockholders of said corporation may organize the same, and said corporation may proceed to business.

SEC. 5. Each share of stock entitle the holder thereof to one vote, in person or by proxy, at all meetings of the stockholders; the holders of a majority in interest of the capital stock, present in person or by proxy, shall constitute a quorum (the corporation shall have a lien on all the stock and property of its members invested therein for all debts due by them to said corporation, which lien may be enforced in such manner as the by-laws shall prescribe).

SEC. 6. The stock, property, and affairs of said corporation shall be managed by a board of directors of such number, not less than three, as may be from time to time determined by the corporators or stockholders. The directors shall be elected by the stockholders at such time and place, and in such manner, and for such terms, as the stockholders shall from time to time determine. Meetings of directors or stockholders may be held within or without the State. No person shall be elected a director who is not a stockholder of the corporation. A majority of the directors shall constitute a quorum of said board for the transaction of business. The directors shall appoint from their own number a president, and they shall also appoint a clerk and treasurer, and such other officers and agents as they may deem proper, to hold their offices during the pleasure of the board. In case of a vacancy or vacancies in the board, the remaining directors may fill such vacancy or vacancies. The capital stock of said corporation may be increased from time to time to such sum as may be determined by the board of directors of said corporation, provided such increase or diminution shall be approved by at least two thirds in interest of the stockholders of said corporation.

SEC. 7. The annual tax upon said corporation shall be the same as is now fixed by law for broker's license: *Provided,* That all property owned by said corporation and situated in the State shall pay the same State and local tax as is assessed upon similar property; and capital stock in said corporation owned by citizens of the State shall be assessed against the holders thereof as choses in action under the equalization law.

SEC. 8. The company shall keep an office for the transaction of business, and the clerk or assistant clerk of said corporation shall reside within the State of Kentucky, but the said corporation may keep offices at such places outside of this State as in the judgment of its board of directors its business may from time to time require: *Provided,* That nothing herein contained shall be construed as granting any lottery or banking privileges.

SEC. 9. This act shall take effect immediately upon its passage.

CHAS. OFFUTT,
Speaker of the House of Representatives.
JAMES R. HINDMAN,
Speaker of the Senate.

Approved March 17, 1884.
J. PROCTOR KNOTT.
By the governor.
JAS. A. MCKENZIE, *Secretary of State.*

[Chapter 601.]

AN ACT to amend "An act to incorporate the Southern Pacific Company," approved March seventeenth, eighteen hundred and eighty-four.

Be it enacted by the General Assembly of the Commonwealth of Kentucky:

SECTION 1. That the act entitled "An act to incorporate the Southern Pacific Company," which was approved March seventeenth, eighteen hundred and eighty-four, be and the same is amended by adding to section 1 thereof the following words, to wit: except subject to and in conformity with the provisions of the laws of the State of Kentucky applicable to railroads, and acquiring no special rights that may be possessed by any railroads in the State except the general and ordinary rights of common carriers as possessed by railroads generally.

SEC. 2. This act shall take effect from its passage.

BEN JOHNSON,
Speaker of the House of Representatives.
J. W. BRYAN,
Speaker of the Senate.

Approved March 21, 1888.
S. B. BUCKNER.
By the governor.
GEO. M. ADAMS, *Secretary of State.*

The committee adjourned till to-morrow, Saturday, March 7, at 10.30 a. m.

WASHINGTON, *Saturday, March 7, 1896.*

The committee met at 10.30 a. m.

Present: Senators Gear (chairman), Stewart, Frye, and Morgan.

CENTRAL PACIFIC RAILROAD.

EXAMINATION OF C. P. HUNTINGTON—Continued.

Senator Morgan had read by the stenographer the last question asked by him in yesterday's session, and which had then remained unanswered, as follows:

Senator MORGAN. The Union Pacific has lost money very largely in consequence of the diversion of traffic from the Central Pacific to the Southern Pacific. Do you not think that it has?

Mr. HUNTINGTON. Well, it has not to my knowledge; and it is not very likely that I would have known it if it had. As I said before, out of the seven or eight lines in this business, all the time the Central Pacific has had more than 50 per cent of the business.

Senator MORGAN. Of all the business?

Mr. HUNTINGTON. Of all the business done by all-rail lines.

Senator MORGAN. How do you ascertain that fact?

Mr. HUNTINGTON. We get it from our traffic men and from the operations of the road. It is in my testimony before the commission. I got the exact figures at that time, and there was no time when the percentage of the Central Pacific business was as low as 50.

Senator MORGAN. Was the percentage of the Central Pacific in this business adjusted in any way between the various companies that touched the Pacific Ocean?

Mr. HUNTINGTON. I so understand.

Senator MORGAN. Do you know?

Mr. HUNTINGTON. Yes; I may say I know. I do not know whether the tonnage is divided or not, or whether the roads have agreed to these different percentages.

Senator MORGAN. To the rates for passengers and freight?

Mr. HUNTINGTON. Yes.

Senator MORGAN. Of all kinds and descriptions?

Mr. HUNTINGTON. So I understand.

Senator MORGAN. What roads were in that agreement?

Mr. HUNTINGTON. I think all the roads.

Senator MORGAN. Name them.

Mr. HUNTINGTON. The Canadian Pacific most of the time; the Great Northern; the Northern Pacific; the Union Pacific, having an independent line across the continent; the Atchison, Topeka and Santa Fe; the Texas Pacific; the Chicago, Burlington and Quincy, I think; the Chicago, Rock Island and Pacific; the Missouri Pacific, and perhaps some others.

Senator MORGAN. Were these agreements in writing?

Mr. HUNTINGTON. I should suppose they were. I do not think I have ever seen any agreement in writing; but it is pretty notorious, I believe, that that agreement was made.

Senator MORGAN. Who made that agreement on behalf of the Central Pacific?

Mr. HUNTINGTON. I presume Mr. Stubbs; he is the head of the traffic department.

Senator MORGAN. Who made it on behalf of the Southern Pacific?

Mr. HUNTINGTON. I do not know; I think probably Mr. Stubbs.

Senator MORGAN. Did Mr. Stubbs make such an agreement on behalf of any other road besides those two?

Mr. HUNTINGTON. I should say not.

Senator MORGAN. He is the traffic agent for both the Central Pacific and the Southern Pacific?

Mr. HUNTINGTON. Yes; he is at the head of the traffic department.

Senator MORGAN. Did that agreement increase the rates of freight as well as percentages—this division or pool?

Mr. HUNTINGTON. It is hardly a pool, perhaps, but an understanding that the rates shall be so and so, and I think there was a division of traffic. I do not have much to do with the traffic department.

Senator MORGAN. But you know how it is?

Mr. HUNTINGTON. Yes; but the heads of the traffic department regulate these things.

Senator MORGAN. Whether we call it a pool or an agreement——

Mr. HUNTINGTON. I do not think it is a pool, because I think each road handles its own receipts. The rates are agreed upon. I do not say that the rates are all the same. I think there is a differential, the Canadian Pacific having the right to put in a lower rate.

Senator MORGAN. Why?

Mr. HUNTINGTON. I will not say directly that it does, but I think that is the custom with all the railroads. The New York Central and the Pennsylvania have the maximum rates; and the other roads have slight differentials in their favor, that is, the right to make lower rates.

Senator MORGAN. Is the rail line of the Canadian Pacific longer than the rail line of the Southern Pacific from Portland, Oreg., to New Orleans?

Mr. HUNTINGTON. No; I think the Canadian Pacific is running from Duluth; and its rail line is shorter than that of the Southern Pacific. The Southern Pacific is about 2,500 miles.

Senator MORGAN. How would it be between Port Townsend and the eastern terminus of the Canadian Pacific?

Mr. HUNTINGTON. The Canadian Pacific does not go to Port Townsend; it goes to Vancouver.

Senator MORGAN. In the same neighborhood?

Mr. HUNTINGTON. There is quite a difference between them. One is on the Gulf of Georgia and the other on Puget Sound.

Senator MORGAN. What is the distance from Vancouver to the eastern rail terminus of the Canadian Pacific?

Mr. HUNTINGTON. I do not know. I should not think it more than 2,000 miles.

Senator MORGAN. It is not as far as from Portland, Oreg., to New Orleans?

Mr. HUNTINGTON. It is not so long, I think, by a thousand miles.

Senator MORGAN. This differential was made up in favor of the road from Portland to New Orleans, and of the road from Vancouver to the eastern terminus of the Canadian Pacific?

Mr. HUNTINGTON. I do not think it is made up in that way. I think that San Francisco is the point.

Senator MORGAN. If San Francisco is the point or base of the calculation of the freight, and also of the division of the income, then that, I suppose, would necessarily give an advantage in the transportation in favor of the Southern Pacific over its line or lines between San Francisco and Portland, Oreg.

Mr. HUNTINGTON. I do not understand the Senator.

Senator MORGAN. Inasmuch as the Southern Pacific would have the haul on its lines from San Francisco, that being the point of starting——

Mr. HUNTINGTON. This is done by water. The Canadian Pacific has a line of steamers from Vancouver to San Francisco.

Senator MORGAN. Then the Canadian Pacific puts its line of steamers into the pool also?

Mr. HUNTINGTON. I take it so. But it is not a pool; it is an agreement for rates. A pool is where the parties to it put into a general pot and divide the income from a certain business, each having a percentage.

Senator MORGAN. And that was not the way in this case?

Mr. HUNTINGTON. No, I think not.

Senator MORGAN. This was only what?

Mr. HUNTINGTON. An agreement as to rates.

Senator MORGAN. What division was given to the Central Pacific in that agreement?

Mr. HUNTINGTON. They gave the Central Pacific more than 50 per cent. Exactly how much more I do not recollect.

Senator MORGAN. Fifty per cent of what?

Mr. HUNTINGTON. Fifty per cent of the business from San Francisco to the Missouri River.

Senator MORGAN. That was not 50 per cent of the freight rates, but 50 per cent of the income?

Mr. HUNTINGTON. Probably. I do not know how it was made up.

Senator MORGAN. How could they make up an estimate by which the Central Pacific would get more than 50 per cent (say, 54 per cent) unless they had first ascertained the income of all these different lines?

Mr. HUNTINGTON. I do not know that they could. I suppose the matter had to be equalized. I am not familiar with the details of the operation.

Senator MORGAN. That agreement included the freight going east, as well as the freight going west.

Mr. HUNTINGTON. I think so; but still it is on my mind that it referred more particularly to the freight going east.

Senator MORGAN. And the agreement is on all the lines you have mentioned.

Mr. HUNTINGTON. Yes.

Senator MORGAN. That agreement gave, you say, to the Canadian Pacific a lower or differential rate?

Mr. HUNTINGTON. Yes; the Canadian Pacific had a lower rate. I do not think that that company was always in the agreement. Sometimes, I think, it was running wild.

Senator MORGAN. By a lower rate, do you mean a lower percentage, or a lower freight rate?

Mr. HUNTINGTON. I mean a lower price for handling the business.

Senator MORGAN. The Canadian Pacific had a right to charge a less price per mile for freight and passengers?

Mr. HUNTINGTON. I think it had a right to charge a less price from Chicago to San Francisco. On account of the greater mileage of that company it had a right to charge a lesser rate, so as to get its share of the business.

Senator MORGAN. When was that common agreement first entered into?

Mr. HUNTINGTON. I think there have been several such agreements for the last twenty-five years.

Senator MORGAN. You began it twenty-five years ago?

Mr. HUNTINGTON. I can not say it was just twenty-five years ago, but it has been done more than once.

Senator MORGAN. Up to what time was it continued; when was it ended?

Mr. HUNTINGTON. I do not know but that it is in force now.

Senator MORGAN. You have not been notified of its being ended?

Mr. HUNTINGTON. I would not naturally be notified of it. The traffic department attends to such matters.

Senator MORGAN. You are the vice-president of the Central Pacific Company, and have been all the time from its first organization?

Mr. HUNTINGTON. Yes.

Senator MORGAN. And you have been the principal business agent of the company?

Mr. HUNTINGTON. Yes.

Senator MORGAN. And you were also president of the Kentucky corporation?

Mr. HUNTINGTON. Yes.

Senator MORGAN. And the Kentucky Company has, either by operation or by lease, controlled all the railroads from Portland, Oreg., to New Orleans?

Mr. HUNTINGTON. I do not know that it has controlled them all. It has controlled a large majority of them.

Senator MORGAN. Is there any gap which anybody else owns in that line except the Southern Pacific?

Mr. HUNTINGTON. I do not think that the Southern Pacific owns the California Pacific. I am pretty sure it does not.

Senator MORGAN. But the Southern Pacific controls the California Pacific?

Mr. HUNTINGTON. I am very sure it does not.

Senator MORGAN. It neither owns nor controls it?

Mr. HUNTINGTON. It may have a traffic arrangement with it.

Senator MORGAN. Who does own it?

Mr. HUNTINGTON. I do not know; there are quite a great number of shareholders.

Senator MORGAN. Who are the principal shareholders in the California Pacific?

Mr. HUNTINGTON. I think that Mr. Searles, Mr. Hubbard, Mr. Stillman, Mr. Charles F. Crocker, Mr. George Crocker, Mr. William Crocker, Mr. Stanford, and myself were the principal owners.

Senator MORGAN. How much did you yourself own in it?

Mr. HUNTINGTON. I do not know how much.

Senator MORGAN. About how much?

Mr. HUNTINGTON. I think in the neighborhood of one-fifth or one-sixth.

Senator MORGAN. How much does the Stanford estate own in it?

Mr. HUNTINGTON. My impression is, about the same.

Senator MORGAN. How much does the Colton estate own in it?

Mr. HUNTINGTON. Colton is dead.

Senator MORGAN. But the estate?

Mr. HUNTINGTON. The estate is divided.

Senator MORGAN. Well, Mr. Colton's successor?

Mr. HUNTINGTON. I do not know; but my impression is, not any.

Senator MORGAN. How much does the Hopkins estate own?

Mr. HUNTINGTON. That estate is settled up. I do not know; I think about the same.

Senator MORGAN. That amounts to three-fifths of this California Pacific that you know of?

Mr. HUNTINGTON. I am not quite positive, but I am sure it is more than one-half.

Senator MORGAN. At all events it is the controlling interest?

Mr. HUNTINGTON. Yes.

Senator MORGAN. Owning that controlling interest, what have you done with the California Pacific? Have you put it into the Kentucky Company?

Mr. HUNTINGTON. No.

Senator MORGAN. Not at all; you kept it out?

Mr. HUNTINGTON. Yes.

Senator MORGAN. So that three of you own three-fifths of the intermediate line between Portland and New Orleans, called the California Pacific?

Mr. HUNTINGTON. Yes.

Senator MORGAN. How long is that line?

Mr. HUNTINGTON. One hundred and twenty-five miles.

Senator MORGAN. What are its terminal points?

Mr. HUNTINGTON. Knights Landing, on the Sacramento. There is a branch of it to Woodland, Calistoga, and Vallejo.

Senator MORGAN. What lines connect with your trunk line from Portland to New Orleans?

Mr. HUNTINGTON. The San Francisco Northern owns from Tehama down. They run in, a little distance on the California Pacific, from Davisville.

Senator MORGAN. I want to know where this California Pacific becomes a part of the main trunk line leading from Portland, Oreg., to New Orleans?

Mr. HUNTINGTON. At Sacramento.

Senator MORGAN. That is the northern point?

Mr. HUNTINGTON. That is where they connect.

Senator MORGAN. Where is the southern point of connection?

Mr. HUNTINGTON. I think it is at Suisun.

Senator MORGAN. Is this California Pacific under the control of the Kentucky Company?

Mr. HUNTINGTON. No.

Senator MORGAN. Is it leased by the Kentucky Company?

Mr. HUNTINGTON. I am inclined to think that it is.

Senator MORGAN. Do you not know that it is?

Mr. HUNTINGTON. I am pretty certain that it is.

Senator MORGAN. You are the president of the Kentucky Company. Do you not know whether you have leased this California Pacific Company, or not?

Mr. HUNTINGTON. I think we have.

Senator MORGAN. Do you not know that you have?

Mr. HUNTINGTON. I am not quite positive.

Senator MORGAN. If you have not leased it, who has?

Mr. HUNTINGTON. Nobody. I am not the president of the California Pacific Company.

Senator MORGAN. But you are the president of the other company?

Mr. HUNTINGTON. Yes; I am president of the Southern Pacific.

Senator MORGAN. If the California Pacific is leased to the Southern Pacific by somebody, by whom is it leased?

Mr. HUNTINGTON. It may be by Mr. Charles Crocker. He is the vice-president and might sign the lease without my knowing it.

Senator MORGAN. You really do know that this California Pacific is leased to the Kentucky Company—the Southern Pacific?

Mr. HUNTINGTON. My impression is that it is. I never saw the lease; I had nothing to do with it.

Senator MORGAN. Having got that kink out of the yarn, I want to know whether this whole line from New Orleans to Portland, Oreg., was put into this agreement, which I call a pool agreement?

Mr. HUNTINGTON. No; my impression is that it was only to San Francisco—from Ogden or Chicago to San Francisco.

Senator MORGAN. Was the part of the line between San Francisco and Portland, Oreg., left out of the agreement?

Mr. HUNTINGTON. No.

Senator MORGAN. Then it is included in it?

Mr. HUNTINGTON. I do not think that it was in. It was not necessarily in. Most likely it was in. But there were two steamer lines running between the upper waters of Oregon and Washington and San Francisco.

Senator MORGAN. Competing lines?

Mr. HUNTINGTON. Yes.

Senator MORGAN. One of them owned by the Central Pacific?

Mr. HUNTINGTON. No; neither of them.

Senator MORGAN. Or by the Southern Pacific?

Mr. HUNTINGTON. No; neither of them.

Senator MORGAN. They are independent lines, are they?

Mr. HUNTINGTON. I think one of them is controlled largely by the Canadian Pacific, and the other by the Oregon Railway Navigation Company.

Senator MORGAN. The Canadian Pacific and the Oregon Navigation Company had two competing lines running to San Francisco?

Mr. HUNTINGTON. Yes.

Senator MORGAN. And they were included in this general agreement?

Mr. HUNTINGTON. I think so.

Senator MORGAN. Would they include these two competing steamship lines, and leave out the railroad line?

Mr. HUNTINGTON. I am inclined to think that the railroad line was in.

Senator MORGAN. Then we have got all in, including the two competing water lines. The point they start at is San Francisco, and it was from that point that you made the estimate of the income of all of these different roads and steamship lines before you ascertained that the Central Pacific was entitled to more than 50 per cent of the net income. Now you state that this began about twenty-five years ago?

Mr. HUNTINGTON. No; I said that it might have commenced that long ago. It is a long way back. All these things generally come to me after they are done. This may have come to me for confirmation; but I trust largely to the men having charge of these matters.

Senator MORGAN. I am quoting not guesses but statements of fact which you make in an equivocal way. I would like you to get as near the facts as you can.

Mr. HUNTINGTON. Yes; I would like to give you all the facts.

Senator MORGAN. Did it commence twenty-five years ago?

Mr. HUNTINGTON. Yes; I think it was as early as 1871 we had an arrangement.

Senator MORGAN. And it is going on yet?

Mr. HUNTINGTON. I can not say. There have been breaks in it. Whether it is going on to-day or not I do not know.

Senator MORGAN. You are the president of one of these great lines and the vice-president of another of these great lines, and, if there should be any break in the arrangement, would you not have knowledge of it?

Mr. HUNTINGTON. Not necessarily. These agreements have certain times to run; and the times run on. I have able men doing this business, who know all about it much better than I can know. I could not sit down and make an agreement of that kind. I would not know how to do it. But Mr. Stubbs, the head of our traffic department, meets the heads of traffic departments of other lines, and they agree to what would be a fair division.

Senator MORGAN. Do they submit their agreement for your ratification?

Mr. HUNTINGTON. I do not know; they may.

Senator MORGAN. Do you not know that they did?

Mr. HUNTINGTON. No; I do not.

Senator MORGAN. Did they not inform you of what they did?

Mr. HUNTINGTON. Probably they did. Mr. Stubbs has been with us for twenty-six years, and he knows his part of the business a great d al better than I know it.

Senator MORGAN. Does he manage the business independently of you?

Mr. HUNTINGTON. No; not independently of me. I have the last say; but if he did not know how to do the business better than I, he would be the wrong man in the place.

Senator MORGAN. How can you have the last say if he does not report the agreements to you?

Mr. HUNTINGTON. He probably does; but I would be very likely to say to him, "Do what you think right in the matter."

Senator MORGAN. Then the power behind the throne would be greater than the throne itself?

Mr. HUNTINGTON. Yes; in certain details.

Senator MORGAN. Well, you know, Mr. Huntington, whether, in regard to these immensely important matters, they did submit the agreement to you or not?

Mr. HUNTINGTON. Not necessarily, in all its details.

Senator MORGAN. That was not my question. I want to know whether you know that the agreement was submitted to you.

Mr. HUNTINGTON. In the main, I suppose I knew what the agreement was.

Senator MORGAN. If any change was made in the agreement did you not know it?

Mr. HUNTINGTON. I think there might have been changes made of which I did not know. I think that if there was any radical change or any new thing they would have advised me of it.

Senator MORGAN. Have these percentages in favor of the Central Pacific been increased or decreased within the last twenty-five years; and if so, why?

Mr. HUNTINGTON. I can not say why. The percentage might have been made more or made less. The traffic department may have made changes.

Senator MORGAN. With your consent?

Mr. HUNTINGTON. I did not consent or dissent?

Senator MORGAN. About how often were these rearrangements of rates made?

Mr. HUNTINGTON. I can not say. This thing is growing all the time. Companies cut rates, and they cut and cut, and they become demoralized and then they get together again.

Senator MORGAN. Is there no agreement for an annual readjustment of rates?

Mr. HUNTINGTON. I do not think there is.

Senator MORGAN. At the time that the Interstate Commerce Commission was created that law gave to the Canadian Pacific a great advantage, did it not?

Mr. HUNTINGTON. Yes.

Senator MORGAN. And you got the Canadian Pacific in in order to break down that competition?

Mr. HUNTINGTON. No; I think the Canadian Pacific was in before the interstate commerce law went into effect.

Senator MORGAN. But you say the agreement was changed from time to time?

Mr. HUNTINGTON. Yes; I believe that the interstate commerce law is construed now so that it does not make any difference in competition.

Senator MORGAN. As it was construed then did it make a difference?

Mr. HUNTINGTON. Yes; but the Canadian Pacific only came in competition with the ocean lines. The ship line is by Cape Horn, by which the cheap and heavy tonnage is sent when time is no special object. The Cape Horn route is very hard to compete with.

Senator MORGAN. As to this 50 per cent or over, which you speak of, in favor of the Central Pacific for freights going east or going west under this combination or agreement, was there any agreement or understanding between the Central Pacific and the Kentucky company, the Southern Pacific, as to how the two companies should divide the freights?

Mr. HUNTINGTON. I do not know whether there was or not, but I expect there was.

Senator MORGAN. What part of it did the Southern Pacific get and what part the Central Pacific?

Mr. HUNTINGTON. That is in my testimony before the United States Pacific Railroad Commission. I looked that up at the time. The Southern Pacific got 20 per cent of the business.

Senator MORGAN. Twenty per cent of the 50 per cent?

Mr. HUNTINGTON. No; it did not get any of that. That was all to the Central Pacific.

Senator MORGAN. Did the Southern Pacific get none of the percentage awarded to the Central Pacific?

Mr. HUNTINGTON. It got whatever the fraction may have been between Sacramento and San Francisco.

Senator MORGAN. Only that?

Mr. HUNTINGTON. Only that. I do not know why it could have got anything else. The ferry across the Straits of Benicia was out of repair for a couple of months, but the railroad could run by way of Tracy, and that did not make any difference, I suppose. I wish to say about this 20 per cent that I mentioned that for a considerable part of it, the Southern Pacific was taking low-priced freights which we took from the Cape Horn route, and which other roads did not compete for.

Senator MORGAN. I wish you would explain about that 20 per cent.

Mr. HUNTINGTON. The 20 per cent was on the overland business. Where it divides, I can not tell you. It was 20 per cent of this transcontinental business, which goes largely by steamer from New York to New Orleans. But a considerable percentage of that (I think 25 per cent of that 20 per cent) is taken from business done by the Cape Horn route, and at very low rates.

Senator MORGAN. Do I understand you now that, under this general agreement of all these companies, there was awarded to the Central Pacific more than 50 per cent of the business?

Mr. HUNTINGTON. I think that all the time they shared with these other companies, the Central Pacific took its pro rata; but I think it was more than 50 per cent of the whole.

Senator MORGAN. That was because the Central Pacific was able to earn that per cent of the business, I suppose?

Mr. HUNTINGTON. I suppose so.

Senator MORGAN. It was not given as a gratuity?

Mr. HUNTINGTON. I should think not.

Senator MORGAN. There was no benevolence or charity in it?

Mr. HUNTINGTON. I think not. We never had money enough to be liberal with; but we had enough to be just.

Senator MORGAN. I want to know, under that arrangement, or under any other arrangement that you made, or that your Southern Pacific Company made, with the Central Pacific, what were the rates or charges for freight which the Southern Pacific got between Mojave and San Francisco, or to its connection with the Central Pacific?

Mr. HUNTINGTON. I can not say what the rates were. Our rates last year (1895) were really less on the whole line than 2 cents a mile for passengers. I can not tell what the rate was on any piece of the road, but the average rate was about 1.97.

Senator MORGAN. On what?

Mr. HUNTINGTON. On all the lines of the Central Pacific and the Southern Pacific—on all the lines that we control. The rate per passenger was a little less than 2 cents a mile.

Senator MORGAN. How much was the freight?

Mr. HUNTINGTON. A little less than 12 mills per ton per mile.

Senator MORGAN. On the whole line?

Mr. HUNTINGTON. On the overland part of it. The rate on all the tonnage was a little less than 12 mills per ton per mile.

Senator MORGAN. I do not understand what you mean about the overland business.

Mr. HUNTINGTON. I mean the transcontinental business.

The CHAIRMAN. Are your local rates to California a little less than 2 cents a mile per passenger?

Mr. HUNTINGTON. On all the lines the average is less than 2 cents a mile.

The CHAIRMAN. Is that as low as the general average for passengers in the United States?

Mr. HUNTINGTON. I think it is. I go into New England occasionally and no rates up there are as low as those. I do not think there are any lines in the United States which have rates so low under the circumstances.

The CHAIRMAN. In other words, you think that railroad passengers in California and on the Pacific Coast generally, are carried as cheaply as they are in the United States, as a general average?

Mr. HUNTINGTON. I believe so. I believe they are the best accommodated people in the world by rail. I have traveled pretty much over Western Europe, and I do not know any place there where railroad travel is as cheap as on our road, while the expenses of operating railroads in Europe are not nearly as much as they are here. Coal with us cost four times as much as it costs in England.

Senator MORGAN. You own coal mines, do you not?

Mr. HUNTINGTON. We own some coal mines, but they do not anything like supply the roads with coal.

Senator MORGAN. What percentage of the coal used on your railroads do your coal mines supply?

Mr. HUNTINGTON. I do not know; I presume one-half of it. It may be more.

Senator MORGAN. Then you are selling your coal pretty high to these railroad companies?

Mr. HUNTINGTON. No; I think we are selling coal at less than one-half than it is being sold for in San Francisco.

Senator MORGAN. Where do you deliver the coal which you supply to the railroad companies?

Mr. HUNTINGTON. At Benicia, Port Costa, and Oakland.

Senator MORGAN. How much haulage is there from the mines to the railroad?

Mr. HUNTINGTON. We are interested in the Cammack mines in Vancouver. The haul is about 1,000 miles to where we deliver the coal. We deliver it at Oakland pier. We carry quite many thousand tons there. We have coal bunkers there which carry, I presume, 20,000 tons; and at Los Angeles we have bunkers which carry 10,000 tons. The ships come there and deliver the coal to the railroad.

Senator MORGAN. How far is this Cammack mine from Portland, Oreg.?

Mr. HUNTINGTON. It is in the Gulf of Georgia; I should say about 300 or 400 miles.

Senator MORGAN. Is the coal brought by water or by rail?

Mr. HUNTINGTON. By water.

Senator MORGAN. When you get it to Portland, Oreg., you deliver it to your own road?

Mr. HUNTINGTON. I think we buy our coal at Portland from dealers.

Senator MORGAN. Where do you send that coal from Cammack?

Mr. HUNTINGTON. To Benicia, Oakland, and Los Angeles.

Senator MORGAN. All the way from Portland, Oreg., you haul it on your own road?

Mr. HUNTINGTON. No; we do not deliver any coal at Portland.

Senator MORGAN. Do you deliver it at San Francisco?

Mr. HUNTINGTON. We deliver it at Oakland.

Senator MORGAN. How do you deliver it at Oakland?

Mr. HUNTINGTON. By ships.

Senator MORGAN. Which bring it from Cammack?

Mr. HUNTINGTON. Yes, and from Tacoma.

Senator MORGAN. Does the railroad company own those ships?

Mr. HUNTINGTON. I think so; I am not certain.

Senator MORGAN. And from there it is distributed at various points on the railroad lines?

Mr. HUNTINGTON. Yes.

Senator MORGAN. It is hauled and distributed over the line wherever you want to use it?

Mr. HUNTINGTON. Yes.

Senator MORGAN. How far south do you have to go to get access to another coal mine?

Mr. HUNTINGTON. We buy coal from the Atchison Company at Deming.

Senator MORGAN. Have you no coal mine of your own except Cammack?

Mr. HUNTINGTON. We have one in Oregon at Carbon Hill.

Senator MORGAN. And you have no other between Portland and New Orleans?

Mr. HUNTINGTON. No; I think not.

Senator MORGAN. So that, whatever coal you do not buy, you supply the railroad with from your mines at Cammack and Carbon Hill?

Mr. HUNTINGTON. Yes; we buy coal also. I should not wonder if we bought a million tons of coal from Australia and England since we have been running the Central Pacific road.

Senator MORGAN. Did you do so because that coal was cheaper?

Mr. HUNTINGTON. Yes. Whenever we can beat them down in prices we do it.

Senator MORGAN. Do you know what a ton of coal costs you at the mouth of the mines at Cammack or Carbon Hill?

Mr. HUNTINGTON. I think the cost is $2.35 a ton.

Senator MORGAN. At the mouth of the mine?

Mr. HUNTINGTON. At the end of the rail from the mine, 12 miles.

Senator MORGAN. Where you strike water transportation?

Mr. HUNTINGTON. Yes; and then there is 40 cents a ton duty for bringing it into the United States.

Senator MORGAN. Then you get your coal for $2.35 at the mines, and you pay 40 cents a ton duty on it, and that is what it costs you?

Mr. HUNTINGTON. That is what is in my mind.

Senator MORGAN. The balance of the cost is transportation and handling.

Mr. HUNTINGTON. Yes.

Senator MORGAN. Of course, when you have to load the coal on trains, you have to break bulk.

Mr. HUNTINGTON. We put the coal into coal bunkers and the railroad company takes it up there.

Senator MORGAN. You can not afford to haul your coal, at that cost for mining and transportation, as far south and southeast as New Orleans?

Mr. HUNTINGTON. Oh, no; we can not.

Senator MORGAN. Why not?

Mr. HUNTINGTON. The transportation of it, even at half a cent a mile per ton, would amount to $12.50 a ton at New Orleans. When we can buy coal at New Orleans we would never think of hauling that coal there.

Senator MORGAN. You could carry it half way to New Orleans at a quarter of a cent a ton?

Mr. HUNTINGTON. We could not and live.

Senator MORGAN. Do I understand you to say that a half a cent a ton would be the cost of transportation?

Mr. HUNTINGTON. I say that to transport coal to New Orleans at half a cent a ton would make the freight $12.50 a ton.

Senator MORGAN. Would it cost that much to put the coal in there?

Mr. HUNTINGTON. No; I don't suppose it would cost that much.

Senator MORGAN. So that your testimony is that after you got the coal to Sacramento you could not afford to haul it on your own road to supply your own engines?

Mr. HUNTINGTON. We could afford to haul it a certain distance, but not to haul it over the Sierra Madre Mountains. We buy coal east of the Sierra Madre from the Denver and Rio Grande people.

Senator MORGAN. You haul the coal until you can get coal at a cheaper market, and then you buy?

Mr. HUNTINGTON. Yes.

Senator MORGAN. Then, this coal problem does not protect you any more than it does the Central Pacific?

Mr. HUNTINGTON. I do not understand your question, Senator.

Senator MORGAN. Does the Central Pacific have advantages over the Southern Pacific in the way of obtaining coal?

Mr. HUNTINGTON. No.

Senator MORGAN. Does it have to pay as much as the Central Pacific does?

Mr. HUNTINGTON. The two companies pay just the same.

Senator MORGAN. So that there is no difference in that?

Mr. HUNTINGTON. I should not say there was.

The CHAIRMAN. What percentage of the coal that is used on the Central Pacific do you buy at the eastern terminus of the road—Ogden?

Mr. HUNTINGTON. I do not know.

The CHAIRMAN. About how much?

Mr. HUNTINGTON. It is but a small part of it.

The CHAIRMAN. The coal which you use on the eastern portion of the road between the Sierras and Ogden you buy at Ogden?

Mr. HUNTINGTON. Yes.

The CHAIRMAN. And the coal which you use west of the Sierra Nevadas you furnish from your mines?

Mr. HUNTINGTON. Yes.

The CHAIRMAN. What percentage of the road is that; is it as much as one-half?

Mr. HUNTINGTON. A good deal more than one-half. I have been working down the price of coal.

The CHAIRMAN. Do you pay more for coal at Ogden than you pay at the seacoast?

Mr. HUNTINGTON. No; we pay more at the seacoast. The coal at Ogden costs us very little more than it costs at the Cammack mine; not so much.

The CHAIRMAN. Where does the coal which you buy at the east come from?

Mr. HUNTINGTON. Somewhere back of the mountains east of Salt Lake. We have some coal mines (the Rocky Mountain Coal Mine Company has) at Evanston.

(Mr. Payson, counsel for the Central Pacific, said that he would submit a tabulated statement as to the coal.)

Senator MORGAN. I would like to have somebody swear to it before it goes into the record. I do not care about voluntary statements.

(Mr. H. E. Huntington was sworn as to the correctness of the table which he would submit, and was directed to state in the table what other corporations in San Francisco paid for coal.)

Senator MORGAN. I am interested in trying to get an explanation about this allowance of more than 50 per cent to the Central Pacific Railroad Company. I think you have already stated, Mr. Huntington (I know you have), that the Central Pacific Company would not have been entitled to it unless it could earn it and did earn it.

Mr HUNTINGTON. I do not know any other reason why it should be given to the Central Pacific unless it could earn it.

Senator MORGAN. Therefore the Central Pacific Company can earn more than any of the roads you have mentioned, if it gets more than 50 per cent of the business. In other words, it is a more profitable road than any of the others?

Mr. HUNTINGTON. I should say that would be the natural outcome.

Senator STEWART. That is, so far as the through business is concerned?

Mr. HUNTINGTON. Yes; of course there is no local business on the Central Pacific.

Senator MORGAN. Mr. Huntington did not qualify it in that way.

Senator STEWART. Well, I should like to inquire as to that.

Mr. HUNTINGTON. So far as the through business is concerned there is hardly any local business on 600 miles of the Central Pacific.

The CHAIRMAN. Was this allowance made to the Central Pacific because it is a shorter line than the other transcontinental lines?

Mr. HUNTINGTON. Yes; and it runs to the great central points of business.

Senator MORGAN. Now, we will get to the local business and also to the through business which you send from the Southern Pacific over the Central Pacific to the east. Is there no agreement and has there been no agreement between the Southern Pacific and the Central Pacific as to a division of that freight which is forced by the Southern Pacific to the Central Pacific?

Mr. HUNTINGTON. I do not think that that is a proper way to state it. The Central Pacific takes freight at San Francisco, and I suppose the division is on the mileage. The Atchison people go into California, and into San Francisco, and make rates the same as we do; but the Southern Pacific has no more to do with it than the New York Central has.

Senator MORGAN. I am not talking about the Atchison and Santa Fe, but about the Central Pacific. You had a separate agreement between the Central Pacific and the Southern Pacific for the rates of freights and for the division of freights coming over the Southern Pacific to the Central Pacific, east or west, whether they came from that direction or from the direction of Mojave. I want to know what that agreement was.

Mr. HUNTINGTON. There was no agreement except as to the division of mileage. I do not know myself how that is.

Senator MORGAN. Did not the Central Pacific pay per mile more than the Southern Pacific paid per mile for the freight charges which passed over the Southern Pacific?

Mr. HUNTINGTON. Oh, no; I am quite sure about that. I do not know, but I am as certain of that as I am of anything, because it would not be a natural thing to do. Whatever one did the other did.

Senator MORGAN. Were not the freights designed for southwestern California, as far south as Mojave from New Orleans, sent to San Francisco for delivery, or were they delivered along the line?

Mr. HUNTINGTON. I do not understand you, Senator.

Senator MORGAN. Did you permit the trains that were sent from New Orleans to any point in California north of Mojave to be delivered there, or did you require the cars to go on to San Francisco?

Mr. HUNTINGTON. If they go on to San Francisco I never heard of it; I would not suppose they did.

Senator MORGAN. Have there not been complaints made to you frequently by the merchants along the line, that they could only get their freights by paying twice; that is, by paying the freight to San Francisco and back from San Francisco to the point of delivery?

Mr. HUNTINGTON. I think not. They have complained that we charge more for a short distance than was charged to San Francisco, and that, I have no doubt, is true.

Senator MORGAN. Was no complaint made by the merchants at Los Angeles about that practice?

Mr. HUNTINGTON. No; they complained, I think, because we charged more for the shorter haul than for the longer haul; but that we could not remedy. The only way for that to be remedied would be for them to move to tide water, where they would have tide-water competition. If we did not charge any more to Los Angeles than we did to San Francisco the company could not live at all, or it would have to go out of the San Francisco business entirely, because ships by the Isthmus route and by the Straits of Magellan and by Cape Horn would do all the business. In doing the San Francisco business, where we come in competition with tide-water business, we figure that whenever we can make anything over the cost of the moving of the train it is for our interest to take the business. But, if we charged the regular rates—rates that would pay the train movement and the fixed expenses—the company could not do that business at all. It could not begin to do it.

Senator MORGAN. I am not asking what the company could do, but what it did do. Do you undertake to say that the Southern Pacific Company has not refused to deliver goods along that line, shipped from New Orleans or from places east of New Orleans to places north of Mojave, until those goods had first gone to San Francisco and been hauled back?

Mr. HUNTINGTON. I never heard of it. I heard, as I stated before, that there were complaints that we charged too much for local rates—that we charged more for short hauls than for long hauls, as we have a right to do under the interstate commerce law.

Senator MORGAN. If there was such a case as that, charging freight to San Francisco and then back again, the complaint was well-founded.

Mr. HUNTINGTON. I do not think it was done; and if it was done, there was some good reason for it.

Senator MORGAN. What good reason could possibly exist for charging a man double freight on goods passing right by his door going to San Francisco and then being hauled back again?

Mr. HUNTINGTON. I do not know.

Senator MORGAN. Could there be any good reason?

Mr. HUNTINGTON. There could be.

Senator MORGAN. What reason could there be?

Mr. HUNTINGTON. When we first started the Central Pacific road there were some complaints. They said we charged full prices to San Francisco and charged the local price back, which made a pretty fair rate; and they said that if we were going to charge that rate we must haul the goods to San Francisco and then haul them back; and I suppose that under those circumstances we would do it. I can not tell anything else. We have got to have enough out of the business to pay the current expenses and the fixed charges.

Senator MORGAN. That complaint was made when you first started in the business?

Mr. HUNTINGTON. Yes.

Senator MORGAN. How long was it continued to be made?

Mr. HUNTINGTON. I have not heard that complaint for a long time.

Senator MORGAN. But the complaint has been made?

Mr. HUNTINGTON. It did not come to me.

Senator MORGAN. Then how do you know anything about it?

Mr. HUNTINGTON. I am talking about what happened when we first started business on the road.

Senator MORGAN. You knew it then?

Mr. HUNTINGTON. Yes; I knew it then—thirty years ago.

Senator MORGAN. When did you drop that scheme?

Mr. HUNTINGTON. I do not know.

Senator MORGAN. Did you ever drop it?

Mr. HUNTINGTON. I think so. I have not heard any complaint of it for years.

Senator MORGAN. Sometimes men get into such difficulties that they are afraid to complain.

Mr. HUNTINGTON. I do not think that people over there are afraid to complain. Some few who have nothing to ship are afraid of the rates.

Senator MORGAN. And the others can be kept down because they do not dare to say anything?

Mr. HUNTINGTON. Not that; but reasoning with them shows that we must have enough earnings to keep the road running.

Senator MORGAN. I am very much interested in getting information from you as to when this arrangement stopped, which you have just detailed, so as to have it put upon the record.

Mr. HUNTINGTON. I can not tell. I have not heard anything about it for twenty years. I think there were probably some complaints of that kind when we first operated the Central Pacific. We charged them at that time probably a dollar a hundred for freight across the mountains. I have paid, myself, $50 a hundred for freight across the mountains.

Senator MORGAN. You have got a local railroad commission in California, have you?

Mr. HUNTINGTON. Yes.

Senator MORGAN. Has not that commission been trying just such questions as this?

Mr. HUNTINGTON. No; I do not think they have. They pledged themselves before election that they would put down railroad rates 25 per cent, and when they were elected they tried to do it. Now, we are trying in the courts whether they can do it or not.

Senator MORGAN. You deny the authority of the State of California to do that?

Mr. HUNTINGTON. I deny the authority of anybody to take a man's property without consideration.

Senator MORGAN. Was not this particular complaint which I am suggesting to you now put into that suit? Is not that a part of the issue—that you had made the very arrangement which you have here admitted, and that you kept it up until the time of filing that suit?

Mr. HUNTINGTON. If it is, I do not know it.

Senator MORGAN. Have you never seen the record in that case?

Mr. HUNTINGTON. No; that belongs to the legal department of the company.

Senator MORGAN. Do you not think that that is one of the grounds of complaint against your company?

Mr. HUNTINGTON. No.

Senator MORGAN. And that that complaint continues up to the present time?

Mr. HUNTINGTON. No. Whatever the court says about it I suppose will be final. We say that they have not any right to confiscate our property, and it is for the courts to say whether they have that right or not.

Senator MORGAN. But Congress has the right to amend or repeal your charter, and make you do it.

Mr. HUNTINGTON. I do not think that Congress should confiscate our property. I do not believe it would.

Senator MORGAN. I know that the railroad people believe that they are stronger than the State government, but I want to know whether they think themselves stronger than the United States Government.

Mr. HUNTINGTON. I do not think that Congress has the right to confiscate my property or anybody else's property.

Senator MORGAN. What property have you got in the rates of freight?

Mr. HUNTINGTON. That is like any other property.

Senator MORGAN. You mean the absolute right to fix rates?

Mr. HUNTINGTON. No.

Senator MORGAN. What right?

Mr. HUNTINGTON. Whenever we charge more than would give a fair return for the money invested, the courts may say that we must stop there.

Senator MORGAN. That is what I am trying to do.

Mr. HUNTINGTON. That is fair enough, Senator Morgan; but when we charge less than 2 cents a mile for passengers and less than 12 mills a mile per ton for freight, and when it is proposed to cut those rates 25 per cent, I say that there is no place in the world where a railroad could live at such rates.

Senator MORGAN. The 12 mills a mile per ton is not the local rate?

Mr. HUNTINGTON. It is the average of all our tonnage.

Senator MORGAN. Local rates and all?

Mr. HUNTINGTON. The average of all our lines is less than 12 mills a mile per ton, so our traffic men say; and I have no reason to doubt the correctness of the statement.

Senator MORGAN. Does that include the haul for the company?

Mr. HUNTINGTON. I suppose it includes everything.

Senator MORGAN. You did not make an estimate on that haul, did you?

Mr. HUNTINGTON. I do not know how the estimate is made out.

Senator MORGAN. I suppose all this long coal haul would be included in the estimate?

Mr. HUNTINGTON. I do not know how it is made up. We are moving coal on our trains, and if we did not charge the freight on it there would be more expense for hauling. It would come back on the coal business all the same. If there is so much out, there must come so much in.

Senator MORGAN. That estimate of 12 mills per ton per mile includes all the movement of the locomotives on your road, for short distances or long distances, hauling trains?

Mr. HUNTINGTON. What do you mean, Senator?

Senator MORGAN. I mean all the movement of locomotives hauling trains on long distances or short distances. Your estimate includes the movement of all locomotives hauling trains.

Mr. HUNTINGTON. It includes the expense of hauling tonnage, and, of course, we haul it with locomotives.

Senator MORGAN. You mean tonnage on which you charge freights?

Mr. HUNTINGTON. Yes.

Senator MORGAN. On which you charge freights to the people?

Mr. HUNTINGTON. I suppose to everybody.

Senator MORGAN. That would include the movement of trains for hauling materials for the railroad company, for coal, for repairs, for the construction of bridges, and everything of that sort?

Mr. HUNTINGTON. The hauling has to be paid for.

Senator MORGAN. And it includes all repair and construction trains that move over the roads. That is the proper way of bookkeeping, I suppose.

Mr. HUNTINGTON. It is the movement of the tonnage.

Senator MORGAN. And the tonnage is whatever you haul over the road, and it makes no difference to whom it belongs, whether to the railroad company or to anybody else?

Mr. HUNTINGTON. No.

Senator MORGAN. How much would the average be per ton per mile if you confined your estimate to what you charge the people?

Mr. HUNTINGTON. I do not understand the question.

Senator MORGAN. Your current income is derived from charges on freight and passengers?

Mr. HUNTINGTON. Yes.

Senator MORGAN. If your estimate of the rates of haul per ton per mile were based upon that income, then you would know how much the people had to pay per ton per mile for freight?

Mr. HUNTINGTON. Yes, I think so; if I understand your question.

Senator MORGAN. But your estimate is not based upon that. It is based on all the tonnage which you haul, whether on account of the company or on account of the people?

Mr. HUNTINGTON. Yes; the percentage of tonnage which we haul for the company is very light in comparison with the whole tonnage.

Senator MORGAN. Whether light or not.

Mr. HUNTINGTON. It is light in comparison with the whole.

Senator MORGAN. How do you know?

Mr. HUNTINGTON. We burn a ton of coal in 60 miles, I believe.

Senator MORGAN. Do you know anything about the hauling of timber and stone and clay and ballast for construction and repairs on your road?

Mr. HUNTINGTON. That is a small percentage of the whole tonnage.

Senator MORGAN. You said yesterday that the Western Development Company was continually building roads.

Mr. HUNTINGTON. No; not the Western Development Company. I said the Pacific Improvement Company. I think that the light work which we are doing now is being done by the company itself.

Senator MORGAN. By what company?

Mr. HUNTINGTON. By the Southern Pacific Company.

Senator MORGAN. You stated yesterday that the Pacific Improvement Company was continuing to build railroads right along.

Mr. HUNTINGTON. I think it is building the coast line, but I think that the Southern Pacific is building a number of pieces of road which the Pacific Improvement Company has nothing to do with.

Senator MORGAN. Is all of the haul for the Pacific Improvement Company included in that estimate? What is the basis of your calculation?

Mr. HUNTINGTON. If the Pacific Improvement Company builds a road it pays for the hauling like anybody else.

Senator MORGAN. But you include that in the basis on which you estimate 12 mills per ton per mile for hauling freight.

Mr. HUNTINGTON. I should think so; that would be the proper way.

Senator MORGAN. Now, Mr. Huntington, it is reasonable to suppose that at least a part of this 12 mills per ton per mile is based on work done for the Southern Pacific, or for companies related to it, is it not?

Mr. HUNTINGTON. It is based on work done for anybody.

Senator MORGAN. Including those companies?

Mr. HUNTINGTON. Yes.

Senator MORGAN. Have you any idea of what would be the estimate on the income of the road derived entirely from the people?

Mr. HUNTINGTON. No; I have not.

Senator MORGAN. It would be very much larger?

Mr. HUNTINGTON. It naturally would be; but when you carry expensive goods, it is worth more to carry them.

Senator MORGAN. So, when you come to fix the rate per ton per mile, you would have to take a larger sum than 12 mills per ton per mile, would you not?

Mr. HUNTINGTON. I should think so. The stuff which the Southern Pacific or the Pacific Improvement Company hauls is cheap tonnage. If the people had the same sort of stuff to carry they would pay the same rates. Of course we charge more in proportion for a bale of silk than we do for a ton of pig iron.

Senator MORGAN. What right do you think you have got to charge the patrons of your road for keeping it up?

Mr. HUNTINGTON. I really would ask where the money is coming from to keep up the road unless we get it out of those who use the road.

Senator MORGAN. I can tell you. It would come out of the dividends which you declare to yourself.

Mr. HUNTINGTON. The Southern Pacific has never declared a dividend.

Senator MORGAN. No; but you have already explained that by saying that you have used the money that should go to dividends in making improvements.

Mr. HUNTINGTON. In keeping the road up.

Senator MORGAN. And in building extensions.

Mr. HUNTINGTON. That is construction, and goes to another account altogether. I say that until the road is up as a first class road, no dividends should be declared.

Senator MORGAN. And until the road is built as far as you want to build it?

Mr. HUNTINGTON. Yes, there is great call for us to build extensions.

Senator MORGAN. The same gentlemen who own the Southern Pacific are building in Mexico too, are they not?

Mr. HUNTINGTON. Yes.

Senator MORGAN. And are they going to wait for that Mexican road to be built before they declare dividends on the Southern Pacific?

Mr. HUNTINGTON. The Southern Pacific has nothing to do with that Mexican road. That is a separate corporation.

Senator MORGAN. Do you not carry the profits and dividends earned by the Southern Pacific into that Mexican road?

Mr. HUNTINGTON. No.

Senator MORGAN. Do you build it out of separate resources entirely?

Mr. HUNTINGTON. Yes, I think so.

Senator MORGAN. Is that the fact?

Mr. HUNTINGTON. I should think so.

Senator MORGAN. What is the fact?

Mr. HUNTINGTON. The Southern Pacific has nothing to do with that Mexican road.

Senator MORGAN. Are not the profits made on the Southern Pacific carried to this Mexican road to some extent?

Mr. HUNTINGTON. Not a dollar. We have had no dividends on the Southern Pacific, and therefore no money has been carried over from the Southern Pacific to this Mexican road.

Senator MORGAN. If you had no dividends on the Southern Pacific, was it because you were not able to declare them, or because you did not want to declare them?

Mr. HUNTINGTON. I wanted to build the road up.

Senator MORGAN. And to extend it?

Mr. HUNTINGTON. We are extending it somewhat in California. But that is not the Southern Pacific. It is the Southern Pacific of California that is doing that.

Senator MORGAN. I think you have got it down pretty distinctly that the profits from the Southern Pacific are going into these improvements instead of going into your pockets. You mentioned something about hauling fruit with great advantage, and you spoke of complaints being made by Delaware and New Jersey peach growers of the low rates of freight which you charged to the California fruit growers. You mentioned that?

Mr. HUNTINGTON. Yes.

Senator MORGAN. Do you recollect the rate of freight from any point on the Southern Pacific, say from Los Angeles, to Chicago for fruit?

Mr. HUNTINGTON. I do not know just what it is.

Senator MORGAN. Is it not $1.20 per hundred pounds?

Mr. HUNTINGTON. It may be as low as that; perhaps it is. We carry great weight besides the fruit. We take 10 tons of freight, or thereabouts, and some 34 tons of car and ice. In other words, we haul more than 3 pounds of dead weight to 1 pound of proper freight.

Senator MORGAN. Take a carload of fruit destined from Los Angeles to Chicago, the Southern Pacific Company would haul it 435 miles, would it not?

Mr. HUNTINGTON. Yes.

Senator MORGAN. From Los Angeles to where you strike the Central Pacific road?

Mr. HUNTINGTON. I do not know how far it is. It is something like that, I should think.

Senator MORGAN. And the Central Pacific haul is 743 miles?

Mr. HUNTINGTON. Something more. The Central Pacific would haul it from Goshen, I suppose, and that would be 200 miles added to the 743 miles.

Senator MORGAN. Do you not know that, on that kind of freight, under an agreement between the Central Pacific and the Southern Pacific, the Southern Pacific gets 54 per cent for hauling that fruit 435 miles?

Mr. HUNTINGTON. No, I do not know that.

Senator MORGAN. If such a thing as that exists, it would be very bad, would it not?

Mr. HUNTINGTON. I do not know. If it does exist I have no doubt that it is all right. I do not know just what they do.

Senator MORGAN. You do not want to correct that?

Mr. HUNTINGTON. Not without inquiry.

Senator MORGAN. Who would you inquire from?

Mr. HUNTINGTON. From our traffic people.

Senator MORGAN. Who?

Mr. HUNTINGTON. From Mr. Stubbs.

Senator MORGAN. Mr. Stubbs always comes in in these transactions.

Mr. HUNTINGTON. Naturally.

Senator MORGAN. Is Mr. Stubbs agent for both companies?

Mr. HUNTINGTON. Yes.

Senator MORGAN. As vice-president of the Central Pacific Company do you think you ought to permit Mr. Stubbs, as traffic agent, to charge 54 per cent in favor of the Southern Pacific for hauling fruit 435 miles, and 46 per cent in favor of the Central Pacific for hauling the same 743 miles?

Mr. HUNTINGTON. That would depend upon what the Southern Pacific does in gathering in the freight and loading it, and perhaps supplying the ice. For instance, in hauling freight from San Francisco to Ogden, we got 80 cents on the Central Pacific (800 miles), while the Union Pacific, in hauling the same freight to Silver Bow, gets $4.25 and vice versa. That was running along a good while, and I did not think it exactly right, but the traffic men said that it was. We hauled it as far for 80 cents as the Union Pacific hauled it for $4.25.

Senator MORGAN. Do you not haul a large amount of fruit from Los Angeles and from places south and east of Los Angeles in California to the interior States east of the Rocky Mountains on the Southern Pacific?

Mr. HUNTINGTON. No; I do not think we do.

Senator MORGAN. It goes the other way?

Mr. HUNTINGTON. Yes. The Texas Pacific people have a good road, and why they do not get this trade I do not know. I do not think that the Southern Pacific hauls any of it. Our people, for some reason, have sent it all the other way. It may be that that is a part of the consideration.

Senator MORGAN. It was not because you could not deliver the fruit from the Southern Pacific as soon as over the Central Pacific on account of crossing the ferry?

Mr. HUNTINGTON. It would not cross any ferry.

Senator MORGAN. I mean by going to Oakland and from there to Ogden?

Mr. HUNTINGTON. I think the time would be about the same either way. It might be a little shorter time over the Southern line.

Senator MORGAN. If the time is about the same, why would it be sent over the Central Pacific instead of over the Southern Pacific?

Mr. HUNTINGTON. I do not know unless it was because our people wanted to do it. You see, the Southern Pacific got a little extra for it. That is usual, perhaps. The Southern Pacific took the freight and packed it up and got a little extra.

Senator MORGAN. It got 54 per cent of the freight.

Mr. HUNTINGTON. If that was so, there was good reason for it, I have no doubt. I do not know the reason myself; but it is a fact that instead of sending fruit from Los Angeles by the Southern Pacific, they send it by the Central Pacific. I think it nearly all goes that way.

Senator MORGAN. That is the choice of the company. The company wants to have it all that way.

Mr. HUNTINGTON. It goes that way. The reason for it I do not know.

Senator MORGAN. This 435 miles of road between Los Angeles and the connection of the Southern Pacific with the Central Pacific runs through the San Joaquin Valley?

Mr. HUNTINGTON. Yes.

Senator MORGAN. How many cars can you haul by one locomotive on that level piece of road?

Mr. HUNTINGTON. We can haul probably five times as many cars as we can haul from Los Angeles to Bakersville. It is a very ugly piece of road from Los Angeles to Bakersville. It has heavy grades up the Santa Clara to the summit of the mountains, and also down the mountains.

Senator MORGAN. Then take Fresno and Bakersville, and that vicinity where these large graperies and vineries and those immense orchards of oranges are, and you would have a level road from there to San Francisco?

Mr. HUNTINGTON. Yes.

Senator MORGAN. And you could haul 60 cars to a train on that road?

Mr. HUNTINGTON. Yes; with the best engine, but we do not haul as many cars as that.

Senator MORGAN. In leaving Bakersville to go to New Orleans with a load of fruit, how many cars can you haul with one locomotive?

Mr. HUNTINGTON. The train has to go over the mountains.

Senator MORGAN. Can you haul 13 or 14 or 15 cars to a train?

Mr. HUNTINGTON. Not over the mountains.

Senator MORGAN. The fruit trade from California to the East is a very important matter, is it not?

Mr. HUNTINGTON. Yes; it is an important item in the business.

Senator MORGAN. It includes the shipping of wines and brandies and all that, does it not?

Mr. HUNTINGTON. I suppose the wines and brandies are shipped at very low rates. There is competition by water upon them.

Senator MORGAN. And they benefit in quality by being shipped by water?

Mr. HUNTINGTON. Yes; some people claim that, but I think a ride by rail would do them good, too.

Senator MORGAN. The people in the section of California from Los Angeles up to San Francisco make very large annual shipments of fruits to market?

Mr. HUNTINGTON. Yes; I think the majority of the fruit comes from south of the Sierra Madre Mountains—from San Bernardino and San Diego.

Senator MORGAN. And all this fruit goes over the Central Pacific?

Mr. HUNTINGTON. Not all.

Senator MORGAN. Well, very nearly all.

Mr. HUNTINGTON. I think most of it does. I never have heard of any fruit going, to a considerable extent, over the Southern Pacific.

Senator MORGAN. Is not the fruit interest the largest agricultural interest in that section of California?

Mr. HUNTINGTON. I think so.

Senator MORGAN. Very much the largest?

Mr. HUNTINGTON. I think so.

Senator MORGAN. The wheat crop has rather petered out?

Mr. HUNTINGTON. There is very little wheat there.

Senator MORGAN. It is the same from the Napa Valley to San Francisco, is it not? that is a fruit country?

Mr. HUNTINGTON. Yes.

Senator MORGAN. So that from Napa Valley clear on down, and nearly as far as San Diego, the main agricultural crop of the country is fruit?

Mr. HUNTINGTON. They raise a good deal of grain in the San Joaquin Valley and in the Salinas; but I should say that the tonnage of fruit was greater than that of grain.

Senator MORGAN. And if the tonnage is greater, the value must be immensely greater?

Mr. HUNTINGTON. I should think so.

Senator MORGAN. What is the average freight between Los Angeles and New York City upon a carload of grapes?

Mr. HUNTINGTON. I do not think we send grapes that way.

Senator MORGAN. Well, on a carload of peaches?

Mr. HUNTINGTON. I do not think we send peaches that way.

Senator MORGAN. On a carload of pears?

Mr. HUNTINGTON. The freight is local to New Orleans.

Senator MORGAN. What has been, for the last three or four years, the average cost a of carload of fruit of any description, sent from Los Angeles, either by the Southern Pacific to New Orleans, or by the Central Pacific to New York.

Mr. HUNTINGTON. I do not know, but I should think about 1 cent a pound.

Senator MORGAN. How much a car?

Mr. HUNTINGTON. It depends upon the amount in the car.. That varies. The rate is so much per hundred pounds.

The CHAIRMAN. What is the average number of pounds required to be shipped for a carload?

Mr. HUNTINGTON. It depends on what the freight is.

The CHAIRMAN. On fruits.

Mr. HUNTINGTON. I do not know what it is. My impression would be 10 tons, because they take a good deal of ice, as fruit has to be sent in a refrigerator car.

The CHAIRMAN. You can not take as many pounds of fruit in a car as you could of wheat?

Mr. HUNTINGTON. Oh, no.

The CHAIRMAN. Why not?

Mr. HUNTINGTON. Because the wheat goes in bulk. Of some goods you can send 20,000 or 30,000 pounds in a car and of others 40,000.

The CHAIRMAN. Within what classification does fruit come?

Mr. HUNTINGTON. My impression is that they do not put more than 10 tons of fresh fruit into a car.

The CHAIRMAN. They carry more canned fruit than that?

Mr. HUNTINGTON. Oh, yes.

Senator MORGAN. What would be the whole weight, including ice, of a car which carries 10 tons of fruit?

Mr. HUNTINGTON. I do not know. I think that for 10 tons of fruit there would be 30 tons of car and ice.

Senator MORGAN. I do not understand you.

Mr. HUNTINGTON. I think that a refrigerator car, properly iced for handling fresh fruit, would weigh over 30 tons and would carry 10 tons of fruit, which would make the whole weight 40 tons.

The CHAIRMAN. With ice?

Mr. HUNTINGTON. I have got the ice in with the car. A refrigerator car, iced, would weigh some 30 tons. At least, I have got that impression.

Senator MORGAN. And you can put 10 tons of fruit into a refrigerator car?

Mr. HUNTINGTON. Yes.

Senator MORGAN. And that is the limit?

Mr. HUNTINGTON. I have got the impression that that is about the way we carry fruit.

Senator MORGAN. With this 10 tons of fruit in an iced refrigerator car what is the freight on a carload from Los Angeles to New York?

Mr. HUNTINGTON. You may say $1\frac{1}{2}$ cents a pound.

Senator MORGAN. A cent and a half a pound on the fruit?

Mr. HUNTINGTON. Yes.

Senator MORGAN. Or on the ice?

Mr. HUNTINGTON. No; we do not charge freight on the ice. We transport the fruit in a certain way.

Senator MORGAN. That would make the cost of transporting the fruit $300.

Mr. HUNTINGTON. Yes; and sometimes it goes to $500. It has been more than that.

The CHAIRMAN. You do not carry your canned fruit in refrigerator cars?

Mr. HUNTINGTON. No; and it is packed very much closer. The fresh fruit is packed loosely.

Senator MORGAN. In sending your refrigerator cars loaded with ice from Los Angeles, do you make rates clear through to New York?

Mr. HUNTINGTON. I think so. That is by agreement with all the other lines.

Senator MORGAN. And the fruit is put in New York at a price stipulated at Los Angeles?

Mr. HUNTINGTON. I understand the price has to be fixed before the start.

Senator MORGAN. In making that haul, if it is to be $400 a car, the Southern Pacific Company would get 54 per cent of that $400?

Mr. HUNTINGTON. I do not know how it would be made up.

Senator MORGAN. Or it would get 54 per cent of whatever was allowed to the Southern Pacific and the Central Pacific for carrying the fruit?

Mr. HUNTINGTON. Yes. I am not familiar with the operations. If I had known that Senator Morgan wanted to know about them I could have had somebody here to inform him more accurately.

Senator MORGAN. Then, for all shipments between Napa and Bakersfield for freights passing over the Central Pacific, the Southern Pacific has the advantage of a level country over which you can haul 60 cars to a train?

Mr. HUNTINGTON. Napa is different. Napa is not in the San Joaquin Valley. There is considerable grade there until we get down to Fairfield or Suisin. My impression is that we can not haul 25 cars on a train from Napa to Bridgeport, at the foot of the grade.

Senator MORGAN. Are not the rates for hauling this crop of fruit prescribed by the Southern Pacific Company?

Mr. HUNTINGTON. Oh, no; we can not fix the rates.

Senator MORGAN. Who can fix them?

Mr. HUNTINGTON. It has got to be a joint arrangement.

Senator MORGAN. A joint arrangement with whom?

Mr. HUNTINGTON. With whatever roads the fruit goes over. It will be with one set of people if the fruit goes to Minneapolis; with another set of people if it goes to Chicago, and with other sets if it goes to St. Louis.

Senator MORGAN. Confine yourself to the Central Pacific and Southern Pacific roads. By whom are the prices for fruit made?

Mr. HUNTINGTON. There is an agreement and division.

Senator MORGAN. Between the Central Pacific and the Southern Pacific?

Mr. HUNTINGTON. Between all the roads interested in the transportation.

Senator MORGAN. I am talking about the Central Pacific and the Southern Pacific. I want to know who prescribes the agreement for carrying fruit as between the Southern and the Central Pacific.

Mr. HUNTINGTON. I suppose Mr. Stubbs or Mr. Smurr.

Senator MORGAN. So Mr. Stubbs would have the right to say, and does say, what the rates and division are to be; and you think it is all right if he does so?

Mr. HUNTINGTON. Yes.

Senator MORGAN. You think it is all right that the people of California should be compelled to take their great crop of fruit over the Central Pacific instead of by competing lines?

Mr. HUNTINGTON. No. The Atchison and Topeka is in there—a competing road, with a most active set of men.

Senator MORGAN. In where?

Mr. HUNTINGTON. In California—in San Francisco and Los Angeles.

Senator MORGAN. But, so far as the Central Pacific and the Southern Pacific are concerned, and so far as they can control the freights, the matter would be left entirely to Mr. Stubbs to say what the rates ought to be?

Mr. HUNTINGTON. I should think so. If I were to have to decide it, I should leave it to Mr. Stubbs.

Senator MORGAN. The matter is to be decided by Mr. Stubbs both as to the rate of freight and then as to the rate for which it shall be carried by the Southern Pacific to the Central Pacific and over the Central Pacific to the point of distribution?

Mr. HUNTINGTON. I should think that would be the result. But the freights would have to be reasonable. They are probably agreed rates. If we wanted unreasonable rates, the Atchison people would come in and take the business.

Senator MORGAN. Can you state any reason why those two railroad companies have not got the monopoly of the transportation of fruit from California under this arrangement?

Mr. HUNTINGTON. There are six or seven or eight railroad companies that compete for that business in San Francisco—not so much, perhaps, for the green fruit.

Senator MORGAN. Do they get it?

Mr. HUNTINGTON. They probably get some.

Senator MORGAN. How much do they get?

Mr. HUNTINGTON. I do not know.

Senator MORGAN. Are they getting any?

Mr. HUNTINGTON. I do not know.

Senator MORGAN. Is it not the policy of the Southern Pacific and the Central Pacific to keep them out?

Mr. HUNTINGTON. We can not keep them out.

Senator MORGAN. Is is not your policy to keep them out, if you can get the business?

Mr. HUNTINGTON. No; we do not want to keep them out. There must be competition; we must do business on business lines, and we make our rates as low as we can do the business for.

Senator MORGAN. Is it not your interest to keep these other roads out?

Mr. HUNTINGTON. I do not know that it would be. I do not know that we could keep them out if we wished. There is no use in our wasting an effort on it, for we know that we can not keep them out if we should try.

Senator MORGAN. Does this general deal that you spoke about, in regard to the business to be divided between all the companies, apply to fruit?

Mr. HUNTINGTON. Yes; I think it applies to all matters.

Senator MORGAN. Is not that the reason why 54 per cent of the general income of all of these rates is given to the Central Pacific under that general agreement?

Mr. HUNTINGTON. I do not know that it is. I do not think it is mentioned.

Senator MORGAN. But is not that the reason?

Mr. HUNTINGTON. If it is, I never thought of it.

Senator MORGAN. The fruit business being the principal business in California, you never thought that a monopoly of it would be of an advantage to you?

Mr. HUNTINGTON. I do not think that the green-fruit is anything like a majority of the tonnage.

Senator MORGAN. How do you distinguish between the green fruit and the other fruit?

Mr. HUNTINGTON. The preserved fruit can go anywhere and upon any line.

Senator MORGAN. You mean the canned fruit?

Mr. HUNTINGTON. The canned fruit and the dried fruit. That has the world's market and can go over any line. The green fruit only goes but a short time, while the other goes all the year.

The CHAIRMAN. The green fruit consists of grapes and citrous fruits.

Mr. HUNTINGTON. Yes; but there is dried fruit and preserved fruit, and they can go anywhere. Grapes, oranges, pears, and peaches are about the only fruit that can not be transported by water. Fruit is not the great tonnage of the State. The great tonnage is wines, and that is now sent over any lines. The green fruit does not cut any great figure in the trade.

Senator MORGAN. About how many car loads of green fruit are sent over the Central Pacific road?

Mr. HUNTINGTON. I do not know how many.

Senator MORGAN. You say that the green fruit does not cut any great figure in the business. How do you know, if you can not tell the number of carloads?

Mr. HUNTINGTON. I know it in a general way.

Senator MORGAN. I want it in a particular way, if I can get it.

Mr. HUNTINGTON. There are a great many prunes raised in California, and the whole prune crop is put up in a way that it can be sent by any line of transportation.

Senator MORGAN. Do your railroad books show the number of cars of green fruit that have gone over the Central Pacific for the last five years?

Mr. HUNTINGTON. I should think so.

Senator MORGAN. Will you give that information to the committee?

Mr. HUNTINGTON. Yes.

Senator MORGAN. I want to know the number of cars of green fruit that have passed over the Central Pacific annually for the last five years?

The CHAIRMAN. And also the number of cars with canned goods.

Mr. HUNTINGTON. Shall I give the weight by pounds?

Senator MORGAN. You may give it by pounds and by the number of carloads. Is not one of the matters which the State railroad commissioners have to regulate this very important matter which we have been discussing about the transportation of fruits from California to the East?

Mr. HUNTINGTON. It comes under general traffic. It is a part of the traffic of the company. The commission is a blind strike at everything.

The CHAIRMAN. Has the board of railroad commissioners of California the power to fix railroad rates?

Mr. HUNTINGTON. That is a question which the United States court is now trying. The court has the whole matter before it now.

The CHAIRMAN. Does the law of California give the railroad commissioners the power to fix rates?

Mr. HUNTINGTON. The law of California says that the commissioners can fix rates; and the question before the courts is whether they can confiscate our property.

The CHAIRMAN. The question before the courts is whether the rates are reasonable.

Mr. HUNTINGTON. Yes; whether or not they can confiscate our property; for there is a lively little set over there which would do so if it could.

The CHAIRMAN. That is the same question that is now before the courts of Nebraska.

Mr. PAYSON (of counsel for Central Pacific). There the question is whether there can be a horizontal reduction of rates by 25 per cent made without hearing the railroad company.

Senator MORGAN. Does the California Pacific Railroad charge track rent to the Southern Pacific Company?

Mr. HUNTINGTON. I do not know how that is done. I think the Southern Pacific Company leases the California Pacific.

Senator MORGAN. Do any of these roads which you or your friends control, or have controlled, make any charge for track rent to the Kentucky company—the Southern Pacific?

Mr. HUNTINGTON. If they lease the road, I suppose they come in under a general lease. I do not know how it is.

Senator MORGAN. Whether it is track rent or a general lease, how much do you realize for the use of those roads out of the Southern Pacific Company annually?

Mr. HUNTINGTON. We never have received any dividends on the shares of the Southern Pacific Company at all.

Senator MORGAN. How much do you realize in favor of each of these companies—how much is paid to them annually?

Mr. HUNTINGTON. I do not know.

Senator MORGAN. About how much?

Mr. HUNTINGTON. I do not know. We never have declared any dividends on the shares.

Senator MORGAN. You did not just give those roads to the Southern Pacific company, did you?

Mr. HUNTINGTON. No.

Senator MORGAN. You hire, then, to the Southern Pacific either by lease or track rent?

Mr. HUNTINGTON. By lease, I think.

Senator MORGAN. How much do you get out of it?

Mr. HUNTINGTON. We never have received any dividends on the shares.

Senator MORGAN. I know perfectly well that you do not intend to declare any dividends on the shares. That is not your plan. To bring the question down to your comprehension, you did give, up to a recent period, $1,300,000 a year for the lease of the Central Pacific?

Mr. HUNTINGTON. The Southern Pacific paid $1,200,000 a year to the Central Pacific and then increased it to $1,360,000.

Senator MORGAN. Up to within a recent period, and up to the end of the first ten years of the lease, this Kentucky company paid to the Central Pacific Company twelve or thirteen hundred thousand dollars a year for the lease of that road?

Mr. HUNTINGTON. Yes.

Senator MORGAN. How much did the Southern Pacific Company pay for the leases for the other roads which it operated?

Mr. HUNTINGTON. I do not know.

Senator MORGAN. About how much?

Mr. HUNTINGTON. I do not know what was paid.

Senator MORGAN. What was the aggregate sum?

Mr. HUNTINGTON. I can not give you that information.

Senator MORGAN. Does it not amount to as much as $9,000,000 a year, which the Southern Pacific pays for the leases of all these different roads?

Mr. HUNTINGTON. I do not know. The Southern Pacific controls, by ownership of shares, all the lines, I think, between Portland and New Orleans, except the California Pacific and possibly the Northern.

Senator MORGAN. Take last year and the year before last. Do not the books of the Southern Pacific—this Kentucky company—show that, during these two years, it has paid, by way of leases for those roads which it controls and which belong to you and your associates, as much as $9,000,000 a year?

Mr. HUNTINGTON. I should think that very likely it ran along there.

Senator MORGAN. Is it not even more than that?

Mr. HUNTINGTON. Well, I should think it would be more.

Senator MORGAN. How much more?

Mr. HUNTINGTON. I do not know. The Southern Pacific paid enough to these companies to pay interest on their bonds and their current expenses and their taxes. I should think it amounted to more than that.

Senator MORGAN. About how much?

Mr. HUNTINGTON. I do not know; but it seems to me that it would run over that.

Senator MORGAN. That has become a fixed charge on the whole length of the line?

Mr. HUNTINGTON. Interest and taxes, of course, have to be paid. These are part of the fixed charges.

Senator MORGAN. Do these different companies that are under your control make enough to pay their way under this arrangement with the Kentucky company?

Mr. HUNTINGTON. Yes.

Senator MORGAN. How much more do they make?

Mr. HUNTINGTON. I would like to send you all our annual reports. They give the amounts exactly. There is always a little surplus.

Senator MORGAN. I do not care about exact figures. I will take round figures.

Mr. HUNTINGTON. My impression is that they make, as an average, a little over a million dollars a year—sometimes more, sometimes less.

Senator MORGAN. For each road?

Mr. HUNTINGTON. No; for the whole of them.

Senator MORGAN. So that the Southern Pacific makes a net profit of $1,000,000 a year out of these roads?

Mr. HUNTINGTON. Not exactly; there are always improvements to be made. The bookkeeping will show that, but the money is hardly ever in the till.

Senator MORGAN. Because you are all the time improving and increasing the value of the property?

Mr. HUNTINGTON. Keeping it up.

Senator MORGAN. And extending it?

Mr. HUNTINGTON. Yes; people in the different neighborhoods come to us and ask us to build roads here and there, and we are desirous to accommodate them and have done so.

Senator MORGAN. The Southern Pacific Railroad is a very good property, is it not?

Mr. HUNTINGTON. I think very well of it. It will take time to work it out.

Senator MORGAN. But this California Pacific. That seems to be in a sort of gang by itself.

Mr. HUNTINGTON. I do not understand you.

Senator MORGAN. "Gang by itself" is a Southern expression. I mean that it seems to be under a different management from the others.

Mr. HUNTINGTON. Yes; it was built up by other parties, and we finally bought it.

Senator MORGAN. Who bought it?

Mr. HUNTINGTON. Stanford and Crocker and Hopkins and myself, and Colton, I guess; and maybe Hammond had a little interest in it. There were some lesser interests. I think there were four large interests.

Senator MORGAN. With your guesses and your maybes and your thinkings, I would like to know how much of your statement is mere guess and conjecture.

Mr. HUNTINGTON. I am quite sure we had a majority, a considerable majority of that company; I can not say exactly how much.

Senator MORGAN. You four being the majority owners of the California Pacific and having power of control over it, why did you not put it into the Southern Pacific to keep it in a "gang by itself?"

Mr. HUNTINGTON. I do not know that I can tell you the reason why. We bought a majority of the shares, and we did not buy all the shares. We have not got them now, by a long way.

Senator MORGAN. But you have the controlling power?

Mr. HUNTINGTON. We have the majority.

Senator MORGAN. The majority could carry the California Pacific into the Southern Pacific. Why did it not do so?

Mr. HUNTINGTON. We made up our minds not to do it, I suppose, and did not do it.

Senator MORGAN. You had some reason for that, had you not?

Mr. HUNTINGTON. I forget the reason; no doubt we had some good reason for it.

Senator MORGAN. Was it not that the possession of the California Pacific gave you the leverage by which you could control both the Southern Pacific and the Central Pacific lines?

Mr. HUNTINGTON. The Sacramento River is always open and is as free and cheap a means of communication as any in the world.

Senator MORGAN. The Sacramento River is pretty well filled up, is it not?

Mr. HUNTINGTON. No; there are 4 feet of water in the Sacramento, and an immense commerce can be done over 4 feet of water. They are doing an immense business now, above Sacramento, over 20 inches of water. I think there was a lawsuit with some parties in San Francisco who held a lot of those shares of the California Pacific, and our people wanted to compromise with them; but I did not. The suit ran along for a good many years, and I think that is the reason why we did not put in the California Pacific.

Senator MORGAN. What lawsuit was that?

Mr. HUNTINGTON. It was what was known as the Haskins and Mayne suit.

Senator MORGAN. It was not the Brannan lawsuit?

Mr. HUNTINGTON. No; that was in the air.

Senator MORGAN. When was that lawsuit ended?

Mr. HUNTINGTON. Three or four years ago.

Senator MORGAN. Then you have had plenty of time since then to put the California Pacific in with the Southern Pacific?

Mr. HUNTINGTON. I do not think that the question has been discussed since then.

Senator MORGAN. How much do you get a year for the California Pacific under lease?

Mr. HUNTINGTON. I do not know.

Senator MORGAN. As nearly as you can think, how much do you get per year?

Mr. HUNTINGTON. I would not say. It is less than a million a year.

Senator MORGAN. How much less?

Mr. HUNTINGTON. I do not know. I will get the exact figures for you in a day or two.

Senator MORGAN. I can not examine you on oath if I have got to wait for those figures. I would like to know now.

Mr. HUNTINGTON. I can not say what it is. I have not seen the lease. It is a matter which our people have dealt with.

Senator MORGAN. Are you a member of the board of directors of the California Pacific?

Mr. HUNTINGTON. I do not believe I am. I may be, but I believe I am not.

Senator MORGAN. Who controls that—Mr. Stubbs?

Mr. HUNTINGTON. He controls the traffic; he is the head of the traffic department.

Senator MORGAN. Who made this contract or lease between the California Pacific and the Kentucky company?

Mr. HUNTINGTON. I have no doubt that it was made between the boards of directors of the two companies.

Senator MORGAN. You do not know anything about it?

Mr. HUNTINGTON. That would be the practice.

Senator MORGAN. It must have been made with your approval as president of the Kentucky company?

Mr. HUNTINGTON. No doubt.

Senator MORGAN. And you approved it?

Mr. HUNTINGTON. Not necessarily; but I have no doubt it was satisfactory.

Senator MORGAN. If you were not under the necessity of approving it, who was?

Mr. HUNTINGTON. Charles F. Crocker. He is the first vice-president. He is at San Francisco and can do whatever the president can do.

Senator MORGAN. And the lease was made with the Southern Pacific and you do not know what it was?

Mr. HUNTINGTON. I do not know the exact figures.

Senator MORGAN. I am not calling for exact figures, but for your best recollection.

Mr. HUNTINGTON. As I have not the exact figure I do not know how to state it.

Senator MORGAN. You have been four or five days doing that very same thing. You can state it from your best knowledge and recollection.

Mr. HUNTINGTON. I do not believe I have it clear as to what the figure is. It seems that I ought to know it.

Senator MORGAN. It seems so to me.

Mr. HUNTINGTON. Yes; it strikes me so.

Senator MORGAN. Do any of those companies that are controlled by your Kentucky company owe more debts than they can pay?

Mr. HUNTINGTON. I should say not; in fact, I am very sure that they can all pay their debts.

Senator MORGAN. Are any of those companies which you and Stanford and Crocker and Hopkins controlled when you were building the Central Pacific, and when you were building the Southern Pacific, able to pay all their debts?

Mr. HUNTINGTON. I think so. I do not think of any of those companies at this time that is not abundantly able to pay its debts. They are growing properties. They were built through a country where there were then very few people, and now they are growing.

Senator MORGAN. Then all these different companies are solvent?

Mr. HUNTINGTON. Very decidedly so.

Senator MORGAN. Every one of them?

Mr. HUNTINGTON. I think so; they are all growing properties and going properties.

Senator MORGAN. If that were the case, what was the necessity to wind up and disincorporate this Contract and Finance Company?

Mr. HUNTINGTON. We got through with that. That was a company organized for a certain purpose. Mr. E. B. Crocker went out of it, and that I think was one reason for disincorporating it. We got through with everything and we organized the Western Development Company and undertook the business. I think there was some interest in that company (I do not recollect what) which went out, and we thought we would close up the concern.

Senator MORGAN. Did you disincorporate the Western Development Company too?

Mr. HUNTINGTON. I think not.

Senator MORGAN. That still lives?

Mr. HUNTINGTON. Yes, sir.

Senator MORGAN. Is that company at work now?

Mr. HUNTINGTON. No.

Senator MORGAN. Then you came to the Pacific Improvement Company?

Mr. HUNTINGTON. Yes.

Senator MORGAN. That is at work now?

Mr. HUNTINGTON. I think they are doing some work on the coast line.

Senator MORGAN. Neither of those companies owns any railroads?

Mr. HUNTINGTON. No; they are not railroad companies; they were contract and operating companies.

Senator MORGAN. To build railroads?

Mr. HUNTINGTON. To build anything—ships, railroads, and canals.

Senator MORGAN. And they built all of those railroads which were put into the Southern Pacific?

Mr. HUNTINGTON. No; there were a good many of them that failed, and that we bought.

Senator MORGAN. The Pacific Improvement Company either built them or bought them?

Mr. HUNTINGTON. Yes; I think so.

Senator MORGAN. These roads which the Pacific Improvement Company either built or bought were organized under and became the property of a separate organization?

Mr. HUNTINGTON. Yes; they have been incorporated with the Southern Pacific of California.

Senator MORGAN. You paid the debts upon them?

Mr. HUNTINGTON. There were debts upon them when we bought them. There was a mortgage on the road from Salinas to Monterey when we bought it.

Senator MORGAN. Has that mortgage been paid?

Mr. HUNTINGTON. No; it is not due yet. The interest on it has been paid.

Senator MORGAN. What was the next road that you bought?

Mr. HUNTINGTON. The Stockton and Copperopolis.

Senator MORGAN. Did that have any debt upon it?

Mr. HUNTINGTON. It had a million dollars of 8 per cent bonds out, and we issued for that half a million of 5 per cent bonds.

Senator MORGAN. Is that mortgage outstanding?

Mr. HUNTINGTON. It is not due yet.

Senator MORGAN. It is outstanding?

Mr. HUNTINGTON. The bonds are out.

Senator MORGAN. That road was bought by one of these companies?

Mr. HUNTINGTON. I think it was bought by the Western Development Company.

Senator MORGAN. Go ahead now.

Mr. HUNTINGTON. There is another little road running out from Galt, and another near there.

Senator MORGAN. Did you buy these two roads or did you build them?

Mr. HUNTINGTON. We bought them.

Senator MORGAN. Is there any mortgage on these two roads?

Mr. HUNTINGTON. Yes.

Senator MORGAN. What other roads did you build or buy?

Mr. HUNTINGTON. The Placerville road from Sacramento to Placerville. That we bought. We built 9 miles at the end of it. We completed it.

Senator MORGAN. Any more?

Mr. HUNTINGTON. We bought a road from Maysville down to Macks Landing. There is a mortgage on it now. Then we bought a little road running over to Iona Valley.

Senator MORGAN. Is there any mortgage on that?

Mr. HUNTINGTON. There is a mortgage on that.

Senator MORGAN. Did you buy any other roads?

Mr. HUNTINGTON. I think there are some others. I do not know. I think that we bought a road from Iona to Los Angeles, and we bought a road from Los Angeles to Santa Monica Bay.

Senator MORGAN. Is there any mortgage on that?

Mr. HUNTINGTON. Yes; there is a mortgage on that. Then I believe we bought the road from San Bernardino to Riverside, and I think a road from San Bernardino up to Red Lines.

Senator MORGAN. Are there mortgages on both these roads?

Mr. HUNTINGTON. I think so; and I think there are some others. The roads were generally in bankruptcy when we took then. We put the prices down in every case from the rates which they had been charging and we made money, but that was owing to our superior way of operating the roads. Before be bought them they had machine shops made up generally of old tools and machinery that could not be worked, and they had master mechanics' salaries and superintendents' salaries, and we brushed all that away and put the roads on a good footing.

Senator MORGAN. Have you got to the last of those roads that you bought?

Mr. HUNTINGTON. All that I think of at this time.

Senator MORGAN. You sold all of these roads to the California Pacific?

Mr. HUNTINGTON. Yes; I think they were consolidated in the California Pacific.

Senator MORGAN. Which became the Southern Pacific of California?

Mr. HUNTINGTON. Yes.

Senator MORGAN. By contract and consolidation?

Mr. HUNTINGTON. My impression is that Judge Sanderson was living when the first consolidation was made.

Senator MORGAN. Was Judge Sanderson a lawyer?

Mr. HUNTINGTON. Yes; a very able lawyer.

Senator MORGAN. Whose lawyer was he?

Mr. HUNTINGTON. He was our general legal adviser. He was the head of the supreme court in the State, and was a man of very superior ability, and of such unquestionable integrity that we thought it best to get the best talent in the State, and we took Judge Sanderson.

Senator MORGAN. All of these roads, having been bought or built by the several construction companies, became their property, subject to the mortgages on them?

Mr. HUNTINGTON. Yes.

Senator MORGAN. And they were in the ownership of the four gentlemen whom you have been naming here—Stanford, Hopkins, Crocker, and yourself?

Mr. HUNTINGTON. The California Pacific was not altogether in our ownership. We got a majority of the shares. We got all the shares in some of the companies and in some we did not.

Senator MORGAN. But in all of them you got a majority of the shares?

Mr. HUNTINGTON. Yes; we would not take the companies unless we had.

Senator MORGAN. And you had the right to control them as stockholders?

Mr. HUNTINGTON. Yes.

Senator MORGAN. And you consolidated all of them?

Mr. HUNTINGTON. I think so.

Senator MORGAN. That consolidation was conducted entirely by and for the construction companies?

Mr. HUNTINGTON. No; I should say for the Southern Pacific Railroad Company more particularly.

Senator MORGAN. There had to be two parties to the bargain?

Mr. HUNTINGTON. Yes; but still it was a good deal the same interest, and we wanted to reduce expenses.

Senator MORGAN. You treated it as a common unit and put it into the Southern Pacific Railroad Company?

Mr. HUNTINGTON. Yes; we consolidated it.

Senator MORGAN. Leaving the mortgages to stand where they were?

Mr. HUNTINGTON. Yes.

Senator MORGAN. And of course in doing that the property remained liable for each of the mortgages upon it?

Mr. HUNTINGTON. Yes.

Senator MORGAN. You owned, therefore, a majority of the stock in each of these minor companies?

Mr. HUNTINGTON. Yes.

Senator MORGAN. How many bonds of these minor companies did you own?

Mr. HUNTINGTON. I do not think we owned any of the bonds. We got the stock of the Stockton and Copperopolis Company and gave a half million dollars in 5 per cent bonds to the people who had $1,000,000 in 8 per cent bonds and who lived in Amsterdam. We gave a half million 5 per cent bonds for the one million of 8 per cents.

Senator MORGAN. Then the bonds of all these various companies were not held by the construction company?

Mr. HUNTINGTON. No; I do not think so. I do not recollect our having any of them at all.

Senator MORGAN. They were out on the country?

Mr. HUNTINGTON. Yes, unless they were absorbed and canceled. I think that in the consolidation we gave Southern Pacific bonds in exchange for some of them. It seems to me that for the Anaheim branch we gave bonds of the Southern Pacific Company.

Senator MORGAN. Are there any of the roads where you have not substituted Southern Pacific bonds for the bonds of the minor companies?

Mr. HUNTINGTON. Yes; the Stockton and Copperopolis road is one. Those bonds are out under that name. They are not due.

Senator MORGAN. Have you any idea of how many Southern Pacific bonds you gave in exchange for the bonds of those small companies?

Mr. HUNTINGTON. No; I think that generally they kept their bonds, and we agreed to pay the interest on them and they gave us their shares. These minor roads were almost all bankrupt. That had all come from the disadvantage of working little roads having all the machinery of a great corporation, and of course, as a rule, they run into bankruptcy.

Senator MORGAN. They gave you their stock?

Mr. HUNTINGTON. I would not say that.

Senator MORGAN. You did say it.

Mr. HUNTINGTON. The California Pacific gave something for the stock.

Senator MORGAN. About how much?

Mr. HUNTINGTON. Ten or twelve per cent; but that is a great many years ago.

Senator MORGAN. Was the California Pacific paid for in money, or stock, or bonds of the Southern Pacific?

Mr. HUNTINGTON. The Southern Pacific does not control the California Pacific to-day. The California Pacific is an independent company.

Senator MORGAN. I am talking about these other little companies. What did you give in exchange for their stock?

Mr. HUNTINGTON. Ten or twelve per cent.

Senator MORGAN. Did you pay that in money?

Mr. HUNTINGTON. No; I think not. I think we made a contract with them to double track the road from Davisville to Sacramento. They wanted us to take the road, because they had it terribly overmortgaged, and we cut the mortgage down.

Senator MORGAN. After getting all these little roads in your grasp you consolidated them all, except the California Pacific, with the Southern Pacific of California?

Mr. HUNTINGTON. I will say got them into our possession, not into our grasp. We bought them and controlled them.

Senator MORGAN. I call that a grasp.

Mr. HUNTINGTON. Maybe that is the right word.

Senator MORGAN. You got them into your control and ownership, and you put them into the Southern Pacific of California?

Mr. HUNTINGTON. Yes.

Senator MORGAN. And then the Southern Pacific of California went into the Kentucky company?

Mr. HUNTINGTON. Yes; they sold their shares.

Senator MORGAN. And you became the owners of the stock in all these little roads which you consolidated and put in; and then you put that stock into the Kentucky concern—the Southern Pacific?

Mr. HUNTINGTON. Yes.

Senator MORGAN. That is the way it occurred; for all of this stock which you put into the Southern Pacific or Kentucky company you paid very little?

Mr. HUNTINGTON. We did not pay but little, and I do not think we got any stock, or hardly any of it, on these purchases.

Senator MORGAN. I do not suppose you would get any, for you had all of it consolidated with the Southern Pacific of California.

Mr. HUNTINGTON. That was done in a very broad and liberal spirit. I do not believe that we got any shares for some of these roads. We thought it a great benefit to the Southern Pacific and to the people along the roads for us to get control of it.

Senator MORGAN. You and Hopkins and Stanford and Crocker were the owners of a very large majority of the stock of the Southern Pacific of California?

Mr. HUNTINGTON. Yes; we had a large majority of that stock.

Senator MORGAN. How much did you four have in the Southern Pacific of California?

Mr. HUNTINGTON. The contract for building the road was made with the Western Development Company, I think, and they took the bonds, I should think, and the stock, I should think—some $40,000,000 of stock.

Senator MORGAN. How many bonds?

Mr. HUNTINGTON. Thirty-eight million dollars of bonds. I think we took the bonds. I do not know whether we took the bonds or were paid so much money for the building of the road; but I think the Western Development Company took the bonds and stock.

Senator MORGAN. Did you take the land grant also?

Mr. HUNTINGTON. No; the bonds were mortgaged on the land grant.

Senator MORGAN. That Western Development Company was the company which was building the Southern Pacific of California?

Mr. HUNTINGTON. I think so. I am pretty certain they set in to build it.

Senator MORGAN. Did they not wind it up?

Mr. HUNTINGTON. No; I think the Pacific Improvement Company took it off their hands.

Senator MORGAN. The same people?

Mr. HUNTINGTON. Not altogether.

Senator MORGAN. The great majority of the Western Development Company was owned by these four men?

Mr. HUNTINGTON. Yes; we always tried to keep a control of these things.

Senator MORGAN. The same four men found it convenient or necessary to transfer that contract for building the Southern Pacific of California from the Western Development to the Pacific Improvement Company?

Mr. HUNTINGTON. I think so.

Senator MORGAN. Did you then wind up the Western Development Company?

Mr. HUNTINGTON, I think so.

Senator MORGAN. And you took a new start upon a new company?

Mr. HUNTINGTON. Yes.

Senator MORGAN. Who owned the stock of the Western Development Company?

Mr. HUNTINGTON. We four men owned it largely. We kept together all the time. We were railroad builders from the start and had to keep control. The only salvation in these things is to get men who go into it to keep together.

Senator MORGAN. Through the Western Development Company and the Pacific Improvement Company you have built the Southern Pacific of California, so far as it has been built?

Mr. HUNTINGTON. The company itself may have done some little work outside of that. We have some little work now in southern California which I think we are doing.

Senator MORGAN. Is it not true that the Western Development Company and the Pacific Improvement Company were organized for the purpose of building the Southern Pacific road?

Mr. HUNTINGTON. No; they were organized for general work.

Senator MORGAN. But they took the contract for the Southern Pacific road in succession, one after the other?

Mr. HUNTINGTON. Yes.

Senator MORGAN. Then you wound up and disincorporated the Western Development Company?

Mr. HUNTINGTON. No; I do not think the Western Development Company has ever been disincorporated.

Senator MORGAN. It has been wound up and ceased work?

Mr. HUNTINGTON. Yes.

Senator MORGAN. Then you took to the Pacific Improvement Company what remained to be done and the assets of the Western Development Company?

Mr. HUNTINGTON. Yes.

Senator MORGAN. They were just transferred to a new company?

Mr. HUNTINGTON. Yes; I do not see any other way to do it.

Senator MORGAN. The Western Development Company and the Pacific Improvement Company together (and one as the successor of the other) have built the Southern Pacific Company in California?

Mr. HUNTINGTON. Yes; in the main. Nearly all, I should say.

Senator MORGAN. And got all the stock and all the bonds of the Southern Pacific Company after building it?

Mr. HUNTINGTON. Not all the stock. They got all the bonds.

Senator MORGAN. How many?

Mr. HUNTINGTON. Thirty-eight million dollars.

Senator MORGAN. How much stock have they got?

Mr. HUNTINGTON. I think $40,000,000.

Senator MORGAN. How much stock was left that they did not get?

Mr. HUNTINGTON. I think the Southern Pacific of California was capitalized at $60,000,000.

Senator MORGAN. How much stock has ever been issued by that company?

Mr. HUNTINGTON. I think something over $50,000,000. We have a much greater mileage, I think, than in the Southern Pacific of California. There may be fifteen or sixteen or seventeen hundred miles.

Senator MORGAN. There still remains stock to be issued by that company?

Mr. HUNTINGTON. The company can increase its stock under the law of the State.

Senator MORGAN. And you are working now to improve and extend the property of the company?

Mr. HUNTINGTON. Yes; we are taking care of it.

Senator MORGAN. Do you still hold those bonds?

Mr. HUNTINGTON. No; I am sorry to say we have not a dollar of the $38,000,000 of bonds.

Senator MORGAN. And you transferred the stock to the Kentucky company?

Mr. HUNTINGTON. It was transferred to the Southern Pacific company.

Senator MORGAN. So you got entirely rid of your California property?

Mr. HUNTINGTON. No; I have the Coton House, where I live in the winter.

Senator MORGAN. I am talking about this stock of the Southern Pacific of California. It has been transferred to Kentucky?

Mr. HUNTINGTON. The franchise is a Kentucky franchise.

Senator MORGAN. Subject to Kentucky laws?

Mr. HUNTINGTON. Yes; and I am glad it is.

Senator MORGAN. I am, too. On that stock, or on the lease of the property (you do not know which), you are drawing dividends—getting lease money or track hire from the Kentucky company?

Mr. HUNTINGTON. For which?

Senator MORGAN. For the Southern Pacific of California.

Mr. HUNTINGTON. They own the shares, and of course whatever goes to the shares go to them. They are the proprietors. There is nothing singular about that. Whatever profits there were followed the shares; but I am sorry to say we have had no dividends.

Senator MORGAN. You do not want to have any?

Mr. HUNTINGTON. If we had any way of getting dividends and keeping up the property at the same time, we would be very glad to take the dividends.

Senator MORGAN. But still you had more than was necessary to keep the property up, and you expended it in extending the property?

Mr. HUNTINGTON. That is construction account; another account entirely.

Senator MORGAN. You consider it such good property that you are extending it as well as improving it?

Mr. HUNTINGTON. I think very well of that property. California is one of the best States in the Union. It has now 1,500,000 of people; and 25,000,000 of people could live there and get fat. It is the best State in the Union to live in; and I believe that, if we hold on to that property twenty-five or thirty years, there will not be as good a railroad property in the United States.

Senator MORGAN. Will it be as good as the Central Pacific?

Mr. HUNTINGTON. Yes; because it runs through a good country; we even "builded better than we knew."

Senator MORGAN. I think you stated that you had no personal interest in the Central Pacific?

Mr. HUNTINGTON. Yes; I have the same interest in it as ever.

Senator MORGAN. That is, a sentimental interest; but I am talking about a money interest. How many shares have you in it?

Mr. HUNTINGTON. Not more than 6,000 shares.

Senator MORGAN. You have had more?

Mr. HUNTINGTON. I do not know that I ever had.

Senator MORGAN. Have you ever sold any stock of the Southern Pacific of California or of any of these companies, or any of the stock of the Kentucky Company as low as 19 cents on the dollar?

Mr. HUNTINGTON. I do not think that I ever sold them at any price.

Senator MORGAN. You have always held that stock at a higher price than that?

Mr. HUNTINGTON. I could not sell it above the market price.

Senator MORGAN. There is none of it for sale at 50 cents on the dollar?

Mr. HUNTINGTON. Yes; I will let the Senator have all he wants at that price.

Senator MORGAN. I do not want to go into debt for it.

Mr. HUNTINGTON. I made my money by going in debt.

Senator MORGAN. I thought you made the most of it by paying your debts. What is the largest amount of stock that you ever owned in the Central Pacific at any time?

Mr. HUNTINGTON. I never owned very much. I owned some stock in the Contract and Finance Company.

Senator MORGAN. I am talking about the Central Pacific Company.

Mr. HUNTINGTON. I would not be positive that I ever had more than a couple of thousand shares.

Senator MORGAN. You have 6,000 shares now.

Mr. HUNTINGTON. I was thinking about old times.

Senator MORGAN. Two thousand shares is about all you owned?

Mr. HUNTINGTON. Until a long time after.

Senator MORGAN. When did you become the owner of 6,000 shares?

Mr. HUNTINGTON. I do not know; it may have been that the Contract and Finance Company may have distributed the shares of the Central Pacific that it owned. The Contract and Finance Company got money and paid all its debts, and it may then have distributed some shares.

Senator MORGAN. Did you say that the 6,000 shares which you now own were distributed to you by the Contract and Finance Company?

Mr. HUNTINGTON. They may have been.

Senator MORGAN. Have you ever bought any of the Central Pacific in the market?

Mr. HUNTINGTON. I do not believe I have.

Senator MORGAN. None at all?

Mr. HUNTINGTON. I do not recollect ever buying any, and I did not sell any except when I wanted money.

Senator MORGAN. You have sold some of the stock of your personal holding?

Mr. HUNTINGTON. I think so.

Senator MORGAN. How much of it have you sold?

Mr. HUNTINGTON. Not a great deal.

Senator FRYE. Did not Mr. Huntington go over that yesterday? He said he sold stock at 19.

Mr. HUNTINGTON. I do not know how much; it is years ago.

Senator MORGAN. You have got the 6,000 shares of Central Pacific stock now, and you think that you got it from the Contract and Finance Company; and you sold some stock just after the passage of the Thurman Act at 19 cents on the dollar?

Mr. HUNTINGTON. I did not say I sold it just after the passage of the Thurman Act. I said that I sold some, but I can not locate the time.

Senator MORGAN. You did locate it yesterday as just after the passage of the Thurman Act.

Mr. HUNTINGTON. I said it might have been after, or it might have been before.

Senator MORGAN. When was it?

Mr. HUNTINGTON. I do not know. I can find out from New York when it was that the price of the stock was 19; and that is the time I sold.

Senator MORGAN. You did not sell part of the 6,000 shares which you have got now?

Mr. HUNTINGTON. No.

Senator MORGAN. Where did you get these 6,000 shares?

Mr. HUNTINGTON. I may have got them from the Contract and Finance Company.

Senator MORGAN. So that you have got more than 6,000 shares from the Contract and Finance Company?

Mr. HUNTINGTON. I do not think so; but I may have got them from that company.

Senator MORGAN. And you do not know how much you sold at 19 cents on the dollar?

Mr. HUNTINGTON. I do not.

Senator MORGAN. And you never have bought any of these shares?

Mr. HUNTINGTON. I do not believe that I ever bought a share of the Central Pacific in the market.

Senator FRYE. Did you not testify yesterday that you took Crocker's stock when he went away?

Mr. HUNTINGTON. Yes; when he went to Europe we bought his stock at 12½ cents on the dollar. He went to Europe and was gone something like two years, and when he came back I asked him to take back his stock. He did not want to take it back, but I told him that we would like to have him come back into the company and go to work; and he finally did so.

Senator MORGAN. So he took his stock back?

Mr. HUNTINGTON. Yes; he took his stock back.

Senator MORGAN. Inasmuch as you are totally unable to recollect about this stock, have you books that will inform us how much of that stock you sold at 19 cents and when you sold it?

Mr. HUNTINGTON. I do not know that I can tell by my books; but I can tell by the stock list in New York. I can tell by the stock list when the price was 19.

Senator MORGAN. I have some questions to ask you as to the statement filed in writing relating to the Pacific Railroad Commission. You said:

I observe that the commission refers to the suits which were brought in California by Sam Brannon and others, as stockholders of the Central Pacific Railroad Company.

I have already stated that suits of a similar character were brought here in New York, where they were under my direct observation. The suits were defended in all the courts, and we were absolutely and entirely successful, and the plaintiffs were entirely defeated by decisions of the highest courts of the State of New York. As to the suits commenced in California, I can only say that if they had been under my observation I would have fought them in the same way and with the same results; but the suits were commenced for blackmail, and settled by others than myself, and for political reasons about which I knew and cared nothing, and when I heard of it I disapproved the settlement.

Who settled these suits?

Mr. HUNTINGTON. Governor Stanford, as I understand.

Senator MORGAN. For political reasons?

Mr. HUNTINGTON. The Governor was never much in railroads and was almost always in politics.

Senator MORGAN. Why do you say that the suits were commenced for blackmail?

Mr. HUNTINGTON. Because there were no good reasons why they should be commenced. They had complaints charging us with everything in the world, and I said to them, "Go to the courts and prove it." I rather flatter myself on my life record; I am pleased with it.

Senator MORGAN. Was that the case of Sam Brannon and R. O. Ives, plaintiffs against the Central Pacific Railroad Company of California and other defendants?

Mr. HUNTINGTON. I do not know about Ives. I have always known it as the Sam Brannon case.

Senator MORGAN. I have here a copy of what purports to be the bill and answer of this case. This is the suit to which you refer as a blackmailing suit, and as making accusations against you which were entirely unfounded and wrong. That is the suit you refer to, is it not?

Mr. HUNTINGTON. Yes; I only remember one Sam Brannon suit.

Senator MORGAN. In that bill it is charged that the total amount which you four gentlemen received in aid of the construction of the Central Pacific road was $156,825,360. There is one item in that which is probably very much exaggerated—the item of land—and I would like to find out about it.

Mr. HUNTINGTON. I will tell you all that I know.

Senator MORGAN. They say that the value of the lands granted by the United States was $50,208,000. Is that an exaggeration?

Mr. HUNTINGTON. I should say so.

Senator MORGAN. How much of it is an exaggeration?

Mr. HUNTINGTON. It is pretty much all an exaggeration.

Senator MORGAN. The lands were worth something?

Mr. HUNTINGTON. The Central Pacific got somewhere above 7,000,000 acres of land.

Senator MORGAN. Is that all?

Mr. HUNTINGTON. It was not eight millions. The California Pacific got 3,000,000 acres, but that was better land. Our 7,000,000 acres was mostly in Nevada and Utah. Have you ever been there, Senator?

Senator MORGAN. Yes.

Mr. HUNTINGTON. Well, what do you think that land is worth?

Senator MORGAN. I have no idea, Mr. Huntington. I suppose that when they get water to irrigate it, it is as fine land as any in the world.

Mr. HUNTINGTON. But there is no water there; that is the trouble. You know what Uncle Ben Wade said about that?

Senator MORGAN. No; I do not.

Mr. HUNTINGTON. He was going through there on the cars one day when he met an old Ohioan who had same cattle out there. He had 1,000 head of cattle. He was an old neighbor of Mr. Wade's in Ohio, and he got quite excited over the country, and said, "If we only had good water and good society, there is no better country in the world;" and Mr. Wade said, "Just the two things they lack in hell." I thought that a very good story.

Senator MORGAN. It seems from the census reports that they are building that country up pretty fast?

Mr. HUNTINGTON. The land is worth very little.

Senator MORGAN. I have here an official statement from Mr. Carroll P. Wright, census commissioner. It has an important summary, which I will have put into the record, calling your attention to only a few figures. It shows the increase in the value of real and personal property in specified States and Territories from 1870 to 1890. In States and Territories which feel the influence of the railroad system, showing the wonderful increase which railroads and the Almighty together have contributed to the property of this country. For instance, we will take Arizona. There is no other railroad line but yours there?

Mr. HUNTINGTON. The Atchison, Topeka and Sante Fe runs through it.

Senator MORGAN. The value of real and personal property in Arizona from 1870 to 1880 was $37,559,000?

Mr. HUNTINGTON. A State larger than New York.

Senator MORGAN. In 1890 it ran up to $147,880,000, being an increase of 361 per cent.

Mr. HUNTINGTON. I am not much surprised at that. That is toward the lower Gila; and there, as I stated, "We builded better than we knew."

Senator MORGAN. The increase of the number of people in Arizona from 1870 to 1880 was 30,782, and that number had increased in 1890 by 19,180, an increase of 47.3 in population. Then, take Utah. In 1880 the valuation of its real and personal property was $97,847,005, and in 1890 it was $235,411,274. The increase in population from 1870 to 1880 was 57,177, and the increase from 1880 to 1890 was 63,942.

Senator FRYE. Does that table give the increase in the valuation of lands in Nevada?

Senator MORGAN. Yes; in every one of the States under the influence of railroads.

Senator Morgan put the paper in evidence, as follows:

DEPARTMENT OF THE INTERIOR, CENSUS DIVISION,
Washington, February 17, 1896.

SIR: Your letter of the 15th instant, addressed to Commissioner Wright, asking a tabulated statement relative to the increase in wealth and population of a number of States directly affected by the transcontinental lines of railroad, was delivered at this office about noon Saturday. In order that the facts desired may be in your hands by the time specified, I at once directed the preparation of the statements, and have the honor to transmit them herewith. This will explain why your letter has not had the Commissioner's personal attention.

Very respectfully,

GEO. S. DONNELL,
Chief of Division.

Hon. JOHN T. MORGAN,
United States Senate.

Increase in true valuatian of real and personal property of specified States and Territories, 1870 to 1890.

States and Territories.	1880 to 1890.		1870 to 1880.	
	Amount.	Per cent.	Amount.	Per cent.
Minnesota	$899 851, 927	113.6	$563, 090, 410	245.9
Iowa	566, 348, 333	32.9	1, 003, 355, 250	139.8
Missouri	835, 902, 945	53.5	277, 077, 103	21.6
North Dakota / South Dakota	644, 147, 805	545.9	112, 400, 248	1, 873.3
Nebraska	890, 685, 514	231.4	315, 722, 517	457.5
Kansas	1, 039, 343, 501	136.7	571, 107, 986	302.2
Texas	1, 280, 576, 766	155.3	665, 947, 458	419
Arkansas	169, 147, 422	59.1	129, 605, 309	89.5
Montana	413, 135, 209	1032.5	24, 815, 478	165.3
Wyoming	115, 773, 710	214.8	46, 983, 252	671.1
Colorado	905, 712, 267	377.5	219, 756, 697	1099.0
New Mexico	182, 459, 897	373.5	17, 650, 207	55.2
Arizona	147, 880, 976	361.0	37, 559, 209	940.0
Utah	235, 411, 234	206.5	97, 840, 005	611.5
Nevada	24, 323, 668	15.6	124, 865, 988	402.8
Washington	698, 608, 726	1127.0	48, 437, 836	346.0
Oregon	436, 396, 194	283.4	102, 441, 068	197.0
California	1, 190, 733, 627	88.7	704, 232, 983	110.2
Idaho	178, 896, 591	616.9	22, 447, 319	374.1

Increase in population of specified States and Territories, 1870 to 1890.

States and Territories.	1880 to 1890.		1870 to 1880.	
	Number.	Per cent.	Number.	Per cent.
Minnesota	521,053	66.74	341,067	77.57
Iowa	287,281	17.68	430,595	36.06
Missouri	510,804	23.56	447,065	25.97
North Dakota / South Dakota	*a* 376,350	*a* 278.41	*b* 120,996	*b* 853.23
Nebraska	606,508	134.06	329,409	267.83
Kansas	431,000	43.27	631,697	173.35
Texas	643,774	40.44	773,170	94.45
Arkansas	325,654	40.58	318,054	65.65
Montana	93,000	237.49	18,564	90.14
Wyoming	39,916	192.01	11,671	128.00
Colorado	217,871	112.12	154,463	387.47
New Mexico	34,028	28.46	27,691	30.14
Arizona	19,180	47.43	30,782	318.72
Utah	63,942	44.42	57,177	65.88
Nevada	*c* 16,505	*c* 26.51	19,775	46.54
Idaho	51,775	158.77	17,611	117.41
Washington	274,274	365.13	51,161	213.57
Oregon	138,999	79.53	83,845	92.22
California	343,436	39.72	304,447	54.34

a North and South Dakota combined. Apportioning the population of Dakota Territory in 1888, North Dakota (36,909 in 1880) increased 145,810, or 395.05 per cent and South Dakota (98,268 in 1880) increased 230,540, or 234.60 per cent.

b Dakota Territory.

c Decrease.

Senator MORGAN. How did you dispose of the lands granted to the California Pacific?

Mr. HUNTINGTON. In building the Southern Pacific of California. The lands could be irrigated by the Colorado, the Gila, and the Salt rivers; and that property is going to be the garden spot of the United States from White River to Seneca Canyon.

Senator MORGAN. You thought so much of it that you took all your personal earnings from the roads you built in Virginia and put them in there?

Mr. HUNTINGTON. Not altogether. I put a couple of million of dollars that I made into these roads.

Senator MORGAN. Your big interest then, as far as railroads are concerned, is the Southern Pacific line?

Mr. HUNTINGTON. It is in the line from Portland south.

Senator MORGAN. That great sweep of railroad embraces the great interest which you hold?

Mr. HUNTINGTON. My great interest in railroads is west of the Mississippi.

Senator MORGAN. It is between Portland and New Orleans? It is on these lines? It is all located right there?

Mr. HUNTINGTON. Yes; it is all good property.

Senator MORGAN. What have you done with the Central Pacific lands?

Mr. HUNTINGTON. We have sold all the lands we could, and have got up to this time less than $8,000,000 for it, we paying ourselves for the surveying and probably other expenses, so that we have not made any more than that out of the land. We got no land in the plains in California. That land was nearly all covered in old Spanish grants, and the land which we got was in the mountains, and in Nevada and Utah. We did not get much land in Utah, because the lands in the mountains west of Salt Lake are worth very little. There is some very valuable land in Bear River Valley east of the Wahsatch Mountains, and right off the Wahsatch from Webber and Ogden and Bear rivers. There, there is a strip of valuable land, 80 miles wide.

Senator MORGAN. Have you sold that land?

Mr. HUNTINGTON. We did not have much land there. It went all to the Union Pacific. We bought that road from the Union Pacific.

Senator MORGAN. How much did you get for all the land you sold?

Mr. HUNTINGTON. I suppose that for the land we sold we have got at the average of $2 an acre.

Senator FRYE. At what amount do you put the full money value of all the lands which the Central Pacific received from the United States?

Mr. HUNTINGTON. I would not put it, I think, at $5,000,000. That amount, paid in, for all the land would be a sum on which the sales of the land would never keep up the interest.

Senator MORGAN. You have spoken very enthusiastically of all the value which your road added to the land of the people in California?

Mr. HUNTINGTON. Yes, but there is. Where water, and soil, and climate come together.

Senator MORGAN. There is water, and soil, and climate on a good deal of the land which you have got?

Mr. HUNTINGTON. Not in Nevada. Across Promontory Mountain you get into the Pequod Mountains and the Cedar Mountains, and I do not think we ever sold any land there except a little which we got in Humboldt Valley. There we have sold some; but when we get out of the valley on the mountains the land is not worth anything.

Senator MORGAN. Whatever value is added by the railroads to any of the land is equally added to yours?

Mr. HUNTINGTON. No doubt the fact of the railroad being there has made the half of the Government lands worth four times as much as the whole of them were worth before.

Senator MORGAN. And the same for your land?

Mr. HUNTINGTON. Yes. The half that the Government kept was worth four times, with the railroad, more than it was worth when there was no railroad.

Senator MORGAN. Besides that, you gentlemen have got from the Government a pretty large land grant on the Southern Pacific line?

Mr. HUNTINGTON. We did get some good land in the San Joaquin Valley; not much. Then we got to the Mojave Desert. I think we are going to have some good land from White River. I think we will get water there from the Colorado River, and make the land valuable, but up to the present time we would have taken 25 cents an acre for it.

Senator MORGAN. Some of the best lands in Alabama have sold at public sale for 15 cents an acre and you can not get them now for $500 an acre. You got some land between San Francisco and the California line?

Mr. HUNTINGTON. The California and Oregon grant was a grant which we did not get. The parties who got it undertook to build the road and failed, and we took it from them and completed the road.

Senator MORGAN. You got the land?

Mr. HUNTINGTON. Yes; that land is worth more.

Senator MORGAN. So that, taking it altogether, including the Central Pacific line and the lines from Oregon south to San Francisco and from San Francisco south through Arizona——

Mr. HUNTINGTON. We do not get any land in Arizona.

Senator MORGAN. You stop at Yuma, do you?

Mr. HUNTINGTON. Yes.

Senator MORGAN. Including all of these lands together, the companies which you now own and control have received from the Government of the United States about how many million acres?

Mr. HUNTINGTON. I should say 15,000,000 or 16,000,000.

Senator MORGAN. Is it not nearer 25,000,000?

Mr. HUNTINGTON. No; I do not think we got that much. I think the Central Pacific got 7,000,000, the Oregon and California about 3,000,000, and I doubt whether the Southern Pacific got more than 5,000,000 or 6,000,000. The question of our lands is in the courts there.

Senator MORGAN. You say that you have sold about $8,000,000 worth of the Central Pacific land?

Mr. HUNTINGTON. Yes; about that.

Senator MORGAN. Did you divide these sales in dividends on the stock?

Mr. HUNTINGTON. No; we issued a land-grant bond of $10,000,000, and when we sold land we redeemed the bonds.

Senator MORGAN. What did you issue land-grant bonds for?

Mr. HUNTINGTON. In building the Central Pacific the contract was that the Contract and Finance Company should have so much money and so much stock; gold went up so high that the money which we received from the sale of bonds fell short, and so the Central Pacific issued land-grant bonds and paid the Contract and Finance Company the balance which was due it.

Senator MORGAN. Then you took the bonds of the United States which were issued to you, and you sold the lands which had been granted to you, and you got money enough to make up the difference between the gold and the par?

Mr. HUNTINGTON. That is not fairly stated.

Senator MORGAN. State it fairly yourself.

Mr. HUNTINGTON. The Contract and Finance Company agreed to do the work for so much assets, and went to work and built the road. In doing that gold advanced. When we commenced, gold was not at a premium; but it went up so that we paid $222 in currency for $100 in gold. We paid for all the work, and all the lumber and material in California, in gold. I know that gold was worth so much, and that the work to be done cost so much.

Senator MORGAN. Did you not know how much gold you would have to use in the work?

Mr. HUNTINGTON. We did not expect to have to pay $222 in currency for $100 in gold. I sold Government bonds as low as 85 for currency, in order to buy gold.

Senator MORGAN. I am not asking about those bonds; I am asking about what you did with the money you got for the land?

Mr. HUNTINGTON. The Central Pacific paid it out for building the road.

Senator MORGAN. In addition to the subsidy which yougot in bonds, and in addition to the money which you got for the first-mortgage bonds, you got the proceeds of the sales of land to the amount of $8,000,000?

Mr. HUNTINGTON. What was the grant for, Senator Morgan, but to build the road?

Senator MORGAN. You can not stop to argue with me, Mr. Huntington, when I am asking you a question. I shall ask you that question again, and I want you to answer it. You may try to dodge as much as you please, but you must answer.

Senator FRYE. Mr. Huntington has a right to answer in his own way.

Senator MORGAN. But he has no right to make an argument in answering.

Mr. HUNTINGTON. I would like to have Senator Morgan know all that I know about this.

Senator MORGAN. I would be mighty glad to know all that you know about it.

Mr. HUNTINGTON. I wish you did.

Senator MORGAN. Come back to the question. What did you do with the $8,000,000 which you got for the land?

Mr. HUNTINGTON. We paid it for building the road, and, as I recollect—and you refreshed my mind the other day when you read that the contract was for so much money and so much stock—in selling the company's bonds and the Government bonds we did not get as much money as we agreed to pay, on account of the high price of gold, and therefore we issued a mortgage on the lands, and gave the money derived from that mortgage to build the road.

Senator MORGAN. On what lands?

Mr. HUNTINGTON. On the lands of the Central Pacific; and the money was given to the Contract and Finance Company.

Senator MORGAN. Did not the Government give the Central Pacific Company as much as it agreed to give?

Mr. HUNTINGTON. Yes; the Government agreed to give so much land and so much bonds. The Government did not give us any more than it agreed to give us, and we did not pay any more than we agreed to pay.

Senator MORGAN. The Government did not give you money at all?

Mr. HUNTINGTON. No; the Government gave us the bonds and the lands. The Central Pacific made a contract with the Contract and Finance Company to build the road for so much money and so much of its own stock. The Central Pacific sold its own first-mortgage bonds and the Government bonds and did not get gold enough to pay what it agreed to pay in gold to the Contract and Finance Company, because gold and currency parted after the contract was made. That being so, the Central Pacific fell in debt to the Contract and Finance Company and had not anything to pay it with excepting the land. On those lands (the lands which the Government had given to build the road) the Central Pacific issued a mortgage and gave the Contract and Finance Company the mortgage to pay that company what it lacked in gold. That seems to me very simple.

Senator MORGAN. Were those lands not under a lien in favor of the United States?

Mr. HUNTINGTON. I should say no; and I believe it has been decided that we had a right to mortgage the lands.

Senator MORGAN. And that does not interrupt the lien of the United States?

Mr. HUNTINGTON. No; if the United States wants to pay off the mortgage on the lands, I should like to have it do so.

Senator MORGAN. You sold the lands and carried the money to the Contract and Finance Company?

Mr. HUNTINGTON. Yes.

Senator MORGAN. Then you got $8,000,000, the proceeds of the sales of lands. You got all the Government bonds and all the first-mortgage bonds; and then you got all of the stock of the Central Pacific Company, which was issued in payment for this contract to build the road?

Mr. HUNTINGTON. We did not get it all; we got whatever we agreed to be paid. The whole stock of the Central Pacific is $100,000,000.

Senator FRYE. And the whole, together, did not build the road?

Mr. HUNTINGTON. No; when we got through the Contract and Finance

Company could not pay its debts out of the assets which it had; and it was only by carrying along the debt from year to year, till the stock appreciated, that we could pay the debt. As soon as people would buy the stock and I could see my way clear to paying the debts of the Contract and Finance Company, I commenced selling the shares, and they went up, until at the end we had something to the good.

The CHAIRMAN. In other words, the Contract and Finance Company held those assets until they advanced sufficiently in value to enable the company to pay its debts, which the Contract and Finance Company had incurred in carrying out this contract to build the road?

Mr. HUNTINGTON. Yes; exactly.

Senator MORGAN. State what it cost the Contract and Finance Company to build the road.

Mr. HUNTINGTON. I have stated to the Senator a number of times that I do not know; but I do not believe that the road could be built for less than $90,000,000 in money.

Senator MORGAN. And you got $116,000,000 in stock and bonds, besides $8,000,000 for land, making $124,000,000?

Mr. HUNTINGTON. Well, that is easy enough said. We bought a large block of this stock at 12½ cents, and I got the man who sold it to take it back two years afterwards at the same price. These are facts.

Senator MORGAN. That does not prove anything about the market price of the stock.

Mr. HUNTINGTON. Do you suppose that he would have sold his stock below the market price? I do not believe that we could have sold that stock at that time on the market at 10 per cent, although I believed then that it would be valuable at some time. I really want to have you know everything about it.

The CHAIRMAN. A resolution has been offered in the Senate by Senator Allen, and referred to this committee, which requires the committee to procure from the Central Pacific Company and from the Union Pacific Company information as to the cost of the construction of these roads, and then we are to ascertain the amount of Government aid furnished to the companies.

Mr. HUNTINGTON. I can give that right here, under oath.

The CHAIRMAN. I want it in the form of communications, to be furnished by the company.

Mr. HUNTINGTON. The Contract and Finance Company got $60,000,000 of Central Pacific stock and $27,000,000 of Government bonds and the land grant, which was worth $8,000,000, and we got nothing more.

Senator MORGAN. Yes; you got $27,000,000 of first mortgage bonds.

Mr. HUNTINGTON. Those are the bonds of the company. We got $240,000 in gold from the city of San Francisco. The building of that road was the cleanest piece of work ever done in the United States.

Senator MORGAN. Mr. Brannan, in his bill in equity, speaks about the bonds of the United States Government, $27,000,000; the first-mortgage bonds of the Central Pacific, $27,000,000; and of the second-mortgage bonds delivered to Stanford, Charles and E. B. Crocker, Huntington, Hopkins, A. P. Stanford, and Marsh and Miller, $15,601,000. Did that amount go the construction of the road?

Mr. HUNTINGTON. I do not know anything about the second mortgage.

Senator MORGAN. That is what is stated here in this bill in equity.

Mr. PAYSON (of counsel for the Central Pacific). That undoubtedly refers to a mortgage on the unaided portion of the line.

Senator MORGAN. It went to the construction of the road. Was that amount turned over to the Contract and Finance Company?

Mr. HUNTINGTON. I do not know. I do not think it was.

Senator FRYE. That had nothing to do with the aided portion of the line at all.

Senator MORGAN. They speak in this bill in equity of second-mortgage bonds, "issued and sold as above charged," $11,787,000.

Mr. HUNTINGTON. I do not know anything about that. What date was that?

Senator FRYE. What are you reading from, Senator Morgan?

Senator MORGAN. From a bill in equity here, I want to know the height and depth and breadth and width of Sam Brannan's offense. One of the charges he brings is—

That from and after the organization of said Contract and Finance Company all the contracts made and entered into in the name of the said Central Pacific for materials to be furnished for, and work to be done in, the construction, furnishing, and equipment of said railroad and telegraph line, were by said Leland Stanford, Hopkins, Huntington, C. & E. B. Crocker, and their confederates, composing a majority of the directors of said Central Pacific, voted to be let, and in fact were let and entered into by said Central Pacific of the one part and the said Contract and Finance Company of the other part, without advertising to let the same to the lowest bidders or bidder, and without in any manner inviting competition therefor.

That is one of the charges he makes. Is that true?

Mr. HUNTINGTON. I do not know. I read that complaint originally. It was got up to see how much money they could get out of us. I believe they got something out of Stanford. It was a blackmail concern originally; and it has been hashed and rehashed and published by a little clique in San Francisco from that time. It has been their breadwinner. But since I have been in control it has not been a breadwinner to anybody.

Senator MORGAN. Was Sam Brannan a stockholder in the Central Pacific?

Mr. HUNTINGTON. I do not know; he might have been and I might not have known it.

Senator MORGAN. He brought this suit as a stockholder?

Mr. HUNTINGTON. Yes.

Senator MORGAN. He had a right to call you to account in the courts.

Mr. HUNTINGTON. I do not say that he had not.

Senator MORGAN. Then why do you say that it was blackmail?

Mr. HUNTINGTON. Because everything we did was right and proper. He had a little interest, I presume, in the company and thought he would get money out of it. They did the same in New York.

Senator MORGAN. You say here, in this memorandum, referring to that suit, "if it had been under my supervision I would have fought them in the same way and with the same result."

Mr. HUNTINGTON. Yes, because I would have shown that everything which we had done was all right. But for some reason or other they did not want to get into the courts. I do not know why.

Senator MORGAN. As vice-president of the company, was not that under your supervision as much as under any other body's?

Mr. HUNTINGTON. Stanford was president and he was in California, while I was in New York. I had nothing to do with it.

Senator MORGAN. You state here in this memoranda which you have submitted:

I have already stated what an absolutely wild and reckless estimate of the cost of the road is contained in the report of the commission in pages 74 and 75, where it is stated as amounting to $36,000,000. They are mistaken in that. They do not know and could not know anything about the cost of constructing the road, while I knew all about it.

You do not know now?

Mr. HUNTINGTON. I do. After we got the profiles we said that we could build the road for about so much in assets, and we expected to make some money.

Senator MORGAN. How much did it cost?

Mr. HUNTINGTON. Sixty million dollars in shares of stock at its face value, $56,000,000 in bonds, and the land grant.

Senator MORGAN. And you spent it all in building the road?

Mr. HUNTINGTON. Yes.

Senator MORGAN. Did you spend any more?

Mr. HUNTINGTON. When we put in money we took it out again.

Senator MORGAN. How much in money had it cost you on the day you finished the road and drove the last spike in it? How much had it cost you to build and equip the road?

Mr. HUNTINGTON. It had cost the proceeds of $27,000,000 of Government bonds.

Senator MORGAN. That is not what I want. I want to know what it had cost you in money.

Mr. HUNTINGTON. That is the only way that I can get at it.

Senator MORGAN. You kept your books, and you know how much it cost you. How much money did you spend in building this road?

Mr. HUNTINGTON. All the money we got.

Senator MORGAN. You did not pay for the work in stock or bonds or lands. You paid for it in money. How much money did you spend?

Mr. HUNTINGTON. All the money which we got, and then we could not pay for it when we got through.

Senator MORGAN. You must not think, Mr. Huntington, that I am a child, and that you can evade answering my questions.

Mr. HUNTINGTON. I do not want to evade answering them.

Senator MORGAN. I will state the question again. You did not pay for the work in stock; you did not pay for it in bonds; you did not pay for it in lands; you paid for it in money.

Mr. HUNTINGTON. Yes; we paid for it in money.

Senator MORGAN. How much money was due for the building of that road at the time you finished it?

Mr. HUNTINGTON. I can not say. I should say somewhere in the neighborhood of $10,000,000 or $12,000,000.

Senator MORGAN. I do not mean the balance which was due. I am talking about what the road cost in money.

Senator FRYE. I think Mr. Huntington answered the question just as it was asked.

Senator MORGAN. Your answer as to ten or twelve millions means how much money you had lost?

Mr. HUNTINGTON. No; it means how much we owed when the road was finished.

Senator MORGAN. Here is a railroad company for which you build a road. How much did you charge that railroad company in money for that road? How much in money did your books show that you had expended in building that road?

Mr. HUNTINGTON. I can not say. I suppose the books of the Contract and Finance Company showed what that company had paid out; and Mr. Crocker's books would show what he paid out on his contract; and the books of the other seven contractors would show what they paid out on this 31 miles of road. But I never saw these items.

Senator MORGAN. I am talking about the Contract and Finance Company.

Mr. HUNTINGTON. I never saw their books.

Senator MORGAN. Therefore you can not state?

Mr. HUNTINGTON. No; but I know that we had not enough to pay our debts out of the assets which were left.

Senator MORGAN. I want to know what it cost the Contract and Finance Company to build the road—whether it broke you or whether it made you?

Mr. HUNTINGTON. It did not break us, and it did not make us.

Senator MORGAN. You know (if you know anything about it) and you say that the commission did not know what they were talking about?

Mr. HUNTINGTON. How could they?

Senator MORGAN. They could know after hearing your testimony; although, if they had to rely on such statements as you have made here, they could not find out.

Mr. HUNTINGTON. I gave them all that I knew. I was in New York while the Contract and Finance Company was building the road.

Senator MORGAN. I am willing to admit, Mr. Huntington, that you have successfully evaded the question, and I will not ask you any more on that subject. I want that to appear on the record.

Mr. HUNTINGTON. The stenographer will also put down, if he will, that Mr. Huntington did his very best to give the Senator all the knowledge which he had on the subject.

Senator MORGAN. That is all right. I would like you to make an explanation here. In this paper which you have submitted to the committee you say:

> As an illustration of the methods adopted by the Commission in ascertaining the cost of work, I would refer to the report at the foot of page 75, where they substituted a wholly unfounded assumption of their own for the testimony of Gen. G. M. Dodge, a well-known and experienced engineer, of undoubted ability and integrity, as to the actual cost of construction of the 47½ miles of the road from Promontory to Bonneville Table. General Dodge testified that the cost of this piece of road was $87,000 cash per mile, which would equal $4,132,500, notwithstanding which fact the Commissioners, for their own purposes, and without evidence, see fit to estimate its cost at $3,000,000. I have no doubt but that General Dodge's statement was right; and it should be understood that there were no important structures on the 47½ miles, and that no rolling stock went with it.

What charge do you bring against the commissioners there when you say that they did this for their own purposes?

Mr. HUNTINGTON. I do not know their purposes.

Senator MORGAN. Do you mean to accuse the gentlemen who composed that commission of having personal interests to subserve in making that report?

Mr. HUNTINGTON. There are many things in it which would seem to show that, like the Sam Brannan complaint, they had some animus somewhere. What it was I do not know. I certainly know that Mr. Anderson and Mr. Littler are very nice gentlemen.

Senator MORGAN. You mean to make an impeachment of the integrity of these officers?

Senator FRYE. Oh, no, Mr. Morgan; I think that Mr. Huntington did nothing of the kind.

Senator MORGAN. I do not care to know what you think of it, Mr. Frye.

Mr. HUNTINGTON. I think a good deal of both those gentlemen; I know Mr. Anderson very well and I know Mr. Littler very well, and I do not think that either of them would do anything wrong.

Senator FRYE. I do not wish Senator Morgan to say that he does not care what I say about it.

Senator MORGAN. In regard to this particular question, I do say it.

Senator FRYE. I require to be treated with politeness.

Senator MORGAN. You get treated with all the politeness you deserve. At the same time, when I am asking a witness a question, and he does not answer it as it should be answered, you have no right to interfere between me and the witness.

Senator FRYE. I do not think it legitimate to inquire of a witness whether he impeaches certain officers. To ask a witness to testify, inferentially, whether or not he is impeaching certain officers would not be tolerated in any court.

The CHAIRMAN. Every Senator here, of course, is on an equal footing, and it is fair to presume that all members of the committee will conduct their examinations with dignity and treat their colleagues with proper respect.

Senator MORGAN. Does the chair think it is proper for Mr. Frye to break into a question which the witness is answering?

The CHAIRMAN. The chair has no right to think anything about it. The chair is simply making a remark.

Senator MORGAN. If the Chair has no right to think anything about it, the Chair has no right to say anything about it, and if the Chair will permit that to be done, I shall make an appeal to the Senate.

The CHAIRMAN. Senator Frye has a perfect right, as your equal and mine, to speak regarding the line of cross-examination.

Senator MORGAN. He has a perfect right to do that, but he has no right to interrupt the witness between a question and answer.

(To Mr. Huntington.) You say in this memorandum:

Notwithstanding which facts the Commission, for their own purpose and without evidence, see fit to estimate the cost at $3,000,000.

Mr. HUNTINGTON. If that language suggests any wrong purpose on the part of the commission I will change it. I do not mean to say that, but I think that the commissioners had a lot of information such as you can get in San Francisco to-day. I think they were filled with stuff taken from the Examiner's story, while good men out there were attending to their own business. That is, I think, where the Commissioners got their information.

Senator MORGAN. The commissioners reported to the Government all these facts from sworn witnesses before them as sworn commissioners.

Mr. HUNTINGTON. I think that Mr. Anderson and Mr. Littler did not intend to do anything wrong; but I think they were filled up with wrong information either under oath or otherwise.

Senator MORGAN. What grounds have you for thinking so?

Mr. HUNTINGTON. Their views about the cost of that road being $3,000,000—they could not know anything about it. General Dodge says it cost $87,000 a mile. He was the engineer and knew all about it. That part of the road was not finished when we bought it, and we changed the line. It had not a wheel on it when we bought it. I think that we put into the road, giving it its proportion of rolling stock and completing it, $1,000,000 after we bought it. Now, that road did not cost as much as the building of our road cost, because we had to send our material around Cape Horn at an enormous cost for freight, and an enormous rate of interest, and we had to unload it at San Francisco and take it to Sacramento, and then haul it back nearly all the way across the continent, so that the Central Pacific would naturally cost 50 per cent more than the Union Pacific. I think Senator Morgan will say that.

Senator MORGAN. Then you mean to say that the commissioners did this for their own purpose?

Mr. HUNTINGTON. If my language means that, I will change it so far. I thought there might be something in it, but I do not know what it is. Perhaps it may have been Mr. Pattison's influence.

Senator MORGAN. Had not Mr. Pattison as much right to his judgment as any of the other commissioners?

Mr. HUNTINGTON. Yes.

Senator MORGAN. What you are inveighing against here is the judgment, not of a partisan, but of the other commissioners?

Mr. HUNTINGTON. Yes.

Senator MORGAN. Have you any reason for saying that Mr. Pattison was influenced by anything improper?

Mr. HUNTINGTON. If you will excuse me, I would rather not talk about Mr. Pattison.

Senator MORGAN. The people of the United States seem to have some respect for him.

Mr. HUNTINGTON. I suppose so.

Senator MORGAN. You say here—

It would be useless to undertake to discuss the tables which were stated to have been prepared by the accountant of the commission in regard to the cost of construction and the consideration received in bonds or stock or cash for such construction. I have already shown by my statements how utterly unfounded are the assumptions of that report in regard to the actual cash cost of the construction of the various properties.

Have you done that; have you shown the actual cash cost of the construction of the various properties?

Mr. HUNTINGTON. Yes; we knew what we had to do it with and we knew the work that we had to do, and we knew what we had when we got through the work. That is the best bookkeeping in the world. I did not follow the details of it.

Senator MORGAN. Then you state, with reference to what it cost you, and not what it cost the Central Pacific?

Mr. HUNTINGTON. To what it cost the Contract and Finance Company; and that company did not have enough when the work was completed to pay its debts.

Senator MORGAN. And you naturally identify yourself with the Central Pacific and with the Contract and Finance Company because you were part of both?

Mr. HUNTINGTON. Yes; and that was the only way to build the road.

Senator MORGAN. I am trying to find out, as if you were a stranger to the Central Pacific Company, how much the building of the road cost the Central Pacific Company?

Mr. HUNTINGTON. It cost so much in stock and so much in bonds and so much in lands.

Senator MORGAN. Do you mean to say it was paid for in those specific articles and not in money at all?

Mr. HUNTINGTON. The Central Pacific paid part in money and part in land and stock of the Central Pacific.

Senator MORGAN. The next question is how much money did the Contract and Finance Company pay out to complete the road?

Mr. HUNTINGTON. We paid out all we got.

Senator MORGAN. Then you have no particular reason for saying how utterly unfounded is the estimate of the Commissioners in this report?

Mr. HUNTINGTON. I have, because I say we paid out all the money that we got, and the cost was very much more.

Senator MORGAN. If that is the best answer that you can make I suppose we can go on. The integrity of this Commission can not be assailed by testimony like that.

Mr. HUNTINGTON. I think it is the best way in the world of arriving at the cost of anything.

Senator MORGAN. You say here—

As to the charge of using money to influence legislation, I will say that no money was ever used by me or anybody connected with our companies with my knowledge for the purpose of influencing legislation, except that, from time to time, different persons have been employed in various States and Territories and at Washington to see that the facts in regard to pending legislative matters were thoroughly and fully understood by the legislators who had to pass upon them.

Do you mean people employed in Washington as your lobby?

Mr. HUNTINGTON. They would be people employed to do certain things for which they received pay.

Senator MORGAN. What certain things?

Mr. HUNTINGTON. What is stated there—to explain things; that is done everywhere.

Senator MORGAN. I do not want to try to prove that you paid money to members of legislatures or to members of the House or Senate. I do not think that has any particular bearing on this particular case at this particular time.

Mr. HUNTINGTON. Still I would like to say as a witness, when that question comes up, that I never did pay any money to anybody directly to influence his vote. Of course I might hire somebody to go and explain a bill to a member of the legislature or to a Member of Congress and get him to vote for it by giving him all the facts in the case. I understand the trouble to be that legislators have so much to do that they can not examine every subject; and while I can not get to talk with them, almost every Member has somebody in his district who knows him and who can sit down beside him and talk the matter over with him. I can not do so if I would, and I have to get it done by others. I see that the great London and Northwestern Railway spent £500,000 to get their charter through Parliament, and nobody supposed that they bought a vote with it.

Senator MORGAN. If they did not buy votes they violated the English custom. We have not yet got to that as a regular business.

Mr. HUNTINGTON. I supposed that it was paid to attorneys.

Senator MORGAN. This report of the commission states that you had paid out a very large sum of money in this way.

Mr. HUNTINGTON. They state it at over $2,000,000. I told them that it must be more than that.

Senator MORGAN. You told them so in your deposition?

Mr. HUNTINGTON. I think I did. One railroad man told me not long ago that in Albany he always calculated to spend $250,000 a year for attorneys to go there and explain matters.

Senator MORGAN. Did that $2,000,000 which you spent come out of your private pocket?

Mr. HUNTINGTON. No.

Senator MORGAN. Where did it come from?

Mr. HUNTINGTON. From the Contract and Finance Company, I suppose.

Senator MORGAN. Did you keep an account of it?

Mr. HUNTINGTON. Every month I sent my accounts to California and had a settlement.

Senator MORGAN. Did you take receipts for the money you paid out?

Mr. HUNTINGTON. Not generally. Mr. Fancher was there, and Mr. Searle was there, and other men. I never took receipts when I found men whom I could trust.

Senator MORGAN. You trust them and say nothing about it?

Mr. HUNTINGTON. Yes.

Senator MORGAN. That is one of the faiths that remove mountains.

Mr. HUNTINGTON. I suppose so.

Senator MORGAN. You are not doing that something now, are you—paying lobbyists to help us?

Mr. HUNTINGTON. No; I am doing it very largely myself—I and Mr. Boyd and Mr. Payson, our regular attorney.

Senator MORGAN. You quit the practice then that you have been speaking of?

Mr. HUNTINGTON. Well, yes; I think so.

Senator MORGAN. You do not find it necessary now in order to get a bill through to pay out $2,000,000?

Mr. HUNTINGTON. That amount was scattered all over the United States, and over twenty-five or twenty-six years.

Senator MORGAN. It was all the better for being scattered. You are not doing that now?

Mr. HUNTINGTON. No; there may be some little expenses of that kind; probably there are. I send my accounts to California.

Senator MORGAN. You say there are probably some little expenses of that kind. What are they?

Mr. HUNTINGTON. I can not say; they are all proper and legal.

Senator MORGAN. I suppose the propriety of them depends entirely upon a man's recognition of what is proper and improper?

Mr. HUNTINGTON. Yes.

Senator MORGAN. Every man judges that for himself?

Mr. HUNTINGTON. Anybody brought up in Connecticut, as I was, would get the right start.

Senator MORGAN. When he had lived to be a pretty old man he might be out of the way?

Mr. HUNTINGTON. I do not know about that. When I get there, I will judge better.

Senator MORGAN. Quite a number of letters were produced in evidence in a suit between you and Mrs. Colton?

Mr. HUNTINGTON. Yes; four or five hundred.

Senator MORGAN. Did you read them?

Mr. HUNTINGTON. I read some letters.

Senator MORGAN. Did you read those letters?

Mr. HUNTINGTON. I read those that I wrote.

Senator MORGAN. Did you read all that were attributed to you in that contest?

Mr. HUNTINGTON. I did not. I looked over them, I presume. The thing was published, but I did not read them.

Senator MORGAN. Have you seen any of them?

Mr. HUNTINGTON. The fact is that I have never read them. They are published once in a while.

Senator MORGAN. When you did read them, did you recognize them?

Mr. HUNTINGTON. Some of them.

Senator MORGAN. You are not prepared to deny that they were all true?

Mr. HUNTINGTON. No; I am not prepared to deny that they were all true.

Senator MORGAN. Have you ever seen those letters since you wrote them?

Mr. HUNTINGTON. No further than that somebody brought me a paper in which they were printed.

Senator MORGAN. I mean the original letters?

Mr. HUNTINGTON. No; I have not.

Senator MORGAN. Has any agent of yours ever seen them?

Mr. HUNTINGTON. No; I think not. When I was in California four different parties came to sell them to me after they were stolen out of my office, or perhaps I should say taken out. I told the parties to sell them to some newspaper. I said that those I had written I did not want to read because I knew what was in them, and that those I didn't write I did not want to read, either.

Senator MORGAN. Here is a certified statement of your real estate and property subject to taxation at the time you began business in Sacramento, 1861, 1862, 1863, and 1864 [handing the paper to witness].

Mr. HUNTINGTON (after looking at the paper). I do not remember anything about it. It may be all right.

Senator FRYE (to Senator Morgan). What is it; an assessment list?

Senator MORGAN. An assessment list of Mr. Huntington's property in Sacramento.

Mr. HUNTINGTON. I do not remember much about it.

Senator FRYE (to Senator Morgan). Does that paper purport to be a certified copy?

Senator MORGAN. Yes, sir; a certified copy under seal.

Mr. HUNTINGTON. I do not remember anything about it. I was in New York mostly those years, excepting that my money was there largely; I do not know anything about this statement.

Senator MORGAN. Did you have any real estate in New York?

Mr. HUNTINGTON. No; I do not think I did.

Senator MORGAN. How much money did you keep on hand there on an average?

Mr. HUNTINGTON. I do not know; I kept some money.

Senator MORGAN. How much?

Mr. HUNTINGTON. I do not remember how much. I always had enough to pay my debts.

Senator MORGAN. You did not owe any debts, did you?

Mr. HUNTINGTON. Yes; I owed a great many debts.

Senator MORGAN. Large ones?

Mr. HUNTINGTON. Yes; I have been owing money in New York pretty much all the time since I went there.

Senator MORGAN. I suppose when you say you had enough to pay your debts that you do not mean to say that you had any great surplus after paying your debts?

Mr. HUNTINGTON. No; I had something. I was doing a pretty large business those years.

Senator MORGAN. Did you have any assessment made on your money in New York?

Mr. HUNTINGTON. I do not think there was.

Senator MORGAN. In accounting for your assets in that examination you have not made any reference to the money you had in New York. I would like to know exactly how much you had and what money you refer to as constituting part of your estate in New York.

Mr. HUNTINGTON. I do not know how much I did have. I was living there then. If I knew how much, I would tell you, and be very glad to do so.

Senator MORGAN. Do you know anything about the contract which was signed or required to be signed by the merchants and shippers of San Francisco, that was called the "pink contract?"

Mr. HUNTINGTON. I do not think I ever heard of it before.

Senator MORGAN. It is printed in an appendix of a report to the senate and assembly of California in 1883, page 133, volume 3. Do you know anything about it?

Mr. HUNTINGTON. No; I never heard of it; or, if I did, it has passed entirely out of my mind.

Senator MORGAN. Have you any recollection of any contract which provided for an examination of shippers' books by the company if it is suspected that the shipper is not acting in good faith in sending all of his goods by the company lines. Has there been any contract of that sort?

Mr. HUNTINGTON. No; I do not think I recollect it. I am quite sure I never heard of it, and still I may have.

Senator MORGAN. And also of breaking up packages en route if the company suspected that they contained anything not in the bills of lading? Do you recollect any contract which contained that?

Mr. HUNTINGTON. I do not.

Senator MORGAN. Do you not know that your company did exact a contract of that kind commonly called the "pink contract" from merchants and others in relation to shipments of freight on your lines?

Mr. HUNTINGTON. No.

Senator MORGAN. And that if they did not sign that contract they would not be entitled to equal accommodation with other people?

Mr. HUNTINGTON. No. I may say, however, that that might be a very proper thing to do.

Senator MORGAN. If they did do it, would it be all right?

Mr. HUNTINGTON. I should think it a very proper thing. Goods are shipped according to their value. In one instance, a case of such weights, paying a half a cent a pound, was shipped from San Francisco, and it contained a case of cutlery which should have been shipped at 3 cents a pound. In another instance, the ship *Eldorado* went on the rocks, and we found a case of kid gloves which was shipped as burlaps. The case of kid gloves would be worth $500 a case, while the burlaps would be worth only $50.

Senator MORGAN. Were rebates of freight allowed to merchants who signed the "Pink contract?"

Mr. HUNTINGTON. Not that I know of. If a man sent 1,000 kegs of nails he got a little better price than if he only sent 1; and if a merchant gave all his business to the company he was entitled to a little rebate. I think he was entitled to it. If a man wants to buy from a merchant a bale of sheeting it would be one price, but if he took 20 bales it would be another price.

Senator MORGAN. Do you know that these reductions and abatements amounted to the sum of $1,022,000 in 1864?

Mr. HUNTINGTON. I do not.

Senator MORGAN. You know nothing about it?

Mr. HUNTINGTON. I do not.

Senator MORGAN. Do not your books show that rebates were made?

Mr. HUNTINGTON. They might. I am not a bookkeeper. I keep away from books as far as I can.

Senator MORGAN. You would be apt to know, as president of the company, whether in a single year (1864) $1,060,000 had been allowed to customers for rebates?

Mr. HUNTINGTON. I would not suppose that any such amount, if any, was allowed. If there was, the matter is all settled from month to month among the traffic men and would not naturally come to me. That is one of the disadvantages of having so many roads. I have often said that if all the roads in the United States could be owned by one company rates could be put down 5 per cent and more money made than is made now. I see that one company has had $7,000,000 of unpaid vouchers for rebates of that kind.

Senator MORGAN. In 1884, or about that time, was there not some arrangement with the merchants of San Francisco that, in order to get rebates, they should send all their shipments by your line?

Mr. HUNTINGTON. I think that there was such an arrangement, but I do not know anything of the details; still, I have heard of it before, somewhere.

Senator MORGAN. You have heard that the merchants of San Francisco signed a contract by which everything should be shipped over your lines in consideration of these rebates?

Mr. HUNTINGTON. If they shipped all their business I should say they would be entitled to a little rebate. In merchandizing, where a man takes 1,000 kegs of nails, he gets a little rebate; and I should think that if a merchant gave all his business to a railroad company it could afford to give him a little rebate. I should say that that would be business anywhere in the world.

The CHAIRMAN. Is there any law in California preventing that?

Mr. HUNTINGTON. I do not know. I think not. We must treat all men alike. If one man comes with 1,000 kegs of nails and another man comes with 1,000 kegs, they must have the same rate of freight.

Senator MORGAN. If two men were to ship 1,000 kegs of nails on your road, and if one of them signed this "Pink contract" and the other refused to sign it, would you have the right to give a better rate to the man who signed it?

Mr. HUNTINGTON. The question was about getting all the business. Of course, if the 1,000 kegs of nails were all they sent, I should think it would be quite wrong to give one a better rate than the other.

Senator MORGAN. I understood you to say that you did have some recollection of it.

Mr. HUNTINGTON. I think I have.

Senator MORGAN. You are not aware that litigation has taken place between your company and the merchants of San Francisco about this "Pink contract?"

Mr. HUNTINGTON. I never heard of it before.

Senator MORGAN. You are not aware that the litigation has got into the newspapers of the State, and has been printed there?

Mr. HUNTINGTON. I do not think I ever heard of it. If I did, it has gone out of my mind. I do not read newspapers very much. I think that half a column a week would cover all my newspaper reading.

Senator MORGAN. As far as I am concerned, I will not ask Mr. Huntington any more questions.

Senator FRYE. This examination has lasted a long while and has gone over a great deal of ground. I suppose that the witness will have the right, after his testimony is presented, to examine it and to make corrections?

Senator MORGAN. I shall insist on their being made in the presence of the committee.

Mr. HUNTINGTON. Of course, I do not pretend to carry the details of business in my mind, and I am asked questions very frequently which I ought to know, but do not know. I have endeavored to give Senator Morgan the best that I know.

The committee adjourned until Friday, March 13, at 10.30 a. m.

CENTRAL PACIFIC RAILROAD.

The following communications were received from Mr. C. P. Huntington and were made part of his testimony:

23 Broad Street, New York, *March 17, 1896.*

Dear Sir: One of your committee requested information regarding the amount of fruit or fruit product in California. I telegraphed to California for the facts and send you herewith the figures they have sent me. I have no doubt they are correct. I believe the object of the member who asked the information was to see how much of the tonnage was not perishable, so that it could have the world's market and take any route, and how much was perishable and necessarily had to take a short route and be limited in the time it could be kept and the distance it could be transported.

Yours truly,

C. P. Huntington.

Hon. John H. Gear,
Chairman Committee on Pacific Railroads,
United States Senate, Washington, D. C.

Statement of tonnage of green fruit from California to the East.

Year.	Deciduous.	Citrus.	Total.
	Pounds.	*Pounds.*	*Pounds.*
1891	83,200,000	37,400,000	120,600,000
1892	97,000,000	19,200,000	116,800,000
1893	149,000,000	65,600,000	214,600,000
1894	167,600,000	43,200,000	210,808,000
1895	123,000,000	99,000,000	222,000,000
Total	620,400,000	264,400,000	884,800,000

Statement of tonnage of dried fruit and wines, California to the East.

DRIED FRUIT.

Year.	Raisins.	Prunes.	Grapes.	Figs.	Other.	Total.
	Pounds.	*Pounds.*	*Pounds.*	*Pounds.*	*Pounds.*	*Pounds.*
1891	37,000,000	23,200,000	5,400,000	50,000	33,000,000	99,250,000
1892	43,800,000	20,000,000	5,200,000	86,000	28,600,000	97,686,000
1893	67,200,000	42,000,000	3,800,000	500,000	30,800,000	144,300,000
1894	86,200,000	40,400,000	4,000,000	800,000	51,800,000	183,200,000
1895	88,200,000	61,600,000	1,000,000	1,400,000	52,400,000	204,600,000
Total	323,000,000	187,200,000	19,400,000	2,836,000	196,600,000	729,036,000

WINES.

Year.	Rail lines, Southern Pacific Company.	Panama route.	Cape Horn route.
	Pounds.	*Pounds.*	*Pounds.*
1891	58,500,000	18,800,000	27,800,000
1892	66,000,000	16,000,000	28,600,000
1893	88,400,000	8,400,000	24,000,000
1894	116,000,000	8,800,000	13,400,000
1895	112,800,000	25,200,000	7,200,000
Total	441,700,000	77,200,000	101,000,000

Note.—Atchison, Topeka and Santa Fe takings unknown; probably not to exceed one-tenth of that shown above as moving over Southern Pacific Company's rails.

23 BROAD STREET, NEW YORK, *March 20, 1896.*

DEAR SIR: I beg to send you herewith statements comparing the passenger and freight earnings on the Southern Pacific Company's lines, with those of the more thickly settled States of the East; also a statement showing comparative earnings on the Southern Pacific Company's lines, and those of certain groups of States; also a statement showing the passenger rates from London on the London and Northwestern Railway, which, I think, will prove interesting and instructive. Statement No. 3 illustrates the density of travel and tonnage, showing the earnings from passengers and freight *per mile of road*, but a more graphic illustration of this as between Eastern and Western States (Atlantic and Pacific coast States) is shown in the diagrams of density of passenger and freight traffic, as set forth in the report of the Interstate Commerce Commission for the year ending June 30, 1894.

As you will see, these statements make a very favorable showing for the Southern Pacific lines, considering the price of fuel; and from the last statement you will perceive that the third-class fares on the London and Northwestern Railway are just about the same as the regular (first class) fares on the Southern Pacific.

Very truly, yours,

C. P. HUNTINGTON.

Hon. JOHN H. GEAR,
Chairman Committee on Pacific Railroads,
United States Senate, Washington, D. C.

P. S.—It includes also the Central Pacific.

No. 1.—*Memorandum comparing company's earnings per ton per mile on Southern Pacific Company's lines with those of the more thickly settled States in the East, as stated in the railroad commissioners' reports of said States.*

	Cents.
Southern Pacific system:	
Year 1894	1.171
Year 1895	1.137
Maine (as average is not published, the principal railroad systems are quoted, year 1895):	
Bangor and Aroostook	1.911
Boston and Maine	1.545
Maine Central	1.412
Massachusetts (Railroad Commissioner's Report for 1894, p. 58)	1.330
Connecticut (Railroad Commissioner's Report for 1894, p. 123)	1.427
Illinois (Railroad Commissioner's Report for 1894, p. 103)	1.213

No. 2.—*Memorandum comparing company's earnings per passenger per mile on Southern Pacific Company's lines with those of the more thickly settled States in the East, as stated in the railroad commissioners' reports of said States.*

	Cents.
Southern Pacific system:	
Year 1894	1.916
Year 1895	2.004
Maine (Railroad Commissioner's Report, year 1895, as average is not published, the principal railroad systems in Maine are quoted):	
Bangor and Aroostook	2.421
Boston and Maine	1.745
Maine Central	2.284
Massachusetts (Railroad Commissioner's Report for 1894, p. 56)	1.800
Connecticut (Railroad Commissioner's Report for 1894, p. 122)	1.802
Illinois (Railroad Commissioner's Report for 1894, p. 102)	2.312

No. 3.—*Memorandum comparing certain statistical data published in the Annual Report of the Interstate Railroad Commission for the year ending June 30, 1894, in respect to Group No. I, constituting the New England States, Group No. IX, constituting Louisiana, Texas, and part of New Mexico, and Group X, constituting part of New Mexico and the States of California, Nevada, Oregon, Washington, Utah, and Idaho, with same data for Southern Pacific Company.*

PASSENGER.	Southern Pacific Company.	Group I.	Group IX.	Group X.
Earnings per passenger per mile .... cents..	2.004	1.854	2.444	2.046
Earnings per passenger train mile .... do...	1.18.291	1.25.607	1.00.670	1.39.400
Earnings per mile of road	$1,667.02	$5,248.58	$1,024.37	$1,616.33
FREIGHT.				
Earnings per ton mile .... cents..	1.137	1.243	1.209	1.343
Earnings per train mile .... do...	1.92.544	1.57.009	1.64.779	1.94.779
Earnings per mile of road	$4,089.02	$5,229.02	$2,883.93	$2,791.85

The statistics for the Southern Pacific Company are for the year 1895.

London and Northwestern Railway Company, passenger rates from London.

Station.	From London.	Rate.			Rate per mile.		
		First class.	Second class.	Third class.	First class.	Second class.	Third class.
	Miles.				*Cents.*	*Cents.*	*Cents.*
Watford Junction	17.50	$0.60	$0.42	$0.33	3.42	2.40	1.88
St. Albans	24	.64	.48	.39	2.66	2.00	1.62
Wolverton	52.50	1.92	1.32	1.05	3.65	2.51	2.00
Kenilworth	99	3.66	2.80	1.95	3.69	2.83	1.97
Crewe	158	5.80	4.62	3.16	3.67	2.92	2.00
Liverpool	200	6.96	5.22	3.96	3.48	2.61	1.98
Kendal	251.25	8.48	6.64	5.00	3.37	2.64	1.99
Keswick	300	10.08	7.86	5.78	3.36	2.62	1.92
Greenore	344.50	10.80	8.40	5.04	3.13	2.43	1.46
Edinburgh	400	13.80	....	7.84	3.45	....	1.96
Perth	450	15.80	....	8.74	3.51	....	1.94
Oban	504	17.28	....	9.82	3.42	....	1.94

WASHINGTON, D. C., *March 13, 1896.*

The committee met at 10.30 a. m.

Present, Senators Gear (chairman), Wolcott, Frye, Brice, and Stewart.

THE UNION PACIFIC RAILWAY.

EXAMINATION OF OLIVER W. MINK.

OLIVER W. MINK, sworn and examined:

Senator WOLCOTT. Mr. Mink, you are one of the receivers of the Union Pacific Railway Company?

Mr. MINK. I am.

Senator WOLCOTT. How long have you been connected with the organization of the Union Pacific Company?

Mr. MINK. I have been one of the receivers since October, 1893. Prior to that time I was connected with the Union Pacific Railway Company and its constituents since 1872.

Senator WOLCOTT. In all, your knowledge of the road extends back for nearly twenty-five years?

Mr. MINK. Certainly.

Senator WOLCOTT. As a receiver what is your particular branch of the business?

Mr. MINK. Personally, I have had charge of the duty of looking after the accounts and finances.

Senator WOLCOTT. That had been your duty for several years?

Mr. MINK. Yes; in the days of the corporation.

Senator WOLCOTT. You have been stationed usually in Boston?

Mr. MINK. Yes; during the days of the corporation. Since the receivership I have been in New York.

Senator WOLCOTT. Have you a table showing the earnings of the road since the receivership?

Mr. MINK. I have.

Senator WOLCOTT. The receivership commenced when?

Mr. MINK. It dates from October 13, 1893.

Senator WOLCOTT. Have you before you a statement showing the earnings from the date of the receivership until December 31, 1895?

Mr. MINK. I have.

Senator WOLCOTT. That covers about how many months?

Mr. MINK. That covers twenty-six and one-half months.

Senator WOLCOTT. What are the portions of the Union Pacific system covered by that statement?

Mr. MINK. The statement that I have here covers all the railroads and other parts of the system in the hands of the receivers.

Senator WOLCOTT. Describe the property.

Mr. MINK. The Union Pacific Railway embraces substantially 1,822 miles; and all of the other companies go to make up what is generally known as the Union Pacific system.

Senator WOLCOTT. Give the names of those constituent lines.

Mr. MINK. Boise City Railway and Terminal Company; Carbon Cutoff Railroad Company; Atchison, Colorado and Pacific Railroad Company; Atchison, Jewell County and Western Railroad Company; Denver Leadville and Gunnison Railway Company; Echo and Park City Railway Company; Junction City and Fort Kearney Railway Company; Kansas Central Railroad Company; Kearney and Black Hills Railway Company; Laramie, North Park and Pacific Railroad and Telegraph Company; Montana Railway Company; Omaha and Republican Valley Railway Company; Oregon Short Line and Utah Northern Railway Company; Oregon Railway and Navigation Company; Oregon Railway Extensions Company; Washington and Idaho Railroad Company; St. Joseph and Grand Island Railroad Company; Kansas City and Omaha Railroad Company; Salina and Southwestern Railway Company; Solomon Railroad Company; Union Pacific, Lincoln and Colorado Railway Company; Union Pacific, Brighton and Boulder Branch; Union Pacific, Denver and Gulf Railway Company. Besides those railroad companies the receivers also have charge of the following miscellaneous companies: Boulder Valley and Central City Wagon Road Company; Boseman Coal Company; Callaway Improvement Company; Green River Waterworks Company; Loveland Pass Mining and Railroad Tunnel Company; Morrison Stone, Lime, and Town Company; Rattle Snake Creek Water Company; Union Land Company; Union Pacific Coal Company, and Wood River Improvement Company.

Senator FRYE. Have you charge of all of the coal mines which the Union Pacific Railway Company owned six or eight years ago?

Mr. MINK. Yes, sir; they are all owned to-day by the Union Pacific Coal Company.

The CHAIRMAN. Are they in your hands as receivers?

Mr. MINK. Yes.

Senator WOLCOTT. As to those railroad companies that you have enumerated; some of them have since passed out of your hands as receivers, have they not?

Mr. MINK. Yes. The Denver, Leadville and Gunnison Railway property was taken out of our hands on the 7th of August, 1894. The Union Pacific, Denver and Gulf Railway property was taken out of our hands on the 18th of December, 1893, and the Oregon Railway and Navigation Company system was taken out of our hands on the 3d of July, 1894.

Senator WOLCOTT. How much railway mileage have you still left as receiver?

Mr. MINK. Something over 5,000 miles.

Senator WOLCOTT. Of those 5,000 miles how many miles are included in what is called the Government aided road?

Mr. MINK. Fourteen hundred and thirty miles, owned by the Union Pacific Company, and 100 miles, owned by the Central Branch of the Union Pacific Railway Company.

Senator WOLCOTT. That 1,400 miles includes the Kansas Pacific?

Mr. MINK. Yes.

Senator WOLCOTT. In this table of earnings which you present do you show separately the earnings of the Government-aided portions of the line?

Mr. MINK. I do not. I can have it done without difficulty.

Senator WOLCOTT. I desire that you shall furnish to the committee a statement showing the earnings and expenses of those portions of the line known as the Government-aided line, so far as practicable, since the receivership.

Mr. MINK. I will do so.

Senator WOLCOTT. The statement that you have here shows, in addition to the 1,400 miles of Government-aided line, the line between Denver and Kansas City, and the line between Denver and Cheyenne?

Mr. MINK. Yes; about 400 miles in addition.

Senator WOLCOTT. So that the whole line concerning which your statement is applicable would be, roughly speaking, from Kansas City to Denver, from Denver to Cheyenne, and from Council Bluffs to Ogden?

Mr. MINK. Yes; including also the line from Leavenworth to Lawrence and Kansas City.

Senator WOLCOTT. What are the gross earnings?

Mr. MINK. The gross earnings of the 1,822 miles of the Union Pacific Railway Company from October 13, 1893, to December 31, 1895, are $32,832,602.

Senator WOLCOTT. A period of how many months?

Mr. MINK. A period of twenty-six and one-half months.

Senator WOLCOTT. And what are the gross expenses?

Mr. MINK. The operating expenses were $21,179,233.

Senator WOLCOTT. Will you file a copy of your statement?

Mr. MINK. Yes.

Senator WOLCOTT. Naturally, you deduct your taxes and the United States earnings withheld?

Mr. MINK. Yes.

Senator WOLCOTT. And you show the interest paid on coupon orders. What is the amount of that interest paid?

Mr. MINK. $3,509,265.

Senator WOLCOTT. What is meant by the phrase "coupon orders"?

Mr. MINK. Orders of the court to pay coupons.

Senator WOLCOTT. On what securities have those payments been made?

Mr. MINK. On the Union Pacific main line, first mortgage 6 per cent bonds, $1,634,070; on the Union Pacific sinking fund eights, $149,200; on the Omaha Bridge eights, $22,600; on the collateral trust sixes, $110,160; on the Eastern Division bonds, first mortgage, Kansas Division and Leavenworth Branch, $67,200; on the Middle Division sixes, Kansas Division and Leavenworth Branch, $121,890; on the consolidated mortgage sixes, Kansas Division and Leavenworth Branch, $351,600; on the collateral trust five per cents, $116,925; on the Omaha Bridge fives, $52,800; on the equipment trust fives, $33,475; on the collateral trust notes, $668,835; and on the Denver Extension, $176,610; making a total of $3,505,365.

Senator WOLCOTT. Were those different coupons paid on the application of the receivers or on the order of the court, of its own motion?

Mr. MINK. Never on the order of the court of its own motion; almost always on the application of the receivers.

Senator WOLCOTT. Who directed those applications? Was it the initial action of the receivers?

Mr. MINK. Generally the initial action of the receivers or of a majority of them.

Senator WOLCOTT. How often have the five receivers met as a united body?

Mr. MINK. The majority of the receivers reside in New York. Our meetings are not daily, but quite frequent. Mr. Clark is in Omaha, Mr. Doane in Chicago, Mr. Coudert is a lawyer in New York, Mr. Anderson resides in New York, and I am in New York constantly. I pretend to live in Boston, but I am most of the time in New York.

Senator WOLCOTT. Give a general idea of how often the receivers meet.

Mr. MINK. I should say they meet formally perhaps twice a week

Senator WOLCOTT. And informally every day, I suppose?

Mr. MINK. Yes.

Senator WOLCOTT. If two of you met, would that be informally?

Mr. MINK. Yes; a majority of the receivers would constitute a formal meeting.

Senator WOLCOTT. Then, as a rule, three of you get together about twice a week?

Mr. MINK. I should say so.

Senator WOLCOTT. Then, on the united action of the receivers these applications to the court are generally made?

Mr. MINK. Yes.

Senator WOLCOTT. The first mortgage sixes come before the Government lien, do they not?

Mr. MINK. They do.

Senator WOLCOTT. These payments have come out of the earnings of the 1,822 miles of the Union Pacific Railway?

Mr. MINK. They have.

Senator WOLCOTT. What is the sinking fund eights.

Mr. MINK. The sinking fund eights are practically a first mortgage on the lands granted to the Union Pacific Railway Company, and are a third mortgage on the main line of the Union Pacific.

Senator WOLCOTT. What lands are there included in the mortgage; is it a large acreage?

Mr. MINK. A considerable acreage. At the end of 1894 there were 3,345,000 acres left unsold.

Senator WOLCOTT. So that the payments of coupons on these sinking fund eights were made to preserve the integrity of the lands which might otherwise be lost?

Mr. MINK. They were. I think that might be called the controlling consideration in their payment.

Senator WOLCOTT. The mortgage was a first mortgage on those lands?

Mr. MINK. Yes.

Senator WOLCOTT. And a third mortgage on the main line?

Mr. MINK. Yes.

Senator WOLCOTT. But their principal security would be on the acreage?

Mr. MINK. I presume so. There is considerable doubt about these sinking fund eights, some claiming that they are also secured on a large part of the equipment; but that claim is not fairly defined.

Senator WOLCOTT. I am trying to help to show that there was an excellent reason for paying this back due interest, in that you would otherwise have lost your title to the lands on which these sinking fund eights were a first mortgage, and there was a claim upon equipment, whether clear or shadowy it makes no difference; and the mortgage also stands as a third mortgage on the railroad.

Mr. MINK. Yes.

Senator WOLCOTT. The Omaha Bridge eights cover the structure between Council Bluffs and Omaha?

Mr. MINK. Yes, and the approaches to the bridge.

Senator WOLCOTT. What do the collateral trust sixes cover?

Mr. MINK. They are simply a note of the Union Pacific Railroad Company, secured by a pledge of bonds.

Senator WOLCOTT. What bonds?

Mr. MINK. There are behind the 6 per cents $1,746,000 of Colorado first mortgage sevens, $1,981,000 of Utah and Northern first mortgage sevens, and $863,000 of Omaha and Republican Valley first mortgage sevens.

Senator WOLCOTT. The loan is how much?

Mr. MINK. The loan was on the 30th of June, 1894, $3,672,000. I believe it has been changed since.

Senator WOLCOTT. When was this money borrowed?

Mr. MINK. The trust deed was made on the 1st of July, 1879, and the indorsement followed shortly after that.

Senator WOLCOTT. Are those bonds held by the public at large?

Mr. MINK. Yes; they are widely scattered.

Senator WOLCOTT. Are they quoted on the market?

Mr. MINK. Frequently. They are now worth in the neighborhood of par.

Senator WOLCOTT. Do these bonds cover any portion of the 1,800 miles of road of the Union Pacific Railway Company?

Mr. MINK. No, sir; they are merely promises to pay of the Union Pacific Railway Company, secured by this pledge of securities.

Senator WOLCOTT. So these obligations would be merely the note of the company, secured by certain of the stocks and bonds and property of other roads than those included in the parent system?

Mr. MINK. Exactly.

Senator WOLCOTT. On what theory did you divert the earnings of the main line to the payment of the interest on those securities?

Mr. MINK. The theory on which the receivers filed petitions asking the order of the court was altogether for the purpose of holding together the system of railroads which was turned over to us under the bill of 1893. The receivers, when they made the application for orders to pay interest on these securities, believed that the business depression which prevailed so generally would not last as it has lasted, and they thought that they would be able, at the end of the year, to do better. We are not paying the interest now on those collateral trust obligations.

Senator WOLCOTT. When did you make the last payment upon them?

Mr. MINK. My impression is that we applied for leave to pay but one coupon; and that was the coupon due on the 1st of January, 1894.

Senator WOLCOTT. In this instance, as in many others, it is a fact, is it not, that the earnings of the parent system were used (whether wisely or unwisely is not to be questioned now) in the payment of obligations outside of the system, and in order to secure the control of all the branches to the parent system?

Mr. MINK. The payments were made out of interest that was received on the collateral trust obligations—the Colorado Central sevens, the Utah Northern sevens, and other high-grade bonds.

Senator WOLCOTT. Then you would say that, as to these payments made by the receivers on account of interest due, the income came from the securities and the receivers were not required to take it from the earnings of the system?

Mr. MINK. That is my impression.

Senator WOLCOTT. The Eastern Division sixes cover, I suppose, a portion of the Government land-aided lines?

Mr. MINK. They do.

Senator WOLCOTT. That is a mortgage in advance of the Government lien?

Mr. MINK. It is.

Senator WOLCOTT. And the Middle Division sixes the same, I suppose?

Mr. MINK. Yes.

Senator WOLCOTT. The consolidated mortgage sixes cover the mileage not included in the Government-aided portion of the road?

Mr. MINK. It does cover that, practically. It is a second mortgage on that part of the road, and you may call it a third mortgage on the road to Denver east of the three hundred and ninety-fourth mile post.

Senator WOLCOTT. You mean that it is a first mortgage on the nonaided portion?

Mr. MINK. Subject to the Denver Extension bonds. It is also claimed to be a first mortgage on some of the property east of the Missouri-Kansas State line in the State of Missouri.

Senator WOLCOTT. So, as receivers, you felt it to be your duty to pay this interest in order that the Union Pacific Railway might be kept a going concern between Kansas City and Denver?

Mr. MINK. Yes; I ought to say that we received from the trustees about $220,000, which they had in hand, and which was authorized to be applied in the payment of interest.

Senator WOLCOTT. The trust 5-per-cent bonds; what are they?

Mr. MINK. They are a collateral trust obligation of the Union Pacific Railway Company like the collateral trust sixes, except that the collateral trust fives are secured by other securities.

Senator WOLCOTT. Given when?

Mr. MINK. The trust was made in 1883. There are outstanding now of these bonds about $4,667,000, and they are secured by $1,169,000 Colorado sevens, $1,809,000 Omaha and Republican Valley fives, and by other securities. These collateral trust bonds, I think, are selling in the neighborhood of 75.

Senator WOLCOTT. That is an obligation of the Union Pacific Railway Company?

Mr. MINK. It is.

Senator WOLCOTT. Secured by obligations of other roads not in the parent system?

Mr. MINK. It is not a mortgage; it is merely a security.

Senator WOLCOTT. Have you kept that paid up to date?

Mr. MINK. No; my recollection is that we paid but one coupon upon that issue, the coupon due in December, 1893.

Senator WOLCOTT. Did you receive from the securities in the pledge a sufficient sum to pay the interest on these trust 5 percents?

Mr. MINK. My impression is that we did not.

Senator WOLCOTT. Speaking in the rough, about how much money was taken from the earnings of the road to pay these coupons?

Mr. MINK. My impression is that all the money charged in the account of the trust 5 percents came out of the earnings of the property.

Senator WOLCOTT. Aggregating how much?

Mr. MINK. Aggregating $116,925.

Senator WOLCOTT. Then this $116,925 would have been applicable to paying the interest on the first-mortgage bonds, that are anterior to the Government lien, if it had not been diverted to pay outside obligations?

Mr. MINK. Yes; it might have been. Of course the bill under which we were acting was a bill not brought by the trustees under the mortgage, but by the stockholders and creditors. The moneys derived by us from the earnings of the railroad or from the securities were held by us and applied as the court directed us to apply them.

Senator WOLCOTT. It is a matter of fact, is it not, that you took, and paid from the ordinary funds of the company, on these trust 5 per cents, moneys which could have been devoted to the payment of the interest on the first-mortgage bonds?

Mr. MINK. Yes.

Senator WOLCOTT. And that those moneys amounted to $116,925?

Mr. MINK. Yes.

Senator WOLCOTT. A payment which you have ceased to continue?

Mr. MINK. Yes, we have ceased making these payments, leaving the collateral trust note holder to resort to his collaterals and to pay his interest out of them.

Senator WOLCOTT. The Omaha Bridge fives and the equipment trust fives were given for the structure of the bridge and for the equipment of the company?

Mr. MINK. Yes.

Senator WOLCOTT. Now, come to the collateral trust notes. What obligation was that?

Mr. MINK. That was a note of the Pacific Railway Company very like that of the collateral trust obligations.

Senator WOLCOTT. Given when?

Mr. MINK. Given in 1891.

Senator WOLCOTT. What time in 1891?

Mr. MINK. I think in September.

Senator WOLCOTT. Within about two years of your receivership?

Mr. MINK. Yes.

Senator WOLCOTT. A note amounting to how much?

Mr. MINK. There was about seventeen millions originally issued. The amount now is about eight and a half millions.

Senator WOLCOTT. The Denver extension bonds—are these the obligations held by the Denver extension mortgagees as trustees?

Mr. MINK. They are the trustees.

Senator WOLCOTT. They hold the pledge?

Mr. MINK. Yes.

Senator WOLCOTT. Has that interest been kept paid up to date?

Mr. MINK. I think the receivers paid the interest on those notes until the 1st of August, 1894. Since that time the trustee has held the collections under the trust for the payment of the interest; and those collections have been quite sufficient to meet the interest obligations. I believe that the last coupon, due on the 1st of February, has been paid.

Senator WOLCOTT. Is it a fact that, since the receivership, the sums used to pay the interest on these bonds have been furnished by the interest and dividends paid by the property pledged?

Mr. MINK. It is not a fact. The collections from the collaterals during the period from October, 1893, and prior to the 1st of August, 1894, were not sufficient to meet that interest. The receivers were called upon to advance considerable sums. The amount I have not in my mind.

Senator WOLCOTT. Give a general impression as to about how much the receivers advanced for that purpose?

Mr. MINK. I think it might have been about $150,000.

Senator WOLCOTT. So that you have advanced to pay the interest on that trust about $150,000?

Mr. MINK. Yes.

Senator WOLCOTT. And about $116,000 on the trust 5 percents?

Mr. MINK. Yes.

Senator WOLCOTT. On what ground did you base your application to the court for an order to make these payments out of the earnings of the system—I mean the payments on these collateral trust notes?

Mr. MINK. So that we might retain the securities pledged for them and which we believed to be of very great value, largely in excess of the collateral trust obligations.

Senator WOLCOTT. The Denver extension bond is a first mortgage from the three hundred and ninety-fourth mile post to Denver, is it not?

Mr. MINK. Yes.

Senator WOLCOTT. And a second or third mortgage on the rest of the road?

Mr. MINK. Yes; the security rests on the western end of the road.

Senator WOLCOTT. When did you cease to pay interest on the first-mortgage obligations of the Union Pacific Railway system that are superior to the Government lien?

Mr. MINK. The last coupon paid upon the main line mortgage was that of January, 1895. The coupons for July, 1895, and January, 1896, are now in default. The trustee under the mortgage filed a bill asking its foreclosure in the early months of 1895. Under that proceeding a petition was filed for the payment of the January, 1895, coupon; and an order was entered upon it, and the coupon was paid. A petition has been quite recently filed for an order to pay the July, 1895, coupon, but no order has yet been made. No doubt it will be made. The interest on the main-line mortgage will probably be paid up to and including July, 1895, within a very short time, and the coupon due on the 1st of January, 1896, will be paid within the next ninety days.

Senator WOLCOTT. Was there any purpose in failing or neglecting to pay these coupons on the first-mortgage bonds?

Mr. MINK. No, sir; absolutely none. You mean by that——

Senator WOLCOTT. I mean, was there any ulterior purpose to close out the Government interest? You are aware that there is an idea abroad that under the plan of reorganization, or otherwise, it might be deemed advisable not to pay the interest on the first-mortgage bonds.

Mr. MINK. I do not think that it was ever deemed advisable not to pay the interest on the first-mortgage bonds, at least so far as the receivers are concerned. We have constantly used our endeavor to have the trustee under the first mortgage move (whenever there seemed to be money enough for the purpose) for leave to pay the interest upon the first-mortgage bonds as soon as we thought the accounts would justify it.

Senator WOLCOTT. This was the particular interest, which should be paid first of all, if you had the funds wherewith to pay it?

Mr. MINK. Yes. In the early days of the receivers, however, I do not think that the need of paying that interest was quite so prominent in our minds. We were appointed under what may be called a general bill, including all these properties, and our hope was that this system of roads might be kept together. We perhaps never dreamed that the disasters of 1893 and 1894 would overtake us. It, therefore, never was the purpose of the receivers to neglect to pay the interest on the first-mortgage bonds; and I am sure there never was such a purpose either on the part of the trustees under the mortgage.

Senator WOLCOTT. I suppose that when the receivers were appointed nobody had any doubt that the earnings of the whole system would not only pay the outstanding obligations, but that, with care and economy, the receivers could bring the whole system together again?

Mr. MINK. At the outset that was the general belief. Of course, as time went by, we began to modify that belief; and we have changed it very decidedly since then.

Senator WOLCOTT. You found that one branch after another has been lopped off from the general system?

Mr. MINK. We have lost two important lines. The Oregon Railway and Navigation line was taken off in the summer of 1894, and the Union Pacific, Denver and Gulf line in December, 1893. We have, nevertheless, endeavored to keep up friendly relations with these lines, and we think that we have succeeded in getting a fair share of the traffic of all of them.

Senator WOLCOTT. I suppose you are aware that the contention has been made that the Government can be foreclosed of its lien altogether, if it fail to assert its rights and to protect its interests, by the failure of the Union Pacific Railway Company to pay the interest on the mortgage superior to the Government lien?

Mr. MINK. I have heard that claim made.

Senator WOLCOTT. So that, by some legal process, the receivers, although the net earnings of the road were sufficient to pay the interest on the first mortgage, failing to do so, these people would be able to foreclose the Government of the United States out of a great many million dollars due from the Union Pacific Railway system. You have heard that claim made?

Mr. MINK. Often. So far as the payment of interest is concerned, there can be no question as to the ability of the main line of the Union Pacific Railway always to earn the interest on twenty-seven millions of dollars—certainly if anything like the present conditions with reference to the branch lines are maintained. Therefore, I have thought there never has been anything in that suggestion, so far as the payment of interest is concerned. The only danger (so far as I have looked at it) has been owing to the fact that a large amount of principal is due.

Senator WOLCOTT. We can take care of the principal when it becomes due. That is another matter. The claim was made, was it not, that the Government can be foreclosed out of its interest in this property because the interest due on the prior mortgage is not paid, and that, therefore, there may be a sale of the property?

Mr. MINK. The claim was made; and the receivers, whenever they thought the accounts justified it, insisted upon applying to the court for leave to pay the coupons due on the first-mortgage bonds, and we have been generally successful.

Senator WOLCOTT. This committee is directly and particularly interested in preserving the interest of the Government in this railroad property. That is the main purpose for the existence of the committee. Can you assure the committee that the interest upon the liens prior to the Government lien will continue to be paid?

Mr. MINK. No, sir. In answering your questions I have limited my answers to the main line. So far as that mortgage is concerned I have made as full and comprehensive an answer as I can.

Senator WOLCOTT. Do you anticipate the meeting of the interest due on the first liens prior to the Government lien?

Mr. MINK. I do. I think the defaults in the interest will be met. Of course the default in principal can not be.

Senator WOLCOTT. I am simply referring to the coupons due.

Mr. MINK. If the Union Pacific system, as now constituted, can be kept together, there is no reasonable doubt as to the payment of the interest.

Senator WOLCOTT. Now as to the other portions of the system.

Mr. MINK. In Kansas my recollection is that no coupons have been paid on the main line on the mortgage, prior to the United States lien, since the coupon of February, 1894. In other words, my present recollection is that the coupons for August, 1894, February and August, 1895, and February, 1896, on the Eastern Division bonds, which cover the first 140 miles, are all in arrears.

Senator WOLCOTT. West from Armstrong?

Mr. MINK. West from Armstrong. The Middle Division bond is a bond covering a piece of road from the one hundred and fortieth mile post to the three hundred and ninety-fourth mile post. I believe that on those bonds the coupons of June and December, 1894, and of June and December, 1895, are in default.

Senator WOLCOTT. Amounting to how much? About what is the deficit?

Mr. MINK. The Eastern Division bonds amount to $2,240,000. The amount of interest in default would be about $250,000. The Middle Division sixes amount to $4,063,000, on which the interest in default would be about $480,000.

Senator WOLCOTT. Then, in fact, for the Eastern Division and the Middle Division the amount of interest in default is about $750,000.

Mr. MINK. Substantially so.

Senator WOLCOTT. Do you hope to meet these payments?

Mr. MINK. The situation in reference to the Kansas Pacific line is very much involved. I do not know whether I can say that we hope to meet the interest or not. We were made receivers under the Ames bill in

October, 1893, and we continued to operate all the lines as receivers under that bill up to the 16th of July, 1894, when a bill was filed by the trustees under the consolidated mortgage of the Kansas Pacific Railway Company, and, under that bill, the claim has been made by the trustees that the revenues from the Kansas Pacific Division became impounded for the benefit of the consolidated mortgage bondholders. Since that time no interest has been paid on account of any of the bonds of the Kansas Pacific Division. If you look at the printed statement you will find on page 33 of the copy of a petition recently filed by the receivers, on which a hearing is now in progress at Omaha, and it contains a statement of the income derived from the operations of the consolidated mortgage Division up to September, 1895. The amount of the surplus earnings, $458,000, is claimed to have been impounded for the benefit of the consolidated mortgage bondholders. Whether the earnings are so impounded as against the rights of the Eastern and Middle divisions I have no opinion.

Senator WOLCOTT. There is a claim that whatever may be the earnings of the Kansas Pacific, none of them are applicable to the coupons anterior to the Government lien.

Mr. MINK. The bill has been filed.

Senator BRICE. Have you stopped paying the interest?

Mr. MINK. The Kansas Pacific is in our hands as receivers under this consolidated mortgage, and no orders have been made by the court.

Senator BRICE. Have you ever applied for such orders?

Mr. MINK. We make no such applications. They are made by the trustees.

Senator BRICE. You leave the matter to the creditors—to individuals?

Mr. MINK. That is our invariable rule when the mortgages are in court.

Senator BRICE. And the mortgages in this Kansas Pacific case are in court?

Mr. MINK. In the case of the Kansas Pacific road every subdivision of the property is now in court by its mortgagees. In the case of the Kansas Pacific we have this situation: First, the shareholders' receivership of October, 1893; then the foreclosure receivership, extending from the 17th of July, 1894, to the 29th of July, 1895, when the trustees under the Denver extension mortgage filed an intervening petition, which may have had the effect of impounding the earnings of that subdivision for the benefit of that mortgage. Afterwards, on the 5th of August, 1895, the trustees on the Kansas Division collateral mortgage filed their bill, and on the 21st of November, 1895, the Eastern Division mortgage trustees filed their bill. In view of that complicated situation, that petition sets out the complications and asks the court to give instructions as to the distribution of the earnings, and the hearings in that case have now commenced.

Senator BRICE. What mortgages on the Kansas Pacific road are superior to the Government lien?

Mr. MINK. The Eastern Division mortgage and the Middle Division mortgage.

The CHAIRMAN. You stated that the trustees made an application to the court to permit the payment of past due coupons?

Mr. MINK. After the filing of bills to foreclose the mortgages, the receivers left to the trustees the applications to the court to have the coupons paid. When the mortgage is not in court (as is the case in the Union Pacific Coal Company) the receivers have usually filed petitions asking the court for authority to pay the coupons.

The CHAIRMAN. In paying those coupons all the holders are paid share and share alike?

Mr. MINK. Yes.

Senator WOLCOTT. Is there an application filed to-day for the payment of past due coupons on the Eastern and Middle divisions?

Mr. MINK. The petition which the receivers filed will in the end result in the determination of the sums which ought to be carried to each division. I have not any doubt that other petitions asking for instructions to pay coupons will be filed.

Senator WOLCOTT. But, as a matter of fact, there has been no application by the trustees of the Eastern and Middle divisions bondholders for the payment of their interest.

Mr. MINK. None that I know of.

Senator WOLCOTT. Who are those bondholders?

Mr. MINK. They are scattered far and wide.

Senator WOLCOTT. Are you advised that the holders of those bonds have joined in the reorganization scheme?

Mr. MINK. Yes.

Senator WOLCOTT. Is it your opinion that it is any portion of that reorganization scheme that the holders of those bonds shall not apply for their interest, so that the Government may be said to be imperiled in its lien by the failure to pay the interest on these bonds?

Mr. MINK. That is not my impression.

Senator WOLCOTT. What is your impression as to the reason why these people have not asked for payment of their interest?

Mr. MINK. My impression is that they have not asked for the payment of their interest because of the complicated situation, to which I have referred, growing out of the various suits.

Senator WOLCOTT. But would you not think that if they were not entitled to any interest out of the earnings of the road on which their mortgage is a first lien, the sooner they knew that fact the better?

Mr. MINK. That is a very reasonable conclusion. However, the situation is so complicated that I feel quite sure that the trustees under the mortgage must have been aware that the court would never entertain a petition asking an order for the payment of interest, unless the account filed by the receivers showed that the interest ought to be paid.

Senator WOLCOTT. You think that the situation is so complicated that the court would be sure not to order payment of interest on these securities?

Mr. MINK. I think that the court would not order payment of interest until it had before it an accounting showing that the interest had been earned, and, in the case of the Kansas Pacific, no such account can be made.

Senator WOLCOTT. If the court would be slow do you not think that the Government would be equally slow to declare those bonds in default?

Mr. MINK. I suppose so.

Senator WOLCOTT. You say that the court would not order interest to be paid out of the earnings applicable to it because of certain complications?

Mr. MINK. I did not intend to say that. The earnings have been derived from the operation of the entire Kansas Pacific division, extending from Kansas City and Leavenworth on the east to Denver on the west. There are four mortgages in court endeavoring to assert their rights; and the fifth mortgage, which has an interest in these earnings, is not yet in court. I think that until the rights of each of these mortgages are determined, the court would be very slow to make an order in any of those cases directing the payment of interest; and it was with that idea in the minds of the receivers that we presented this complicated situation to the court and asked for instructions.

Senator WOLCOTT. When did you file your petition?

Mr. MINK. Six or eight weeks ago.

Senator WOLCOTT. So that for more than a year the trustees of this Eastern Division first mortgage failed to make application to the court for the payment of their interest, and have not made such application up to this time?

Mr. MINK. My impression is that no such applications are pending.

Senator BRICE. Who are the trustees under that mortgage?

Mr. MINK. My recollection is that the trustees under the Eastern Division mortgage are H. M. Alexander and Judge J. F. Dillon. Judge Dillon has only recently been made a cotrustee.

Senator WOLCOTT. Cotrustee with whom?

Mr. MINK. With Mr. Alexander.

The CHAIRMAN. In keeping the accounts of the Kansas City and Denver Division, is there any difference made? Do you keep them as part of the aided portion of the road, separately from the nonaided portion, or are the accounts all kept in one pool?

Mr. MINK. They are all kept in one account. We do keep, for the benefit of the United States Commissioner of Railroads, an account of the earnings of the aided portion as distinct from the earnings of the nonaided portion of the road, and I presume we will endeavor to use that at the hearing which is now on at Omaha. I do not know, however, that we can induce the trustees under the Denver Extension mortgage to accept that account as representing what that division is fairly entitled to, the earnings not having been divided in proportion to distance.

The CHAIRMAN. I was going to ask you that question, whether they are divided in proportion to distance or by a general average?

Mr. MINK. By a general average, so far as the revenue is concerned. I think that the mileage is always a factor, so far as expenses are concerned—the locomotives mileage, train mileage, car mileage, and general expenses are the factors.

Senator WOLCOTT. As to the Middle Division mortgage trustees, who are they?

Mr. MINK. I have no memorandum here of the trustees under that mortgage. My record says that there are two vacancies, but my recollection is that those vacancies were filled some time ago, and that Mr. John A. Stewart and Judge Dillon were made trustees.

Senator WOLCOTT. What are the professional relations of Judge Dillon to the receivers?

Mr. MINK. Judge Dillon is counsel to the receivers.

Senator WOLCOTT. So that your own counsel is the trustee in this first mortgage?

Mr. MINK. Yes.

Senator WOLCOTT. And he has not made any application, either as your counsel or as trustee, for the payment of any of this back interest?

Mr. MINK. I believe not. His application would not come to us until after it was filed in court.

Senator WOLCOTT. But Judge Dillon, as counsel to the receivers, as well as trustee under this mortgage, would notify one of the five receivers of such application if he made it?

Mr. MINK. He might or he might not.

Senator WOLCOTT. It is his duty to do so, is it not?

Mr. MINK. I think not.

Senator WOLCOTT. Do you not consider it your duty to keep advised of all the applications for payment of interest that are filed in court?

Mr. MINK. Judge Dillon, if he prepared a petition, would prepare it only after a conference with his cotrustee. That petition would go to the files of the court, and we perhaps might not know about it until it came back to us on reference to a master.

Senator WOLCOTT. Do you not advise your counsel as to whether you want to resist a reference or not, or as to whether you want to enter an appearance?

Mr. MINK. All petitions of that character are referred to the master as a matter of course.

Senator WOLCOTT. And you are not usually advised until after reference to a master?

Mr. MINK. No, sir.

Senator WOLCOTT. And you have not been advised of a reference to a master in the matter of the Kansas Pacific line?

Mr. MINK. No; we have not.

Senator BRICE. Who are the trustees under the consolidated mortgage?

Mr. MINK. Russell Sage and George J. Gould.

Senator BRICE. That is the only one in which you are receivers?

Mr. MINK. That was the first mortgage to file a bill of foreclosure.

Senator WOLCOTT. What does this consolidated mortgage cover?

Mr. MINK. It is a first mortgage on the lands east of the three hundred and eightieth milepost in Kansas. It is a second mortgage on the lands west of the three hundred and eightieth milepost in Kansas and Colorado, and it is a second mortgage on the line west of the three-hundred and eightieth milepost, subject to the Denver Extension bonds. It is also substantially a fourth mortgage on the road east of the three hundred and ninety-fourth milepost. I say "substantially," because there are some small issues of bonds not worth referring to. It is therefore subject to the first mortgage of the Eastern Division, next to the lien of the United States, and next to the Denver Extension bonds.

Senator WOLCOTT. Then it is the objections of Messrs. Gould and Sage, trustees, that are preventing the payment of interest on those bonds?

Mr. MINK. It is not their objections. It is the complications that grow out of the matter.

Senator STEWART. Have you considered the question whether Judge Dillon's position is not a little peculiar, being counsel for the receivers and a trustee for the mortgage? Do not those duties come in conflict?

Mr. MINK. I believe I never thought of it. My recollection is that Judge Dillon's appointment as one of the trustees is of a very recent date. I think it is a matter of three or four months ago.

Senator WOLCOTT. Then the action of Messrs. Gould and Sage would make an apparent foreclosure possible, and would make it possible that the Government interest on this Kansas Pacific Branch would be wiped out?

Mr. MINK. In part, possibly that may be so. I can not express an opinion upon it. It involves a legal proposition. As a business question, however, I do not think that it is of much consequence, because the Kansas Pacific consolidated mortgage makes it necessary to take care of the interest on these first-mortgage bonds.

Senator WOLCOTT. Nevertheless, it has not been done up to this time and there is an apparent default?

Mr. MINK. Yes It is a fact that, so far as the Kansas Division is concerned, prior to the 17th of July, 1894, when Gould and Sage filed their bills to foreclose the mortgage, the proportion of the earnings attributable to the Kansas Pacific Division was very much less than the proportion of the interest charges which were attributable to that division plus the interest charges local to that division. The deficit on page 29 amounts to something like $400,000. The receivers have suggested that perhaps it would be advisable that this deficit shoud be made good out of funds which are claimed to have been impounded.

Senator WOLCOTT. The net earnings of your whole 1,800 miles of road are amply sufficient to pay this interest, are they not?

Mr. MINK. They are sufficient to pay the first-mortgage interest.

Senator WOLCOTT. To pay the interest on the mortgage superior to the Government lien?

Mr. MINK. Yes.

Senator WOLCOTT. You have not hesitated to take money from your whole road to pay promissory notes of the company, have you?

Mr. MINK. We have not hesitated to take money which came into our hands under the bill, and to pay those promissory notes, on the order of the court.

Senator WOLCOTT. These moneys came in under the head of earnings of the road?

Mr. MINK. They came in from the property, which was made up in part from the railroad property and a great part of it from securities to which the mortgage did not attach, and on the revenues from which the mortgage gave no claim.

The CHAIRMAN. What source of revenue was there, other than the earnings of the road?

Mr. MINK. All those securities pledged under this collateral trust. I have here a memorandum of miscellaneous income derived from the 13th of October, 1893, to the 30th of September, 1895, and the income from those sources amounted to $663,130.

The CHAIRMAN. And what is the whole amount that would be applicable to the payment of interest outside of those miscellaneous items?

Mr. MINK. $3,516,000.

Senator WOLCOTT. This Union Pacific system is composed of two trunk lines parallel with each other until they reach Cheyenne and Denver, where they connect with a northern and southern line, with an extension of one of them to Ogden?

Mr. MINK. Yes.

Senator WOLCOTT. You work it all as one system?

Mr. MINK. Yes.

Senator WOLCOTT. And you think it is essential to keep it as one system?

Mr. MINK. In my judgment it is very desirable.

Senator WOLCOTT. You would make any sacrifice rather than lop off one half of it—the Kansas Pacific?

Mr. MINK. I think that the line should be held together. It is certainly for the interest of the United States to have the Kansas Pacific property held with the Union Pacific.

Senator WOLCOTT. Why should you have hesitated to have made a payment of this interest out of your general earnings if you had not been prevented by the action of Sage and Gould as trustees?

Mr. MINK. I had no hesitation in the matter that has any significance. Our duty, as receivers, is to administer the property under orders made by the court. After the bill was filed to foreclose the consolidated mortgage on the Kansas Pacific a claim was made that the earnings of that division were impounded for the benefit of the mortgagee. The rights of any prior lien holder can be easily determined on intervention.

Senator WOLCOTT. But they have gone a couple of years without any intervention?

Mr. MINK. They have.

Mr. WOLCOTT. Nobody has taken pains to present the matter to the court until you took the initiative?

Mr. MINK. That is my recollection.

Senator WOLCOTT. Who is the counsel for Sage and Gould?

Mr. MINK. Mr. Winslow S. Pierce.

Senator WOLCOTT. He is the counsel of record for the consolidated mortgage?

Mr. MINK. That is my recollection.

Senator BRICE. On this branch of the subject I have only one question to ask. It is apparent, from what examination has been had, that on the threshold of this whole matter there is a cloud on the action of the receivers, and of the trustees, and counsel, and on the whole fabric. It is true (and I think you should explain to the committee) that there is practically but one mind in charge of all the various phases of the case, and that the divisions and partitions between them are merely technical—I mean between the mortgage trustees and the counsel. You should explain why you have not paid this interest, and whether the nonpayment arises out of any attempt to create and make a default. I think you ought to give a full explanation of that if you have not already done so. I think, in justice to the receivers, you ought to explain that situation.

Mr. MINK. I am indebted to you, Senator Brice. So far as the interest obligations of the Kansas Pacific line are concerned, Mr. Pierce (who is now sitting in the room) has suggested to me that, as he remembers it, the trustees under the Denver Extension mortgage, who are the holders as pledges of a large number of the Eastern Division and Middle Division bonds, had filed an intervening petition asking an order for the payment of one or more coupons. I merely mention that, and reserve the right to correct my testimony if I find it to be a fact. So far as the action of the receivers in relation to the payment of interest on mortgages prior to the lien of the United States is concerned, I can only say that the aim, the constant aim and purpose, of the receivers (three of whom were appointed or were supposed to have been appointed—two of them certainly—at the instance, and for the benefit, of the United States), has been always to have the moneys applied for the payment of this first mortgage interest from the day that the disasters of 1893 had begun to impress us as being irretrievable.

Prior to that time, as I have already mentioned, our hope and purpose was to hold together all these various properties. But after the summer of 1894 we began to realize that it was impossible to do it. We then bent our energies and attempts so to shape the policy of the trustees where possible (of our own people, certainly) as to pay all the interest on the first-mortgage bonds. Two of the receivers—Mr. Coudert and Mr. Doane—were charged with the duty of protecting the interests of the United States in this property. The United States, for some reason, has so far failed to become a party to the record. It seems to me that its rights, if they are in jeopardy, ought to be subject to the decrees of the court.

Senator WOLCOTT. That is the opinion of a great many people who have securities that are junior to the first-mortgage bonds.

Senator BRICE. I am directing your attention to these apparent facts. You earned four and a half million dollars net one year, and five and one-eighth millions net another year, and the total interest obligations in each of those years, including everything held by the Government and everything behind the Government lien, fell much short of those apparent total earnings. And yet, not only did the receivers fail to pay the interest on the bonds on other divisions of the road, but they failed to pay the interest on the first mortgage bonds.

Mr. MINK. The answer to that is very simple. To begin with, in October, 1893, when we were made receivers of these properties, we took them in with almost no money in the purse of the corporation. We began to pay on the 1st of December, 1893.

Senator BRICE. As that is a very serious matter, the explanation of which is absolutely necessary to this committee, so that it may be submitted to the Senate, I suggest that you frame your answer at your own convenience and have it put in the record.

Mr. MINK. I thank you very much; I will do so.

Senator WOLCOTT. I think it is due to anybody who knows anything about this system, as I do, to say that no one who is familiar with it questions your single-minded devotion to the interests of the property, or that you desire to keep it together as a going concern for the building up of the interests of the country. In Mr. Ames's lifetime you were regarded as his first adviser and friend in that matter?

Mr. MINK. Yes.

Senator WOLCOTT. You have been with the company for nearly a quarter of a century?

Mr. MINK. Yes; and I have been very much interested in the progress of the property and very much concerned about its disasters.

Senator WOLCOTT. I will not question you as to the necessity of five receivers for this property; but, as we are on that branch of the inquiry, I would like to know whether the court has yet fixed the compensation of the five receivers?

Mr. MINK. The court has not yet fixed their compensation. It has made orders by which we are drawing on account.

Senator WOLCOTT. The fact is, I suppose, that if this railroad is burdened with five receivers, two-fifths of them, at least, are imposed upon it by the action of the Attorney-General of the United States, or at his suggestion?

Mr. MINK. I do not like to answer that question. The appointment of two additional receivers was made at the instance of the United States. I think that it has been a very great advantage to the receivership to have the counsel and aid of Mr. Coudert and Mr. Doane.

Senator WOLCOTT. And the advice and counsel of five more men—if skilled and friendly and cautious—would be of help also?

Mr. MINK. It might be, but I think the receivership at present is sufficiently large.

Senator WOLCOTT. You think that five receivers are enough?

Mr. MINK. The interests of the United States would seem to me pretty well represented in the receivership.

Senator WOLCOTT. You think that five receivers are enough?

Mr. MINK. Yes.

Senator WOLCOTT. As to the integrity of the system in its operation, is it operated in connection with, or by close track relations with, the Chicago and Northwestern road?

Mr. MINK. It is.

Senator WOLCOTT. Has the contract been published which shows under what circumstances the two roads exchange business?

Mr. MINK. My impression is that the contract has been published a number of times.

Senator WOLCOTT. That is my impression. Would you be a custodian of such a contract if it existed?

Mr. MINK. I would be the custodian either of the original or of a copy. Technically, Mr. Millar, the assistant comptroller, would be its custodian.

Senator WOLCOTT. If there are any agreements in writing, I would be glad for the committee to have them, so as to see what the relations are between the Chicago and Northwestern and the Union Pacific companies.

Mr. MINK. I will furnish them to the committee.

The CHAIRMAN. What is the character of this contract with the Chicago and Northwestern?

Mr. MINK. It is a contract for close and harmonious operation and for a division of rates.

Senator WOLCOTT. Have you as yet any agreement with the Missouri Pacific?

Mr. MINK. Not that I know of. My impression is that our relations with the Missouri Pacific are not more intimate than they are with the Alton road.

The committee here took a recess until 2.30 p. m.

After the recess the examination of Mr. Mink was continued.

Senator WOLCOTT. I find on looking over some of the past testimony that Mr. Monroe gave the gross earnings of the Union Pacific Company in 1892 as upward of $20,000,000; of 1893, as upward of $17,000,000; and of 1894 and 1895, as upward of $14,000 each. Does that include the 1,825 miles of the system?

Mr. MINK. They are the earnings of the 1,822 miles owned by the Union Pacific Railway Company.

Senator WOLCOTT. When does the financial year of the Union Pacific Company end?

Mr. MINK. It runs with the calendar year.

Senator WOLCOTT. Are the earnings of 1896 a little larger than those of 1895 for so far?

Mr. MINK. I think they are a shade better. I have no statement of the earnings of the aided portion of the railway for any part of 1896 as distinct from the earnings of the whole family of roads; but on the entire system the earnings for January and February of 1896 exceed those of January and February, 1895, by about $179,000. Of course a good deal of that is due to the fact that there has been one more day in February of this year.

Senator WOLCOTT. Then the earnings for this year are practically about the same as those for last year?

Mr. MINK. They are practically the same.

Senator WOLCOTT. From your long experience of these properties, what, in your opinion, is the earning capacity, based upon present conditions, of the Union Pacific Railway proper—the 1,825 miles?

Mr. MINK. That is a very difficult question to answer. But, on the assumption that the relations which have so long existed between the Union Pacific and its branch lines are to be maintained and preserved,

I should say that a company might safely take over that property and reorganize it and assume the charges set out in the plan of the reorganization committee, say, $4,000,000. I think it would stand that as a fixed charge.

Senator WOLCOTT. The past years have been years of remarkable and unusual depression?

Mr. MINK. Yes; since the summer of 1893.

Senator WOLCOTT. Are you aware that everybody in that section of country hopes and believes in increased prosperity for it, and do you share that feeling?

Mr. MINK. I do, in a great part.

Senator WOLCOTT. Of course, I realize that you can not ask investors to put money in with any glowing hopes for the future, and yet, in all human probability, nothing can be worse than the existing conditions.

Mr. MINK. Nothing can affect the earnings of the Union Pacific and throw them below those of 1893 and 1894 unless it was to be a complete revolution in regard to the make-up of the whole system. In that event, I think it would be almost impossible for anybody to make an estimate of the earning capacity of the road.

Senator WOLCOTT. Suppose you lose the Oregon Short Line?

The CHAIRMAN. They have lost it now.

Mr. MINK. No; we have never lost it.

The CHAIRMAN. Are you receiver for it?

Mr. MINK. Yes.

Senator BRICE. You would lose it under the reorganization plan?

Mr. MINK. Yes.

Senator BRICE. If the reorganization plan were carried out, you would not have the Oregon Short Line in this system?

Mr. MINK. No.

Senator BRICE. Then the question must be put upon the system as left by the reorganization plan?

Mr. MINK. It is very difficult for me to answer the question.

Senator WOLCOTT. But you indorse the general scope of the reorganization plan?

Mr. MINK. I think that, with given conditions, as they exist to-day, the property will stand the annual charge of four millions, but it would not do so if the branch lines were taken away.

Senator WOLCOTT. Do you expect to lose the Oregon Short Line?

Mr. MINK. There is a strong probability that we shall retain it; but it is very difficult to say what the outcome will be. To-day the Union Pacific Company owns fifteen millions of the twenty-six millions of stock issued by the Oregon Short Line. That stock is held by J. P. Morgan & Co., as trustees. Under the scheme of reorganizing the Oregon Short Line, if Morgan & Co. should pay the assessment on the stock held by them, we should own about one-third of the stock.

Senator BRICE. But there is no provision in the reorganization scheme for retaining the Oregon Short Line?

Mr. MINK. There is no such provision.

Senator BRICE. Therefore, in the scheme which you present to this committee for the reorganization of a new company, there is no contemplation of having the Oregon Short Line as a portion of the system?

Mr. MINK. There may be no expressed plan. It, nevertheless, should be a part of that plan, in the end to control that branch line system; otherwise the plan based upon a fixed annual charge of four millions could not be carried out.

Senator WOLCOTT. How much would it fall short if it were an independent company, standing alone; what charges would it bear?

Mr. MINK. I can only make an estimate. No one could make any forecast of what the result would be, but I made some figures within a day or two in an endeavor to determine that matter for myself; and I have brought them with me. In 1894 the net earnings of the Union Pacific after the payment of taxes were $4,300,000. Now, the gross earnings of the Union Pacific Company from traffic interchanged with branch lines in every direction amounted to $5,500,000. It is very hard to make any estimate of what the net percentage of the expense of moving that business was; but, assuming that it was 50 per cent, that would leave $2,700,000 which went to our revenue derived from these branches.

Senator WOLCOTT. But you do not do business on your own lines at 50 per cent of the gross earnings?

Mr. MINK. No, the cost of operation is very much above that; but I put it on the basis of 50 per cent because the branch lines have borne the expense of one of the terminals, and the business done from the branch lines is subject to only a minimum cost. If the operation of this branch-line business cost 50 per cent of the gross receipts, then we had $2,700,000 of net income from the branch lines. I suppose that the loss of these lines would not deprive us of all of this traffic. We should be always in the market for some of the east-bound and west-bound traffic of the branch lines, and the question is what proportion of it we should receive. Assuming that we might lose half of it, that would still leave us a net income of $1,375,000 from these branch lines, and if you deduct that from the $4,300,000 of the present receipts it would bring the estimate of net earnings to about $2,900,000.

Senator WOLCOTT. Does that answer the question?

Mr. MINK. As well as I can answer it now, with the light I have.

Senator WOLCOTT. All the through freight from California has only one terminal; is not that true?

Mr. MINK. That is true.

Senator WOLCOTT. How much would you lose if you lost all the branch-line business; and how much would you lose if you lost one-half of it?

Mr. MINK. My estimate is that the cost of moving this interchange traffic does not exceed 50 per cent; but if, as has been suggested here, the cost is the same as the average cost of moving all our traffic, say 70 per cent, then if we lost it all, the loss would be $1,655,000 net.

Senator WOLCOTT. And if you lost half of it, it would be about $825,000?

Mr. MINK. Yes.

Senator WOLCOTT. You have not the Union Pacific, Denver, and Gulf business now, have you?

Mr. MINK. We have a large part of it.

Senator WOLCOTT. But not so much as when you controlled it?

Mr. MINK. I think we have got a very large profit there.

Senator WOLCOTT. Do you think you have got as much as if you controlled it?

Mr. MINK. No; we have lost something by losing the control of it.

Senator WOLCOTT. Do you not think, as a matter of fact, that your road has lost all it can lose?

Mr. MINK. No, sir; I think that the loss of the Oregon Short Line would be almost irretrievable.

Senator WOLCOTT. But, from the terminals of the road, and from the country through which it runs, and from the ordinary direction of its freight, you know that it is utterly impossible that that freight could be all taken away from you.

Mr. MINK. I suppose not.

Senator WOLCOTT. In what way would the Oregon Short Line get through to the East if not through your line?

Mr. MINK. By way of the Rio Grande line. The activity of those strong lines east of Denver—the Burlington, the Rock Island, the Santa Fe, and others—would be, of course, brought into play against the Union Pacific; and I think, therefore, that the loss of the Oregon Short Line business would be a great misfortune for the Union Pacific.

Senator WOLCOTT. But the Union Pacific would lose that business by the reorganization plan which you indorse.

Mr. MINK. I beg pardon; I did not mean to indorse it.

Senator WOLCOTT. That reorganization plan is suggested here as a plan that expressly excludes from the apparent future of the property any consideration of the Oregon Short Line, does it not?

Mr. MINK. Any specific consideration.

Senator WOLCOTT. Would you say, generally speaking, that you think that $4,000,000 of net profit could be realized under the reorganization plan?

Mr. MINK. I think so.

Senator WOLCOTT. Does that leave the stock of the Union Pacific Railway of any value?

Mr. MINK. The Union Pacific stock is absolutely valueless.

Senator WOLCOTT. I mean the stock of a new concern which would be able to pay $4,000,000 of fixed charges a year, what would be the value of that stock?

Mr. MINK. A merely nominal value.

Senator WOLCOTT. You think that $4,000,000 a year would exhaust the earning capacity of this property?

Mr. MINK. No, sir; I might not want to put the maximum capacity at those figures. The stock would have some value of course, but the amount earned in excess of that $4,000,000 is not likely to be very great in my judgment; not greater than the needs of the corporation.

Senator WOLCOTT. Go back to 1892, before the bad years, and give us the net earnings of the 1,822 miles of the Union Pacific Railroad.

Mr. MINK. The steed which carried us so bravely along in 1892 has stumbled since then.

Senator WOLCOTT. Yes, and the mints have been closed to silver since then.

Senator BRICE. The "crime of 1873" has had its effect.

Mr. MINK. The steed's knees are barked, and he will not sell for so much in the market.

Senator WOLCOTT. Do you think that the prosperity of that country has forever left it?

Mr. MINK. No, sir; not forever.

Senator WOLCOTT. Do you think that the maximum earning of the road is practically measured by its present earning?

Mr. MINK. I think that, with the changed conditions, and with the enormous number of railroad lines traversing that country, it is not possible that the earnings of 1892 will be repeated for a good many years to come.

Senator WOLCOTT. What were the net earnings of the Union Pacific Railroad Company in 1891 and 1892?

Mr. MINK. The net earnings of 1892 were $8,500,000. The net earnings of 1893 were $6,200,000. The net earnings of 1892 were very much larger than the net earnings of 1891, which were $7,800,000. The net earnings of 1890 were $7,200,000.

Senator WOLCOTT. We should feel very badly in the West if we thought these earnings had permanently suffered. You have had no new railroads out there to compete with yours since 1893 which you did not have in 1892?

Mr. MINK. Yes; we have the Burlington. I think that the Burlington has finished its line through to Billings since 1892, and has become a great competitor. The Great Northern line has gone to the coast since 1892.

Senator WOLCOTT. With the exception of some roads at the north of your line, there are no new lines in competition with you within the last two years?

Mr. MINK. No; with the exception of the two I have mentioned.

Senator WOLCOTT. So, practically, if prosperity returns to that section of country, there is no reason why the earnings of the Union Pacific should not be as good in the future as in the past?

Mr. MINK. The trend of prices in the market indicates a very well-grounded opinion that they never will be. Four million dollars a year would be a safe and reasonable figure for a reorganization committee to assume as fixed charges for that road.

Senator WOLCOTT. How much is the first-mortgage incumbrance on such portions of the road and terminals as are not embraced in the Government-aided line; in other words, what is the face of the bonded indebtedness of so much of the road as is not included in the Government-aided portion of the road—I mean the mortgages, not the collateral obligations?

Mr. MINK. About $20,000,000.

Senator WOLCOTT. Suppose that your road was bonded at $100,000,000 at 4 per cent; $20,000,000 of your obligations would cover the terminals and the nonaided portion of the road?

Mr. MINK. Yes.

Senator WOLCOTT. Would the road not bring more than that if it was put up at sale?

Mr. MINK. I am not able to answer that question. If the bondholders' judgment of the value of the property is worth anything it would indicate that it would bring pretty nearly that.

Senator WOLCOTT. Therefore you would have a value of $80,000,000 left in your road.

Mr. MINK. That is assuming that the reorganization plan is carried out.

Senator WOLCOTT. I am leaving out of view all the reorganization plan. I am assuming that we should start in with this property at $100,000,000, and that we will be able to acquire that portion of it not covered by Government aid at $20,000,000. That would leave us $80,000,000, which the other part of the property would be worth, if we could place our 4 per cent bonds at par. What is the amount of the bonded indebtedness separate from the Government lien on the Government-aided portion of the road?

Mr. MINK. Thirty-three million five hundred thousand dollars.

Senator WOLCOTT. And what is the amount of the Government indebtedness?

Mr. MINK. About $52,000,000.

Senator WOLCOTT. So that, apparently, if these securities, in the order of their priority, could be exchanged at par for a 4 per cent security (which you say would be a perfectly safe and adequate security) you could practically pay the whole of the mortgage superior to the Government lien and the whole of the Government debt, could you not?

Mr. MINK. I do not know that I meant to say that.

Senator WOLCOTT. But is not that the result?

Mr. MINK. That might be the result.

Senator WOLCOTT. I find the total of the bonded indebtedness superior to the Government lien, and the Government indebtedness to be $85,500,000.

Mr. MINK. I think that an issue of $100,000,000 of 4 per cent bonds (if negotiations could be had between the present lien holders and the reorganization committee) by which all the present liens could be taken up and a new issue of consolidated bonds to the amount of $100,000,000 put out in place of them, could be safely carried by the reorganized company.

Senator WOLCOTT. I am leaving out of view for the moment the fact that there are subsequent incumbrances and the fact that there are stockholders, and I am trying to reach an actual value of the property, based on its earning capacity. You say that it is good for four millions net a year, at least?

Mr. MINK. I do.

Senator WOLCOTT. If that be so, it is good for an issue of $100,000,000 of bonds at 4 per cent?

Mr. MINK. Yes.

Senator WOLCOTT. That being true, it is good for 4 per cent on all the lines prior to the Government lien and on almost all the total amount of the Government debt, principal and interest, less the sinking fund, is it not?

Mr. MINK. I think that that is so; I limit my answer, however, in this particular. I do not know that, in the negotiation of these bonds by the reorganization committee, it would be right or proper to put out the bonds of the new company, dollar for dollar, against all the various debts which we have enumerated, because that would leave the reorganized company without any resources whatever. Every dollar would be invested in the debts of the old company; and if you are going on to take care of the future, the reorganized company must go into the business with something in its treasury. The plan of the reorganization committee contemplates a reserve of something like $13,000,000 and I think that that is a very reasonable reserve.

Senator WOLCOTT. The infirmity of the whole business lies in the fact that there is nobody forthcoming to give the $100,000,000 and to wipe out existing securities; but they desire, by assessment and otherwise, to protect their own securities and to assess other subordinate securities; and they desire to make a good concern of it by recognizing many existing securities which are subordinate to the Government lien. Is not that true?

Mr. MINK. Does that not, after all, make it perfectly clear that the best way for the United States to solve the question and to obtain the value of its interest in the property is to do as an ordinary creditor would do—go into a conference and treat and negotiate for a place in the reorganization committee? That is what any ordinary lien holder would do. That is what the lien holders all over the country are doing to-day. You take a default and almost immediately the bondholders come together and organize a committee charged with the duty of arranging the business, and the action of such a committee is affirmed by the stockholders. I think (and my confidence in the matter is very strong) that if the interest of the United States could be intrusted to a commission made up of conspicuous and prominent citizens charged and empowered to negotiate for a settlement, and able to meet the other lien holders and to treat with them as people treat in the ordinary, every-day transactions of life, this matter could be settled inside of six months.

Senator WOLCOTT. It is possible, however, that the unpleasant experience that the Government is passing through, whereby it is asked to sacrifice about 50 per cent of its claim, may make it reluctant to submit its interest to another reorganization concern.

Mr. MINK. The Government may not be required to sacrifice anything.

Senator WOLCOTT. I am trying to get your idea of what the Government should do. You say that the Government should trade away its interest, and that the customary way is for people to get together and negotiate. Is it an ordinary thing to organize syndicates and to underwrite?

Mr. MINK. I think it is very ordinary.

Senator WOLCOTT. Is this reorganization committee underwritten?

Mr. MINK. I do not know.

Senator WOLCOTT. Have you heard that it is underwritten?

Mr. MINK. If I have heard it, it has made no impression on my mind.

Senator WOLCOTT. Do you know Mr. Schiff?

Mr. MINK. I have not met him.

Senator WOLCOTT. Do you know that he is the financial agent of the reorganization committee?

Mr. MINK. Yes.

Senator WOLCOTT. Do you know the Schieff interest in the reorganization plan?

Mr. MINK. I do not; I may have known it when I read the plan.

Senator WOLCOTT. Have you seen the confidential circulars which have been issued to subscribers?

Mr. MINK. I believe not; I have really paid very little attention to this matter, except as occasional inquiries have been made of me in my official capacity. I have, in a measure, encouraged the deposit of bonds for the reorganization committee, because I have thought where bonds like those of the Union Pacific Railroad Company have been held in very high estimation for twenty-five years and have been scattered all over the world, it was the most natural thing in the world that they should be deposited with some committee charged with the duty of representing them. To that extent I have interested myself in them, but beyond that I have no interest in them.

Senator WOLCOTT. Your relation to the Union Pacific has been simply fiduciary?

Mr. MINK. My relation to the Union Pacific is almost nothing to-day. My duties as receiver take up all my time.

Senator WOLCOTT. I will not question you as to the wisdom or unwisdom of the reorganization system from the point of view of the Government becoming a trader, because if I did I should have to go through all the different securities and to get you to show me where other creditors, with so important a lien and so prior a lien as that of the United States, have made such a great sacrifice as the Government is called upon to make by this proposed scheme; therefore I will confine myself to questions as to the value of the property and as to the burdens that it bears. Did you read the testimony of Mr. Anderson, your coreceiver?

Mr. MINK. I read part of it. I was not well when Mr. Anderson was here.

Senator WOLCOTT. Did you notice that he makes a recommendation that the two properties—the Union Pacific and the Central Pacific—should be sold together to the highest bidder?

Mr. MINK. That was his recommendation as a Government director

Senator WOLCOTT. Will you give the committee the benefit of your opinion as to that recommendation of Mr. Anderson?

Mr. MINK. As I understand it, his idea was that the liens of the United States on the main lines of the Union Pacific and on the main line of the Central Pacific should be foreclosed and the property acquired, either in the interest of some reorganization committee or in the interest of the United States, and then put up at auction.

Senator WOLCOTT. Yes.

Mr. MINK. I think very well of that proposition, except that, when I read the recommendation, I thought it would completely sacrifice the interest of the United States in the Kansas Pacific line.

Senator WOLCOTT. Otherwise would you approve of it?

Mr. MINK. I think that the two roads would make a very strong line.

Senator WOLCOTT. Would you favor putting the Central Pacific and the Union Pacific together?

Mr. MINK. I think they would make a wonderfully strong, effective road.

Senator WOLCOTT. From your point of view, what would you think of it?

Mr. MINK. Really, I have no very strong convictions about it, because I have scarcely thought of it except during the last few days.

Senator WOLCOTT. You are not of the opinion, I take it, that the Government could economically operate these roads?

Mr. MINK. I am not.

Senator WOLCOTT. You do not share in that view?

Mr. MINK. I do not think that the United States ought to engage in railroad business.

Senator WOLCOTT. You do not believe in the plan of the Government operating railroads?

Mr. MINK. I do not.

Senator WOLCOTT. Do you think that the Union Pacific property would bring a better price if it were sold in conjunction with the Central Pacific than if it were sold separately?

Mr. MINK. It is very hard to venture an opinion on that. I think it very doubtful. I think that if the Union Pacific Railroad property could be reorganized, and if substantially the same sort of relation could be made with the branch lines as formerly, it would make a reasonably successful system of railroad.

Senator WOLCOTT. What would you think of the idea of selling the interest of the Government in the Union Pacific, separately from its interest in the Kansas Pacific and separately from its interest in the Central Branch of the Union Pacific?

Mr. MINK. I think that the Government would realize more money by the sale of both properties together. I think that the interest of the United States in the Kansas Pacific line is worth, relatively, a very small sum. I think, on the other hand, that the interest of the United States in the main line is worth something. That, also, is very hard to decide. But the interest of the United States in the Central Branch of the Union Pacific is almost valueless.

Senator WOLCOTT. The line from Kansay City to Denver is a good line?

Mr. MINK. It is a very good line, but it has tremendous competition. There are a great many lines through to Denver. If the lien of the United States was foreclosed on that line, and if it had no connection with the West, I should suppose that the 384 miles of the road east would be worth almost nothing.

Senator WOLCOTT. You spoke of the proposition for reorganization. What do you understand the present proposition to be, which has been made in the interest of the Union Pacific reorganization?

Mr. MINK. I may be mistaken, but I have got the impression more from reading the newspapers than from communication with others. I understand that the plan most favored to-day is a plan by which the principal of the subsidy debt should be met, first, by the application of the sinking fund, and that then the balance of the principal should be paid, and that thereupon the unreimbursed interest account should be extended fifty years and should carry interest at 2 per cent; that is what I understand to be the proposition that meets with most favor.

Senator WOLCOTT. How do you understand that this deferred settlement is to be secured?

Mr. MINK. By a second mortgage on the property of the 1,822 miles of road, subject only to a prior lien, not of $100,000,000, but of $75,000,000.

Senator WOLCOTT. Would this second mortgage consist solely of deferred interest, or would it be shared with other bonds?

Mr. MINK. It would consist solely of the deferred interest account.

Senator WOLCOTT. Would you consider that a good security?

Mr. MINK. I think it would be safe, because, as I understand it, the proposition was that the charges for transportation for the Government should be withheld, and should be applied toward meeting the installment of interest on this mortgage. If the unreimbursed account is to amount to $40,000,000 (it will not be quite so much), 2 per cent on that would impose an annual charge on the property of $800,000. The United States, I think, can always make itself secure for that interest by reserving its transportation account.

Senator WOLCOTT. There is, in the minds of a great many people, a serious objection to such a relation between the Government of the United States and railroads as would induce the Government to ship the bulk of its business by a particular line of road. Many of the officials of competitive and parallel lines are largely of opinion that the Government should be free to ship by any of the lines which can carry its business. Do you think that that relation would present to these other lines an element of unfairness?

Mr. MINK. I suppose that that opinion would be entertained by rival and competing lines. It might, or it might not, be well founded.

Senator WOLCOTT. It would be of interest to the Union Pacific Company to have the Government in such relations with it as that the Government would ship its materials by it?

Mr. MINK. Most assuredly; but the fact is that the location of the Union Pacific Road, in connection with the locations of the New York Central, the Pennsylvania, the Lake Shore, and the Michigan Central, is so favorable that, in my judgment, those roads will always obtain a very large part of the transportation of the Government, particularly of the mails.

Senator WOLCOTT. So that the road would be very apt to receive the Government transportation, irrespective of its connection with the Government?

Mr. MINK. Yes.

Senator WOLCOTT. So that, practically, that relation between the Government and the railroad would cut no figure in the matter?

Mr. MINK. No, except that it might present an element of security to the Government.

Senator WOLCOTT. If the Government did not have to take out its interest on these bonds in trade, would it still be secure by that 2 per cent interest?

Mr. MINK. It would, on the assumption that the first or prior mortgage would be limited to $75,000,000 at 4 per cent. That would impose an annual charge of $3,000,000. Then there would be behind that this second lien of $40,000,000 at 2 per cent, imposing an annual charge of $800,000; and that, of course, would be the maximum charge on the road. I understand that in this plan of reorganization, on the basis of $100,000,000, $13,000,000 is reserved for improvements—a very necessary and proper reservation.

Senator WOLCOTT. You think that that proposition is about the best which the property can stand?

Mr. MINK. I think that the annual charge on the property ought not to exceed $4,000,000.

Senator STEWART. State again just how the principal of the Government claim is to be paid.

Mr. MINK. The proposition was this, that the principal of the debt, amounting to $33,000,000, should be met first by the application of the sinking fund held under the Thurman Act.

The CHAIRMAN. Fifteen million dollars?

Mr. MINK. Yes; if that is the sum. That then the difference between this $15,000,000 (supposing that to be the amount of the sinking fund) and the $33,000,000 was to be raised by the reorganization committee and paid in cash, so that the principal of the debt should be extinguished, that thereafter the interest (say $40,000,000) should be extended fifty years and should carry interest at 2 per cent.

Senator STEWART. Was there any provision for a sinking fund to pay off the bonds at the end of fifty years?

Mr. MINK. There is no provision for a sinking fund.

Senator STEWART. That would be quite important.

The CHAIRMAN. It is simply an agreement to pay at the end of fifty years?

Mr. MINK. Yes; on that theory (the Hubbard plan) there would be imposed on this reorganized property just about the same maximum charge which I have first supposed—nearly $4,000,000 ($3,800,000).

Senator WOLCOTT. Have you read the testimony of your colleague, Mr. Anderson?

Mr. MINK. I have not read it.

Senator WOLCOTT. Mr. Anderson testified, on page 47 of the record, as follows:

> Senator WOLCOTT. If a mortgage drawing 3 per cent interest on the 1,400 miles covered by the Government loan would be a good proposition for the Government to accept, better than $35,000,000 in cash, please tell us why a mortgage drawing 2 per cent, covering the whole amount of principal and interest with a sinking fund, is not better than 50 per cent of the amount in cash. Does the difference of 1 per cent furnish a reason why the Government should settle at 50 cents on the dollar?
>
> Mr. ANDERSON. It does. A 2 per cent bond is only worth two-thirds of a 3 per cent bond. A 3 per cent bond such as you describe may be worth 60 cents on the dollar, and a 2 per cent bond would be worth only 40 cents on the dollar, as the security is not very good.

Would you say that a fifty-year bond drawing 2 per cent interest is only worth two-thirds as much as a 3 per cent bond?

Mr. MINK. That is pretty hard to tell; one can only determine the value by the exchange; but my judgment would be that a 2 per cent fifty-year bond would sell not far away from two-thirds as much as a 3 per cent fifty-year bond.

Senator WOLCOTT. What do you think a 3 per cent bond would be worth as a second mortgage on this property?

Mr. MINK. It would be worth from 50 to 55, subject to the mortgage of $75,000,000 at 4 per cent.

Senator WOLCOTT. Then a 2 per cent bond subject to that mortgage would be worth about 35?

Mr. MINK. I think not far from that; but of course this is speculation, pure and simple.

Senator WOLCOTT. Then, as a matter of fact, looking to market value (which is the way for business men to look at it), they are asking the Government to settle for the principal of its debt, and to settle its interest claim at about 35 cents on the dollar. In other words, you are offering the Government the principal of its claim and 35 per cent of its interest?

Mr. MINK. I think they are not offering so much as that. As I understood the offer, it would resolve itself into something like this—I may be wrong: The reorganized company would be required to pay the difference between the $15,000,000 in the sinking fund and the $33,000,000 of the debt, or $18,000,000. The value of the 2 per cent bond would be about $14,000,000, and the two together would figure up about $32,000,000.

Senator WOLCOTT. What is the present principal of the debt?

Mr. MINK. Thirty-three million dollars.

Senator BRICE. Eighteen million dollars for principal and $40,000,000 for interest would make $58,000,000. I understood you to say that the debt was $52,000,000?

Mr. MINK. That is quite true. I did say that the debt was $52,000,000 after deducting the sinking fund. I think I was in error in saying that, since I included in the deductions an item of something like $2,000,000 of premium paid on the bonds held in the sinking fund, and which I suppose should not be deducted.

Senator BRICE. Give the amount of the Government debt as nearly as you can estimate it, and have it put in your testimony, because these figures vary as presented by different witnesses, and you can make an accurate statement and send it to the committee.

Mr. MINK. I will.

Senator STEWART. If there was a provision to pay annual installments on the principal of the $40,000,000 of bonds sufficient to liquidate the amount at the end of fifty years, what would then be the difference in the value of these bonds, and how would that affect the value of the security?

Mr. MINK. It would affect the value of the bonds very noticeably.

Senator STEWART. You put the value now at 35. How would you put it if there was a provision of this kind?

Mr. MINK. It is difficult to say. The bonds might be worth, in that event—supposing they were to be sunk entirely within fifty years—from 50 to 55.

Senator WOLCOTT. As a matter of fact, the Government would never have a foreclosable interest on this second mortgage, would it?

Mr. MINK. I can not answer that question, because it involves a legal proposition.

Senator WOLCOTT. The Government would have an interest that would be subject to $75,000,000 in cash. Practically it is like taking the note of the reorganized company, which would first have $75,000,000 to pay, and of course nobody would seriously contend that the Government, having once settled its claim, would ever again put its hands in its pocket and pay out $75,000,000 in cash.

Mr. MINK. And it was because not only of this consideration, but because of other considerations that suggest themselves to me, that I have formed the opinion that the best way to handle the matter would be to intrust it to commissioners and to let them meet all the other creditors and negotiate.

Senator WOLCOTT. You mean commissioners appointed by Congress?

Mr. MINK. Yes; if Congress would give them the power.

Senator WOLCOTT. Do you not think that it would be a fairer proposition for the Government if the company was to secure the Government by a first lien on its property—make the Government a sharer in the general first lien?

Mr. MINK. It seems to me that that is possible. I have always supposed that the fund reserved in this reorganization scheme was to be reserved with that object in view.

Senator WOLCOTT. Do you not think that a proper reorganization scheme ought to contemplate a cash payment, so that, with the sinking fund, the principal of the Government debt should be paid, and that, as to the interest, the Government should have some security that it could share with the first-mortgage bondholders?

Mr. MINK. If they could bring that about and bring the debt within $100,000,000, it would be a very desirable settlement; but whether you could induce the other bondholders to scale their obligations, having superior liens, could only be determined by negotiation.

Senator WOLCOTT. What proportion of the security holders of the Union Pacific Railway Company are in sympathy with this reorganization plan?

Mr. MINK. I understand the bulk of them; I have an impression that 70 per cent of them favor it.

Senator WOLCOTT. Including the stockholders?

Mr. MINK. No; only the mortgage bondholders. The percentage of the stock in favor of the reorganization plan is very much higher, over 90 per cent.

Senator WOLCOTT. Do you not think that some scheme could be devised whereby something should be paid to the Government in cash on the accrued interest, and whereby the Government should have a first-mortgage security for any deferred payment due?

Mr. MINK. That would be proceeding on the theory that the Government lien was unquestionably worth its face.

Senator WOLCOTT. Not necessarily, if you give the Government a lower interest. You might give the Government a security not bearing its face value.

Mr. MINK. That suggestion might be adopted. I have not considered it.

Senator WOLCOTT. Do you favor the general procedure of this reorganization committee?

Mr. MINK. I have been on friendly terms with General Fitzgerald and the other members of the committee, and I have not hesitated to speak to them about details, but I have not charged myself in any formal way with any opinion for which I would be responsible.

Senator WOLCOTT (referring to the paper presented by Mr. Mink, giving a statement of the financial operations of the receivers). Under this heading of "Other expenditures, $1,513,065," what items generally are chargeable to it?

Mr. MINK. We have charged off there some judgments and deficiencies due to the operation of one or two small and unimportant lines which were not in our hands as receivers, but which, under the court's order, we have been charged with. We have also charged $134,000 for deficiencies which arose from the operation of what are known as crippled lines, lines which do not pay operating expenses, but which contribute advantages to the Union Pacific which are sufficiently important to justify the assumption of these properties. We have also included in this the proportion of the equipment trust obligations, which have been paid under the court's orders. These are all the items which I can enumerate here now. They are all (except the unimportant items relating to the operation of crippled lines) items which would be necessarily charged against revenue.

Senator WOLCOTT. They do not include any extraordinary expenses, I suppose?

Mr. MINK. They do not include extraordinary expenses, since all of the expenses charged against the revenue of the road are under the head of operating expenses.

Senator WOLCOTT. Since the appointment of the receivers, do you pay rebates?

Mr. MINK. Not with the knowledge and consent of the receivers.

Senator WOLCOTT. Are you of opinion that no rebates have been paid since the appointment of the receivers?

Mr. MINK. If there have been, they have been paid without our knowledge and consent.

Senator WOLCOTT. And you are of the impression that none have been paid?

Mr. MINK. That, I know, is the specific order of the receivers.

Senator WOLCOTT. Are you of opinion that none have been paid?

Mr. MINK. I must entertain that opinion.

Senator WOLCOTT. Do you?

Mr. MINK. I do.

Senator WOLCOTT. Does your road expend any money in politics since the appointment of the receivers?

Mr. MINK. Not a penny, so far as I know.

Senator WOLCOTT. There is no authorization on the part of anybody connected with the road to mix with political matters?

Mr. MINK. Absolutely none.

Senator WOLCOTT. Your superintendents are not authorized to spend any of the company's money in political matters, are they?

Mr. MINK. No.

Senator WOLCOTT. Your superintendent at Denver, Mr. Deuel, is he authorized to spend money in political matters?

Mr. MINK. No, sir.

Senator WOLCOTT. Would you be apt to know it if he did?

Mr. MINK. I would be apt to hear it; but I do not know of any such expenses and I believe there are none. That is my firm and honest conviction.

Senator STEWART. You have stated that the combination of the two roads—the Union Pacific and the Central Pacific—would make a strong combination. How would that combination affect the other roads? Would it tend to a monopoly? Would the other roads be opposed to it?

Mr. MINK. You mean the other transcontinental lines?

Senator STEWART. Yes, and those on this side which run part of the way and have connection, more or less, across the continent. How would they regard the combination?

Mr. MINK. I should suppose that they would regard such a combination with disfavor, because my judgment is that that would make a line of very great strength. The geographical position of the Union Pacific and the Central Pacific is a very strong one. It is the natural direct line across the continent. It is the line which, under normal conditions, would carry the passengers; and it seems as if the traffic followed the movement of passengers. I think, therefore, that other lines would look with disfavor on such a combination. The Union Pacific and the Central Pacific would, in my judgment, be a very strong line.

Senator STEWART. How would it affect the business of the country, favorably or unfavorably?

Mr. MINK. I should say that it would affect the business of the country favorably. My belief is that a strong railroad line always affects favorably the country adjacent to it. My impression is that the strong communities are generally along those lines which are prosperous; but whether the one is the cause and the other the effect I am not able to say.

Senator STEWART. Do you think that such a combination of the two roads would have the effect of preventing competition, or would it increase competition?

Mr. MINK. It would probably have the effect of stimulating and increasing competition.

Senator STEWART. If these lines were joined together clear across the continent, would they be likely to let other railroad lines in on equal terms?

Mr. MINK. I should say not. If you mean to ask whether they would open up junction points, I should say that they would prevent it as far as possible.

Senator STEWART. Would it not be desirable for the community that other roads should have equal terms at junction points?

Mr. MINK. Of course I do not mean that the junction points would be closed, except as to competitive traffic. I think that it is an almost invariable rule to close the gateways against competitors.

Senator WOLCOTT. You are not referring to the physical exchange of business; you are referring to the rating of business and to the exchange of traffic?

Mr. MINK. Yes.

Senator WOLCOTT. In other words, every railroad, very properly, carries its freight to the greatest possible distance along its own lines?

Mr. MINK. Yes.

Senator WOLCOTT. That is natural and legitimate, is it not?

Mr. MINK. Yes.

Senator WOLCOTT. Then you had no reference to the question of the physical connection of lines?

Mr. MINK. No. The physical connection would be made, and there must be such physical connections; but none of the competitive traffic would be interchanged.

Senator WOLCOTT. About the agreement between the Union Pacific and the Chicago and Northwestern; will you furnish the committee with a copy of it?

Mr. MINK. I will do so.

Senator WOLCOTT. I would like, when you furnish other statements, to have you show, also, the market price of the obligations of the Union Pacific Railway Company, secured on Government aided portions of the lines, which are subject to the Government mortgage, and also the market value of the stock, figuring the proportional amount of stock which should apply to 1,400 miles out of the 1,825 miles. In other words, I want to show the present public estimate of the equities of the Union Pacific.

Mr. MINK. I understand your question, but it is a very difficult one to answer. I will make the best attempt to answer it I can.

Senator WOLCOTT. If the question becomes too difficult, you need not answer it; but if you can reasonably do so, I wish you would, so that the Senate can see what the general public thinks of this property.

Mr. MINK. Take the Government lien of the United States in so far as it covers the equipment. Originally, the United States subsidy bonds were issued on certificates made by a Commissioner appointed in pursuance of the act of Congress. The certificates related to specific property, including equipment. The bonds were issued upon these certificates, and thereupon they became a lien upon the property enumerated in the certificates, and consequently against the equipment. I understand it to be a doctrine, very generally entertained and accepted, that if an instrument is silent in regard to this matter the afterwards acquired rights do not run. There is no reservation or provision in the act of Congress respecting any after-acquired property of the Union Pacific. "The lien runs against the property," to use the language of the Supreme Court, "for and on account of which it was issued." The extent, in a lineal direction, of the line has been passed on by the Supreme Court, and the extent is only to the three hundred and ninety-third milepost. The suggestion in my mind is that, having been passed on in a lineal direction, it would not reach in any other direction to the property described in the certificate.

The CHAIRMAN. It did not have the words "on all property acquired hereafter?"

Mr. MINK. It did not. I believe that to be a fair proposition, and I know it is the proposition resting on the minds of the junior lienholders.

THE UNION PACIFIC.

The following communication and exhibits were received from Mr. Oliver W. Mink and were made part of his testimony:

THE UNION PACIFIC SYSTEM,
New York, March 21, 1896.

DEAR SIR: Referring to the questions asked me on the 13th relating to the revenues derived from the operations of the properties owned by the Union Pacfic Railway Company during the receivership and the extent to which they have been applied in payment of interest, I beg now to submit the following statement:

On October 13, 1893, the properties of the Union Pacific Railway Company were placed in the hands of Messrs. S. H. H. Clark, Oliver W. Mink, and E. Ellery Anderson as receivers under what is known as a preservative bill. Almost immediately thereafter the Attorney-General filed in the proceeding a bill of intervention, from which I quote the following paragraph:

> And the Attorney-General of the United States further gives the court to understand and be informed that, in his opinion, the protection of the interests of the United States and of all other creditors of the Union Pacific Railway Company requires an increase in the number of receivers as hereinafter suggested; that the number of receivers is not sufficient for the performance of the grave and serious duties imposed upon them, and will not inspire that public confidence that a larger number would secure; that the lien of the United States is by far the largest held by any single person or corporation, and calls for the protection of impartial receivers selected for that purpose, and their association with the receivers who have been nominated to and appointed by this court upon the nomination of the said parties complainant, and whose views and interests (except of said Anderson) are, as the Attorney-General is informed and believes, in unison with those of the complainants.

The prayer in said bill was as follows:

Wherefore, and to the end that the said property may, pending the foreclosure and sale or reorganization, be managed to the best interests of the United States of America as well as of other creditors and stockholders, and to the end that the best advice and judgment accessible to the court may not only be had in its operation, but as to the continuance of existing contracts, which by reason of the said receivership may require for their enforcement judicial aid, and as to the true principles and methods of reorganization and for the protection of all interests in the property, the said Attorney-General for the United States respectfully requests the said court to permit the United States to defend herein and to appoint two receivers, in addition to, but with equal powers to those already heretofore appointed, who shall assist the three receivers now in office in performing their grave and responsible duties, and the Attorney-General prays for such other and further relief as under the foregoing facts and circumstances the United States may be entitled to.

On this bill of intervention Messrs. John W. Doane, of Chicago, and Frederic R. Coudert, of New York City, were appointed additional receivers on November 13, 1893.

The proceeding under which the receivers were thus appointed covered all the properties of the Union Pacific Railway Company, and is generally referred to as the Ames cause.

The preservation of the system as a whole having been one of the purposes, if not the main purpose, of the proceeding, the receivers applied, under proper directions of the court, a part of the moneys coming into their hands to the payment of obligations secured by pledges of collateral, which pledges were believed to largely exceed in value the obligations running against them. Moreover, the security for such obligations represents the control of many of the corporations the lines or properties owned by which had been placed in the hands of the receivers under the general or preservative receivership proceeding. Notwithstanding these considerations, however, the financial and industrial depression became so widespread and pronounced that the receivers soon felt called upon to no longer recommend the court to authorize such payments, and no such payments were made after September, 1894. At or about the same time this general policy was further complicated by the action of the trustees under the consolidated mortgage of the Kansas Pacific Railway Company, who filed, on July 16, 1894, a bill for the foreclosure of that mortgage.

The receivership thus established (that is, the Ames receivership) continued without break until July 16, 1894, when the bill above mentioned to foreclose the consolidated mortgage on the Kansas Pacific line (and which covered all the lines from Kansas City and Leavenworth on the east to Denver on the west) was filed. Thereafter the Ames receivership extended without break (excluding, of course, the road covered by the Kansas Pacific consolidated mortgage) to August 1, 1894, when, on an intervening petition of the trustees of the Omaha Bridge mortgage, the property covered by that mortgage was practically separated from the rest of the property included in the Ames receivership. Thereafter the Ames receivership, as thus reduced, continued without further break until November 19, 1894, when the Denver Pacific mortgage was brought into court under a suit of foreclosure, whereupon the subdivision which it covered passed from the control of the Ames receivership. Thereafter there remained in the Ames receivership only the main line of the Union Pacific, extending from Omaha to a point 5 miles west of Ogden, the administration of which thus remained in the Ames receivers until January 21, 1895, when a bill to foreclose the mortgage covering that division was filed, whereupon it passed from the possession of the receivers in the Ames cause.

On this last-named date, January 21, 1895, therefore, all of the various subdivisions of the Union Pacific Railway had been taken out of the Ames receivership and been passed over to the receivers named in the orders entered in the various foreclosure suits. In each of such foreclosure suits the courts have named the receivers who were named in the original or Ames cause.

Independently of the proceedings instituted on July 16, 1894, by the trustees under the Kansas Pacific consolidated mortgage the trustees under the following mortgages, which are secured by liens on the Kansas Pacific line prior to the lien of the consolidated mortgage, have instituted the following proceedings:

April 15, 1895, suit to foreclose the Middle Division first mortgage.

July 29, 1895, intervening petition seeking the payment of certain interest on the Denver Extension mortgage bonds.

August 5, 1895, suit to foreclose the Kansas Division and collateral mortgage (a mortgage subordinate to all other mortgages resting on the Kansas and Denver Pacific divisions).

November 21, 1895, suit to foreclose the Eastern Division first mortgage.

The complications which have resulted from these various preceedings, particularly in so far as they relate to the mortgage subdivisions of the Kansas Pacific line, were so involved that the receivers filed, on December 14, 1895, a petition setting forth to the court such facts and circumstances as in their judgment would bring about their reasonable solution, a hearing under which has recently been completed at Omaha, and the matter now stands submitted to the special master in chancery for his report. Until a report shall have been made and approved by the court no allotment of the revenues derived from the operation of the several Kansas Pacific mortgage subdivisions, in respect of which foreclosure suits or intervening petitions are pending, can well be made. Meanwhile the operations of the entire Kansas Division from July 17, 1894, to this date have been included in a separate account, the balance of which is subject to such distribution as the court shall order upon the petition now in the hands of the special master. I inclose with this a copy of the receivers' petition thus referred to.

I also inclose the following exhibits:

Exhibit A.—Statement of the financial operations of the Ames receivership of the Union Pacific Railway from October 13, 1893, to December 31, 1895, inclusive, apportioned to the three grand divisions, namely, the Union Division or Main Line, the Kansas Division (including the Leavenworth Branch), and the Denver Pacific or Cheyenne Branch, though it should be understood that the property of the Union Pacific Railway Company, having been placed in the hands of the receivers as a whole, the rights of the different subdivisions, or the mortgagees thereof, prior to their appearance in court, remain to be determined. The apportionment ought, therefore, to be looked upon as more or less suggestive. The statement does not include the operations of any of the mortgaged subdivisions after bills in foreclosure were filed in respect thereof.

As I was questioned respecting the payments made on account of the so-called collateral trust obligations, I may say in passing that our payments for interest on such obligations were as follows:

Collateral trust 6 per cent bonds	$110, 160
Collateral trust 5 per cent bonds	116, 925
Collateral trust 6 per cent notes	668, 835
Total	895, 920

Against these payments it may be well to note that the income derived from investments, a part of which is pledged for such collateral obligations, amounted to $740,944.52. None of these investments is bound by the lien of any of the above-mentioned mortgages which are in foreclosure, and no part of the income derived from these investments could be claimed by the receivers in the respective foreclosure suits as properly applicable to the payment of the interest accruing on these mortgages.

EXHIBIT B.—Statement in detail of the item appearing in Exhibit A entitled "Income from investments."

EXHIBIT C.—Statement in detail of the item in Exhibit A entitled "Deficit of crippled lines."

EXHIBIT D.—Statement of the financial operations of the Kansas Pacific consolidated mortgage property for the period from July 17, 1894, the day following the date on which the bill to foreclose that mortgage was filed, to December 31, 1895, the balance at the credit of which ($556,916.45) is subject to such deductions as may be made by the court in favor of the Middle Division mortgagees, the Kansas Pacific Denver Extension mortgagees, the Kansas Division and collateral mortgagees, and the Kansas Pacific Eastern Division mortgagees when passing on the receivers' petition of December 14, 1895.

The overdue obligations on account of bonds secured by mortgages resting on the Kansas Division are as follows:

Consolidated mortgage:	
May 1, 1894, coupons	$351,600
November 1, 1894, coupons	351,600
May 1, 1895, coupons	351,600
November 1, 1895, coupons	351,600
Middle Division mortgage:	
June 1, 1894, coupons	121,890
December 1, 1894, coupons	121,890
June 1, 1895, coupons	121,890
December 1, 1895, coupons	121,890
Denver Extension mortgage:	
May 1, 1894, coupons	176,610
November 1, 1894, coupons	176,610
May 1, 1895, coupons	176,610
November 1, 1895, coupons	176,610
Eastern Division mortgage:	
August 1, 1894, coupons	67,200
February 1, 1895, coupons	67,200
August 1, 1895, coupons	67,200
August 1, 1895, principal	2,240,000
February 1, 1896, interest	67,200
Total	5,109,200

I do not include the claims of the Kansas Division and collateral mortgagees, since their rank is not such as to make it a factor of consequence now, nor do I include the claims of the Leavenworth Branch and income bondholders, since the amounts involved are inconsiderable.

EXHIBIT E.—Statement of the financial operations of the receivers in respect of the Omaha Bridge Division.

The overdue obligations of bonds secured by mortgages resting on that division are as follows:

First mortgage:	
April 1, 1894, principal	$122,000
April 1, 1895, principal	192,000
Renewal mortgage:	
October 1, 1893, coupons	11,675
April 1, 1895, coupons	26,400
October 1, 1895, coupons	26,400
Total	378,475

EXHIBIT F.—Statement of the financial operations of the Denver Pacific or Cheyenne Branch mortgage receivership for the period from November 20, 1894, the day following that on which the bill to foreclose that mortgage was filed, to December 31, 1895, the balance at the credit of which is $194,620.92.

It is difficult to state the amount of overdue interest on the Denver Pacific or Cheyenne Branch bonds, as controversies are likely to arise respecting a large amount of such overdue interest. The amount of Denver Pacific bonds now outstanding is $975,000. Of these the trustees under the Kansas Pacific consolidated mortgage hold all but $4,000. As the interest on the consolidated mortgage bonds has been paid to November 1, 1893, it may be that the trustees under that mortgage will claim that the interest due on the Denver Pacific bonds which has matured since that day should be paid to them. The amount of such Denver Pacific coupons is as follows:

May 1, 1894	$34,125
November 1, 1894	34,125
May 1, 1895	34,125
November 1, 1895	34,125
Total	136,500

EXHIBIT G.—Statement of the financial operations of the Union Pacific Main Line mortgage receivership from January 22, 1895, the day following that on which the bill to foreclose that mortgage was filed, to December 31, 1895. The balance at the credit of that division, as shown by the statement, $2,039,658.82, has been reduced by the payment begun to be made on January 20 last of the January 1, 1895, coupon, and interest thereon, $51,735.10, amounting in all to $868,605.10. A petition is now pending in which the trustees seek an order directing the receivers to pay the July, 1895, coupon, $816,870. An installment of the principal of this debt, amounting to $6,475,000, became due on January 1, 1896, and there are also overdue the coupons which matured on the same day, $816,870.

I ought, perhaps, to call the committee's attention to the fact that during the entire period of the receivership the United States has retained against the various receiverships the sums which, by the acts of 1862, 1864, and 1878, it claimed the right to retain as against the corporation. The sums thus retained are shown in the various exhibits, and are as follows:

Ames receivership	$1,523,868.30
Kansas Pacific consolidated mortgage receivership	199,778.81
Omaha Bridge receivership	3,425.62
Denver Pacific or Cheyenne Branch receivership	6,340.24
Dexter-Ames or main line mortgage receivership	1,038,881.89
Total	2,772,294.86

The balances standing at the credit of the various receiverships, as shown on the inclosed statements, are as follows:

Ames receivership		$703,031.37
Kansas Pacific consolidated mortgage receivership		556,916.45
Omaha Bridge receivership		22,001.32
Cheyenne Branch mortgage receivership		194,620.92
Dexter-Ames receivership	$2,039,658.82	
Less the January 1, 1895, interest payment	868,605.10	
		1,171,053.72
Total		2,647,623.78

There are now overdue the following bonds and coupons secured by mortgages having liens altogether superior to that of the United States:

Union Pacific Main Line:	
Bonds due January 1, 1896	$6,475,000
Coupons due July 1, 1895	816,870
Coupons due January 1, 1896	816,870
Total of Union Division prior-lien defaults	8,108,740
Kansas Pacific, Eastern Division:	
Coupons due August 1, 1894	67,200
Coupons due February 1, 1895	67,200
Coupons due August 1, 1895	67,200
Bonds due August 1, 1895	2,240,000
Interest due February 1, 1896	67,200
Kansas Pacific, Middle Division:	
Coupons due June 1, 1894	121,890
Coupons due December 1, 1894	121,890
Coupons due June 1, 1895	121,890
Coupons due December 1, 1895	121,890
Total of Kansas Division prior-lien defaults	2,996,360
Grand total of defaults secured by liens altogether prior to that of the United States	11,105,500

The various exhibits which are inclosed will show that since the appointment of the receivers in October, 1893, they have been authorized, in the Ames cause, to pay the following amounts of interest:

Union Division:	
Main line sixes	$1,634,070
Sinking fund eights	149,200
Omaha Bridge eights	22,600
Union Pacific Railroad Company collateral trust 6 per cent bonds	110,160
Kansas Pacific:	
Eastern Division sixes	67,200
Middle Division sixes	121,890
Consolidated sixes	351,600
Union Pacific Railway Company collateral trust 5 per cent bonds	116,925
Omaha Bridge fives	52,800
Union Pacific Railway Company:	
Equipment trust fives	33,475
Collateral trust 6 per cent notes	668,835
Kansas Pacific Denver Extension sixes	176,610
Total	3,505,365

And they have also been authorized to pay in the main-line foreclosure cause the interest coupon of January 1, 1895, with interest thereon, $868,605.10. This payment, not having been made until January 20, last, is not included in the inclosed statements, which extend only to December 31, 1895.

They have also been authorized to pay in the foreclosure causes on account of the equipment trust obligations of the Union Pacific Railway Company the following sums:

For principal of bonds	$861,000.00
For coupons	133,775.00
For interest on delayed payments	57,939.75
Total	1,052,714.75

Yours, very truly,

OLIVER W. MINK,
For the Receivers.

Hon. JOHN H. GEAR,
Chairman Senate Committee on Pacific Railroads,
Washington, D. C.

Exhibit A.

RECEIVERS UNION PACIFIC RAILWAY.

Statement of the financial operations of the "Ames receivership" from October 13, 1893, to December 31, 1895, inclusive, apportioned to the various divisions of the Union Pacific Railway.

	Union and Omaha Bridge Divisions.	Kansas Division and Leavenworth Branch.	Cheyenne Branch.	Total.
INCOME.				
Gross earnings	$14,471,680.84	$2,109,504.11	$691,837.27	$17,273,022.22
Operating expenses	9,603,794.98	1,528,141.01	568,654.52	11,700,590.51
Taxes	436,427.60	170,395.97	22,127.36	628,950.93
Operating expenses and taxes	10,040,222.58	1,698,536.98	590,781.88	12,329,541.44
Surplus earnings	4,431,458.26	410,967.13	101,055.39	4,943,480.78
Income from investments	424,042.55	274,594.04	42,307.93	*a b* 740,944.52
Interest on Kansas Pacific consolidated bonds repaid by the trustees	....	220,000.00	....	220,000.00
Proceeds of Union Depot Co., Spokane Falls, note	13,760.07	8,910.50	1,372.88	*a* 24,043.45
Proceeds of Pueblo Union Depot and Railroad Co., note	5,036.24	3,261.28	502.48	*a* 8,800.00
Miscellaneous income	937.76	607.26	93.56	*a* 1,638.58
Total income	4,875,234.88	918,340.21	145,332.24	5 938,907.33
CHARGES.				
Discount and interest	2,334.96	1,512.04	232.97	*a* 4,079.97
Deficit, Leavenworth, Topeka, and Southwestern Rwy. Co	7,247.20	4,693.01	723.07	*a* 12,663.28
Payment, McDonald coal judgment	5,828.68	3,774.44	581.54	*a* 10,184.66
Payment, Harris accident judgment	4,568.60	2,958.46	455.82	*a* 7,982.88
Commission and expenses of paying coupons abroad	839.24	2,373.57	18.27	*a* 3,231.08
Deficit of "Cripple lines"	82,672.94	53,535.89	8,248.51	*a b* 144,457.34
Union Depot Co., Spokane Falls, bonds purchased	13,760.07	8,910.50	1,372.88	*a* 24,043.45
United States earnings, included above in gross earnings, but withheld	1,352,483.20	149,648.58	21,736.52	1,523,868.30
Total charges to this point	1,460,734.89	227,406.49	33,369.58	1,730,510.96
Balance applicable to interest on bonds	3,405,499.99	690,933.72	111,962.66	4,208,396.37
Interest on bonds ordered paid by the court:				
First mortgage 6s	1,634,070.00	....	....	1,634,070.00
Sinking fund 8s	149,200.00	....	....	149,200.00
Omaha Bridge 8s	22,600.00	....	....	22,600.00
Collateral trust 6s	63,044.57	40,825.30	6,290.13	*a* 110,160.00
Eastern Division 6s	....	67,200.00	....	67,200.00
Middle Division 6s	....	121,890.00	....	121,890.00
Consolidated mortgage 6s	....	351,600.00	....	351,600.00
Trust 5 per cent	66,916.18	43,332.40	6,676.42	*a* 116,925.00
Omaha Bridge 5s	52,800.00	....	....	52,800.00
Equipment trust 5s	19,157.74	12,405.83	1,911.43	*a* 33,475.00
Collateral trust note 6s	382,774.27	247,870.25	38,190.48	*a* 668,835.00
Denver Extension 6s	....	176,610.00	....	176,610.00
Total interest ordered paid	2,390,562.76	1,061,733.78	53,068.46	3,505,365.00
Balance, surplus	1,014,937.23	*c* 370,800.06	58,894.20	703,031.37

a Apportioned to the various divisions on a road milage basis.
b For detail see accompanying statement.
c Deficit.

Office of the Receivers, *Boston, March 11, 1896.*

Alex. Millar, *Assistant Comptroller.*

EXHIBIT B.

RECEIVERS UNION PACIFIC RAILWAY.

Statement of income from investments of the Union Pacific Railway, consolidated, from October 13, 1893, to December 31, 1895, inclusive.

Name of income.	Amount.
Atchison Union Depot and Railroad Co. coupons	$112.50
Cheyenne County (Colo.) judgment coupons	3,668.00
City of Wichita (Kans.) coupons	1,111.46
Colorado Central R. R. Co. coupons	70,280.00
Echo and Park City Rwy. Co. coupons	14,400.00
Hotel department income	3,112.66
Junction City (Davis County, Kans.) coupons	150.00
Kansas City, Wyandotte and Northwestern R. R. Co. trust receipts, interest	3,660.20
Kansas City and Northwestern R. R. Co. coupons	2,425.00
Leavenworth Depot and R. R. Co. coupons	7,875.00
Leavenworth Depot and R. R. Co. dividend	1,000.00
Northern Pacific Terminal Co. coupons	1,500.00
Occidental and Oriental Steamship Co. dividend	25,000.00
Omaha Bridge 8 per cent coupons	160.00
Omaha Bridge renewal coupons	16,100.00
Pacific Express Co. dividends	72,000.00
Pullman-Union Pacific Association cars, three-fourths of net earnings	303,738.03
Union Depot Co. (Kansas City) dividend	7,500.00
Union Depot and R. R. Co. (Denver) dividends	54,000.00
Union Depot Co., of Spokane Falls, coupons and interest	14,391.67
Union Pacific Coal Co. coupons and registered interest	109,775.00
Union Pacific collateral trust note interest	21,600.00
Utah and Northern Rwy. Co. 7 per cent coupons	7,385.00
Total income from investments	740,944.52

OFFICE OF THE RECEIVERS, *Boston, March 11, 1896.*

ALEX. MILLAR, *Assistant Comptroller.*

EXHIBIT C.

RECEIVERS UNION PACIFIC RAILWAY.

Detail of the item of deficit of certain "cripple lines" from October 13, 1893, to July 31, 1894, and their apportionment to the various divisions of the Union Pacific Railway, on a road mileage basis.

Name of line.	Union division, including Omaha Bridge.	Kansas division, including Leavenworth branch.	Denver Pacific.	Total Union Pacific Railway Company.
Union Pacific, Brighton and Boulder Branch	$3,254.55	$2,107.53	$324.71	$5,686.79
Junction City and Fort Kearney Rwy	24,068.32	15,585.74	2,401.36	42,055.42
Omaha and Republican Valley Rwy	42,989.41	27,838.33	4,289.18	75,116.92
Salina and Southwestern Rwy	6,640.99	4,300.45	662.59	11,604.03
Kansas City and Omaha R. R., 18 per cent of $55,523.21, deficit from Oct. 13, 1893, to Dec. 31, 1894	5,719.67	3,703.84	570.67	9,994.18
Total of above five lines *a*	82,672.94	53,535.89	8,248.51	144,457.34

a Including only operating expenses and taxes, less amount of gross earnings.

OFFICE OF THE RECEIVERS, *Boston, March 11, 1896.*

ALEX. MILLAR, *Assistant Comptroller.*

EXHIBIT D.

RECEIVERS KANSAS PACIFIC CONSOLIDATED MORTGAGE PROPERTY.

Statement of the financial operations of the receivers of the Kansas Pacific consolidated mortgage property during the period from July 17, 1894, to December 31, 1895, inclusive.

Receipts:			
Earnings			$4,235,206.98
Expenses		$2,817,514.91	
Taxes		304,242.93	
			3,121,757.84
Surplus earnings			1,113,449.09
Expenditures:			
United States earnings, included above in gross earnings but withheld		199,778.81	
Union Pacific equipment trust obligations paid pursuant to court Order No. B 25		263,178.69	
Denver Extension land expenses	$206,975.21		
Less prepayments	113,400.07		
		93,575.14	
			556,532.64
Balance, surplus			556,916.45

OFFICE OF THE RECEIVERS, *Boston, March 11, 1896.*

ALEX. MILLAR, *Assistant Comptroller.*

EXHIBIT E.

RECEIVERS UNION PACIFIC RAILWAY, OMAHA BRIDGE DIVISION.

Statement of the financial operations of the receivers of the Union Pacific Railway, Omaha Bridge Divisions, during the period from August 1, 1894, to December 31, 1895, inclusive.

Receipts:		
Earnings		$488,454.94
Expenses	$270,708.32	
Taxes	32,187.10	
		302,895.42
Surplus earnings		185,559.52
Expenditures:		
United States earnings, included above in gross earnings but withheld	3,425.62	
J. Pierpont Morgan and Edwin F. Atkins, trustees (court order No. 108)	160,132.58	
		163,558.20
Balance, surplus		22,001.32

OFFICE OF THE RECEIVERS, *Boston, March 11, 1896.*

ALEX. MILLAR, *Assistant Comptroller.*

EXHIBIT F.

CHEYENNE BRANCH MORTGAGE RECEIVERSHIP.

Statement of the financial operations of the receivers of the Cheyenne Branch mortgage during the period from November 20, 1894, to December 31, 1895, inclusive.

Receipts:		
Earnings		$830,924.59
Expenses	$549,770.20	
Taxes	27,557.49	
		577,327.69
Surplus earnings		253,596.90
Expenditures:		
United States earnings, included above in gross earnings, but withheld	6,340.24	
Union Pacific equipment trust obligations paid pursuant to court order No. A 15	52,635.74	
		58,975.98
Balance, surplus		194,620.92

OFFICE OF THE RECEIVERS, *Boston, March 11, 1896.*

ALEX. MILLAR, *Assistant Comptroller.*

EXHIBIT G.

DEXTER-AMES RECEIVERSHIP.

Statement of the financial operations of the receivers of the Union Pacific Railway, Union Division, during the period from January 22 to December 31, 1895, inclusive.

Receipts:		
Earnings		$10,004,993.41
Expenses	$5,840,649.21	
Taxes	345,003.17	
		6,185,652.38
Surplus earnings		3,819,341.03
Expenditures:		
Interest ordered paid by the court	3,900.00	
United States earnings, included above in gross earnings, but withheld	1,038,881.89	
Union Pacific equipment trust obligations, paid pursuant to court order No. 19	736,900.32	
		1,779,682.21
Balance, surplus		2,039,658.82

OFFICE OF THE RECEIVERS, *Boston, March 11, 1896.*

ALEX. MILLAR, *Assistant Comptroller.*

TESTIMONY OF MR. S. H. H. CLARK.

Mr. S. H. H. CLARK, sworn and examined.

Senator WOLCOTT. How many years have you been connected with the Union Pacific Railway Company?

Mr. CLARK. Since June, 1867, with an intermission of a period between October, 1884, and November, 1890.

Senator WOLCOTT. During which time you were with the Missouri Pacific?

Mr. CLARK. Yes.

Senator WOLCOTT. You are now one of the receivers of the Union Pacific?

Mr. CLARK. I am.

Senator WOLCOTT. Mr. Anderson described you in his testimony as the "operating receiver." Is this your title?

Mr. CLARK. No; I think not. I presume he used it simply as a convenient term.

Senator WOLCOTT. You have charge of the traffic and operation of the road?

Mr. CLARK. Of operation.

Senator WOLCOTT. You are entirely familiar with the property and its branches?

Mr. CLARK. To a great degree, yes. I ought to be if I am not.

Senator WOLCOTT. Are the relations of the Union Pacific to the lines with which it connects at Council Bluffs—the Rock Island, the Wabash, the Burlington, and the Northwestern—alike?

Mr. CLARK. I can not say that they are exactly alike; they are friendly.

Senator WOLCOTT. Have you special arrangements with any one of these lines; and if so, what are they?

Mr. CLARK. There is an agreement made by my predecessor with the Chicago-Northwestern Company by which the relations between that company and the Union Pacific are perhaps more harmonious and probably somewhat more advantageous to the Union Pacific property than exist with the other companies connected with the Union Pacific.

Senator STEWART. Do you speak of your predecessor as receiver or as president of the company?

Mr. CLARK. My predecessor as president, Mr. Charles Francis Adams.

Senator WOLCOTT. Are these relations more advantageous to the Chicago-Northwestern Railroad than to other roads?

Mr. CLARK. I should say so, to a certain extent. It is difficult to determine just to what extent.

Senator WOLCOTT. You do not think that the Chicago and Northwestern road is a sufferer by the agreement, do you?

Mr. CLARK. No, sir.

Senator WOLCOTT. Did you renew it at the time of the receivership?

Mr. CLARK. It was not renewed; it was simply allowed to stand, by assent, so to speak.

Senator WOLCOTT. Are you familiar with this plan of reorganization?

Mr. CLARK. I am not.

Senator WOLCOTT. You have looked into it, more or less, I suppose?

Mr. CLARK. Very little.

Senator WOLCOTT. I notice that on this scheme there are Mr. Hewitt and Mr. Depew. Have those gentlemen been heretofore identified with the management of the Union Pacific system.

Mr. CLARK. Mr. Hewitt only, and only as a director of the company, so far as I know.

Senator WOLCOTT. And Mr. Depew?

Mr. CLARK. I do not know Mr. Depew at all. I have seen him, but I have never met him personally.

Senator WOLCOTT. You know of no connection which he has with the Union Pacific?

Mr. CLARK. I do not.

Senator WOLCOTT. Do you know how it happens that these two gentlemen are on this reorganization scheme?

Mr. CLARK. I do not.

Senator WOLCOTT. You know that their names are on the reorganization committee and have been published?

Mr. CLARK. Yes, sir.

Senator WOLCOTT. Did you know that Mr. Depew was an owner of the securities of the Union Pacific Company?

Mr. CLARK. I did not.

Senator WOLCOTT. Have you now any information on that subject?

Mr. CLARK. I have not.

Senator WOLCOTT. Has it occurred to you that the Chicago-Northwestern influence was rather conspicuous in this reorganization plan?

Mr. CLARK. I must say it has occurred to me.

Senator WOLCOTT. But you have given it no special thought?

Mr. CLARK. No, sir; no significance.

Senator WOLCOTT. And you do not know of the reason for it?

Mr. CLARK. No; I do not. I never have heard a reason suggested for it.

Senator WOLCOTT. Are all your agreements with the Northwestern road wholly evidenced in the one document to which Mr. Mink has made reference?

Mr. CLARK. Yes, sir.

Senator WOLCOTT. There is nothing outside of that?

Mr. CLARK. Nothing outside of it.

Senator WOLCOTT. Does that document cover the question of exchanging cars?

Mr. CLARK. I think so. It has been some time since I read the document.

Senator WOLCOTT. As a matter of fact, you run their through sleepers between Ogden and Chicago?

Mr. CLARK. Yes.

Senator WOLCOTT. And you do this for no other road?

Mr. CLARK. For no other road—that is, regularly; of course special cars come through.

Senator WOLCOTT. And your relations with that road are extremely close?

Mr. CLARK. They are friendly.

Senator WOLCOTT. They are pretty close. There is no impropriety about the closeness of the relations of the two roads. I simply want to ascertain if the two roads continue in the same friendly conditions as heretofore.

Mr. CLARK. I may answer that by saying that we are more harmonious with that line than with some other lines. We are friendly with all connecting lines.

Senator WOLCOTT. Do you know whether, under the reorganization plan, the Union Pacific would be practically absorbed by the Chicago and Northwestern?

Mr. CLARK. I do not.

Senator WOLCOTT. Whether it is so or not you are not advised?

Mr. CLARK. I know nothing about it.

Senator WOLCOTT. If the reorganization plan, as suggested, should be a practical absorption of the Union Pacific by the Northwestern it would give to the Northwestern a through road from Chicago to Ogden, would it not?

Mr. CLARK. I should say so.

Senator WOLCOTT. What, in your opinion, is the earning capacity of the 1,822 miles of the Union Pacific road?

Mr. CLARK. That is a very difficult question to answer.

Senator WOLCOTT. I recognize that.

Mr. CLARK. My judgment, Senator, on that point is worth no more than yours.

Senator WOLCOTT. It is worth very much more.

Mr. CLARK. I think not. The earning capacity of the road depends entirely upon conditions. The conditions that exist to-day are very peculiar. If they were continued I could form an opinion, but if these conditions do not continue nobody can tell anything about it.

Senator WOLCOTT. The conditions could not be much worse than they are now.

Mr. CLARK. I think they could be very much worse, Senator.

Senator WOLCOTT. I do not see how.

Mr. CLARK. The conditions all over this country are changed, and we are meeting new conditions which never existed before, but which we will have to meet hereafter. There are no more railroads to be built, for one thing, and there are no more lands to be acquired by mere settlement, so to speak. We are meeting the problem of overproduction. All these things enter into the matter.

Senator WOLCOTT. What is your general impression as to the earning capacity of the Union Pacific road?

Mr. CLARK. With the conditions existing to-day, and with the future prospects as they appear to me, the 1,822 miles of that road will earn in the neighborhood of $4,000,000 net annually. The road earned more last year, but that was because of the exceedingly close economy practiced. The receivers did not buy a steel rail in 1895 and they did the business of the road at the lowest possible expense in all its departments. That can not continue with good judgment even for another year. We need steel rails.

Senator WOLCOTT. Is the road in bad condition?

Mr. CLARK. No; I would not operate it if I thought it in bad condition.

Senator WOLCOTT. But it needs more renewals than you give?

Mr. CLARK. More than we gave it last year.

Senator WOLCOTT. But as the conditions are at present, the road is good for $4,000,000 net a year?

Mr. CLARK. Yes; in that neighborhood.

Senator WOLCOTT. What would be your counsel and advice as to the best method of settlement of the Government claim in the interest of the Government?

Mr. CLARK. In my humble opinion as a layman a commission of straightforward, upright business men ought to be appointed by Congress, who should go out into that country, examine it thoroughly, going back to its construction, taking into account all those things that have occurred, and then make a report of the facts. If I were one of the security holders I would be willing to say in advance that I would take the judgment of those men for my portion.

Senator BRICE. Suppose, Mr. Clark, that you were constituted sole commissioner; you have made all the examinations and have a full knowledge of all the facts; you have been president of that railroad company and have been managing the railroad property. What would you recommend; what do you think would be the best thing to do?

Mr. CLARK. That is my plan.

Senator WOLCOTT. What, in your opinion, is the present value of this Government debt, and how should it be realized to the best interests of the Government and of the company?

Mr. CLARK. I claim that the Government debt has been paid.

Senator WOLCOTT. Do you think that nothing is due?

Mr. CLARK. Yes; there is an equity which should be considered and canceled by payment.

Senator WOLCOTT. How much should be paid?

Mr. CLARK. I feel that the Government debt has been paid in the cheap transportation which the Government has had as against what it cost before the road was constructed. That is a matter of equity and justice, I consider. So with the Government lands. Millions of acres have been brought into the market by the construction of the railroad.

Senator WOLCOTT. On that theory there is no question, I take it, but that the Government has been benefited a great deal more than the road has cost it, if that is what you mean?

Mr. CLARK. That is what I mean.

Senator WOLCOTT. But we are confronted by the fact that there is a debt to the Government in dollars, and that that debt has got to be met.

Senator FRYE. Without regard to equity?

Mr. CLARK. On the shylock process?

Senator WOLCOTT. It has to be met as an existing debt, and I want to know how, in your opinion, it should be met.

Mr. CLARK. I hope you will excuse me from giving an opinion.

Senator WOLCOTT. You know more about this property than any man living, and I wish you would give us some suggestions.

Senator STEWART. Suppose you owned the debt, Mr. Clark, what would you take for it?

Mr. CLARK. I believe that the Government can afford to be fair in the matter.

Senator STEWART. What would you take?

Mr. CLARK. I would take the principal, if I could get it, and I would scale the interest to a fair figure.

Senator WOLCOTT. You would take the principal in cash. How would you scale the interest? Would you scale it for a cash sum?

Mr. CLARK. I think that the better plan. That is the only business way to do it.

Senator WOLCOTT. You would throw off some of the interest and settle it in that way? I am inclined to think that that is correct. But which do you think would be the simpler proposition for the railroad company—to give a security worth 35 per cent in cash for the interest or to pay that 35 per cent in cash in full settlement?

Mr. CLARK. I do not know that I fully understand your question.

Senator WOLCOTT. You heard my questions to Mr. Mink. We spoke of a mortgage to be given at 2 per cent for the interest.

Mr. CLARK. Yes.

Senator WOLCOTT. Mr. Mink was of opinion that the bonds secured by this mortgage (a second mortgage) would be worth about 35 cents on the dollar. Instead of offering the Government a mortgage worth 35 cents on the dollar, do you not think it would be a better proposition for the company to find a way to pay that 35 per cent in cash instead of in bonds worth 35 per cent?

Mr. CLARK. If the company could do so; yes.

Senator WOLCOTT. Do you not think it is as feasible for the company to pay 35 per cent in cash as it is for it to become indebted to the Government for the full amount in a mortgage worth only 35 per cent in cash?

Mr. CLARK. I am not sufficiently familiar with financial affairs to express an opinion on that subject.

Senator WOLCOTT. Is the company in the habit of paying rebates since your receivership?

Mr. CLARK. No, sir.

Senator FRYE. What percentage of the full debt of the company to the Government would be the entire principal due the Government and 35 per cent of the interest?

The CHAIRMAN. We made a calculation and found it would be a fraction over 67 per cent of the whole debt.

Senator WOLCOTT. As I understood Mr. Mink's testimony (he is in the room and can correct me if I am wrong), the general outlook which he had in view and which might be formulated into a proposition was this: that from the principal of the debt due to the Government the sinking fund should be deducted and the difference should be paid in cash, and that the interest should be secured by a second mortgage at 2 per cent on the property of the 1,822 miles of the road. Is that correct, Mr. Mink?

Mr. MINK. Yes, sir.

Senator WOLCOTT. Eighteen million dollars in cash and $14,000,000 in value, making $32,000,000. (To Mr. Mink): What is the total of the Government debt?

Mr. MINK. Thirty-three million five hundred thousand dollars.

Senator WOLCOTT. And the interest?

Mr. MINK. Including the interest yet to accrue, about $38,000,000—call it $40,000,000.

Senator WOLCOTT. What is the amount of the sinking fund to be applied to that $33,500,000?

Mr. MINK. Fifteen million two hundred thousand dollars.

Senator WOLCOTT. That would make $18,000,000 cash to be paid to the Government and $38,000,000 in second-mortgage bonds. Thirty-five per cent of that would be about $40,000,000?

Mr. MINK. Yes.

Senator WOLCOTT (to Mr. Clark). You say that there are no rebates being paid now?

Mr. CLARK. There are not.

Senator WOLCOTT. Is the road in politics at all now?

Mr. CLARK. No, sir.

Senator WOLCOTT. Is the road spending any money in politics?

Mr. CLARK. No, sir.

Senator WOLCOTT. You never dabble in politics yourself?

Mr. CLARK. No; thank God, I never have been a politician.

The CHAIRMAN. You have been connected with the Union Pacific many years?

Mr. CLARK. Yes.

The CHAIRMAN. What time did you commence your connection with that road?

Mr. CLARK. I commenced service with the Union Pacific in June, 1867.

The CHAIRMAN. Shortly after the road was completed?

Mr. CLARK. Long before.

The CHAIRMAN. You have seen that country develop all through the line?

Mr. CLARK. Indeed, I have. Omaha contained a population at that time of about 14,000, and beyond Omaha there were hardly any inhabitants.

The CHAIRMAN. The country has developed in farming and pastoral pursuits?

Mr. CLARK. Yes.

The CHAIRMAN. Also in mining?

Mr. CLARK. Yes; but in a pastoral and grazing sense it has deteriorated.

The CHAIRMAN. That is but a recent incident. What percentage in business is estimated to come to the Union Pacific line proper from the country lying adjacent to the line, or tributary to the line?

Mr. CLARK. Mr. Monroe, who has charge of the traffic matters, says it is 25 per cent.

The CHAIRMAN. The rest of the business is from through business?

Mr. CLARK. Yes.

The CHAIRMAN. Coming from the Oregon Short Line and other connecting lines?

Mr. CLARK. Yes.

The CHAIRMAN. The construction of other lines of railroad has reduced the tonnage from the adjacent country, has it?

Mr. CLARK. Immensely.

The CHAIRMAN. And you consider that the present Union Pacific line furnishes only 25 per cent of the business, and that if these other lines which have been added to the Union Pacific system were cut off you would have to depend largely upon your local traffic?

Mr. CLARK. Precisely so. There are other connections besides the Union Pacific for all of these roads, and if they were to use their other connections exclusively the Union Pacific would be, in railroad parlance, "bottled up."

The CHAIRMAN. There is the Northwestern on one side and the Burlington on the other?

Mr. CLARK. And the Oregon Short Line.

The CHAIRMAN. They all have connections outside of the Union Pacific which they could use?

Mr. CLARK. Yes.

The CHAIRMAN. So the value of your property must depend largely upon your maintaining amicable relations with those lines?

Mr. CLARK. Almost wholly.

The CHAIRMAN. Do you consider that the country that the line runs through has absolutely reached its highest point of advancement in a degree?

Mr. CLARK. I do.

The CHAIRMAN. Almost all of the land left being inarable and unpasturable?

Mr. CLARK. Yes; I mean it will be years hence before that country will show any great improvement.

The CHAIRMAN. And a large part of the value of the country will depend upon ability to irrigate it?

Mr. CLARK. Yes.

The CHAIRMAN. On the other hand, the coast country will naturally develop immediately?

Mr. CLARK. Yes; and I think you may include the new States of Utah and Idaho as progressing in the way of development—also Colorado. But along the present line of the Union Pacific there is no real prospect of a further increase of business.

The CHAIRMAN. And the proximity of parallel lines of road of course takes a large percentage which you had been able to get formerly?

Mr. CLARK. That is so.

The CHAIRMAN. Can you tell, in round numbers, what the Union Pacific has cost?

Mr. CLARK. My recollection is that it cost something over $60,000 a mile.

The CHAIRMAN. For how many miles?

Mr. CLARK. About 1,830 miles.

The CHAIRMAN. Then it cost a little over $100,000,000?

Mr. CLARK. Yes.

The CHAIRMAN. What could that line be replaced for to-day?

Mr. CLARK. For less than half.

The CHAIRMAN. Probably for $50,000,000?

Mr. CLARK. Yes; I should think so. I think that $30,000 a mile would duplicate that property.

The CHAIRMAN. Is the motive power first-class now?

Mr. CLARK. No, sir; we have a variety of engines. The original engines, those that have been there for a number of years, are small, light, and old-fashioned. We have, however, a very fair percentage of good, strong-power engines.

The CHAIRMAN. How many cars can you haul with those old-fashioned engines?

Mr. CLARK. That depends entirely upon the grade. Between Omaha and Denver one of those small engines can probably haul twenty cars.

The CHAIRMAN. And to Cheyenne?

Mr. CLARK. Not over eight.

The CHAIRMAN. What is the traction power of your larger engines?

Mr. CLARK. Our biggest engines are what we call the 1,400 and 1,600 class. They are 20 by 24 cylinder. These engines will pull about two and one-half times as much as the others.

The CHAIRMAN. They will carry twenty cars instead of eight?

Mr. CLARK. Yes.

The CHAIRMAN. What is about the average percentage of operating expenses on your road?

Mr. CLARK. I should say 70 per cent.

The CHAIRMAN. Why are they so much higher than on other western roads? For instance, the Northwestern and other roads in Iowa?

Mr. CLARK. The Northwestern is not a parallel case.

The CHAIRMAN. Well, take the Burlington, where they have got high grades and high curves as compared with the Northwestern.

Mr. CLARK. It depends, of course, on fuel and labor and the amount of traffic. These elements all enter into the question of operating expenses.

The CHAIRMAN. Where do you get your coal?

Mr. CLARK. Largely at Rock Springs, Wyo.

The CHAIRMAN. You have to haul that coal East and West?

Mr. CLARK. Yes; mostly to points East.

The CHAIRMAN. Does the company own those mines?

Mr. CLARK. Yes.

The CHAIRMAN. About how much does the coal cost you?

Mr. CLARK. I take it about $3 a ton.

The CHAIRMAN. And this high rate of operating expenses—70 per cent—comes from high grades and light locomotives?

Mr. CLARK. Yes; and from the cost of coal, and from bad-business.

Senator FRYE. Does the coal delivered at Rock Springs on board the train cost $3 a ton net?

Mr. CLARK. No; but with the cost of transportation to the point of using added it costs the company $3 a ton.

The CHAIRMAN. Are your water facilities good?

Mr. CLARK. Very much better than formerly. We have put down artesian wells which furnish a sufficient amount of fairly good water.

The CHAIRMAN. You have no arrangement, as general manager and superintendent of the company, by which you give one road connecting with the Union Pacific greater facilities than you give other roads?

Mr. CLARK. Only in the case of the Northwestern.

Adjourned.

WASHINGTON, D. C., *Thursday, March 19, 1896.*

The committee met at 2.30 p. m.

Present: Senators Gear (chairman), Stewart, and Brice.

PACIFIC RAILROAD FIRST-MORTGAGE BONDS.

STATEMENT OF LEONARD C. BLAISDELL.

Leonard C. Blaisdell, of Indianapolis, Ind., counselor at law, sworn and examined:

The CHAIRMAN. You may proceed and make your statement.

Mr. BLAISDELL. The statement which I have to make under oath respecting the subject-matter of claims represented by myself as attorney in fact of claimants against the United States, will be found expressed in case 18003 in the Court of Claims. It is therein set forth that by virtue of the action of the Secretary of the Treasury and of the First Comptroller of the Treasury on April 22, 1884, the rights, privileges, and franchises of these creditors of the Union Pacific, the Central Pacific, and other Pacific railroad companies (to which were granted loans by the United States in aid of the construction of these roads and telegraph lines to the amount of $64,623,512), were made subject to the rights of the lawful and just holders of the lien prior and paramount to that of the United States, as expressed in the eighth section of the act of 1864, and as further expressed in the eighth section of what is commonly named the Thurman Act.

That, on the said date, a contract or agreement was entered into with myself, by which the United States undertook to issue call bonds on the said Pacific Railroad Companies, payable January 1, 1885, at the subtreasury in the city of New York. It was further agreed that the amount of interest on the accrued indebtedness, so described as of lien paramount to that of the United States, should be converted into United States sinking fund bonds bearing the rate of 5 per cent interest, to date from March 3, 1883, and made payable by the United States on August 16, 1894. I further state that the complete statement in relation to all the particulars of this transaction has been heretofore made repeatedly, and finally under the determination of the late President, Harrison, and will be found in pamphlet form with the Executive, and also copies with the Secretary of the Treasury, with the Secretary of the Interior Department, and in the Department of Justice. Certified copies under oath will be found in all the Departments.

The CHAIRMAN. Have you a copy of that document?

Mr. BLAISDELL. Yes; I will furnish full printed copies.

Senator STEWART. I would like to know what this controversy is about.

Mr. BLAISDELL. I did not expect to present the matter in full at this time. I expected to get an appointment to do so. We would have to go to our rooms and bring our papers.

Senator STEWART. What is the nature of the claim you were speaking of?

Mr. BLAISDELL. The nature of the claim is, that while we admit that the Government is the actual holder of the sinking fund, we claim every dollar in the sinking fund by virtue of the Government being our agent to collect that money. The Government is a trustee.

Senator STEWART. And you are the bondholders?

Mr. BLAISDELL. We are bondholders in this way: In this same meeting, on April 22, 1884, I held in my hand the bonds of the Union Pacific, of the Central Pacific, and of the other Pacific railways named in the Thurman Act, which are secured by mortgage, and which are expressed therein as a lien prior and paramount to that of the United States.

Senator STEWART. We all understand that.

Mr. BLAISDELL. That is the way we are bondholders.

Senator STEWART. To what amount are you bondholders?

Mr. BLAISDELL. To the amount of $64,644,000.

Senator STEWART. You represent those bonds?

Mr. BLAISDELL. We do.

The CHAIRMAN. Are you the attorney in fact?

Mr. BLAISDELL. I am the attorney in fact and of record?

Senator STEWART. For all the bondholders?

Mr. BLAISDELL. Yes; for all of them.

Senator STEWART. What do they want?

Mr. BLAISDELL. They want this money.

Senator STEWART. With reference to this sinking fund, what legal right do you claim?

Mr. BLAISDELL. Just this, that the purposes of the sinking fund, by law, would be subserved in the period of thirty years (the life of the bonds), and that at the end of the thirty years the amount due should be settled up.

The CHAIRMAN. You seem by this document to have the case in the Court of Claims?

Mr. BLAISDELL. Yes; but we do not bring before you the question which we have before the Court of Claims.

Senator STEWART. Do I understand that these bonds were issued by the United States?

Mr. BLAISDELL. No; they were issued by the Pacific railroads.

The CHAIRMAN. They are the first-mortgage bonds?

Mr. BLAISDELL. Yes; the bonds issued by the Pacific railroads as first-mortgage bonds are what we are claiming.

Senator STEWART. What relation have you directly to the sinking fund; what claim have you on it?

Mr. BLAISDELL. I have a claim on it of this character; I was a party to loaning every dollar which has come into that sinking fund, exclusive of what was collected and is to be collected under the Thurman Act, which amounted to $19,000,000 or $20,000,000.

Senator STEWART. Did you have any contract with the Government or anybody else, independent of your contract with the railroad companies, under which these bonds were issued?

Mr. BLAISDELL. Yes.

Senator STEWART. What contract have you?

Mr. BLAISDELL. It is expressed in the transaction between myself and the officers of the Government—the First Comptroller, the Secretary of the Treasury, and another Cabinet officer, and, I may say, the entire Cabinet, with the exceptions of the Secretary of War, the Secretary of the Navy, and the Postmaster-General.

Senator STEWART. Are these first-mortgage bonds due?

Mr. BLAISDELL. Yes; the Central Pacific bonds all matured in 1892 and the Union Pacific bonds matured in 1894.

Senator STEWART. Under what law did the First Comptroller and those other officers of the Government make any special contract with the bondholders of the Pacific railroads?

Mr. BLAISDELL. The statement made to me was, that it was under the general provisions of the law which had been made with reference to the Pacific railroads, but the specific act, on which this meeting took place and this transaction took place, was that decision of the Supreme Court by which the Secretary of the Treasury had been instructed that the Government could make no further demands on the roads for moneys, for the reason that the accrued interest on the bonds of the paramount lien remained unpaid, and the companies claimed the right to pay that interest before the Government could demand any money. The particular decision can be found in 196 United States Reports.

Senator STEWART. The companies did pay the interest until they defaulted?

Mr. BLAISDELL. They paid a certain portion of the net earnings.

Senator STEWART. Did not the companies pay the interest on the first-mortgage bonds until the recent default?

Mr. BLAISDELL. No, sir.

Senator STEWART. When did the different roads default?

Mr. BLAISDELL. The decision of the First Comptroller was on the 22d of April, 1884.

Senator STEWART. What roads defaulted then?

Mr. BLAISDELL. All of them.

Senator STEWART. You mean in paying interest to the first-mortgage bondholders?

Mr. BLAISDELL. Yes; the question was put to Judge Brewster, the Attorney-General, by Judge Folger, the Secretary of the Treasury. Judge Folger said: "We have here what represents payment; but I put the question to you, Judge Brewster, and ask you whether these bonds which act in the way of accrued interest constitute payment within the meaning of the law?" And Judge Brewster said they did not.

Senator STEWART. I thought that these roads kept on paying interest on their first-mortgage bonds?

Mr. BLAISDELL. Not a cent has been paid except in that way. Somewhere from $20,000,000 to $27,000,000 has gone into the Treasury, and the Government has given to the railroad companies credit for the money that has gone into the sinking fund. Some of the bookkeeping calls it payment of interest; but the Supreme Court has said that it is just simply a fund there.

Senator STEWART. This is a new statement of the whole thing.

Mr. BLAISDELL. I expect it is. I expect that it overturns every theory on that subject.

Senator STEWART. You pretend to say that these Pacific railroad companies have paid no interest on their first-mortgage bonds?

Mr. BLAISDELL. Practically speaking, not one cent I admit what they paid into the Treasury, but, as to any actual payment to the actual bondholders, there has not been a cent of interest paid on the first-mortgage bonds.

Senator STEWART. I ask you if you mean it to be understood that the companies have paid no interest on their first-mortgage bonds?—I do not mean on the Government subsidy bonds.

Mr. BLAISDELL. I answer the question by saying just what Secretary Folger said: "They have executed their bonds and lodged them with the Secretary of the Treasury, and pay accrued interest." I mean the bonds issued by the Pacific railroads and not the bonds issued by the Government in aid.

Senator STEWART. And you say that there has not been a cent of interest paid on them?

Mr. BLAISDELL. Except by Government credits. Credits have been given to them.

Senator BRICE. Inasmuch as the holders of each one of the bonds did, in fact, get his interest every six months, and has done so for thirty years, where did they get that interest from?

Mr. BLAISDELL. I do not say that they did get it.

Senator BRICE. But I do, for I have held some of the bonds and have been paid the interest on them.

Mr. BLAISDELL. And you do not know that more than $64,000,000 of these bonds have been floated which never have been guaranteed by an act of Congress? I admit that any amount of bonds may have been floating, on which the companies have been paying interest.

Senator BRICE. Who holds these bonds?

Mr. BLAISDELL. The Government, for the actual owners.

Senator BRICE. Where are they stored?

Mr. BLAISDELL. In the office of the Secretary of the Treasury.

Senator STEWART. Where are the bonds that you speak of?

Mr. BLAISDELL. I will not say where they are, but I know where they ought to be. They were left in the custody of the Secretary of the Treasury, and they were to be redeemed.

Senator STEWART. Let us see if we understand each other. In the aggregate there were $64,000,000 of subsidy bonds, and the same amount of first-mortgage bonds. Drop everything but the first-mortgage bonds issued by the company. Do I understand you, no interest has been paid on these first-mortgage bonds?

Mr. BLAISDELL. Not to the lawful holders. There has been to the Government, but not to the lawful holders.

The CHAIRMAN. Who are the lawful holders?

Mr. BLAISDELL. The heirs at law of Charles Durkee.

The CHAIRMAN. Did he own them all?

Mr. BLAISDELL. Every one of them.

The CHAIRMAN. How did he acquire them?

Mr. BLAISDELL. By purchase.

The CHAIRMAN. From whom?

Mr. BLAISDELL. From holders to whom the companies had issued them.

The CHAIRMAN. Are these bonds in evidence anywhere?

Mr. BLAISDELL. I claim that they ought to be in vaults 75 and 85, in the Treasury Department.

The CHAIRMAN. You claim that they were deposited there?

Mr. BLAISDELL. Yes; by order of Secretary Folger.

The CHAIRMAN. You claim that they were issued by the Pacific railroad companies?

Mr. BLAISDELL. Yes.

The CHAIRMAN. And put in trust of the Government?

Mr. BLAISDELL. Put into the hands of the Secretary of the Treasury.

The CHAIRMAN. For the benefit of any one person or of a given number of persons?

Mr. BLAISDELL. No; but as the court describes it in its opinion, "for the benefit of the lawful and just holders."

The CHAIRMAN. You claim here to be the holders of these bonds through some heirship or contract representing the estate of Charles Durkee?

Mr. BLAISDELL. Yes.

The CHAIRMAN. Then why do you not go to the Secretary of the Treasury and make application to him to carry out the law?

Mr. BLAISDELL. That is what we are asking Congress to do.

The CHAIRMAN. If you and the parties in interest own these bonds, it seems to me that you should go to the Secretary of the Treasury and demand payment from him.

Mr. BLAISDELL. There is a difficulty in talking to you about this matter without knowing that I was going to talk about it. I should have brought the record along with me; not only the Thurman Act but the act of March 3, 1887—an act which I drafted, and which Senator Cullom got through for the purpose of protecting these particular interests.

Senator BRICE. This is a very important matter, and you should have your documents and an opportunity to present them.

Mr. BLAISDELL. I did not expect to be rushed into this subject at all.

Senator BRICE. The witness ought to lay before the committee his propositions in proper order.

Senator STEWART. Yes; and submit a statement in writing.

Mr. BLAISDELL. I will do that.

Adjourned until Saturday, March 21, at 11 a. m.

WASHINGTON, D. C.,
Saturday, March 21, 1896.

The committee met at 11 a. m. Present, the chairman.

INTEREST ON FIRST-MORTGAGE BONDS.

STATEMENT OF MR. LEONARD C. BLAISDELL—Continued.

Leonard C. Blaisdell appeared before the committee, and submitted the following statement:

My own personal relation to this matter of Pacific railroad bonds began about the year 1882. During that year and the succeeding one of 1883 there was a considerable amount of correspondence between myself and the Department of the Treasury. The principal part of such correspondence was between myself on the one part, and the late Secretary of the Treasury, the Hon. Charles J. Folger, and the late First Comptroller of the Treasury, the Hon. William Lawrence.

The subject of that correspondence was confined strictly to a single question proposed by me, to wit: "What bonds of indemnity to the United States were signed by Charles Durkee, late governor of the Territory of Utah, during his lifetime, and which bonds had been canceled?"

The greater part of this correspondence occurred during the year 1882. During its pendency, however, while there was no satisfactory answer to my question, there was manifested on the part of the officials with whom I corresponded a desire to encourage my further inquiries.

At this juncture, or the beginning of the year 1883, it was officially communicated to me "that one of the two or more bonds of indemnity, signed by Charles Durkee, was in behalf of Franklin H. Head and pertained to Indian agency; that such bonds had been duly canceled." This not being satisfactory (to me) I made further inquiry as to what connection, if any, Mr. Durkee appeared to have with either the construction or security for construction of any part of the Pacific railroad lines.

The reason I had for pressing my inquiries further was that my investigation before this time had fully satisfied me that, no matter in what form consisted the bulk of the estate of Charles Durkee, it had been sequestered from its lawful heirs. I had informed the Department that the probate records of Kenosha County, Wis., disclosed the fact that a "bargain or assignment" of matters of estate not mentioned in inventory had been made between Caroline Durkee (the widow of Charles Durkee) and one Harvey Durkee (an executor of the estate), and that such procedure had been in fraud of the rights of next of kin, claimants as heirs at law, under the ordinance of 1787.

I am satisfied that it was this information alone, unsupported by anything that I personally knew about the assets of said estate, that caused me to receive soon afterwards instructions in official manner, from both the Secretary of the Treasury and the First Comptroller, what course I should pursue, and to report to the Department when I should have complied with instructions and completed the arrangements I was directed to make.

The directions were to commence a suit in equity procedure in a United States court having jurisdiction over the person of one of the executors of the will of the late Charles Durkee, and that when such suit should have been instituted to report forthwith to the head of the Treasury Department for further advices.

Therefore, having complied literally with these instructions and filed the suit in the supreme court of Cook County, in Chicago, on the 15th day of April, 1884, on the 22d day of that month and year I was presented by the Hon. Joseph G. Cannon to the Treasury clerk, Amos Webster. Mr. Cannon requested Mr. Webster to look over the papers I had to present to him, and, further, to immediately call together such officials as the papers seemed to require to make the required investigations, which all related to Pacific railroad bonds and Charles Durkee's obligations to the United States on bonds of indemnity.

Within a short time there came into the Treasury building Judge Lawrence, First Comptroller; Judge Folger, Secretary of the Treasury; Judge Brewster, Attorney-General; Secretary of State Frelinghuysen, and several other officers, each bearing in hand a large bundle of papers. Mr. Webster presented me, and with little delay I, with all these officials, was ushered into a room I understood to be the office of Judge Lawrence; and he further continued the introduction by making the statement that I was the person who had been making all the inquiries of the Department respecting the relations, if any, that the estate of Charles Durkee bore to the affairs and business of such Department.

Immediately Judge Lawrence began to interrogate me as to what knowledge I had acquired relative to the subject-matter of the proposed investigation. After ascertaining that I knew practically nothing of Charles Durkee's ownership of Pacific railroad or other bonds (at that time), he proceeded to examine the power of attorney, court papers, and official letters which I had brought with me; and at the conclusion of his examinations he addressed Judge Folger in a formal way, declaring that the powers of attorney presented under the provisions of the ordinance of 1787 constituted me the legal representative of the estate of the late governor of the Territory of Utah, and that any business he might have with such estate could be legally transacted with myself. Then Judge Folger arose and stated what the business was that he desired to transact and the purposes to be effected, if found practical, in the joint meeting of officials present and myself.

Judge Folger, then directing his conversation to the Attorney-General, Judge Brewster, rapidly recited the enactments of 1862, 1864, and of 1878, respecting Pacific railroads, and concluded by stating that there had been in all some forty or more suits between the Government and these corporations over the question of what constituted "net earnings" and the resultant rights or privileges of the Government to collect moneys from the said corporations for the purposes named in the last enactment mentioned, or the Thurman Act.

At about this stage of the proceedings Judge Folger turned his attention to the vast number of papers, files, and records of various kinds that lay on the tables, picking up different ones in his hand as he continued his remarks to Judge Brewster. "These," he said, pointing to the first collection, "are the first-mortgage bonds issued by the Union, the Central, and other Pacific railroad corporations, as under the provisions of the act of 1864." Next, he said, "We have here a large amount of bonds, issued by the same corporations, which have been issued to secure payment of interest accrued on the principal bonds. These first-mortgage bonds differ from all others, in that they are guaranteed by act of Congress, as lawfully paramount to the rights and interests of the United States in respect of its mortgage against the same corporations, and each and every one," said he [holding some of them up in his hands, so as to be seen by all present], "are assigned to one, sole, assignee—Charles Durkee."

Then, exhibiting some of the interest bonds, Judge Folger explained that these, as well as the first-mortgage bonds, were issued in the form of call bonds, by the terms of which, on any default being made in the payment of the same on the demand of the legal holder or his legal representatives, the right of foreclosure immediately vested in the holder. "Therefore," said he, "I have contended against the practice heretofore adopted, of treating these bonds as payments of interest, however good they may be as securities, and have contended that they do not, within the meaning of the law, constitute payment of the interest. To you, Judge Brewster, I present the question for your decision." Judge Brewster promptly replied: "Judge, I fully concur in your conclusion. That is my judgment also." Then Judge Folger immediately turned himself about, and, facing me, said: "You have just heard the decision of Judge Brewster, the Attorney-General. What do you want done with these bonds?"

I answered: "I should prefer to leave the whole matter to your discretion, Judge Folger. I can not determine what disposition shall be made of these bonds; that is for you to say."

"Let me put the question in this way: Do you want these mortgages foreclosed?"

Mr. BLAISDELL. "That depends upon how much money can be realized out of them without foreclosure."

Judge FOLGER. "I think that the amount of the Central's bonds, with the interest accrued, might be collected by giving plenty of time."

Mr. BLAISDELL. "What is the amount of the Central's bonds?"

Judge FOLGER. "$25,885,120."

Mr. BLAISDELL. "You think that amount could be realized on a call, do you?"

Judge FOLGER. "Yes, sir."

Mr. BLAISDELL. "Let it be called then."

Judge FOLGER. "At what date?"

Mr. BLAISDELL. "At the end of the fiscal year."

Addressing then the accounting officers, Secretary Folger said:

"Make an estimate of the value of this bond with the interest to accrue to that date."

It was made, but while being made other conversation was going on between the Secretary and myself, he giving me information and instructions to guide me.

Receiving the paper from the accounting officers on which the estimate had been made, he remarked with apparent surprise:

"Why, that amounts to almost as much as the sum total of all the original bonds. I fear that if so much is called at one time there will be a failure. Could you not extend the time on a part of the payments?"

"Certainly," I said "I am not so anxious to get it all at once as I am to at once get good security for the whole. Take as much time as you desire to make the calls in, provided only that we hold the United States securities for our money instead of Pacific railroad bonds."

Judge FOLGER. "How would the 1st of January next (1885) do?"

"That will do," I said. "I was only solicitous to get the job off my hands and into yours, and the only care that I have is to see that the security shall pass from the Pacific railroads to the United States, so that I shall look to the Government, and not to the Pacific railroads for the payment."

The accounting officers, at this stage of proceedings, picked up their pencils and made a new computation of interest, adding interest to January 1, 1885.

Judge FOLGER. "But you must remember that there is a great deal more of this indebtedness to be looked after. What are you going to do with the balance of it; that of the other roads?"

Mr. BLAISDELL. "Well, we want to collect it."

Judge FOLGER. "Should there be an attempt to collect the whole amount due, as under the terms of the forfeiture, the property of these corporations would fail to make anything near the amount required, and the Government would get absolutely nothing. I would like to arrange it to save something for the Government."

Mr. BLAISDELL. "How will this do. Secure to us the entire principal of the mortgages, and you take just as long time for the Government to pay the accrued interest as you desire?"

Judge FOLGER. "I will fix the date of the maturity of the accrued interest at that of the maturity of the last bond, or August 16, 1894. At what date shall we begin to compute the interest on the Pacific railroad interest bonds?"

Mr. BLAISDELL. "I notice you said that the last payment of interest had been made March 3, 1883. Fix it at that date."

Judge FOLGER. "Very well. Now what rate of interest shall this fund bear?"

Mr. BLAISDELL. "What rate of interest do sinking-fund bonds now bear?"

Judge FOLGER. "Five per cent per annum."

Mr. BLAISDELL. "Will you make it 5 per cent?"

Judge FOLGER. "I think we can."

"Do that then," said I.

Judge FOLGER. "Now what depository do you propose to receive the principal in?"

Mr. BLAISDELL. "New York City subtreasury."

Judge FOLGER. "Why New York City; why not Washington?"

Mr. BLAISDELL. "I think it less likely to get mixed up with other funds."

Judge FOLGER. "Very well, that will do. Now, is there any more interest to be paid by the corporations?"

Mr. BLAISDELL. "No, sir. From these dates they will all be excused from the payment of any more interest."

Judge FOLGER. "But I would like in some way to secure to the Government some more net earnings."

Mr. BLAISDELL. "Well, I do not know that I have anything to do with that."

Judge FOLGER. "Not directly, but indirectly it would aid the Government, if you make a demand upon the Union Pacific for the whole of its net earnings—as a matter of default—for payment of interest."

Mr. BLAISDELL. "Very well, you can fix that to suit the case."

Judge FOLGER. "On what date now should the payment of all interest, as by the corporations, cease?"

Mr. BLAISDELL. "On what date did you receive the last interest?"

Judge FOLGER. "March 3, 1883."

Mr. BLAISDELL. "Let it cease on that date, then."

To this proposition Mr. Folger agreed.

This closed the transactions and the conversation with me, excepting that, when he was about to retire, I asked him what I should have to show that these transactions had occurred. Addressing Judge Lawrence, he said: "You, Judge, will see to it that Mr. Blaisdell is supplied with the proper certificate of ownership of these bonds, and a copy of the proceedings and transactions between himself and the Government, omitting nothing essential to the protection of the interests which he represents."

Mr. BLAISDELL (to Judge Lawrence). "When shall I receive these papers and certificates?"

Judge LAWRENCE. "Oh, you return for them in about a month. I think we will have everything ready about that time."

In about five or six weeks I returned to Washington again, and being accompanied by Hon. J. G. Cannon, made a personal application for the papers promised. Judge Lawrence manifested a degree of indifference and ignorance on the subject which called forth from Mr. Cannon this remark: "Why, Judge Lawrence, were you not present, and knowing to all that transpired in the interview with Mr. Blaisdell?"

Judge Lawrence replied: "Certainly I was; but you know, Mr. Cannon, the business was of such a nature that it was not proper to make it the subject of open conversation, and you see that this room is filled with promiscuous people. Let Mr. Blaisdell come in in the afternoon, and we will have a private talk, and I will tell him all about it."

Then beckoning with his hand to Joseph A. D. Thompson, Deputy First Comptroller, he said: "Go with these gentlemen and introduce Mr. Blaisdell to Mr. William Armstrong, the Commissioner of Railroads, and tell that officer that hereafter it will be his duty to report Pacific railroad matters and accounts to Mr. Blaisdell." Mr. Lawrence added, as instructions to Mr. Armstrong, "that he should take particular pains to instruct Mr. Blaisdell as to his rights and prerogatives."

Mr. Armstrong turned to those pages in the last railroad report which referred more especially to the rights and privileges of holders of liens prior and paramount to that of the United States and recited to me the text important to my protection. Afterwards, handing me the report, he said, "You are entitled to this report, take it along."

From that time to the present, all Commissioners of Railroads have continued to furnish me with railroad reports as they have been published, and have uniformly forwarded them to my address, whether at Champaign, or Chicago, Ill.

Although satisfied personally with the treatment received from Mr. Armstrong, I felt disappointed, and returned again to Judge Lawrence, and expressed to him my great dissatisfaction and disappointment in not discovering anything in the reports that identified the late Governor Durkee, of Utah, with any of the matters in which, by reason of the transactions of April 2, 1884, I had become concerned in as a legal representative for lawful creditors.

I insisted that Judge Lawrence should so far comply with the known order of Judge Folger (who then had retired on account of sickness) as to deliver to me certificates, or other form of written evidence, that I was the legal representative of the creditors of the Government in these matters. He then promised me, that as soon as the terms and agreements made with respect to Pacific railroads in the matter should have been fully carried into effect, and accountings fully completed, that he would supply me with certified copies of every transaction that had occurred in the matter with me.

Accepting this promise as having been made in good faith, I then returned to my home in Champaign, Ill. The time from the second to the third visit to Washington was about six or seven months. During this time a number of letters passed between myself and the Treasury

Department. Generally my letters were answered in person by Judge Lawrence. The answers were generally brief, and uniformly evasive on every question of vouchers and certificates.

I came the third time in January, 1885; waited on Senator Cullom, who wrote a letter of introduction to the Assistant Secretary of the Treasury, Jonathan Tarbell, requesting such officer to give me special attention for the time I had to spend with him. This he did, and we spent the entire day in the examination of large bundles of papers brought to us by clerks, with the view of selecting the most important, and of finding, if practicable, "how and when Pacific railroad bonds were assigned to Charles Durkee, deceased, and the papers showing rights of his heirs."

The result was disappointing to Mr. Tarbell, as well as myself, and he proposed to continue the examination the next day. Owing, however, to my engagements in the suit that had been placed under my management, by an arrangement with the Secretary of the Treasury, that was still pending in Chicago, I felt compelled to return and trust the further investigation to Mr. Tarbell, who promised to do for me the best he could. I returned that night to Chicago.

The Secretary of State, Mr. Frelinghuysen, however, having a personal knowledge of the proceedings of the Secretary of the Treasury, April 22, 1884 (having been present), voluntarily prepared some State papers to be used in the case, to which he attached the great seal of State, and affixed his signature, saying that the purpose of so doing was to enable me to save all the testimony I had received, and to attach thereunto all that I should thereafter receive, in testimony of the transactions had with myself.

It was mutually agreed between myself, Secretary Frelinghuysen, and Secretary Tarbell that search for the documents should continue after I should leave, and that as fast as discovered, they should be forwarded to me.

There were a few more documents sent me after this, but I never received the certificate of ownership of the bonds.

W. Blaisdell dictated to the stenographer the following additional particulars:

THE ENTIRE INDEBTEDNESS EXPRESSED IN UNITED STATES STATUTES.

First. The first-mortgage indebtedness and the subsidy indebtedness being paid, there exists no further liability against the United States.

Second. The United States statutes have provided and the Supreme Court has decided that there is but one class of creditors with higher claim than that of the United States. (See section 8 of the Thurman Act, and sections 4 and 5 of the act of March 3, 1887.)

Third. No records of the Government show any other claim purporting to be a paramount lien to that of the United States except the claim represented by L. C. Blaisdell.

Fourth. The act of March 3, 1887, is a complete statutory preparation and provision directing the Secretary of the Treasury to clear off such paramount lien.

If the parties claiming to hold paramount lien bonds are correct in their statements, how can the last report of the Secretary of the Interior be correct?

The Secretary of the Interior says that all these bonds are now matured; that the Government holds the second lien and must protect the property against the first lien. And the statutes declare that the United States has but one lien security—the first lien.

See act of May 7, 1878, preamble, pages 318 and 319, section 3743 of the Revised Statutes:

All contracts to be made by virtue of any law and requiring the advance of money, or in any manner connected with the settlement of public accounts, shall be deposited in the offices of the First Comptroller of the Treasury of the United States, the Second Comptroller of the Treasury of the United States, or the Commissioner of Customs, respectively, according to the nature thereof, within ninety days after their respective dates.

Section 306, Revised Statutes of the United States, on liabilities outstanding three years or more, provides:

That such sums as shall stand to the credit of any disbursing officer for any purpose, in liquidation of an indebtedness due to the United States which have for three years or more remained outstanding, unsatisfied, and unpaid shall be deposited by the Treasurer to be covered into the Treasury by warrant, and to be credited to the credit of the parties in whose favor such certificates, drafts, or checks were, respectively, issued, or to the persons who are entitled to receive pay therefor, and into an appropriation account, to be denominated "outstanding liabilities."

Secretary Foster, in a statement made to one of the Congressional committees, said that it has been the practice of the Treasury Department to treat the interest accrued on the paramount lien obligations of the said Pacific railroad corporations as not maturing until the maturity of the last one of the bonds. A reference to the reply made by the Senate Judiciary Committee, which examined Mr. Foster, will show, as I have been informed, that the committee held to the opposite view and stated that the obligation of the Government in relation to payment of interest accrued on such paramount lien should date from the time when the Government assumed the direct responsibility of payment of the bonds of such lien, to be determined by the date of such assumption.

By reference to the act of March 3, 1887, we shall see that in that act the Secretary of the Treasury is directed to satisfy the claims of the lawful creditors of the paramount lien, as expressed in the act of May 7, 1878. This is the construction which the claimants place on these statutes as applied to their rights. The legal representative of the claimants begs leave to state that, had this been done, as directed in such act, it would have been a saving to the Government of all the interest which has accrued in the period of nine years that has passed since the enactment of that law. And, furthermore, that it would have been to the advantage of the Government, in this respect, that it would have become subrogated to the rights of the paramount lien, by which all the property of the branch lines—worth much more than the main lines—would have become security for the payment of the Government interest. This, in the aggregate, would amount to a saving of more than $100,000,000.

The CHAIRMAN. Is there anything else that you desire to add to your statement?

Mr. BLAISDELL. I have nothing more to offer at present. Our plan is to submit the statute quotations, when we can be questioned by members of your committee. I do not care to offer anything more until the committee begins its interrogations.

The CHAIRMAN. Have you citations from statutes?

Mr. BLAISDELL. In abundance. Anything that you want to ask. We have them already printed, and will put them in the record if the chairman permits us to do so.

The CHAIRMAN. You may hand them to the stenographer and have them printed in the proceedings of the committee.

The following papers were handed in by Mr. Blaisdell, and were ordered to be printed:

Case 18003. In Court of Claims. L. C. Blaisdell *v.* The United States. Application for rule on the Secretary of the Treasury to show cause why judgment should not be entered against the United States, and in favor of the Petitioners and Claimants *v.* The United States.

[Final statement of Case 18003. In Court of Claims. L. C. Blaisdell *v.* The United States.]

This case was brought before the honorable court through the intervention of the Committee on Claims of the Fifty-fourth Congress, from whose files it will appear that the plaintiff had been duly presented by a Member of that Congress, the Hon. Wm. M. Springer, of the State of Illinois.

It was filed in the first instance by the present claimant, L. C. Blaisdell, in behalf of not only the heirs at law of the decedent, Charles Durkee, but in behalf of all creditors of the lien prior and paramount to that of the United States, as designated in the several acts of Congress, 1864–1878, and of the act of March 3, 1887.

Thus it appears on the face of the petition that it was a claim filed and founded upon acts of Congress, which acts were in the petition definitely and at length set forth in form and substance, and made exhibits for the purposes of conveying to the mind of the court the foundation upon which all rights claimed by the complainants in the case were to be ascertained. The rights of the complainants, whatever they shall be ascertained by the honorable court to be or to have heretofore been, are fully defined in the Pacific railroad laws set up, designated, and pleaded in the preliminary and informal petition; in the more complete petition following on the case or matter of the petition being by the court taken for consideration as in ex parte; and must finally appear, not necessarily from any or all of the answers of the several Departments, bureaus, and officers of the Government, the information thereby conveyed to the court, but through the information conveyed to the mind of the court through statutes of the United States, and specific acts of Congress defining the particular rights and character of rights set up and appearing in this petition.

It will only be necessary to merely call the attention of this honorable court to the acts of Congress that have been duly presented to it as the authority for bringing this claim against the United States—to complete all the testimony in support of the claim herein presented—that can be required of the complainants in the case to present.

The information that has been filed with this honorable court by the attorney of record in the case—and that particular portion of it which classifies as "official matter," certified by the several Departments, Bureaus, and officers of the Government—disclose a state of facts which precludes the possibility of there being hereafter, at any time, by or through any Department, Bureau, or officer of the Government, a state of facts to it presented that shall run counter to or in any material form modify the conclusions which the court may draw from that which has been already thus presented.

A summary of these facts thus presented, and that have been on file with this honorable court for the greater part of the two years last preceding the present date, shows to the honorable court all the essential information necessary that it shall have obtained before proceeding to enter final judgment in the cause of the complainants versus the United States.

As they embrace a large part of the history of the Pacific railroad system, their operations, duties, and obligations were as expressed in the United States Statutes; and so great a portion of the detailed information is to be conveyed to the court through official reports of the Auditor of Railroad Accounts in the first instance (and Railroad Commissioners' reports in the latter instances), it is deemed in order to present first the annual report of the Auditor of Railroad Accounts to the Secretary of the Interior for the year ending June 30, 1878.

On page 6 of this report occur the words:

"The act of Congress approved May 7, 1878 (chap. 96, p. 56, 20 Stat. L., 1877–78), entitled 'An act to alter and amend the act entitled "An act to aid in the construction of a railroad and telegraph line from the Missouri River to the Pacific Ocean, * * * approved 1862,'" * * * and "to alter and amend act of 1864," in amendment of said first-named act, requires:

"That the net earnings mentioned in said act of 1862 of said railroad companies, respectively, the Central Pacific Railroad Company of California and the Union Pacific Railroad Company, shall be ascertained by deducting from the gross amount of their earnings, respectively, the necessary expenses paid within the year in operating the same and keeping the same in a state of repair, and also the sum paid by them, respectively, within the year in discharge of interest on their first-mortgage bonds."

On the first proposition, to wit, the amount paid by these companies "within any given year in operating their railroad and telegraph lines and in keeping the same in a state of repair," it is not proposed to make any remarks. But the second proposition, namely, "with the amount paid by them, respectively, within the year or at any other time, in discharge of interest on their first-mortgage bonds," with this proposition we do propose to deal.

It is made the basis of the rights set up by the complainants against the United States that the interest accrued upon these first-mortgage bonds, to wit:

Union Pacific	$27,236,512
Central Pacific	25,885,120
Denver Pacific Railroad and Telegraph Company (Western Pacific)	1,970,560
Kansas Pacific	1,600,000
Central Branch Union Pacific Railroad Company	1,600,000
Sioux City and Pacific Railroad Company	1,628,320

A total first-mortgage debt and indebtedness lien prior and paramount to that of the United States of $64,623,512, with interest accrued thereon at the rate of 6 per cent per annum, was, until the dates, respectively, March 3, A. D. 1883, and January 1, A. D. 1885, the debt and the expressed indebtedness of these railroad and telegraph companies, jointly and severally, to such parties and persons as were expressed and designated in "certain files and records of the Treasury Department," and which were referred to in these terms by Hon. William Lawrence, First Comptroller of the Treasury, in Comptroller's decision by said William Lawrence, under the date of December 3, A. D. 1884, and at such date became, by contract, an indebtedness of the United States.

That the names of "the lawful and just holders of" the said "lien prior and paramount to that of the United States" have not appeared of record within the knowledge of this honorable court, and have never yet been produced (so far as known) before any committee of either House of Congress nor reported in any railroad report required by law to have contained them, constitutes no evidence and no rebuttal of the testimony that first mortgage creditors answering to that description do not exist, for we can not consistently believe that when such mortgages of such description and of such character of lien have been so well provided with protection in the expressed provisions of the acts of Congress—1864, 1878, and 1887—that the very "liens" or incumbrances thus openly recognized by such acts of Congress could exist independently of an expressed ownership of such character of mortgages in the Department of the Treasury and the Department of the Interior, both of which said Departments contain the most conclusive evidence and recorded proofs that such bonds do exist.

The Departments just named have, it is true, failed to produce the "evidence" called for by the complainants in the first instance, and by the honorable court in the second instance, that such mortgage bonds do exist; but these acts of Congress just referred to, more especially the preamble to the act of May 7, 1878, declare that the Union Pacific Railroad Company named in this and the other said acts of Congress, and the Central Pacific Railroad Company and others therein named, "did and have issued" an amount of "their own bonds" equal to the amount so issued (as therein expressed) to them, and each of them, by the United States.

Furthermore, rights of owners of bonds thus issued are not, in law or equity, to be defeated by the neglect and refusal of the said several Departments, or any officer, bureaus, or heads of such Departments to make and preserve proper "files and records" of the various transactions that may have occurred in either one.

In pleading for the protection of the rights of this class of creditors of the United States, I shall submit for the consideration of the honorable court the general proposition that rights thus guaranteed by acts of Congress are not to be defeated by "the neglect and refusal of officers of the Government (more particularly the heads of the two Departments last named) to keep, preserve for the use of this court, and to present the true and perfect record of such transactions occurring therein as have involved the credit of the United States to the total amount named in the said Pacific Railroad bonds."

The truth of this last proposition, I believe, is not questioned by any head of any Department of the Government, so far as I have yet been informed, to wit, the records of the Treasury Department do disclose the "public debt statement; that all interest accrued upon the said bonds are payable by the United States." To whom payable is not disclosed. That the principal of the bonds ($64,623,512) is also "payable by the United States." To whom payable is not disclosed.

Nor is it disclosed (by record or information to Congress given) when, in the history of these bonds, that portion of them became due and payable which represented "interest indebtedness accrued for the period of time which intervened between issue of the principal bonds and the date of April 22, 1884." The plaintiff in the case has alleged the fact of the transposition of a specific and well-defined and expressed indebtedness of these corporations into an indebtedness of the United

States. The Treasury Department corroborates the fact stated, that such indebtedness has become the indebtedness of the United States, but does not show when it so became (debt payable by the United States).

The Interior (Railroad Department thereof) carries the same debt account under the title or name of "Bond indebtedness," and charges the same item against the United States as such, which the Treasury Department terms a cash and "sinking-fund indebtedness." The information is thus disclosed to the honorable court that there is a vast discrepancy between the "public debt statement" of the Secretary of the Treasury and that disclosed in the Department of the Interior. The sinking fund, as shown by the Commissioner of Railroads, does not show to exceed $27,000,000 (less than $20,000,000 in 1884), while the Treasury Department (unless the Pacific Railroad Committee under Mr. Outhwaite have misstated) shows $64,000,000 of "sinking-fund indebtedness of the Government," by reason of these Pacific railroad obligations, in addition to that shown in the Department of the Interior.

To prove that there is a gigantic discrepancy and erroneous statement of the public liabilities in this respect, as between these two departments the honorable court has but to summons Mr. Outhwaite as witness, who, with thirteen other members of that committee (in 1888), declared "that the amount of $64,623,512 in cash" was, on the 1st day of January, 1885, an "outstanding liability" of the Government by reason of the amount of cash having been, on that date, deposited with the Secretary of the Treasury "for the definitely ascertained indebtedness of the several Pacific railroad companies to their lawful creditors" of the lien prior and paramount to that of the United States.

If the liability of the United States, or my statement of its liability in this respect, and as alleged in my petition, both the original and amended, has been disputed by any answer, plea, or demurrer filed with this honorable court, I am as yet not made aware of the fact. The statement has gone before the Department of the Treasury, signed and sworn to as set forth in my affidavits, and stands unchallenged so far as I know.

The order of the court for the information that would deny the truth of the statement has gone forth, and does not bring the information that would deny it.

The statement has stood in form and in print before the eyes of every Secretary of the Treasury from the date of January 12, 1889, and not one has attempted to deny it or make any official answer tending to deny the truth, substantially, of my statements, as in petition contained. The President of the United States (Benjamin Harrison, while Chief Executive) caused all my statements to be placed before himself, in official capacity, and in official capacity referred them "for the official action" (note the words) of the Secretary of the Treasury. The Supreme Court, in 99 United States Reports, supports the statement of my petition, that the United States is debtor to the "sinking fund" and in favor of "the lawful and just holders of paramount lien," as stated, "to the full amount of the deposits made under the provisions of such sinking fund as contained in the act of May 7, 1878." The committee referred to last has the information that the sum of $64,623,512 is and has been withheld from the "possession of the lawful and just holders of such paramount lien, by each and every Secretary of the Treasury, on the plea, or notion, rather, that such officer held a discretionary authority to make of such fund a sinking fund."

Congress, by act of March 3, 1887, directed that officer "to clear off such paramount lien or incumbrance by payments (by payments, mark the words, out of the sinking fund and provided that the entire amount be paid, whether the sinking fund was more or less than the amount due to the lawful owners of such bonds, or the "lawful creditors of the paramount lien aforesaid."

For this disobedience of the requirement—the direct, positive, and special order of Congress—the present incumbent in that office is answerable. He can not and does not answer either Congress or this honorable court that he knows not the lawful creditors of the United States; that he has no legal knowledge of them that he is bound by law to take cognizance of.

He appears to rest contentedly upon "want of information, such information as would create an official liability on his part to answer" the demands made by me on the United States Treasury. He acts, or, rather, neglects to act; and rests upon the assumption that his neglect and refusal to answer me in official manner, either by affirmation or by denial of the claims I have filed, prevents the consummation of my purpose to enforce an accounting from him; and he acts as if he expected that the entire body of Congress and the Supreme Court, including this honorable court, would unitedly be unable to compel him either to affirm or deny my right to an accounting, and thus prevent not only myself and my clients from obtaining the benefits of those acts of Congress upon which we rely for protection, but that all possible creditors of such lien, as Congress provided should be secured to "its lawful holders" (should others than myself and clients proved to be the "lawful beneficiaries"), would be powerless and the courts named and Congress itself be powerless to enforce against his will the payment of the sums due.

With these statements I have concluded to include the following motion: That the

Secretary of the Treasury be, and, with the approval of this honorable court, is hereby ordered to show cause, by his personal appearance before this honorable court, at the next ensuing rule day, why judgment should not be rendered in behalf of the United States for the benefit of the petitioners and claimants in said case and cause, No. 18003, in accordance with the statement of claims against the United States made to this honorable court.

Very respectfully submitted by

———— ————,
Attorney of Record in Case No. 18003.

To the Honorable Chief Justice and Judges thereof.

Supplemental to the Revised Statutes of the United States, vol. 1, 1874-1881.

AN ACT to alter and amend the Act entitled "An act to aid in the construction of a railroad and telegraph line from the Missouri River to the Pacific Ocean, and to secure to the Government the use of the same for postal, military, and other purposes," approved July first, eighteen hundred and sixty-two, and also to alter and amend the act of Congress approved July second, eighteen hundred and sixty-four, in amendment of said first-named act.

SECTION.
Pacific Railways.
1. Net earnings, how ascertained.
2. Compensation due from United States to be retained; how applied.
3. Sinking fund.
4. Credits to and payments into fund.
5. Secretary of Treasury to remit into sinking-fund percentage on net earnings.
6. No dividend to be voted, &c., in case of default.
Liability of officers to repay dividends illegally made.
Penalty on officers, &c., for voting, &c., to pay illegal dividends.

SECTION.
7. Application of sinking fund.
8. Priorities in application of sinking fund.
9. Liabilities to United States constitutes a lien on property of companies.
Companies not prevented from disposing of property in ordinary manner.
10. Enforcement of rights of United States.
11. Forfeiture of franchises on failure to comply with this act.
12. This and former acts subject to alteration, repeal, &c.
Existing remedies not affected.
13. This act deemed as amending former acts.

PREAMBLE.

Whereas on the first day of July, Anno Domini eighteen hundred and sixty two, Congress passed an act entitled "An act to aid in the construction of a railroad and telegraph line from the Missouri River to the Pacific Ocean, and to secure to the Government the use of the same for postal, military, and other purposes;" and

Whereas afterward, on the second day of July, Anno Domini eighteen hundred and sixty-four, Congress passed an act in amendment of said first-mentioned act; and

Whereas the Union Pacific Railroad Company, named in said acts, and under the authority thereof, undertook to construct a railway after the passage thereof, over some part of the line mentioned in said acts; and

Whereas, under the authority of the said two acts, the Central Pacific Railroad Company of California, a corporation existing under the laws of the State of California, undertook to construct a railway, after the passage of said acts, over some part of the line mentioned in said acts; and

Whereas the United States, upon demand of said Central Pacific Railroad Company, have heretofore issued, by way of loan and as provided in said acts, to and for the benefit of said company, in aid of the purposes named in said acts, the bonds of the United States, payable in thirty years from the date thereof, with interest at six per centum per annum, payable half yearly to the amount of twenty-five million eight hundred and eighty-five thousand one hundred and twenty dollars, which said bonds have been sold in the market or otherwise disposed of by said company; and

Whereas the said Central Pacific Railroad Company has issued and disposed of an amount of its own bonds equal to the amount so issued by the United States, and secured the same by mortgage, and which are, if lawfully issued and disposed of, a prior and paramount lien, in the respect mentioned in said acts, to that of the United States, as stated, and secured thereby; and

Whereas, after the passage of said acts, the Western Pacific Railroad Company, a corporation existing under the laws of the State of California, did, under the authority of Congress, become the assignee of the rights, duties and obligations of the said Central Pacific Railroad Company, as provided in the act of Congress passed on the third day of March, Anno Domini eighteen hundred and sixty-five, and did, under the authority of said act and of the acts aforesaid, construct a railway from the city of San Jose to the city of Sacramento, in California, and did demand and receive from the United States the sum of one million nine hundred and seventy thousand five hundred and sixty dollars of the bonds of the United States of the description before mentioned as issued to the Central Pacific Railroad Company, and in the same manner and under the provisions of said acts; and upon and in respect of the bonds so issued to both said companies, the United States have paid in interest to the sum of more than thirteen and one-half million dollars, which has not been reimbursed; and

Whereas said Western Pacific Railroad Company has issued and disposed of an amount of its own bonds equal to the amount so issued by the United States to it, and secured the same by mortgage, which are, if lawfully issued and disposed of, a prior and paramount lien to that of the United States, as stated, and secured thereby; and

Whereas said Western Pacific Railroad Company has since become merged in, and consolidated with, said Central Pacific Railroad Company, under the name of the Central Pacific Railroad Company, whereby the said Central Pacific Railroad Company has become liable to all the burdens, duties and obligations before resting upon said Western Pacific Railroad Company; and divers other railroad companies have become merged in and consolidated with said Central Pacific Railroad Company; and

Whereas the United States, upon the demand of the said Union Pacific Railroad Company, have heretofore issued by way of loan to it, as provided in said acts, the bonds of the United States, payable in thirty years from the date thereof, with interest at six per centum per annum, payable half yearly, the principal sums of which amount to twenty-seven million two hundred and thirty-six thousand five hundred and twelve dollars; on which the United States have paid over ten million dollars interest over and above all reimbursements; which said bonds have been sold in the market or otherwise disposed of by said corporation; and

Whereas said corporation has issued and disposed of an amount of its own bonds equal to the amounts so issued to it by the United States as aforesaid, and secured the same by mortgage, and which are, if lawfully disposed of, a prior and paramount lien, in the respect mentioned in said acts, to that of the United States, as stated, and secured thereby; and

Whereas the total liabilities (exclusive of interest to accrue) to all creditors, including the United States, of said Central Pacific Railroad Company, amount in the aggregate to more than ninety-six million dollars, and those of the Union Pacific Railroad Company to more than eighty-eight million dollars; and

Whereas the United States, in view of the indebtedness and operations of the said several railroad companies respectively, and of the disposition of their respective incomes, are not, and cannot, without further legislation, be secure in their interests in and concerning said respective railroads and corporations, either as mentioned in said acts or otherwise; and

Whereas a due regard to the rights of said several companies respectively, as mentioned in said act of eighteen hundred and sixty-two, as well as just security to the United States in the premises, and in respect of all matters set forth in said act, require that the said act of eighteen hundred and sixty-two be altered and amended as hereinafter enacted; and

Whereas, by reason of the premises also, as well as for other causes of public good and justice, the powers provided and reserved in said act of eighteen hundred and sixty-four for the amendment and alteration thereof ought also to be exercised as hereinafter enacted. Therefore, be it enacted, &c.

SECTION 1. That the net earnings mentioned in said act of eighteen hundred and sixty-two, of said railroad companies respectively, shall be ascertained by deducting from the gross amount of their earnings respectively the necessary expenses actually paid within the year in operating the same and keeping the same in a state of repair, and also the sum paid by them respectively within the year in discharge of interest on their first mortgage bonds, whose lien has priority over the lien of the United States, and excluding from consideration all sums owing or paid by said companies respectively for interest upon any other portion of their indebtedness.

And the foregoing provision shall be deemed and taken as an amendment of said act of eighteen hundred and sixty-four, as well as of eighteen hundred and sixty-two.

This section shall take effect on the thirtieth day of June next, and be applicable to all computations of net earnings thereafter; but it shall not affect any right of the United States or of either of said railroad companies existing prior thereto.

SEC. 2. That the whole amount of compensation which may, from time to time, be due to said several railroad companies respectively for services rendered for the Government shall be retained by the United States, one-half thereof to be presently applied to the liquidation of the interest paid and to be paid by the United States upon the bonds so issued by it as aforesaid, to each of said corporations severally, and the other half thereof to be turned into the sinking-fund hereinafter provided for the uses therein mentioned.

SEC. 3. That there shall be established in the treasury of the United States a sinking-fund, which shall be invested by the Secretary of the Treasury in bonds of the United States; and the semi-annual income thereof shall in like manner, from time to time, be invested, and the same shall accumulate and be disposed of as hereinafter mentioned. And in making such investments the secretary shall prefer the five per centum bonds of the United States, unless, for good reasons appearing to him, and which he shall report to Congress, he shall at any time deem it advisable to invest in other bonds of the United States.

All the bonds belonging to said funds shall, as fast as they shall be obtained, be so stamped as to show that they belong to said fund, and that they are not good in the hands of other holders than the Secretary of the Treasury until they shall have been endorsed by him, and publicly disposed of pursuant to this act.

SEC. 4. That there shall be carried to the credit of the said fund, on the first day of February in each year, the one-half of the compensation for services hereinbefore named, rendered for the Government by said Central Pacific Railroad Company, not applied in liquidation of interest; and, in addition thereto, the said company shall, on said day in each year, pay into the treasury, to the credit of said sinking-fund, the sum of one million two hundred thousand dollars, or so much thereof as shall be necessary to make the five per centum of the net earnings of its said road payable to the United States under said act of eighteen hundred and sixty-two, and the whole sum earned by it as compensation for services rendered for the United States, together with the sum by this section required to be paid, amount in the aggregate to twenty-five per centum of the whole net earnings of said railroad company, ascertained and defined as hereinbefore provided, for the year ending on the thirty-first day of December next preceding.

That there shall be carried to the credit of the said fund, on the first day of February in each year. the one-half of the compensation for services hereinbefore named, rendered for the Government by said Union Pacific Railroad Company, not applied in liquidation of interest; and, in addition thereto, the said company shall, on said day in each year, pay into the Treasury, to the credit of said sinking-fund, the sum of eight hundred and fifty thousand dollars, or so much thereof as shall be necessary to make the five per centum of the net earnings of its said road payable to the United States under said act of eighteen hundred and sixty-two, and the whole sum earned by it as compensation for services rendered for the United States, together with the sum by this section required to be paid, amount in the aggregate to twenty-five per centum of the whole net earnings of said railroad company, ascertained and defined as hereinbefore provided, for the year ending on the thirty-first day of December next preceding.

SEC. 5. That whenever it shall be made satisfactorily to appear to the Secretary of the Treasury, by either of said companies, that seventy-five per centum of its net earnings as hereinbefore defined for any current year are, or were insufficient to pay the interest for such year upon the obligations of such company in respect of which obligations there may exist (see act March 3rd, 1887,) a lien paramount to that of the United States and that such interest has been paid out of such net earnings, said Secretary of the Treasury is hereby authorized, and it is made his duty, to remit for such current year so much of the twenty-five per centum of net earnings required to be paid into the said sinking-fund, as aforesaid, as may have been thus applied and used in the payment of interest as aforesaid. (Note: For example, if the sum of 19 million dollars shall appear to the satisfaction of the Secretary of Treasury as having been applied by the corporation to the liquidation of "interest accrued on mortgages of the paramount lien," it is the duty of said officer of the Government to remit an equal amount of the sums due to the United States on subsidy debt, from said corporations; which would in practice, eliminate the entire subsidy debt, when the whole amount due to the United States should be covered by the equal sums paid in interest upon the bonds whose lien are paramount to that of the United States.)

SEC. 6. That no dividend shall be voted, made, or paid for or to any stockholder or stockholders in either of said companies respectively at any time when the said company shall be in default in respect of the payment of either the sums required as aforesaid to be paid into said sinking-fund, or in respect of the payment of the said five per centum of the net earnings, or in respect of the interest upon any debt the lien of which, or of the debt on which it may accrue, is paramount to that of the United States. (This prohibits and makes unlawful the dividends, and all distributions constituting in effect dividends to stockholders, or to persons acting in trust for stockholders, for no interest appears (from records) to have been paid to, or for any first mortgage, or paramount-lien creditor.)

And any officer or person who shall vote, declare, make, or pay, and any stockholder of any of said companies who shall receive any such dividend contrary to the provisions of this act, shall be liable to the United States for the amount thereof, which, when recovered, shall be paid into said sinking-fund. (Note: Under such terms and provisions a suit in equity brought by the United States for the recovery of the value of the interest accrued on the bonds of the paramount lien ($116,000,000), would be the lawful remedy to apply in this case.) (Note 2nd: Under the terms of Act of March 3rd, 1887, the position of the Government as First Mortgage Creditor being attained by conforming to its provisions, there could be no doubt but that a judgment, equal to the amount stated, could be recovered against said corporations by the United States; to say nothing about the principal of the mortgage.)

Penalty. And every such officer, person, or stockholder who shall knowingly vote, declare, make or pay any such dividend, contrary to the provisions of this act, shall be deemed guilty of a misdemeanor, and, on conviction thereof, shall be punished by a fine not exceeding ten thousand dollars, and by imprisonment not exceeding one year.

SEC. 7. (See the connection with Sec. 3.) That there shall be established, etc. That the said sinking-fund so established and accumulated shall, at the maturity of said bonds so respectively issued by the United States, be applied to the payment and satisfaction thereof, according to the interest and proportion of each of said companies in said fund, and of all interest paid by the United States thereon, and not reimbursed, subject to the provisions of the next section.

SEC. 8. That the said sinking-fund so established and accumulated shall, according to the interest and proportion of said companies respectively therein, be held for the protection, security, and benefit of the lawful and just holders of any mortgage or lien debts of such companies respectively, lawfully paramount to the rights of the United States, and for the claims of other creditors, if any, lawfully chargeable upon the funds so required to be paid into said sinking-fund, according to their respective lawful priorities, as well as for the United States, according to the principles of equity, to the end that all persons having any claim upon said sinking-fund may be entitled thereto in due order. (Note: But one claim has been filed against said fund; that claim is set forth in petition No. 18,003. But one party (the United States) was, at such time, or is now, known to have held, or to have sought to hold, an interest in the said sinking-fund, other than the parties claimant under said petition. Therefore, said fund is not "lawfully chargeable upon the funds by said section 8 of act May 7th, 1878, required to be paid into said sinking-fund," because, see further, section 8 requires payment to be made according to "lawful priorities," and "lawful priorities" other than recorded claimants before the Treasury Department, and said court, do not exist.)

SEC. 9. That all sums due to the United States from any of said companies respectively, whether payable presently or not, and all sums required to be paid to the United States or into the Treasury, or into said sinking-fund under said act, or under the acts hereinbefore referred to or otherwise, are hereby declared to be a lien upon all the property, estate, rights and franchises of every description granted or conveyed by the United States to any of said companies respectively or jointly, and also upon all the estate and property, real, personal and mixed assets and income of said several railroad companies respectively, from whatever source derived, subject to any lawfully prior and paramount mortgage, lien or claim thereon. (Note: The only question of the title of the United States becoming, by force of the defaults made, clear and perfected is: Is there a "prior and paramount mortgage, lien or claim thereon?") and (Note 2nd: The only question of the title to claim as set up in Court of Claims, No. 18,003, is: Is there, or can there be, any title paramount to that of the United States, and to that set up in said claim, set up in said Court, adversely to the claimants therein?) (Note 3rd: If there is, and if such claim can be so set up, it is the business of such claimants to set it up, and not mine, or that of the Government to entertain outside talk about it.)

But this section shall not be construed to prevent said companies respectively from using and disposing of any of their property in the ordinary, proper and lawful course of their current business, in good faith and for valuable consideration.

SEC. 10. That it is hereby made the duty of the Attorney-General of the United States to enforce, by proper proceedings against the said several railroad companies respectively or jointly, or against either of them, and others, all the rights of the United States under this act and under the acts hereinbefore mentioned, and under any other act of congress or right of the United States.

And in any suit or proceeding already commenced, or that may be hereafter commenced, against any of said companies, either alone or with other parties, in respect of matters arising under this act, or under the acts or rights hereinbefore mentioned or referred to, it shall be the duty of the Court to determine the very right of the matter without regard to matters of form, joinder of parties, multifariousness, or other matters not affecting the substantial rights and duties arising out of the matters and acts hereinbefore stated and referred to.

SEC. 11. That if either of said railroad companies shall fail to perform all and singular the requirements of this act and of the acts hereinbefore mentioned, and of any other act relating to said company, to be by it performed, for the period of six months next after such performance may be due, such forfeiture shall operate as a forfeiture of all the rights, privileges, grants and franchises derived or obtained by it from the United States.

And it shall be the duty of the Attorney-General to cause such forfeiture to be judicially enforced

SEC. 12. That nothing in this act shall be taken to be or construed in any wise to affect or impair the right of Congress at any time hereafter further to alter, amend, or repeal the said acts hereinbefore mentioned; and this act shall be subject to alteration, amendment, or repeal, as, in the opinion of Congress, justice or the public welfare require.

And nothing herein contained shall be held to deny, exclude, or impair any right or remedy in the premises now existing in favor of the United States.

SEC. 13. That each and every of the provisions in this act contained shall severally and respectively be deemed, taken, and held as in alteration and amendment of said act of eighteen hundred and sixty-two and of said act of eighteen hundred and sixty-four respectively, and of both said acts. [May 7, 1878.]

[United States First Comptroller's Decisions, Vol. V, pp. 206-207.]

LOST BOND CASE.

The law, in theory at least, attributes to the Government absolute impeachability. The law commands what is legally right. "The king can do no wrong" is a maxim of law. The Government is immortal, and in doing what the law authorizes can do no wrong. Man in his present state is mortal and sometimes "prone to evil" and "born unto trouble as the sparks fly upward." If the finder of a lost bond present it to the Treasury Departmant the possession of it by the officers of the Department raises no legal presumption of payment. The law presumes, and the fact is, that such a record will be kept of it as will protect the rights of the real owner. The usage as to the bonds now in question, and as to all bonds presented for payment, or for the issue of a duplicate as to which there is a question of controverted ownership, is to stamp them thus: "Treasury Department, Office of the Secretary, April 22, 1884. Held for decision of ownership," and a proper record is made to protect the rights of claimants. In legal contemplation, the possession of such bond by the Government involves no danger of its destruction or other act to the prejudice of the rightful owner. He is protected by the stamp and record to which reference has been made. The highest guaranty is given that the rights of the real owner will be protected. The Government keeps a record of its public debt open to the inspection of every person interested. * * * (206.)

The Government, in its statement of the public debt, periodically published, makes known the amount of mature and unpaid public securities. It is the duty and the interest of the Government to ascertain and pay the owners of lost bonds.

* * * The Government has a well-defined duty in becoming the custodian of lost bonds; the purpose of its custody is reasonable, necessary, and just. * * * The Government becomes a bailee without charge to the owner. * * * (2 Schouler, Personal Property, 15; id., 488; 2 Kent, 636; Nicholson v. Chapman, 2 H., Bl. 254; Wentworth v. Day, 3 Metc., 352; Marvin v. Treat, 37 Conn., 96.) The public credit will be improved by maintaining the right and duty of the Government to act as custodian, and thus public policy, good morals, and the rights of owners of bonds be promoted.

A learned author in referring to "goods unclaimed in the hands of some trustee or bailee, deposits in a bank for example, where, as often happens, the rightful owner or creditor is not aware of his rights," says: "It may be, in such a case, that the owner is in ignorance of his rights, and would still assert his rights should any notice reach him; or it may be he has died."

AFFIDAVIT OF ATTORNEY OF RECORD.

Charles Durkee, who, as stated by the Secretary of the Treasury, in the presence of numerous witnesses, was the "lawful and sole assignee of all the first-mortgage bonds of the Union Pacific, Central Pacific, and other Pacific railroad companies, had died seized in legal possession thereof." The fact was unknown to his "next of kin" and lawful heirs. Such next of kin, as were represented by attorney with powers of attorney to do all things which they, or either of them might, if personally present at the doing thereof, had made L. C. Blaisdell their legal representative for all purposes pertaining to the collection of undiscovered assets of said decedents' estate.

As such representative he was called by order of the Secretary of the Treasury to be present on the 22d day of April, 1884, and, obeying such order, he was present and witnessed and took part in all the transactions occurring whereby the United States has become the legal custodian and trustee for the heirs of the said decedent, empowered to retain custody of said bonds for the lawful purposes of collection.

In the case No. 18003 in Court of Claims said Blaisdell charges the United States as being the "lawful custodian" of the first-mortgage bonds of the paramount lien to that of the United States of the Central Pacific, the Union Pacific, and other Pacific railroad companies, as designated in the acts of Congress, and stated by the late Secretary of the Treasury, in the presence of witnesses named, to the said Blaisdell, on the said April 22, 1884.

In the said claim against the United States, said claimant, for himself, asserts that the records of the Treasury Department disclose the fact that himself, and no other person, has ever filed a claim in the Treasury Department against the United States, as for moneys received by the United States, pursuant to any contract or agreement not designated in the Thurman Act, or any other act of Congress; that the sums severally, to wit: $64,623,512 in gold and upward of $70,000,000 in Pacific Railroad "call bonds" have, by the Secretary of the Treasury, been "called into the Treasury (subtreasury) in the first instance (January 1, 1885), and in the second instance, made use of the United States to float the particular amount of the $70,000,000 and upwards" of call-bond indebtedness agreed upon.

That at the maturity of the last of such call-bond indebtedness (or August 16, 1894), the entire amount of investment so made, with interest from March 3, 1883, became due and payable by the United States to the "accredited legal representatives as accredited in the transactions with the Treasury Department April 22, 1884."

That the said sum in gold, with interest payable in gold, at 6 per centum for the time held by the United States, was, at the time of the maturity of said call bonds, also due to said creditors.

Your affiant refers the honorable court to the files of the Treasury and Interior and State Departments and to the Department of Justice and Court of Claims for detailed and more particular information, and concludes this affidavit by the statement that a few days prior to the end of the last fiscal year, by promises representing that the Secretary of the Treasury, Mr. Carlisle, would cause to be closed up, in due form of law, and presented to the Court of Claims, the true balances of sinking-fund account, showing the amount and character of all liability of the United States for or arising from the several acts of Congress on the question of "bond liabilities of the United States growing out of aid and securities advanced or assumed by the United States for said railroad corporations."

A certain motion for accounting of sinking fund was withdrawn, that contrary to the promise made, and by which said promise said plaintiff was induced to withdraw his motion for the enforced appearance and answer of said Secretary of the Treasury before said Court of Claims, said Carlisle, Secretary of the Treasury, has defaulted, and has given neither to the court nor to said affiant any satisfactory excuse therefor.

For which cause, and other substantial matters of law and fact, to be offered in plea hereafter, your petitioner, L. C. Blaisdell, in appearance for those whom he represents as clients in the matters now pending before the Treasury Department, prays the relief to be granted unto him by the honorable court that an order of the court shall issue to John G. Carlisle, Secretary of the Treasury of the United States, charging him with accountability for all the funds that by statute the United States stands chargeable with for the liquidation of the entire indebtedness named in the act of March 3, 1887, as "of lien prior and paramount to that of the United States," according to the terms and tenor of said act; for which relief, and other proper relief thereon, your petitioner will ever pray.

Bond Ownership: Case of no Ownership Found.

PLEA OF L. C. BLAISDELL.

Repeating from page 206, First Comptroller's Decisions, Vol. V, the words of First Comptroller in decision: "The law commands what is legally right," and applying this decision to act of March 3, 1887, wherein said law directs the Secretary of the Treasury to pay off by payments out of the Treasury of the United States, the parties entitled to payment as upon a "lien prior and paramount to that of the United States." Such direction is peremptory command of this Government that "the Secretary of the Treasury shall do what is commanded," and we can not avoid the conclusion that such contemplated payment is right, for all the means of ascertaining rights have been, by the law, placed within the reach of successive Secretaries of the Treasury for the period of eleven, almost twelve, years, during which period the claims of the clientage of said L. C. Blaisdell have ever been before the Department, as they are now, supported by competent testimony of their legal representative, and undisputed in any official manner, that the claims are supported by the "good faith and credit of the Government;" by all the acts of Congress made for the relief and protection of creditors of such class; by various decisions of the Supreme Court in relation to the application of the sinking fund; by the findings of fact of the Court of Claims in preliminary procedure; and by the recommendation of the preceding President in the act of referring, for the official action of the Secretary of the Treasury, the claims of the claimants as filed with such Chief Executive, and submitted for his consideration, according to the provisions of said act of March 3, 1887.

The Comptroller, Lawrence, has quoted, and has sought to apply (apparently) to this claimant attorney, the phrase, "The king can do no wrong." This man, of all others the most directly and completely responsible for all wrongs that have, since the date of the transactions, been inflicted on the rightful owners of the bonds in question, would have this Government assume that his own act in disobedience of law, of statute, of Treasury rules and regulations, and in disobedience of the official order of the late Secretary of the Treasury; he would have the people of the United States believe that there was no act of the Secretary of the Treasury as I have stated; that there was no decision of the late Judge Brewster as I have stated; that he did not himself present me to the Secretary of the Treasury, saying that he had examined my powers of attorney and found them to be sufficient for the purpose of constituting me the proper legal representative of the lawful creditors in the matters about to be settled, in the premises; that he did not know what my representative rights were ascertained to be on said April 22, 1884. In brief, this man has, by all the personal influence he has been able to exert, sought to defeat the rights of the lawful and just creditors of the United States in their cause. The example of this man has been most pernicious. Emboldened by his example, succeeding First Comptrollers have said that they had no official knowledge of any record of the transactions in the Treasury Department, such as would establish proof of my averments.

The singular circumstance about it all is, that said Lawrence never in all these years, by word of writing or orally, to me addressed, made denial of any part of my statements. True, it has come to my knowledge in recent years that he thought I was mistaken as to the character of the bonds I was interested in, "that they were coupon bonds, the number and classification of which had been lost, or that such was his impression." But he did not state this as a fact, but as his opinion. I wish to introduce before this honorable court the testimony of a written contract signed by Kennedy, the law partner of Judge Lawrence, which contract had for its purpose the setting up of the very claims which I have set up before the Treasury Department and Court of Claims, and to ask the honorable court to construe its meaning and application to the true condition and status of my rights, and to take notice that such contract had the indorsement of Judge Lawrence several years after the said April 22, 1884.

I ask the honorable court to decide whether this contract does not disclose an admission on the part of Judge Lawrence that, so far as he had the knowledge or information to judge, my averments were substantially true. Remembering that Judge Lawrence was present; that he was First Comptroller; that he was the very officer whose orders and directions brought into that conference all other officers; that he had been in correspondence for months with myself, preparatory to bringing about the interview, that he knew the purpose of the same, that he took the very first and initiatory step himself in the procedure then had, and remembering that both by statute and by the special order of Judge Folger, and advice officially given by Judge Brewster he was charged with the duty of preserving and transmitting to me a certified copy of the proceedings of such meeting. Remembering all these points, I ask the honorable court to construe this purported contract with the view of determining and a view of answering the question: Did this First Comptroller judicially ascertain and officially recognize my representative rights to be, as I have, in petition before the Court of Claims and in application to the Treasury Department for an accounting, represented them to be?

The second part of my plea before this honorable court is that the act of March 3, 1887, before referred to, was in itself a recognition of rights, the nature and extent of which appears in the act itself, and the legal representative of which rights received due official indorsement as such in the very presentation and adoption of the act by Congress. Senator Cullom, of Illinois, attached that portion of the interstate commerce bill which relates to Pacific railways to his bill before offering the same to be voted on, with the full knowledge that such provisions as were contained therein for the security, benefit, and protection of holders of liens prior and paramount to that of the United States (in such matters as treated thereof) were provided at the earnest solicitation of your orator, acting in the same office, or position, that I now hold in the record.

I am credibly informed, and believe it to be true, that the passage of that act was regarded by the friends of the executive and official heads of the several railroad corporations concerned, as having been passed with the full knowledge of its main supporters; that it was a measure looking directly to the protection of the personal interest in paramount liens, represented at that time solely and exclusively by said Blaisdell, attorney of record for creditors of the paramount lien.

The question, "Who are the legal representatives or the lawful and just holders of lien prior and paramount to that of the United States in this matter," has never been raised in any due and legal form by any officer of any department representing the Government. It only assumed the form of a question because the attorney of record for the creditors found it necessary to have his legal rights duly recognized by the Court of Claims by due investigation.

Accordingly, when it had become apparent that there was a studied, long practiced, and determined evasion of my rights by the Treasury Department, and that many things were officially circulated tending to induce the general public to the belief that my claims were either unfounded in law and fact, or rested solely upon my own assertions, I applied to the Court of Claims and requested that court to send for the Committee on Claims, and to grant me a hearing of my preliminary statement of claim. This was duly granted, the court ordering my petition to be filed, and filed as ex parte, on the showing of facts made by me under oath and in due form for record.

From time to time I continued to present items of information to this court, until in March last the original petition was succeeded by an amended petition, and the original powers of attorney, under which I had appeared (with Messrs. Dudley & Michiner), were supplemented and succeeded by new powers of attorney from all, or so many of the original clients and heirs at law of Charles Durkee (the assignee of the bonds), as, in the opinion of counsel and court, were required to be made more explicit. Such powers of attorney were made irrevocably to myself, exclusive of all other attorneys heretofore associated with me. I, therefore, upon such powers of attorney (on file with the Court of Claims), take the privilege of referring this honorable court to its files for information thereon.

Representing (as I believe the record will sustain me in so doing) that I am sole legal representative for all interested parties in the estate, or such part or residue of estate of the late Charles Durkee as may be represented by bonds of the Pacific railroads or bonds of the United States; representing, as I believe I hold authority to do, those important interests of "lawful and just holders" of the indebtedness represented by the bonds in question, I submit to this honorable court the act of March 3, 1887; the act of May 7, 1878, and the records of the matter contained in the Court of Claims, under the title of L. C. Blaisdell *v.* The United States, or, more properly speaking, the motion that the court will order the Court of Claims to send up to itself the substantial portions of the records of the matter as appear on its files, or the whole thereof, as, in the opinion of the court, may be deemed best suited to the purpose of informing the court of the true condition of the Treasury of the United States in relation to obligations of the same, expressed in United States Statutes.

And the court having been duly informed, application is hereby made (under motion for the purpose), with the leave of this court first granted, for a final hearing before it, on the question of the "rights" of all legal and equitable creditors, other than the United States, interested in the distribution of the funds contained, or to be derived from the lawful distribution and application of the sinking funds, such as are provided by law for the payment of any mortgage or lien debts, lawfully paramount to that of the United States, to the parties to be designated by decision of this honorable the Supreme Court of the United States.

For which favors and relief your orator, for his clients and himself and all interested parties, will ever pray.

L. C. BLAISDELL,
Attorney of Record in Treasury Department,
in Court of Claims, and Elsewhere, for "Interested Parties.

[Certified copy of case. United States First Comptroller's Decisions, Lawrence, 1884, Vol. V.]

In the matter of the application of a private person for a certified copy of certain records and files of the Treasury Department.

DECISION.

The permission, now asked to withdraw papers, is refused. Copies will be furnished when the regulation on the subject is submitted.

TREASURY DEPARTMENT,
First Comptroller's Office, December 3, 1884.

DECISION BY WILLIAM LAWRENCE.

[See pp. 444 and 445, Vol. V.]

Mr. Lawrence herein says: "An application is made by a private person to the First Comptroller for permission to withdraw certain papers filed in this office relating to a claim pending therein; or, if such permission can not be granted, for copies thereof."

Applications of the character stated are frequent. It is deemed advisable to present in this connection, for general information, a regulation of the Treasury Department on this subject that has long been in force, and which a blank circular letter of the Department says "must be strictly observed in each and every case." The regulation is as follows:

"No copy of any paper shall be furnished to private individuals except on application to, and with the previous written consent of the Secretary, one of the assistant secretaries, the chief clerk, or the head of the proper bureau; and no account, document, or paper of any kind, on file in the Department, shall, on any occasion, be withdrawn by agents, attorneys, or other persons. Upon application for copies of papers on file, or any record of the Department, the rule established in the Treasury order, dated October 20, 1830, must be observed, to wit: 'Copies of accounts or other papers on file or of record in the Department *are to be furnished only to such persons as may be interested in them or at their request; if they relate to suits in which the United States are interested, such copies must be transmitted to the United States attorney having charge of such suits, subject to the inspection of the parties applying for them;* and when transmitted to the district attorneys they must be sent through the Solicitor of the Treasury, that he may be duly apprised of all the facts communicated to the opposite party.' *An affidavit showing the necessity of copies must be furnished in all cases.*"

[Provisions of statutes prescribing mode of authenticating copies of books, records, papers, and documents in the Executive Departments and elsewhere, and their effect as evidence.]

SEC. 461. Land titles: Copies in cases where such papers would in any wise affect the title to lands shall be furnished by the Secretary of the Interior for the person so applying.

SEC. 461. Exemplification of patents, etc.: All exemplification of patents or papers on file or of record in the General Land Office, *which may be required by parties interested in the same, shall be furnished by the Commissioner upon the payment by such parties at the rate of fifteen cents per hundred words, with additional sum of one dollar for Commissioner's certificate.*

SEC. 632. Cases of appeal in equity or admiralty causes: In cases of an appeal, as provided by the preceding section, copies of the proofs and of such entries and papers on file *as may be necessary on hearing of the appeal may be certified up to the appellate court.*

SEC. 698. Transcripts on appeals: Upon the appeal of any cause in equity, etc., a transcript of the record, as directed by law to be made, and copies of the proofs and of such entries and papers on file *as may be necessary on the hearing of the appeal, shall be transmitted to the Supreme Court. Provided, That either the court below or the Supreme Court may order any original document or other evidence to be sent up, in addition to the copy of the record, or in lieu of a copy of a part thereof.* And on such appeals no new evidence shall be received by the Supreme Court except in admiralty and prize causes.

SEC. 883. Copies of any records, documents, books, or papers in the office of the Solicitor of the Treasury, certified by him under the seal of his office, or when his office is vacant, by the officer acting as Solicitor for the time, *shall be evidence equally with the originals.*

(Read also sec. 884 and sec. 885.)

SEC. 886. When suit is brought in any case of delinquency of a revenue officer, *or other person accountable for public money*, a transcript from the books and proceedings of the Treasury Department, certified by the Register and authenticated under the seal of the Department, *shall be admitted as evidence*, and the court trying the cause shall be authorized to grant judgment and award execution accordingly. And all copies of bonds, contracts, or other papers relating to or connected with the settlement of an account between the United States and an individual, when certified by the register or (proper auditor), as the case may be, to be true copies of the originals on file, and authenticated under the seal of the Department, may be annexed to such transcripts, and shall have equal validity, and be entitled to the same degree of credit which would be due to the original papers if produced and authenticated in court: *Provided*, That where suit is brought upon a bond, *or other sealed instrument*, and the defendant pleads non est factum, or makes his motion to the court, verifying such plea or motion by his oath, the court may take the same into consideration, and, if it appears to be necessary for the attainment of justice, may require the production of the original bond, contract, or other paper specified in such affidavit.

SEC. 887. Transcripts as evidence in trial of indictments: Upon the trial of any indictment against any person for embezzling public monies it shall be sufficient evidence, for the purpose of showing a balance against such person, to produce a transcript from the books and proceedings of the Treasury Department, as provided by the preceding section.

[Note: It is claimed in said suit that a true transcript from the proceedings of the Treasury Department will show that in each and every affidavit, oath, or certificate made by any officer relative to "accounts between the United States and the Pacific Railroad companies" as relates to their "creditors of the statutory paramount liens" and certifying credits in favor of said companies as having discharged portions of their subsidy debt, or indebtedness to the United States, by or through the deposits by said companies made into the sinking fund designated by act of May 7, 1878, was and remains a certificate, affidavit, and oath erroneously made, and made in fraud of the "lawful and just holders of liens prior and paramount to that of the United States," and the court is requested to take notice further that section 8 of said named act of May 7, 1878, is a statutory prohibition of any such entry of credits, in any such manner, or out of said sinking fund, whilst the said companies, or either of them, shall remain (as they do) in default as for the payment of "interest accrued" on such paramount lien bonds or any portion thereof.]

The inference is that the officers of the Government who have made entries of credits to the Pacific railroad companies through certificates to them issued as for payments made in reduction of the debt due by them to the United States, thus denying to "lawful creditors" their own statutory credits, are constructively guilty of acts of embezzlement; for misappropriation of funds, or making use of them in any manner not directed by law, is embezzlement, as described in the statute.

This part of the subject I leave with the court, just where the statute and the record leave it, and proceed.

[Note: On sec. 886. Suit No. 18003 in Court of Claims is a "suit brought on a bond and other sealed instruments;" and the defendant, the United States, has not pleaded non est factum, and the attorneys charged with the defense of the United States in said suit have not made their motion to the court, or in any manner verified, under oath, any plea or motion relating to the subject-matter of this suit; therefore it can not be necessary, or be considered to be necessary for the attainment of justice by the Court of Claims, to require either the production of the original bonds as assigned to Charles Durkee, deceased, by the Pacific railroad companies named, or the original contract with the United States made by the claimant, or other paper not specified by affidavit of the defendant attorneys, to be necessary to complete my proofs.]

For proof of evidence of "Demand in suits for recovery of balances due," see section 890, Post-Office Department.

SEC. 899. When original records are lost or destroyed: When the record of any judgment, decree, or other proceeding of any court of the United States is lost or destroyed, *any party or person interested therein may, on application to such court, and on showing to its satisfaction that the same was lost or destroyed without his fault, obtain from it an order authorizing such defect to be supplied by a duly certified copy of the original record, where the same can be obtained; and such certified copy shall thereafter have, in all respects, the same effect as the original record would have had.*

[Note: It is assumed, but not pleaded, answered, or put in form of demurrer by the defense, that the original record of proceedings had at the meeting in First Comptroller's Office in 1884 have been lost or destroyed; that the bonds named in petition can not be discovered in the Treasury Department; that the name of the assignee thereof (if there was an assignee) can not be discovered in any record of the Treasury or other Department; and yet the testimony filed with the Court of Claims for the claimants disclose the statement in writing, signed by one Thomas Robinson, as custodian of files and records pertaining to this said assignee, Charles Durkee, deceased, that all the records, vouchers, letters, and other matter pertaining to accounts between said Charles Durkee and the United States are to be found in vaults Nos. 75 and 85, in the Treasury Department; this statement bearing the date of January 19, 1885.]

This statement is in direct response to the question of his superior officer, Jonathan Tarbell, which question is also found on the same slip of paper now on file in the Court of Claims; and the same paper refers to the legal representative for whom said Tarbell bespeaks the assistance of said Robinson in discovering the very bonds which it is said can not be discovered in the Treasury Department.

SEC. 900. When any such record is lost or destroyed, and the defect can not be supplied as provided in the preceding section, any party or person interested therein may make an application to the court to which the record belonged, verified by affidavit, showing such loss or destruction; that the same occurred without his fault or neglect; that certified copies of such record can not be obtained by him; and showing also the substance of the record so lost or destroyed, and that the loss or destruction thereof, unless supplied, will or may result in damage to him. The court shall cause said application to be entered of record, and a copy of it shall be served personally upon *every person interested therein, together with a written notice that on a day stated therein, which shall not be less than sixty days after such service, said application will be heard;* and if, upon such hearing, the court is satisfied that the statements contained in the application are true, it shall make and cause to be entered of record an order reciting the substance and effect of said loss or destroyed record. Said order shall have the same effect, so far as concerns the party or persons served, as above provided, but subject to intervening rights, which the original record would have had if the same had not been lost or destroyed.

SEC. 908. The edition of the laws and treaties of the United States, published by Little & Brown, shall be competent evidence of the several public and private acts of Congress, and of the several treaties therein contained, in all the courts of law and equity and of maritime jurisdiction, and in all the tribunals and public offices of the United States, without any further proof or authentication thereof.

[Note: The Comptroller, Lawrence, has evidently confounded a real, personal, and to himself well-known "applicant for a well-known purpose," based upon rights well known to himself, with an informal and general instruction to the general public, and the general civil service or Executive officers of the Government, in this so styled "Certified copy case." The evidence of a personal witness, however, will show to the court that Judge Lawrence presented the volume from which these extracts are taken to the affiant and attorney for claimants in the case pending (as alleged) before the Treasury Department, with the statement "that he had written up said affiant's case in his (Lawrence's) First Comptroller's Decisions;" and by his remarks thereon gave his hearers to understand that he meant to designate said L. C. Blaisdell as the "private person" who had "applied for (not certain files and records, etc., in these words), but who had, in the interim between the 22d day of April and the 3d day of December, 1884, applied to Lawrence, as First Comptroller, for the delivery of papers, files, and documents named in his affidavit as the bonds of the Union Pacific, the Central Pacific, and other railroad companies, and for the complete orders of the head (Hon. Secretary Folger) of the Treasury Department concerning said bonds; and for the certificate of ownership of such bonds, to be certified to applicant, as the attorney in fact for the legal representatives and creditors under said mortgage bonds."]

[Summary and application of the foregoing decision of First Comptroller; rules and regulations of Treasury Department, etc., to the subject-matter to be construed by the Supreme Court.]

The foregoing recites in order as follows: That some time during the year 1884 "an application was made by a private person to the First Comptroller of the Treasury for permission to withdraw certain papers filed in said office relating to a claim pending therein; or, if such permission can not be granted, for copies thereof."

On the call of the Court of Claims for evidence from the Treasury Department (issued 15th of March, 1895), such Department fails to furnish to the court the information that should enable it to determine who such "private person" was who made the application stated in this book as the subject of the First Comptroller's decision, December 3, 1884.

The affidavit of said "private person" is now on file in the Court of Claims, and it states that such person was L. C. Blaisdell.

In like manner the so-termed answer or response of the said Department, to the call for the information made by the court, fails to furnish "any such statement in writing, as section 188 of the Revised Statutes requires shall be made," in all such cases, to wit: It fails to give or to set forth any fact in corroboration or in denial of the following facts stated in the petition in Case No. 18003: First. Whether said Blaisdell was the identical person who made the application referred to in said First Comptroller's decision of December 3, 1884. Second. Whether the "certain papers and files of the Treasury Department," as stated in the petition, were or were not such files and papers as the said Blaisdell has named in his affidavit. Third. Whether said Blaisdell was, at such time, attorney for claimants with a "claim pending in the Treasury Department." Fourth. Whether the permission to withdraw papers related to the papers known as the "Original first-mortgage bonds of the Union, Central, and other Pacific railroads." Fifth. Whether the permission refused and the privilege granted in the said order, or decision of said First Comptroller, designated and was intended to apply to said Blaisdell, or some other person.

All of which questions, unanswered by said Department, under the said call of the court, said Blaisdell, standing on his rights, as representing all known and recognized creditors of the United States, in respect of the matters and things concerned in the said undiscovered and unrevealed records of the Treasury Department, now presents, as an original question, to the honorable Supreme Court, with the prayer that it will determine: 1. The personality of the party to whom said Comptroller's decision was intended to apply. 2. The class and particular "papers and files or records of the Treasury Department" such purported decision is held to apply to; and, finally, should they be found to be, and to include the first-mortgage bonds of the said Union and Central Pacific railroad companies and other matter, as set forth in claimants' petition, now on file in the Court of Claims, the prayer of the applicant is for the Court of Claims to be instructed by the Supreme Court in accordance with its findings of fact thereon, to the end that it may discover the "lawful and just holders of the lien or liens prior and paramount to that held by the United States in respect of the debts of the aforesaid corporations."

For which favors and such further relief as your honorable court may graciously grant, your orator and petitioner shall ever pray.

L. C. BLAISDELL,
For claimants in said Case No. 18003 in Court of Claims, and for the use and benefit of such other parties as may be found entitled to some part of said funds, as claimed.

Affidavit of L. C. Blaisdell, to be appended to powers of attorney, filed in Case No. 18003, Court of Claims.

AFFIDAVIT.

Personally appeared before me, John T. Plummer, a notary public in and for the county of Marion, State of Indiana, Leonard C. Blaisdell, attorney of record in Case No. 18003, Court of Claims, who, being on his oath first duly sworn, states as follows:

In reply to the statements in official report contained, of the Acting Secretary of the Treasury and of the First Comptroller of the Treasury, as appears from the inclosed and accompanying papers of the date of May 14, 1895, wherein said report mentions letters, to wit, dated August 23, 1884; dated September 30, 1884; dated March 31, 1884, etc. I will not undertake to say exactly what those letters contained, not having preserved any copy of the same, nor any copies of the letters written by me during said year of 1884.

I am sure, however, that on the 22d day of April, A. D. 1884, I presented to the then chief clerk of the Treasury Department a number of letters, and that most, if not all of such letters, were retained by said clerk ostensibly for the purpose of using them as vouchers for calling together the heads of the several Departments and the accounting officers whom I have named in my petition.

I am sure that the letter on file with this honorable court, containing a reference to the Treasury rule, said to have been adopted in October, 1830, and adhered to in the Treasury Department as a rule ever afterwards, had no application (properly) to me, or to the matters pending between myself and the Treasury Department at that time.

Yet there was an attempt to make it apply to me, as may be seen by the fact that I am the person addressed.

In conformity with the requirements that I should then make an affidavit for the use of the Treasury Department I made it, and it should appear appended to some one of the letters written by me within the year, and before the decision of the First Comptroller of the 3d day of December of that year.

In conformity with the well-known usage, and the provision of the United States Revised Statutes for the reproduction of "lost bonds, and of papers and files" relating thereto, I make this my statement in affidavit concerning the same, to wit:

It was in conformity to official advices contained in one or more of the said letters retained by the Treasury Department (as aforesaid), that I appeared before the head of that Department, in the First Comptroller's office, on said date of April 22, 1884. (Hon. J. G. Cannon, who introduced me to the chief clerk, is a witness who can testify the purpose of such introduction.)

It was in conformity to the specific information referred to in these "lost letters" (to me addressed) that I acted in coming before the Department at such time.

It was in conformity to "information" contained in said "lost letters" that I at the time contended with the First Comptroller of the Treasury, William Lawrence, that he had no lawful authority to withhold from me the "certificate of ownership" of the "First-mortgage bonds" of the Central and the Union Pacific railroad companies.

It is in conformity with such information, as follows: That Charles Durkee died seized and possessed of the bonds of these and other railroad companies to the amount of $64,623,512. That after his decease bonds termed interest call bonds "accumulated in the Treasury Department for the period of twenty years and upward," assigned to Charles Durkee, or legal representative. It is in conformity with such information (given to me by the late Secretary Folger April 22, 1884) that I have stated "that 6 per cent per annum interest had accrued, without the payment of any part thereof, on such bonds, up to the date of said April 22, A. D. 1884.

It is in conformity with the knowledge obtained through these official letters retained by the Treasury Department, and others filed with this honorable court which have already been certified for my use, that the Treasurer of the United States, Conrad N. Jordan, acknowledged officially to me the obligation of the Government to settle in the Treasury Department all the liabilities attaching to the United States by reason of the transactions aforesaid, and in which matter said Jordan acknowledged that the said sum of $64,623,512 was due and payable by the United States to me, as legal representative of lawful and just creditors of the United States. I furthermore add that Mr. Jordan himself suggested to me the propriety of procuring "an enabling act," as he termed it, through which he said it would be his duty, when the same should have been enacted, to pay off the obligations thereunto attaching to the United States by reason of those matters and things which have been alleged in my complaint; and for reference I give the Hon. Shelby M. Cullom, United States Senator from the State of Illinois, and state as follows: Mr. Cullom and myself at different times, and in the Senate Chamber of the United States at various times discussed in private the modes of reaching an accounting from the Government in those matters and things which did not appear of record in the railroad reports. I told him at various times what the trouble was; that accounts which had been duly rendered to me while acting in my lawful capacity as legal representative of the holders of these first-mortgage bonds were withheld from me, and were not lawfully reported to Congress as they should be.

I told him that there ought to be some action of Congress taken to protect such interests as those I represented.

He told me that he would do what he could to get the proper action taken; that I should write up and send to him what I considered would be the proper action for Congress to take.

I did so, and he procured the enactment of the act of March 3, 1887, appending the same, as I understood, to other enactments relating to the interstate-commerce bill.

Senator Allison, of Iowa, also conferred with me about the matter, and was cognizant of the relation that I sustained toward the subject-matter of this act.

But the one person whom I have regarded as being most at fault has been William Lawrence, of Bellefontaine, Ohio. This man I know to have been directed by the late Hon. Charles J. Folger, "to keep and preserve all necessary files and records of the Treasury Department," and all other files of all other Departments involved in the transactions of the said April 22 in the First Comptroller's Office; and furthermore charged him "with the delivery" to myself of "certified copies" of the same; and it is true that I have often reminded this same Judge Lawrence of his obligations in this respect, and that he was reminded of the same by myself and the Hon. J. G. Cannon on the occasion of my returning in five or six weeks after the date of said April 22; and it is true that he did not dispute the fact, but sought to create the impression on those around him that he did not know much about the matter I was talking about; and it is true that Mr. Cannon expressed some surprise at his assumed ignorance of these matters, and used the words, "Why, Judge Lawrence, were you not there? Don't you know all about it?" And then he said he did, but that it was not proper to speak openly of what occurred there, but that he would see to it that all proper information was given me. It is true also that at the same time he (Judge Lawrence) called Joseph A. D. Thompson, Deputy First Comptroller, and directed him to go with me to see William Armstrong, the then Commissioner of Railroads, and to inform that gentleman that he must make reports to me. It is true that Mr. Armstrong acknowledged my right to receive these reports, and presented me with the very one he was then using in his office. It is true that all succeeding Commissioners of Railroads have recognized their accountability to me as the legal representative of the first-mortgage interest in these respective railroad properties.

It is true that said William Lawrence offered to make a contract—and did, in terms, make a contract—to become my attorney to prosecute my rights, and only failed to become so because the man who was interested with me in the matter, as a financial supporter, refused to sign the contract without Judge Lawrence should tell him, in affidavit, what did actually take place in that "meeting of April 22, 1884."

It is true that he said in a letter to Simon P. Douthart, of Dearborn street, Chicago, that he "did know all about what then occurred, but that he never would reveal it until I should employ him, and pay him, as for services of an attorney.

It is true that he made a similar statement in a letter to C. W. G. Merriam, of Chicago (attorney).

To conclude my affidavit, I believe that said William Lawrence knew for many years afterwards, and now knows, unless age has dimmed his memory, all the facts in relation to the foundation of the present suit of L. C. Blaisdell *v.* The United States, and that his deposition should be taken.

It is true, likewise, of U. T. Wymond, ex-United States Treasurer; of Eugene B. Daskam, chief clerk; of William Fletcher, an accounting officer, and of Charles V. Parkman, or the stenographer, who, as Judge Lawrence has told me, took down every word that was spoken by myself and all present in the said meeting of April 22, A. D. 1884. This affidavit is submitted, that the honorable court may use its pleasure concerning the obtaining of affidavits or of depositions from the parties whose names are herein mentioned.

CRIME AGAINST THE GOVERNMENT.

See sections 5403 and 5408, United States Revised Statutes.

"SEC. 5403. Every person who willfully takes away any record, paper, proceeding, or document, filed or deposited with any clerk or officer in any public office, or with any judicial or public officer, shall, without reference to the value of the record, paper, document, or proceeding so taken, pay a fine of not more than two thousand dollars, or suffer imprisonment at hard labor not more than three years, or both.

"SEC. 5408. Every officer, having the custody of any record, paper, document, or proceeding specified in section 5403, who fraudulently takes away, or withdraws, or destroys, any such record, paper, or proceeding filed in his office, or deposited with him, or in his custody, shall pay a fine of not more than two thousand dollars, or suffer imprisonment at hard labor not more than three years, or both; and shall, moreover, forfeit his office and be forever afterward disqualified from holding any office under the United States."

(The above relates to "destroying or removal, from place of lawful deposit, the files and records of the Treasury Department.")

I charge it to be the fact that William Lawrence, who was First Comptroller of the Treasury, under a commission dated July 15, 1880, to the date of March 24, 1885, did, under the special direction and by official consent of the late Secretary of the Treasury, the Hon. Charles J. Folger, in the presence of witnesses (of whom I am one), on the date of April 22, 1884, in the office of said First Comptroller of the Treasury, assume the custody, care, control, and safe-keeping of all such "files and records:" First, of the Treasury Department; second, of the Department of the Interior; third, of the Department of State; fourth, of the Department of Justice; as did, in law and fact, designate, describe, determine, and constitute the true, lawful, and just holders of mortgage or lien debts of the Central Pacific, the Union Pacific et al. railroad companies, by reason of which said liens on their property rights and franchises the United States, under acts of Congress, have become obligated to "clear off, by payments, out of the Treasury of the United States," all such class and character of indebtedness; and I charge the fact to be furthermore true that each and every successor in office of the said William Lawrence have, in official letters, repeatedly declared their inability to furnish, either to myself or to any interested parties whomsoever, any of the "files and records" of the said office, so as aforesaid, left by the Secretary of the Treasury aforesaid, in the care, keeping, and custody of the First Comptroller, or the "certified copies thereof," and that valuable papers, records, documents, and proceedings, all pertaining to the settlement of the indebtedness of said Pacific railroad companies, and in which affiant hold an interest by right of representation as attorney of record in said settlements, have become "lost or destroyed through the violation by said William Lawrence" and others of the rules and regulations of the Treasury Department, and of the Revised Statutes of the United States (see sections 277, 307, 313, 236, 191, 305, 306, 308, 197, 188), and I charge that the "neglect of official duties" by the said William Lawrence while incumbent in said office, and by his willful intention, has prevented the "lawful and just holders of the said paramount lien to that of the United States" from receiving the benefit, security, and protection of those statutes of the United States enacted by Congress for their especial protection of rights and interest in the "files and records" of the Treasury Department, and as relating to their respective interests in the aforesaid liens, and that such official neglect has been followed by similar defaults and neglects of other executive officers of the Treasury Department (as see statutes cited), as a necessary consequence of the defaults of said First Comptroller, for which offenses this attorney of the record prefers against the said William Lawrence, ex-First Comptroller of the Treasury, Conrad N. Jordan, incumbent in office and ex-Treasurer of the United States, now assistant treasurer presiding over the subtreasury in the city of New York, that they, and each of them, are guilty of crimes against the Government of the United States, as defined in the Revised Statutes, sections 5403 and 5408 thereof.

The United States, the defendant in this case, was charged with all those special obligations under the terms of the statutes which would pertain to any lawfully constituted security holders who, by virtue of the mere fact of being "security holders" in trust for the cestu qui trust, would not permit the trustee to obtain payment of the moneys due from debtor to creditor, and afterwards to deny any part of the trust which the statute, without personal contract or written contract, would impose. It is admitted and I understand that the United States is now charged with the duty of "making the amount and character of payments out of the Treasury of the United States," that is declared in this petition for relief; the petition itself is so framed that if, in the judgment of the court, no relief can be extended to the claimants, the power of the court over the subject-matter is not thereby exhausted, but it may continue the case with an amended petition, which shall undertake to afford that relief contemplated as to the original claimants for the benefit of such persons as the court may ascertain to be the "lawful and just holders of the securities" (the bonds in question), and which have in the original petition been alleged to have vested in Charles Durkee.

It is assuming an absurdity, which the court should not tolerate from the defense, that the United States Government first knew me as a claimant on record against the Government. I was not. It was not until the Treasurer of the United States personally confessed to me the facts that he, the said Conrad N. Jordan, as Treasurer of the United States, held himself accountable to me in the sum of $64,623,512 (the sum named to him in the question) that I sought the aid of legislation to provide for its payment.

That it was not until this officer had suggested the idea—to me personally—that legislative relief be sought for my own relief and for his authorization to pay this demand that I applied to the Senator (Hon. S. M. Cullom) of Illinois for such legislation.

May it please the honorable court, that Senator can tell the court for himself what was the purpose of the act of March 3, 1887; that act which directed the Secretary of the Treasury to clear off, by payments out of the Treasury of the United States, the sums due to "the lawful and just holders of the lien prior and paramount to that of the United States." (See, also, Thurman Act.)

And still, with all the recognition of my representative rights in such lien, officially attested in the acts of the accounting officers in the premises, by the Secretary of the Treasury, by the Attorney-General, by the First Comptroller, and by the corporations whose act of making payments in response to such demands ought to stop the mouths of all objectors, with all this recognition of rights, the present Secretary of the Treasury would ignore me as a false pretender without rights before his Department, and as one who had not even filed a claim against it in form so as to make it the subject of an investigation.

"UNEXPLAINED POSSESSION OF MONEYS."

I have been instructed "that unexplained possession of moneys in the hands of one not the lawful owner is larceny." Possession gained by whomsoever, whether he be the Treasurer, subtreasurer, or the President of the United States, of moneys by law payable only to other parties than the United States (if Blackstone knew about law), was a grand larceny, and as the Government is incapable of committing such an act, the act attaches to the officers as a personal offense against the United States.

LEONARD C. BLAISDELL.

Subscribed and sworn to before me, the undersigned, this 24th day of May, 1895.

[SEAL.] JNO. T. PLUMMER, *Notary Public.*

SUPPLEMENTAL INFORMATION BY AFFIDAVIT.

It is stated as information by one who stood in intimate relation to Charles Durkee, and to whom he committed such information in keeping as a secret which he had not given to either of his executors as appointed in his will, that shortly before his death he called this party to his bedside, and said "that he had had his suspicions aroused by certain things that had transpired within the last six months; that one of his intended executors—if not both—had evil designs on his estate, and that he had taken the precaution to put his more valuable papers and evidences of estate into a certain 'tin box,' which he pointed out to the witness, and that he wished this witness to observe that it was 'sealed' and directed to 'The Metropolitan National Bank of the city of New York;' that he charged it as his dying request upon this witness that she should keep watch over his executors, to see that this box was safely consigned to said 'Metropolitan National Bank, in said city of New York.'"

* * * * * * *

This statement was made the subject of consideration in the Cabinet meeting of April 22, A. D. 1884, Chester A. Arthur being President. At the conclusion of the conference in relation to the same it was agreed between this affiant (L. C. Blaisdell) and Secretary Folger, on behalf of the Government, that the said Secretary should have the necessary authority to call for and to receive, in the name of the said Blaisdell, the said "tin box," if the same could be found in aforesaid bank, or the contents, or any part of the contents that such box might have contained; and that the same should be taken possession of by the Solicitor of the Treasury and held for the "joint use and benefit of the heirs at law of Charles Durkee and the United States.'

* * * * * * *

In the presence of this affiant and another witness, the Solicitor of the Treasury, about the year and during the month of August, 1888, in his office, stated that papers of the character described in the above had been delivered by the said Metropolitan National Bank, presumably so, he judged, from the circumstance of the assignment of said bank being found on the books of the Solicitor, and containing, ostensibly, "the assignment of all such matters as were designated" by the order of the Secretary of the Treasury of April 22, A. D. 1884. This affiant was not at such time as learned in the law, or the rules and regulations governing the Departments, as he believes himself now to be, and believes that the very attorney, whom he had with him to assist him, was then in collusion with the enemies of the Government and the defendants in this case, No. 18003, to prevent affiant from seeing said assignment and judging for himself whether it contained the matters and things which he himself and the Secretary of the Treasury had specified, and put into an order of the Secretary of the Treasury that it should contain, to wit, the private papers of said Durkee that should show the assignment and delivery to said Durkee by Pacific railroad corporations, designated in said suit, of all the bonds so designated in the petition in said case.

Affiant here again states, as under oath, that such order of said Secretary of the Treasury was to contain the private papers, and all the private papers, whether letters, deeds, bonds, or assignments or other character of evidences of indebtedness to Charles Durkee aforesaid, which had at any time come into the possession or under the control of the said Metropolitan National Bank of the city of New York aforesaid; that said Secretary made the proposition to receive from affiant such character of orders and to execute the same at once; and that said Secretary left the room with the last words on his lips which affiant ever heard him utter, saying, "I will see that the order is at once transmitted to the subtreasury in the city of New York."

LEONARD C. BLAISDELL,
Attorney of Record of Case 18003, Court of Claims.

STATE OF INDIANA, *County of Marion, ss:*

Subscribed and sworn to before me, the undersigned notary public, in and for the aforesaid county and State, this 24th day of May, 1895.

[SEAL.] JOHN T. PLUMMER, *Notary Public.*

In Court of Claims. L. C. Blaisdell *v.* The United States. Applicant for rule on the Secretary of the Treasury to show cause why judgment should not be entered against the United States and in favor of the petitioners and claimants against the United States.

[Final statement of Case 18003. In Court of Claims. L. C. Blaisdell *v.* The United States.]

This case was brought before the honorable court through the intervention of the Committee on Claims of the Fifty-fourth Congress, from whose files it will appear that the plaintiff had been duly presented by a Member of that Congress, the Hon. William M. Springer, of the State of Illinois.

It was filed in the first instance by the present claimant, L. C. Blaisdell, in behalf of not only the heirs at law of the decedent, Charles Durkee, but in behalf of all creditors of the lien prior and paramount to that of the United States, as designated in the several acts of Congress, 1864, 1878, and of the act of March 3, 1887.

Thus it appears on the face of the petition that it was a claim filed and founded upon acts of Congress, which acts were in the petition definitely and at length set forth in form and substance, and made exhibits for the purposes of conveying to the mind of the court the foundation upon which all rights claimed by the complainants in the case were to be ascertained. The rights of the complainants, whatever they shall be ascertained by the honorable court to be or to have heretofore been, are fully defined in the Pacific Railroad laws set up, designated, and plead in the preliminary and informal petition; in the more complete petition following on the case or matter of the petition being by the court taken for consideration as in ex parte; and must finally appear, not necessarily from any or all of the answers of the several Departments, Bureaus, and officers of the Government, the information thereby conveyed to the court, but through the information conveyed to the mind of the court through statutes of the United States, and specific acts of Congress defining the particular rights and character of rights set up and appearing in this petition.

It will only be necessary to merely call the attention of this honorable court to the acts of Congress that have been duly presented to it as the authority for bringing this claim against the United States, to complete all the testimony in support of the claim herein presented that can be required of the complainants in the case to present.

The information that has been filed with this honorable court by the attorney of record in the case—and that particular portion of it which classifies as "official matter," certified by the several Departments, Bureaus, and officers of the Government—disclose a state of facts which precludes the possibility of there being hereafter, at any time, by or through any Department, Bureau, or officer of the Government, a state of facts to it presented that shall run counter to or in any material form modify the conclusions which the court may draw from that which has been already thus presented.

A summary of these facts thus presented, and that have been on file with this honorable court for the greater part of the two years last preceding the present date, shows to the honorable court all the essential information necessary that it shall have obtained before proceeding to enter final judgment in the cause of the complainants versus the United States.

As they embrace a large part of the history of the Pacific railroad system, their operations, duties, and obligations were as expressed in the United States statutes; and so great a portion of the detailed information is to be conveyed to the court through official reports of the Auditor of Railroad Accounts in the first instance and Railroad Commissioner's reports in the latter instances, it is deemed in order to present first the annual report of the Auditor of Railroad Accounts to the Secretary of the Interior for the year ending June 30, 1878.

On page 6 of this report occur the words:

"The act of Congress approved May 7, 1878 (chap. 96, p. 56 Statute II, 1877-78), entitled 'An act to alter and amend the act entitled "An act to aid in the construction of a railroad and telegraph line from the Missouri River to the Pacific Ocean, * * * approved 1862,"' * * * and "to alter and amend act of 1864," in amendment of said first-named act, requires:

"That the net earnings of said act of 1862, of said railroad companies, respectively, the Central Pacific Railroad Company of California and the Union Pacific Railroad Company, shall be ascertained by deducting from the gross amount of their earnings, respectively, the necessary expenses paid within the year in operating the same and keeping the same in a state of repair, and also the sum paid by them, respectively, within the year in discharge of interest on their first-mortgage bonds."

On the first proposition, to wit, the amount paid by these companies "within any given year in operating their railroad and telegraph lines, and in keeping the same in a state of repair," it is not proposed to make any remarks upon; but the second proposition, namely, "with the amount paid by them, respectively, within the year or at any other time, in discharge of interest on their first-mortgage bonds," with this proposition we do propose to deal.

It is made the basis of the rights set up by the complainants against the United States that the interest accrued upon these first-mortgage bonds, to wit:

Union Pacific	$27,236,512
Central Pacific	25,885,120
Denver Pacific Railroad and Telegraph Company (Western Pacific)	1,970,560
Kansas Pacific	1,600,000
Central Branch Union Pacific Railroad Company	1,600,000
Sioux City and Pacific Railroad Company	1,628,320

A total first-mortgage debt and indebtedness of lien prior and paramount to that of the United States of $64,623,512, with interest accrued thereon at the rate of 6 per cent per annum, was, until the dates, respectively, March 3, A. D. 1883, and January 1, A. D. 1885, the debt and the expressed indebtedness of these railroad and telegraph companies, jointly and severally, to such parties and persons as were expressed and designated in "certain files and records of the Treasury Department," and which were referred to in these terms by Hon. William Lawrence, First Comptroller of the Treasury, in Comptroller's Decision by said William Lawrence, under the date of December 3, A. D. 1884, and at such date became, by contract, an indebtedness of the United States.

That the names of "the lawful and just holders of" the said "lien prior and paramount to that of the United States" have not appeared of record within the knowledge of this honorable court, and have never yet been produced (so far as known) before any committee of either House of Congress, not reported in any railroad report required by law to have contained them, constitutes no evidence, and no rebuttal of the testimony that first-mortgage creditors answering to that description do not exist, for we can not consistently believe that when such mortgages of such description and of such character of lien have been so well provided with protection in the expressed provisions of the acts of Congress—1864, 1878, and 1887—that the very "liens" or incumbrances thus openly recognized by such acts of Congress could exist independently of an expressed ownership of such character of mortgages in the Department of the Treasury and the Department of the Interior, both of which said Departments contain the most conclusive evidence and recorded proofs that such bonds do exist.

The Departments just named have, it is true, failed to produce the "evidence" called for by the complainants in the first instance, and by the honorable court in the second instance, that such mortgage bonds do exist; but these acts of Congress just referred to, more especially the preamble to the act of May 7, 1878, declare that the Union Pacific Railroad Company named in this and the other said acts of Congress, and the Central Pacific Railroad Company and others therein named, "did and have issued" an amount of "their own bonds" equal to the amount so issued (as therein expressed) to them, and each of them, by the United States."

Furthermore, rights of owners of bonds thus issued are not, in law or equity, to be defeated by the neglect and refusal of the said several Departments, or any officer, bureaus, or heads of such Departments to make and preserve proper "files and records" of the various transactions that may have occurred in either one.

In pleading for the protection of the rights of this class of creditors of the United States, I shall submit for the consideration of the honorable court the general proposition that rights thus guaranteed by acts of Congress are not to be defeated by "the neglect and refusal of officers of the Government" ("more particularly the heads of the two Departments last named) to keep, preserve for the use of this court, and to present the true and perfect record of such transactions occurring therein as have involved the credit of the United States to the total amount named in the said Pacific Railroad bonds."

The truth of this last proposition I believe is not questioned by any head of any Department of the Government so far as I have yet been informed, to wit, the records of the Treasury Department do disclose the "public-debt statement; that all interest accrued upon the said bonds are payable by the United States." To whom payable is not disclosed. That the principal of the bonds ($64,623,512) is also "payable by the United States." To whom payable is not disclosed.

Nor is it disclosed (by record or information to Congress given) when, in the history of these bonds, that portion of them became due and payable which represented "interest indebtedness accrued for the period of time which intervened between issue of the principal bonds and the date of April 22, 1884." The plaintiff in the case has alleged the fact of the transposition of a specific and well-defined and expressed indebtedness of these corporations into an indebtedness of the United States. The Treasury Department corroborates the fact stated, that such indebtedness has become the indebtedness of the United States, but does not show when it so became (debt payable by the United States).

The Interior (Railroad Department thereof) carries the same debt account under the title or name of "bond indebtedness," and charges the same item against the United States as such, which the Treasury Department terms a cash and "sinking-fund indebtedness." The information is thus disclosed to the honorable court that there is a vast discrepancy between the "public-debt statement of the Secretary of the Treasury and that disclosed in the Department of the Interior. The sinking fund as shown by the Commissioner of Railroads does not show to exceed $27,000,000 (less than $20,000,000 in 1884). While the Treasury Department (unless the Pacific Railroad Committee, under Mr. Outhwaite, have misstated) shows $64,000,000 of "sinking-fund indebtedness of the Government," by reason of these Pacific Railroad obligations, in addition to that shown in the Department of the Interior.

To prove that there is a gigantic discrepancy and erroneous statement of the public liabilities in this respect, as between these two Departments, the honorable court has but to summon Mr. Outhwaite as a witness, who, with 13 other members of that committee (in 1888), declared "that the amount of $64,623,512 in cash" was, on the 1st day of January, 1885, an "outstanding liability" of the Government, by reason of that amount of cash having been on that date deposited with the Secretary of the Treasury "for the definitely ascertained indebtedness of these several Pacific railroad companies to their lawful creditors" of the lien prior and paramount to that of the United States.

If the liability of the United States—or my statement of its liability in this respect, and as alleged in my petition, both the original and the amended—has been disputed by any answer, plea, or demurrer filed with this honorable court, I am as yet not made aware of the fact. The statement has gone before the Department of the Treasury, signed and sworn to as set forth in my affidavits, and stands unchallenged, so far as I know.

The order of the court for the information that would deny the truth of the statement has gone forth and does not bring the information that would deny it.

The statement has stood in form and in print before the eyes of every Secretary of the Treasury from the date of January 12, 1889, and not one has attempted to deny it or make any official answer tending to deny the truth, substantially, of my statements as in petition contained. The President of the United States (Benjamin Harrison, while Chief Executive) caused all my statements to be placed before himself, in official capacity, and in official capacity referred them "for the official action" (note the words) of the Secretary of the Treasury. The Supreme Court, in 99 United States Reports, supports the statement of my petition, that the United

States is debtor to the "sinking fund" and in favor of "the lawful and just holders of paramount lien," as stated, "to the full amount of the deposits made under the provisions for such sinking fund as contained in the act of May 7, 1878." The committee referred to last has the information that the sum of $64,623,512 is and has been withheld from "the possession of the lawful and just holders of such paramount lien by each and every Secretary of the Treasury, on the plea, or notion, rather, that such officer held a discretionary authority to make of such fund a sinking fund."

Congress, by act of March 3, 1887, directed that officer "to clear off such paramount lien or incumbrance by payments (by payments, mark the words) out of the sinking fund," and provided that the entire amount be paid, whether the sinking fund was more or less than the amount due to the lawful owners of such bonds, or the "lawful creditors of the paramount lien aforesaid."

For this disobedience of the requirement—the direct, positive, and special order of Congress—the present incumbent in that office is answerable. He can not and does not answer either Congress or this honorable court that he knows not the lawful creditors of the United States; that he has no legal knowledge of them that he is bound by law to take cognizance of.

He appears to rest contentedly upon "want of information, such information as would create an official liability on his part to answer" the demands made by me on the United States Treasury. He acts, or, rather, neglects to act; and rests upon the assumption that his neglect and refusal to answer me in official manner, either by affirmation or by denial of the claims I have filed, prevents the consummation of my purpose to enforce an accounting from him; and he acts as if he expected that the entire body of Congress and the Supreme Court, including this honorable court, would unitedly be unable to compel him either to affirm or deny my right to an accounting, and thus prevent not only myself and my clients from obtaining the benefits of those acts of Congress upon which we rely for protection, but that all possible creditors of such lien, as Congress provided should be secured to "its lawful holders" (should others than myself and clients prove to be the "lawful beneficiaries"), would be powerless, and the courts named, and Congress itself, be powerless to enforce against his will the payment of the sums due.

With these statements I have concluded to include the following motion: That the Secretary of the Treasury be, and with the approval of this honorable court is hereby, ordered to show cause, by his personal appearance before this honorable court, at the next ensuing rule day, why judgment should not be rendered in behalf of the petitioners and claimants in said case and cause, No. 18003, in accordance with the statement of claims against the United States made to this honorable court.

Very respectfully submitted by

——— ———,
Attorney of Record in Case No. 18003.

To the Honorable Chief Justice and Judges thereof.

[In the Court of Claims of the United States. Term 1894-1895. Leonard C. Blaisdell, attorney in fact, etc., et al., *v.* The United States. No. 18003. Filed March 6, 1895.]

AMENDED PETITION.

The claimants, Leonard C. Blaisdell, attorney in fact for the following-named heirs at law of Charles Durkee, late a citizen of the United States, now deceased, to wit:

George Durkee, Joseph Durkee, Charles C. Durkee, Harvey Durkee, Martha K. Durkee, Bessie Durkee, John Durkee, Charles E. Durkee, Harriet Fluent, Mary L. Hendrix, Caroline C. Johnson, Charles L. Boardman, Harriet Boardman, Henry Boardman, Jessie H. Moneghan, May A. Fargo, Ellen Church, Mary L. Furness, Laura A. Huntington, Louiza Hoag, and Harriet L. Blaisdell (who is the wife of Leonard C. Blaisdell), for their amended petition herein say:

I.

That they are all citizens of the United States; that their said attorney in fact resides at Champaign, in the State of Illinois; that they are the sole and only heirs at law of said Charles Durkee, deceased; that they and their said attorney in fact have always yielded true allegiance to the United States, and that they are the sole owners of the claim herein sued upon.

II.

That the said Charles Durkee, during his life, was lawfully possessed and was the owner of certain prior and paramount lien bonds of the Union and Central Pacific railroad companies, which bonds had been issued by said companies through their officers and agents in the construction and equipment of said railroads, and which bonds were of the value and amount of sixty-four million six hundred and twenty-three thousand five hundred and twelve dollars ($64,623,512.00), and that said bonds subsequently were deposited in the Treasury Department of the United States, or in a subtreasury, to be held by the United States in trust for the use and benefit of the owners thereof, and their payment was guaranteed by the Government of the United States, and the claimants say that, by virtue of being the heirs at law of said decedent, and by virtue of the premises, they became at his decease the lawful owners of the bonds aforesaid.

III.

That the Government of the United States, pursuant to law, collected of and from the said Union and Central Pacific railroad companies the said sum of sixty-four million six hundred and twenty-three thousand five hundred and twelve dollars ($64,623,512.00), and now holds the same for the protection, security, and benefit of the lawful and just holders of any mortgage or lien debts of such companies, respectively, lawfully paramount to the rights of the United States, but the United States have neglected, failed, and refused to pay the same over to these claimants as the heirs at law of said decedent, and who are the lawful owners of the said bonds, and are lawfully and justly entitled to the sum of money aforesaid, although often requested so to do by the claimants, and that, notwithstanding the premises, that sum is now retained in the Treasury or in a subtreasury of the United States.

IV.

And the claimants say that they are justly entitled to the sum aforesaid, on account of said bonds and of the premises hereinbefore stated, and that the said sum is justly due and owing to them from the United States, and is wholly unpaid.

V.

And the claimants further say that they have made the allegations in their said amended petition as specific and accurate as they are able to do from the data in their possession, the accurate and specific information therein being in possession of the defendant, and they wish to reserve their right to further amend said petition should the allegations herein be properly amendable in the light of further information.

Wherefore The claimants demand judgment against the United States in the sum of sixty-four million six hundred and twenty-three thousand five hundred and twelve dollars ($64,623,512.00) and all proper relief in the premises.

LEONARD C. BLAISDELL,
Attorney in Fact and one of the Petitioners.

DUDLEY & MICHENER, *Attorneys.*
CHANEY & GARRISON, *Counsel.*

DISTRICT OF COLUMBIA, *City of Washington, ss:*

Before me, a notary public in and for said District, personally appeared Leonard C. Blaisdell, who, being duly sworn, upon his said oath says that he is one of the petitioners in the foregoing petition, has read and understands the same, and that the allegations set forth therein are true to the best of his knowledge and belief.

L. C. BLAISDELL.

Subscribed and sworn to before me this 4th day of March, A. D. 1895.

[SEAL.] L. P. SQUIER, *Notary Public.*

Mr. Blaisdell continued his statement as follows:

I think that the proposition that the Government is a trustee over the funds in the sinking fund for the security, benefit, and protection of the lawful creditors of the paramount lien will not be dissented from by the honorable committee. Nor do I hesitate to say that I believe the committee will not dissent from the proposition that the Secretary of the Treasury is (under the provisions of the act of March 3, 1887) charged with the duty of using the sinking fund for the satisfaction of the paramount lien obligations; nor from the proposition that such officer has not satisfied one dollar of such obligations; nor from the proposition that claimants have been before the Treasury Department, appearing for the satisfaction of such obligations for more than ten years past. Nor will the committee dissent from the proposition that the Government should either cause these obligations to be satisfied according to law or renounce the trust and allow such paramount lien creditors to resort to the courts in suits against the Pacific Railroad corporations to enforce their rights.

Adjourned.

WASHINGTON, D. C., *March 24, 1896.*

The committee met at 11 a. m. Present, Senator Gear, chairman.

THE UNION PACIFIC.

STATEMENT OF MR. JOHN ROONEY.

Mr. John Rooney, of New York, representing bondholders of the Union Pacific Railroad Company, not parties to the reorganization plan, appeared before the committee and submitted the following statement:

Bill for Government commissioners to execute a plan, indicated by Congress, for the compulsory redemption of the first and Government debts at par in cash; the payments to be made by the present junior bondholders and the stockholders, who shall invest the requisite amounts in interest-bearing mortgage bonds.

This plan, propounded in the bill which we had the honor to submit, is simply the application to the collection of the Government mortgages of the methods pursued every day by private interests in railroads. Practically there can be no competitive cash bidding for such colossal properties. The best market of the creditors, requiring the adequate payment of their claims, consists in the junior bonds and stocks interested to save their equities from foreclosure. In the case of these railroads, the earnings furnish to the junior claimants a desirable investment, which it would be folly for them to reject, at the risk of losing their great interest in the probable increased revenues of these properties.

With these certain elements, based upon the present actual earnings of the aided divisions, on which Congress can predicate the Government plan of reorganization, why resort to the aleatory method of authorizing certain officials to assess the value of the Government's mortgages? These properties are worth just what the stocks will pay for them under the pressure of foreclosure. This can not be ascertained except by process of foreclosure, modified as to all junior interests by providing them with substantial securities to represent their proportions of the redemption of the superior liens. It is upon such an assured basis that this bill proceeds, providing for the execution of the necessary administrative details by commissioners.

The method adopted in this bill is simply the normal course contemplated by the contracts for the benefit of creditors who have stipulated for a superior mortgage and which is followed by business men every day in the year. Why should the Government alone divest itself of these remedies? These great properties are not worth merely what any three or four worthy officials may declare them, upon problematical data, to be potentially worth, but what the law of the land, acting in its ordinary course upon subordinate and imperiled interests, may actually ascertain it to be worth to them.

In corroboration of the practical nature of this remedy we submit the following concrete considerations, which bear forcibly upon the minds of stockholders called upon to make investments in such new securities as are provided in this plan:

Present increase of revenues.—The recent reports for the completed year 1895 show a rate of increase in Union Pacific earnings which enhances the importance to the stockholders of saving their shares by paying the Government debts through subscriptions to substituted bond issues of intrinsic value.

Increase of price of junior securities has always followed the payment of heavy assessments and the restoration of the solvency of the companies. In this way the stock has generally promptly recouped itself for its outlay, which, in this case, would be a result additional to the investment in a desirable security.

Success of the assessment plan when employed by individual mortgage holders now invoked for the Government and its fellow-interests. The New York Times of February 9 contains such apposite material on this point that we venture to quote from it:

"If the Government had simply asked payment in the same way that a corporation asks payment for an issue of its securities—that is, by certified checks—it would never have been anything but a question of how many times over the loan would have been subscribed; for the sum of $100,000,000 is but a drop in the bucket as compared with the wealth of the country. See the proof of it. Three bankrupt corporations have just called upon certain classes of their security holders for new money, in the way of assessments and otherwise—not to buy Government bonds, but to preserve an equity of more or less doubtful value in these bankrupt properties—and all of these demands have already been met or are being met, as follows: Reading, $28,000,000; Atchison, $14,000,000; Erie, $10,000,000.

"Here is a total of $52,000,000 cash, paid up by a limited number of people under most discouraging conditions; in the case of the Reading the new assessment following one of $15,000,000 levied in $1889. We leave out the numerous other assessments of millions levied within the past eighteen months or two years—as the Richmond Terminal, of $18,000,000."

Many similar instances could be added.

In the face of these amounts of assessments raised upon the stocks of roads inferior, in most instances, to these bond-aided properties, and with new stock merely, instead of good bonds, being given to the subscribers, it would be inefficient on the part of the Government not to direct its commissioners to pursue this rightful remedy.

Since our last statement before the committee several plans of reorganization have been based on the requirement of payments from the stock to avoid forfeiture. The Oregon Short Line, one of the Union Pacific connecting roads, has levied $12 per share on its stockholders. The Northern Pacific requires its stockholders to pay $15 per share. For these assessments the stockholders receive only new stock. Contrast these onerous levies with the subscription to well-secured interest-bearing bonds on these Pacific railroads.

In view of these everyday financial occurrences, it is not surprising that the statutes of New York establish this equity of redemption as an individual right of each stockholder. Under these acts each stockholder has the privilege of redeeming the prior mortgages, in the proportion which his stock bears to the total issue. (Stock Corporation Laws of 1892, sec. 49.)

It is not to be expected that junior claimants will voluntarily offer the best terms of redemption. Therefore, the plain, straightforward course by which all mortgages are collected should not be deviated from in favor of the junior claims on these aided railroads. The correlative of foreclosure is payment, and this bill merely provides the machinery to facilitate the inferior interests, in making their proportionate payments into a common fund, for the discharge of the mortgages of which the Government is a holder.

Under our plan the Government has absolutely no concern with these items. If the Government were going to operate the roads these elements would be measurably involved. But we propose that the Government and the first mortgages be paid in cash—by subscriptions to the new securities of a reorganized company, to be issued for those cash payments. The annual interest charge for these new securities is based upon the official returns of the annual earnings of the subsidized divisions, excluding nonaided line, terminals, and bridge. When the Government is paid by the present stockholders—who take transfers of the first and second mortgages—those stockholders secure the retention of their present interests in the aided lines.

Their interests in the nonaided lines will not have been affected, and of course they retain them likewise. They can reorganize them or let their securities remain as they are. But, in any event, the aided and nonaided lines, the terminals, and the bridge remain united in the same ownership as at present. Hence there is no use in discussing whether the Supreme Court was right in holding that the Government lien covers the bridge; nor is it important to consider the earnings of the nonaided line, which are only one twenty-fourth of the whole; nor to attempt to value terminals, which would be of little value unless used by the aided divisions. Indeed, it is this very ownership of these truncated morsels which renders it more desirable to the juniors and stocks to subscribe to the new issue of bonds, in order to utilize those weaker properties. After their compliance with the terms of this reorganization, they would own and operate exactly the same railroad properties which they now own and operate. Only the personnel of the creditors would be changed—from the Government to the individual stockholders.

The occasion for contemplating consolidation in the interest of the Government arises from the fact that there is an excess of revenues on the Union Pacific beyond the amount necessary to pay the Government, while on the Central Pacific there is a deficiency. If the surplus on the Union and Kansas Pacific (about $900,000) could be utilized as the basis for capitalizing a further amount of four-and-a-half bonds, twenty millions more of the Central Pacific debt could be paid to the Government. This could be effected by the commissioners providing in the plan for the sales of both roads as an entirety. They could provide for the formation of a single corporation to own both roads. This company should issue mortgage bonds predicated upon the earnings of both lines as an entirety. There would then be $7,500,000 of annual net revenues, ample to apply to the interest, at 4½ per cent, on $165,000,000 of debt—the net aggregate of the first and Government mortgages on the three roads. The subscription to these bonds by the present stockholders and junior bondholders would furnish the condition for their avoidance of foreclosure and obliteration. Of this amount the commissioners are, by the act, required to reserve ten millions, to secure the independent outlet to the Pacific.

The present road from San Jose to the Pacific would not be of much value if a new road were built, so that its owners would probably be willing to make a proper arrangement for its use with the new company. But if it had to be built, the Government commissioners could turn over to the new company ten millions of the interest-bearing bonds, retaining an additional ten millions (to bear interest when earned), as explained in our previous statement.

The practical question would be the distribution of the stock of the consolidated company, as between the present stockholders of the Union and Central. As the Union Pacific would furnish the greater proportion of revenues to the consolidated company, as well as a lesser debt, it would seem that its stockholders should have a proportionately increased amount of the consolidated stock. This could be reached by an arithmetical calculation. There is nothing in the bill as now drafted which militates against consolidation. But as it would be so valuable to the Government, we have suggested a clause to cover it in the list of amendments appended.

Attorney-General Olney has held, in an elaborate written opinion, that the transportation credits of the Central Pacific are applicable only to the interest account on the subsidy bonds—not to the principal of those bonds. Hence, the failure of the Central Pacific to pay the currency sixes, which fell due January 16, 1895, constitutes a default, for which the road is foreclosable by the United States.

It must be apparent that the coercive method, adapted in this bill from the prevailing system of railroad reorganization, is certain to produce the best possible price for the prior-mortgages. It is not to be supposed, in the nature of things, that the junior interests in these properties are coming forward voluntarily to offer the firsts and the Government the highest price of which the property is susceptible for their interests. As there are just about enough earnings to sustain the capitalization for bringing the firsts and the Government "out whole," it is not surprising to find the juniors and stocks maneuvering to get the prior mortgages to share these present earnings with them, instead of their awaiting a partial resumption of the old scale of revenues.

As matter of fact, they will derive considerable advantage from the reduction in the rate of interest upon the new issues, substituted for the present 6 per cent. And with the income bonds (which the commissioners would likely accord them, in lieu of their present fixed-charge securities, and in addition to the new superior mortgages which they would receive for their subscriptions) they would get all out of the property to which they are equitably entitled. In any event, the Government, through its commissioners (being its own committee of reorganization), would act directly upon each junior bondholder and stockholder, endeavoring to protect the future of his investment. No syndicate could interpose between the Government and the just payment of more than $100,000,000 into its Treasury, as well as the protection of its prior lienors, the first-mortgage bondholders.

No legislation is better than the proposed sacrifices of the first and Government mortgages, because we hold that the Government would be better off not to go on at the present time, but to wait for another year. The Government will not lose anything by waiting for another session of Congress.

Propositions are being pushed before Congress to enable their promoters to avail themselves of the minimum condition of earnings as the basis for obtaining the most favorable terms from the Government. The recent percentage of improvement in transportation business is expected by the commercial community to increase, so that, in all probability, the junior bonds and stocks will make better propositions to Congress next year.

Meanwhile, the financial relations of these roads to the Government will, in all likelihood, remain in statu quo. In the opinion of the Government counsel, Hon. George Hoadley, there can be no foreclosure against the United States as to the right of retention of Government earnings; he holds that the Government liens were never subordinated in this respect to the first mortgages, thus retaining a very considerable prior security to the United States. Furthermore, the President is required by the act of 1887 to take up overdue first-mortgage bonds when safety for the Government liens requires.

The total amount of the first mortgages on all the roads which have matured and will mature before January, 1897, is $11,000,000. If there should be a serious attempt to foreclose the first mortgage, the President would be constrained to execute the act of 1887 by directing the payment "out of the Treasury" of the overdue installments.

Of course, if Congress adopts the assessment plan for the full payment of the firsts and the Government, no more could be required, and, therefore, nothing could be gained by awaiting next session. But no action is better for the firsts and the Government than selling to these subordinate debtors, on terms fixed by them, under the most adverse conditions of the properties.

This bill simply provides the machinery for the Government, which individual holders of prior mortgages provide for themselves.

Individual holders select committees to frame plans of reorganization, whereunder junior interests may absolve themselves from extinction by foreclosure, through assessment payments for the benefit of superior incumbrances. This bill provides for the appointment of commissioners to perform those functions, under the directions prescribed by Congress in this act.

The first step of the commissioners would be the issuing of notices to the junior bondholders and stockholders, as follows:

That the first and Government mortgages are in process of foreclosure. [The first-mortgage foreclosures on the Union and Kansas Pacific are now pending. The other proceedings would have been theretofore initiated.]

That before a day named they should comply with the act of Congress requiring them to subscribe to new issues of bonds sufficient to discharge the Government holdings of first and second incumbrances, and such individual holdings of first mortgages as do not exchange. [The issues and rates of interest to be fixed in the notices, subject only to the exigency that they be productive of the full amount required.]

That the present first-mortgage individual holders notify the commissioners before a day certain (to precede the return date of the foregoing notice to stockholders) whether they elect to accept the new issues or the cash payment.

Should any of the junior interests fail to make the subscriptions at the dates named, the commissioners would offer their interests to the investing public. In return for their subscriptions they would receive not only the issues of new bonds, but, in addition, they would be allotted the same stock interests which the present holders had forfeited (to be enforced by the foreclosure) by the failure to subscribe.

Upon the sale under foreclosure the commissioners would bid in the property for the amount of ———, the Government firsts +, the individual firsts who agreed to exchange +, and the Government mortgages.

This would be a minimum of $113,000,000, payable in firsts and Government claims.

The new company would be formed, and would issue the new securities to the commissioners in exchange for their deeds of the properties. The commissioners would deliver the new securities, according to the subscriptions and allotments made. The payments therefor in cash would be turned into the United States Treasury.

We propose, in case the committee so desire, to take the amount of the Government claim—principal and interest—with such additional as may be needed to take up the first-mortgage bonds, or to take up the first-mortgage bonds belonging to those bondholders who may refuse to exchange them for the new issue. And we will undertake to do so for 20 per cent, and to pay cash for the whole amount of the Government debt, principal and interest.

Mr. Rooney presented the following plan, and said that in a few days he would submit other papers to the committee:

REORGANIZING THE ROADS AS AN ENTIRETY—CONSOLIDATION.

The occasion for contemplating consolidation in the interest of the Government arises from the fact that there is an excess of revenues on the Union Pacific beyond the amount necessary to pay the Government, while on the Central Pacific there is a deficiency. If the surplus on the Union and Kansas Pacific (about $900,000) could be utilized as the basis for capitalizing a further amount of 4½ bonds, twenty millions more of the Central Pacific debt could be paid to the Government. This could be effected by the commissioners providing in the plan for the sales of both roads as an entirety. They could provide for the formation of a single corporation to own both roads. This company should issue mortgage bonds predicated upon the earnings of both lines as an entirety. There would then be $7,500,000 of annual net revenues, ample to apply to the interest at 4½ per cent on $165,000,000 of debt, the net aggregate of the first and Government mortgages on the three roads. The subscription to these bonds by the present stockholders and junior bondholders would furnish the condition for their avoidance of foreclosure and obliteration. Of this amount the commissioners are by the act required to reserve ten millions to secure the independent outlet to the Pacific. The present road from San Jose to the Pacific would not be of much value if a new road were built; so that its owners would probably be willing to make a proper arrangement for its use with the new company. But, if it had to be built, the Government commissioners could turn over to the new company ten millions of the interest-bearing bonds, retaining an additional ten millions (to bear interest when earned), as explained in our previous statement.

The practical question would be the distribution of the stock of the consolidated company as between the present stockholders of the Union and Central. As the Union Pacific would furnish the greater proportion of revenues to the consolidated company, as well as a lesser debt, it would seem that its stockholders should have a proportionately increased amount of the consolidated stock. This could be reached by an arithmetical calculation. There is nothing in the bill as now drafted which militates against consolidation. But, as it would be so valuable to the Government, we have suggested a clause to cover it in the list of amendments appended.

PREFERENCE OF PROCEEDINGS ON CALENDARS OF COURTS.

This would insure the utmost promptitude in the disposition of this matter, so that it could be disposed of in sixty to ninety days after the appointment of commissioners, if we are to judge by the celerity with which stockholders have paid similar assessments. An amendment is inserted in our bill to cover this point.

TEMPORARY EMPLOYMENT OF THE ACT OF 1887—NO SYNDICATE REQUIRED.

The mere affirmance of the act of 1887 by the present Congress would most likely render the execution of its provisions unnecessary, because the first-mortgage bondholders would perceive that it was in the power of the commissioners to protect the Government. Moreover, the Government plan of reorganization would be acceptable to the first-mortgage bondholders, as it offers them better terms than many of them have already indicated a willingness to accept. In any event, the redemption of the first-mortgage debt, accruing in 1896, would be merely temporary until this reorganization was completed, when the new substituted bonds could be sold. The bill enables the commissioners thus to protect the Government reorganization, either through the act of 1887 or by advances obtained from stockholders who had subscribed to the plan.

THIS PLAN IS BOUND TO PRODUCE THE BEST ATTAINABLE PRICE FOR THE FIRST AND SECOND MORTGAGES.

It must be apparent that the coercive method, adapted in this bill from the prevailing system of railroad reorganization, is certain to produce the best possible price for the prior mortgages. It is not to be supposed, in the nature of things, that the junior interests in these properties are coming forward voluntarily to offer the firsts and the Government the highest price of which the property is susceptible for their interests. As there are just about enough earnings to sustain the capitalization for bringing the firsts and the Government "out whole," it is not surprising to find the juniors and stocks maneuvering to get the prior mortgages to share these present earnings with them, instead of their awaiting a partial resumption of the old scale of revenues. As matter of fact they will derive considerable advantage from the reduction in the rate of interest upon the new issues substituted for the present 6 per cent. And with the income bonds (which the commissioners would likely accord them in lieu of their present fixed-charge securities, and in addition to the new superior mortgages which they would receive for their subscriptions) they would get out of the property all to which they are equitably entitled. In any event, the Government, through its commissioners (being its own committee of reorganization), would act directly upon each junior bondholder and stockholder endeavoring to protect the future of his investment. No syndicate could interpose between the Government and the just payment of more than $100,000,000 into its Treasury, as well as the protection of its prior lienors, the first-mortgage bondholders.

AMENDMENTS TO BILL.

Section 1, second line, after "President," insert the words "not more than two of whom shall be of the same political party, and none of whom shall have been in any manner officially connected with any of said companies."

Section 2, at the end insert the following words: "All suits to enforce liens on the bond-aided railroads shall, in furtherance of this act, have absolute preference at all stages on the calendars, and on hearings in the Federal courts, and the time for return of all process and the filing of all pleadings shall be shortened, so that the roads may be sold under this Government plan of reorganization not later than October 1, 1896."

Section 3, fourth line, before the word "company" insert the word "consolidated." On the fourteenth line of the same section, after the word "railroads," insert the words "as an entirety."

Section 4, eighth line, after the word "Government," insert "this company shall possess all the corporate powers heretofore granted by Congress to the bond-aided railroads, and also such powers as may be requisite to enable it to carry out the purposes of this act."

PACIFIC RAILROAD DEBTS—PLAN FOR THE PAYMENT IN FULL OF FIRST AND SECOND (GOVERNMENT) MORTGAGES—BILL AND STATEMENT PRESENTED ON BEHALF OF FIRST-MORTGAGE BONDHOLDERS.

PACIFIC RAILROAD REORGANIZATION.

Preserving all junior interests on condition of their redemption of prior liens.

To the Congress of the United States:

In presenting the accompanying "Bill to provide for the collection of the liabilities of Government-aided railroads to the United States," the undersigned respectfully submit the following explanation of its provisions:

The guiding principle of the measure is to provide for the payment to the Government and its fellow-bondholders of the full amount of their claims. This result is to be attained by requiring the junior interests in these properties to subscribe for issues of bonds, based on the present earnings of the railroads, thus providing the cash funds for the satisfaction of the first and second mortgages. The bill establishes the usual efficient machinery for accomplishing this result, such as is employed by private individuals in like exigencies.

In considering the practical application of this measure it should be premised that the Government is in effective control of the first as well as the second mortgages on these roads. Besides the Government holdings of $16,568,000 of the first-mortgage bonds in the sinking funds, Congress has, by the act of 1887, empowered the President to pay the overdue first mortgage debt "out of the Treasury." Therefore, while enacting measures for the collection of the entire debts to the United States, Congress starts with the benefit of its previous legislation, protecting the Government's interest against the attacks of foreclosing bondholders. The Government, being the practical controller of both the first and second mortgages in default, dominates all proceedings for the foreclosure and sale of the properties, and can utilize those proceedings to obtain full payment for itself and its fellow-bondholders. That is, in effect, what the present bill proposes to accomplish.

We are not dealing with dilapidated or impoverished estates, but with 2,302 miles of railroad, in first-class condition, and earning net about $7,500,000 per annum.

This is the minimum of earnings for the past ten years; yet it is sufficient to pay the interest, at 4½ per cent (about the normal rate on this class of security), on $166,000,000 of mortgage bonds. The first and second mortgage debts of the Union, Kansas, and Central Pacific railroads (less company sinking funds) aggregate about $165,000,000. Therefore, even under the present unfavorable conditions, the earnings can be capitalized (treating the roads as an entirety) at an amount sufficient to pay the two superior incumbrances in full.

Considering that the average net earnings for the past ten years have been about $10,500,000 per annum, it is apparent that there is more than ample warrant for this proposed basis of reorganization. Let us, however, examine the financial condition of each road separately, to ascertain the extent of its ability to pay the interest upon issues of bonds equal in amount to its present first and second mortgages.

UNION PACIFIC—SUBSIDIZED DIVISION.

The first and Government debts of this road are about $68,000,000. The net earnings for the current year are about $3,800,000. The sum required to pay the interest on the above debt, at 4½ per cent, is $3,060,000, being $740,000 less than the current net earnings of the subsidized portion of the line. The average annual net earnings of these rails for the past five years have exceeded $5,000,000. Assuming that the Union Pacific main line were recognized separately from the Kansas Pacific Division, under this general plan, then, in that event, the settlement of United States mortgage claims is doubly assured by the large net returns of that route by itself.

KANSAS PACIFIC—SUBSIDIZED DIVISION.

The first and Government debts of this road aggregate about $19,000,000. The net earnings for the current year are about $1,000,000. The sum required to pay the interest on the above debts, at 4½ per cent, is $855,000, being $145,000 less than the present deteriorated earnings of the aided portion of this line. The average annual net earnings for the past five years have exceeded $1,300,000.

CENTRAL PACIFIC—SUBSIDIZED DIVISION.

The net first-mortgage and Government debts, secured on the bond-aided portions of this line, are approximately $80,000,000. The net earnings for the current year (under the lease to the Southern Pacific) are about $2,750,000. The sum required to pay the interest, at 4½ per cent, on the above debts, is $3,870,000. The average annual net earnings for the past ten years during the lease, have somewhat exceeded $3,000,000.

AMOUNT OF SUBSCRIPTION TO NEW BONDS REQUIRED TO SATISFY GOVERNMENT AND INDIVIDUAL HOLDINGS ON MAIN LINES.

The foregoing data indicate that the first-mortgage bondholders (including the Government as the largest holder) and the United States as the second mortgagee, can be adequately reimbursed by the operation of this bill. It provides that the Government commissioners, who are to manage its administrative details, shall notify the bondholders and stockholders that they may retain their interest in the properties and participate in their future earnings upon subscribing to issues of bonds sufficient in amount to pay off the first and second mortgages. The penalty for not uniting in such subscriptions will consist in exclusion from any further interest in the property, and the allotment of such nonassenting interest to other subscribing parties. In ascertaining the probability of thus obtaining these payments, the amount required may be practically reduced by the sum of the present first-mortgage debt (less the Government holdings of those bonds), inasmuch as the first-mortgage bondholders will, doubtless, exchange their present holdings about falling due for these fifty-year 4½ per cent bonds amply secured. Many of them have already expressed their willingness to accept a 4 per cent bond with inferior security. Forty-one million one hundred and thirteen thousand dollars of the new issues of bonds may, therefore, be deemed exchangeable for the present first-mortgage bonds. The balance of the new issues, consisting of the Government's first-mortgage holdings and its entire second mortgages, aggregating $124,000,000, are under this plan to be placed with other creditors and the stockholders. The total junior lien bonds and stocks of the three roads available for this purpose aggregate $161,089,000.

Let us examine the resources of the Government for thus placing these new issues, through the action to be taken by its commissioners, under the provisions of this bill.

RIGHTS OF SUBSCRIPTION TO THE NEW ISSUES OF BONDS—UNION AND KANSAS PACIFIC.

There are about twenty millions of bonds having incumbrances on these roads, inferior to the Government liens, and $60,800,000 of capital stock outstanding on these properties. The total amount of first-mortgage and Government debts of these roads is $87,000,000. Considering that the present first-mortgage bonds (excluding the Government holdings thereof, which are to be paid in cash) would be exchanged for the new issues, the net balance required to be taken up by the subscriptions of the junior securities and stockholders would be $62,000,000. To accomplish this result, the holders of twenty millions of bonds and of more than sixty millions of stock would be enlisted as subscribers. The investment of capital in these new issues must be favorably regarded, considering the present showing of $900,000 of surplus revenues of these roads over and above the aggregate amount requisite to pay the interest account. The very much greater average annual revenues for ten, or five, years past will also form an essential element in the estimate of investors. But the position of these new securities is favorably affected by other special considerations.

The present stockholders are deeply interested in their equity in the property—in the future earnings. While the investment of their capital in a well-secured interest-bearing bond is of itself desirable, it is doubly so when that investment leaves them in possession of stockholdings showing a dividend even under the present minimum conditions, and with a practical warrant for increased returns to the stockholders under fairly restored conditions.

On the other hand, if they fail to furnish the money wherewith the first and Government mortgages may be paid off, their stock will be forfeited, and will be allotted to other parties in interest who are willing to take the new bonds, and thus satisfy the superior claims on the railroads. There is no ground for apprehension that they will suffer any such result to transpire, as the success of similar plans during the past few months amply evidences.

Without entering upon details, the following illustrations may suffice: The New York and New England Railroad stockholders paid $20 per share, cash assessment, without receiving any new security of the reorganized company to represent their new capital, but so subscribed merely to save their nondividend-paying stock from forfeiture. The stockholders of the Minneapolis and St. Louis Railroad Company paid $25 per share, in cash, to take up foreclosing bonds, which were thereupon transferred to the subscribing stockholders, as proposed substantially by this plan. The stockholders of the Erie Railroad have almost unanimously paid $12 per share, in cash, on nearly $78,000,000 of stock, receiving in return only stock in a new company. In the above instances and many others apparently hopeless stockholdings have afforded the resources for redeeming the properties from insolvency.

But in the case of the Pacific railroads the inherent merits of the properties invest the proposed new issues of bonds, as well as the stock interest, with special considerations favorable to the resumption of much larger earnings. During the receiverships large sums have been spent on betterments, and the roads are now in good physical condition. The recent decision of the Supreme Court of the United States relieves them of the incubus of the Western Union and enables them to utilize their fine telegraph system. It should also be noted in this connection that, pursuant to the suggestion of Government officials, the bill makes provision for the reorganized companies to secure an independent connection with the Pacific Coast, which is expected to increase their through traffic. The contemplation of these elements of value has already induced a large number of Union Pacific stockholders to furnish proof of their confidence in the future of the property by subscribing $15 per share, under a plan heretofore presented to them, and agreeing to accept in return only preferred stock at par out of an issue of $75,000,000, and subject to a mortgage of $100,000,000. In fact, the memory of large dividends received upon this stock is still too vivid in the minds of the holders for them to permit any lapse of their interests. The much larger part of the total stocks of the Union and Central Pacific roads is held in England and other parts of Europe, therefore the demand for money involved in these subscriptions will not measurably affect the domestic money markets, but will, on the contrary, benefit the foreign exchange conditions with Europe. Moreover, nothing unreasonable is required of any interest, but the requirements are proportioned to the grade of security belonging to each claimant and merely furnish the facilities through which the junior holders in the roads may preserve their aliquot interests through the usual equitable course of redemption. Indeed, these rights of subscription to such valuable securities will probably command a premium, as the stock itself has recently doubled in price. Therefore, no doubt need be entertained that under the skillful management of Government commissioners, wielding legitimate powers, the negotiation of the new issues of bonds will be financially assured and the Government fully repaid in cash, with the partial exception now to be noticed.

CENTRAL PACIFIC.

All that has been heretofore said applies to the Central Pacific, with this modification: The current net earnings (under the lease), \$2,750,000, are not sufficient to pay the interest, at 4½ per cent, on more than about fifty millions of bonds, after deducting the ten millions set apart for acquiring the Pacific Coast connection. Hence there would remain about thirty millions of debt from the Central Pacific to the Government still unsatisfied. This would, however, be represented by that amount of the new issue of bonds in the hands of the United States, to bear interest when justified by the earnings of the road (with provision for capitalizing the unpaid interest account down to the time of the commencement of cash-coupon payments). Provisions for this purpose to be inserted in the mortgages, to be drafted under the direction of the commissioners. But if the anticipation of increased revenues by reason of independence from the Southern Pacific be justified, there would not be a long interval before the bonds thus retained became interest bearing. By the above arrangements the reorganization would provide the resources upon the security of the road for assuring its independent operation, and meanwhile the interest of the United States in the property would be represented by \$22,000,000 in cash, received on subscriptions to the new bonds, and \$30,000,000 in the new bonds, secured as above set forth.

RECAPITULATION.

The financial result would be the payment, in cash, to the Government of \$92,568,000, as follows:

First-mortgage bonds, held in sinking funds (individual first-mortgage holders exchanging for new four-and-a-halfs)	\$16,568,000
Union Pacific second mortgage, in full	41,000,000
Kansas Pacific second mortgage, in full	13,000,000
Central Pacific second mortgage, partial	22,000,000
Mortgage bonds, representing balance of Government interest in Central Pacific	30,000,000

We have endeavored by the foregoing statement to outline our estimate of the practical workings of this bill. But the measure proceeds on the principle that it is to the interest of all the first and second mortgagees to leave the administrative details of the reorganization to the Government commissioners, binding them, however, by the essential limitation that those mortgages shall be paid in full, as far as the present resources of the properties admit, and for the balance that they shall have all possible security. The adoption of this measure would secure those results in a businesslike way and with such safeguards as would be beyond the cavil of criticism.

New York, February 3, 1896.

H. LIVINGSTON ROGERS,
Agent for Bondholders.

L. J. MORRISON, *Of Counsel.*

A BILL to provide for the collection of the liabilities of Government-aided railroads to the United States.

Be it enacted by the Senate and House of Representatives in Congress assembled:

SECTION 1. That three commissioners shall be appointed by the President, by and with the advice and consent of the Senate, whose duty it shall be to represent and manage the interests of the United States in bond-aided railroads for the collection of all sums due and to become due therefrom to the Government, subject to the provisions and limitations of this act.

SEC. 2. That the Government commissioners shall proceed to enforce all the rights, liens, and claims of the United States, upon the said railroads, the sinking funds, and all other property in or to which the United States has any claim or equity, the intent of the said enforcement being to obtain the payment in full and in cash to the Government of all the aforesaid liabilities; and the said commissioners shall not make any arrangement, or give quittances, except upon the basis of the receipt of the entire amounts, principal and interest, payable to the United States from the said railroads, respectively, as hereinafter set forth.

SEC. 3. That in furtherance of the above object the Government commissioners shall, upon taking office, issue notices to the creditors and stockholders of the railroad companies, severally, and with such assessments and penalties as they may prescribe, that the United States will proceed to obtain decrees of foreclosure and sale of the said railroads, and that the commissioners will thereat purchase the said railroads in trust for a company or companies, which shall consist of all the present creditors and stockholders who subscribe to the Government plan of reorganization, which plan shall be constituted as follows:

It shall provide for the issue of new mortgage bonds, bearing a lower rate of interest than the present prior liens, and to such amounts and in such series as are warranted by the net earnings of the said railroads. The said new issues of obligations shall include at least the amounts of the present first-mortgage bonds and the sums secured by the Government liens.

The holders of all obligations of the said companies and the stockholders thereof shall have the right, upon subscribing to the said new issues of mortgage bonds, to receive allotments of the same, and the present stockholders shall, in addition, have the right to retain their proportionate stock interests in the railroads as reorganized. In case of the failure of some of the said creditors or stockholders to subscribe for the new securities, as aforesaid, the commissioners shall make arrangements with other creditors or stockholders who may be willing to subscribe, and they shall be allotted the bonds and stocks of the reorganized companies proportionately to their additional subscriptions.

The amounts received by the commissioners on account of subscriptions to the new securities shall be applied to the payment of the Government and other holdings of first-mortgage bonds, and likewise to the payment of the Government liens. First-mortgage bondholders other than the Government shall have the right to subscribe for and receive new issues of bonds and to pay for the same with their present first-mortgage holdings, which shall thereupon be canceled.

The commissioners shall turn into the Treasury all net sums received by them on subscriptions to the new issues of bonds, and upon full payment of all the amounts due to the United States from each railroad company severally, or on account of each Government lien severally, the commissioners shall, on behalf of the United States, deliver a full release of such Government lien. In case the subscriptions to the said bonds do not equal the total amount secured by the liens severally, the commissioners shall deliver releases pro tanto, and the Government liens for the balances shall thereafter be represented by the amount of bonds remaining in the hands of the commissioners until the same are sold at par.

SEC. 4. That deposits of the obligations and stocks of the said companies shall be received by the commissioners pursuant to the above-described notices. The commissioners shall use deposited bonds that are available for the purchases of the said railroads at the foreclosure sales. The commissioners shall thereupon transfer the title or titles of the railroads so purchased to a company, or to companies, composed of the subscribers to the new securities, to be issued for the payment of the Government. And for the above purposes the commissioners shall have the power to employ counsel, clerks, and all proper agents, whose compensation, as well as that of the commissioners, shall be paid from assessments on the bondholders and stockholders, or out of the proceeds of sale, and according to the usual manner in cases of the reorganization of railroads.

SEC. 5. That for the purpose of effecting the full payment of the Government as aforesaid, the commissioners shall request the President to enforce the provisions of the act of 1887, in reference to the payment of the first-mortgage bonds of the said railroads, or may make arrangements with any subscribers toward the payment of the Government liens as aforesaid, for advances of the amounts necessary to protect the Government liens during the progress of the reorganization.

SEC. 6. That in determining the amounts of the new issues of mortgage bonds, the commissioners shall provide a sufficient amount thereof to complete the main line of Pacific Railroad from Omaha to the Pacific Ocean. And the said bonds so executed by the purchasing company or companies shall be used by them for the construction of any part of the said continuous line or for the purchase of any existing line adapted to said connection.

SEC. 7. That upon the payment in full to the Government as aforesaid of any of the said liens belonging to the United States, all acts and parts of acts in reference to the earnings of the said railroads severally, or establishing special relations between them and the Government, shall thereupon cease and determine.

Adjourned.

The following statements were subsequently received from Mr. Mink:

A.

THE UNION PACIFIC SYSTEM.

Statement of the financial operations of S. H. H. Clark, Oliver W. Mink, E. Ellery Anderson, John W. Doane, and Frederic R. Coudert, receivers of the properties owned by the Union Pacific Railway Company, during the period from October 13, 1893, to December 31, 1895.

Name of company.	Gross earnings.	Income from investments.	Other receipts.	Total receipts.	Operating expenses.	Taxes.
Union Pacific Railway:						
Ames receivership	$17,273,022.22	$740,944.52	$254,482.03	$18,268,448.77	$11,700,590.51	$628,950.93
Consolidated mortgage receivership	4,235,206.93	....	....	4,235,206.93	2,817,514.91	304,242.93
Dexter-Ames receivership	10,004,993.41	....	....	10,004,993.41	5,840,649.21	345,003.17
Denver Pacific mortgage receivership	830,924.59	....	....	830,924.59	549,770.20	27,557.49
Omaha Bridge mortgage division	488,454.94	....	....	488,454.94	270,708.32	32,187.10
Total	32,832,602.09	740,944.52	254,482.03	33,828,028.64	21,179,233.15	1,337,941.62

Name of company.	Interest paid on coupon orders.	United States earnings withheld.	Other expenditures.	Total expenditures.	Surplus.
Union Pacific Railway:					
Ames receivership	$3,505,365.00	$1,523,868.30	$206,642.66	$17,565,417.40	$703,031.37
Consolidated mortgage receivership	....	199,778.81	356,753.83	3,678,290.48	556,916.45
Dexter-Ames receivership	3,900.00	1,038,881.89	736,900.32	7,965,334.59	2,039,658.82
Denver Pacific mortgage receivership	....	6,340.24	52,635.74	636,303.67	194,620.92
Omaha Bridge mortgage division	....	3,425.62	160,132.58	466,453.62	22,001.32
Total	3,509,265.00	2,772,204.86	1,513,065.13	30,311,799.76	3,516,228.88

ALEX. MILLAR, *Assistant Comptroller.*

OFFICE OF THE RECEIVERS, *Boston, Mass., March 24, 1896.*

AMES RECEIVERSHIP.

Memorandum showing detail of item "other expenditures" October 13, 1893, to December 31, 1895, inclusive, Ames receivership, as shown in statement of financial operations, dated Boston, March 13, 1896.

Commission and expense of paying coupons abroad		$3,231.08
Discount and interest		4,079.97
Harris accident judgment (court order, Ames, No. 203)		7,982.88
McDonald coal judgment (court order, Ames, No. 97)		10,184.66
Union Depot Company, Spokane Falls bonds purchased		24,043.45
Leavenworth, Topeka and Southwestern Railway deficit, October 13, 1893, to January 6, 1894, inclusive (court order, Ames, No. 24)		12,663.28
Deficit, cripple lines:		
October 13, 1893, to July 31, 1894, inclusive (court order, Ames, No. 138—		
Union Pacific, Brighton and Boulder Branch	$5,686.79	
Junction City and Fort Kearney Railway	42,055.42	
Omaha and Republican Valley Railway	75,116.92	
Salina and Southwestern Railway	11,604.03	
October 13, 1893, to December 31, 1894, inclusive (court order, Ames, No. 158), Kansas City and Omaha Railroad	9,994.18	
		144,457.34
Total		206,642.66

ALEX. MILLAR, *Assistant Comptroller.*

OFFICE OF THE RECEIVERS, *Boston, March 24, 1896.*

CONSOLIDATED MORTGAGE RECEIVERSHIP.

Memorandum showing detail of item "other expenditures," July 17, 1894, to December 31, 1895, inclusive, consolidated mortgage receivership, as shown in statement of financial operations, dated Boston, March 13, 1896.

Union Pacific Railway equipment trust obligations paid pursuant to Kansas Pacific (court order No. B-25)		$263,178.69
Denver extension land expenses, October 13, 1893, to February 28, 1895, inclusive	$206,975.21	
Less repayments	113,400.07	
		93,575.14
Total		356,753.83

ALEX. MILLAR, *Assistant Comptroller.*

OFFICE OF THE RECEIVERS,
Boston, March 24, 1896.

DEXTER-AMES RECEIVERSHIP.

Memorandum showing detail of item "other expenditures," January 22 to December 31, 1895, inclusive, Dexter-Ames receivership, as shown in statement of financial operations dated Boston, March 13, 1896.

Union Pacific Railway equipment trust obligations paid pursuant to Dexter-Ames (court order No. 19) $736,900.32

ALEX. MILLAR, *Assistant Comptroller.*

OFFICE OF THE RECEIVERS,
Boston, March 24, 1896.

DENVER PACIFIC MORTGAGE RECEIVERSHIP.

Memorandum showing detail of item "other expenditures," November 19, 1894, to December 31, 1895, inclusive, Denver Pacific mortgage receivership, as shown in statement of financial operations dated Boston, March 13, 1896.

Union Pacific Railway equipment trust obligations paid pursuant to Denver Pacific (court order No. A-15) $52,635.74

ALEX. MILLAR, *Assistant Comptroller.*

OFFICE OF THE RECEIVERS,
Boston, March 24, 1896.

OMAHA BRIDGE MORTGAGE DIVISION.

Memorandum showing detail of item "other expenditures" August 1, 1894, to December 31, 1895, inclusive, Omaha Bridge mortgage division, as shown in statement of financial operations dated Boston, March 13, 1896.

Net earnings Omaha Bridge mortgage division from August 1, 1894, to October 31, 1895, inclusive, paid to J. Pierpont Morgan and Edwin F. Atkins, trustees, pursuant to Ames (court order No. 108) $160,132.58

ALEX. MILLAR, *Assistant Comptroller.*

OFFICE OF THE RECEIVERS,
Boston, March 24, 1896.

B.

Statement of the Union Pacific Railway Company's debt to the United States, the estimated value of the United States sinking fund January 1, 1897, and the amount required to meet the interest on the debt January 1, 1897.

Principal of debt to the United States:		
Union Division bonds	$27,236,512.00	
Kansas Division bonds	6,303,000.00	
Total debt		$33,539,512.00

Value of the company's sinking fund January 1, 1896, as follows, viz:		
Union Pacific first-mortgage bonds at par	$6,367,000.00	
Central Pacific first-mortgage bonds at par	3,230,000.00	
Sioux City and Pacific first-mortgage bonds at par	716,500.00	
Kansas Pacific Eastern Division first-mortgage bonds at par	553,000.00	
Kansas Pacific Middle Division first-mortgage bonds at par	925,000.00	
Western Pacific first-mortgage bonds at par	350,000.00	
United States 5 per cent bonds due 1904 at 112½	1,030,218.75	
United States currency sixes, $74,000, at	77,790.00	
Atchison and Pikes Peak first-mortgage bonds at 50 per cent	512,500.00	
Total value of sinking-fund investments January 1, 1896		$13,762,008.75
Cash in sinking fund January 1, 1896		1,191,179.03
Probable increase in sinking fund from interest and transportation during the year 1896, viz:		
From interest collections	$690,000.00	
From transportation accounts	575,000.00	
		1,265,000.00
Total estimated value of the sinking fund January 1, 1897		16,218,187.78
Accumulated interest January 1, 1897, including interest at 6 per cent to that date on all overdue bonds:		
Union Division interest	$47,019,425.13	
Kansas Division interest	11,234,763.09	
Total accumulated interest to January 1, 1897		58,254,188.22
Interest repaid to January 1, 1896 (excluding sinking fund):		
Union Division	$14,814,908.51	
Kansas Division	5,250,575.54	
Total repayments to January 1, 1896	20,065,484.05	
Probable repayments on account of interest during the year 1896:		
Union Division repayments	575,000.00	
Kansas Division repayments	65,000.00	
		20,705,484.05
Balance of interest account January 1, 1897		37,548,704.17
Interest to accrue on debt maturing subsequent to January 1, 1897, from that date to respective dates of maturity, viz:		
Interest January 1, 1897, to January 1, 1898, at 6 per cent on $17,342,512.	$1,040,550.72	
Interest January 1, 1897, to January 1, 1899, at 6 per cent on $3,157,000.	378,840.00	
Total	1,419,390.72	
Present value on January 1, 1897, of last-named sums, reckoning interest at 2 per cent	1,020,147.76	
and	364,269.23	
Respectively, amounting to		1,384,416.99
Amount necessary to meet the payment of the interest on the debt January 1, 1897, exclusive of the sinking fund		36,933,121.16

NOTE—The above statement does not include $556.026.05 due from the United States standing on the receivers' Union Pacific system books at Omaha on December 31, 1895.

ALEX. MILLAR, *Assistant Comptroller*.

OFFICE OF THE RECEIVERS, *Boston, March 24, 1896*.

C.

RECEIVERS UNION PACIFIC RAILWAY COMPANY.

Statement showing the earnings, expenses, taxes, and net earnings of the aided and non-aided portions of the Kansas Division during the period from October 13, 1893, to December 31, 1895, inclusive.

Kansas Division.	1895.		1894.		October 13 to December 31, 1893.	
	Aided.	Nonaided.	Aided.	Nonaided.	Aided.	Nonaided.
Earnings	$2,000,114.24	$744,421.97	$2,074,716.87	$639,469.04	$507,057.40	$165,119.48
Expenses	1,255,951.26	608,253.86	1,368,168.26	536,980.16	286,636.26	106,105.53
Taxes	119,725.14	50,479.64	116,414.84	10,866.09	19,925.99	9,863.47
Expenses and taxes.	1,375,676.40	658,733.50	1,484,583.10	547,846.25	306,562.25	115,969.00
Net earnings	624,437.84	85,688.47	590,133.77	91,622.79	200,495.15	49,150.48

ALEX. MILLAR, *Assistant Comptroller*.

OFFICE OF THE RECEIVERS, *Boston, March 16, 1896*.

D.

THE UNION PACIFIC RAILWAY COMPANY.

Earnings and expenses by months for the years 1890 to 1895, inclusive.

EARNINGS.

Month.	1895.	1894.	1893.	1892.	1891.	1890.
January	$970,520.07	$1,039,115.99	$1,404,791.44	$1,427,180.01	$1,288,365.89	$1,193,633.82
February	940,343.64	1,006,963.49	1,260,776.43	1,299,071.47	1,200,352.87	1,264,983.05
March	1,075,573.36	1,078,896.39	1,426,937.81	1,463,973.44	1,499,228.61	1,679,273.88
April	1,083,343.78	1,104,231.91	1,372,203.89	1,468,447.13	1,515,743.55	1,710,067.54
May	1,156,180.20	1,201,079.60	1,510,993.18	1,506,147.92	1,520,078.82	1,958,716.27
June	1,188,052.02	1,202,995.23	1,530,287.16	1,744,513.06	1,613,290.54	1,789,436.30
July	1,192,507.91	1,094,369.98	1,338,113.49	1,689,878.10	1,612,702.21	1,704,886.84
August	1,209,586.14	1,442,800.64	1,324,973.21	1,885,449.26	1,735,523.28	1,915,717.58
September	1,368,532.65	1,497,066.39	1,607,010.98	2,191,098.72	2,947,249.55	1,905,782.90
October	1,646,406.15	1,706,522.50	1,756,470.08	2,072,940.59	2,148,357.06	2,032,406.94
November	1,362,813.84	1,333,110.45	1,544,901.64	1,940,965.14	1,963,289.32	1,910,294.95
December	1,142,431.48	1,110,645.17	1,299,332.80	1,670,836.82	1,643,556.78	1,313,008.29
Total	14,336,291.24	14,817,806.74	17,376,792.11	20,361,401.66	19,687,738.48	20,438,208.36

OPERATING EXPENSES (INCLUDING TAXES).

Month.	1895.	1894.	1893.	1892.	1891.	1890.
January	$867,924.29	$738,487.09	$888,869.54	$904,883.65	$871,452.11	$929,175.28
February	675,113.40	733,497.31	820,330.49	849,628.48	851,306.38	913,006.55
March	696,624.90	854,764.53	974,578.47	880,122.79	923,883.19	1,063,116.14
April	695,367.70	795,144.77	904,059.13	941,016.14	1,017,862.40	1,169,086.74
May	725,445.94	968,201.52	989,488.62	958,428.58	985,066.27	1,185,583.09
June	770,742.38	903,946.13	932,052.22	940,235.87	1,007,819.45	1,049,148.46
July	781,043.14	710,086.66	854,825.21	884,150.57	1,035,313.05	913,617.25
August	739,067.44	871,944.99	814,776.21	1,040,688.93	1,015,004.84	1,029,674.87
September	783,072.98	886,248.16	852,515.41	1,082,900.72	959,511.55	1,044,854.52
October	861,367.82	1,104,379.51	1,044,062.41	1,126,146.91	1,129,310.43	1,341,691.52
November	801,618.37	1,120,281.32	1,044,508.64	1,076,893.53	1,049,292.52	1,313,145.81
December	1,036,745.55	815,747.50	1,046,453.95	1,126,037.27	995,464.59	1,211,349.07
Total	9,434,134.00	10,502,729.49	11,166,520.30	11,811,133.44	11,841,286.78	13,163,449.30

SURPLUS EARNINGS (TAXES DEDUCTED).

Month.	1895.	1894.	1893.	1892.	1891.	1890.
January	$102,595.78	$300,628.90	$515,921.90	$522,296.36	$416,913.78	$264,458.54
February	265,230.15	273,466.18	440,445.94	449,442.99	349,046.49	351,976.50
March	378,948.46	224,131.86	452,359.34	583,850.65	575,345.42	616,157.74
April	387,976.08	309,087.14	468,144.76	527,430.99	497,881.15	540,980.80
May	430,734.26	232,878.08	521,504.56	547,719.34	535,012.55	773,133.18
June	417,300.64	299,049.10	598,234.94	804,277.19	605,471.09	740,287.84
July	411,464.77	384,283.32	483,288.28	805,727.53	577,389.16	851,269.59
August	470,518.70	570,864.65	510,197.00	844,760.33	720,518.44	886,042.71
September	585,459.67	610,818.23	754,495.57	1,109,098.00	987,738.00	860,928.38
October	785,038.33	602,142.99	712,407.67	946,793.68	1,019,046.63	690,715.42
November	561,195.47	212,829.13	500,393.00	864,071.61	913,996.80	597,149.14
December	105,685.93	294,897.67	252,878.85	544,799.55	648,092.19	101,659.22
Total	4,902,157.24	4,315,077.25	6,210,271.81	8,550,268.22	7,846,451.70	7,274,759.06

ALEX. MILLAR, *Assistant Comptroller.*

BOSTON, *March 24, 1896.*

Letter received from the Secretary of the Treasury by the chairman of Pacific Railroad Committee regarding L. C. Blaisdell's testimony, to be read in connection with that testimony. (See pp. 407 to 441, inclusive.)

TREASURY DEPARTMENT, OFFICE OF THE SECRETARY,
Washington, D. C. April 8, 1896.

SIR: In reply to your inquiry of the 31st ultimo I have to inform you that there is no evidence on file in this Department as to the ownership of the first-mortgage bonds of the Union Pacific and Central Pacific Railroad companies, nor has there ever been an agreement made by Secretary Folger with the owners of said bonds regarding their investment in the sinking fund of the Union and Central Pacific Railroad companies.

Respectfully, yours,

C. S. HAMLIN, *Acting Secretary.*

Hon. JNO. H. GEAR,
United States Senate.

INDEX TO PACIFIC RAILROAD HEARINGS.

UNION PACIFIC.

CENTRAL PACIFIC.

SIOUX CITY AND PACIFIC.

ALL THE PACIFIC RAILROADS.

FIGURES, TABLES, AND EXHIBITS.

www.ingramcontent.com/pod-product-compliance
Lightning Source LLC
Chambersburg PA
CBHW031823270326
41932CB00008B/521

* 9 7 8 3 7 4 4 7 4 6 4 4 1 *